MW01532344

MANAGING
OFFICE
AUTOMATION
A Complete Guide

MANAGING OFFICE AUTOMATION
A Complete Guide

MARY M. RUPRECHT, P.h.D.

President, Mary M. Ruprecht & Associates, Inc.

KATHLEEN P. WAGONER, C.M.C.

Professor, Ball State University

JOHN WILEY & SONS

New York   Chichester   Brisbane   Toronto   Singapore

Copyright © 1984, by John Wiley & Sons, Inc.

All rights reserved. Published simultaneously in Canada.

Reproduction or translation of any part of
this work beyond that permitted by Sections
107 and 108 of the 1976 United States Copyright
Act without the permission of the copyright
owner is unlawful. Requests for permission
or further information should be addressed to
the Permissions Department, John Wiley & Sons.

Library of Congress Cataloging in Publication Data:

Ruprecht, Mary M.
 Managing office automation.

 Includes index.
 1. Office practice–Automation.   I. Wagoner,
Kathleen P.   II.   Title.
HF5547.5.R925   651   83-17046
ISBN 0-471-88731-5

Printed in the United States of America

10 9 8 7 6 5 4 3 2 1

To my family:

Greg, Debbie, Sharie, Brad, and my parents, Chic and Mary

To my family:

"J," Neil, and Carol

FOREWORD

This book is designed to help you understand the principles of managing in the office environment as it becomes increasingly automated. That management skill will be an indispensable responsibility in every organization as the demand for white-collar work grows and as long as the need to increase productivity in the office exists.

This is not merely a book about computers, or about data processing in the office. Rather, it strives to explain how all technologies can be combined to improve the work done in the traditional office. It especially emphasizes the development of applications and systems that address managerial, secretarial, and clerical functions formerly handled manually or by simple electromechanical devices.

The term *office* is rapidly becoming outmoded and archaic. It no longer fits its old description of a room in which the business of an organization takes place. The office function now exists wherever business information is created, stored, replicated, and distributed.

The computer-based word processor was—and is—far more than just a faster typewriter. It was the first integrator of office functions. It opened the door to the electronic office, first by enabling two devices to exchange information electronically, eliminating the need to recreate data each time. Soon computers were working hand-in-hand with word processors and phototypesetters. Software-based systems then became prevalent, enabling word processors to perform computing functions and computers to type. By the end of the 1970s, an avalanche of other breakthroughs inundated the office: communications, personal computers, shared resource systems, OCR, intelligent printing, local networks, and intelligent typewriters.

Although these technological strides will continue to be of importance in the 1980s, much of the technology is now in place for a springboard into the 1990s. The future challenge for those who work in the information processing environment will involve, first of all, analysis of office tasks, applications, and procedures. Then, systems and software must be designed to perform them faster, at lower cost, and with higher quality and accuracy, and to present information to all who must use it in a manner that is easy to find and easy to use. That is the mission of the information manager of today.

Today's offices look different. Open-plan layouts are prevalent. Employees' workstations are now tailored to individual job needs and to accommodate the tools of the electronic office.

Techniques of management and working patterns have shifted. More management time is spent in planning and in long-range problem solving and less in day-to-day operation (because many of those functions are automated).

The skill levels of white collar workers are becoming more highly specialized. Those who work in future offices will need both the skills and the tools to be far more productive than are their counterparts of today.

Perhaps the biggest opportunities for productivity improvement lie in the area of making managers and executives more productive and more effective. The first area includes the automation of routine administrative duties; the second area deals with providing executives with the means to solve problems and to retrieve the information needed to complete assignments. Automation of the above-listed tasks will continue to reduce the amount of executive time spent performing them, and thus allow more time to be spent on priority matters.

The authors' purpose is to provide you with the basic knowledge and requirements of management, personnel, procedures, and systems in this dawning era of the integrated office.

John B. Dykeman
Executive Editor and
Associate Publisher
Modern Office Technology

PREFACE

The maxim "Nothing is more certain than change" is applicable to all aspects of our lives, but it is particularly meaningful in the office world of work. In order to adapt most effectively to this change, we must examine continuously and carefully the extent of change and its consequences. At the same time, if we are to have any control over change and the working environment, we must determine our goals and desired outcomes and plan for them to progress in the most appropriate and orderly way. Without goal setting and planning, change is often piecemeal and disruptive.

Managing Office Automation is designed to provide you with an overall approach to managing the changing office; identifying present and evolving technologies; and achieving an integrated automated office.

The rapid change in technology and the need to maintain a competitive edge have necessitated embracing new concepts of operational policies and procedures and new management styles and philosophies within the automated office.

Managers who are both flexible and farsighted will survive the changing times. Our goal is to provide direction and a plan so that you will be able within your work situation to

—improve productivity by maximizing staff and technology;

—receive information more rapidly at the point of need;

—enhance your decision-making skills;

—plan for integrating technologies;

—accept the changing environment and provide training to promote such acceptance;

—study existing workloads;

—present your thoughts to others;

—incorporate human considerations into plans for change;

—ergonomically design your office;

—select equipment that best fits the application (from word processing to global networks);

—prepare procedures for greater effectiveness;

—budget for ongoing success;

—consider some future trends, both sociological and technological in nature.

Part One provides a history of and an evolutionary perspective on the traditional office and its transition to automation. Part Two opens with an overview of changing career patterns and the opportunities available in most office-related organizations. Part Two continues with a complete overview of the information processing flow and all its major parts—input, processing, and telecommunications (which will make integration possible), together with replication and distribution. In addition, records management and administrative functions and their role in the office of the future are examined.

The full potential of office automation will not be achieved easily. Part Three focuses on the issues of office automation, including such necessary steps to achieve automation as conducting feasibility studies, presenting these results to management, and considering the ergonomics of the working environment.

Part Four centers attention on major management considerations—strategies for implementing the integrated electronic office; an in-depth look at the human, structural, procedural, and technological issues involved in office automation; and the very important people aspects involved with change. An understanding of such personnel aspects as selection, evaluation, compensation, and training will help today's manager become more promotable. Supervisory/management techniques and human relations, together with an understanding of the importance of continuing development and growth, will help managers to successfully undertake new roles. The last section of Part Four discusses measuring and budgeting productivity.

In addition, to help readers attain a broad outlook, the book closes with a chapter concerning the future of office automation. Finally, the last section of the book lists tools to assist the information manager in implementing an office automation program.

The appendices include sample forms for developing office automation objectives; preparing project proposals; conducting feasibility studies; determining implementation schedules; designing job descriptions and performance appraisals; creating equipment requests for proposals and equipment evaluation checklists; producing procedures manuals and control forms; and scheduling training and continuing education seminars. Lists of professional organizations and trade journals for professional development are also provided.

We, the authors, recognize the need for improving communication and the use of information in the office. Only through attention to these factors can improvement in overall productivity be achieved. We sincerely hope this book will assist management in planning for the "office of the future" and moving on to total automation in a logical, budgeted manner.

With a clear understanding of the transition to automation, a positive approach to change can result.

We have been extremely fortunate to have had the assistance of so many interested individuals in creating this book. Although the "office of the future" seldom evokes the same image in all minds, we received many helpful ideas from the feedback provided by our reviewers. We wish to express our thanks to the following educators:

Dr. Jeanne L. Holley, associate professor, School of Business Administration, University of Mississippi, University, Miss.; Dr. Richard Kelly, Professor, Business Education and Office Administration, Ball State University, Muncie, Ind.; Mrs. Helen Martin, School of Applied Science, Miami University, Oxford, Ohio; Dr. Sam Murphy, associate professor, Administrative Services, West Texas State University, Canyon, Texas; Dr. L. Marilyn Stinson, associate dean, College of Business, St. Cloud State University, St. Cloud, Minn.; Dr. Patsy Nichols, Murray State University, Murray, Ky.

We also wish to thank the following reviewers from the business world for providing real-world input: L. Millard Collins, IBM, Dallas, Texas; and Mart Nelson, Blythe-Nelson, Dallas, Texas.

We gratefully acknowledge the wise counsel and many helpful contributions of Mr. John B. Dykeman, executive editor and associate publisher of *Modern Office Technology*.

Our special personal thanks to Karen Crabtree and Scott Kelso for keyboarding; Cil Haugen for organizing and maintaining research files; W. J. Wagoner for proofing and verifying content; Sharie and Brad Kimball for preparing and detailing figures; Greg Ruprecht for drawings and illustrations; Dr. Leonard B. Kruk for patience and support; Debbie Ruprecht for coordination and organization of permissions; and Marilyn Gloss for the hours spent in the coordination and revision of the final product.

Mary M. Ruprecht
Kathleen P. Wagoner

CONTENTS

PART ONE

INTRODUCTION

CHAPTER 1

THE INTEGRATED AUTOMATED OFFICE

OBJECTIVES

In this chapter you will learn about

1. The development of the traditional office function.
2. The traditional office and its costs.
3. The need for more effective management of resources.
4. The evolution of specialized work within the office.
5. The need to delegate administrative work to make management personnel more productive.
6. How the convergence of word processing, data processing, and telecommunications will develop into the integrated office.
7. The total support approach and the part it plays in the integrated office.
8. The need for total support in today's business world.
9. The benefits of integrated technologies.
10. The components of the electronic office and the framework of total support systems.

As office technology advances, it is important to understand and to recognize both the differences and similarities between the traditional office of yesterday and today and the integrated electronic office.

THE TRADITIONAL OFFICE STRUCTURE

Traditionally, the office has been the place where business paperwork is handled. The traditional office usually includes secretaries, stenographers, typists, and clerks who support people who work at specific office tasks.

Traditionally, top and middle management personnel frequently had full-time secretarial support on a one-to-one basis. Although these full-time assignments should have been justified based on work volume, they more likely were related to the manager's level in the organization. A full-time secretary has long been a status symbol of a high-level management position in the organization. Secretaries, typists, and clerks seldom appeared on organization charts, because their service was to assist others in carrying out their duties and functions.

In addition, office services generally existed as separate, unrelated operations—such as the mail room, printing services, or typing pool.

As office systems became more sophisticated and the volume of business information exploded, this traditional structure encountered an increasing number of problems and disadvantages. This explosion, along with the urgent need to increase white-collar productivity, caused many executives and managers to look for ways to restructure their secretarial and clerical support at all management levels.

PROBLEMS WITH THE TRADITIONAL OFFICE

There are several disadvantages to the traditional one-secretary-to-one-manager structure. While many managers may be expert in their own work, they usually are neither concerned with nor familiar with secretarial work and what makes a secretary productive. The manager's main concern is that the secretary get the work done. Another disadvantage is that much of a manager's time is spent working with other people or away from the office. In both cases, a lack of competent supervision exists.

In addition, secretarial work is relatively unstructured, differing greatly from one setting to another. Some secretaries perform clerical tasks such as filing, photocopying, handling mail, and running errands, while others have considerable responsibility assisting their employers with higher-level tasks such as arranging meetings, preparing itineraries, researching needed information, and recordkeeping.

Secretarial workloads vary. Some are overloaded with work; others have such light duties that they have idle time. Other secretaries have peak and valley workloads, and still others may have work so diverse that they find it difficult to perform one task without being interrupted by a new one, making it hard to complete any of their tasks promptly.

Idle time and interruptions have often characterized the traditional office structure as an environment that fosters a low level of productivity. According to a research study of 13 companies, idle time (waiting-for-work time) amounts to approximately 18 percent of traditional secretarial time.[1] When managers become involved in other duties, meetings, or telephone calls, they may not be able to organize work for their secretaries to perform. For example, a sudden meeting might prevent a manager from preparing a report that the secretary has to type and mail the following day. The secretary must wait for the report to be readied or use that office time to do other tasks.

Today's management can no longer afford such costly routines. Business has recognized the need for a new approach to increased productivity through supervised office procedures and electronic office systems.

The traditional office is one of the last frontiers that business must study for the specific purpose of increasing productivity. The first advances in technology were directed at improving secretarial/clerical staff duties, which are often unsupervised and labor-intensive. The work (e.g., typing, filing, and calendaring) has been performed manually by office personnel—a time-consuming, inefficient, and expensive process.

ECONOMICS OF THE OFFICE FUNCTION

Because clerical and secretarial work was secondary to the principal purpose of an organization, management in the past did not pay much attention to the office's organization, control, and purposes. The cost of running an office has continually risen, but office productivity has not increased at a corresponding rate. However, the need to control costs has forced management to reevaluate office functions in terms of their contributions to profitability and effectiveness.

During the 1960s, factory-worker productivity jumped 80 percent; farm workers enjoyed similar productivity growth through mechanization. During the same period, office-worker productivity rose a mere 4 percent.[2]

Today, the office is the most labor-intensive sector in our society, and labor costs have continued to go up at a rate of 7 percent annually during the latter part of the seventies and even higher during the early part of the eighties.[3]

[1] Harold Tepper, "The Private Secretary: A Company Liability," *Management Review*, February 1973.
[2] "Productivity and Information Management," *Fortune*, special advertising section, March 12, 1979.
[3] John Dykeman, "The Need to Automate: Greater Than Ever," *Modern Office Procedures*, April 1980, p. 8.

According to the Automatic Data Processing Reorganization Project, the information industry now accounts for more than half the Gross National Product (GNP). In 1955 this information industry was only a quarter of the GNP.[4]

The office work force now represents about 22 percent of the U.S. labor base, and the percentage is growing. The total white-collar work force accounts for about 53 percent of adult employment and more than 70 percent of the nation's salaries and wages. Both percentages are projected to increase dramatically in the years ahead.

The U.S. Bureau of Labor Statistics estimates that white-collar workers will account for 55 percent of the total employment by 1985, and some observers believe that the figure will rise to 90 percent by the end of the century.[5] The white-collar work force is broken into four categories: (1) managerial/administrative; (2) professional/technical; (3) sales; and (4) clerical. The clerical work force amounts to about 22 percent of the total.

Attrition contributes to increasing overhead costs because training new employees takes a long time. It also takes a long time for a trainee to become a fully productive and contributing employee. The U.S. Bureau of Labor Statistics reveals that the average employee turnover ranges from 19 percent to 28 percent annually.

While office employment and overhead costs have soared, prices of office hardware have decreased about 10 percent annually, bringing computers within the reach of the smallest businesses. It is estimated that the performance of computers has increased 10,000-fold in 15 years, while the price of each unit of performance has declined 1,000,000-fold since 1960.[6] It should be noted, however, that software costs are increasing because of the highly skilled labor necessary for development requirements.

The automation approach to increasing productivity has been aimed at the repetitive and routine tasks of office-support employees. However, functions such as sorting, compiling, accounting, filing, mailing, and billing are being taken over by microprocessors that handle both words and numbers efficiently and at less cost.

MAKING MANAGEMENT MORE PRODUCTIVE

Management has become aware of its own needs to become more productive. Too often management expends excessive effort and time on routine clerical tasks that could, with proper planning, be delegated to an office

---

[4] "Productivity and Information Management."

[5] "White Collar Productivity—The National Challenge," *Philadelphia Inquirer*, February 7, 1983, p. 2.

[6] Howard Anderson, "Office '80s—The Systems Era," *The New York Times*, special advertising section, October 1979.

support staff. If such tasks were delegated, management could spend more time on proper management functions such as planning and organizing.

Electronic technology is providing the basis for the integrated office, also called the automated office or the office of the future. These terms describe the automation and integration of previously discrete office functions such as dictating, typing or keyboarding, storing and retrieving information, communicating, and distributing information.

In many cases, word processing equipment was originally used in the traditional office as a secretarial tool. However, to meet the service and support needs of management and staff, a total office support structure that goes far beyond the use of word processing must supplant the one-to-one secretary to boss relationship. This level of support requires trained secretarial personnel. Yet, at a time when management's support needs are increasing, the supply of such trained personnel is decreasing. Although the white-collar work force grew 29 percent in the seventies (from 37.9 million workers to 48.9 million), the number of people in the 18-to-24 age bracket available for entry-level office jobs will drop by 20 percent within the next decade.[7] There is already a shortage of qualified employees in many areas of the country.

The cost of obtaining and retaining top-quality people is increasing steadily. Turnover rates (i.e., the number of people leaving and changing jobs) are high. Historically, maintaining an office has constituted 20 to 30 percent of overhead costs. It is not uncommon now for the cost of these same services to reach 50 percent of overhead. Studies reveal that office costs are rising 12 to 15 percent per year and that office costs will double within the next decade.[8] These dramatic increases in cost result from many factors, one of which is the increasing demand for secretaries in the office and the shortage of qualified workers.

According to the U.S. Bureau of Labor Statistics, this shortage stems in part from women leaving office support jobs for careers that in the past have been predominantly male-oriented. In addition, women are starting to progress up the corporate ladder, leaving their former secretarial positions open.

Office automation promises to increase both secretarial and managerial effectiveness. While most efforts to automate have focused on secretarial work, the greatest potential for improvement lies in the work performed by executives, managers, and professional (or "knowledge") workers. According to studies conducted by the Xerox Corporation, secretarial and clerical workers represent only 20 to 40 percent of the total office labor cost. Executives, managers, and professionals account for the larger share, from 60 to 80 percent.

[7] John Dykeman, "The People Factor: Again, It's a Priority Concern," *Modern Office Procedures*, March 1980.
[8] John J. Connell, "Office of the 80's Productivity Impact," *Business Week*, special advertising section, February 18, 1980.

The time secretaries spend on typing duties represents only 14 percent of their total time worked; although automation achieves a 15 percent improvement of that 14 percent, the benefits are still minimal. If automation achieves a 15 percent improvement in the executive area (60-80 percent), a far larger gain is realized.

Typically, there has been no big capital investment in office technology to support the activities of office workers. The capital investment in the farm worker approaches $70,000 in equipment such as tractors, combines, and pickers. The average factory worker is supported by $35,000 of investment in manufacturing equipment. The office worker, on the other hand, is supported by a capital investment of $4000, which buys little more than a desk, chair, typewriter, and wastebasket. The difference in capital investment for office workers, as opposed to investments to support farm and factory workers, is reflected quite directly in the relative productivity levels of the three groups.[9]

Thus the traditional office does not attain a high level of productivity, partly because of the limitations of the manager-secretary relationship, problems of secretarial idle time, the shortage of high-quality office personnel, and the lack of major investment in high technology and office equipment.

NEW OFFICE STRUCTURES

Today, the office function can be performed in any location within an organization. The purpose of an office is to process and communicate information effectively and efficiently. The traditional office structure does not often achieve that purpose.

However, automation alone will not make people more productive. New organizational and reporting structures within the office are necessary to provide proper incentives and attitudes to change work habits and update skills. Both management and support personnel require this change in thinking to accept new structures and procedures at all levels in the organization.

THE HUMAN FACTOR: A PRIORITY CONCERN

The impact of office automation on the behavior and attitudes of people is one of the most important aspects of implementing a new system, yet it is often overlooked. Management must address such questions as "How is office mechanization going to affect personnel attitudes, personnel selection, and personnel placement policies?" "Which organizational design or reporting structure is best suited for automation?" "What are appropriate job descriptions and what are the paths for promotion in the company?" "How are employees trained and prepared for the changed envi-

---

[9] Connell, "Office of the 80's."

ronment?" "How does working with the tools of the integrated office require changes in workstations, work hours, and the jobs themselves?"

The integrated office will be far more complex to manage than was the Computer Department when it was introduced more than 20 years ago, primarily because the integrated office affects far more people in the business environment. The electronic office also has a more direct effect on traditional reporting relationships, such as secretary to boss, and the resulting interdependency.

The new office environment requires an understanding of the changes in technology, office organizations, and the nature of office work itself. Therefore, there will be an increasing demand for people with the background and knowledge to make the transition from the traditional to the integrated electronic office. Career opportunities will be plentiful—not only in the office structure itself, but also in many other related businesses and professions.

The main ingredients of a strategy to address the human concerns of office automation are programs to

1. Involve and inform employees prior to the implementation of a new system.
2. Explain new policies, procedures, and organizational changes.
3. Train employees in equipment operation.
4. Set up a continuing program to monitor employee feedback.
5. Set up continuing communications about progress, performance, and changes.

SETTING THE GOALS

A careful and thorough study of information needs and flow is necessary to determine which equipment (from the great variety available) will most effectively meet an organization's needs. Increased productivity, personnel satisfaction, and other organizational goals in the electronic office can be achieved only by a managed approach that coordinates all the traditional secretarial and clerical functions of filing, typing, taking dictation, photocopying, making travel arrangements, and so on.

The truly integrated electronic office is not a destination, but a journey. An effective office information system always will be under development. The journey begins, of necessity, with changing job functions through the application of technology, but it should become based more and more upon the main purpose of the office: *to process and communicate information more effectively and efficiently.*

HISTORICAL EVOLUTION OF THE INTEGRATED ELECTRONIC OFFICE

Three distinct disciplines are converging to form the electronic office: office automation, electronic data processing, and communications. Office automation includes the process of automating the input and creation functions, such as dictating, typing or keyboarding; the processing and replicating functions, such as reproducing copies; filing; and the distribution functions. Data processing is the use of the computer for the storing, retrieving, sorting, merging, calculating, analyzing, and reporting of (generally) numerical data according to programmed instructions. Communications involves the transmission of information over telephone, telegraph, network, or satellite communication facilities.

In order to understand the total scope of the integrated electronic office, we must trace the evolution of these disciplines.

OFFICE AUTOMATION

The evolution of office automation can be traced best through the stages of development of typewriters and of dictation equipment.

Typing

The need to process words quickly led to a number of inventions for machine-based writing during the 1700s and the 1800s. The idea of a typewriter is believed to have been originated by Henry Mills, an English engineer to whom Queen Anne granted a patent for an early typewriter in 1714. Historians have also found references to writing machines invented in Switzerland, France, Austria, and Italy during the eighteenth century. Most of these models possessed a common fault: they were as slow as or slower than writing by hand. In 1853, the handwriting speed record was only 30 words per minute; in addition, handwriting was often difficult to read.

The first practical commercial device (using piano-style keys) was developed in 1867 by Christopher Sholes, Carlos Glidden, and W. W. Soule (see Figure 1). An improved version called a "typewriter" was patented in 1868. By 1873 the improved model was beginning to look like today's typewriter. It had a four-bank keyboard with letters and characters ar-

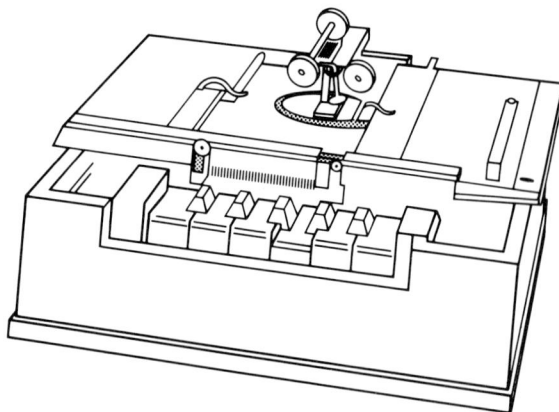

Figure 1 Artist sketch of the typewriter invented by Christopher Latham Sholes in 1868. Note the piano style keys and single element.

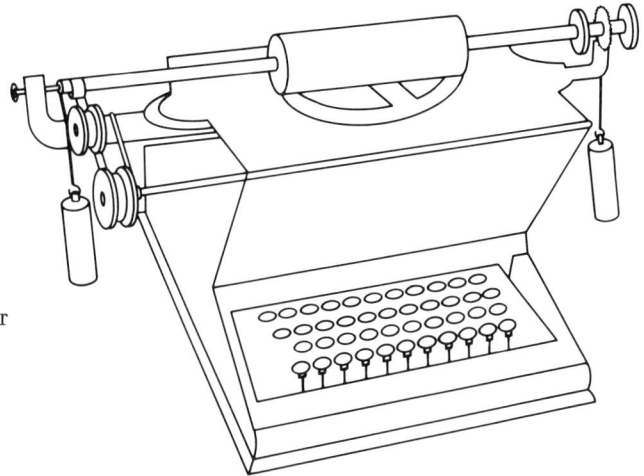

Figure 2 Artist sketch of Christopher Latham Sholes' "typewriter" sold to Remington in 1873. Note the standard keyboard.

ranged in what has ever since been called the standard keyboard (see Figure 2).

The advent of the typewriter opened new roles for women in business. In 1881, the New York City YWCA began teaching eight young women to type. Demand for the typing course graduates was high, and the revolution began. Those who were trained to operate typewriters were called "typewriters." Thousands of women, eager to gain employment, found skill as a typewriter provided a means of entry into the business world. (It is estimated that today two-thirds of all office and clerical jobs are held by women.) No doubt, part of the demand for women typewriters was their willingness to work for low wages—less than $20 per week. Wage levels for comparable work performed by male office workers continued to exceed those of female workers until the enactment in recent years of equal opportunity legislation (the Civil Rights Act of 1964 and The Equal Employment Opportunity Act of 1972).

Touch Typing. Today's 10-finger touch technique was introduced in 1881 but did not replace the "hunt-and-peck" method until 1888. In a speed contest, one contestant who used 10 fingers and had the keyboard memorized so that he could keep his eyes on the copy easily bested his opponents. Eventually, the public became convinced that touch typing was the most efficient method.

Dvorak Simplified Keyboard (DSK). Christopher Sholes' arrangement of the keyboard involved placing the most-used characters as far apart as possible in the type basket, in order to avoid clashing typebars. Except for a few changes, that original QWERTY (the left-hand top-row characters) arrangement has remained the standard keyboard for over 100 years. Critics claim that this keyboard overloads the commonly weaker left hand, overworks certain fingers, and underutilizes home-row stroking.

After many years of study and two grants from the Carnegie Corporation, August Dvorak introduced a new typewriter keyboard in 1932. His carefully researched improvements produced a keyboard that makes it possible for 70 percent of the work to be done on the home row and a majority of the stroking to be done by the stronger right hand; in addition, a better-balanced workload for the fingers helps avoid fatigue and errors.

Although tests have shown the Dvorak Simplified Keyboard (DSK) to be markedly superior to the standard keyboard, relatively few people are aware of its existence. There has been little support for its adoption as the new standard. Only a few manufacturers offer it as an option.

Electric Typewriters. Thomas Edison received a patent for an electric single-element printing wheel in 1872, and through the years a number of companies attempted unsuccessfully to combine electric power with typewriting. Finally, in 1935, IBM produced the first commercially successful electric office typewriter. Today, nearly all business typewriters are electric.

Automatic Typewriters. The first automatic typewriter was developed by the Hooven Company around 1917. In 1932 the American Automatic Typewriter Company produced its Auto-Typist using player-piano roll technology. The Hooven and Auto-Typist were the first machines widely used for repetitive letter writing. During the early 1940s, IBM developed an electric typewriter that used punched paper tape as a recording medium; although not used for text editing, it contained the practical elements for such application. Around 1944, the product was spun off to an independent company later purchased by the Friden Corporation. Friden is credited with making the first significant entry into the office strike-on composition market with its Justowriter.

The next major advancement in typewriters came in 1961, when IBM introduced the single-element Selectric typewriter. Selectrics differed from other existing typewriters in using a type ball (containing all characters) to type on the page. Striking a key causes the ball to rotate the selected character toward the page, then strike the ribbon to print the character. On the Selectric, the type ball moves across the page; on conventional typebar typewriters, the typewriter carriage moves the sheet after each typebar strikes the character (through the ribbon) onto the paper.

IBM also introduced the Selectric principles into its input/output terminals for computer systems. Other companies began to adopt the Selectric as a terminal for computer systems in the late 1960s and early 1970s.

IBM's experience with the Selectric next led to the development of automatic typewriters for general office use. In 1964, IBM introduced the MT/ST (Magnetic Tape Selectric Typewriter), which for the first time combined the electromechanical typewriter with a magnetic tape storage medium that stored keystrokes on the tape, and permitted operators to make corrections, erase and rewrite, and automatically type out a stored document at 175 words a minute. Magnetic tape recording gave impetus to development of stand-alone text editors, and through its use, changes in text could be made with new ease and flexibility. The introduction of the MT/ST in 1964 is generally regarded as marking the beginning of word processing (see Figure 3).

Figure 3   The first representative of magnetic word processing, the MTST and MTSC. (Courtesy of IBM Corporation)

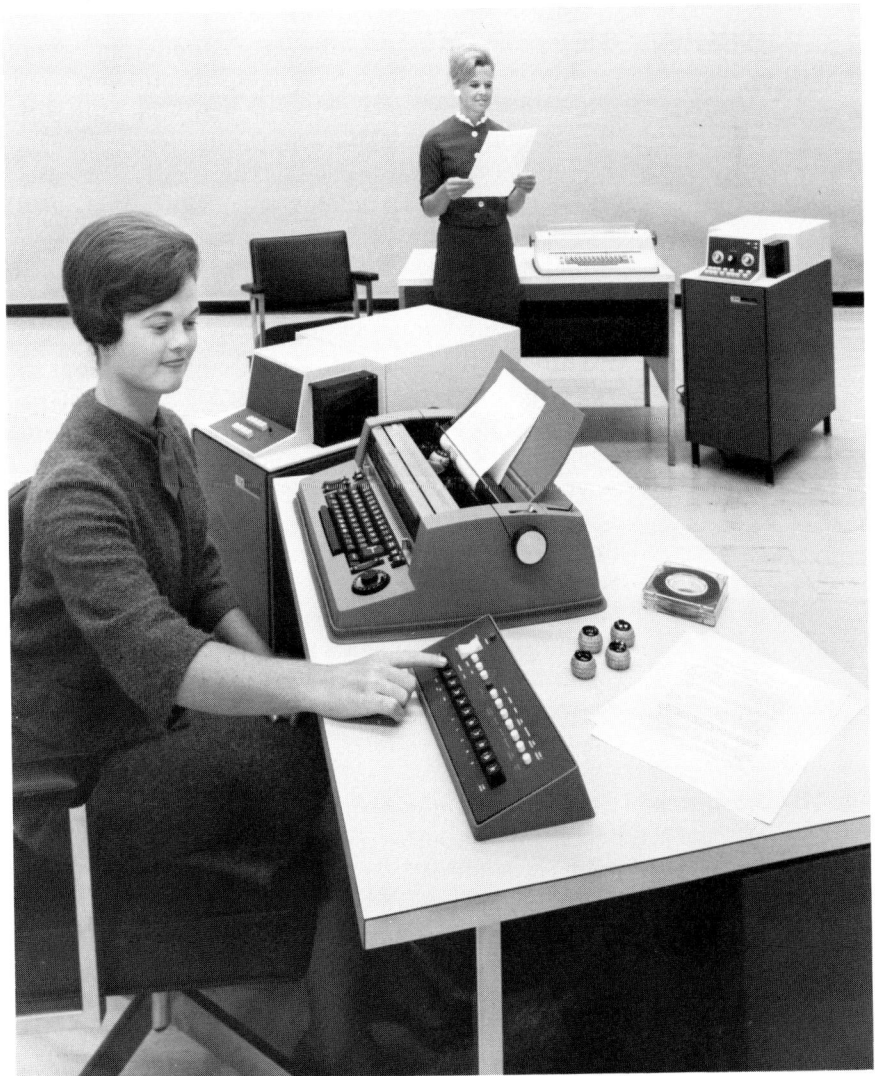

Since 1964, more advances and innovations in typewriters have taken place than in the 96 years since the Sholes machine was patented. Shortly after magnetic tape machines appeared, word processors using magnetic cards were introduced. The magnetic card stored the equivalent of a page of text and simplified the handling and finding of stored text, especially in the use of letters, memos, and short documents. Many of the developments resulted from the application of computer technology to word processing systems. Systems that have evolved since the MT/ST include stand-alone text editors, CRT text editors, shared/distributed logic typewriting systems, computerized text processing, floppy disc storage, and intelligent electronic typewriters. These systems will be discussed in detail in a later chapter.

Dictation Equipment   Modern dictating machines descended from earlier research by both Alexander Graham Bell and Thomas Edison, who were interested in developing equipment to record the sound of the human voice. Edison developed the commercial phonograph, the forerunner of the wax cylinder Ediphone, which was used by thousands of secretaries through the 1950s. In May 1886, Bell and two associates received a patent for a dictating machine that they called the Graphophone. Two years later the Volta Graphophone Company began production of the office dictating machine in Bridgeport, Connecticut. The company was later reorganized and by 1923 became known by its present name, the Dictaphone Corporation.

Through the years, dictating equipment has steadily improved. The voice quality was enhanced first by the use of plastic belts, then by the availability of transistorized machines, and finally by the introduction of magnetic recording media, such as standard cassettes, minicassettes, and microcassettes.

The use of magnetic tape offers convenience and cost advantages through fast-forward and fast-reverse features for easier revision as well as automatic erasing. Magnetic-tape cassettes have come into common use because of ease of handling and operation. It is believed that the most significant advancements made in dictation development are (1) cassettes, (2) miniaturization, (3) centralized dictation, and (4) management control devices. Various types of dictation systems will be discussed in greater detail in a later chapter.

The Computer   The historical development of business-oriented computers is generally described as a series of stages or generations. The first generation of computers (1946 to 1959) utilized vacuum tubes. The second generation (1956 to 1965) incorporated transistors. The third generation (1965 to 1970) is characterized by integrated circuits and solid-logic technology. The fourth generation (1970 to the present) has been more evolutionary than revolutionary and has incorporated not only improved technology but also increased use of software packages developed for specific purposes.

Further developments in computer technology paved the way toward its present role in office automation. Until the early seventies, the computer was primarily a number processor used for accounting tasks such as payroll, inventory, receivables, order invoicing, and so on. However, programs for text editing and manipulation, called computer word processing or text processing, now exist. To achieve a quality appearance similar to typewriting, manufacturers introduced special letter-quality printers or terminals in place of the all-capital printout of the regular high-speed printers (see Figure 4).

Computer word processing. IBM launched computer word processing in the early 1960s with the introduction of a text-editing system called Datatext. The system was designed to store characters in computer memory in order to retrieve them at a later time for editing on a video-display screen. The advantage of computer-based systems is their huge storage and manipulative capability. Moreover, such systems can automatically retype or print repetitive text such as form letters.

Around 1965 the firm introduced ATS (Administrative Terminal System), which utilized the large IBM 360 computer system. This was followed by the development of two programs: ATMS (Advanced Text Management System), for the operation of the advanced 370 computer system; and TERMTEXT/Format, a program that accepts text prepared on a termi-

Figure 4 Early example of computers with lowercase printers depicted by the IBM 1401 Data Processing System. (Courtesy of IBM Corporation)

nal system and composes it into fully made-up pages for output to a line printer or phototypesetter. In conjunction with ATMS, a STAIRS (Storage and Information Retrieval System) software program has been developed to enhance the necessary storage and retrieval functions related to the use of ATMS. These programs are used primarily by organizations with large in-house mainframe computers or by organizations utilizing service bureaus on a time-shared basis. Today, all major computer manufacturers offer some type of software package for text or word processing.

Since 1971 a number of minicomputer systems dedicated to word processing or offering word processing in conjunction with data processing have become available. In 1981, microcomputers based on microprocessor technology began to be used widely in business offices. For the first time, executives were not required to be data processing technicians in order to manage and operate their own computers. Lower prices made computers affordable. Simple operating instructions and prepackaged programs made turnkey computer systems possible. As users became more familiar with their systems, they looked for additional ways to utilize them. Soon most vendors offered programs that offered basic word processing capabilities (see Figure 5).

Figure 5 Companies such as Digital Equipment began offering computers with word processing capability. (Courtesy of Digital Equipment Corporation)

Computer technology is still advancing rapidly. Since 1976, most word processing systems have been based increasingly upon computer components (such as processors, memories, video displays, and high-speed printers). As a result, word processing has been merging with data processing and telecommunications. Eventually, the three will combine into one integrated function that will be called information processing—a term already being widely used.

Although the technology behind word and data processing is practically the same, the nature of work in the two environments is not. Substantial differences still exist between a data processing system and an office automation system. An office system is still many subsystems. Data processing is a far more disciplined environment than the office environment. The ability to handle the unexpected is something the office system must offer. Data processing is more likely to schedule the jobs to be done; that choice is not available in the office, and a manager of an office support function is not likely to say that his or her department is not prepared to handle an urgent job.

Tele-communications
The patent for a telegraph granted in England in 1837, Samuel Morse's patent for his telegraph in 1840, and the laying of the first transatlantic cable in 1858 laid the foundations for transmission of information by wire. Later, radio waves, microwaves, and similar processes would be used for high-speed data communication.

The next step was the worldwide proliferation of teletype and TWX. The next leap followed in 1957, when the first artificial earth satellite sent back information from space. Today, a cluster of satellites makes it possible to relay transmissions from one point to another. Satellites have reduced the costs of communications to a fraction of what they once were, because of the large volume of communications that satellites can handle at one time. Many offices today are already transmitting large amounts of information by teleprinters, teletypes, or facsimile machines; many also have their own private wires. In the office of tomorrow, much more is likely to be transmitted through various forms of electronic mail, because of the advantage of capturing the information at the point of origin. The advent of networks both internal (local area networks) and external (global networks) to the office marks a significant development in office communications and will be detailed in later chapters.

AUTOMATING AND INTEGRATING OTHER OFFICE FUNCTIONS

In addition to word processing systems, consideration must be given to how word processing in the automated office integrates other kinds of equipment. For example, OCR (Optical Character Reader) equipment (which can read printed or typed characters and then convert them into digital input to a data or word processor) is becoming a viable means for input to computer, word processing, and photocomposition operations. Photocomposition, when interfaced with word processing equipment, puts the word-processed material into type in preparation for printing, and eliminates the need to rekey the text again at the phototypesetting stage.

The increasing accumulation of paper stemming from the increasing volume of business transactions has led organizations to turn to microfilm to reduce their physical storage needs and increase their ability to retrieve those records quickly. Word processing may again be the key to converting today's information to microfilm. Keystrokes, recorded as digital impulses, can be converted to computer-compatible storage, and then to COM (computer output microfilm). The magnetic media storage can also be used as an economical preparation of COM: the normal printer output of a computer is reduced to one of several available microforms by a special output device that takes the place of the line printer.

Most of today's office functions are affected by keyboarding, usually through word processing. Information can now be captured on automatic typewriters and directly input into the total system for processing (see Figure 6).

MAJOR ELEMENTS OF THE ELECTRONIC OFFICE

The benefits to both management and staff are the main motivation for executives to investigate and adopt office automation. Technological developments necessarily bring about change. Economic justification is one main advantage to embracing change. Increased productivity is another. Other classic management benefits include savings in time and personnel and increased accuracy, quality, and throughput. Once these benefits have been defined, management must understand the role of equipment and be assured that change can be implemented with minimal disruption to normal business.

However, successful change depends on workers' acceptance and their willingness to modify work habits. Victor Hugo said, "Greater than the tread of mighty armies is an idea whose time has come." The electronic office is an idea whose time has come because it can be economically justified. Office automation offers the potential integration of office systems, including input/creating, processing/replication, distribution/communication, and storage and retrieval—all of which enhance the delivery of information to management—and is therefore economically effective.

A brief summary of the major elements of the electronic or automated office follows. In-depth discussion of these elements is presented in later chapters (see Figure 7).

Input

Input involves the creation of ideas and the placing of those ideas into an information flow cycle through dictation or OCR.

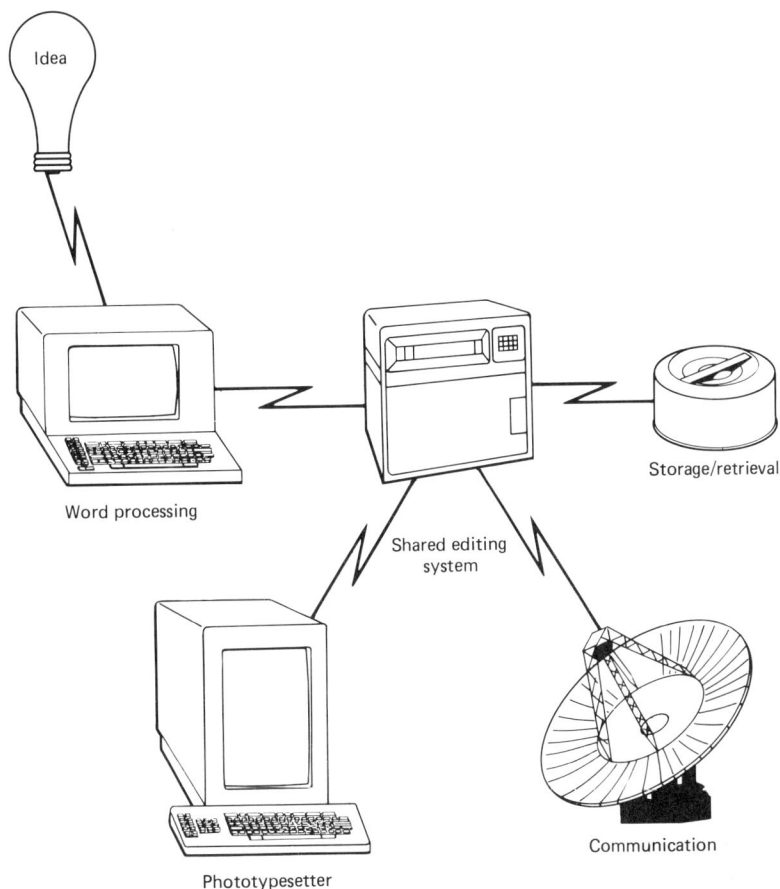

Figure 6 Information created, dictated to word processing, placed in a system for storage, retrieval, distribution, or communication to another technology for duplication, replication, or communication.

Processing   The processing part of electronic systems includes word processing or keyboarding, and the replication of that information in preparation for distribution.

Word Processing.   Word processing is a systems approach to document preparation involving the keyboarding or typing of correspondence, reports, statistical matter, and the like. Word processing is a system because it is made up of three interrelated and interdependent elements: skilled people, revised procedures, and automated equipment. When combined and managed effectively, word processing will increase the productivity and overall quality of typewritten communication. Word processing equipment captures typewritten keystrokes and records them in the form of digital impulses on magnetic media. Because these keystrokes, or im-

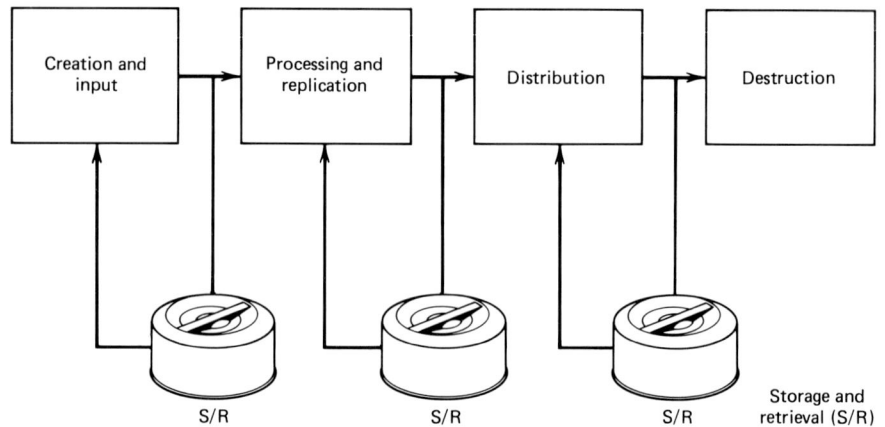

Figure 7 The flow of information in all systems requires the elements of creation and input, processing and replication, distribution, and/or destruction with the ability to store and retrieve at every point in the flow.

pulses, are captured at the point of origin and are available, word processing plays a key role in the integrated office. Once captured and verified, the information need not be rekeyed for subsequent processing and/or replication. Replication can take place through reprographics such as printing, phototypesetting, or duplicating, or through COM (computer output microfilm) and other forms of communications.

Replication Replication is the process of reproducing multiple copies by copying or duplicating, or by in-house printing equipment. Material for reproduction may be prepared in final form (camera-ready copy), or in keystrokes (when captured through word processing), which may be revised and reformatted and prepared for final printing through specialized phototypesetting equipment. "Intelligent" copiers can take digitally stored text and data, reformat it, set it in a program-selected type style, and then produce the required number of copies. This elimination of duplicate effort is an important key to labor savings.

Distribution Distribution includes the dissemination of information through electronic mail, telecommunications, fax, or telex, or through the network.

Storage and Retrieval The managing of business information stored on paper or on magnetic media involves the entire life cycle of records, including their creation, maintenance, and disposition. Word processing and records management are closely interrelated. Word processing is concerned with the preparation of documents. Records management is the systematic handling of these documents from creation to destruction. Once text is keyboarded, it does not necessarily have to be converted into human-readable records for distribution or storage purposes. The more advanced word processing systems provide fast and efficient indexing of documents as well as digital output to a computer and eventual output as COM (computer output microfilm).

Administrative Support

One of the organizational elements of the automated office is administrative support, which can be defined as the performing of tasks of a nontyping nature for management. The main function of the administrative support secretary is to take on more of the paperwork and quasiclerical duties currently handled by management, such as preparing travel and meeting arrangements. Administrative secretaries are also expected to work with the other components of the electronic office: for example, dictating to the word processing center, sending communications via telecommunication devices, working with the computer center to obtain information, and interpreting reports for management.

THE TOTAL SUPPORT PHILOSOPHY

A good office structure effectively and profitably supports management and enables management to meet its goals. A successful support system provides management with the best possible information upon which to make accurate and profitable business decisions. It employs the most cost-effective combination of hardware, software, and people to process information in a timely manner to make these necessary business decisions.

THE NEED FOR A SUPPORT SYSTEM

The complexity of the contemporary business world, the overabundance of paperwork, and the increasing documentation and recordkeeping required to meet the needs of today's society demand that better ways be found to meet organizational objectives. Interestingly, while businesses are striving to meet these informational demands, society is also recognizing the need for the individual worker's growth and development. Management is seeking a way to accommodate both areas of concern—which will, without doubt, benefit both management and employees.

Any attempt to meet the ever-changing information needs of management and staff in an unstructured office support environment will be neither effective nor acceptable. It is now necessary to structure the office function in order to assure the required support and provide the information that is necessary for management to meet its goals. This calls for the development of the total support approach.

As a concept, the total support system considers that all functions formerly considered separate are in fact interrelated: typing, nontyping (such as filing, handling mail and telephones, researching information), reprographics, records management, data processing, and communications. The term support system describes a planned structure for integrating all the services into a support staff under centralized supervision and control. The support structure provides avenues for total communication among the support-staff personnel through regularly scheduled meetings using a team approach. The administrative-secretarial personnel, the word processing staff, and the records management, reprographics, and communications employees, as well as all those in other activities of a service-support nature, first meet as individual teams and then together to discuss problems, make suggestions for procedural improvements, and plan in advance for timely completion of proposed projects.

To date, white collar employees have comprised the only occupational group to escape meaningful analysis, efficiency, and cost-reduction methods. There is, however, proof that secretaries and clerks are manageable and measurable resources. Programs have been designed to evaluate job performance and provide a basis for recommendations to improve support-staff efficiency.

At the same time, management now recognizes that many office employees must create and manipulate the same information and data base throughout the organization. For example, secretaries may type individualized form letters to large groups of customers whose names and addresses are already stored in the computer. The parallel or duplicated use of the same information elsewhere in the organization requires coordination and integration of the various functions.

WORK SPECIALIZATION

Historically, work specialization seemed to belong in the more structured environment of manufacturing and industrial organizations. Management traditionally has not applied work specialization techniques in the office, because the office functions were performed as needed, without much supervision, and at a low cost.

Increased office costs, the need to use similar data for a variety of tasks, and the need for carefully defined career progressions make work specialization a necessity. The total support philosophy provides a framework for bringing work specialization into the office.

Work specialization can be defined as the assignment of a limited number of specific activities to people with the appropriate level of competency. For example, under the total support approach, duties such as routine filing, running errands, photocopying and collating reports, opening mail, bursting data processing reports or computer printouts, routine telephone backup, and so on, would be assigned to an entry-level trainee as clerical support functions.

The next level of administrative duties of a nontyping nature would be handled by administrative secretaries—for example, screening telephone calls, maintaining calendars and schedules, reading mail and preparing routine correspondence, researching data for reports, and so on.

Duties of a typing nature, such as formatting, proofreading, composing, typing, and so on, would be assigned to a word processing specialist. An even more advanced specialization mode would be the coordinating function of the next highest career level: developing standards, coordinating workflow, preparing productivity reports, training, and so on.

Work specialization creates a greater concentration of work in fewer jobs, thus developing specialists. For example, an upper Midwest corporate office of a store chain implemented the total support approach (with administrative support, word processing, a service center with clerical support, and a project center). The administrative secretaries perform nontyping secretarial assignments, such as maintaining personnel files, handling vendors, departmental filing, screening telephone calls, and dealing with the public, as well as providing more direct assistance to managers. The word processing specialists perform all typing requirements for the company, including letters, reports, ad preparations, and forms. The clerical-project specialists burst computer reports, summarize monthly telephone reports from other locations, handle all project mailings, and are involved in projects that occur periodically and are time-consuming. The support service center handles all location mailing, microfilming, mail delivery, and building maintenance. The net result: specialization permitted the same number of support personnel to serve a managerial staff 38 percent larger than before.

Job specialization requires that titles be related to job duties and responsibilities. For example, a vice-president of marketing would be responsible for all marketing functions. However, the specialized activities of advertising and sales, which would fall within the scope of marketing, would need to be managed by specialists in these areas with such titles as advertising director and sales manager. The same logic applies to finance, administration, and the other functions of the organization. A vice-president of administration would be responsible for all of the administrative activities of an organization; however, highly trained individuals are necessary to manage such specialized areas as administrative support, word processing, and telecommunications. These people would have such titles as manager of administrative support, word processing manager, and telecommunications manager.

TEAM EFFORT   All individuals need to work together in a team effort at each level in an organization. All team members must not only take responsibility for their areas, but also must actively communicate and coordinate their jobs with all related functions in other areas, to meet the objectives of the organization. A total support system attempts to bring the elements of office service closer together.

Businesses can succumb to the glamour of the new technology without thoroughly analyzing the needed changes in office procedures and structure, as well as the effects on personnel. At the same time, meeting the challenges of change requires an open-minded approach to a different way of administering the office environment.

This open-minded approach to new systems requires a commitment by management to different procedures, structures, and methods of working. For example, a Midwest law firm has converted from the traditional office structure of assigning one secretary to one or two attorneys to assigning support teams to specialized areas of law. This change required the firm's management committee to implement working groups of teams of lawyers working with teams of secretaries. The word processors previously at each secretarial workstation were replaced with electric typewriters, and all document typing was assigned to the word processing centers located on each floor of the office.

The support structure now consists of specialized teams of paralegals, administrative legal secretaries, word processing secretaries, and runners (or clerical support). Several qualified secretaries became paralegals. The resultant savings amounted to approximately $100,000 per year. Career progressions have been clearly defined, and employee turnover has been substantially reduced.

BENEFITS OF THE TOTAL SUPPORT APPROACH

When management implements new systems and work habits, it expects a better level of service. The total support approach provides many of these benefits.

Better Work Distribution
Supervising day-to-day activities in the total support structure results in more even work distribution and less idle time than supervision over the traditional one-to-one structures. Moreover, when working teams assume responsibility, management is assured of more constant support—even when illness and vacation periods occur. Because of better distribution of work in a team mode, the total number of secretaries may often be reduced, with resulting cost-reduction benefits.

The flexibility of the team approach is a distinct business advantage. For instance, managers who under the old structure were forced to hold work while their secretaries were sick or on vacation can now give the work to another cross-trained secretary. Support for management is always available with a team. Likewise, if a large project must be completed by a certain deadline, several members of a support team can work together to relieve the stress and pressure that traditionally would have fallen on one secretary.

Through better distribution of work and better utilization of time, more work, as well as work of a new and different nature, may be absorbed. As a result, management will have better information for decision making and more time to perform its proper functions.

MORE OBJECTIVE PERFORMANCE RATING Within a support environment, secretaries are evaluated on their own performance by a support supervisor rather than by executives they support. Their work is objectively judged by supervisors who know and understand the difficulty of the work and the conditions under which it is performed.

CAREER PATHS Work specialization can provide office personnel with visible career progressions. For example, employees can see the different job levels, in such areas as clerical support, administrative support, and supervisory roles, to which they might aspire. These visible career opportunities often provide job satisfaction and incentive for secretarial and clerical personnel who otherwise would have considered that their positions had no future.

An array of new jobs has opened up as a result of word processing: word processing operators or specialists, word processing supervisors and managers, systems analysts and designers, and word processing training specialists.

COORDINATED BUYING The total support approach also may bring about cost savings through improved control of equipment purchases. Typewriters, dictation equipment, and photocopiers are often purchased as a result of a secretary's perceived need, not as a result of a studied organizational requirement. The manager of the support function should be the point of control. When individual executives have authority to buy equipment, the role of the support supervisor is limited: this situation sometimes results in equipment purchases that do not fit the overall information needs of the organization. The total support approach, through overall office planning and control, ensures better utilization of equipment and may ultimately save an organization thousands of dollars.

IMPROVED JOB DESCRIPTIONS An important part of the managed approach is the writing of detailed job descriptions and desk procedures. Better job descriptions aid in hiring people with the right qualifications to fulfill organizational needs. Desk procedures serve as both training tools and guidelines for backup either by other members of a team or by temporary help. Whenever work continues smoothly under circumstances of change and uncertainty, productivity is improved and overhead costs reduced. Every dollar saved, whether because of an overhead cost reduction or because of time savings, adds directly to net profit.

PROFESSIONAL DEVELOPMENT Both management and staff can achieve greater personal fulfillment through performing new and challenging tasks rather than traditional routine work. All employees are provided with opportunities for ongoing professional development and growth. As they develop and take on more responsibilities, they become likely candidates for career progression opportunities.

DOLLAR SAVINGS   White-collar automation has largely been aimed at secretaries and typists—the largest single group of white collar workers. Dataquest Authoritative Research has projected that by 1986 there will be one word processor or electronic typewriter for each secretary/typist in the United States. The continuing payoff will come with improved productivity of professional workers. These savings will be detailed in a later chapter.

PART TWO

OFFICE AUTOMATION— WHAT IS IT?

CHAPTER 2

CAREER OPPORTUNITIES

OBJECTIVES

In this chapter you will learn about
1. The various career opportunities within the electronic office.
2. Career paths and some specific career opportunities.
3. Associations that offer educational and professional information.
4. Model support staff organizational plans for career options.
5. Sample career patterns for the total support approach and related fields.

Today's rapidly changing world requires that people change the way they regard their careers. Traditionally the mode has been one of periodic adjustments. Now, however, planning for contemporary change is necessary. Within the past few decades, the rapid rate of social and technical developments has propelled present-day society through several lifetimes of change in a single generation. Those born in the Industrial Age have lived to witness the Space Age, the Technological Age, and are now entering an electronic era that is introducing a highly automated society.

Adjusting to this rapid progression poses a challenge, especially when it involves exploring job alternatives and career planning. In the past, the office occupations often provided little or no planned career progression. One simply took events as they happened and made the best of the situation.

OFFICE CAREER OPPORTUNITIES

With the broadening scope of office activities in the automated environment, more opportunities for career options are opening.

Also, career opportunities in the fields that support the office are increasing: for example, sales representatives of the new technology and those who sell the services and supplies that support these new products, environmental designers who adapt the traditional office to the electronic office, educators who teach future and present employees the new approach to conducting business, and consultants to the office automation industry. Some of these career opportunities are illustrated in Figure 1. Many new careers will be discussed in detail in later chapters.

Administrative Management	*Manufacturing*	*Professional*
Management information System (MIS) executives	Vendor executives	Consultants in
Human resources personnel	Marketing managers	Space design
Administrative managers	Marketing support representatives	Equipment
Training directors	Systems engineers	Training
Office services	Customer field engineers	Procedures
Supervisors	Sales representatives	Personnel
Systems analysts		
Support coordinators		Educators
Word processing analysts		
Data entry specialists		
Information specialists		
Communications specialists		

Figure 1   Integrated electronic office career opportunities. Numerous career opportunities are available in the office automation industry.

The opportunities and challenges are endless, and one must recognize that electronics and technology are now a part of life. There is no turning back; indeed, people's lives and careers can be greatly enhanced by the new information age.

The changes in the office will be pervasive and profound. Technology is creating a new information age that will change forever the way an office operates and the way information is handled. High technology is indeed proliferating in the office environment. From the typing team to the executive suite, keyboards, video screens, satellite communications, traditional telephone lines, and computers are being integrated into an electronic environment.

EMPLOYEE REQUIREMENTS

This environment requires employees to be knowledgeable not only about technology but also about applying to operations principles of information processing and communications. People with these skills are essential to the implementation of a total support system. One must be able to analyze problems and devise solutions that end users can understand and that meet users' needs. This requires another ability: to communicate with others and to involve them in the planning process.

Interpersonal communication skills are important whether one chooses to participate in the design and implementation of a totally integrated electronic office; to market products, supplies, or services connected with the electronic office; or to educate, train, and assist others involved in the implementation process.

To explore opportunities, careers, and progression patterns in the office and its many related fields, we must review some traditional thinking related to office jobs to gain a perspective about the opportunities available.

EMPLOYEE ATTITUDES

Manpower consultant Roy Walters, head of a New Jersey management firm, lists the following as the 10 most boring jobs:

1. Assembly line worker.
2. Elevator operator in push-button elevator.
3. Typist in office typing pool.
4. Bank guard.
5. Copying machine operator.
6. Keypunch operator.
7. Highway toll collector.
8. Car watcher in tunnel.
9. File clerk.
10. Housewife.

When interviewers from *U.S. News and World Report*[1] spoke to workers in seven of these occupations, not a single one found his or her job boring or monotonous. Factors that people consider important in their careers vary widely. It is important for a smoothly operating office that management select and hire individuals who not only have an aptitude for the jobs, but also consider the work enjoyable and rewarding.

People often have misconceptions about certain jobs because of their own misunderstandings or the prejudicial opinions of others. Often those who actually work in the jobs have entirely different attitudes. One misconception concerns the jobs of word processing specialists. Their work has been described as dull and boring, yet recent research has shown many word processing specialists believe just the opposite. Note that 67 percent of each group in Figure 2 indicated that what they liked best in their jobs was the variety of work.

EMPLOYMENT "LIKES" CITED BY WORD PROCESSING SPECIALISTS AND ADMINISTRATIVE SUPPORT SECRETARIES*

Word Processing Operators/Correspondence Secretaries	
Variety of work	67%
Machine capability and efficiency	57%
Fellow employees in the center	51%
Opportunity to control work environment	44%
Status of working in a center	27%
Compensation program	20%
Administrative Support Secretaries	
Variety of work	67%
Machine capability	6%
Fellow employees in center	64%
Status of working in a center	28%
Opportunity to control work environment	55%
Compensation program	15%
Enjoy challenge	14%

* Write-in responses.

Figure 2 Employment "likes" cited by word processing specialists and administrative support secretaries. Source: Jolene D. Scriven, Jeanne L. Holley, Kathleen P. Wagoner, Richard D. Brown, *National Study of Word Processing Installations in Selected Business Organizations*, Delta Pi Epsilon, Inc., St. Peter, Minnesota, 1981, pp. 128 & 238. (Courtesy of Delta Pi Epsilon)

[1] "Those Boring Jobs—Not All That Dull," *U.S. News and World Report*, December 1, 1975, pp. 64–65.

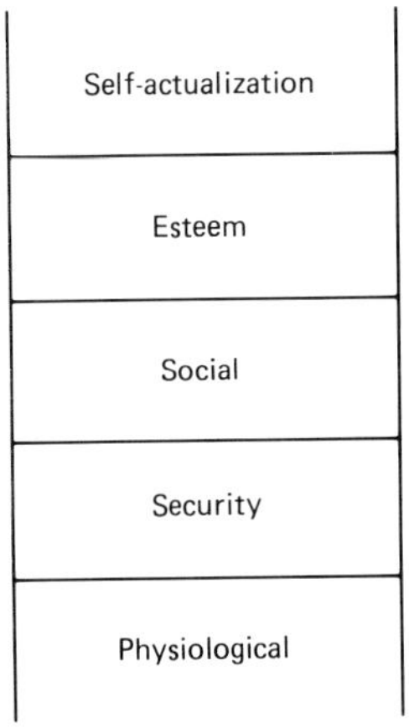

| Self-actualization |
| Esteem |
| Social |
| Security |
| Physiological |

Figure 3 Maslow's hierarchy of needs. More emphasis in the automated office is being placed on job satisfaction and meeting human needs.

EMPLOYEE NEEDS

Many of the other likes or satisfiers relate to much of what is known about human needs. Abraham Maslow identified a hierarchy or ladder of needs and theorized that people can attempt to satisfy a higher-level need only after satisfying at least some of the needs on the lower levels (see Figure 3).

Once a need is fulfilled, individuals often move to the next higher-level need to be motivated. Also, personal circumstances cause individuals to move up and down in the hierarchy. For example, upon the birth of a child, an employee is likely to become more concerned with security and less concerned with self-fulfillment.

Recent studies show that job satisfaction can control how long people live, how healthy they are, and whether they feel happy with their lives. A major life insurance company states that living to a healthy old age is often determined by the amount of job satisfaction and the recognition received from others for accomplishments.

CAREER AND LIFE PLANNING

Identifying what it is one wants to do, not only for the present but also for some steps beyond that, is life planning. Each person is in command of his or her career—career and life planning and control of one's destiny are the individual's responsibility.

Career and life planning is something most people are going to have to do extensively, according to Richard Nelson Bolles, author of the renowned *A Practical Manual for Job Hunters and Career Changes: What Color Is Your Parachute?* The point is that rather than allowing themselves to drift, people should be self-managers in terms of career choices and career changes.

Some people may not be aware of what they want from their lives; however, when a person decides to work for the better part of a lifetime—

and a variety of circumstances causes most individuals to do so—planning must be a part of a person's life goals. The forces that cause an individual to choose a career may vary. For example, those forces may be economic, because of the need for money; societal, because of the need for status; or psychological, because of the need to be wanted or to be busy. Individuals should do as much planning as possible, taking into consideration their needs and the facts that should influence their decisions.

With appropriate planning, a career path with steady advancement goals can be achieved. People have a better chance to achieve their personal goals if they understand the goals of the organization in addition to their own job goals, if they acquire a relevant education, and if they remain open-minded about accepting changes.

Education for a career is a requirement. The importance of education as preparation for a career in the office is emphasized by the dramatic increase in the use of computers and automated business machines. The demand for unskilled labor is continually decreasing. The Bureau of Labor Statistics predicts that more than 80 percent of today's office jobs will require technical specialization and a high skill level.

Those trained and educated in occupational skills have an advantage in the job market. A survey conducted during the recession of 1975, examining unemployment in relation to the level of an individual's formal education, indicated that the jobless rate for high school dropouts was 15.2 percent; for high school graduates, 9.1 percent; for those with some college training, 6.9 percent; and for college graduates, 2.9 percent. These figures suggest that the demand for college graduates can be expected to grow at three times the rate of the demand for all workers in the American labor force.[2]

To select a goal on which to focus career and life planning, it is necessary first to decide what role one wishes to pursue in the office of today and tomorrow. The electronic office is here to stay, and it is critical to approach that entity in an open-minded manner in order to maintain the flexibility to work within this new environment at all stages of its development. One out of every five people works in an office, so the likelihood of an office career is great for many people. Office workers represent 50 percent of the total growth in white-collar workers. The office and all its related support areas offer one of the greatest growth areas and potentials ever known.

International Data Corporation projects that a total of $1 trillion will be spent between 1982 and 1987 for information processing equipment. These survey results indicate that, even in the face of recession, the areas surrounding the electronic office will provide expanded opportunities for office jobs, for service, and for sales of technology produced.

---

[2] Estelle L. Popham and Blanche Ettinger, *Opportunities in Office Education*, (Louisville, Ky.: Data Courier, Inc., 1976), p. xiv.

CAREER OPTIONS WITHIN THE OFFICE

Opportunities for people with the right skills and understandings abound within the office in such specialized areas as word processing, administrative support, records management, office services, data processing, and telecommunications. As previously mentioned, opportunities also exist in related fields such as the selling of equipment, supplies, or related services; serving as consultants for office activities; designing office space and workstations; and educating and providing training.

Several charts of job titles and career progressions in the integrated office are illustrated in this chapter. People who pursue any type of career in the integrated office must possess flexibility, responsiveness, adaptability, and a service orientation.

WORD PROCESSING

Word processing is an excellent starting position for office careers, offering valuable training for people at the entry level, and exceptional advancement potential for those who gain experience. The demand nationwide for skilled operators has accelerated rapidly. This growth may be seen clearly in the data gathered by the Association of Information Systems Professionals (formerly known as International Information/Word Processing Association) in its annual salary survey. In 1974, there were 4714 employees included in nine word processing positions; in 1977, 10,715 word processing employees; and in 1982, 20,637 employees in 15 information/word processing positions.

Typically those who build a career in word processing start at the entry level, with keyboarding, and progress to positions such as coordinators and supervisors. Other job opportunities include

1. Word processing manager—manages, budgets, and controls word processing operations.
2. Word processing supervisor—supervises work flow, evaluates the word processing staff, and establishes procedures for ongoing operations.
3. Word processing coordinator—coordinates work flow on a daily basis, determines priorities, and monitors work distribution in an equitable manner.
4. Proofreader—ensures the accurate production of typewritten documents within the word processing center.
5. Word processing specialist—types and produces dictated work and assignments submitted in longhand, hard (printed) copy, and in other forms.
6. Word processing operator/trainee—performs work of an entry-level nature in the word processing environment.

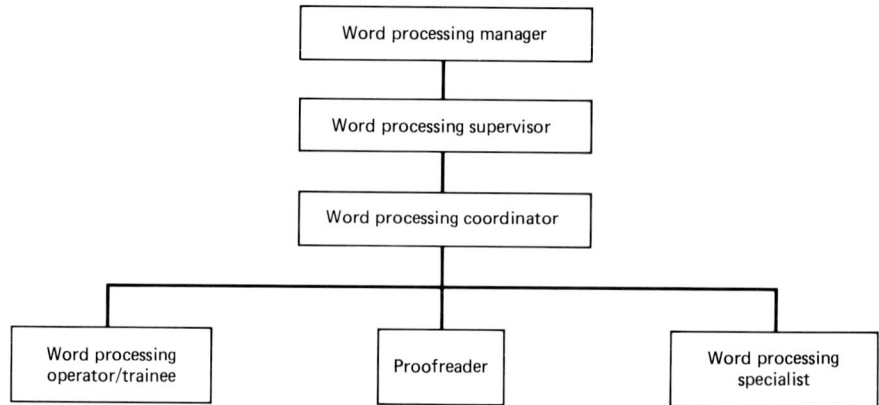

Figure 4 Word processing organizational structure. Note the options for upward mobility providing the opportunity for career planning.

Traits and characteristics desirable in those individuals pursuing a career in word processing are flexible thinking, technical orientation, team consciousness, curiosity, persistence, carefulness, verbal and grammatical skills, audio acuity for transcription, and enjoyment of working with machines. Figure 4 shows a word processing organizational structure with job titles and career progressions.

ADMINISTRATIVE SUPPORT

Administrative support generally includes most of the nontyping functions previously performed by the traditional secretary. However, as the office evolves and equipment prices fall, electronic workstations for the administrative secretary are likely to proliferate, with terminals performing the traditional functions via a computerized network. Within the administrative support function are a variety of career opportunities, such as

1. Manager, secretarial services—assumes total responsibility for the managing of activities of word processing and administrative secretaries.
2. Manager, administrative support—assumes full responsibility for all administrative support activities, including administrative secretaries and support clerks; coordinates their activities with company goals; and provides training programs and procedures.
3. Supervisor, administrative support—schedules and maintains work load distribution among the staff, providing liaison with the users of the system; implements procedures and enhancements to the system.
4. Senior administrative secretary—supports management and functions as a group leader; makes day-to-day decisions for the principals he or she supports; composes and edits created work.
5. Administrative secretary—composes from instructions; dictates composed material; edits materials prepared by word processing special-

```
┌─────────────────────────────────┐
│     Secretarial services manager │
└─────────────────────────────────┘
                │
┌─────────────────────────────────┐
│   Administrative support manager │
└─────────────────────────────────┘
                │
┌─────────────────────────────────┐
│ Administrative support supervisor│
└─────────────────────────────────┘
                │
┌─────────────────────────────────┐
│   Senior administrative secretary│
└─────────────────────────────────┘
                │
┌─────────────────────────────────┐
│       Administrative secretary   │
└─────────────────────────────────┘
                │
┌─────────────────────────────────┐
│ Associate administrative secretary│
└─────────────────────────────────┘
```

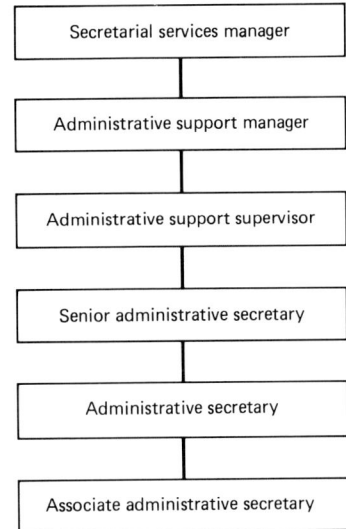

Figure 5 Administrative support structure. Career progression as illustrated provides motivation for longer term employment.

ists; handles the mail, telephone, and filing; operates on established guidelines with minimal day-to-day direction.

6. Associate administrative secretary (entry-level position)—handles routine functions of the office, such as opening mail, answering telephones, and filing; operates on established guidelines under the daily supervision of a more experienced person.

Traits and characteristics desirable in individuals selecting administrative support as a career are adaptability, communicativeness, organization, and initiative. Figure 5 shows an administrative support organizational structure with job titles and career progressions.

RECORDS MANAGEMENT Records management has become a diversified and technically specialized field. The automated office has caused a specific differentiation among the three major areas of records management: (1) filing and micrographics, (2) archiving, and (3) destruction of records. The application of technology to filing and micrographics is requiring higher technical skill levels than in the past. It also opens up additional job opportunities. A brief list of job opportunities in records management includes

1. Record's manager—supervises and trains personnel in the maintenance of central files, supervises work of employees and evaluates performance, improves personnel relations in the records management department.

2. Records coordinator—coordinates with corporate records management staff the various facets of the records management program.

3. Records supervisor—supervises the records center clerks and staff, as-

sumes responsibility for records protection and security, evaluates records staff performance.

4. Records clerk/trainee—operates daily under the close supervision of a trainer or supervisor and performs simple sort, file, and retrieve functions.

Filing is the process of arranging and storing materials according to some definite plan for immediate access and for permanence, with the activity performed as a part of a daily routine. Most filing jobs are clerical in nature and provide the following career opportunities:

1. Specialized file clerk—performs the following duties:
   Correspondence—maintains a file of general correspondence, sorts and files, answers inquiries about correspondence, maintains a followup file, labels files, retrieves correspondence.
   Sorting—handles notices of change, distributes change to unit clerks, alphabetizes information on new accounts, sorts outgoing communications.
   Unit—maintains an alphabetical unit of customer cards, answers inquiries, processes reports, checks file for titles, removes cards in accordance with retention procedures.
   Coding—codes information obtained from reports.
   Records—receives company records and examines them for contents and categorization.
   Senior file clerk—sorts, codes, and files unclassified material by subject headings or partly classified material by finer subheadings.
2. Junior file clerk—performs filing of material already classified by a senior clerk, works closely with records management staff.

Micrographics describes the process of recording information in a micro form through microfilming. Sometimes the process is used to reproduce hard copy in a microform; other times the process is used to produce information directly from a computer, as with COM (computer output microfilm). A brief list of micrographics jobs follows:

1. Micrographics supervisor—supervises micrographics technicians and works closely with records management staff.
2. Micrographics technician (entry-level position)—operates micrographics technology in the preparation of microforms under close supervision of a unit head.
3. Archivist—preserves the archives established to preserve records for the benefit of the scholar and of posterity. Archivists often are involved in appraisal, or evaluation of worth, and are concerned with the arrangement and care of the archives.

Traits and characteristics desirable in individuals selecting records management as a career are that they be good team members and be detail-

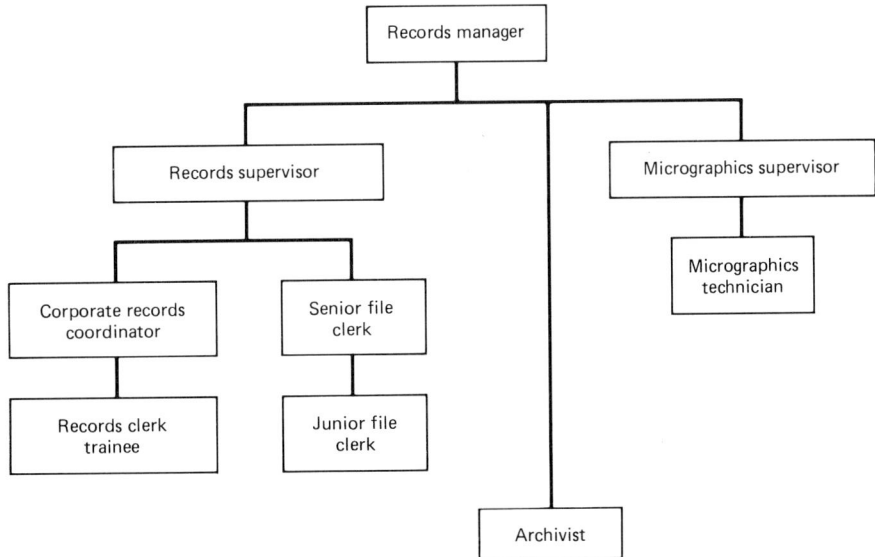

Figure 6 Records management organizational structure. Note the variety of jobs available with the introduction of automation to records management.

minded, logical, systematic, and security conscious. Figure 6 shows a records management organizational structure with job titles and career progressions.

OFFICE SERVICES Job opportunities in office services have evolved over the past decade into a separate area with specific positions. Since the advent of work specialization within the office, activities historically unattended have been identified, and objectives for those activities have been clearly defined. Because of the need for improved productivity and control of overhead, these office services activities are gaining the attention of management and becoming managed. This management process has brought on additional budgeting, controlling, and reporting of ongoing activities, as well as more paperwork. Part of the process is the establishment of supervisory roles for the following areas:

1. Building maintenance supervisor—assumes total responsibility for the supervision of maintenance staff, including cleaning staff, electricians, and building maintenance personnel.
2. Fleet maintenance coordinator—assumes responsibility for the maintenance of company cars, trucks, and other vehicles used by the management and professional staff.
3. Travel services supervisor—supervises the staff responsible for trans-

portation and hotel reservations; controls priorities, and coordinates day-to-day demands.

In a large organization, additional positions might include

1. Travel services reservationist—makes reservations, either by computer terminal or telephone, for rental cars, airplane transportation, and hotel accommodations, utilizing established procedures as directed by a supervisor.

2. Travel services clerk (entry-level position)—delivers tickets, car keys, and communications related to the travel services area; sometimes acts as a receptionist for this department.

3. Food services supervisor—supervises the staff responsible for maintaining the cafeteria services in an organization and may serve coffee and other refreshments throughout the organization twice daily; has responsibility for budgeting, controlling, and training new employees in this department.

4. Security supervisor—assumes total responsibility for coordinating the scheduling of security guards, establishing training, and developing security procedures.

The number of organizations with their own in-house printing centers has been expanding greatly. Consequently, new positions for knowledgeable managers to not only supervise day-to-day operations but also coordinate the entire reprographics process with other aspects of office automation are developing. Such individuals must give attention to detail yet be concerned with quality and artistic appearance of their products.

Traits and characteristics desirable in office services personnel are that they be dependable, service-oriented, open-minded, responsive, and adaptable. Figure 7 shows an office services organizational structure, with job titles and career progressions. Figure 8 shows the actual office services organizational structure of a major insurance corporation, with representative departments reporting to office services.

DATA PROCESSING
Career opportunities continue to increase in data processing. However, within the integrated electronic office, employees will be working daily in the processing of information and communicating with other support systems. In the past, data processing has sometimes been a separate function reporting directly to executive management. Of ever-increasing importance will be the convergence of the data processing and word processing functions with telecommunications. Systems analysis and systems programming will require a broader understanding of all types of office automation.

Traits and characteristics of persons pursuing a data processing career are responsiveness, flexibility, practicality, systematic, and logic. Figure 9

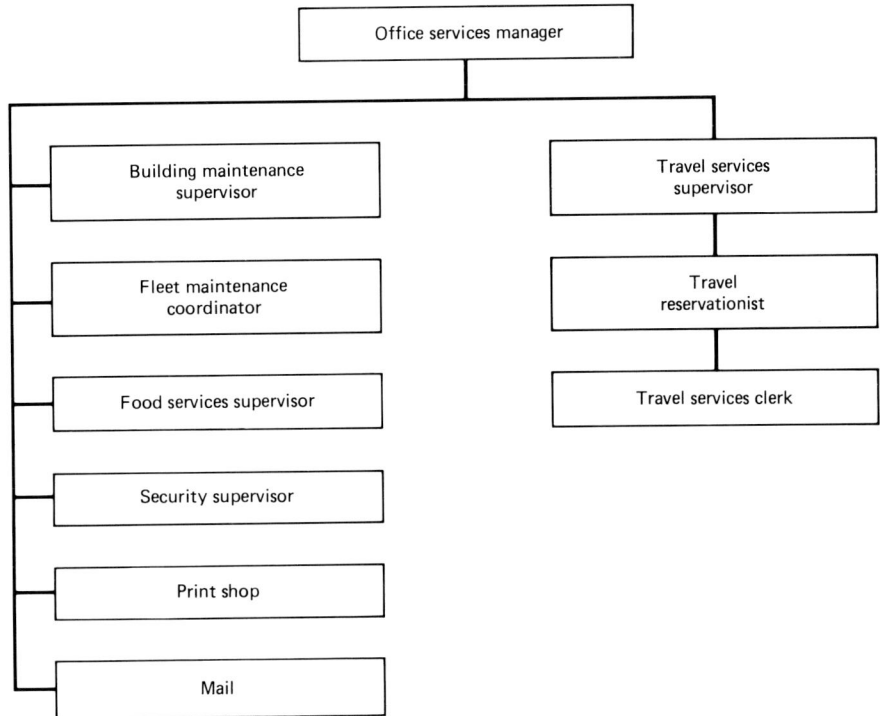

Figure 7 Office services organizational structure. Note the wide assortment of service functions represented.

shows a data processing organizational structure, with job titles and career progressions.

TELE-COMMUNICATIONS The field of telecommunications offers great opportunities, because communications technology will integrate the electronic office. The demand for knowledgeable, highly trained technical experts will continue to increase. Career opportunities will cover a variety of jobs

1. Telecommunications manager—assumes total responsibility for the management of the staff who plan, install, maintain, and create networks of communications and monitor the transmission lines for the communication functions of an organization.
2. Electronic mail supervisor—assumes the responsibility for supervising the day-to-day operation of the electronic mail system, which includes teletype, telex, TWX, facsimile; and coordinates these activities and word processing and data processing.
3. Technician—works with specific procedures within the various units

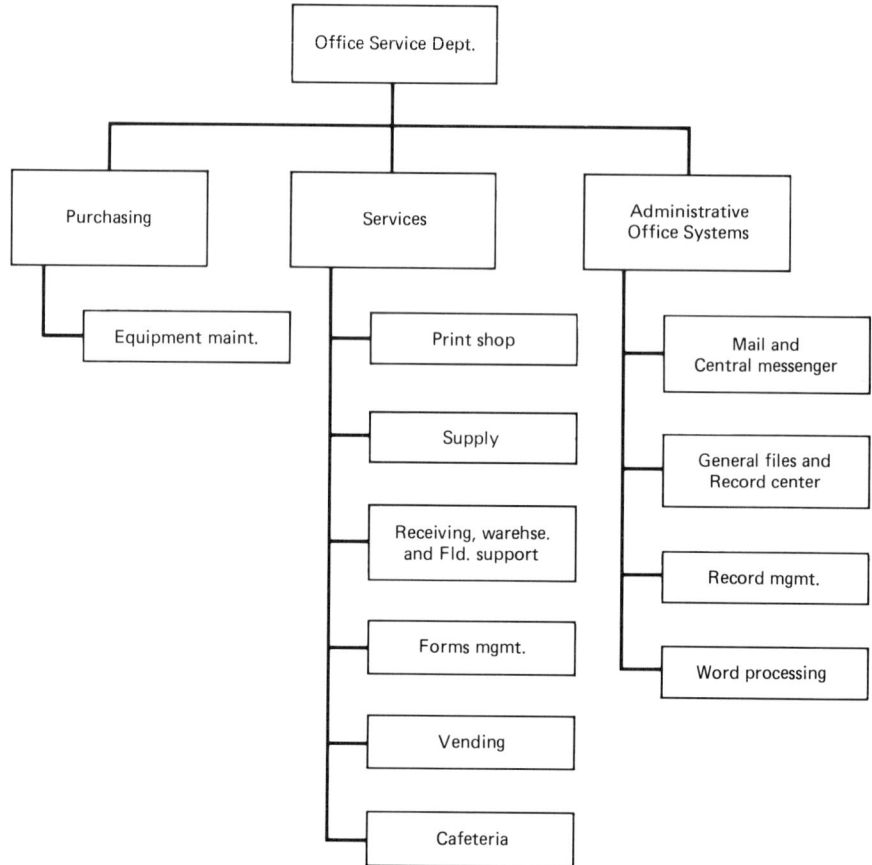

Figure 8 Office services structure of a major insurance corporation.

of telecommunications under supervision. Control clerk/trainee (entry-level position)—performs functions as directed by other staff members.

Perhaps the most important characteristics in telecommunications personnel are their abilities to solve problems and make decisions. They should also be technically oriented, creative, and detail-minded. Figure 10 shows a representative telecommunications organizational structure, with job titles and career progressions.

Within the areas of word processing, administrative support, records management, office services, data processing, and telecommunications, there will be an ongoing need for analysts. In small organizations, managers and supervisors will often perform the analysis function. In large organizations, specialized analyst positions offer career opportunities.

Data processing

Systems analysis	Computer operations	Systems programming
Systems manager	Operations manager	Programming manager
Senior analyst	Senior operator	Senior programmer
Systems analyst	Operator	Programmer

Trainees in each area

Procedures clerks

Systems clerks

Systems librarians

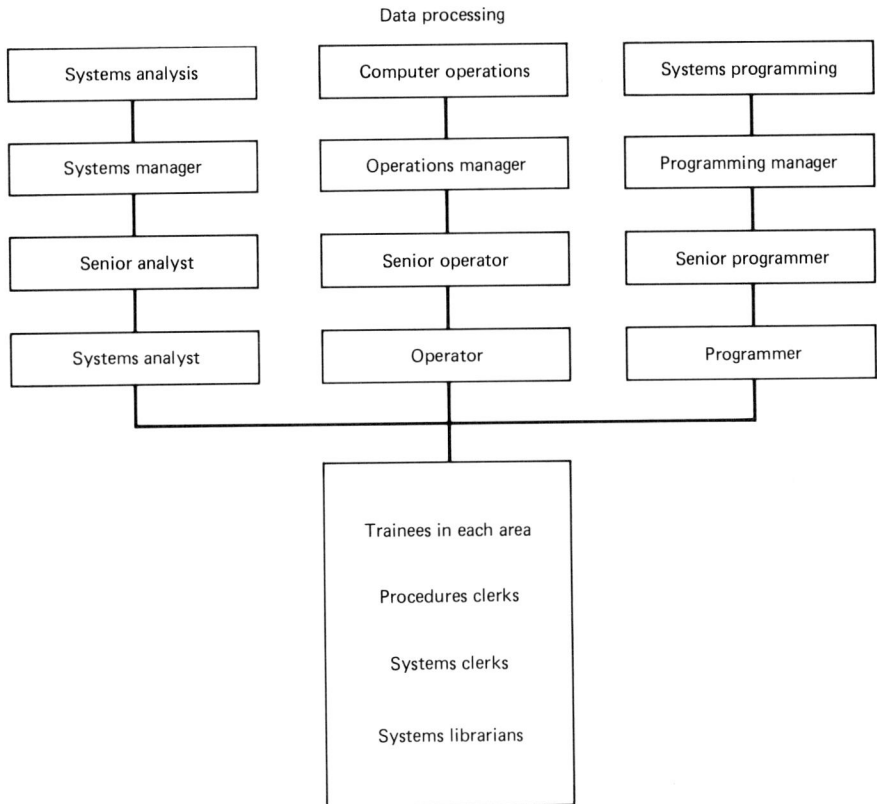

Figure 9 Data processing organizational structure. The traditional data processing structure represents specialized departments

Figure 10 Telecommunications organizational structure. Traditional structure usually encompassed the telephone maintenance within a company. Note the addition of electronic mail.

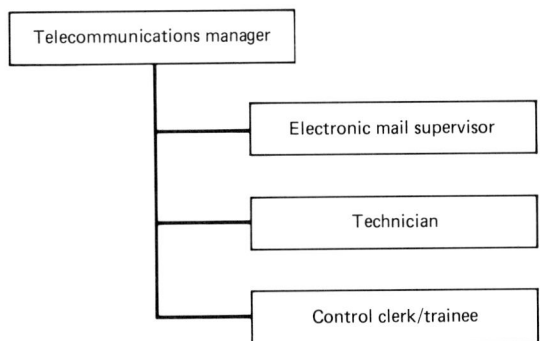

Telecommunications manager

Electronic mail supervisor

Technician

Control clerk/trainee

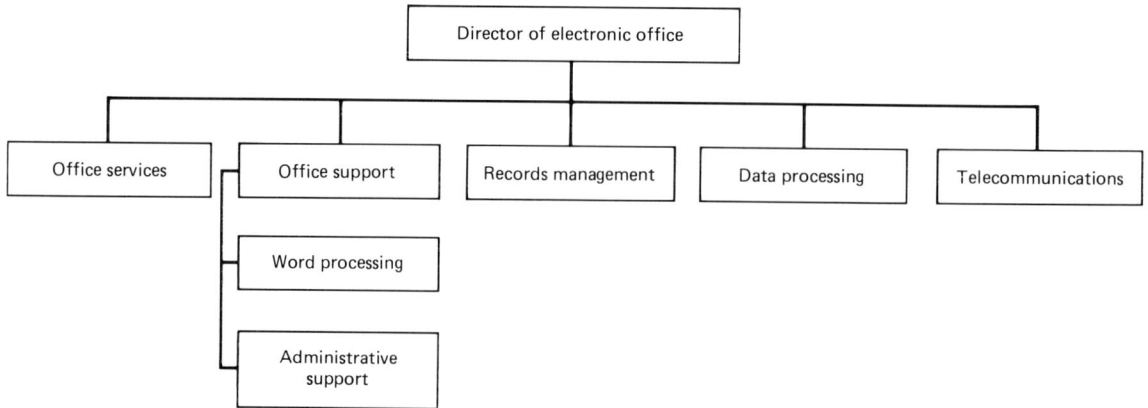

Figure 11 Integrated electronic office structure, depicting the team approach to automation.

Without analysts, the components of the integrated office will function as individual units, and not as a cohesive organization. Total communication in an organization means that communication and interaction flow through its structure. Figure 11 shows one way that interaction can be achieved.

PREPARATION FOR NEW CAREERS IN OFFICE AUTOMATION

New career paths in office automation are opening for those aspiring to achieve executive levels. Extensive study and/or degrees in business administration and technical or scientific fields is necessary. The managers of the integrated electronic office must be flexible and be able to adapt changing policies and procedures to the office structure. They should be able to manage people, technology, and information.

Change requires that all people (and especially those who want to advance) continue their education. As the technological revolution continues, those who are knowledgeable must keep themselves up to date. Some will seek formal education and advanced degrees; others can join professional associations that provide opportunities to share experiences and knowledge with others in similar positions and organizations.

A representative list of professional associations that are related to the integrated electronic office and provide continuing growth and education is given in the Appendix. Each of these associations provides its membership with specialized publications; many have annual conventions and

T 3:15-4:45 p.m.
Data Processing Terminology — W129
(Repeated Thursday morning)
• Charles M. Williams, Ph.D
Associate Professor, Information Systems
Georgia State University
Atlanta, GA
Information technologies are merging, and both dp and wp managers must learn to speak each other's language as a first step toward integrating systems. Williams, who has extensive systems experience, will define common jargon and technical terms.

IT 3:15-4:45 p.m.
The Hiring Challenge: Identifying Operator Skills — W128
• John W. Meroney
Federal Management Advisory Service Consultant
Price Waterhouse & Co.
Office of Government Services
Washington, DC
Information/word processing managers must constantly be concerned with staffing requirements. What skills should an entry-level operator possess? Meroney will discuss both the tangible skills and the intangible extras to look for when hiring.

PO **NEW** 3:15-4:45 p.m.
Management Considerations for Developing the Knowledge Worker — W132
• Truett E. Airhart
Senior Vice President
Zytron Corp.
San Antonio, TX
The work force is almost equally divided between knowledge and clerical workers, yet the costs for knowledge workers are almost triple the costs of clerical workers. In this session, Airhart will cover the overall effect of applying information technologies to improving knowledge worker productivity. It is estimated that such improvement can provide savings of $125 billion by 1985.

PO **NEW** 3:15-4:45 p.m.
Establishing Job Descriptions and Personnel Structure — W131
• Kathleen P. Wagoner, Ph.D
Professor, Business Education and Office Adminstration
Ball State University
Muncie, IN

• Mary Ruprecht
Consultant
Mary Ruprecht & Associates
Duluth, MN
Ruprecht and Wagoner will present an approach to developing work elements for job descriptions in the information processing environment. They will explore personnel department policies and government guidelines. The speakers will provide examples of phraseology and weighing factors to establish new job titles and descriptions which provide upward mobility and career progression.

SA 4-7 p.m.
Educators Advisory Council Meeting and Panel Discussion — W120
4:45-6 p.m.
Free time to visit exhibits

WEDNESDAY EVENING

5:15- :15 p.m.
IWP Chapter Officers Meeting
6:30-7:30
IWP Manufacturers Advisory Council Meeting

THURSDAY MORNING

All sessions take place at Atlanta Hilton
8:30-11 a.m.
Conference Registration, Atlanta Hilton
10 a.m.-2 p.m.
Manufacturers Exhibit Open
10:30-10:45 a.m.
Coffee break

SA **NEW** 9-10:30 a.m.
Business Education: The Challenge of Office Automation — TH101
• Joyce Arntson
Coordinator, Business Center
Saddleback College, North Campus
Irvine, CA
• William Mitchell, Ph.D.
Chairman, Department of Business Education and Information Management

University of Wisconsin
Eau Claire, WI
The shift in emphasis by business to automated technologies is providing many challenges for the business educator. Information processing, word processing, image processing, and administrative support all must be integrated into the secondary and post-secondary curricula of the 1980s.

T 9-10:30 a.m.
Data Processing Terminology — TH104
For session description see pg. 13.

P 9-10:30 a.m.
Planning the Office Environment — TH102
For session description see pg. 11.

PO 9-10:30 a.m.
Human Resources and Office Automation: A Workshop — TH103
For session description see pg. 11.

IT 9-10:30 a.m.
Implementing Office Automation — TH105
For session description see pg. 11.

IT 9-10:30 a.m.
Productivity Measurement for Information/Word Processing — TH106
For session description see pg. 9.

PD **NEW** 10:45-11:45 a.m.
WRAP UP SESSION: Motivation and Management Psychology — TH107
• Heartsill Wilson, Ph.D.
Professional Speaker
Denver, CO
Dr. Heartsill Wilson has a national reputation as an expert on motivation, one of the most important management techniques. He is exciting, stimulating and knowledgeable. His upbeat dynamic presentation is guaranteed to leave you with a new outlook on your job and career.

11:45 a.m.-2 p.m.
Free time to visit exhibits

Figure 12 Annual convention brochure. (Courtesy of International Information/Word Processing Association)

exhibits, as well as workshops and seminars. Figure 12 illustrates one type of program (courtesy of Association of Information Systems Professionals—formerly known as International Information/Word Processing

Association). Some of these organizations offer only national member-ships whereas others have local chapters throughout the country; a few have campus chapters and/or student memberships. Several conduct sur-veys and research to keep their memberships aware of developments in their fields.

Many professional organizations sponsor major national conferences and equipment exhibits that are open to nonmembers as well as members. Such conferences provide opportunities to keep up with the state of the art. Most associations will send convention and membership information to interested people, upon written request.

Other groups, as well as consultants, retailers, and vendors, offer two-, three-, and five-day seminars and programs for more intensive study on topics such as integrating word and data processing and increasing office productivity. Others are designed to provide training in supervisory skills and management effectiveness (see Figure 13).

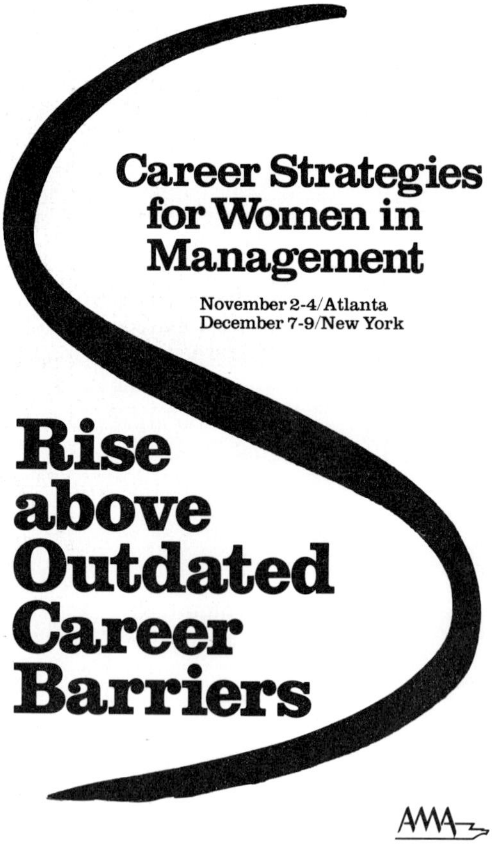

Career Strategies for Women in Management

November 2-4/Atlanta
December 7-9/New York

Rise above Outdated Career Barriers

AMA

Figure 13 A special intensive program brochure. (Courtesy of American Manage-ment Association)

OTHER OPPORTUNITIES IN OFFICE AUTOMATION

As indicated in Figure 1, substantial career options are available in firms that offer products and services for the integrated office. There are many positions with equipment vendors, supplies dealers, furniture companies, and professional groups.

In the foreseeable future, equipment manufacturers will continue to offer expanded career opportunities. This technological explosion will open many additional careers for technicians, sales staff, trainers, marketing support representatives, and for systems engineers, field engineers, scientists, engineers, and administrators. As major companies diversify their products and enter the competition in the office marketplace, they will be opening up entirely new departments and subsidiaries. Typical job opportunities in companies selling systems to offices include

1. Marketing/sales manager for branch, district, region.
2. Market support manager, supervisor, or representative.
3. Customer support manager, supervisor, or representative.
4. Systems consultant, analyst, or engineer.
5. Applications specialist.
6. Special markets representative or analyst.
7. Communications specialist.
8. Sales representative.

In addition to the technical vendors, traditional furniture vendors are expanding and diversifying their marketing horizons to include office furniture specially designed to meet the needs of the electronic office. Within these areas, management is seeking marketing representatives who are knowledgeable about the requirements of the integrated office, the behavioral effects on personnel who must work in the new office, and the expectations of decision makers in the electronic office.

Vendors are manufacturing supplies for the technology and its surrounding office activities. The birth of these marketers of supplies has also created new job opportunities related to the integrated office.

As in the past, there is no one route to the top; however, many have come up through the ranks through the production of goods. Now, many will be involved in providing information and support services.

Those who have in the past achieved success have done so because they have been able to view the total picture and all related activities. Figure 14 indicates the skills that will be needed by tomorrow's information manager.

Those who achieve success in the integrated electronic office will do so because they have a broad view of the information and communication

**SKILLS AND PERSONAL CHARACTERISTICS
REQUIRED OF TOMORROW'S INFORMATION MANAGER**

Administrative ability—to plan, organize, and coordinate information flow; to demonstrate effective decision making and creativity.

Interpersonal skills—to demonstrate leadership and behavior flexibility by commanding all skills necessary to communicate and work with employees, peers, and management.

Stability of performance—to demonstrate tolerance of uncertainty and resistance to stress and such characteristics as energy, self-objectivity, and career orientation.

Technical knowledge—to demonstrate recognition of how to use information and the importance of information flow; to demonstrate an understanding of office operations and other support functions, as well as the technological tools available to improve the flow of information.

Intellectual and analytical ability—to demonstrate a range of interests and general mental ability; to demonstrate the ability to analyze the equipment marketplace and workflow procedures and to make appropriate recommendations for equipment and procedures.

Figure 14 Basic generalist skills needed by information managers. Tomorrow's information manager will need a broad range of special skills. Note the emphasis on interpersonal skills and flexibility in working with employees. (Courtesy of H. T. Smith)

needs within the office and the entire organization, and are flexible and open-minded to the changes required to lead that organization to the automated approach to doing business.

CHAPTER 3

INFORMATION FLOW AND MANAGEMENT

OBJECTIVES

In this chapter you will learn about
1. Information as a resource, and the pros and cons of information resource management.
2. The information cycle and flow.
3. The components necessary to maintain and manage information flow: input, processing, replication, distribution, storage, retrieval, archiving, and destruction.
4. The major forms of information—data, text, voice, and image.
5. Transaction processing and communications processing.
6. Networking and its function in the electronic office.

Information is as important a resource as personnel, materials, and capital. Managing and processing information constitutes the most important challenge facing the business world. All offices deal in some form of communication. Most managers and supervisors spend about 75 percent of their time communicating some form of business information. Because of this great volume of information processing, information management has become a growing field.

Information management is the supervision and control over a system that creates, gathers, processes, replicates, distributes, stores, and/or destroys the information utilized by an organization, from inception to destruction. Organized procedures and established standards enable an organization to control the amount and quality of its information. Without information management, unorganized, unending information (that can-

Figure 1 Information processing flow. Note the interaction of each stage of information processing.

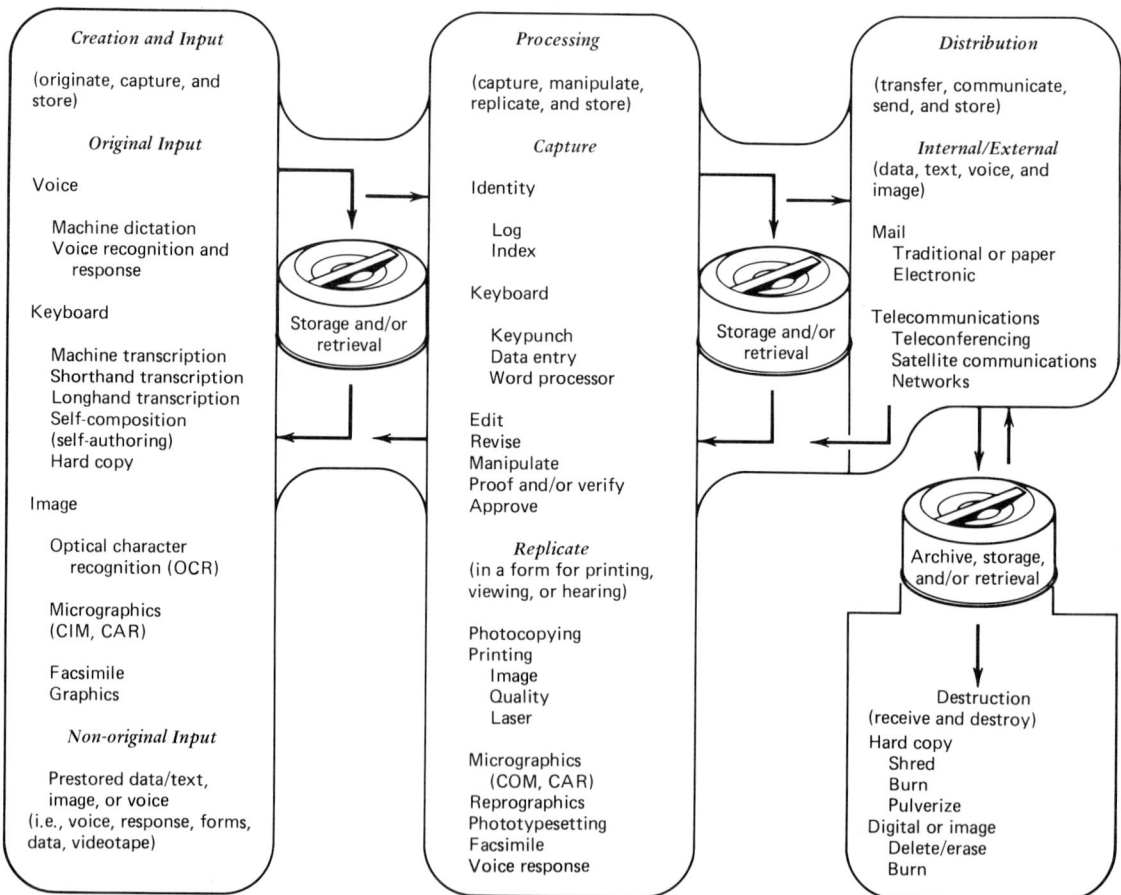

not be used effectively or destroyed safely) will ultimately overwhelm management and render it incapable. The purpose of information management is to monitor and control information flow within an organization and to maximize its usefulness while minimizing its cost.

The following requirements are necessary for an effective information system:

1. Accuracy. Information should be correct. It should be in a form that is easily understood, usable, and correctable quickly, should error occur.
2. Accessibility. Information should be processed in such a way that it is easily stored and easily retrieved for later use.
3. Speed. Information should be retrieved and distributed fast enough to be current.
4. Economy. Information should be provided on an economical basis consistent with volume and urgency.

This chapter presents an overview of the information processing cycle and the information flow within the modern office; these subjects will be treated in detail in later chapters. It is necessary, however, to view the total concept of the entire information cycle in order to understand how each component relates to the whole (see Figure 1).

It is also necessary to understand the information float that exists within the cycle. Information float is that period of time when information is in transmission from the point of origination until its receiver has accessibility.

The opportunities for improved productivity are great—but so are the challenges they present to those responsible for producing and managing information.

CREATION AND INPUT

Creation and input involves the origination, capture, and storage of information at the point of entering a system. The ideas of executives and others in an organization can be put into action in various ways, through either original or nonoriginal methods. Original input can be further divided into voice, keyboard, and image. Nonoriginal input consists of information already in existence in an organization.

ORIGINAL INPUT   In terms of office management support systems, original input includes data or ideas entered in raw form before correction or review. The ultimate objective of information flow management is to process raw information into a refined form for storage, analysis, distribution, and use. This refined form usually includes letters, memos, and reports.

Ideas originate as a mental process, but some type of business tool or process is necessary to turn ideas into action. Original methods such as voice or telephone, shorthand or direct dictation to a secretary, person-to-person conversation, keyboarding or self-authoring, or imagery such as optical character readers into word processors are most often used. All types of input modes usually involve at least two people—the originator and the processor. A recent survey of American executives revealed that input consisted of the following forms and the percentage of the time each was used:

Longhand text: 75 percent.
Machine dictation: 10 percent.
Shorthand: 10 percent.
Other (such as OCR image): 5 percent.

This survey illustrated the need for additional acceptance for modes of input that make better use of the executive's time. The integrated electronic office encompasses even greater dimensions of original input than those surveyed. As illustrated in Figure 1, these dimensions can be subdivided into the categories of voice, keyboard, and image.

Voice   Voice input technology includes machine dictation and voice recognition and response.

Machine dictation is the most efficient method for organizations using word processing centers. It is gaining acceptance in more offices, because of the potential for time and money savings. The dictating machine enables a manager to dictate a letter, report, and memo directly to a word processing center on an "immediate response" basis, regardless of the availability of the secretary. Dictation machines offer another great advantage for modern management: they handle work on the spot. They can answer correspondence or write memos or reports without having to rely on a secretary's availability. Dictation is faster than the other methods—over 60 words per minute. A secretary can more easily transcribe machine-dictated material. Studies have shown a transcribing rate of 20-30 words per minute. In addition, most machine transcription equipment allows a secretary to control the voice speed, rate, tone, and volume. Despite its advantages, studies have shown that managers are still reluctant to use machine dictation.

Voice recognition and response are closely related and are still a developing technology. Devices that can recognize speech often are used in conjunction with devices that can generate voice. An example would be using speech for data entry and verification as you would in a pay-by-phone application, in which the telephone is both the input and the output device.

According to George Glaser, consultant, of Los Altos, California: "It is highly unlikely that voice recognition systems will ever compete with OCR or key punching for high-volume entry of data. A proficient key-punch operator can enter between 15,000 and 18,000 characters per hour but it is literally impossible to speak digits or characters at that rate, even in short bursts."

However, it is expected that both voice recognition and voice response will advance significantly in the next five to ten years.

Keyboard The keyboard is the major point of input for both text and data, as evidenced by its role in typing and data entry. Keyboard input is the second major category of original input. Keyboarding is utilized as a result of machine transcription, shorthand, longhand, self-authoring, or retyping hard copy.

Machine Transcription. Machine transcription is the process of transcribing information from dictation authored by a principal of an organization, using a dictation device. The principal dictates into a centralized, portable or desktop dictation device, and a secretary transcribes that material.

Shorthand. In this mode, which utilizes the traditional boss-secretary relationship, the manager originates the idea and the secretary usually serves as support by catching errors, correcting grammar, or calling to the manager's attention ambiguities or omissions. Although taking shorthand is twice as fast as creating work in longhand (30 words per minute), it ties up two people. In addition, interruptions during dictation and deciphering legibility of the shorthand may further lessen efficiency. Shorthand also requires the secretary to perform the intermediate step of taking the thoughts in brief form prior to transcribing into document form.

Longhand. Longhand text usually means handwritten notes submitted for further processing. Many executives prefer to write their ideas out in longhand. They prefer putting the ideas on paper so they can see them and modify them before giving them to reviewers or typists. Their tools are simple—pen and paper—and they have only themselves to consult. When handling correspondence, managers pencil in facts, answers to questions, dates, and so on in the margins of letters received from others. Trained secretaries can then interpret these "notes" into a response letter (see Figure 2).

Longhand origination is slow—usually an average of 15 words per minute are created, not including thinking time. Legibility can be a problem; secretaries' time can be wasted in deciphering longhand jottings. Despite

SWOWP/AS

1 November

Mrs Mary M Ruprecht, CMC
President
Mary M Ruprecht & Associates, Inc.
140 W. Myrtle St.
Duluth MN 55811

SOUTHWESTERN OHIO WP/AS GROUP MEETING - DECEMBER 12

It is my pleasure to contact you, Mrs. Ruprecht, regarding your
availability to speak to our local group at its December
membership meeting. We would be very interested in your
addressing our group on the subject of the issues involved in
Office Automation.

Speakers are asked to make a presentation of about 1 hour and to
remain for a short question and answer period. For your
information, our group appreciates any handout materials provided.

We hope you will be able to join us and look forward to hearing
from you at your earliest convenience.

[handwritten margin notes: mg / Tell them okay! / 1 hr is fine. / Send handout packet #3 / need a slide projector.]

Program Coordinator
SWOWP/AS Group

Southwestern Ohio Word Processing/Administrative Support Group   P.O. Box 30155, Cincinnati, Ohio 45230

Figure 2 Outlining of thoughts on the margin facilitates ease of letter preparation by support staff. (Courtesy of Southwestern Ohio WP/AS Group)

Mary M Ruprecht & Associates, Inc.

Word Processing & Management Consultants

140 West Myrtle Street
Duluth, Minnesota 55811

Offices:
Minnesota:
  218-727-5150
Ohio:
  513-232-5155

3 November

Program Coordinator
Southwestern Ohio WP/AS Group
PO Box 30155
Cincinnati OH 45230

SOUTHWESTERN OHIO WP/AS GROUP MEETING – DECEMBER 12

I will be happy to participate in your membership meeting on
December 12.

The presentation topic you suggest is fine. I will provide a
handout packet. Please let me know whether you want me to bring
enough copies for all attendees or whether you will handle
duplication of an original packet.

I will require a 35mm slide projector, screen, and a podium with a
microphone.

I'm looking forward to meeting your group and will await your
confirmation of all arrangements.

Mary M Ruprecht
Mary M Ruprecht, CMC
President

encl

mg

Figure 2 *(Continued)*

these shortcomings, however, studies have demonstrated that longhand text origination is utilized extensively in today's office.

Self-Composition.   Self-composition covers those documents that are self-authored on a keyboard.

Hard Copy.   Materials that have already been printed or typed are sometimes referred to as hard copy. Hard copy can be keyboarded by a secretary or specialist for entry into a system; however, properly prepared hard copy may also be scanned into a system through OCR (or image processing).

Image   Image input is the original input into a system of previously prepared information that may be in the form of scanning through optical character recognition (OCR), computer input microfilm (CIM) of stored microforms, computer-assisted retrieval (CAR) of information in a computer, facsimile information that has been transmitted into an organization but not yet input to a system, and forms of graphics.

The most familiar example of image copying is OCR (optical character recognition). OCR machines scan and read printed or typed characters and convert them into digital impulses for input directly to a word processing or data processing system. In addition, OCR permits the capture of input data at the point of origination and eliminates the need for additional keying before input to word processing operations.

See Chapter 4 for further discussion of image input.

NONORIGINAL INPUT   Nonoriginal input consists of that information which exists in an organization in some form and has not as yet been entered into a system. An example of a source of nonoriginal input is the recall of prestored data. It is important to establish priorities for the entry of text and/or data into an information processing system.

Often, procedures will specify which special work will supersede the normal priority channels, and how that work is authorized.

The input function begins the total information flow cycle. The key ingredients for success in the total system are procedures and guidelines that set up efficient and productive input processing channels.

STORAGE/RETRIEVAL

Storage is the systematic preservation of information within the system in some form. Retrieval is the recalling of that stored information for reuse. The storage/retrieval function can be performed through either manual or electronic systems.

MANUAL STORAGE/ RETRIEVAL Manual storage includes the filing of hard copy, microforms, or computer or word processing media. Manual retrieval is accomplished via an indexing system that uses alpha, numeric, topical, or color coding systems to locate the needed material. The manual systems involve extensive labor. For example, to find information in a given file, an office employee would have to (1) determine how an item is indexed and classified, (2) go to the files or storage area, (3) look for the appropriate file folder, (4) retrieve it, (5) prepare an out guide to take the material back to the work area in order to use it, and (6) eventually return it to the storage area. By contrast, the on-line system involves only keyboarding key words and viewing the desired material as it appears on a screen.

ELECTRONIC STORAGE/ RETRIEVAL Electronic storage/retrieval is accomplished from on-line memory. Information is directly stored in the central processing unit (CPU) of the computer for instant recall by the proper code. This automatic filing system within the computer can use alpha, numeric, or topical coding. Computer-assisted retrieval (CAR) can also be accomplished through CIM (computer input microfilm), COM (computer output microfilm) and other micrographics systems.

There are two main forms of magnetic media storage. External storage usually includes removable magnetic media—for example, mag cards, floppy disks, magnetic tape. Fixed storage is performed inside the automated system, where it usually is not handled by the operator. These storage devices include hard disk, magnetic tape drives, core memory, bubble memory, or other types of mass storage devices. (Some hard disks and magnetic tapes are removable.)

Managing information and storage retrieval systems requires controls, including procedures for indexing, securing, accessing, modifying, retrieving, and purging.

As an outgrowth of the need for flexibility, data base management systems (DBMS) are being developed as an affordable software for smaller computers. In the past, DBM systems, costing from $50,000 to $200,000, were packaged for large computers. A newer approach is to provide the flexibility of the large-computer DBM systems tailored to microcomputer capabilities, thereby reducing costs to fit the growing market (see Figure 3).

Data base software can significantly reduce the costs of information storage and retrieval in several ways. DBMS (1) maintains an internal data directory, keeping descriptions of data and relationships among the data; (2) allows data to be accessed in a form that is appropriate, rather than forcing a new program to be written; and (3) provides great flexibility and economy in altering the initial system to meet new needs.

It is important to note that the storage and retrieval functions may occur at various points within the flow or cycle with different applications and

Shared Distributed Data bases

Partitioning. In a distributed data base configuration, partitioned segments of the central data base are assigned to the remote nodes that originate the data contained in those segments and need it for day-to-day operations. Data contained in the segments can be shared by network nodes and may be located by a directory in the DBMS.

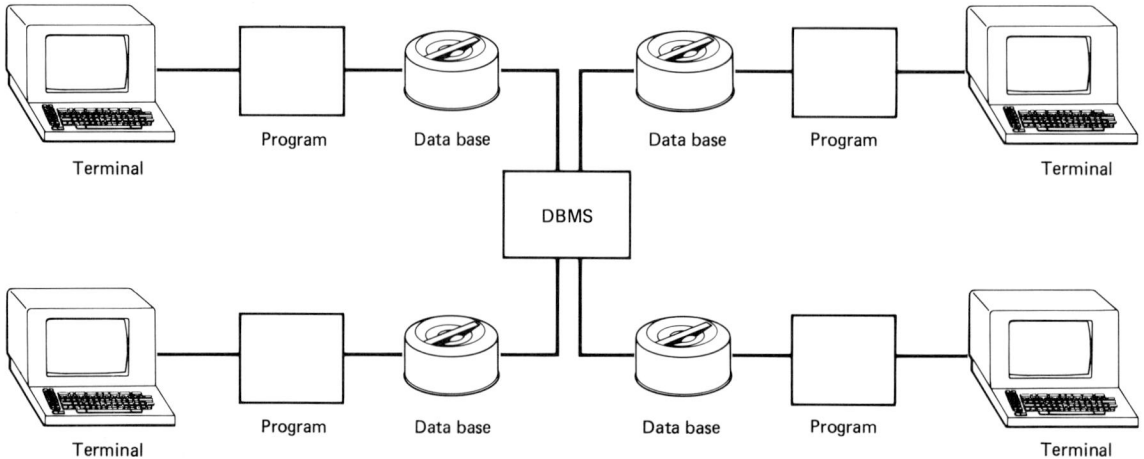

| Terminal | Program | Data base | | Data base | Program | Terminal |

DBMS

| Terminal | Program | Data base | | Data base | Program | Terminal |

Figure 3 Shared distributed data bases. *Source:* Executive Guide to Data Communications.

configurations of the integrated office. There may be some variation in the same office from time to time, depending upon deadlines and other tasks to be performed.

PROCESSING

Processing is the component in the cycle of information flow for the manipulation of those ideas that have been input to the system to be replicated and distributed in the form of communication (see Figure 4).

Until recently, data processing was concerned with processing transactions. The primary use of computers had been in processing data transactions—a sale, a paycheck, a change in inventory, and so on. All accounting activity is concerned with data processing transactions. Word processing may also process transactions; however such transaction processing is of a list processing or records processing nature. More importantly word processing is also communications processing because it conveys an idea or interpretation of information to the receiver.

Processing is the stage in information flow at which information—be it text, numbers, images, voices, or anything else—is transformed from source information (as input) into forms and formats suitable for storage and use by people for whom the processed information is intended. Pro-

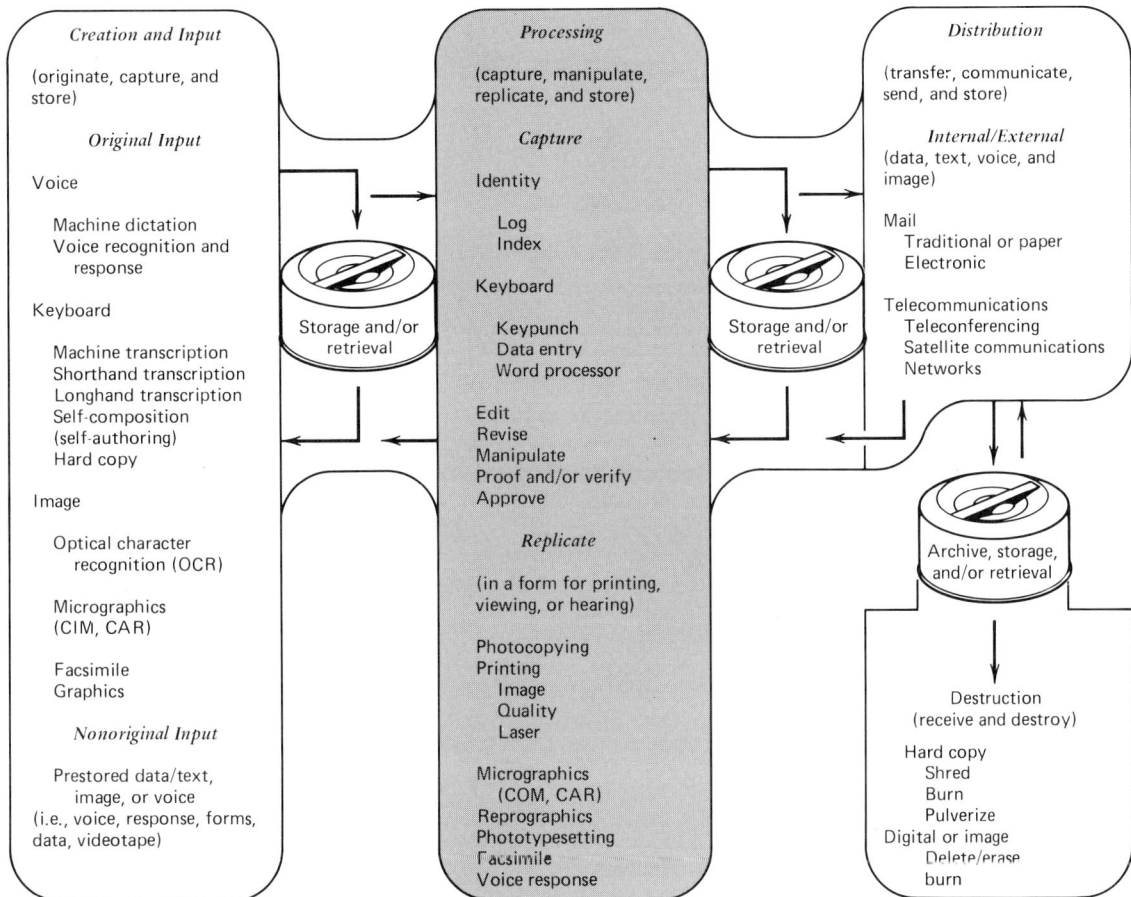

Figure 4 The processing component of the information flow includes capturing, manipulating, replicating, and storing of information.

cessing attempts to convert all input information into electronic memory to be read and displayed and stored, and/or replicated (see Figure 5).

The first step in the text processing function is the transcribing, or keyboarding, of information from its original state into the system. For example, the longhand notes of a manager would be raw input until they are entered into the information processing cycle. Usually a secretary would have to turn those longhand notes into typed copy that would be keyboarded or read into OCR and transmitted to the word processor. It is at this entry point that the information is logged into the system and assigned an index designation for future distribution and/or retrieval. The keyboarding function is one of the most critical in the entire text information flow (see Figure 6).

Once in the system, information can be edited, corrected, changed, and formatted. Many organizations have predetermined formats for corre-

Creation and Input	Processing	Distribution
(originate, capture, and store)	(capture, manipulate, replicate, and store)	(transfer, communicate, send, and store)
Original Input	*Capture*	*Internal/External* (data, text, voice, and image)
Voice	Identity	
Machine dictation	Log	Mail
Voice recognition and response	Index	Traditional or paper Electronic
Keyboard	Keyboard	Telecommunications
Machine transcription Shorthand transcription Longhand transcription Self-composition (self-authoring) Hard copy	Keypunch Data entry Word processor	Teleconferencing Satellite communications Networks
	Edit Revise Manipulate Proof and/or verify Approve	
Image	*Replicate*	
Optical character recognition (OCR)	(in a form for printing, viewing, or hearing)	Archive, storage, and/or retrieval
Micrographics (CIM, CAR)	Photocopying Printing	
Facsimile Graphics	Image Quality Laser	Destruction (receive and destroy) Hard copy
Nonoriginal Input	Micrographics (COM, CAR)	Shred Burn
Prestored data/text, image, or voice (i.e., voice, response, forms, data, videotape)	Reprographics Phototypesetting Facsimile Voice response	Pulverize Digital or image Delete/erase Burn

Storage and/or retrieval

Storage and/or retrieval

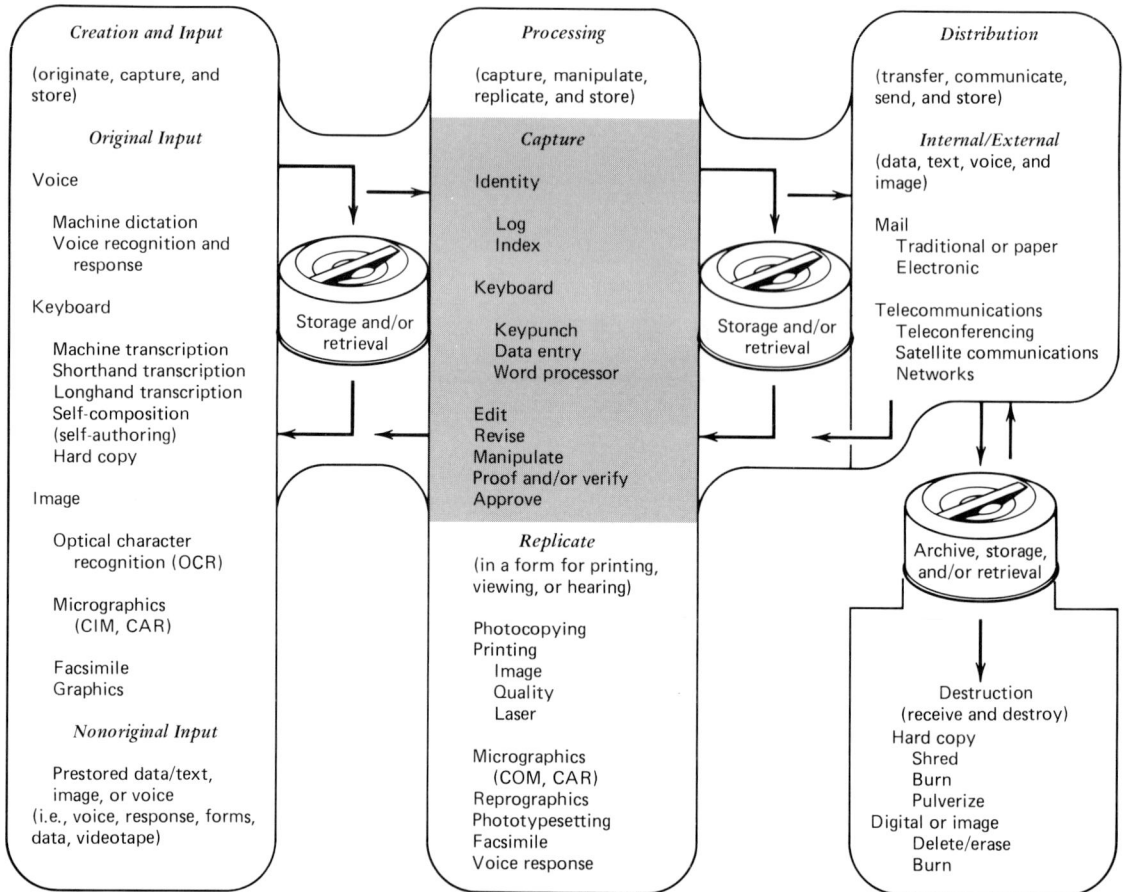

Figure 5 Capturing of information includes identifying, entering, and revising information.

spondence, reports, letters, memos, and so on. The editing function is important. Many managers (who concentrate on problem solving and decision making) may not take time to be grammatically correct, may make spelling errors, or may be wordy when originating material. Once entered, material can be edited or rewritten, checked for errors or revised. The editing function can be performed either by the word originator (the manager) or by a designated word processing operator who proofreads and edits, or by both.

Along with being edited, the material or information can be manipulated. Manipulation involves changing the information into different formats, changing the order of paragraphs, juggling columns of numbers in tables, and possibly trying to come up with the most attractive and workable form in which to present the information to others.

Figure 6 Operator performing the editing function. (Courtesy of CPT Corporation, Minneapolis, MN)

After the final format of the material is specified and selected, copy should be printed out and the material carefully proofread. Proofreading involves looking for errors in spelling, sense, grammar, spacing, and any other type of procedural error that will detract from the accuracy and quality of the copy.

Once the document is processed and approved, it can be prepared for final output and/or replicated in final form for distribution.

REPLICATION

Replication is the transfer of already captured information into another form. That form may or may not be distributed at this point of the process (see Figure 7).

Much information generated within an organization needs to be used by many people, and different people require that same information in various forms and formats. Replication may take many forms such as

1. Photocopying.
2. Printing.
   ▶ Laser.
   ▶ Image.

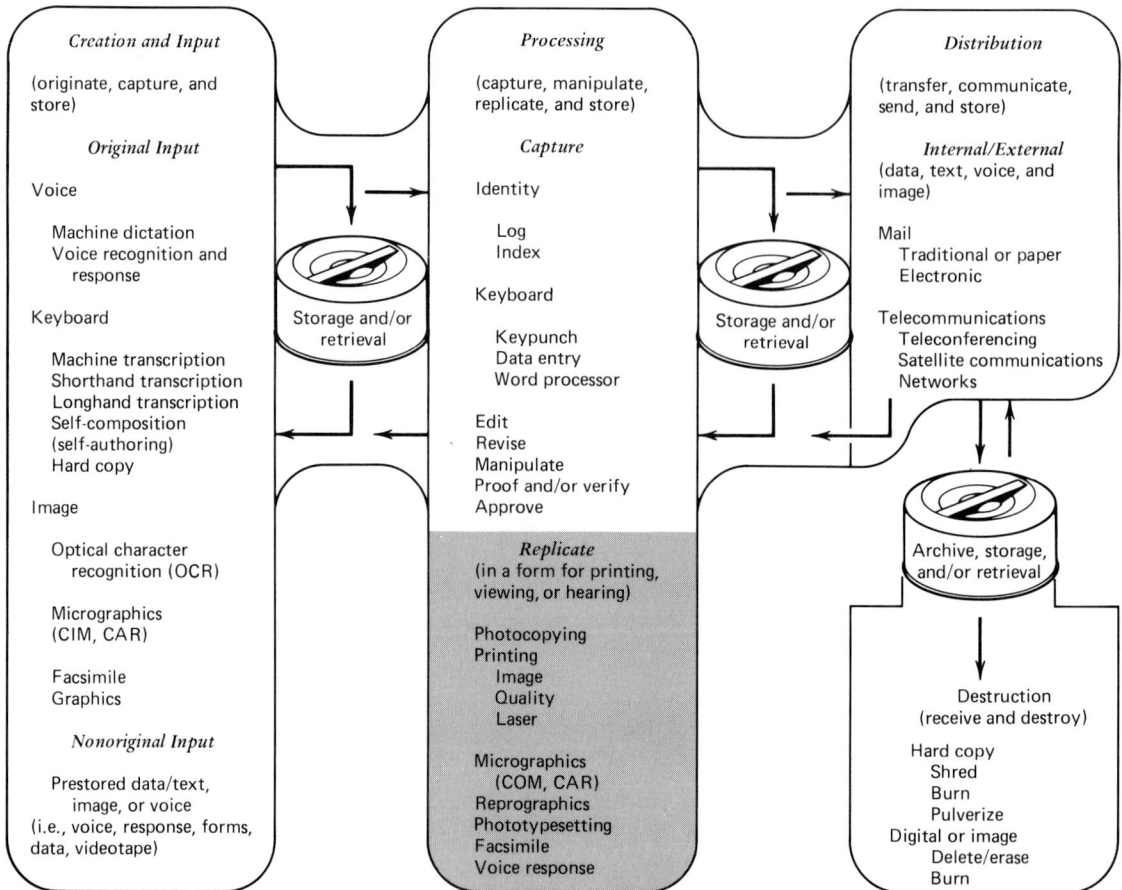

Figure 7 Replicating information is the transfer of information into another form.

3. Micrographics.
4. Reprographics.
5. Phototypesetting.
6. Facsimile.
7. Voice.

**PHOTOCOPYING/
DUPLICATING**   Photocopying is the process of making multiple copies of an original or from an original source without the need for an intermediate master. Formerly, the term *duplicating* referred to the reproduction of copies on spirit, stencil, or offset duplications. With the introduction of high-speed, plain-paper copiers, the term "copier/duplication" became accepted. The most recent advances in copying/duplicating are image and laser printing.

MICROGRAPHICS Micrographics is the reproducing of information in miniature form, such as roll or cartridge film, microfilm, micropositives, and so on. Computer output microfilm (COM) is a process in which microfilm and microfiche are produced directly from computer output without intermediate hard-copy (typing on paper) and microfilming steps.

REPROGRAPHICS Reprographics is the term applied to the process of reproducing or duplicating information, usually onto paper or microforms. Copying, duplicating, and printing are all parts of reprographics.

PHOTOTYPE-SETTING In phototypesetting, information is put into type through the process of exposing characters on photosensitive material such as photographic paper or film. When phototypesetters can accept information previously recorded by word processors, the need to rekeyboard is eliminated.

FACSIMILE Facsimile is a system of telecommunications that scans an original image, converts to an electrical signal, and then converts the electrical signal to a replica of the original image at the receiving terminal.

VOICE RESPONSE Voice processing is still in its infancy. Voice response devices are components of computers, with limited vocabularies, that can respond by generating such voice answers as the message that tells you the telephone system is not working.

DISTRIBUTION

Distribution is the moving of information from one place to another and is the third major facet of the information processing flow (see Figure 8).

Distribution takes place when information is sent to recipients to provide information and/or to elicit an action or response. Information includes letters, memos, reports, manuals, catalogs, brochures, etc. Distribution can be either internal or external to the organization. Internal distribution can be more flexible when an organization has terminals and/or word processing workstations that can communicate with each other. Electronic distribution often eliminates the need for hard copy, since some internal information can be sent through in-house communication networks. Electronic internal distribution also is less expensive, since it takes less effort to accomplish and many additional costly steps are eliminated. Internal distribution may also be handled through the traditional methods of mail service, messengers, and couriers.

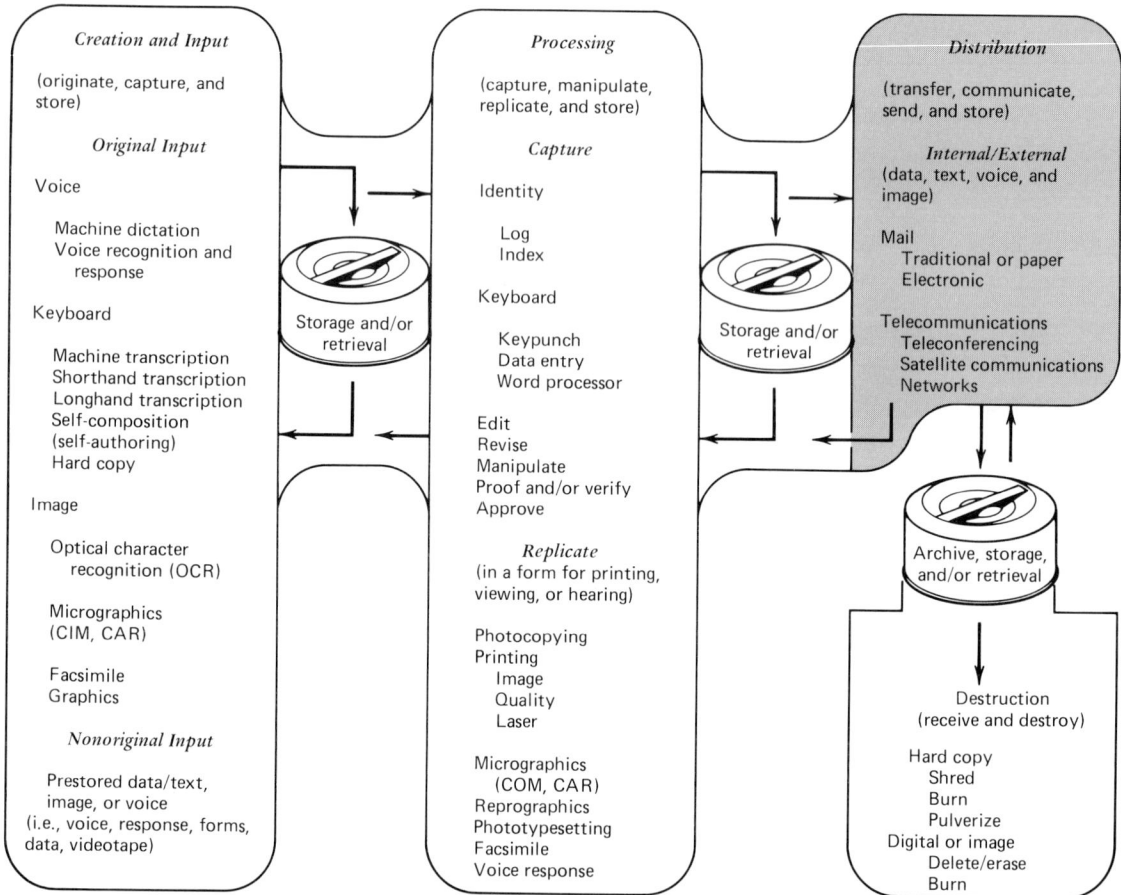

Figure 8 Information distribution can be internal or external.

External distribution involves communication with outside sources. External information is mainly hard copy (i.e., paper copy such as letters or reports), although with the growth of communications systems and networks, more companies are using telecommunication rather than paper. Information can be received in a variety of forms—hard copy, video terminal display, or directly onto magnetic storage. In this way, output materials can be viewed, typed, retyped, copied, printed or heard by the recipient. There are many forms of distribution, including electronic mail, telecommunications, teleconferencing, networking, and satellite communications.

ELECTRONIC MAIL Mail comes in two forms—traditional and electronic. Mail is a distribution method. Traditional mail is the manual method of transmitting communication from the sender to the receiver via the U.S. Postal Service, messengers, private couriers, and parcel delivery services. Traditional mail (the system we all use) has been improved in some offices through the use of electronic mail.

Electronic mail is the transmission of information internally to and from users via electronic mailboxes or externally by digitizing information and communicating the messages by facsimile, communicating word processors, computer-based message systems, public-carrier-based systems, public postal electronic services, or private and public teletype. Electronic mail potentially could link all office communications through integration of data and all office communications through integration of data and word processing networks. Electronic mail is discussed in depth in a later chapter.

TELECOM-MUNICATIONS Telecommunications is the transmission of information between one information processing system and another, between a computer and remote terminals, or among terminals/workstations, depending on the capabilities of the systems and terminals. If an organization has telecommunications, it may have the ability for data (digital and sensor), voice, text, and image (graphics and facsimile) communication. On-line telecommunications provides instant distribution of information from one location to another, within the same building or half a world away. Telecommunications systems also include the technologies of (1) teleconferencing, (2) satellite communications, and (3) networking.

Teleconferencing Teleconferencing, another information distribution method, involves the processing of data, visual, and audio via telephone lines so that the picture and voice appear on a screen in two or more locations. Teleconferencing could potentially eliminate the need for executive travel in the future. Teleconferencing will be discussed in greater detail in a later chapter.

Networking Another means of information distribution is networking. A network is a series of points interconnected by communications technology. Networking enables various information processing devices such as word processors and data entry units, storage devices, printers, processors, and other peripherals to send, receive, exchange, store, or reproduce information. Networking is one of the more significant catalysts to the office of the future.

The fully automated environment will not deal with separate technologies but rather with networks of technologies. Information introduced into the network through any one device could be available to every other point on the network. Thus, information in a company's computer files will be available to word processing and administrative personnel and information in text files will be available to computer personnel. Both can supply information to the Reprographics Department. The office of the future will consist of networks of separate yet interdependent technologies.

The introduction of integrated networks is important for several reasons. First, networks make available an increasingly powerful array of office technologies to every office worker in every office location. The tendency in the past has been to move the "automatable" work out of the regular office and into a technology center. Data processing provides the classic example of moving components of office work into a separate "center" of operations. The capabilities of the technology were made available to the specialists in the technology center but not to the managers and professionals. The introduction of networks changed this trend, since networks brought the power and capabilities of modern office technologies into one's work place. Networks provide technological power to people.

Second, networking is important in that individual technologies are subordinate to the network. Since offices tend to be organized around separate technologies (Data Processing Department, Word Processing Department, Micrographics, and so on), the introduction of networks will fuse these separate and independent subsets. Each technology still can operate certain stand-alone functions, but the primary thrust will be the greatest potential gained from integration.

Third, networks require a level of coordinated planning never before encountered. Instead of planning by separate department or subunit, the networked office will need to be placed from the top down (although implemented from the bottom up) in order to coordinate all the office functions into a unified whole.

The fourth reason that networks are important is that as more information is processed in the network, less paper is created. Electronic processing and video display units will rapidly replace the need for paper for many normal office functions. Although the paperless office is a long way off, the need for paper will diminish as the use of networks increases.

A network that interconnects office machinery and systems will increase the speed with which information is communicated. See Figure 9 for an example of one office system network. Remember that communicating information is of prime importance; we must be as concerned with communicating as with processing.

Satellite Network.   Another distribution system is a satellite network. Satellite networks are a telecommunications system. They provide communication through transmission of television and digital signals to all locations with a proper receiver. Earth antennas linked to a satellite in space allow the transmission of business data. Usually, satellite systems have a wider scope than telecommunications, since the former can be

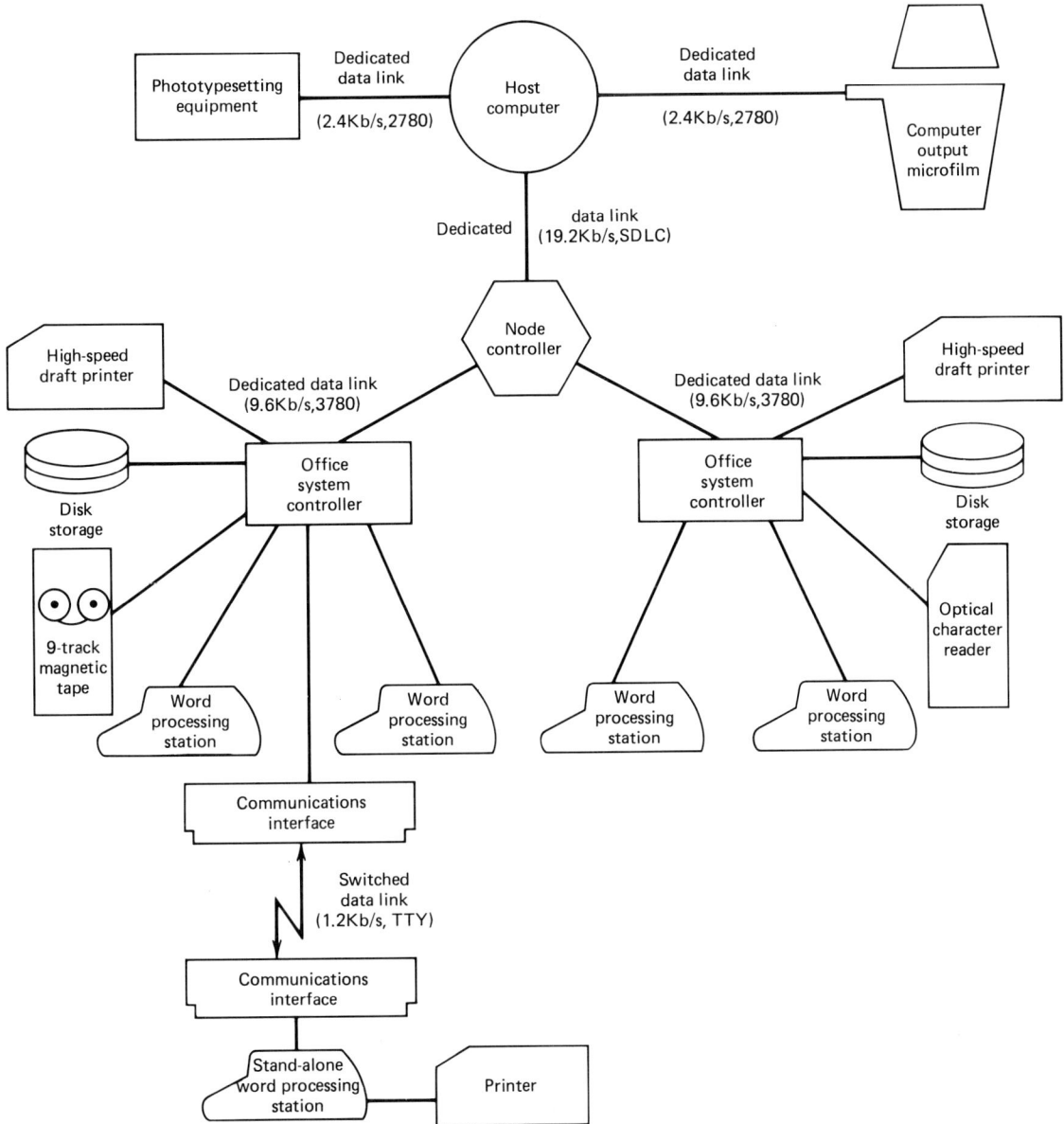

Figure 9 Example of hierarchical distributed office system network. (Courtesy of Modern Office Procedures, copyright Penton/IPC, Division of Pittway Corp.)

global whereas some of the latter are only local. Telecommunications will be discussed in detail in a later chapter.

Automation has been added to the origination, production, and reproduction of documents to increase productivity and decrease costs. However, efficiency ends there, unless the document can also be distributed quickly and efficiently. Studies have shown that 75 percent of the time spent on a document from its origination to final destination was spent in distribution.

According to estimates, the world's information is doubling every six years. With this explosion, traditional methods of distribution are becoming inadequate. The need to improve the distribution function of the office area remains one of the most critical challenges. Unless the information compiled is available immediately and delivered rapidly to the appropriate person, efficiency will decline while costs continue to increase. However, this stage does not conclude the flow of information. It is necessary to provide for storage, retrieval, archiving, and destruction or purging to complete information's life cycle.

ARCHIVING/DESTRUCTION

Archiving is the storage of records that are no longer frequently required but that may be required in the future. Those records still have to be preserved, in an area designated for inactive records, permanently or for a specified inactive retention period. Information preserved in an archive is considered a vital record that has evidential or informational value. Evidential value includes those records that show how an organization came into being, how it developed, how it was organized, what its function has been, and the results of its activities.

Informational value includes those records that provide information that should be preserved for future generations. The decision as to what material to retain and what to destroy should be made by a person or team trained in archiving and versed in the types of records that an organization needs and wants to retain. Clearly, not all information or records can be retained permanently.

Archiving can involve off-line archiving of hard-copy or magnetic media (microforms or computer tapes, disks, and so on). Usually, archiving is not done on line because it would take too much computer time and storage capacity and could increase computer processing time.

After records have been retained for their legal and useful life, they should be destroyed. Destruction can be accomplished through shredding, pulverizing, or burning hard copy and purging, erasing, or deleting magnetic media or on-line storage. A disposition schedule and method of destruction should be established as a part of defined organizational procedures so that no accidental destruction of documents can occur.

TECHNOLOGIES OF THE 1980s AND 1990s

All the components of the information cycle previously discussed are presently operating in many offices. Many technologies (some are quite new and others currently under development) will come into wider use as office automation develops.

Interactive WP/DP software.

Business graphics.

Electronic typewriters.

Microcomputers.

Bubble memories.

Video disk products.

Touch-sensitive screens and keyboards.

Voice recognition.

Managerial workstations.

Intelligent copier/printers.

Laser printers.

Audio/video communications.

Document distribution systems.

Data base file systems.

On-line public data bases and networks.

SUMMARY

The various office subsets outlined in this chapter are basic to making the automated office a reality. All of the concepts described in this chapter are involved in the transition from the traditional office to the automated office and will be developed in detail in the following chapters. One must remember, however, that the issues are not only technological but also organizational, behavioral, and managerial—and that each must be kept in perspective.

CHAPTER 4

INPUT

OBJECTIVES

In this chapter you will learn about
1. Original and nonoriginal input.
2. Forms of voice, keyboard, and image input.
3. Categories of dictation equipment.
4. Appropriate methods of input for a particular setting.
5. Various types of voice-based technology.
6. Sources of information to be keyboarded.
7. OCR as a method of input.

Creation and Input

(originate, capture, and store)

Original Input

Voice

  Machine dictation
  Voice recognition and
    response

Keyboard

  Machine transcription
  Shorthand transcription
  Longhand transcription
  Self-composition
    (self-authoring)
  Hard copy

Image

  Optical character
    recognition (OCR)

  Micrographics
  (CIM, CAR)

  Facsimile
  Graphics

Nonoriginal Input

Prestored data/text,
  image, or voice
(i.e., voice, response, forms,
data, videotape)

Storage and/or retrieval

Processing

(capture, manipulate,
replicate, and store)

Capture

Identity

  Log
  Index

Keyboard

  Keypunch
  Data entry
  Word processor

Edit
Revise
Manipulate
Proof and/or verify
Approve

Replicate
(in a form for printing,
viewing, or hearing)

Photocopying
Printing
  Image
  Quality
  Laser

Micrographics
  (COM, CAR)
Reprographics
Phototypesetting
Facsimile
Voice response

Storage and/or retrieval

Distribution

(transfer, communicate,
send, and store)

Internal/External
(data, text, voice, and
image)

Mail
  Traditional or paper
  Electronic

Telecommunications
  Teleconferencing
  Satellite communications
  Networks

Archive, storage, and/or retrieval

Destruction
(receive and destroy)

Hard copy
  Shred
  Burn
  Pulverize
  Digital or image
  Delete/erase
  Burn

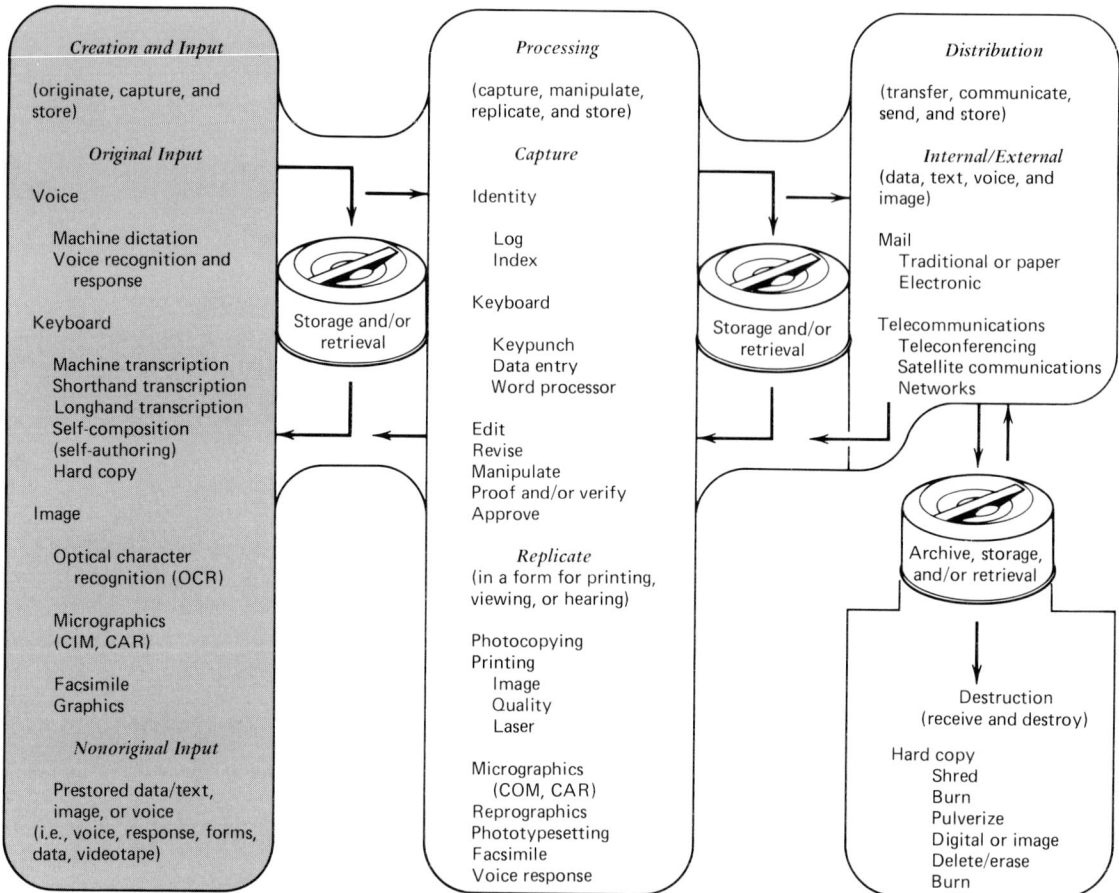

Figure 1 Creation and input includes original and nonoriginal input.

Input into an office system includes any source data or ideas to be processed. Some data may be used in the original form; some may require correction or change. Input can be divided into two major kinds: original and nonoriginal (see Figure 1). Original input can be defined as information that enters the system for the first time, such as

1. Documents first written in longhand by a principal and keyboarded into the system by a secretary, typist, or operator.
2. Documents self-composed by the author, secretary, typist, or operator.
3. Documents created by the principal using machine dictation; the recorded dictation is then transcribed by a secretary, typist, or operator.
4. Written or verbal instructions that give a form letter code or paragraph codes that instruct a secretary, typist, or operator to create a letter from prestored (nonoriginal) input.

Nonoriginal input can be defined as that information already existing in a system: for example,

1. Prerecorded and prestored documents such as letters, contracts, and so on (often called boilerplate), to which variable fill-in information can be added via the keyboard. Collection letters to delinquent accounts is one example.
2. Prerecorded paragraphs or sections that can be selected by the principal and assembled into a complete letter or other document. Certain engineering specifications are common to many projects; selecting appropriate ones and including them in a new contract or proposal saves preparation and rekeyboarding time.
3. Information sorted in another system that is transmitted—from a data processing system to a text processor, for example.
4. Previously typed material that can be read into a system via page reading or scanning (OCR).
5. Any other material generated at a remote location and telecommunicated into the local system.

Those methods that presently account for the major part of input will be explored in depth, so that you can better understand the management considerations in decision making concerning their usage.

ORIGINAL INPUT

Original creation as just defined can further be divided into three major categories: voice, keyboard, and image.

VOICE Voice consists of machine dictation and voice-based systems.

Machine Dictation Attempts to increase office productivity originally focused on the secretarial/clerical work force. Recently, however, as the need for increased managerial/professional productivity has been recognized, more attention has been directed to the use of machine dictation, which assists executives to input ideas into the system in the fastest, most economical way.

Equipment and Its Use. Dictation equipment can be broken down into four categories: portables, desk-top units, wired, and remote systems. Each has specific characteristics and uses.

Portable dictation units offer their users the advantage of recording ideas, notes, memos, and so on, right on the spot, where the need to get thoughts and ideas recorded is the greatest, because they are still fresh. Current models are compact—most are pocket size, weighing 6 to 12 ounces (see Figures 2 and 3). The portables are best suited for travel,

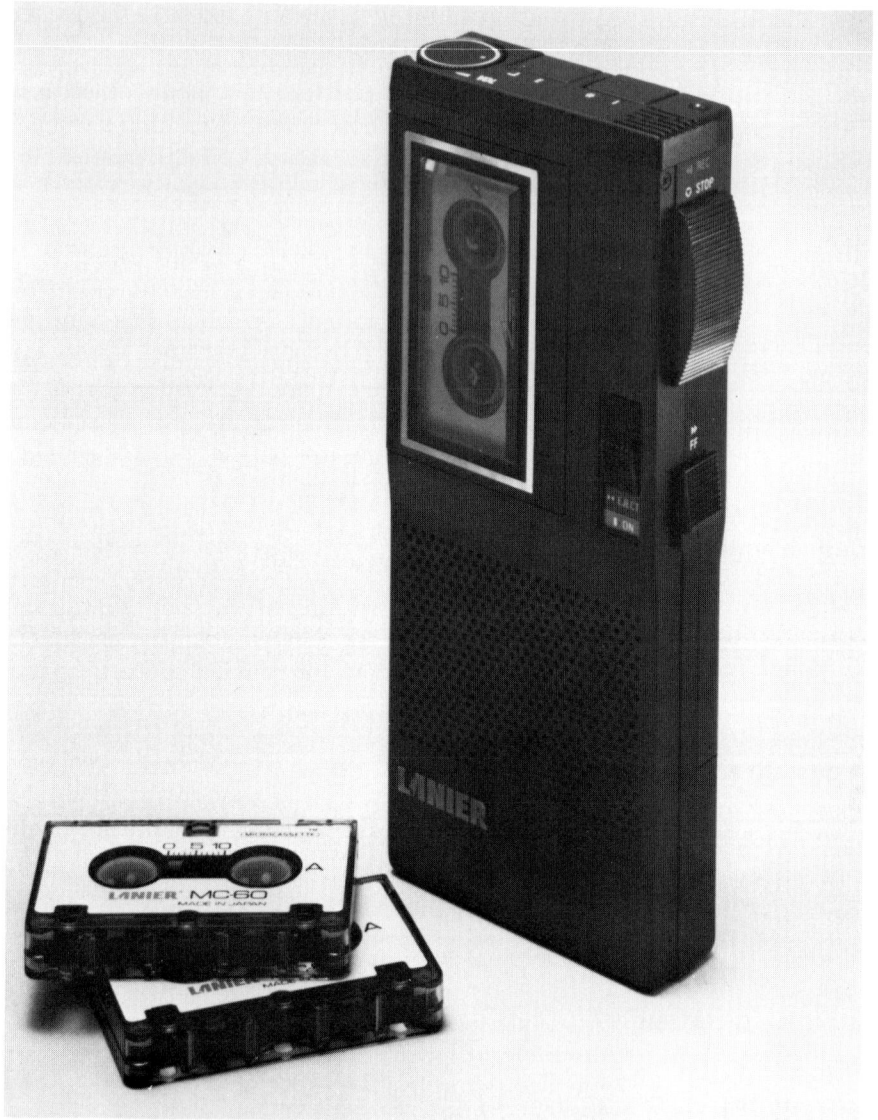

Figure 2 A portable dictation unit provides compact pocket size equipment. (Courtesy of Lanier Corporation)

field work, or use at home. They use either micro, mini, or standard magnetic tape cassettes.

Desktop units are suited to office organization structures that require the originator to dictate and have a secretary available to transcribe promptly for one or a few principals, or whenever one originator does a large volume of dictation. Desktop units use the same media as portables—micro, mini, or standard cassettes (see Figure 4).

Figure 3 A portable dictating unit. (Courtesy of Dictaphone Corporation)

For both portable and desktop dictation units, the cassette must be removed and placed in a transcription unit for typing. However, several dictation units can also function as transcribers when equipped to do so. Most portables or desktops can record conferences, speeches, interviews, and telephone calls.

Hard-wire, or private wire, dictation systems consist of handsets wired directly to a central recorder. The handset closely resembles a telephone but is equipped with dictation controls. Systems that serve only a small number of originators, such as three to six, are sometimes called work

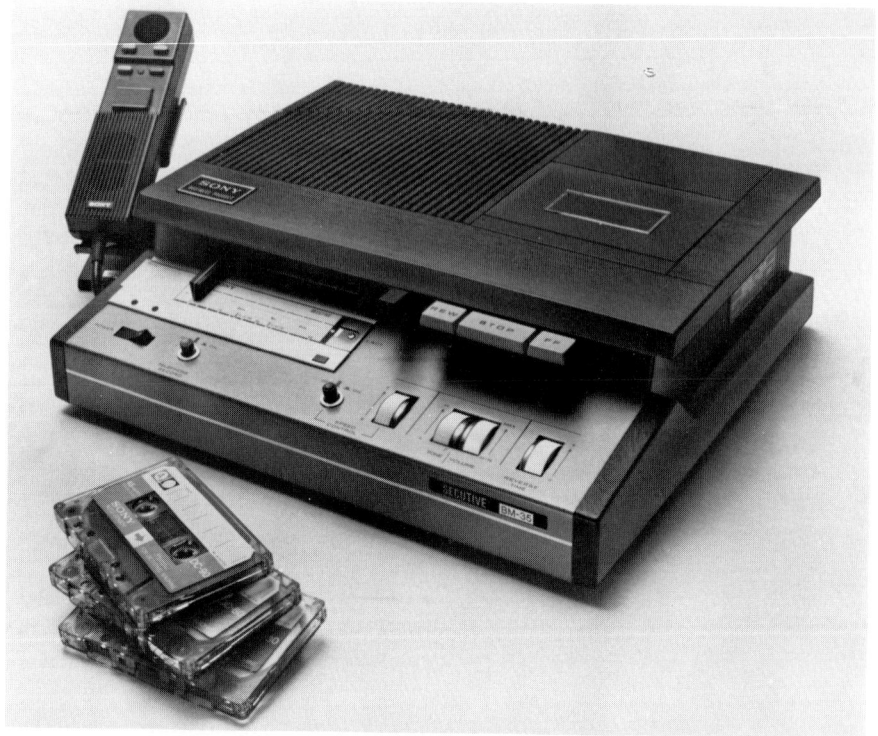

Figure 4   A desktop dictating unit. (Courtesy of Sony Corporation)

group systems; several of them include intercom capabilities (see Figure 5).

Usually used in large to medium dictation/transcription operations, most centralized dictation systems utilize the existing telephone system. This arrangement makes every telephone in the organization a potential dictation unit. By dialing the dictation center's number, an originator is connected to a recorder. Touch-Tone® systems are well suited for these systems, because of the ease of pressing buttons to control dictation functions, such as review, erase, and stop (see Figure 6).

Central systems offer distinct advantages. They offer dictation to all who require it, including the infrequent user who would not otherwise have a separate unit because its use cannot be justified. In the center, workloads can be spread among several transcribers, reducing turnaround time for completed work and improving service to all users.

Central systems have provisions for handling rush and priority work. They also enable users to call in dictation from phones outside the company.

Central dictation equipment is suited to situations in which individual

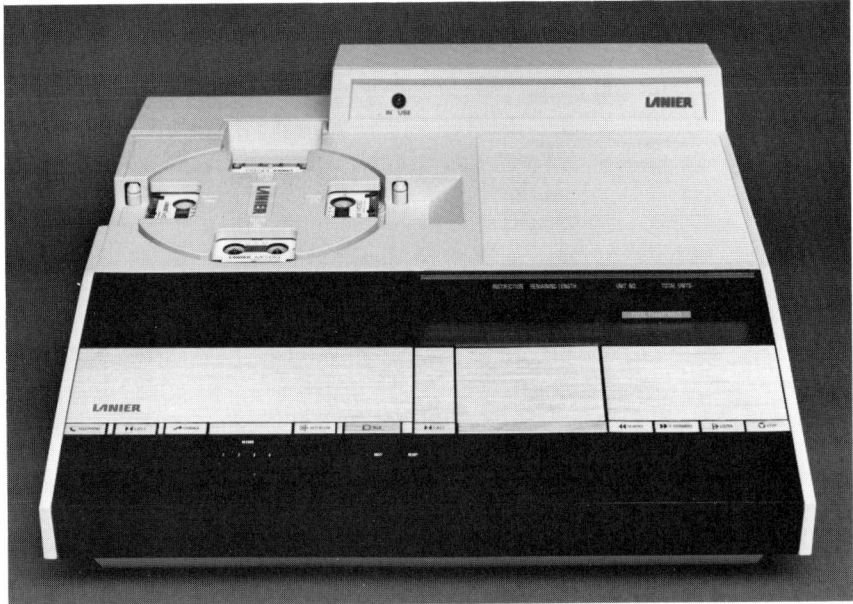

Figure 5 A messenger dictating unit. (Courtesy of Lanier Corporation)

Figure 6 A central recorder provides ease of use from remote locations. (Courtesy of Dictaphone Corporation)

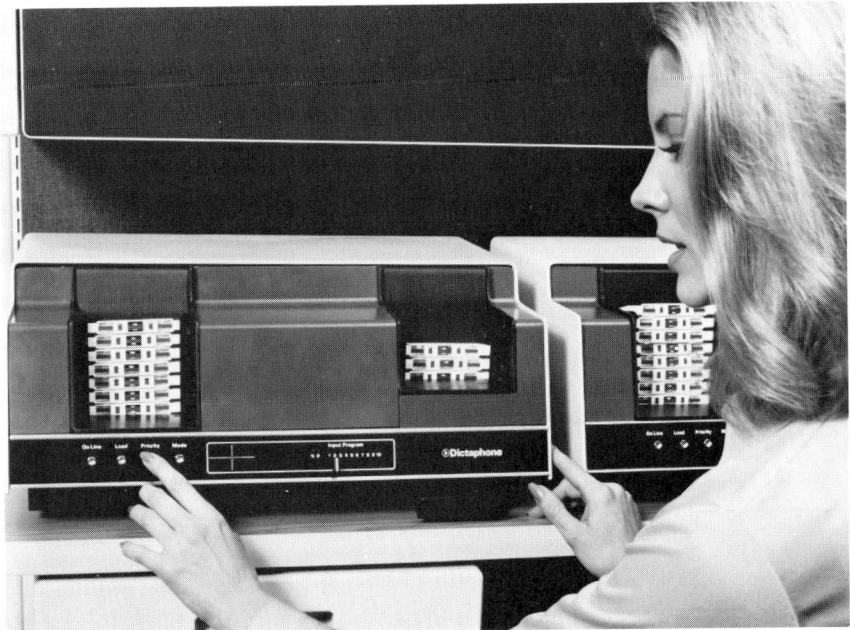

secretaries serve several executives. Groupings can be small or large. The type of equipment selected generally depends upon the number of people served, the frequency and volume of dictation, and the size of work group involved. Also, departments having highly specialized work often install a dedicated system to handle their written communications.

Off-premise dictation enables users of a system to dictate from any telephone outside of the location of the central recording or receiving system. The ability to phone in dictation from a remote location is useful when people are working away from the office. Off-premises systems are often used by traveling executives and sales representatives. They also serve an office whose operators keyboard in their home by enabling office managers to dictate to the home of the transcriber.

Selecting Equipment.   When selecting dictation equipment, administrators should first identify their requirements for efficient standard operations, and then consider specific features needed for the organization's special applications. The features should be evaluated in terms of benefits to the principal and to the transcriptionist.

For example, portables should be pocket size, so that they will be easy to carry around. Lightweight units equipped with micro and mini cassettes can be used for recording short notes. Machines using standard cassettes and having indexing capabilities (to indicate the end of one text segment and the beginning of the next) as well as cueing (for author instructions) are preferable for heavy-duty letter writing. Equipment used to record research should allow one-button control of operations so that the author can keep one hand free to handle publications and other materials. Of course, the transcriptionist must have a transcription machine that can not only accept the media produced by the portable, but also alert the operator to indexing signals.

A company with many occasional users might consider establishing a lending library to furnish portables. The person in charge of the machines would be responsible for keeping track of loans and returns, as well as for seeing that they are maintained in good working order (replacing batteries and erasing tapes, etc.) before they are reassigned.

Desktop dictation units should be equipped at least with a microphone and transcription machines with earphones and footpedal. Combination units will need all three accessories.

Combination units are usually bought in pairs and not moved between the author's and secretary's desks. To change a combination unit from dictating unit to transcriber requires unplugging a machine, exchanging its microphone for earphones and footpedal, transferring it to another desk, and plugging it in—each time a different person needs to use it (see Figure 7).

The selection of desktop machines requires careful evaluation of the principal's and secretary's needs. At a minimum, the principal requires one-button control on the microphone for record, stop, playback, and

Figure 7 A dual function desktop unit can be used by either secretary or principal. (Courtesy of Lanier Corporation)

possibly rewind. A fast playback feature allows the author to review recorded material quickly. The person should also be able to search to the last word dictated, in order to resume dictation promptly. End-of-text indexing and instruction cueing with the ability to note changes and insertions in the margins of the text (placed on a second tape track) are also important when dictation is moderate to heavy.

Other features that might be useful, depending upon individual preferences, are lights under the microprocessor control that show how much tape has been used or where cues are located. Audible fast-forward that indicates where dictation is stored and voice activation (the tape starts to move when a person speaks and stops when there is a pause) are further aids to efficiency.

More sophisticated microprocessor-based units offer telephone recording of messages when the principal is out of the office (see Figure 8).

Units used in conferences and meetings should produce excellent-quality sound so that individual voices can be differentiated easily no matter where the person is located in the room. In order to reduce machine downtime, it is also desirable to obtain a unit that can run a self-diagnosis and display a word or code explaining the cause of equipment failure.

From the transcriptionist's point of view, one of the most important features is sound quality. When a word originator steps away from the microphone, the speech should be nearly as clear as when he or she speaks directly into it. Comfort of earphones is equally as important (see Figure 9).

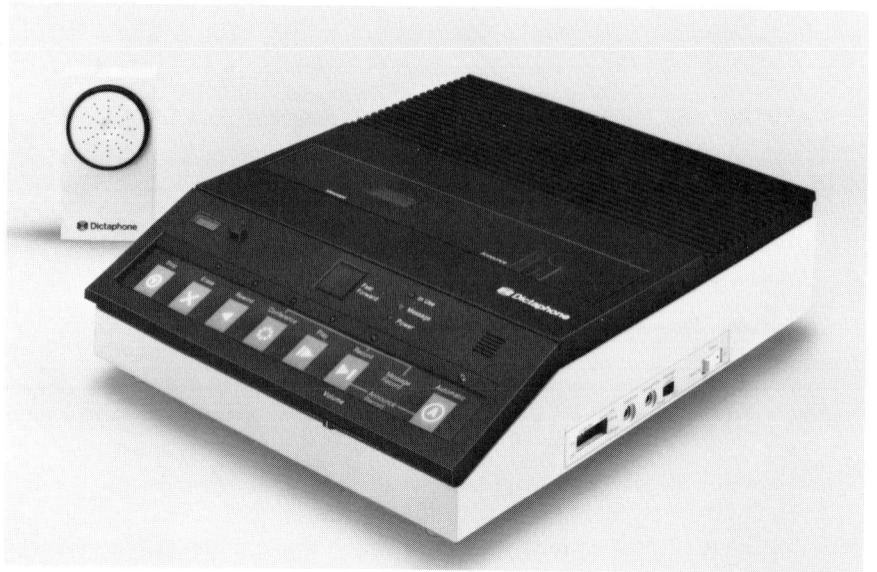

Figure 8   Telephone answering device. (Courtesy of Dictaphone Corporation)

Figure 9   Note the cushioned earphones of the transcription unit. (Courtesy of Lanier Corporation)

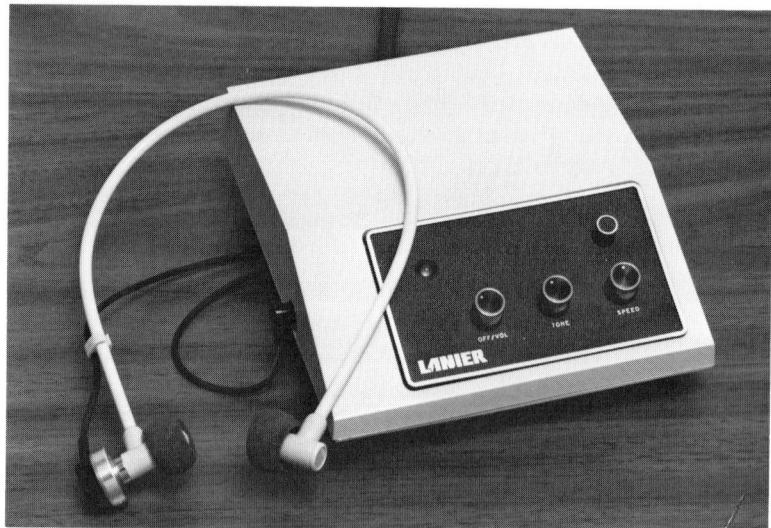

Manufacturers of transcription equipment also offer time-saving play-back features. These include scanning capability, so that the transcriber can listen to instructions before recording, and variable speech control that speeds up dictation yet keeps it understandable.

Many of the same considerations for evaluating desktop units apply to off-premise and centralized systems.

Advanced Features.   Machines have been introduced that perform several dictation-related functions automatically. These include

▶ Triple-duty portable units used for dictating while traveling and for dictating and transcribing while in the office.

▶ Portable desktop units equipped with a digital clock and alarm that can be used by timekeepers such as lawyers and accountants, to note the amount of time they spend dictating for a particular client. The alarm also serves to remind people of important appointments.

▶ Dictation/transcription/telephone answering/voice message systems that handle dictation and answer the telephone while the principal is away from the office (see Figure 10). When the principal returns, the message can be played back at his or her convenience. This capability saves callers' time dialing and redialing telephone numbers when individuals are away from their telephones. Similarly, users are assured of receiving their messages.

▶ Conference recorders that employ several microphones to record onto different tracks of the same tape. This capability enables the transcriptionist to determine which person is talking by listening to each track separately.

Figure 10   Telephone answering devices are particularly useful for storing messages when a principal is away from the office. (Courtesy of Lanier Corporation)

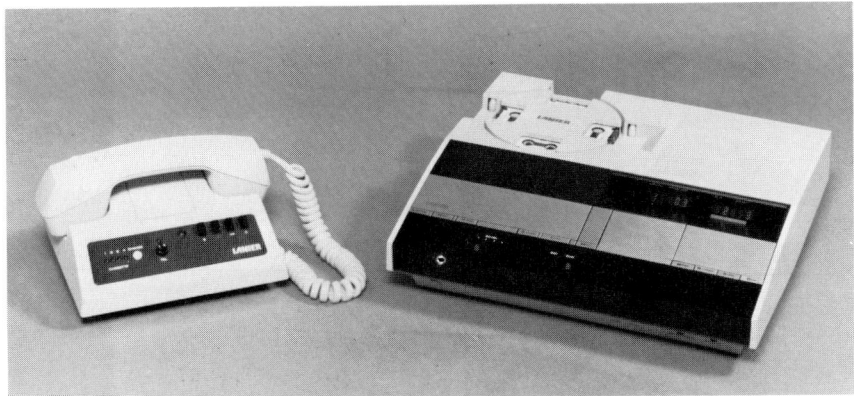

▶ Supervisor monitoring systems for central dictation systems that keep track of all work that flows through a center. These systems can show the status of work in progress and print a summary of work done in the center by a variety of criteria (department, originator, typist, type of work, time, and so on).

System Expandability.   Expandability allows more dictation/transcription stations and recorders to be added as a company or department grows. Organizations might also want to consider utilizing a system moni-

Figure 11 Nucleus central system is a management device for monitoring workload. (Courtesy of Dictaphone Corporation)

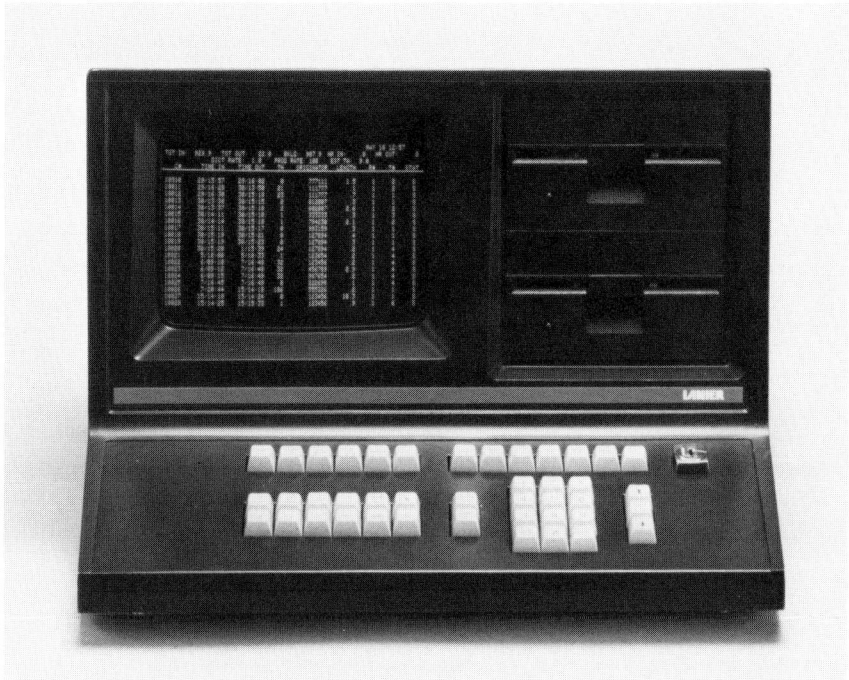

Figure 12 Supervision III is another vendor's management tool. (Courtesy of Lanier Corporation)

tor (with CRT and floppy diskette storage) that allows workflow to be controlled, data to be tracked, productivity measured, and reports to be generated for management purposes (see Figures 11 and 12).

Compatibility. Compatibility in dictation units is determined by the media and indexing methods used. If machines have been provided by one vendor and use the same type of media (micro, mini, or standard cassettes) and identical indexing methods (index slips, electronic cue, audible signal, digital counter, or tape markings), all transcriptions stations will be able to handle work prepared on any dictation unit. However, where several manufacturers' brands are used in combination, several precautions should be taken.

Machines should be equipped with the same type of recording media, where possible. Otherwise, transcription units should allow fitting with adapters that accept cassettes of different sizes. Likewise, indexing methods should be similar. Generally speaking, tapes in various sizes and shapes with different indexing/cueing mechanisms should be avoided in a combination system. Administrators installing two or more brands of equipment should require demonstrated proof that tapes are interchangeable before purchasing.

It is important to check with other customers in your area to ascertain how satisfied they have been with a supplier before contracting for a machine. Dictation equipment can be obtained directly from branch offices of the manufacturer or from office equipment dealers. Discounts, trial periods, and service varies between and among dealers and manufacturer branches.

User Training. After dictation equipment has been selected and installed, it must be used and used properly. User training programs are necessary for both the operators and principals.

Many manufacturers offer self-training programs. These are in the form of comprehensive manuals that are often accompanied by cassette tapes (which can be played on the dictation equipment) that not only give instruction, but also offer practice exercises and dictation organizer forms. One system has built-in audio instructions that play out each time a person dictates into the system.

Along with training programs, a company must develop standardized procedures for ongoing dictation equipment use. Instructions about procedures and equipment use should appear in manuals given to all involved employees to use for reference (see Figure 13).

Figure 13   Dictation procedures and guidelines.

1. Organize thoughts
   (a) Decide objectives first.
   (b) Select points and sequence to meet objective.
   (c) Gather reference material if necessary to refer to (files, reports, names and addresses).
   (d) Organize ideas into paragraphs.
   (e) Make notes on scraps of paper or in margin of letter.
   Do your thinking and organizing off-line rather than on-line
2. Give necessary identification
   (a) Name.
   (b) Case or code number.
3. Identify document and retention instructions
   (a) Letter (type or final).
   (b) Memo (draft—hold one week for revision).
   (c) Report (format indefinite—figures to be revised monthly).
   (d) Manuscript (hold for revisions until completion).
4. Format
   (a) Single/double space.
   (b) What kind of letterhead (personal, company, titled officer, interoffice).
   (c) Number of copies.

Figure 13 (*Continued*)

(d) Envelopes.

(e) Indicate special format within document (asterisk/footnote items will be dictated at conclusion of document).

5. Guidelines
   (a) Dictate complete names and addresses for all outgoing letters.
   (b) Spell out all proper names and unusual jargon.
   (c) Specify unusual punctuation: parentheses, underscoring, semicolon, colon, quotes, exclamation point.
   (d) Specify paragraphs.
   (e) Spell out mechanical instructions: i.e., paragraphs to be indented beyond the regular margin.
   (f) Specify number of columns for statistical reports:
       Simple columnar and statistical work can be dictated—completed format should be delivered to the center.
   (g) Foreign names and addresses should be sent to the center in writing when used infrequently, and if used frequently, should be maintained on file in the Center.

6. Suggested phonetic alphabet

Spelling Names

A—Alice	J—James	S—Samuel
B—Bertha	K—Kate	T—Thomas
C—Charles	L—Lewis	U—Utah
D—David	M—Mary	V—Victor
E—Edward	N—Nellie	W—William
F—Frank	O—Oliver	X—X-ray
G—George	P—Peter	Y—Young
H—Henry	Q—Quaker	Z—Zebra
I—Ida	R—Robert	

Especially important for differentiation are

D and V and B	C and Z	N and M	Y and I
P and T and B	C and G	F and S	T and V

7. Courtesies
   (a) Use relaxed normal conversation tone.
   (b) Especially when reading material, speak at your normal speed and tone.
   (c) Avoid mumbling, smoking, chewing pencil or gum, fumbling with instrument.
   (d) Enunciate clearly—particularly plural endings and tenses and word endings such as *ing*, and *ed*.
   (e) Use appropriate inflections and pauses.
   (f) Address secretary as "Secretary."
   (g) Use "please" and "thank you" where appropriate—adds personal rapport.

8. Instructions for closing
   (a) Signature (originator or designator).
   (b) Title, if appropriate.
   (c) Copies to whom (indicated or blind).
   (d) Enclosure or attachment.
9. Checklist for improvement of communication
   (a) Avoid wordiness.
   (b) Avoid excessive use of stock phrases.
   (c) Use natural expressions—say it in your own words.
   (d) Apply the five C's of communication:
       Clearness
       Conciseness
       Correctness
       Completeness
       Courtesy
   (e) Exhibit the "You" attitude—avoid the "I" strain.
   (f) Use short words, sentences, and paragraphs—not choppy but not so long and complex as to be difficult to interpret.
   (g) Use positive statements—avoid negative words and phrases.
10. Dictation of request for stored material

   Certain items are used repeatedly and have been stored on permanent tape.

   To request an item that has been stored on permanent cassette,
   (a) Dictate or write your name and department or code number.
   (b) Dictate or write the item reference number.
   (c) Dictate any variable information required in the order in which it appears in the document. The date need not be dictated unless the item should be back-dated.
   (d) You may also send a typed or handwritten list of variable information, indicating reference numbers of permanent material desired.

Figure 13 (Continued)

Justifying Machine Dictation. Applying work standards to the origination of work clarifies the need for machine dictation. In addition to data gathered from studies, answers to the questions shown in Figure 14 will provide information to help evaluate and select the proper dictation equipment.

Variable Dictation Variable input to prestored material or nonoriginal input provides the second basic use of voice in the input phase. Authors can dictate via electronic dictating equipment to a secretary, who in turn can merge original input (by keyboarding new data) with prestored boilerplate and thereby create a new document.

To buy or what to buy, and why

WITH A RAPIDLY GROWING selection of dictation equipment, recording media, and systems configuration, choosing the right combination may be a puzzle to executives unfamiliar with it. For those in this situation, here is a list of questions designed to point the prospective buyer in the right direction.

Studies have established the basic benefits of dictation, regardless of the type of equipment used. Executives can machine-dictate six times faster than they can handwrite. And transcribing from dictation equipment is usually twice as fast as transcribing from shorthand notes. (Add automated typing to the procedures, and revised copy prints out at 5 to 10 times faster than if it were done on a standard office electric.) Selecting the proper dictation/transcription equipment will help increase productivity.

Document work volume

1. How many documents, reports, letters, memos, and other typed documents are originated within your offices?
a. _____ more than 10 a day.
b. _____ less than 10 a day.

c. How much typing volume does the entire work load represent in terms of lines or pages? _____ (lines or pages) per _____ (day, week, month).
2. How many people perform the typing function in your offices?
a. _____ secretaries who work for only one manager or executive.
b. _____ secretaries who serve several executives or authors.
c. _____ typists in a steno or word processing center.
d. _____ administrative support secretaries in conjunction with a WP center.
e. Is secretarial and typing service available promptly when it's needed? _____
f. Does the secretary have to interrupt a project to answer a call or to leave the workstation and telephone unattended?

Work away from the office

3. a. How many personnel who travel must originate memos, reports, or other documents while away from the office? _____
b. How many documents, etc., are generated daily by personnel who travel? _____
c. How much work does the away-from-the-office correspondence amount to? _____ more than 25 documents a day. _____ between 5 and 10 documents a day. _____ less than 5 documents a day.

Other uses

4. a. Do business ideas come to you at odd hours or places? _____
b. Would it be advantageous to record a two-way telephone conversation? _____
c. Do you ever need to record meetings, speeches, or interviews? _____
d. Do you have manuals, training programs, and other work that could be recorded on cassette

tapes for employee or customer orientation and education? _____

Control

5. a. How many individual typing jobs come into your correspondence center daily, _____ weekly, _____ monthly, _____ (including dictation and copy typing)?
b. Do you maintain a log? _____
c. Even with a log, are there frequent requests for status of work or for completion times? _____
d. Can you easily locate work in process by originator, recorder, transcriptions? _____
e. Can you easily identify priority work? _____
f. Can you easily determine the amount of work back log? _____
g. Does your center have an effective departmental charge-back system?

Answers

1. a. Generating a large amount of daily paperwork requires a remote system with multiple recorders. If a substantial portion is specialized (such as pathology reports in a hospital), look into the advantages of dedicated recorders or dedicated systems. b. If many people originate only a few documents daily or occasionally, there's a good possibility that a central system is feasible to handle the steady stream of work from all parts of the office. If there are only a few originators in the office, and the volume is small, consider the advantage of a work group system. Even if there's only a handful of people producing a document a day, dictation equipment can save valuable executive time. c. You need an accurate answer to this question before you can use the information in the questions above. With the answers to both, you're in a better position to determine secretarial support requirements,

Figure 14 To buy or what to buy, and why. (Courtesy of Dictaphone Corporation)

and whether a center, work group, or individual secretarial support—or combinations—will suit your office needs best.

2. Answers on these questions will give you a scorecard on your present office structure. They'll also give you a clue to the style of management. a. There's a possibility that management still prefers the 1-to-1 ratio. In this situation there may be more receptiveness towards individual desktop dictating and transcribing machines. b. This structure can lend itself to either work group systems or individual desktop dictation/transcription units. But the final decision rests on the volume and frequency of dictation. c. Word processing center structures are best prepared to accept remote dictation systems, but centers should also accommodate dictation sent in from desktop and portable dictating machines. d. Administrative secretaries are often required to dictate some material in support of their principals' activities. Be sure to count them as possible authors when conducting your survey of dictation needs. e. A "no" answer here is an indicator that backup or overload resources are needed to bolster a secretary burdened with serving one or more principals. If she requires individual transcription equipment for normal duties, it's more important than ever that recording media be compatible with equipment in other offices or in the WP center so other equipment is available to handle extra work. f. Secretaries with varied duties whose activities are frequently interrupted are likely to delay correspondence service to their principals. These circumstances point to a greater need for a remote system to a transcription center that devotes full time to producing typewritten work.

3. Answers to question 3 are intended to identify your needs for portable dictation units and the need to record phone dictation from authors when they are away from the office. For traveling executives and salespersons who need to file reports of daily activity, portables offer the most practical solution. Minicassettes or microcassettes are small enough to carry in a briefcase until the user returns to the office to have them transcribed, or they can be easily mailed in. For urgent work that needs to be reported daily, a desktop or tank-type recorder dedicated to phone-in dictation insures prompt transcription the same day, or the following day if it is phoned in overnight.

4. Answers to these questions tell you what other recording equipment or features will make your people more productive and effective. a. A pocket portable is ready to capture a sudden inspiration or an urgent memo, whether you're in a customer's office, a convention floor, plane, car, or in bed. b. Recording critical details in a phone conversation may assure you of getting the facts accurately. c. Your need to record meetings, speeches and interviews points to the need for a cassette device that offers long recording times of up to 30 or 45 minutes per side. d. Using cassettes as an educational tool isn't new, and dictation equipment offers a handy and practical solution.

5. The more jobs coming into a word processing center, the greater the need to know where they are. With more jobs come more requests from users for status reports and delivery schedules. Without the proper controls, record-keeping and job-tracking has become a time-consuming task, even in centers with good manual logging procedures. The purpose of these questions is to help you determine how a word management computer can reduce the time needed to look up data on job status, eliminate manual record-keeping, provide an accurate report of backlog and priority work, and provide data you need for department charge-back without time-consuming recordkeeping and report preparation.

Figure 14   (Continued)

Voice-Based Systems   Voice response and voice recognition are still in their infancy. To date, their applications have been publicized far beyond their realities. Although people cannot carry on conversations with computers (as in the popular "Star Trek" television series), computer systems can recognize and respond to human voices on a limited basis. There are two types of voice systems:

▶ *Voice-recognition systems*, which "recognize" spoken words and convert them to digital signals to an attached system or display device (see Figure 15).

VOICE RECOGNITION

1. Inquirer dials computer system, "talks" to system, enters I.D., makes inquiry; or microphone can be wired directly into system.
2. Computer matches inquirer's voice against prestored voice patterns.
3. As inquirer speaks, computer system executes commands after matching voice to memory.
4. Output—one possible output form could be display of (a) vocal command for visual verification, (b) answer to command or inquiry.

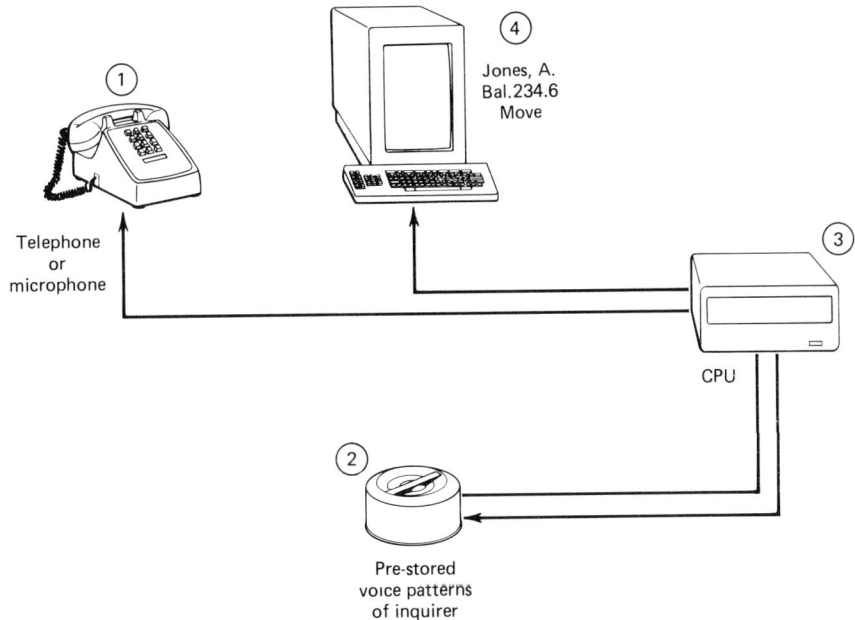

Figure 15 Voice recognition devices that recognize spoken words and convert them to digital signals.

▶ *Voice-response systems*, which "respond" to an inquiry by converting the answer (which is stored digitally in computer memory—an account balance, for example) to a voice response (see Figure 16).

Voice recognition and voice response are closely related, both in their technological base and in their applications. Developments in certain signal processing and data compression techniques are making products of both types more practical and economical than ever before. Manufacturers of voice products offer either recognition or response capability, but not both.

Voice-recognition systems are used for three basic functions: to enter commands, to enter data, and to enter queries. The system is programmed to recognize specific types of entries and to perform certain functions accordingly.

VOICE RESPONSE

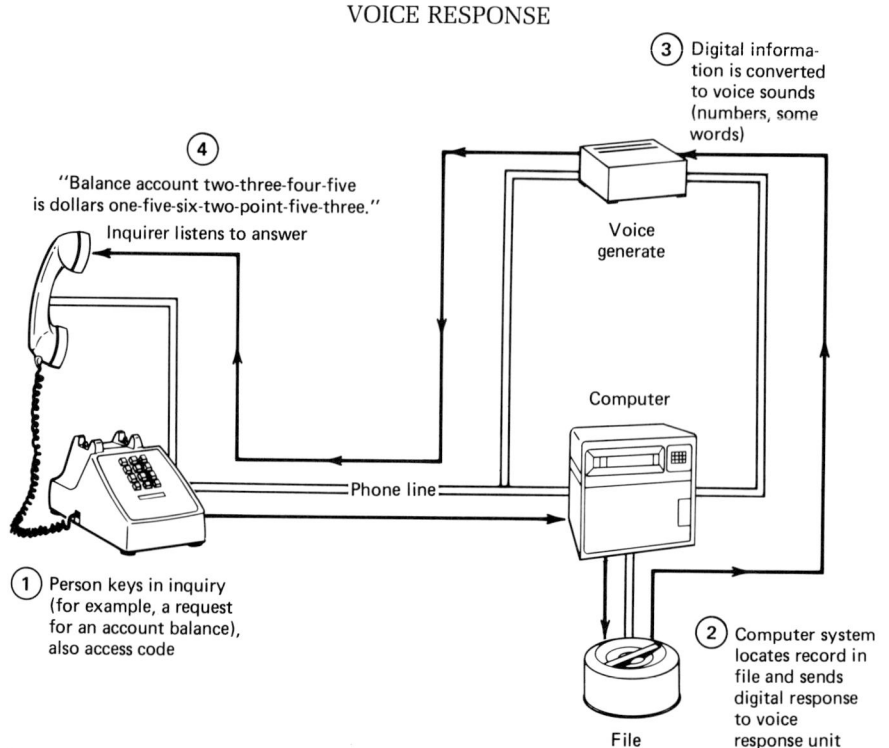

Figure 16 One version of voice response converting digitally stored information to voice response.

Voice-response systems also are used for three basic functions: to respond to queries, to confirm correct recognition of voice input, and to prompt an operator. The system is programmed to answer in a synthesized, voicelike response.

Several other types of voice-based systems can be identified. Voice identification is a system that verifies that the person making the inquiry is who he or she claims to be—a task usually referred to as speaker verification or authentication. In operation, a person wishing to gain entry to a secured location is asked to speak a designated number of words selected by the system from a small vocabulary previously recorded for the purpose. The system matches the spoken input against the stored voice profiles for that speaker. If the match meets certain established criteria, the identity of the individual is assumed to be verified and access is granted.

Voice mail is a system that stores and forwards the digitized voice message for transmission to a receiving point, in much the same way that other communications systems deliver other kinds of electronic message. Messages can originate at any telephone and can be delivered to and stored at other telephone(s), and then retrieved from storage by the telephone user.

Language training is another possible system. Voice-input devices will some day provide important tools for learning foreign languages and for rehabilitating persons who suffer from speech disabilities. The objective is to "score" a student's pronunciation of selected words or phrases against a teacher-defined standard.

Language translation is yet another possibility. The capability to translate from one language to another or, in a related but nonetheless awesomely difficult task, to translate from the spoken word to text, has been the ultimate aim of the voice recognition community (among others) for a long time.

Future voice recognition technologies will be discussed in a later chapter.

KEYBOARD   The keyboard is the major point of input for both text and data, as evidenced by its role in typing and data entry.

Keyboarding, or typing, is the primary means of entering original information into the systems used in today's office. The information to be keyboarded generally comes from one of five sources: (1) machine dictation, (2) shorthand, (3) longhand text and data, (4) self-keyboarding, and (5) hard copy.

Machine Dictation   Machine dictation (described in detail earlier in this chapter) is defined as that information recorded onto an electronic dictating device. This source of input traditionally has been used for short documents consisting of well-formatted material. With the increasing demand for improved white collar productivity, machine dictation has found increased acceptance. It is necessary to prepare and train those who will be inputting into a system via voice technology in the art of dictation and preparation.

Using a dictating machine reduces the average cost of a letter by 25 percent compared with dictating the same letter to a secretary. Figure 17

Figure 17   Note the cost of machine dictated letter vs. shorthand. (Courtesy of Dartnell Corporation)

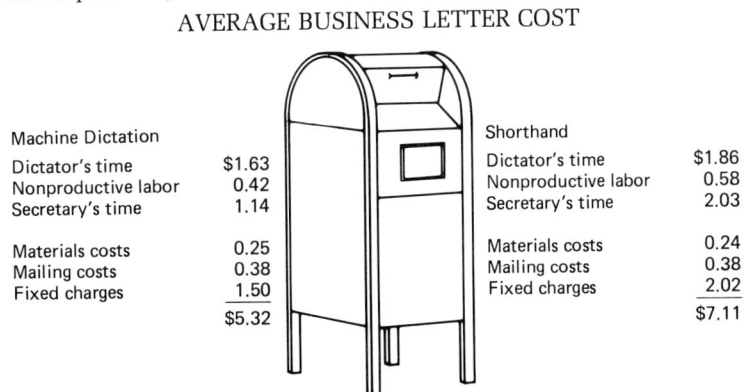

AVERAGE BUSINESS LETTER COST

Machine Dictation		Shorthand	
Dictator's time	$1.63	Dictator's time	$1.86
Nonproductive labor	0.42	Nonproductive labor	0.58
Secretary's time	1.14	Secretary's time	2.03
Materials costs	0.25	Materials costs	0.24
Mailing costs	0.38	Mailing costs	0.38
Fixed charges	1.50	Fixed charges	2.02
	$5.32		$7.11

shows the cost factors for each method, as determined by the Dartnell Corporation.

Machine Shorthand

Another form of keyboard input is machine shorthand. Although the standard shorthand machine has been used for years primarily by court reporters to take notes on court and other formal sessions, the integration of technologies is causing those interested in the improvement of office productivity to take a new look at machine shorthand. Today an originator's idea can be captured as keystrokes on magnetic tape and transcribed using CAT (computer-aided transcription), as shown in Figure 18.

Those who are proficient in the use of machine shorthand learn a system whereby they take notes and record them in digital form on magnetic tape cassettes. Higher input rates are achieved through a special shorthand system that allows the rapid recording of words by depressing one or more keys at a time. The transcript does not require a person's time for rekeyboarding, since a computer can read and translate the magnetic impulses into words. The transcript can then be displayed on the screen for needed editing and revisions before the final copy is printed or stored electronically for later retrieval.

Shorthand

Shorthand is the face-to-face dictation by an originator to a support staff person, or secretary. A certain measure of comfort, security, and status has been associated with face-to-face dictation. The originator has enjoyed

Figure 18 Machine shorthand equipment captures keystroke on magnetic tape and transcribes it through a computer. (Courtesy of Stenograph Corporation)

knowing that the responsibility for the final document has been delegated to a secretary. The secretary transcribes the shorthand dictation into the system via keyboard.

Historically, the kinds of documents dictated (in addition to letters) have included complex documents requiring ongoing explanation to the secretary and longer-than-average documents or multiple documents given simultaneously to the secretary. However, with advancing technology, more emphasis is being placed on transcription skills than on shorthand notetaking speed.

Although shorthand remains a helpful skill, its use is decreasing. Nevertheless, in today's office, it still provides a means for a secretary to gather information prior to keyboarding into an office automation system. There are still occasions when a secretary needs to take short notes from a principal, from a telephone conversation, or from a short meeting, when electronic recording devices are not available.

Longhand Text and Data

Longhand text and data is manually prepared by the originator and subsequently keyboarded by someone else into a system. Creating information utilizing longhand is still commonly used as a method of input. This usage is counterproductive, because of the slow rate of speed with which information is created. As standards shown in later chapters indicate, longhand involves creating information at approximately 10 words per minute, whereas machine dictation allows creation of ideas at an average of 80 words per minute.

Longhand could and sometimes must be used to create specially formatted documents in which information is easier to sketch than to verbalize, such as columnar materials with special requirements for margins, tabs, and spacing; statistical material; and all other documents not appropriate for machine dictation, shorthand dictation, or original keyboarding. For example, if information from many sources must be condensed into a limited space, the condensation process is primarily mental, and writing by hand may be the easiest way to rework the information.

Self-Composition

Self-composed documents are those documents keyboarded by the originator, who can be an author or a secretary. Often executives give secretaries the necessary general information and instruct them to create the letter or document for them. Experienced support personnel are well qualified to perform this responsibility and often self-compose a large percentage of originators' documents. Management workstations and personal and/or portable terminals and computers provide originators who have keyboarding skills the opportunity to self-compose, or self-keyboard, at the point of origination of the idea. By having these ideas captured in a digital form, support staff personnel can retrieve, edit, revise, replicate, and subsequently distribute them throughout an information and communication system.

Frequently, paraprofessionals or technical specialists keyboard highly technical forms or documents that require fill-in entries. For example, paraprofessional or managerial staff may directly enter the following applications into the system:

▶ An Accounting Department (many federal forms).
▶ A Personnel Department (Equal Employment Opportunity reports).
▶ A legal environment (a paralegal has the knowledge and skill to produce probate and estate planning forms, real estate matters, or corporate documents).

Self-composition will increase as an input method as management workstations and personal computers proliferate in the office environment in the next decade. According to a Dartnell Corporation survey, many executives predict that a rough draft letter may be composed on a desktop computer in the near future. This would permit editing and transcription to take place when either the dictator or the secretary is free of other tasks.

Hard Copy   Hard copy is material that has already been typed or printed (such as excerpts from magazines, books, and/or documents that have not been previously stored in the system but were typed). Traditionally, hard copy has been given to a keyboard specialist to enter into the system.

In addition to actual keyboarding, operators' skills must include the ability to organize, structure, format, and logically present information. These skills, which are required to keyboard effectively and productively, will be transferrable to the evolving electronic office. These attributes also will be required of all individuals who will be entering information into future office systems, including those that will utilize voice recognition devices.

Hard copy may also be entered into a system through image processing. It is believed that future technologies will virtually eliminate the need for rekeying "hard copy" data and text. Voice and image will be the medium to introduce "hard copy" into a system through the advancing technologies.

IMAGE   Image constitutes the input of previously captured data via use of technology such as optical character recognition (OCR), micrographics (CIM, CAR), facsimile, or graphics.

Image input into a system will take many forms as the advancing technologies of word processing, data processing, OCR, micrographics (COM, CIM), CAR, facsimile, graphics, and video and computer teleconferencing are integrated into office automation. Each of these is discussed in greater detail in this and subsequent chapters so that you may see how and where they fit.

OCR One of the fastest methods of input, and most discussed in today's office, is OCR (optical character recognition). OCR can be defined as the process by which a system scans typewritten pages and stores the scanned characters in digital form. OCR devices can scan and read printed or typed characters and convert them into storage or input directly to word processing or data processing screens, for immediate editing or formatting.

The first reference to a machine that converted printed characters into code occurred in 1912, when a man named Goldberg patented a machine that directly read characters and converted them into telegraph code. With Goldberg's device, telegraph messages could be sent over wire without human intervention. The machine could read a typed message and convert it to paper tape, in turn generating the proper Morse code for message transmission.

In 1914 the first known operating OCR reading machine was invented by Fournier d'Albe as an aid to the blind. This reading machine scanned a printed page and provided the user with a meaningful oral output.

In 1946, RCA developed the "electric pencil." In 1948, Mort Taube suggested that signals from the electric pencil could be coupled with a facsimile device to transmit a printed page to remote terminals.

OCR for data entry did not become viable until electronic data processing equipment was developed in the mid-1940s. With the birth of the electronic data processing industry, it became obvious that data entry expense would be significant in the business world.

The first practical OCR scanner for data entry was developed when Intelligent Machine Reader Corporation (IMR) manufactured and installed a commercial OCR for *Reader's Digest* in 1954. This application converted typewritten documents into punched cards for input into a computer in the magazine's subscription department.

IMR also developed a prototype OCR page reader in 1959 for the U.S. Air Force in Rome, New York, which read full upper- and lower-case alphanumeric fonts.

Today OCR is accepted as a mature technology with a proven track record of cost reduction in the highly labor-intensive area of data entry. The greatest advantage of OCR lies in its power of interface with other technology in the modern office. In addition, OCR permits the capturing of input data at the point of origination. Through conversion to digital impulses at that point, OCR eliminates the need for again keying the same information before entry into word processing operations. However, most input material must be in a form that can be read by the OCR scanner. More recently, OCR units have been announced that reduce the formatting requirements.

The OCR/WP Information Flow. In an OCR-oriented word processing system, the initial document generation procedure would be as follows:

1. Information for the document is submitted to a processor (secretary) in verbal or hard-copy form.

2. Information is typed or transcribed on a typewriter with OCR-readable type styles and character lift-off capability, such as the IBM correcting Selectric typewriter.

3. The typed document is returned to the OCR reader.

4. The scanned document is called to the screen for editing and reformatting.

5. A revised printout is made.

6. The document is returned to the originator for revision.

Figure 19 illustrates the information flow when OCR and word processing are combined.

The ability to scan typewritten material into text editing machines via OCR is gaining increased acceptance. Most office automation equipment manufacturers offer an OCR reader as an optional peripheral device. Many word processing users are installing these units to increase productivity, maintain traditional office structures, perform media conversion, and provide a link between text editing equipment and dissimilar machines.

Many vendors use OCR as a means of media conversion when upgrading from one system to another. The hard copy from a word processing

Figure 19 A word processing system using optical character recognition. (Courtesy of Hendrix Corporation)

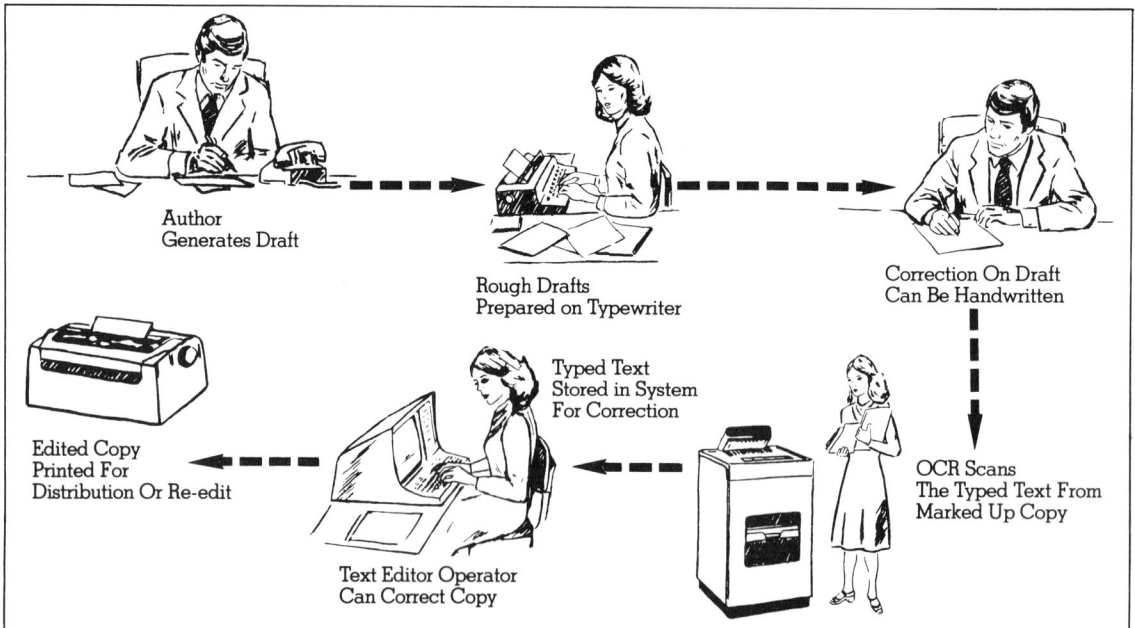

Author
Generates Draft

Rough Drafts
Prepared on Typewriter

Correction On Draft
Can Be Handwritten

Edited Copy
Printed For
Distribution Or Re-edit

Typed Text
Stored in System
For Correction

OCR Scans
The Typed Text From
Marked Up Copy

Text Editor Operator
Can Correct Copy

printer with an OCR-readable font can be read into another system via OCR.

Office automation applications for OCR include text and data original entry into a system. The segment of the OCR industry that serves as input to word processing, text editing, and typesetting systems is a spin-off of the page reader, with some significant differences. First, compared to the large page reader systems, they are low in cost. Second, the machine can be programmed to read a variety of typewriter fonts. Third, interfaces are available for a wide range of word processing and typesetting machines. Fourth, they are relatively slow compared with their high-performance relatives.

The OCR readers in this market segment range from $8000 to $50,000. Some have no capability to handle rejected characters other than to flag the condition. Some are hand-fed, some have automatic feeders. The list of options varies widely. The extension of the word processing world to encompass the electric typewriter universe is what provides the driving force and vigor of this segment of the OCR industry.

One study by Compuscan, Inc., showed that 75 to 80 percent of the word processing operator's time is devoted to keying text and only 20 to 25 percent is devoted to the editing and printing capability of word processing. When an OCR input reader is installed, keying is shifted from the higher-cost word processing operator and equipment to the typist and typewriter. By removing the original text-entry function from the word processing system, it is conservatively estimated, 50 to 75 percent of the receiving word processing center's productive hours may be released and made available for text editing. An OCR reader is illustrated in Figure 20.

The growing acceptance of OCR stems primarily from its relative ease of use and flexibility. In addition, manufacturers have made considerable improvements in machine reliability, speed, and functions during the past few years. Recent enhancements include

1. Input into text editing equipment may be performed in background, leaving the operator free to perform other tasks.
2. Ability to read many fonts, including underscores.
3. Recognition of formats as well as characters.
4. Output to a variety of technical devices.
5. Information transmission through communications channels.

Justification.   OCR units offer a cost-effective means of boosting word processing production by permitting both equipment and personnel to be more fully utilized. Standard electric office typewriters already in use can become input stations for word processing, thus freeing the more expensive text editing equipment to perform editing, merging, formatting, and printing tasks they were designed to handle. Trained word processing operators can devote their time to these tasks exclusively, accomplishing

Figure 20 Hendrix Typereader. TR2: Optical Character Reader (OCR). (Courtesy of Hendrix Corporation)

them in less time. By permitting access to word processing with a typewriter, OCR extends systems usage throughout an organization.

An organization will find OCR suitable for its needs if at least one of the following situations exists:

1. Three or more text editing units are in use.
2. More than 40 percent of the word processing operation is involved in original keyboarding.
3. Rush and overflow jobs occur so frequently that text editing equipment is often overloaded.
4. Document originators are in dispersed locations.
5. The quality of technical material requires a specialized typist who must be situated near the document originator.
6. Word processing output needs to be typeset, fed into a data processing machine or computer, sent as a telex message, or transmitted to a distant location.

Benefits. OCR use in an office automation environment provides benefits such as unattended input of typed text off-line; simplistic media conversion; point-to-point communications at 5-10 pages per minute; input to a computer; manipulation of data at time of input; basic editorial and proofing changes at time of input; and release of word processing equipment for editing, revision, playback, playout, and document assembly (see Figure 21).

The benefits of OCR used to input hard copy to a system include elimination of redundant keyboarding, elimination of transcription errors, reduced equipment costs, reduced turnaround time, elimination of redundant forms, reduced training costs, ease of operation, increased word processing equipment utilization with minimized expansion costs, and workload distribution throughout the organization.

Future plans of OCR vendors include dramatic reductions in cost and size; improved sensors to capture typed images more easily from a wider usage of sources; graphic arts capability for charts, graphs, and schematics; high-speed final copy; communications; and the capability of identifying different or variable types of characters in one document.

OCR high-speed input increases performance. Manufacturers' improvements that are making an impact on OCR ease of use include the ability to read conventional typewritten copy with the following characteristics: single-spaced lines; 10- and 12-pitch type spacing intermixed; OCR fonts and common typefaces; free format layout; skewed or wavy lines; wrinkled, dog-eared, and smudged copy; and typewritten insertions.

The OCR Challenge. Effective use of OCR offers a major challenge to the word processing or secretarial services supervisor. Quality control must be maintained among the dispersed typists and typewriters. Standardized procedures for everyone must be established and followed. Workflow and turnaround time requirements must be understood by both secretaries and the word processing center. A hit-and-miss approach will

Figure 21 Benefits of using optical character recognition devices.

1. OCR extends word processing input capability to everyone in an office with an electric typewriter that can be equipped with OCR type. This means that even occasional users can use word processing when the need arises.
2. Scanning an OCR-typed page eliminates the need to keyboard information into a system a second time.
3. Page scanning is faster than keyboarding. If a large number of pages had to be keyboarded on a word processing device, rather than scanned, the word processing machines would be tied up in keyboarding for days, instead of the few hours it would take to scan.

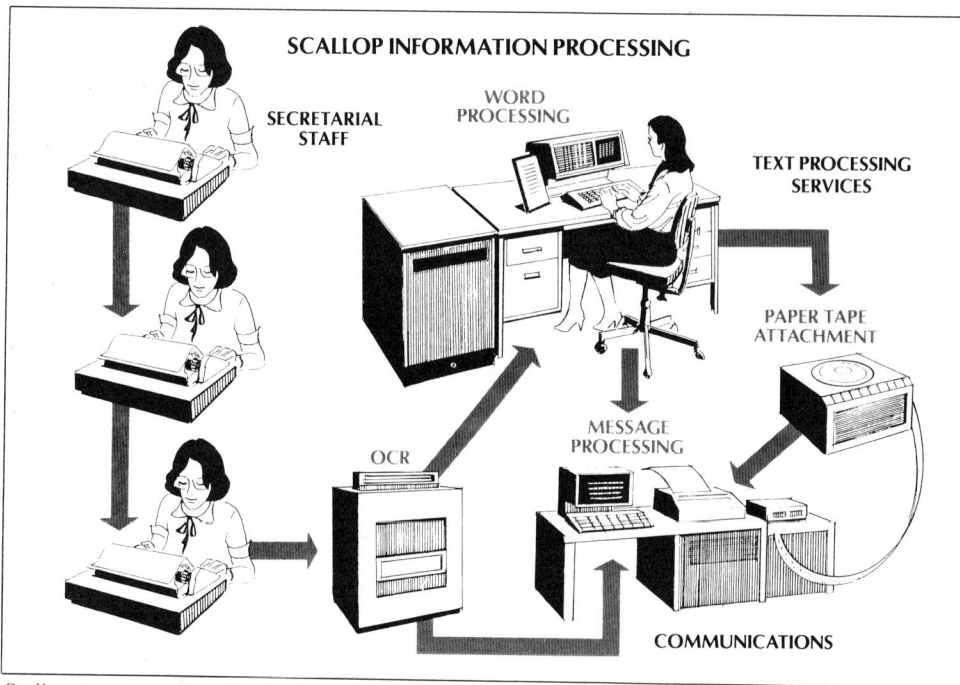

Scallop uses a mixed configuration to deal with information processing. OCR ties word processing, communications, and phototypesetting (not shown) together.

When Scallop Corporation purchased an OCR (optical character recognition) unit, its aim was to reduce the retyping of messages in the Cables Department. When corporatewide usage of OCR is attained, Scallop will have reduced the retyping of 2845 messages per month—one-third of the total messages prepared.

The Hendrix Typereader 2 OCR can communicate via modem with three of the four CPT 8100 word processors at Scallop headquarters, thereby reducing average turnaround time of documents from three to eight days.

The acquisition of word processing equipment has boosted productivity. In July 1979, fewer than 500 pages of text were produced by seven staff members. In June 1981, 2813 pages were processed by four staff members.

Scallop Corporation, headquartered in Manhattan, is a member of the Royal Dutch/Shell Group of companies. Approximately 420 employees work at the main office. Other offices are in Houston and Washington, D.C.

Today, WP equipment can speak with communications and phototypesetting equipment via modems.

Figure 22   One corporation's approach to OCR. Reprinted from the December 1981 issue of *Modern Office Procedures*, copyright 1981 by Penton/IPC, Division of Pittway Corporation.

not be cost effective or productive. An example of successful utilization of OCR is represented in Figure 22.

Other Image Technologies Several other areas of technology involve images—microfilm, graphics, bit mapping, and facsimile. Each of these could involve either original or nonoriginal input, depending upon whether the source of creation of the information has been internal or external to the organization. All of these technologies will be discussed in greater detail in later chapters. Keep in mind, however, that although in the early stages of office automation each of these may be a form of output, in a fully developed system with the appropriate sophisticated level of technology, each of these could serve as input to a system.

NONORIGINAL INPUT

Nonoriginal information is any piece of information that has already been created. All data or ideas are original input at some point. However, much information in an organization is used and reused in a variety of ways at different locations. Traditionally, information was moved from one point to another by physically carrying a piece of paper. If the information needed to be changed in form, the solution had been to recreate or rekey it. Neither of these activities is cost effective or efficient.

The determination of whether information is original or nonoriginal (already existing in the organization in some form) is important in designing an integrated system. This information needs to be picked up. The *goal should be to reuse information without reentering or recreating it.*

Various strategies can be used to achieve this goal. One way is to establish a common data base in a central file processor to eliminate duplicate data in several places, to provide access to needed data, and to facilitate integrated processing. A second way is to use COM (computer output microfilm) and CIM (computer input microfilm) as a means of developing a microform-based information storage and retrieval system. A third way is to retrieve information previously received through facsimile and data that is transformed into graphics from a storage and retrieval system directly into the information flow cycle.

The input function starts the flow of information and communication. It involves the capture of the idea from the originator and the conversion of that idea into a communication that informs, requests a response, or initiates an action. A successful information system often depends on the procedures and guidelines for the input of data to the system.

CHAPTER 5

INFORMATION PROCESSING

OBJECTIVES

In this chapter you will learn about
1. The interrelation between data processing, word processing, and information processing.
2. The evolution of data processing and word processing.
3. Similarities and differences between word processing and data processing.
4. Various ways to integrate word processing and data processing into information processing.
5. Trends in merging data and word processing.
6. How data processing, word processing, and information processing expand the modern office.
7. The components involved in the processing function of the information processing cycle.

The full potential of the completely automated-office concept cannot be achieved until office systems (i.e., word processing) are integrated with the data processing and communications functions. The most fundamental step in achieving this network is through the merger of data processing and word processing into one integrated system of information processing. Figure 1 illustrates the placement of processing in the total flow.

This chapter explores this merger and other related technological disciplines and their effects on the implementation of the information cycle in the electronic office.

DEFINITIONS AND OVERVIEW

In a marriage of data processing and word processing. the similarities between the two operations are most important. However, the real differences between them are equally important. Data processing usually deals with the manipulation of numbers through various computations to deliver meaningful totals and create useful statistical information from raw numbers. Word processing manipulates information in language through entry and revision, to make the originator's meaning clearer to the intended recipient or audience. It changes words and their sequence, as well as their presentation, but it does not add new intelligence.

The fundamental distinction between word processing and data processing is that data processing deals with numerical data and word processing deals with alphacharacters in text form. Word processing focuses on communication (written or oral) between two or more people. Data processing acts more upon statistics and tabular data: figures, account numbers, lists, and so on. Data processing tends to be repetitive and performed periodically (end-of-month billings), and the output tends to appear in a specific format (computer printout form).

Only part of the information stored in a computer's memory (e.g., John Doe's credit account balance) may be relevant to a data processing user at a given time. In contrast, usually the entire message (e.g., a letter) is relevant to the user of a word processing center.

Word processing, because it deals in changing text, is often performed as needed (when a letter needs to be written) and has a variable format based on what the user demands in each given situation (letter, brief, report, etc.).

The distinctions between the two systems also are illustrated in their applications. Data processing business and accounting applications are usually developed once and repeated (e.g., weekly or monthly payroll), and only parts of the whole data file or base are processed and distributed. Word processing applications are usually written, then revised several times—and then the information can be produced in total form only once or may have multiple distribution. Data processing is originated through the use of forms or source documents at the input level; word processing

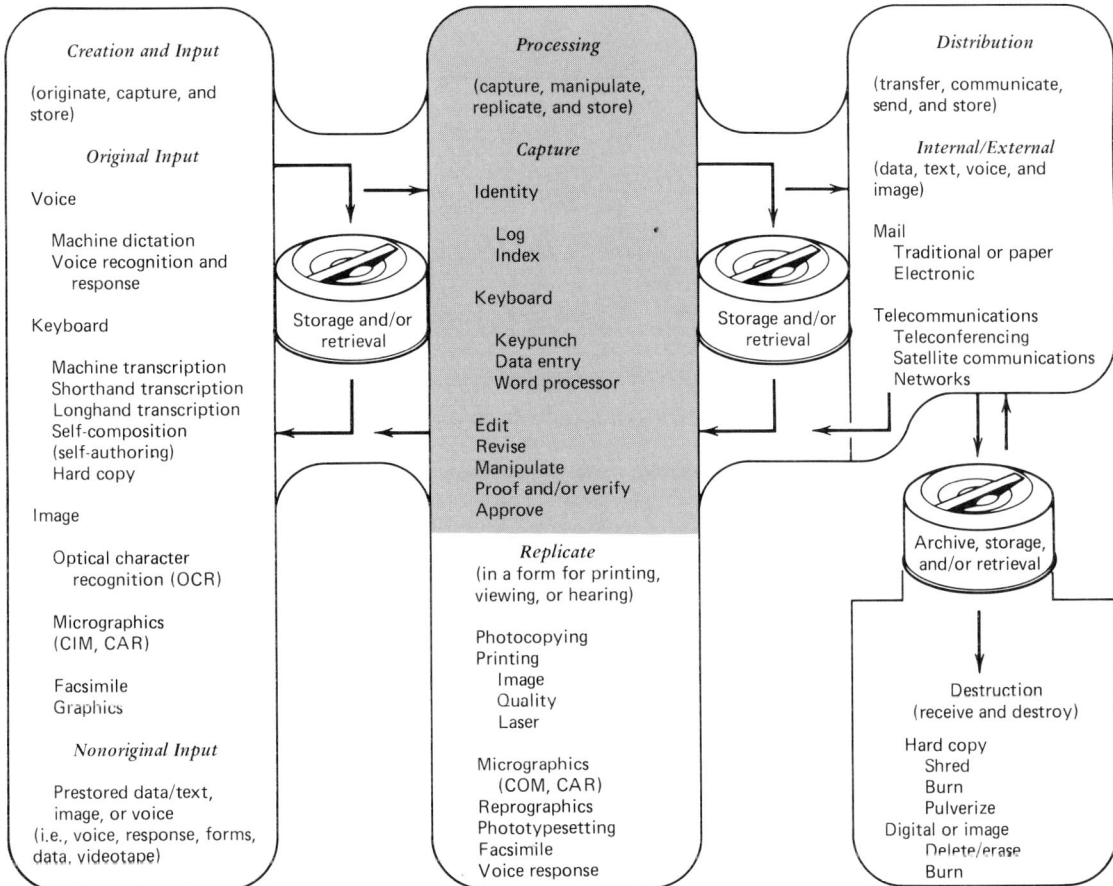

Figure 1 Information processing flow showing the placement of the processing cycle.

input is by voice (dictated material), longhand origination, or marked copy (e.g., a received letter with notations in the margin). Data processing produces computer printout, whereas word processing produces mailable or camera-ready copy. Data processing relies on numbers and logic; word processing on grammar and syntax. See Figure 2 for comparison of some basic distinctions.

THE EVOLUTION OF DATA PROCESSING/WORD PROCESSING

Present-day word processing and data processing systems trace their ancestry back to the lowly mechanical typewriter that revolutionized the office and proved that a keyboard could be effective in business and not

Characteristic	Data Processing	Word Processing
Type of information	Processes data	Processes words
Primary applications	Numerical calculations for payroll, inventory accounting, billing airline reservations, large mailing lists, and so on	Creating and revising letters, memorandums, news releases, small mailing lists, in-house publications, and so on
Turnaround	Usually 24 hours or longer (depending on application)	Usually 2–4 hours (depending on application)
Quality of output/print	Usually of draft quality	Usually of professional letter quality
Processing information	Acquires data, manipulates it, and provides decision, tabular report, or completed forms for management	Acquires data and/or text, manipulates it, and provides final output documents (reports or correspondence for management)
Scheduling	Strict schedules; user must fit the system	Flexible schedules; fits the needs of the people
Priorities	Applications giving highest return on cost	Priorities by urgency of documents
Personnel	Computer operators, programmers, systems analysts. Highly skilled, technically oriented, work alone, not people-oriented.	Administrative secretaries, correspondence secretaries, WP supervisor/manager/coordinator; highly skilled, people-oriented.
Corrections/revisions	Must fit into schedule	Must meet turnaround needs

Figure 2 Word processing/data processing distinctions chart.

just in music. The typewriter replaced traditional pen-and-ink copying methods and assisted office workers to double and triple their output. In the 1930s, the introduction of automatic typewriters made possible repetitive typing of form letters and contracts; they used a punched-paper roll "storage" mechanism similar to those used at that time in player pianos. The evolution of the automatic typewriter continued through the 1950s, with several additions such as five- to eight-channel punched-paper tape and electromechanical logic to allow switching between two tape readers.

The availability of compact and magnetic storage/recording media fostered the explosion of computer technology in the 1960s. In 1964, IBM ushered in the age of word processing by introducing the Magnetic Tape Selectic Typewriter (MT/ST). The MT/ST allowed performance of traditional functions with greater ease and more speed than before. Magnetic tape allowed materials to be erased and rerecorded. The tape also allowed greater storage capacity and longer use.

New and better machines using low-cost electronics exploded onto the market during the 1970s. New companies in word processing and data processing were born, and competition between suppliers was and continues to be fierce.

The 1970s saw fast and furious activity in both fields, with the introduction of new video display units and of diskettes, faster processing and printer speeds, and more production. Still more companies continued to enter the market with better technologies, and the current trend toward integrating office functions such as word processing and data processing is moving technology ahead even further.

Data processing and word processing evolved in widely different ways. For example, data processing managers had an advantage in that technology's early days. The investment that companies would make in data processing hardware was substantial and, as a result, data processing had top management's immediate attention and management's immediate support. Since data processing usually dealt with accounting or financial projections, changes were implemented by such top management personnel as the company president or controller.

In contrast, the word processing manager, who appeared as much as 20 years later, dealt with smaller hardware investments that often escaped management's immediate attention and support. Because word processing was unfamiliar then, the word processing manager had to sell top management on the advantages of word processing. In addition, the word processing manager had to sell the word processing concept to the users of the system as well as to the support staff who converted from the traditional office to the new equipment and procedures. Often, word processing advocates met resistance from both management and clerical levels and had to struggle against overwhelming opposition to introduce innovations to the office. Some word processing pioneers did not give up, and these modern-day survivors have established the connection with data processing.

Recently, some data processing and word processing capabilities have been growing in a different way. Low-cost personal computers have proliferated in many organizations without the awareness or approval of either top management or data processing and word processing management. Users acquire them to meet a need, but they seldom become a part of an organization's integrated approach to office automation. The "personal" computers usually serve only one user well. That is when the user can work more effectively with a personal data base and does not require

Figure 3   One vendor's personal computer. Xerox 820-II is a stand-alone system or a professional work station. (Courtesy of Xerox Corporation)

the exchange of data with the daily mainstream of business data processing operations (see Figure 3).

SIMILARITIES BETWEEN DP AND WP   Data processing and word processing share many similar characteristics. The similarities between the two fields are the very basis for the merger. Both DP and WP are

1. Primarily concerned with producing information.
2. Based on computer technology.
3. Software driven.

4. Dependent on people.

5. Support functions that make users more productive.

6. Technologies that use keyboarding as the primary means of entering data into the system.

7. Creating new jobs.

8. Providing needed capabilities.

Producing information for use by the originator is the primary objective of both data and word processing. Both functions are involved with the preparing of that information for communication. For example, data processing may involve distributing personnel information to a number of branch offices or word processing may involve communicating a management memo to other word processors in various cities.

Both disciplines are based on *microprocessor technology*, which means that a similar evolution to a point of merging is possible. Word processing software is performing applications previously performed on data processing software (e.g., mathematical calculations). Data processing software provides the capability of performing text processing functions.

Both technologies are becoming *software driven*, as are many other office systems. Software allows more flexibility in the processing of information.

Both technologies are *dependent upon the people* who operate them.

Data processing and word processing *perform support functions* to make users more productive. Greater demand is being placed on these disciplines to (1) produce information more quickly, (2) provide communications more accurately, (3) generate graphics to facilitate understanding of the enormous amounts of information handled by management, and (4) create a responsive environment to meet management decision-making needs.

Both technologies *use keyboarding* as the primary means for entering data into a system.

The information explosion and the advancing word processing and data processing technologies have *created new careers* in both fields.

Most organizations need both data and word processing. In order to fulfill the financial projections, billing demands, computations, and so on required in the modern office, organizations require data processing systems. An integration of data and word processing would allow both of these functions to be performed simply, along with myriad other functions such as electronic mail.

Data and word processing functions can be successfully combined. However, we more likely will first see devices with a primary function (word processing, for example) that communicates with data processing for common file access. The device will be able to perform either function separately rather than concurrently.

DIFFERENCES BETWEEN DP AND WP   In spite of the similarities between data and word processing, there are significant differences that may serve as constraints. These differences include

1. Time constraints.
2. Focus of the systems.
3. Mode of operation.
4. Diversified past.
5. Nature of the software.
6. Output format.
7. Personnel knowledge.
8. Management style.
9. Education.

One difference involves the deadline and scheduling requirements of the systems. In word processing the final product (i.e., document) must meet the schedule established by the user. For example, a letter may be needed to be typed, proofread, and mailed within three days or three hours. In data processing, the end product (data output) schedule is determined by total processing requirements and conveyed to the user. In addition, many times the demand for data is set on a calendar. For example, end-of-the-month billings are predetermined, as well as statement accountings at mid-month.

A second difference lies with the focus of the two systems. Word processing as a specialized application is attitudinally centered around traditional secretarial work. It is based on pleasing both the support staff that must operate the word processing center and the users who rely on the center for work output. Data processing as a specialized application is functionally centered. It focuses on producing data output at regular intervals and of a repetitive nature. The users of a word processing center are usually top and middle management who need correspondence, reports, and so on drafted and completed. The users of information output of a data processing center are scattered and vary from clerical to influential individuals (e.g., president of the firm or the controller).

A third difference lies in the mode of operation. Word processing operates in a mode using words, sentences, paragraphs, and finally documents. Data processing uses a mode centered on characters, numbers, lists, and computations. Data processing handles primarily alphanumeric data in a structured predictable format. Word processing handles text— mostly alpha characters—in a somewhat unpredictable form. Data processing usually works with data only once, and the result is often updated in files and/or printout. Word processing usually revises material several times and works from uncontrolled input. These differences in operation mode may create some problems in the integration process.

A fourth difference is the diversified past of the two fields. Data processing and word processing have been operating under different systems and procedures since their inceptions. They have developed unique hardware and software requirements. Their managers are trained in different modes of organization. To integrate, data and word processors will have to stress their common past rather than these differences.

A fifth difference involves the nature of the software. Word processing usually has predetermined software to accomplish various functions. Data processing, by contrast, has been dependent upon custom programming or specialized software packages. Each will need to adapt to make the integration complete.

A sixth difference involves the output format. Data processing is usually in draft form and designed to be viewed internally (i.e., traditional computer output). The purpose of data processing is to manipulate data to create useful information. Word processing is oriented toward developing a final document. Since most output from word processing ends up in public hands (e.g., letters), word processing is concerned with appearance.

A seventh difference has to do with the effect on personnel. When offices first incorporated data processing systems, many of the office personnel were unaware of data processing, since it was a specialized function that affected specific areas such as accounting or financial projections. In contrast, word processing not only affects the heart of the office—the support staff—but also reaches into the work habits of every user of the system. Thus, when it is implemented in an office, everyone is immediately aware of its presence. Therefore, word processing systems require a more complete and careful nurturing, whereas data processing systems can often be implemented and accepted with less overall personnel resistance.

An eighth difference between the data processor and the word processor lies in standardization. The data processing manager usually invested in one system, one vendor, and one communications network to meet the needs of the firm. He had proprietary authority to decide on peripheral equipment. Because of the large investment in hardware and equipment, the data processing revolution created many new jobs (programmers, data entry clerks, documentation clerks, systems analysts, and so on). Data processing from the beginning offered diverse career paths and upward mobility.

Word processing, conversely, rarely spawned managers who possessed the broad authority that data processing could claim. Since the word processing manager decisions were for smaller dollar amounts, the expenditure rarely captured the attention of top management. Without top management's support, change is difficult. As word processing evolved into a system, serious incompatibilities and interface problems began to surface, and the word processing manager of today has difficulty in exerting the management control necessary to offset change.

A final difference between data processing and word processing involves education. Data processing has been around long enough so that management and workers generally have specialized education and courses available to provide in-depth background. As a result of their overall knowledge of data processing functions, data processing personnel can move freely from job to job and even go into word processing fields. By contrast, education and training in and even awareness of word processing and its capabilities is just now beginning. The individuals who are most knowledgeable about the capabilities of word processing systems are those who have experience in the field. However, many of these word processing professionals have little or no formal educational training in management and office management and thus find it hard to move from first-line supervision of word processing to management of other aspects of office automation.

Data and word processing share many elements in common, yet have some conflicting characteristics. Current developers in the field of data/word processing integration are stressing the similarities in an effort to make the transition to a data/word processing network smooth. However, the inherent differences between the two systems will have to be acknowledged and dealt with to ensure complete integration.

THE EMERGENCE OF INFORMATION PROCESSING

Data processing and word processing are becoming indistinct operations—they lie on a converging pattern (see Figure 4). Many business applications need to combine both in varying proportions. Because word processing and data processing share something in common (computer technology), a convergence of the two functions is inevitable. Both deal with information, hence the growing use of the term *information processing*.

The common link, computer technology, allows the two to "alter their personalities." Through software, both computers and word processors can perform each other's basic applications. Software programs give the devices that ability. Therefore, although one can argue that the two systems are different, it is possible to develop a connection between data processing and word processing through changeable software programs on a computer. And the differences are becoming fewer and the similarities greater with each passing year.

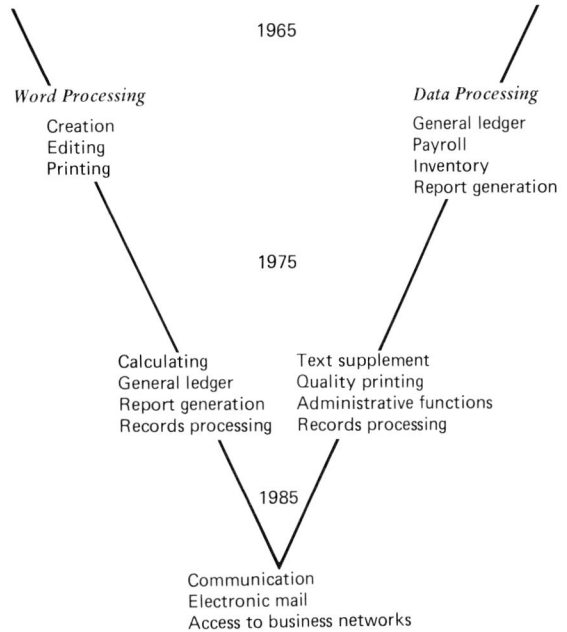

Figure 4 Converging pattern of word processing and data processing.

THE EMERGENCE OF DP/WP INTEGRATION CONCEPT

The basic purpose of data processing/word processing integration is to forge the two separate fields into one information processing system. Integration theoretically maximizes office efficiency by better utilizing equipment, personnel, and management/support staff time.

Several specific benefits can result from integration.

1. One advantage is the ability to use stored information in data files in a wide variety of word processing applications. Formerly, when the two systems were separate, someone from word processing center had to go to the data processing center, request hard copy of necessary information, return, and then reinput and process the information before it could be edited and revised, and then finalized. The disadvantages of such a system are obvious. Now, new systems enable the user to transmit the received data from the computer file to the word processor. Operators can enter certain codes and then immediately display data or information on their video screens, or load it into the word processor file for further revision and reporting. Conversely, the linking of the

word processing function to the data processing function will enable data processors to receive information from word processing.

2. Another advantage to integration is that the user will have access to advanced functions that provide extensive text manipulation capabilities. Presently, the range of computer capabilities available to the Word Processing Department is fairly limited. The text abilities available to the Data Processing Department on their computers is also limited. When the two systems are combined, the overall ability to manipulate information will be enhanced.

3. A third advantage to the Word Processing Department will be increased storage ability for textual material. Currently, word processors often fail to provide adequate storage capacity, so that word processing operators are forced to delete material to make room for incoming material or maintain a large and expensive inventory of diskettes for external storage. When the two functions are fused, the overall storage ability of the word processing center will be increased significantly.

Integration allows direct exchange of information between word processing and data processing. Traditionally, documents in either department had to be physically transported to the other department. With integration, transmitting documents directly to the destination saves both time and dollars.

4. Finally, integration will produce a net support-cost reduction. The most significant advantages related to economy will be the elimination of dual sets of hardware, since, with integration, a terminal will be multifunctional, thereby producing more productivity per workstation. The user will be performing administrative functions directly on a video display terminal, thereby eliminating the time spent in giving verbal instructions to a support staff person. With the improved productivity and multifunctional workstations, fewer people will be required.

THE EVOLUTION OF WP/DP CONVERGENCE

Integration did not develop overnight. Several factors have influenced its development.

One factor is cost. The cost of people (both those who originate the information and those who process it) has continued to rise at a rapid rate. Some estimates place the rate of labor cost increases at as much as 10 percent a year through the 1980s. At the same time, the cost of machine functions continues to decrease, because of the refining of microprocessors, floppy disks, and memory. This trend in the people/machine ratio has made management in most organizations aware of the need to address the integration issue.

A second factor in producing change is the lower cost of technology and increased availability of software. New equipment, in addition to bringing down costs, offers the user many more options and much greater convenience through integration of the word/data processing functions. Software packages provide advanced word processing functions, the ability to access files, and high-speed communications—all without high programming costs. Convenience features, such as video display screens, are increasingly available at nominal expense. As a result, it is now possible to provide at the departmental or work group level at least some functions that were formerly available only through the Data Processing Department.

The use of word and data processing systems have made those users more sophisticated and skilled people. Sizable number of users have now managed successful word/data processing centers. These managers can now implement new integrated systems with confidence. The lessons learned in implementing a word processing approach—in particular, the necessary short- and long-range planning required for implementation—will dictate an evolutionary approach to the integration of word/data processing.

To actually integrate data and word processing, organizations must adopt a planned approach. For example, a planned approach must include the following steps:

1. Formation of a project team of personnel experienced in data processing, word processing, and other involved applications or technologies, such as communications. If the firm does not have such people, it should consider the services of an outside consultant qualified and experienced in integration techniques.

2. The team should identify through internal study and data gathering the applications most likely justified.

3. If the firm already has both data and word processing systems, analysis should determine how the systems can interrelate. (For example, does word processing keyboard information that is a part of the data processing data base, either before it is entered or from hard-copy computer printout? If so, what steps to network them effectively should be taken and what alternatives are available?)

4. Then, once the factors are identified, the project team should assign each potential area to an analyst team for cost analysis.

5. When that analysis is completed, the project team must prepare a prioritized list of short-term data and word processing applications for implementation.

6. Finally, the task force must prepare a strategic long-term plan for implementing more complex systems, such as electronic mail. See Figure 5 for an action plan checklist.

1. Form an experienced project team.
2. Identify the readily justified application.
3. Determine which applications relate to each technology.
4. Assign individual applications to various task force members.
5. Prepare a list of priority applications.
6. Prepare a long-range plan.

Figure 5   Strategic long-term action plan checklist for implementing systems.

Before integration takes place, all of the options for hardware equipment, software programming, model, style, and design must be carefully researched. Short- and long-term planning, with an eye to changing organizational needs and the development of new technology, is the key to successful implementation.

OBSTACLES TO IMPLEMENTATION

Integration of data and word processing is not easy; many obstacles must be identified and dealt with. One such obstacle is equipment incompatibility. The inventors of data and word processing systems developed them independently. Although conventional word processing hardware may resemble small computers, the keyboards, software, codes, and commands are often quite different. Operators have difficulty in moving from one system to another because of the differences. True integration will result more quickly when single workstations can function as word processors and data processors with no significant mode change apparent to the operator.

A second limitation involves the limited data-entry methods and memory capacity of conventional word processors. The capability of a word processor to handle data processing material is limited by structural inherencies. The single most severe limitation in the past was the word processor's lack of sizable memory capacity. Although the technology now has advanced to dual density and Winchester hard disks, there is no way, for instance, for a word processor to handle the large data bases held in the memory of a data processor. In addition, word processors cannot calculate data or recall activity lists as fast as conventional data processing equipment. Although larger, more powerful main memories (128K, 256K, and 512K) are lessening this restriction, it still exists.

Word processors use quality printers that do not normally allow high-speed printing. With the evolution and enhancements of laser printers, this limitation will recede in importance.

These structural limitations on word processors will have to be resolved before integration can occur in the electronic office.

Finally, the integration movement will have to battle the attitudinal barriers to change. For example, a number of myths and misconceptions must be identified and corrected. One myth is that the mainframe can do everything, including manipulate text. This simply is not true. Word processing was developed because the computer originally could not fill this need with total success. A mistaken impression still exists that word processing involves only keyboarding text, and not editing, formatting, turnaround time, and final quality. Another myth is that integrating word processing and data processing will cost either data or word processing an area of managerial influence. Ideally this situation would never occur if integration is accomplished as desired.

Word processing personnel hold similar myths about data processing. For example, many think that data processing people are the only ones who know anything about computers. What word processors fail to realize is that a word processing system is a form of computer system. Word processors also mistakenly believe that all office problems will be solved with the introduction of word processing. That, unfortunately, is not the case. A reality is that the integration movement is hampered by both the fears and the ambitions of the people involved and that this conflict is particularly intense at supervisory and managerial levels. Many managers fear losing authority if applications are combined. Employees fear job loss for the same reason. For the office of the future, only the integration of these two related fields will create an efficient workplace.

OVERCOMING OBSTACLES

A strong executive and leader (totally involved, dedicated, and knowledgeable in office automation) is the key to a successful integration. That person must be able to judge proposals and determine if they will benefit the organization or if the proposal is prompted by personal ambitions. Without strong and involved leaders, certain departments and individuals often attempt to develop systems independently and investigate hardware only for their own use. Although the study of requirements of individual operations is necessary, it should not continue unmonitored, because it often results in duplication of an application or solution already developed elsewhere, or in the development of a system completely incompatible with the overall direction of the organization.

THE ISSUE: DECENTRALIZATION OR CENTRALIZATION?

In the integration process, managers must decide whether to centralize or decentralize. Users of data and word processing systems do not care how their work is processed or completed so long as it is done effectively and efficiently. This combination of user demand and user apathy makes organizing a converged system even more difficult. Data processing and word processing also share internal industry conflict. Everyone wants control over the data processing or word processing center. The user wants a certain amount of control to guarantee results on time. This conflict is a major consideration when discussing decentralization versus centralization.

Centralization occurs when one or more large computers are located at a single site with large and complex support staff organization. To retrieve information from the centralized system, one needs to access the central facility (see Figure 6). Decentralization, in contrast, involves the locating of minicomputers and terminals, as well as word processors with stand-alone intelligence, in departments of an organization with communication lines to each other and the main computer (see Figure 7).

The main justification for a centralized system is the economies-of-scale idea—that is, a large central organization is less expensive and more efficient than many smaller units. However, the rapidly falling prices of stand-alone intelligence are making it easier to prove that decentralized processing (on-line and off-line) is cost effective.

The current trend is toward decentralized or distributed systems. The present state of the art is to dedicate small-computer capability to a specific application, geographic location, office, or plant. When access to other data is required, the system connects over communication lines to other small computers or to the central host computer. The various means of developing a communicating network of decentralized systems will be discussed in a later chapter.

Decentralized systems may be of many levels—small mainframes, minicomputers, or microcomputers. The volume and speed requirements of the applications usually determine the type installed. Personal business computers are examples of independent decentralized systems. Depend-

Figure 6 Centralized facility using a large central computer.

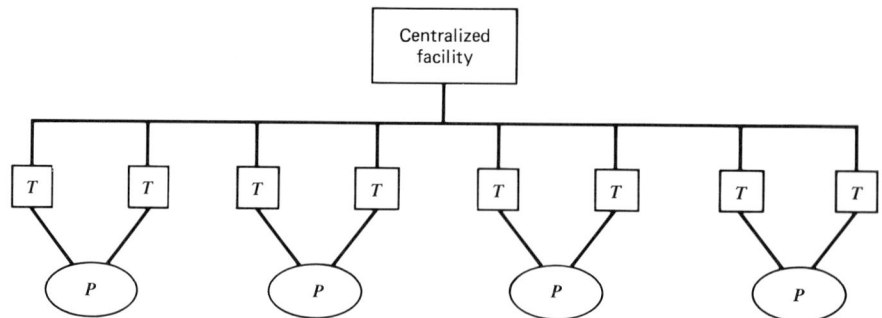

T = terminal
P = printer

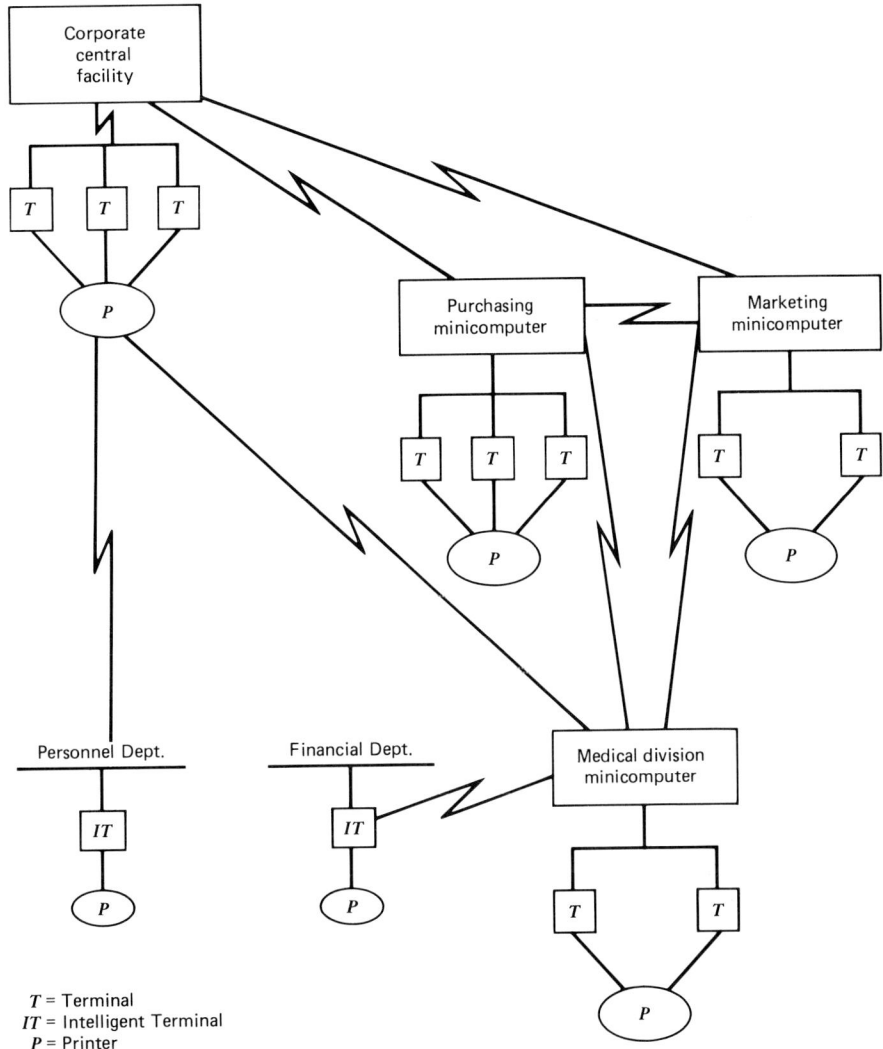

Figure 7 Decentralized facility using several minicomputers for closer user accessibility.

ing upon the size of the computer, decentralized processing powers may be available for a small group, or even for the individual.

PROCESSING SYSTEMS

Processing systems can be broken down into four categories—keyboard and a printer, stand-alone display, shared system, and mainframe computer-based system.

COMBINED KEYBOARD/ PRINTER

The newer keyboard/printer systems include a one-line display to simplify editing, but the basic product is a combined keyboard/printer device (see Figure 8). Products in this category are equipped with microprocessors to aid in editing of information. Some of the devices are available with auxiliary memories on cards, tapes, or floppy diskettes. Many of these types of equipment are also available with communications support that allows them to input into an integrated electronic system.

Component alternatives in this type of workstation are

▶ Input, storage, output.
▶ Input, memory, storage, output.
▶ Input, memory, output.

These components can be defined as follows:

1. *Storage media.* Removable media for storing typed documents: for example, mag card, tape cassette, floppy disk (diskette), paper tape, hard disk.

Figure 8 Electronic typewriter. Note the one-line display. (Courtesy Exxon Corporation)

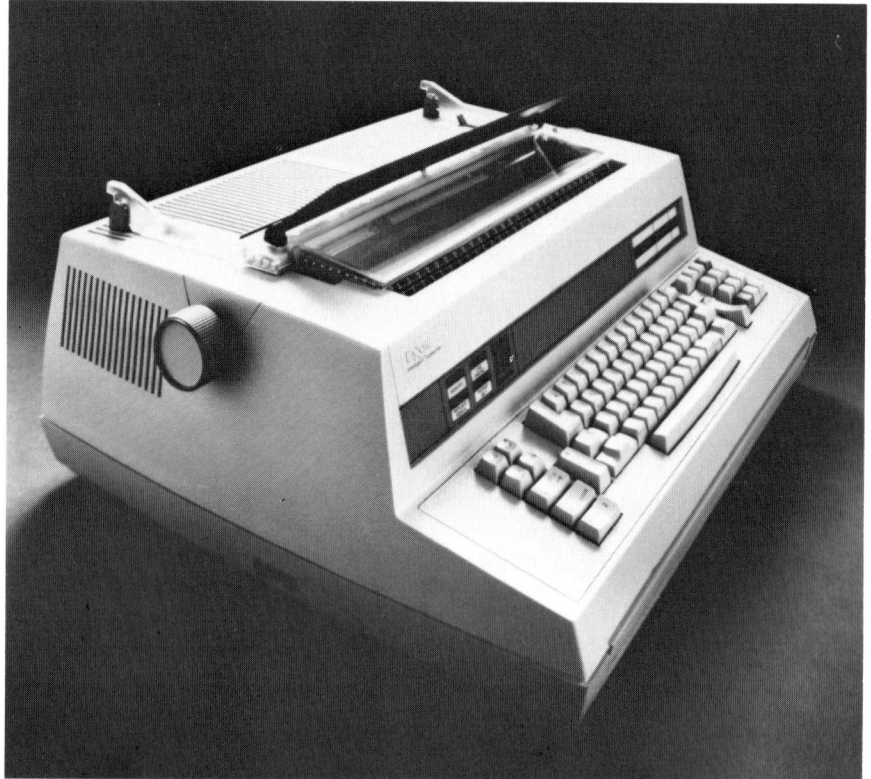

2. *Memory.* Electronic work area or "buffer" housed within the typing unit. Nonremovable from the unit.

3. *Output.* Accomplished when stored text (from storage or memory) is printed. Usually expressed in characters per second (cps) or lines per minute (lpm).

STAND–ALONE DISPLAY

A display-based unit provides the operator with fuller text editing capabilities, more on-line storage, and faster and easier operation than keyboard/printer units can offer, because of the screen and the automatic features of the equipment (see Figure 9).

Very often, stand-alone display systems allow for simultaneous keyboarding and printing and often allow for background processing. The operator is therefore able to perform several tasks at one time—for example, performing records processing in the background while keyboarding a document while at the same time printing out another document. Most of the newer systems in this category of equipment are software loaded and therefore easily updated by the user. The expansion of stand-alone display systems often involves sharing stand-alone printers. A number of operators on display-based systems can input and edit, with one printer supporting several operators instead of one printer for each display unit. This is a cost-effective approach, since rarely can one keyboard operator keep a printer continually busy.

Figure 9   A stand-alone, display-based typewriter. The Displaywriter. (Courtesy of IBM Corporation)

The components of this type of equipment are

▶ Input.
▶ Memory.
▶ Storage.
▶ Video.
▶ Output.

Video means a visual screen called a cathode ray tube (CRT) used especially by operators to edit and reformat documents. A primary consideration is the size of the screen (several lines, half-page, or full-page).

Output occurs on a quality printer which has a three-inch-diameter printwheel. Print speeds range from 30 to 45, 55, and 60 characters per second.

SHARED SYSTEM   Since many shared logic systems were originally developed by companies in the data processing field, these systems evolved from a modification of hardware previously developed for data processing applications. These shared systems were therefore able to support multiple displays for processing of both data and words, and thus several users could share resources such as single storage or a single printer and communications facilities (see Figure 10).

Figure 10 A shared system. (Courtesy of Digital Equipment Corporation)

In the evolution of word processing technology, several vendors introduced shared systems as new products while others upgraded data processing products with word processing software and quality printers. Therefore, multiple application systems have been developed that can simultaneously support one station performing data entry, one station performing data processing, and a third station performing programming functions. The shared-system approach has resulted in a lower-cost unit per keyboard once a specific cutoff size has been reached. For example, if a justification for four keyboards has been arrived at, it becomes significantly less expensive for expansion purposes to consider a shared system.

The components of this type of equipment are

► Input.
► Memory.
► Storage.
► Video.
► Output.

Memory, storage, and printer are shared by several operators.

Figure 11   Mainframe-based computer word processing equipment. (Courtesy of Wang Laboratories, Incorporated)

MAINFRAME COMPUTER BASED There are primarily two types of mainframe-based word processing systems—the in-house computer application software and the external time-sharing service bureaus (see Figure 11). In both types the intelligence and storage reside in a mainframe computer accessed by communicating terminals.

SUMMARY

The integration of the various types of processing technologies is the key objective of the electronic office system implementation. With the integration process comes greater productivity through the elimination of duplication of effort, recopying, rekeying, retyping, and rehandling of information.

The continuing proliferation and increasing power of word processors, small business computers, microcomputers and multifunctional terminals, most of which are enhanced with communications capability, ensures the continuing development of integrated office systems, all of which will be an integral part of the business information and communication networks in the electronic office.

CHAPTER 6

COMMUNICATING INFORMATION
(Telecommunications)

OBJECTIVES

In this chapter you will learn about
1. The relationship between computers and communications.
2. Analog and digital communications.
3. The driving forces in integration.
4. Equipment considerations for communications.
5. Networking and its relationship to telecommunications and the electronic office.
6. The applications of data communications.
7. Management considerations for implementing telecommunications.

AN OVERVIEW

Telecommunications can be defined, in simplified terms, as the electronic transfer of data from one point in an information system to another. In today's office, however, telecommunications is viewed as the tool for linking computers and/or other systems to expedite the exchange of business information, which in turn enables the organization to make good decisions quickly, render better service, or achieve a competitive edge. Telecommunications represents the connecting of every new type of technology and computer development. Its ultimate goal would be to create a totally interconnected world. Currently, telecommunications is far from that goal. However, if change continues at the same pace that we have witnessed in the last 20 years, telecommunications could achieve global integration in this century.

Telecommunications today is highly technical and requires in-depth study. However, certain basic understandings are useful and it is helpful to focus on areas of major importance. This chapter provides an overview of the basic aspects and presents important management considerations about integrating technologies.

Communications and computer technologies advanced along parallel but unrelated paths (see Figure 1). However, one important turning point was reached in 1876 with the invention of the telephone. The first electri-

Figure 1 Chart of communications and computer technologies on parallel paths.

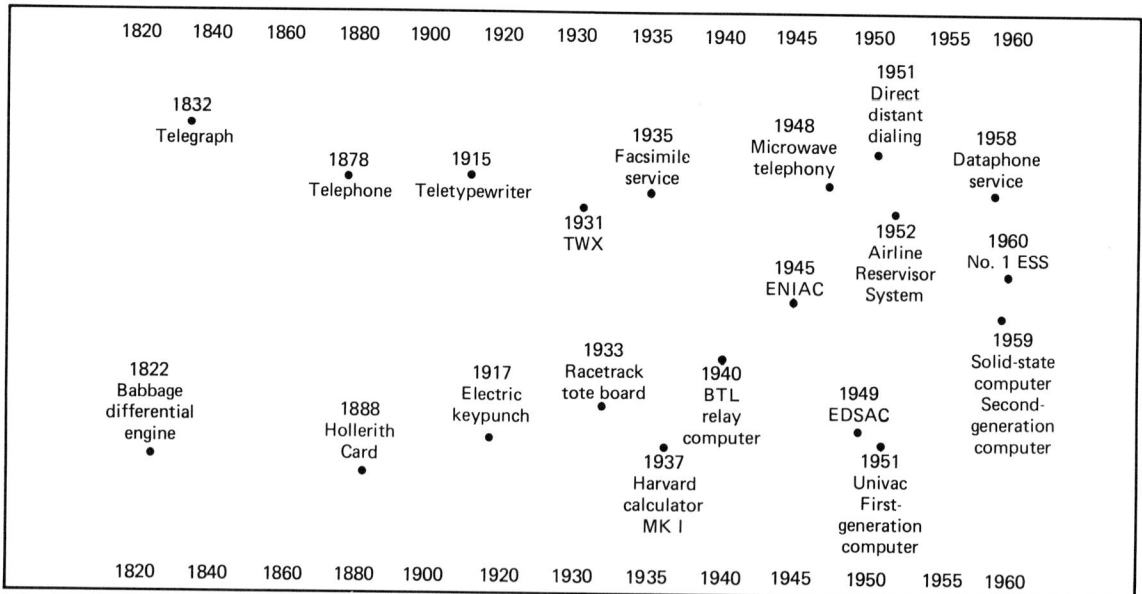

Analog

Figure 2 Digital
square wave and
analog sine wave.

Digital

cal communications, the manual telegraph and later the teletype, were digital.

Digital communications involves a discretely variable signal, for example, the on/off state of a telegraph signal. The telephone changed the form of data transmission from the digital square wave to the analog sine wave, providing a more powerful base for advances in voice communications technology (see Figure 2).

Analog communications involves a continuously variable signal, such as a phone call. The telephone was the beginning of analog communications, and analog has been the dominant form of communications because a vast network was built to handle telephone communications.

From 1930 to 1960, the foundation was laid for the electronic computer systems as we know them today. Many previous tools developed by man, such as the wheel, the steam engine, and the airplane, were to magnify man's physical power; the computer was the first important new tool to magnify and expand man's intellect since the development of the printing press. The extension of power of this new tool has resulted from combining communication and computer technology. The common carrier (public phone) lines became the link between the computer and outlying locations. Various names have been created for the convergence of computers and telecommunications: the French refer to it as *télématique*, a Harvard professor uses *communications*, and the English call it *telematics*.

TECHNOLOGICAL ASPECTS

ANALOG AND DIGITAL COMMUNICATIONS

Business computers, which are digital devices, were not designed to be used over the telephone network, an analog device. To permit computers to communicate over telephone lines, a modem (modulator/demodulator) is required on each end. Modems convert digital information to and from analog form. As the need for computer data transmission has grown, many digital communication devices have become available. The Bell system has offered Dataphone Digital Service (DDS), Rolm Corp. has its Computerized Branch Exchange (CBX) and various Private Branch Exchange (PBX) vendors have begun to develop systems to carry both analog and digital information. The latter has often digitized the human voice.

The system to be selected depends upon where the system will be installed. A large corporation with a need to communicate among branches may have a requirement for a digital PBX. A firm with mostly voice communications and little digital communication from one office or area to another may find an analog system well suited to its needs, although most new systems now use digital switching.

Most existing local telephone networks are analog and are likely to remain so for some time. This is a major hurdle in the design of a new communications system. The growth in the use of computers and other digital devices will require the planners of future systems to include digital transmission devices.

DRIVING FORCES

There are four driving forces in convergence or integration: integrated circuits, software, optical fibers, and communications satellites. An understanding of each and its role in the development of an integrated information network will be helpful.

Integrated Circuits

Electronic circuits, such as LSI (large-scale integration) are now mass produced by etching the circuits onto silicon chips (see Figure 3). Increasing quantities of logic circuitry have been incorporated into newer chips called VLSI (very large-scale integration). The power of this electronic technology will continue to grow, and the prices are expected to drop even further. This growth in power and lower costs will impact our working lives and our home lives.

For example, if you go away on a business trip and keep your furnace turned down to save energy, you will return to a cold house and must wait several hours for it to warm up. With a home information system based on solid-state technology connected to your telephone, you could dial your home phone and with the punch of a few buttons cause the furnace to come on so that your house would be warm when you arrive. How does the chip work in this example? What role does it play? How does it relate to information processing?

Computer Software

LSIs and VLSIs are rapidly increasing in speed and reliability, but decreasing in size and cost. Software is the essential ingredient in stored program control systems such as switching systems in telecommunications or systems to convert signals into digital form and manipulate them in a complex manner. Computer software is appearing in individual terminals and in large national or international communications systems, and it increases the capabilities immensely at both levels.

Figure 3 Silicon chip. (Courtesy of Intel Corporation, Santa Clara, California)

LSI and VLSI are impressive—in addition to performing marvels in electronic miniaturization, their designers have been able to load that chip with a tremendous capability to execute many commands. For example, it would take a room full of 1950 computers and all their capabilities to perform what is being done today on a little personal computer. The developments in integrated circuitry are responsible for this phenomenal improvement.

It is this concentration of computing power in such a small space and at such a low cost that puts stand-alone computing intelligence at remote locations and enables the latter to exchange data with mainframe hosts.

Fiber Optics   In fiber optics, strands of hair-thin glass fibers transmit light. Communications signals are converted to light pulses, then sent over the fiber. AT&T is currently using optical fibers in its telephone networks. See Figure 4 for more information on fiber optics.

There are many advantages to fiber optics. First, it uses no electrical current. Since fiber optics transmits light, not electrical current or voltage, the potential spark hazard is absent. This makes fiber optics particularly well suited for working environments where flammable and explosive

---

CLEAR AS SAND

Bell Canada provides some interesting facts about fiber optics:

▶ They are made mostly of silica or sand—one of the most abundant materials on earth. Copper, on the other hand, is a finite resource that is gradually being depleted.

▶ The fibers used in fiber optic cables are six one-thousandths of an inch thick.

▶ Fibers made of glass are so pure that if you looked through a window of the material one kilometer thick, it would appear as transparent as a pane of glass. If the water of the Pacific Ocean were as clear, you could see bottom at the deepest point.

▶ Fiber has the same tensile strength as steel wire of the same diameter.

▶ Fibers are flexible. You can bend a fiber optic strand into a circle one-quarter of an inch thick in diameter and it will not snap.

▶ Fibers conserve energy. A telephone system using glass would use one-third the electricity required by today's networks.

Figure 4 Facts about fiber optics. *Source:* Alan G. Rockhold, "Fiber Optics, A New World of Communications:," *Infosystems*, August, 1981, p. 58.

material is present. Light is also a more efficient transmitter of signals than electricity.

Unlike electrical signals transmitted over wire, optical fibers are impervious to electromagnetic interference and radio frequency interference. Furthermore, they do not generate interference, a characteristic especially important in data communications, where line interference can cause erroneous messages.

Optical fibers provide secure transmissions. The absence of interference on the line gives fiber optics unmatched data transmission security. Since electromagnetic fields are the basis for remote "bugging," it is useless on fiber optics lines. The only way to steal information is to tap into the light-carrying fiber, which would immediately produce a noticeable signal loss at the receiver's end.

Optical fibers are lightweight and compact. This is a key attraction for the telecommunications industry. One optical cable of 144 fibers can carry 96,768 two-way phone conversations, yet it is only an inch in diameter and weighs only six ounces per foot. In crowded urban areas, where cable conduits may already be filled to capacity, expansion is still possible by replacing wires with fibers.

Finally, optical fibers have high data transmission rates. Being smaller and lighter, optical fibers have far greater information-carrying capacity than their wire counterparts. With the use of laser beam and glass fiber technology, businesses can better utilize the increased computer logic capability that will be available in the next few years. With the safety, versatility, power and space savings afforded, fiber optics is believed to be the cable of the future.

Communications Satellites

Communications satellites have the advantage of sending or accepting digital signals from one point to another point on the other side of the city, country, or globe.

Significant recent progress in satellite transmission technology has for the first time made feasible the widespread local use of the vast communications potential of satellites. The advances in electronic circuitry and storage technologies have contributed in a major way to this progress. So also have the improved antenna systems resulting from the experience of the Apollo space program.

In the past, cost was the major barrier to use of satellite-based communications on a regular and frequent basis. The high cost resulted partly from the huge capital investments required by earth stations, microwave radio relays, and cables necessary for transmission between the satellite and end user. Technological advance has permitted a consistent downward trend in cost per circuit per year. It is now economically feasible to install a local rooftop antenna linked to a satellite to transmit business data (see Figure 5).

The full potential of satellite communication has yet to be determined. Great strides in technology are leading to the increased use of telecommunications.

EQUIPMENT CONSIDERATIONS

Sending information between devices requires careful planning, because the sending and receiving devices must be able to recognize the same machine languages, speeds, codes, and so on. As previously mentioned, a modem is just one consideration in attaining compatibility in communications. Other important characteristics of communications must be included in planning a system that is compatible and can perform the applications and functions required by its users.

Protocol

The term *protocol* is used to refer to the way (technical customs and guidelines) that a message is packaged and handled between two pieces of equipment. Since the equipment in a communications system is likely supplied by different vendors, it is important to be sure that components operate on the same protocol. Only equipment that operates on the same protocol can intercommunicate directly. Equipment that uses different protocols must transmit and receive through an intermediate interpretation device or program, often called a translator or "black box." These devices will be discussed later in this chapter.

Modes of Transmission

There are two primary modes of transmission—*synchronous*, also referred to as bisynchronous, and *asynchronous*. The difference is in the

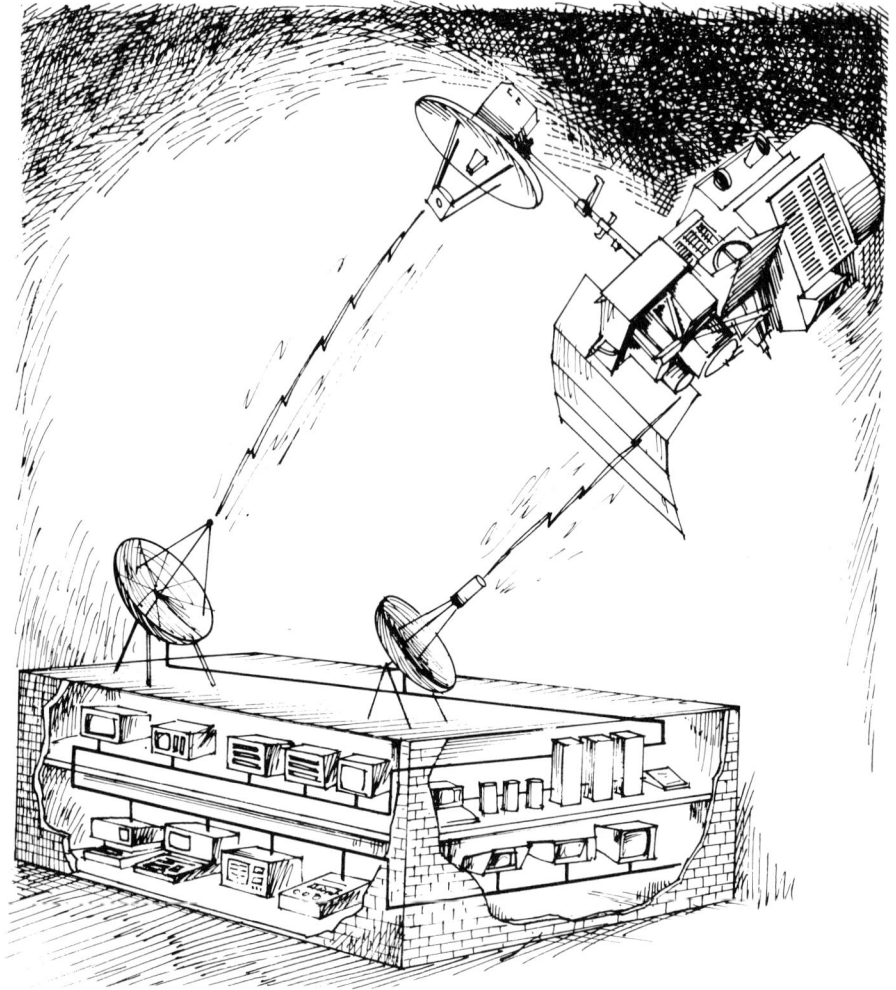

Figure 5 Satellite transmission illustrating cable and microwave radio relay for communications.

timing of character transmission—that is, the method of moving characters or impulses through the communications lines. To put it simply, with asynchronous communications, a "start" signal precedes and a "stop" signal follows each character to check synchronization; and characters move one at a time along the line. With synchronous transmission, each character must arrive at a predetermined time, requiring synchronization between sender and receiver (see Figure 6).

Duplex   A telecommunication path may connect two points only or it may connect several points, as with a conference line or a line connecting several work-

Asynchronous						Bisynchronous	
S	S	S	S	S	S		
T 11000 T		T 11010 T		T 10100 T			
A	O	A	O	A	O	S S S	
R	P	R	P	R	P	Y Y Y	10101000010001111010101
T		T		T		N N N	

Figure 6   Difference in asynchronous and bisynchronous transmission.

stations or terminals to a CPU. Transmission may be *full duplex* or *half-duplex*. Full duplex transmission means that signals can go in both directions at the same time. Half-duplex transmission means that signals can go in either but only in one direction at once. The purpose of the transmission should be considered. Half-duplex is satisfactory for most transmissions between computers and terminals. However, for on-line inquiry handling and for videoconferencing, full duplex transmission is preferred because people find it desirable to watch each other's faces when talking.

Speed of Transmission

Generally, synchronous transmission can be faster, with speeds of transmission (bits per second) of 300, 600, 1200, 2400, 4800, and 9600. Speeds for asynchronous are 110, 300, 1200, and in some instances 2400. The speed of transmission (or baud rate) is a cost factor when transmission is to occur over long-distance lines.

Data transmitted over regular voice-grade phone lines is usually sent at 110-1200 bits per second. Transmission speeds above 1200 bits per second normally require a dedicated line. However, with half-duplex transmission, up to 4800 bits per second is fairly routine. The public network in the United States supports 4800 bits per second on a dial-up line.

Character Codes

Another essential consideration is the character coding system used for transmission. The most widely used code has been *ASCII* (American Standard Code for Information Interchange), a seven-bit alphanumeric code. Another common code is *EBCDIC* (Extended Binary Coded Decimal Information Code), an eight-bit alphanumeric code. Because EBCDIC is used on all IBM computers, as well as on those of a number of other major computer vendors, it is also used widely for a variety of communications applications.

Formatting Codes

In addition, the coding systems for formatting generally differ from one vendor to another. Even though two manufacturers use compatible (ASCII or EBCDIC) transmission codes, they will use different coding to denote underscoring, centering, beginning and end of a document, and so on.

When designing a system, keep in mind that asynchronous equipment cannot communicate smoothly with bisynchronous equipment. *Devices must be equipped to communicate at the same rate of speed, or bits per second, and comparable codes are required.* Because different vendors offer different forms of communications, careful consideration must be given to determining the most desirable means of meeting needs. The eventual goal, of course, is to establish a "seamless" network in which information moves smoothly throughout the organization from any piece of equipment to another.

Black Boxes   In the meantime, "black boxes" have been developed to interface or connect dissimilar pieces of electronic office equipment. The name "black box" comes from the color and overall shape of the early models. Many of them are intelligent (microprocessor-based) devices that are programmed to convert or translate various protocols (codes and modes) from one to the other and vice-versa. There are several different categories of such equipment. See Figures 7 and 8 to gain a better understanding of the functions of such units.

NETWORKING   The most dramatic advance in office automation technology has been the ongoing development of methods and devices to interconnect data pro-

Figure 7 Various kinds of black box interface devices to ease communicating among dissimilar equipment. *Source:* Willoughby Ann Walshe, "Black Boxes Supply the Missing Link," *Word Processing & Information Systems,* March, 1982, pp. 18–19.

Modems. Also known as acoustic couplers, modems perform the function of converting digital data into analog form and back again, thus enabling terminals and remote computers to communicate over ordinary telephone lines.

Port extenders. These devices can turn a machine's single communications outlet into dual or triple channels, making it possible for the machine to be interfaced with several devices.

Line protectors. Such items as isolators, power-line protectors, power interrupters, and telephone circuit protectors, to prevent lost or garbled data caused by electrical problems.

Protocol converters. Translation of communications code (from ASCII to EBCDIC, for example) and modes (asynchronous to synchronous, and vice versa) is the forte of these black boxes.

Media converters. Through media converters, information stored on floppy diskettes created on one text-editing unit can be converted into data acceptable by another electronic office machine, such as a text-editing device of a different make, a computer, or a photocomposition system.

cessing, word processing, dictation systems, OCR, micrographics, photo-typesetting, management workstations, records management—all of which have developed separately and with their own technology. Tele-communications is the medium whereby all of these separate technologies will become interconnected. Through it, information introduced into one device will become available to every other device on the network.

A network is a system that interconnects a wide assortment of information processing devices (computers, text processors, files, printers, OCR, etc.) through a communications line or data base. The advantage of networking is that it allows information to be sent to or shared among all points on the network. It allows workstations on the network to access common files or local ones, and information to be sent to all or selected points on the network.

The introduction of networks is important to the electronic office for many reasons. Networks provide the capabilities of an increasingly powerful array of office technologies to every office worker in every office location. The tendency in the past was to apply technology in the office by moving the work out of the regular office and into a technology center. For

Figure 8 Various black boxes. (Courtesy of Word Processing & Information Systems)

Figure 8 (Continued)

Figure 8 (Continued)

example, data to be processed was taken to a data processing center, where processing data was the sole function. The capabilities of the technologies were made available to the specialists in the technology center but not to the general work force. The introduction of networks changed all this, since networks brought the power and capabilities of various modern office technologies to each workstation. In short, networks provide technological power to everyone.

A second reason why networks are important is that individual technologies become part of and are subordinated to the network system. This fact has important organizational and operational implications. Traditionally, offices tended to be organized around separate technologies, with data processing departments, word processing departments, telecommunication departments, and so forth. Each department had charted its independent route, established its own priorities and operating ground rules, and was accustomed to defending its turf. With the introduction of networking, each of these technologies becomes a subset to the overall network or system and must tailor its operations to organizational requirements for information and to the technical requirements of the network. Each technology can continue to perform certain stand-alone operations, but the primary thrust will be toward the integration of all technologies.

The third reason for the importance of networks is that networks for the totally integrated electronic office will require coordinated planning. The task of linking diverse office functions requires a level of office planning never before encountered. What is clear is that in order for this planning effort to work, it must originate from the top down and include all office disciplines, and require the participation of all areas affected.

The fourth reason that networks are important is that as more and more information becomes available within the network, the need for paper records will lessen. This will not result in the totally paperless office, but as more efficient ways of processing, storing, retrieving, and communicating information are found, there will be less need to store paper.

On a practical level, networking will provide four major data requirements.

1. *Access*—normally incompatible terminals and computer systems will be able to communicate through software translation facilities.
2. *Transport*—data or messages will be sent through the network either on a call basis or on a store-and-forward basis, in which messages are collected, batched, and later sent to recipients.
3. *Control*—customizing software will allow users to define their formats, design forms, set up validating procedures, and so on.
4. *Storage*—both customizing routines and user data will be stored in the same network.

The benefits of such a system will come from permitting incompatible devices to communicate; from the economies of shareable resources and data; from the easy entry into networking; from flexibility. in growth, because facilities are shared with other users; and from the fact that network management flows from the top down.

Local Area Networks

The identification of the importance and benefits of networking has caused a growth of interest in Local Area Networks (LAN). The Yankee Group, a Massachusetts-based research organization, indicates that most business machines communicate within a local building complex. In addition, more than 45 percent of voice communications take place within the same building complex. These kinds of statistics are causing the identification of local area network applications, including terminal-to-host communications, host-to-host communications, shared access to special-purpose devices (data base machines, graphics systems, etc.), environment control, communicating word processing, and all types of microcomputers to enhance electronic mail, teleconferencing, and voice communications.

A Local Area Network (LAN) is an interlinked arrangement of computers (usually microprocessors) that permits a single computer in the net to operate both independently and directly access others in a net over a limited area. The distance limits are imposed by the technical characteristics of the system, and range from 1500 feet up to three miles. The potential for increased office productivity is tremendous. See Figure 9 for an example of a LAN that boosts office productivity.

Careful planning is required to achieve the desired results and meet the needs and applications. Important areas of planning include the topology, or structure, and the manner of transmission. Networks are characterized by their topology and by the physical transmission media. An understanding of these areas will provide a broad perspective of future telecommunications.

Topology.   The topology is the physical and logical structuring or configuration of the network: in other words, the way in which devices are connected to one another and to the traffic processing system.

Computers and various types of terminal devices are generally interconnected in one of three major arrangements, or topologies—the star network, the bus network, and the ring network.

The oldest arrangement, called the *star network*, or hub, passes all communications through some form of switcher at the hub of the configuration. Individual devices have no direct connection with each other. The hub may be some form of central processor, such as a private branch exchange (PBX) or a mainframe or host computer (see Figure 10). As with any centralized controller, a problem at the hub or CPU can create problems throughout the network.

The *ring network* topology connects individual devices in a loop or ring, via a string of signal repeaters. A signal repeater at each station or mode on the net permits signals to travel greater distances. However, this

Office Productivity with a Local Area Network
A person in the marketing department is asked that perennial business question: how much did it cost to make a sale last quarter to sell 1,000 units of product "X"? The answer has implications far beyond the sales department. Using a proper program on a LAN, the researcher can obtain data from the accounting, sales, advertising, and other departments within minutes. This information can then be correlated and analyzed right on the researcher's own microcomputer, and the answer obtained within a few minutes more.

Office Productivity without a Local Area Network
The alternative to the LAN's use in the example is a far more familiar situation in most offices. It includes several requests for information by memo, diary copies of the memo, at least two general conferences, four individual meetings, meeting and conference minutes (with copies to each department's representative), and request for data retrieval (plus a diary copy) for the company's data processing department. The information might be available within a month. That's a far cry from the minutes or very few hours it would take to compile, analyze, and prepare the results through a local area network. The boost in productivity is enormous.

Figure 9 An example of a local area network of improving productivity. *Source:* Henry Holtzman, "Local Networks Form Information Web," *Modern Office Procedures,* June, 1982, pp. 71–72.

system resembles in operation some kinds of Christmas tree lights (see Figure 11). If one device in the ring goes down, the entire network is out of operation. That also means that the entire network is down each time a new device is added to the ring. A ring network is capable of using fiber optic cable for high-performance transmission.

The *bus network* consists of a length of coaxial cable (called a "bus") to which individual devices are attached by means of simple cable taps. Note in Figure 12 the manner in which devices tap into the communications cable, as compared with the manner in which they go through the devices in the ring network illustated in Figure 11. There is no centralized center hub, and signals from one station move along the bus in both directions to all stations tapped into the cable.

The advantage of the bus network is its high reliability, because there are no active components such as repeaters along the transmission line. The failure of one station has no effect on the rest of the network's operations. There is no downtime when new stations or devices are added to or removed from the network. Its disadvantage lies in its present inability to use fiber optic cable; although whether this is a true disadvantage depends upon the applications and needs of the organization.

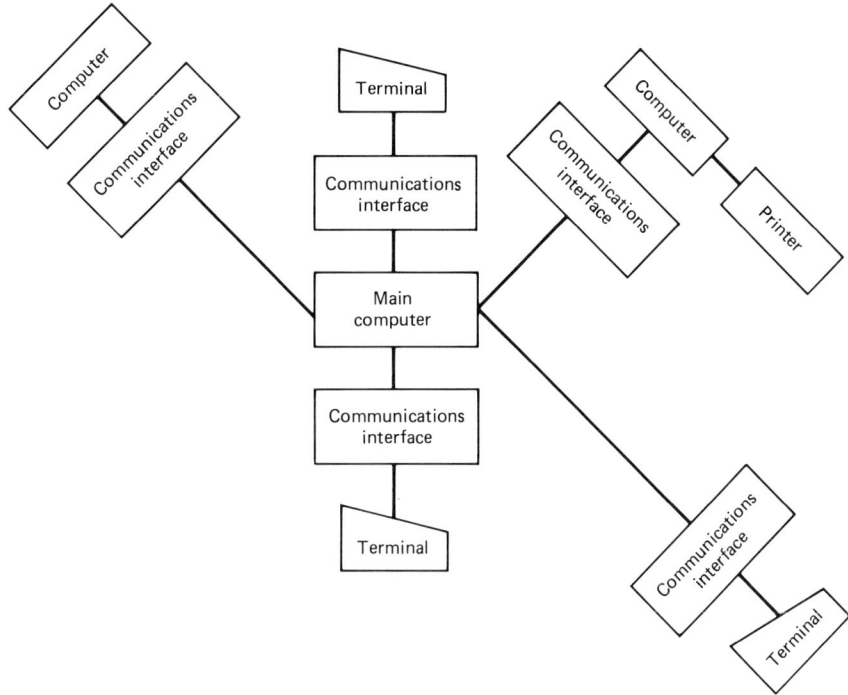

Figure 10 Star network.

Figure 11 Ring network.

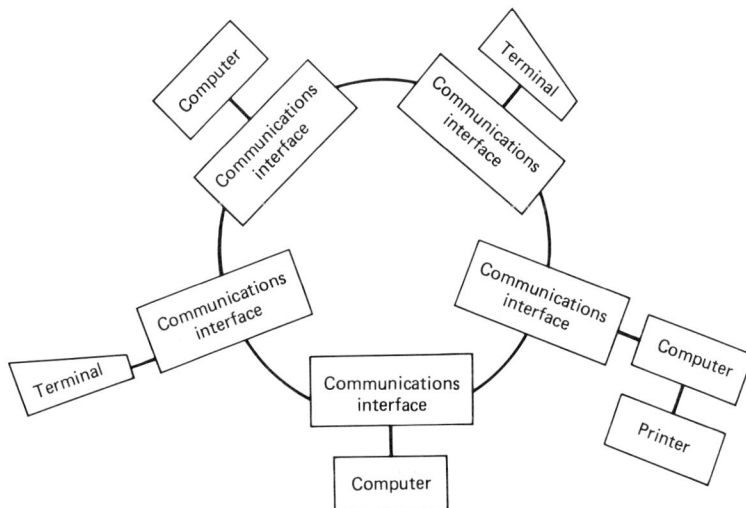

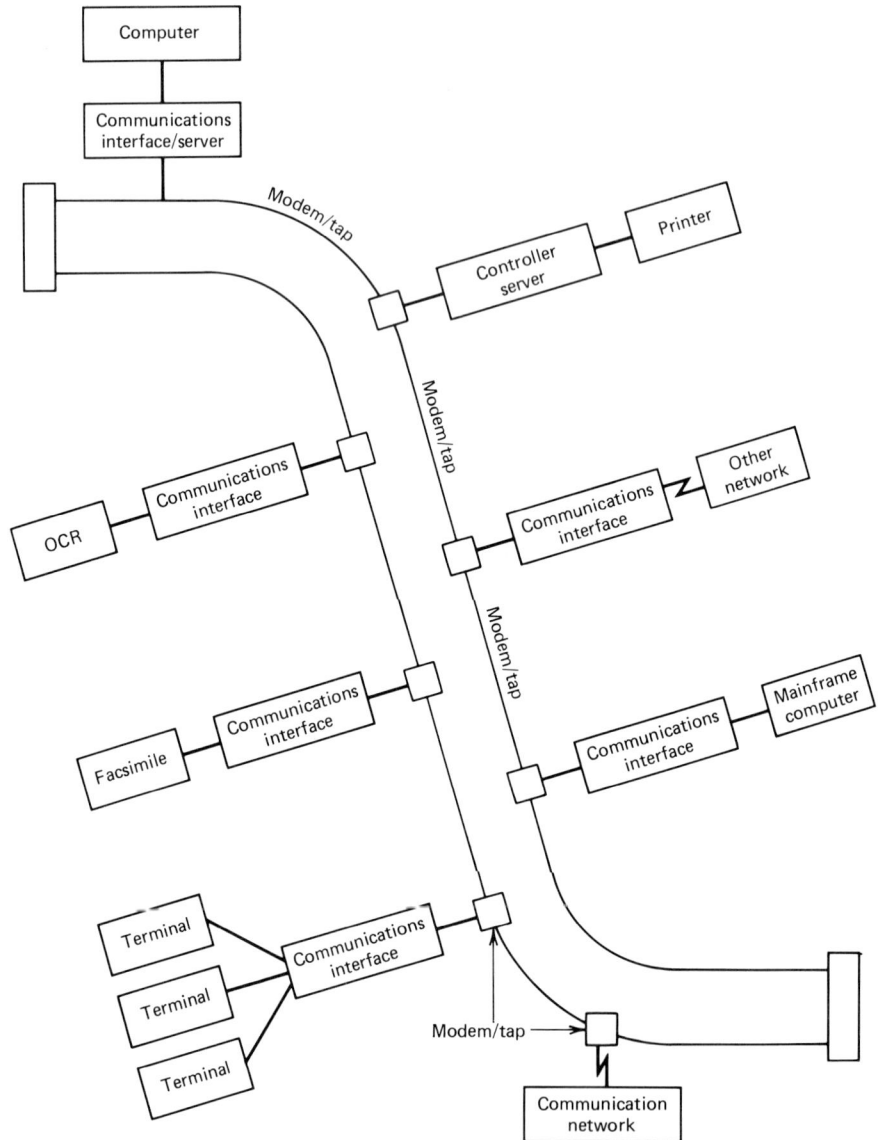

Figure 12 Bus network.

Physical Media.   Essentially, there are three major forms of physical media for the transmission of data—twisted-pair wiring, baseband single-channel cabling, and broadband multichannel cabling.

Twisted-pair wiring is used in telephone-type PBX systems. Its future and that of fiber optics, already in use by AT&T, in local area networks is very likely related to the recent deregulation of AT&T and the products marketed by American Bell, Inc., (ABI) the spin-off that will offer enhanced data communication services. ABI has announced its Advanced Information System/Net 1 Service, which has software to handle protocol conversions necessary to link previously incompatible terminals. The company has estimated it could perform these conversions for 84 percent of all terminals on the market.

Baseband networks involve systems using one digital pathway ranging from around 1 million bits per second to 50 million bits per second. Baseband systems allow a single stream of data to be transmitted on a communication medium. Baseband systems support one channel or path at a time. Baseband networks typically use a three-eighths-inch coaxial cable with carrier wire surrounded by copper mesh. There are both advantages and disadvantages to baseband. Advantages are that the cost of cable is relatively low, reconfiguring the network is easy, network interfaces are inexpensive, and the technology is quite simple. Disadvantages are that the network has a limited scope of application, the number of devices that can be attached is also restricted, completely on-line communications eliminate network availability, and transmissions are subject to a fluctuating quality that is not conducive to voice communications.

Broadband differs from baseband in a number of ways. Broadband uses common cable television (CATV) cable, is analog, and employs modems. Broadband signaling allows multiple streams of data to be transmitted simultaneously at different frequencies on a communications medium, usually coaxial cable. Advantages of broadband include a higher bandwidth, which enables the network to handle data, voice, and video; flexibility and multifunctionality; and easy expansion and reconfiguration. Disadvantages relate directly to cost. Broadband brings with it the high cost of broadband modems, additional hardware requirements, and a possible overdependency on one network for voice, data, and other services.

The terms *broadband* and *baseband* as related to local area networks define only the medium, not the application, and both must be considered when determining the design of a local area network. The baseband and broadband local network approaches differ primarily in their transmission throughput capabilities and their associated cost. The ultimate basis for comparing these facilities is their ability to effectively perform the required applications in a specific office situation. Neither approach is inherently superior; each has its place, according to needs.

Where large volumes of data need to be transferred quickly from one large computer to another, or where realtime video data is needed, the extra cost of a broadband local network may be very worthwhile. Where office communication consists of intermittent to moderate data from a large number of small office workstations, a baseband local network may be the best choice.

Global Networks   Beyond local networking, external communications systems offer further advantages to an organization. Demand for global networks, or the integration of many networks, will increase. Figure 13 shows an evolutionary process from networks within disciplines to the integration of networks by the year 1990. The primary issues to be addressed in this evolutionary process are standardization and software developments. Without them, integrated networks will be impossible.

Standardization.   At first, purchasers of computers were forced to stay with the same vendor for additional equipment to avoid incompatibility. However, the major buyers of office automation are determined to avoid that situation and are asking the office systems industry to standardize the way in which its products communicate with one another. They want an "open" system that will support diverse equipment.

Product standardization, however, is a two-edge sword for manufacturers. Since many consumers will refuse to buy systems that are incompatible or different, manufacturers will be forced to cooperate. In order to maintain market share and expand their sales, vendors will need to conform; however, conformity makes it easier for one competitor to steal sales from another's customers.

Figure 13   The next decade will witness the evolution of integrated networks within disciplines. In the late 1980s and early 1990s, networks will cross boundaries and evolve toward the integrated network.

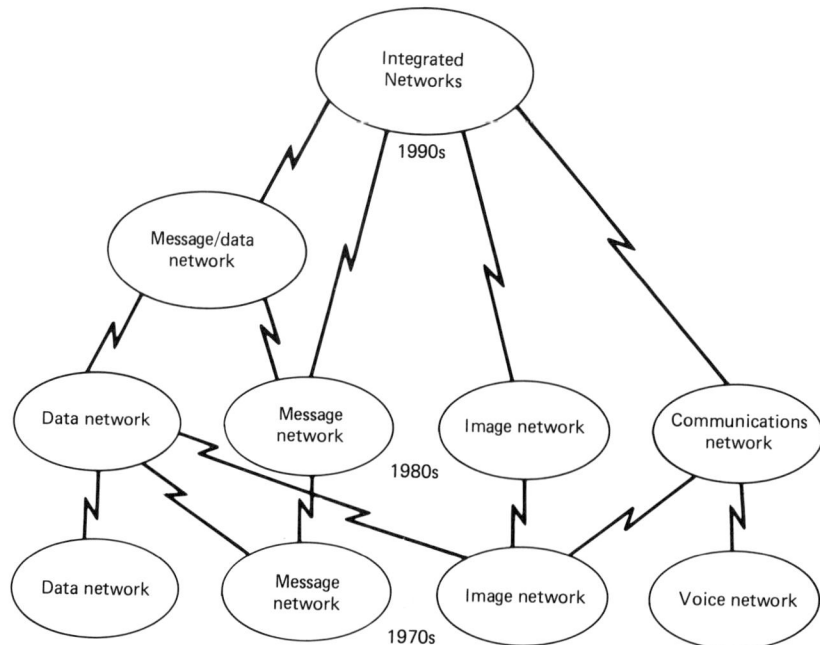

Software. Networking provides the vehicle to transport information and communication; however, it is software that binds together communications, word, and data processing. The goal of networking is to provide a tool whereby chief executives, managers, analysts, and staff can go on-line to extract, process, and communicate information from local and/or remote data bases. As technology increases the accessibility of information, the availability of software to convert this information into usable form by management becomes essential. In order for the information to be useful, office workers must be able to locate, process, and compare the data; look for trends; find statistical significances; and compare actual against projected values. As users of the automated office mature and realize the wealth of accessible data, they will have greater need for instantaneous retrieval and use of the information. Therefore, easy-to-use Englishlike software must be developed in order to permit managers, executives, and office personnel to use the data.

PROCEDURAL CONSIDERATIONS

Standards and procedures must be developed to transmit information. These include

1. Determining the appropriate mode for transmission (communicating word processors, electronic mail, etc.)
2. Identifying the message speed and format required to access the mode of information.
3. Selecting the appropriate route to expedite the delivery of the information transmitted.
4. Verifying the accuracy of the data upon its arrival at the designated destination.
5. Determining that the information is in an appropriate form to be useful to management (see Figure 14).

APPLICATIONS OF DATA COMMUNICATIONS

The applications for communications between office automation components are infinite—between word processing and phototypsetting, word processing and computers, and so on. In addition, telecommunications plays an important role in developing new and better ways to combine office functions formerly carried out as separate and discrete functions. Two of the most exciting examples of new communications capabilities are voice mail and teleconferencing. For example, voice mail and teleconferencing are changing the traditional usage of telephones, meetings, and travel.

Standards and procedures must be developed to move information.

1. Transmission technique must be chosen.
2. Message speed and format specified for transmittal.
3. A route selected to designate destination.
4. Verification of accuracy and receipt of data must be made.
5. A plan for using the information received must be detailed.

Figure 14   Basic procedures for transmitting information.

VOICE MAIL   In the ongoing management effort to improve productivity, a great deal of concern has been addressed to the time wasted as a result of telephone interruptions. The fact that trivial calls disrupt the workday, the traditional telephone-tag (the repeated calling back and forth between parties who keep missing each other), and the need for accurate message-taking and accurate response to messages and instructions have all led to demands for alternatives to traditional telephone usage.

With the introduction of voice mail, some of the problems will be eliminated or at least ameliorated. Voice mail involves the storing of messages in digital form for convenient delivery at a later time. Voice mail differs from electronic mail—the transmitted voice is stored and retrieved at a later time by a recipient who listens to the message rather than reading it on a video display terminal or printout.

Each user of a voice mail system has a "mailbox" that records and stores voice messages in digital form from other users. To retrieve the messages, users simply call the audio "mailbox" from a telephone. In addition, the user may then respond to the message by speaking into the phone immediately, and the system will automatically deliver the reply to the original caller. In addition, the same message can be sent to several persons. For example, all persons to be involved in a meeting could be simultaneously notified. A user can also dictate a message and specify who is to receive it, and when, simply by pressing keys on a Touch-Tone® phone pad.

The principal benefits of voice mail include elimination of telephone tag and improved communications. For example, sales representatives on the road or distant branch offices who were frustrated by busy signals at the home office can now get their messages through no matter what the time of day. One company has found that voice mail reduces long-distance charges by 40 percent.

Although a relatively new technology in this decade of communications growth, several companies have introduced voice mail capability. Early leaders in the field have been ECS Telecommunications, Inc., Wang, and IBM.

TELECONFERENCING With the quest for increased management productivity has come increased attention to how to make more effective use of management's time. Studies of 15 companies by the management consulting firm of Booz, Allen, and Hamilton, Inc., show that managers spend an average of 46 percent of their time in meetings and meeting-associated travel. In recent years, travel costs and the (labor) cost of travel time have risen dramatically.

Far-sighted management has begun to look at teleconferencing to help reduce both travel cost and time expenditures related to meetings. Figure 15 indicates the time and travel benefits that can be achieved. Figure 16 indicates the many forms of cost associated with travel.

Although teleconferencing can take many forms, it consists basically of electronic communication among three or more people at two or more separate locations. Separate locations can mean separate desks within a large office building, separate buildings within the same locale, or many miles apart. According to Thomas B. Cross of Cross Communications Company of Boulder, Colorado, 20 million meetings are held every day in the United States; 80 percent of all meetings last less than 30 minutes; 60 percent of all meetings could be handled by voice communications; and 35 percent of all meetings are for the exchange of information only. Many of these undoubtedly could be conducted via electronic communications.

Because meetings vary considerably in length, purpose, and specific requirements, different types of teleconferencing are appropriate for different types of meetings. The three basic teleconference types, written, audio, and video, can be used separately or in combination.

AETNA OVERCOMES DISTANCE WITH TELECOMMUNICATIONS

"Since our facilities became operational (March 2, 1981), more than 28,100 people have participated in some 4700 meetings via videoconferencing," reports Richard H. Jackson III, director of corporate communications with Aetna Life & Casualty.

The insurance company faced the problem of linking people at two locations about 10 miles apart—the home office in Hartford, and the other for computer programmers, engineering staff, and various administrative services in Windsor, Connecticut.

"Teleconferencing is a practical alternative to shuttle buses and lost work time," notes Jackson. He further estimates that travel time saved (in dollars) in 1981 topped $322,000.

Each location has two rooms available for 45-minute meetings from 7:30 A.M. daily, and each room has a table for six with a flush-to-table microphone at each seat. A light board and control panel are built into the table, allowing meeting leaders to control display of graphic materials. At the front of each room are three 25-inch television monitors. The bottom two are "people monitors" for viewing participants in the corresponding teleconferencing room; the top screen is for viewing graphics from either room.

A phone for both regular and conference calls is tied to the system. Rooms are also equipped with a slide projector, a facsimile machine, and a chalkless board. Each room is fully activated at all times; there is no need to turn cameras or microphones on or off. Some provision for handicapped users has been made: private audio level control via an earphone is available at one seat in each room, for the hard of hearing; telephones can be lowered, for those confined to wheelchairs.

The facsimile machine may be used to send or receive printed documents between locations. This simple process takes two minutes.

Figure 15 Aetna's savings through the use of teleconferencing. *Source:* Coleman, L. Finkel, "What Teleconferencing Can Do and Cannot Do For Your Meeting," *Management Review,* July, 1982, p. 10.

Written Methods   Written teleconferences involve the transmission of words, numbers, or graphics. Teletype, used for years, is one form. Computer teleconferencing, facsimile, and the Electronic Blackboard all involve higher levels of technology.

Computer Teleconferencing.   Teleconferencing through a computer requires no special facilities or equipment other than a terminal at each location. The advantage of computer teleconferencing is that it can provide a forum to conduct a conference without the simultaneous involvement of all participants and without relying on the human voice. Members of a working group do not have to be on their terminals at the same time. They can send either entries for everyone's access or private notes indentified for a specific individual. (Both entries and notes can be stored

TRAVEL COSTS CAN TAKE MANY FORMS:

1. Increase in monetary cost of 30 to 40 percent per year (airfare, hotel, and meals).
2. Inconvenient travel schedules caused by a decrease in the number of flights.
3. Last-minute travel plans are becoming a thing of the past.
4. How much is your time worth? On the average, a person spends two hours in transit for a two-hour meeting, so what is the cost of this nonproductive time?
5. Most important to some, what effect does this traveling have on your personal life?

Figure 16 Forms of cost associated with travel. *Source:* Gregory W. Paulsen, "Corporate Teleconferencing: An Investment for the Future," *The Office,* November, 1980, p. 85.

by subject matter or keyword, for later retrieval.) Computer teleconferencing also eliminates the need for prescheduling, since massive amounts of information can be sent to individuals for response at their convenience. In the event of rush meetings or if decisions are necessary, meeting participants can be scheduled and precise information can be exchanged swiftly (for example, as now available in the national computer conferencing network linking various parts of the nuclear power industry).

Some firms in the data services and communications industries offer their network capabilities to end users on a subscription basis. They are sometimes called value-added networks (VAN). The user communicates with its own remote locations via the VAN, with other computer information sources, or even with other users of the same network. (Tymnet, Graphnet, Autonet, and FaxPak are typical of VANs available.)

Facsimile. Facsimile, also called fax, involves the transmission of an exact copy over communications lines. The ability to transmit photographs, charts, and signatures, as well as text and data, sets facsimile apart from other forms of communication. Facsimile equipment can be either analog or digital. Digital systems can transmit a typical 250-word letter in 20 seconds; analog systems require four to six minutes to transmit a single page. Facsimile is becoming an important part of the office network in combination with other technologies (such as satellite transmission). Fax can also be used in combination with other forms of teleconferencing, including the transmission of a hard copy of whatever appears on a video monitor (see Figure 17).

Electronic Blackboard. The Electronic Blackboard can be set up in each meeting location so that any participating individual can write on it and

Figure 17 A typical video conferencing room contains: A—video camera; B—speaker; C—visual aid equipment; D—screens; E—microphone; F—control console; and G—facsimile.

the writing will appear on a monitor (screen) in any number of other locations (see Figure 18). In addition, microphones and speakers at each location permit discussion of the written material. This form of teleconferencing is inexpensive; it is also easy to install and can be accomplished over standard dial-up telephone lines.

Audio Methods   Audio teleconferences involve only transmission of sound. Here again, time and travel cost savings represent major benefits. Another benefit is uniformity of information—all participants receive the information at the same time. A California electronics distributor conducts a nationwide teleconference every Monday morning with its 30 branch sales locations. The result: current information about sales promotions, policy and procedural changes, and other vital information for all managers. (Meetings held weekly in person would be impossible, because of time and travel costs.)

Video Methods   Video teleconferences involve pictures as well as sound and are transmitted by film, videotape, or "live" action. Variations of video include *full-motion video systems*, which work in the same way as closed-circuit

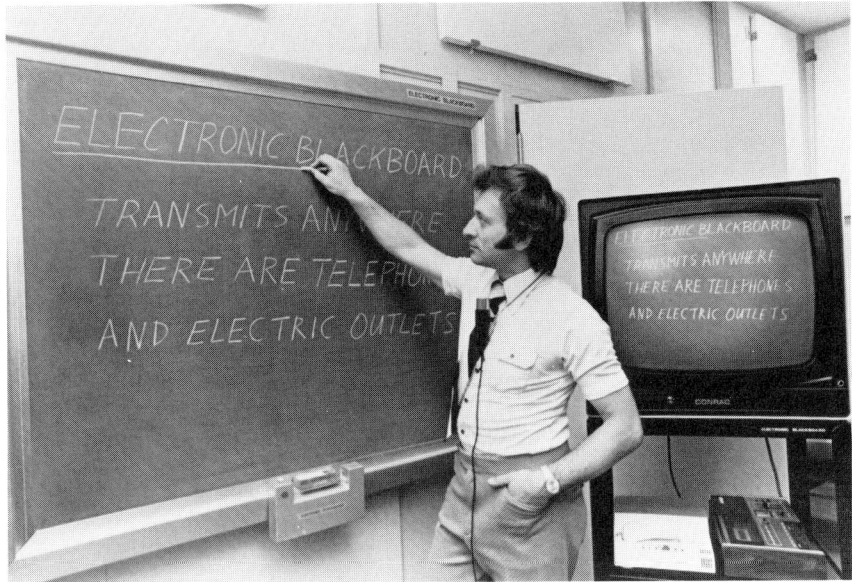

Figure 18 Gemini Electronic Blackboard transmits graphics communications. Sketches, equations, or other graphics transmitted via the new Bell System electronic blackboard could be worth the proverbial thousand spoken words to many schools and businesses. Electronic blackboard, demonstrated by Bell Labs designer, transmits handwriting over ordinary telephone and provides for instant display on a video monitor at distant locations. A portable conference telephone provides accompanying audio communications. *Source: Bell Labs; Gemini is an AT&T Trademark.*

television. All activity is captured and transmitted to the distant location. Current costs for the bandwidth necessary to transmit full-motion video are very high; this system will become more economically feasible when satellite transmission is more commonplace.

With *fixed-frame video*, a new picture is transmitted several times per minute; the monitor displays an image for a number of seconds until the next frame is received. Full-frame video can be transmitted in black-and-white or in color, and at much lower cost than full-motion video. The choice, of course, depends upon the amount of activity expected in a meeting.

Hotel chains such as the Hilton and Holiday Inns have installed teleconferencing facilities in many cities. AT&T has fully equipped public meeting rooms and studios in major cities. Many large organizations are also installing teleconferencing rooms. According to research by Quantum Science, the number of installed teleconferencing rooms will rise to 3400 in 1985, from the 1981 figure of 575.

Although travel costs undoubtedly can be decreased (estimates range from 20 to 50 percent), final evaluation of success cannot be on cost alone. Management's acceptance of teleconferencing and continued willingness to participate, along with its satisfaction with the results obtained through the new types of meetings, are also important criteria in judging success.

MANAGEMENT CONSIDERATIONS

TOTAL VIEW   Because of the many technological considerations in telecommunications and the need to phase in any new plan, it is natural to tend to think in terms of an enlargment of present-day operations. However, Brian R. Blackmarr, an office automation consultant, recommends viewing local networks as an information processing element, rather than as an extension of current data/word processing-based communications. An information processing network, to be totally effective, should allow the handling of audio (phone) and image (graphics) information, as well as the character-based data commonly utilized in data and word processing. In addition, a full information processing network may need to handle realtime video data for applications such as security monitors or teleconferencing.

Careful consideration also should be given to both present and probable future technology and levels of need. It is important to avoid short-range decisions; on the other hand, both technology and an organization's needs constantly change. Every effort should be made to direct sufficient and proper attention to the identification of needs.

IDENTIFYING NEEDS   Identification of the need for telecommunications should extend to many areas; to name a few: telephone, meetings, and distribution of information in a more timely manner.

Telephone. Most phone calls are convenient for one person—the person who made the call. Studies indicate that most of the time spent in making a phone call to communicate a simple piece of information is taken up with niceties. Voice-forward and message switching can reduce the number of phone calls, eliminate lost handwritten messages, and reduce casual conversation. This will reduce the redialing, busy signals, call backs, and misunderstood messages that make up a great deal of office communications.

Meetings. Questions need to be answered regarding the need to provide service and communication to remote locations. Are there already terminals or methods of communication in place to facilitate voice mail or computer conferencing? How many meetings occur in the routine office practice? If these meetings could be reduced by 50 percent, what opportunities for improved worker productivity would there be? Are there task force groups brainstorming for long-term planning? How much travel and time is involved? How often does your organization conduct meetings and communications with offices or personnel working in different time zones? What have the delays cost your organization? Does this cost in hours or dollars saved warrant investigation of computer conferencing?

Distribution of Information. Where does information originate and how is it used? How do managers use reports from computers? Do they handwrite a summary report from those reports?

How much of the same information is used by many people in different locations? How long does it presently take to move information from one point to another? How important is instantaneous access to information? What do delays cost the organization? Do the advantages gained balance the cost and effort to establish a data base and/or network?

BENEFITS   The benefits to be derived from telecommunications relate to many aspects of an organization—job satisfaction, employee motivation, increased flow of communications, greater use of information, company competitive advantage through better information, availability of information for long- and short-term planning, and so on.

THE CHALLENGE   Since the major part of the office labor dollar is spent gathering, processing, and transmitting data in a company, the challenge for management is to control and leverage this valuable information. Telecommunications, with all that it offers for the future, is a major tool to assist management to meet this challenge. Efficient telecommunications management is particularly important today, because telecommunications costs in most corporations are rising more rapidly than the inflation rate.

James Martin, well-known computer author and lecturer, suggests that a number of stages mark the development of telecommunications management.

Stage 1. No centralized management. Lines and equipment are leased haphazardly by user departments.

Stage 2. Centralized planning and management of the corporate telephone facilities. Optimization of separate data networks by data processing system designers.

Stage 3. An attempt to combine the various data networks into an integrated data transmission facility, possibly including a message switching system.

Stage 4. An attempt to combine the data and voice facilities into an overall optimized plan.

Stage 5. A study of all forms of corporate communications, including internal mail and memo typing, executive travel, and use of information resources.

Stage 6. Cost optimization of all forms of corporate communications.

To achieve Stage 6 takes a very complex operation. Few corporations have contemplated it yet, let alone succeeded. The technology becoming available will make it increasingly profitable.

CHAPTER 7

REPLICATION AND DISTRIBUTION

OBJECTIVES

In this chapter you will learn about
1. The roles of replication and distribution in the information processing flow.
2. Convenience copiers and their selection to meet users' needs.
3. The advantages of typesetting and the benefits of integrating phototypesetting with other office systems.
4. The growth of computer graphics in the office.
5. The new electronic printer/copiers and the changes that they are creating in office functions.
6. Management techniques and technology to assist with the handling of incoming and outgoing mail.
7. Electronic mail and its various uses.

Both the replication (taking already captured information and changing into another form) and distribution (moving of information from one point to another) processes are major parts of the information processing flow (cycle) (see Figure 1). Both replication and distribution must be considered as parts of a total support system and integrated office. This chapter discusses each of these processes and their relationship to the integrated electronic office. As with other functions, users' needs should be the basis for the design of the system. But for that system to be totally effective, the human aspects must also be included.

Reprographics is the replication of information through a variety of means, with the ultimate objective of distribution in some form to another party. In today's office, the existing services for moving paper are an important part of this distribution process. Although these services will

Figure 1   Replication is a vital component of the total information cycle. Note the various forms of printing, viewing, or hearing.

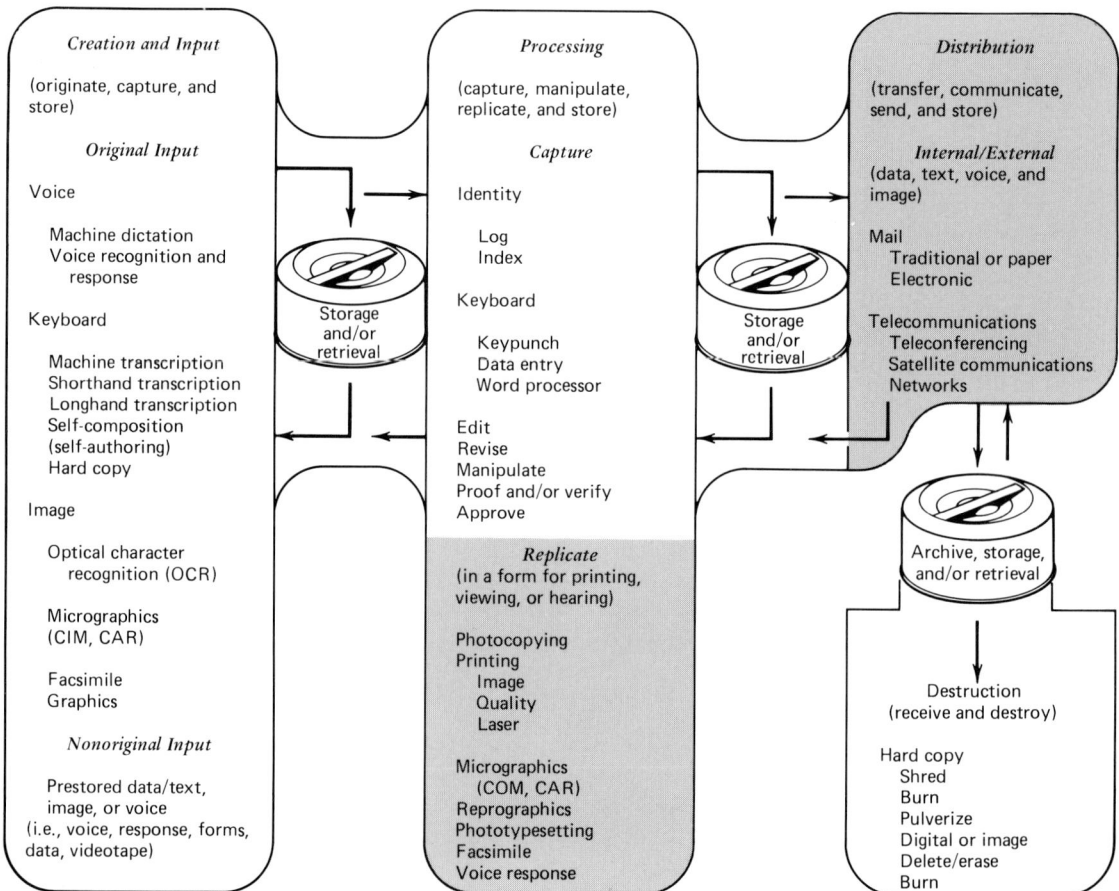

never be totally replaced, more and more information will be distributed electronically in the future. Both traditional and electronic mail applications will be studied.

Traditional copying and mail functions have been given low priority by management. Today, these specialized activities must be studied, proceduralized, and controlled in order to utilize them most effectively. When the mailroom is properly managed, automation of mail functions can save time and money and facilitate good communications. When the mailroom is improperly managed (which often includes the copy center), both support and management employees tend to bypass it (e.g., make their own photocopies, deliver their own internal mail), lowering overall productivity in the office.

The goal of the mail function is simply to provide accurate, efficient, cost-effective service in the delivery of information. This process is handled in three main areas that will be addressed in this chapter—internal and external mail delivery, and outgoing mail.

REPROGRAPHICS

Replication occurs in several ways—through copying, printing, or facsimile, and more recently through intelligent copiers or electronic printers. All of these methods are categorized as reprographics—a method of producing additional hard copies for distribution. In addition, the original information may be reworked to make it more meaningful to the end user, as through the use of computer graphics. Micrographics, discussed in a later chapter, may also be used to replicate the information. Voice input can be replicated or changed in form as it moves through the information process.

The appropriate method of replication or reprographics depends upon the needs and objectives to be accomplished. Key considerations in determining the best method include (1) number of copies needed, (2) the quality and appearance desired, (3) whether the information will be used internally and/or externally, (4) whether an exact copy is required, and (5) whether a change in format is desired.

Reprographics is a rapidly expanding field because new developments are providing lower costs, increased output, higher quality, and greater flexibility. The increase in basic features in the copier market, coupled with the decline in price for most convenience copiers, has provided an electronic or automated tool that can lead to improved productivity.

CONVENIENCE COPIERS According to Pitney-Bowes, a Stamford, Connecticut, manufacturer of copiers and other office equipment, an estimated 90 percent of today's offices have convenience copiers—up from 80 percent in 1974 and 60 percent in 1970. Although demand is greater and use is up, business executives continue to place demands on reprographics vendors for improved reliability, greater image quality, and increased speed.

According to David Kearns, chief executive officer of Xerox Corporation, "Over a trillion pages of business documents were produced in the United States in 1980. The estimate for 1985 is 1.4 trillion pages, a gain of more than one-third in just five years."

Copiers are usually classified by the way they work. They can be divided into dry or wet processes, depending upon whether dry or liquid chemicals are used. Recently, several convenience copiers have adopted a newer process called LTT (liquid toner technology).

Convenience copiers are usually dry processors and fall into three general types—thermal, dual spectrum, and electrostatic. Thermal and dual spectrum, along with a majority of coated paper copiers, have traditionally been the least expensive, running in the hundreds rather than the thousands of dollars. Electrostatic copiers are of two basic types—transfer electrostatic, usually called xerography; and direct electrostatic (electrofax). The main difference between them is that xerography uses plain paper, whereas direct electrostatic uses paper coated with a photosensitive conductor, such as zinc oxide.

Coated-paper copiers (see Figure 2) use specially treated paper that is heavier and more expensive than plain paper. Coated paper is less attractive than plain paper and can easily pick up unwanted marks from objects. The advantages of coated-paper copiers include a relatively low purchase price and simple construction. Coated-paper units are not designed to produce large volumes of copies and tend to be most widely used by offices that make from 500 to 2500 copies per month, usually one to five copies at a time. With a greater number of inexpensive plain-paper models entering the market, coated-paper copiers have declined in popularity.

Plain-paper copiers (see Figure 3) can use a variety of paper stocks, including company letterhead. Consequently, they are more versatile than the coated-paper copiers, and they produce higher-quality copy. Plain-paper copiers usually copy faster than coated-paper copiers; per-copy costs are lower; and they are generally used by organizations that make from 2000 to 25,000 copies per month.

It is important to assess copier requirements carefully and select the units with the capabilities to fulfill them. Most users believe that reliability of a copier and vendor reputation are key factors in the decision. Recent developments, such as fiber optics and microprocessor controls, have led to the development of features and options that greatly enhance performance and reliability. See Figures 4 and 5 for small and large copier models.

Fiber optics technology replaces traditional lens-and-mirror arrangements with low-cost microscopic glass rods that carry a concentrated light

Figure 2 Coated paper copiers, declining in popularity, are usually used for short runs (1 to 5 copies). (Photo, Courtesy of Savin Corporation)

source. Fiber optic units are compact and reliable, since the rods do not require maintenance. This design results in a lower manufacturing cost, a reduction in the physical size of copiers, and increased reliability because of the need for fewer parts. These units give the user superior performance, especially in the low-volume machines, at a competitive price. An additional benefit is the energy savings made by light intensity and lower operating temperatures.

Microprocessors in copiers permit self-diagnostics, which enable copiers to recognize mechanical problems and alert the user via a visual display. Many of the more simple and frequent problems can be rectified by a trained key operator, while more serious problems are pinpointed for the service technician. Microprocessors also allow service representatives to obtain the history of a particular copier and to service that machine to some extent over ordinary telephone lines.

Since the overall objective of most office automation projects is improved productivity, vendors are addressing the needs of copier control systems. Control systems are available that provide low-cost methods to monitor and account for copier machine usage (see Figures 6 and 7).

Figure 3 Plain paper copiers with low per copy costs are generally used by organizations making less than 25,000 copies per month. (Photo, Courtesy of Savin Corporation)

Prevention of unauthorized access to copiers can reduce operating costs through restriction by coded cards, key counters, or key boards. These devices are usually placed on top of the copier. Many systems can be programmed to collect information for each user with regard to number of original documents copied and the total number of copies produced. Display screens or registers can indicate variable data. Summary programs will provide printouts of copier activity by user for charge-back purposes. Permanent records can be maintained on media such as paper, magnetic tape, or diskette.

Copier Selection The selection of a copier should follow a measurement of volumes and a workload analysis that provide the required data to determine the features and characteristics the copier should have.

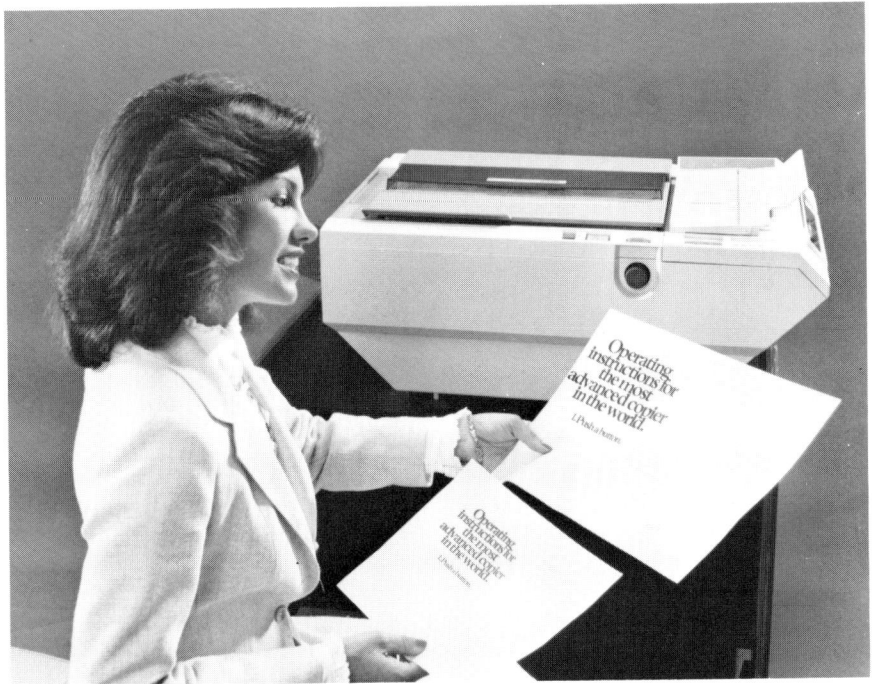

Figure 4 Copiers with enhanced features. (Courtesy of Xerox Corporation)

Figure 5 Kodak Ektaprint 150PS Copier-Duplicator. (Courtesy of Eastman Kodak Company)

Figures 6 and 7   An auditron requires the user to insert the unit into a copier before a copy is made, thus allowing control over use of the machine. (Photo, Courtesy of Xerox Corporation)

The evaluation process should include

1. A determination of the number of copies per month that the machine will be expected to make.
2. Identification of the location of the copier in relation to the location of the users, to determine how much time will have to be spent walking to and from the machine or standing in line waiting to use the machine.
3. A determination of what kind of copying will be done on the machine.
4. Whether a reduction in the size of copies is required.
5. Whether automatic document feed is desirable.
6. The number of copies that will have to be sorted.
7. How frequently duplex (two-sided) copying is required.
8. Identification of the largest sizes of paper that will be copied.
9. How fast a turnaround of copies is required, to determine desired copier speed.
10. Whether the copier will be used to make transparencies for use on an overhead projector.
11. Whether communicating to the copier from word processing units already in place is required. If so, identification of the requirements must be accomplished.
12. Whether monitoring or management controls are needed.

Upon accumulation and analysis of the collected information, management should contact vendors to select the copier model to fit the needs.

Considerations should include the amount in the budget for copiers and cost justification factors.

Controlling copier misuse is the most important factor in the management of a copier facility. The best copier becomes a money eater if misuse becomes rampant. The most common forms of copier misuse are

1. Nonbusiness copying—personal use.
2. Unwarranted copying—copying internally produced documents instead of using carbons and multipart forms and "pack rat" copying of material that *might* have future use.
3. Excess copying—making more copies than are needed.
4. Printing—using the copier as a printing press for forms.
5. Recopying—rejecting less than "perfect" copies and rerunning originals.
6. Operator error—excess copying caused by incorrect control settings, loading of paper and supplies, or inadequate in-house maintenance.

Management can take several steps to make a copier installation productive and cost-effective. The first is to educate user and management personnel about copying guidelines, stressing the costs of copies and the hazards of a paperwork explosion. Depending upon the volume, a full-time or part-time operator might be assigned.

TYPESETTING

Type has had a great impact on human history since Johann Gutenberg developed the printing press in the fifteenth century. Historically, there have been four methods of typesetting: handset, casting, typewriter composition, and photocomposition. The first two involve molten metal that takes the form of the letter to be produced and hence is called *hot type*. Although all four methods can still be found in print shops, most composition today is done by the last two, which are called *cold type*.

Typewriter, or strike-on, composition can be used directly for preparation of camera-ready copy. Machines used especially for strike-on composition are the VariTyper, Justowriter, or IBM's Composer. Although the latter machines use special type sizes and typefaces, the variety is limited and they require considerable amounts of labor time. Unless volume is small, therefore, photocomposition, or phototypesetting, has become the preferred method.

Advantages of Typesetting

Typesetting has a number of advantages for replication purposes. For example, there are three major reasons for using typeset copy rather than typewritten copy. They are

1. Appearance—copy that is typeset looks better.
2. Legibility—copy that is typeset is easier to read.
3. Cost—the compactness of typeset copy reduces costs.

Compaction of text is the primary advantage offered by typesetting. Some 40 percent of the space is saved. For example, a 100-page typewritten manual can easily become a 60-page typeset manual. Reducing the length of the line increases reading comprehension, because the eye does not have to spend as much time traveling back from the right edge to the left edge of the copy. Compaction also results in dramatic savings in reproduction and distribution costs from less paper, fewer printing plates, and less ink, collating, and binding. Production time and printing personnel time may also be reduced. See Figure 8 for a comparison of the two.

Phototypesetting

Phototypesetting, or photocomposition, began in the 1940s and has evolved through four stages of development, which are shown in Figure 9. The four basic types of phototypesetters are distinguished by how characters are stored and how they are generated. The most significant aspect from the point of an integrated office system is the digital storage and,

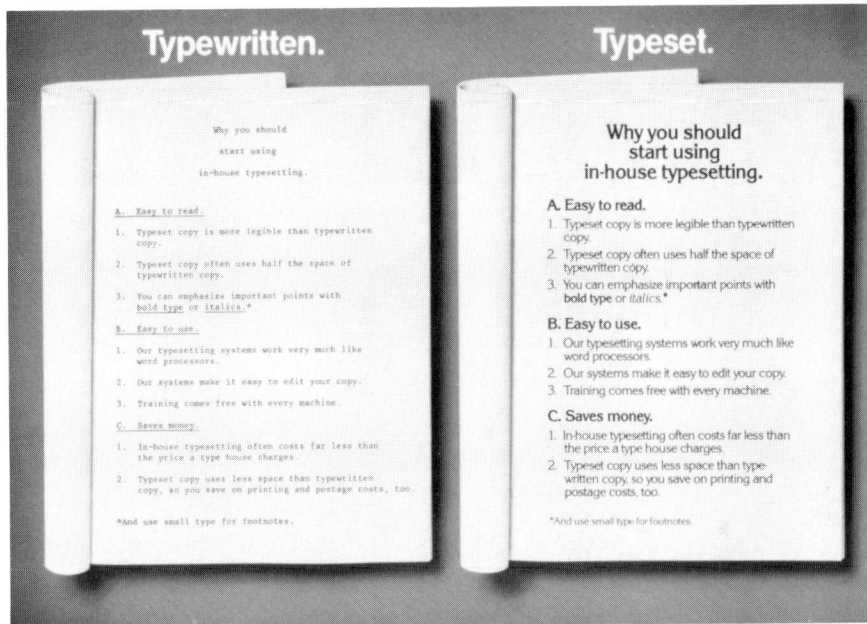

Figure 8 Typewritten document vs. phototypeset document showing results of compaction of print. (Courtesy of Verityper)

even more recently, the use of computer-controlled laser scanning or imaging. When input is stored digitally, whether on a word processor or a computer, and then interfaced to a typesetter, there are many additional advantages.

The purpose of integrating word processing and phototypesetting functions is to obtain higher-quality documents, to use less paper, and to eliminate the need for rekeyboarding of information. In summary, the primary incentives for businesses to bring typesetting processes into the office environment are economy control, quality, and aesthetics (or image) of the documents.

The typesetting function is similar to the inputting and editing function of word processing because material is keyboarded into a terminal with a screen and transferred to a magnetic medium such as a tape or a diskette. Modifications or editing changes can be made on stored information in the same way as they are made in the editing cycle of a word processing installation.

The primary difference between preparing information for a phototypesetter and for a word processing unit is that the document to be typeset must contain instructions or typesetting codes that inform the typesetter of the size of characters, the amount of space required, headlines, bold print, script, and so on. Therefore, phototypesetting requires additional

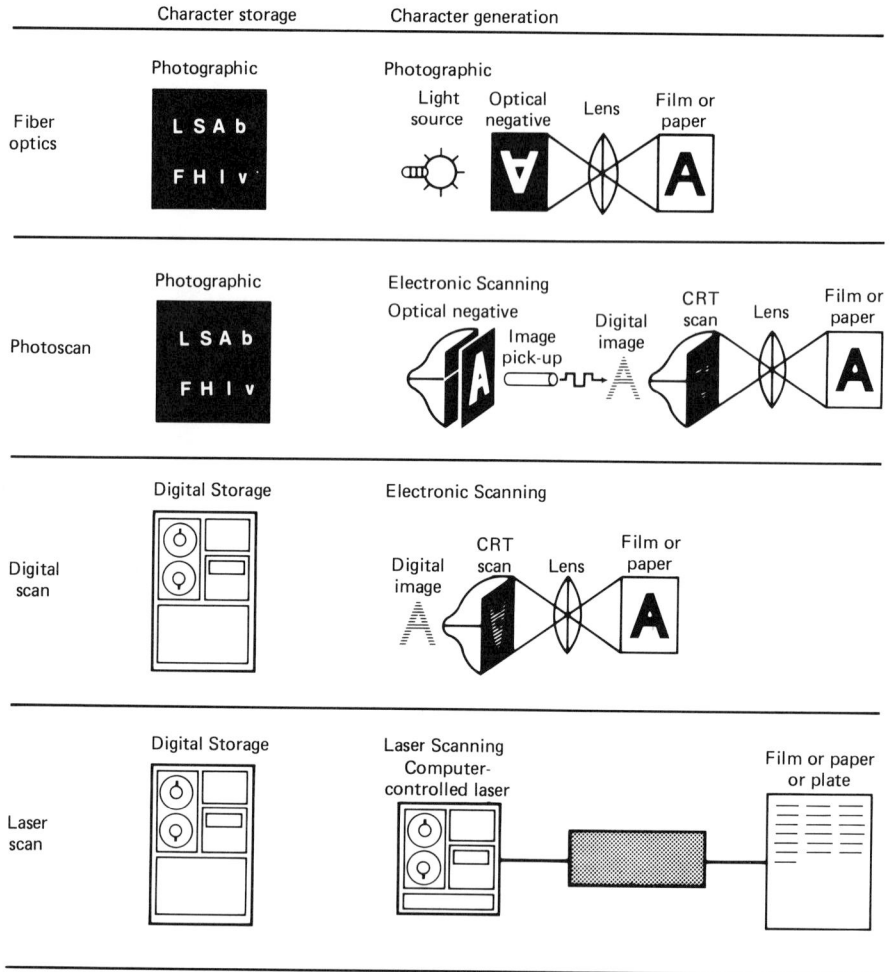

Figure 9 Stages of phototypesetting. *Source:* Edward M. Gottschall, Graphic Communications 1980's, International Typeface Corporation, Inc., 1981, p. 143.

operator training and expertise above those skills required by word processing operators.

Justification for integrating phototypesetting and word processing is now being sought by many reprographics administrators. Some of the cost avoidance and cost justification factors are related directly to the benefits that can accrue by typesetting certain identified applications in an organization, such as lengthy documents, brochures, and publications.

Benefits of Integrating Phototypesetting

1. *Copy compaction.* Generally, the amount of space occupied by typeset type will be 30 to 50 percent less than that occupied by typewriter type.

2. *Savings on printing costs.* Compacted typeset copy requires less paper, less ink, less time on the printing press. The longer the document, the greater the savings.

3. *Lower binding costs.* A 200-page publication can only be assembled in so many ways—all of them more expensive than saddle stitching, which could be used if the 200 pages were reduced to 100 typeset pages.

4. *Reduced distribution costs.* Smaller publications require less postage. Bulk shipments are significantly cheaper.

5. *Ability to meet tighter deadlines.* Copy changes can be made until the final printing plate is burned.

6. *Flexibility of output form.* After keystrokes have been captured by the system, they may be output to a character printer, wide-track printer, twin-track printer, high-speed line printer, or high-speed typesetter without rekeying.

7. *Savings on keyboarding time.* Some studies claim that as much as 69 percent of the cost of a typeset job can be charged to keyboarding. If no rekeyboarding is needed, 69 percent of typesetting costs can be saved. Between 40 to 50 percent is more realistic, however, because the cost of typesetting also depends upon complexity as well as length, and typesetting codes must be inserted. But none of these factors will impact cost as much as automation.

8. *Security.* Engineering publications, financial information, and the like no longer have to be sent outside for typesetting.

9. *Fast turnaround.* No waiting to get on a commercial typographer's production schedule. Set what you want when you want it.

10. *Broader capabilities.* With hundreds of type faces to choose from—and different sizes and different weights—many in-house typesetters start doing slides and visual aids.

11. *Improved readability.* One study claims that typeset copy is 38 percent more readable than typewriter copy. In any event, the ability to vary sizes, weights, and styles—added to compaction—undoubtedly makes typeset copy easier to read.

12. *In-house advertising.* More and more corporations are producing their own four-color advertising literature. Gone are the days when in-house printing was limited to forms.

13. *Top quality.* There is no reason why the quality of in-house type cannot be as good as that of commercial typographers. But quality typesetting involves more than mechanically reproducing captured keystrokes. A host of technical capabilities contribute to the quality of a typeset job.[1]

[1] *Typeworld,* August 1980, p. 13.

Input to phototypesetting equipment can be handled in a variety of methods. Information can be communicated from a word processing machine to a typesetter or keyboarded on a typewriting device and scanned to a phototypesetter through an optical character reader. Another method for inputting information to phototypesetting equipment is through preparing diskettes on a word processing system and converting the stored keystrokes via a black box interface to the phototypesetter. Should any of these methods not have any typesetting codes inserted, the typesetting operator would then do so. Often it is more effective to have the typesetting operator insert all codes, because such a specialized individual working full time will be far more familiar with all codes and can be far more productive.

Phototypesetting is an integral part of the electronic office, and in many large organizations and medium-sized institutions, phototypesetting enjoys an equal status with word processing systems.

Photocomposition in the new office environment will require the marriage of the two technologies. With the predefinition of formats, the transmission of text from word processors without typesetting parameters (the necessary format commands would be entered on the prototype unit) and the use of black boxes or electronic interfaces will provide the solution to the marriage of the various technologies.

The use of the phototypesetter as an in-house information processor will continue to grow and phototypesetters will be in greater demand in the electronic office than in the traditional office environment. Phototypesetting is a logical extension of today's information processing requirements.

IN-HOUSE PRINTING

As the entire information flow presented in this book begins to fit into an integrated system, the in-plant printing center will become more common. Equipment costs and ease of operation of many of the traditional printing hardware—typesetters, platemakers, copiers, printing presses, and binding and finishing equipment—are offering a new combination of cost effectiveness and capabilities that can be handled in-house. This trend is already well established. At the beginning of the 1970s there were about 25,000 in-plant operations; today there are over 83,000. Virtually all of the *Fortune 500* companies have their own in-plant facilities, and many other organizations are developing them.

The heart of the in-house operations in the 1980s will be computer technology. Through computer technology, digitized information can be input, edited, paginated, typeset, and transmitted to a multiple-copy output station, via both the computer and office systems workstations. In-house operations will be organized in different ways in different configurations. Some organizations will interface outside service bureaus and printers. All, however, will have the same objective of improved communications.

Offset Printing Equipment

Although photocopiers are the most common reprographic equipment used in offices of all sizes, organizations with high-volume printing requirements may need offset equipment. Original copy to be printed on offset equipment may be produced on a typewriter, on strike-on composers, or by phototypesetting equipment. With offset printers, the original is reproduced on either a paper or a metal plate and copies are then produced from the plate. Paper plate equipment, often referred to as a duplicator or fast copier, produces high-quality, economical copies for limited runs—usually fewer than 1500 copies. Quality is even higher with photo offset equipment that uses metal plates (see Figure 10).

Unlike paper plates, metal plates can be reused and can generate many

Figure 10 Offset Printer. (Courtesy of Addressograph Multigraph)

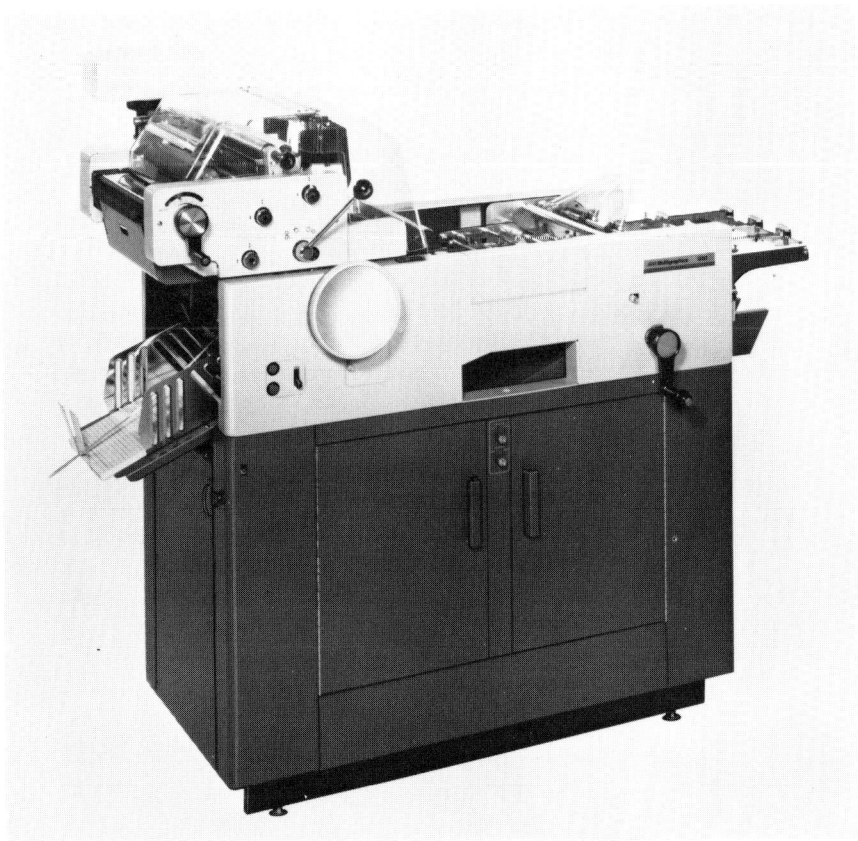

thousands of copies. On very large runs, the cost per copy will be extremely low.

Offset equipment is best situated in an organization's print shop and only operated by qualified personnel. As the newer, high-volume copiers become more cost-effective, they will replace offset equipment for many large organizations' applications. The speed, high-quality images, and ease of operation will provide major incentives for changeover to high-volume photocopiers and intelligent copier printers.

COMPUTER GRAPHICS

A graphic representation is the best way to discover, understand, and communicate the meaningful data often hidden in output tabulations. People do not naturally think in strings and arrays of numbers, but rather in images.

Recent advances have put computer graphics within reach of even the smallest businesses. With desktop workstations, graphics peripherals are becoming more intelligent, less expensive, and easier to use, and are economical in making graphic presentations of business situations. Technology now enables offices to produce low-cost computer graphics, dynamic graphic displays, and walk-away hard copy in black-and-white or color.

Over the past 10 years, manufacturers have made many efforts to bring business computer graphics into the office. Plotter-produced graphs have become more common, but until recently cost-effective interactive graphics systems were not available to the average businessman. Computer graphics are now offered by desktop systems, meaning that a large capital expenditure for graphics is not necessarily a hard-and-fast rule (see Figure 11).

How the computer knows where to place the lines on a graph is not difficult to understand. The computer simply references coordinates or points and draws to and from those points. Where does it get the coordinates? A typical example, simplified, is shown in Figure 12. Picture a grid over a drawing, like that shown in Figure 12. Each point on the drawing can be referenced using a set of two coordinates. These points are stored in a table inside the computer, like this:

Table 1

A (4,7)
B (3,5)
C (4,2)
D (5,5)

Figure 11 Desktop personal computer with graphics capability. (Courtesy of Apple Computer, Incorporated)

Then the operator tells the computer which points to connect with which others by entering a table into memory, like this:

Table 2

A,B
B,C
C,D
D,A
A,C
B,D

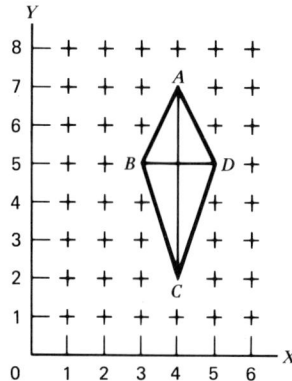

Figure 12 Typical example of computer drawing. *Source: Modern Office Procedures,* "Computer Graphics for Everyone," July, 1982, p. 40.

First, the computer looks at Table 2 and finds A as the first entry. Then it goes to Table 1 and searches for A. When it finds A, it also finds the corresponding coordinates, (4,7). The plotter pen (or CRT cursor, if that is the output device) goes to that point. Then the computer goes back to Table 2 and finds the rest of the first entry, which is B. The computer goes back to Table 1 to find B's coordinates. Then the line is drawn from A to B, now that the computer knows where they both are. This process is repeated for each entry in Table 2, producing the graphic output.

Of course, the actual computer operation to draw this kite figure would take about one-and-one-half seconds, even with all the table searching and switching back and forth. The software is designed to perform plotting in the most efficient way possible, so that each search takes only nanoseconds (a nanosecond is 1 billionth of a second).

The uses for interactive graphics are many and varied. Operators can use it to define drawing scale, to enlarge or reduce a symbol, to letter a drawing (suddenly, the laborious task of hand lettering becomes a simple job of typing the words), to change drawing scale and reproduce the drawing at the new scale, and to erase or change a line simply by touching it. Quick changing of the graphic image to permit rapid investigation of alternate possibilities is the strong point of graphic displays.

The two major types of technology used for display are refresh and storage. Refresh is divided into two categories—stroke writing and raster scanning. In stroke writing, an electron beam is used on the screen in only the positions needed to draw the image, much as a pencil is used on paper. Raster scanning involves an electron beam sequentially tracing the entire screen face. An electronic signal brightens the beam at the required positions for the display. These are called refresh techniques, because they must be repeated frequently to "refresh" the image and keep it from fading too rapidly, which would cause the image to flicker. Raster scanning uses more memory because every point on the screen must reference memory—but it can provide color displays, along with selective image erasing, which are not practical with stroke writing systems.[2]

Display is also divided into two categories—storage tubes and plasma panels. Storage tubes use two electron beams, one for writing the image and one for sustaining it. An image can be stored for several minutes without refreshing, but to change anything on the image, one must erase the entire image and replace it with the new one. Plasma panels use a matrix of electrodes to position each display element uniquely, so that selectively erasing lines or even entire sections of an image is easy. The glass panel provides a bright image requiring no external refresh circuitry.

Buyers must make their own decisions about which features of the display technology best meet their particular requirements, about whether color display is a desirable feature, and about whether to seek three-dimensional capabilities. Color display can add an important benefit to graphic displays, clarifying and sharpening detail definition.

The market for computer graphics equipment will grow tremendously in the next few years, according to research by International Data Corporation.

It is forecast that the graphic hard-copy market will account for the third largest portion of the overall graphics market—some $760 million by 1984. Shipments will jump from 24,000 to approximately 100,000 in 1984. This increase will reflect desktop pen plotters and color printers/plotters expanding the graphic hard-copy market into areas that had not been reached before.[3]

ELECTRONIC PRINTING/COPYING

Terminology in the electronic office is becoming blurred because functions once different, distinct, and separate are beginning to blend into electronic networks. Historically, there was a typewriter pool, a copier center, a computer operation. Today a particular job is just as likely to be handled in the reprographic support center as in the data processing support center or the word processing support center. From a replication and distribution point of view, the boundaries dividing copiers, duplicators, and printers are becoming less distinct as microprocessor intelligence provides new alternatives in electronic capture, storage, transmission, and distribution of document-based information.

Current nomenclature refers to laser-driven printers, electronic printers, intelligent copier/printers, and/or page printers. Essentially, all of these systems involve a method of electronic printing to serve the needs

---

[2] "Computer Graphics for Everyone," *Modern Office Procedures*, July 1980, p. 39.
[3] *Typeworld*, August 1980, p. 13.

of organizations that produce computer-generated reports, large volumes of business letters, numerous invoices, instructional and procedural manuals, and short-run publications. Although quite expensive, these systems offer considerable integration potential. Some special capabilities of electronic printers in the electronic office include

1. The ability to store (or be loaded with) a number of different type fonts (shapes, styles, sizes, bolds, itals, and so on), and the ability to change fonts on-line during printout to print multifont text automatically. Size reduction is also possible.

2. The ability to store and then reproduce business forms for those myriad government forms, contracts, or reports; this ability extends to filling in the form with variable data simultaneously during printout. Prime advantages relate to elimination of a large inventory of preprinted forms that consume space, and associated time-space overhead reductions.

3. The ability to produce bar or pie charts in solids, cross hatches, or shades of gray; to produce linear or log-continuous line charts; and to produce (or be programmed to produce) special characters such as company logos and trademarks, as well as special line-graphics illustrations or technical diagrams.

4. The almost "offset" quality of the character image, and the ability to produce (with appropriate software) multicolumn text with graphic illustrations interspersed throughout. This "printed" page reproduction capability costs considerably less than conventional offset means, and allows the office to "publish" high-quality reports or documents.[4]

The functions of electronic intelligent copier/printers can encompass input, data storage, imaging, and output, as well as communications capability. Wide flexibility in the input and output phases is what makes electronic intelligent copier/printers a viable component of the electronic office and of the overall networking capability that will ultimately encompass and tie all communications together. Several systems already in use are demonstrating the role of such equipment.

The IBM 6670 Information Distributor, which prints with a laser beam, can receive and send documents electronically over regular telephone lines and thus link WP/DP functions and remote sites, as well as interface with other systems (see Figure 13). This device can

1. Condense large computer printouts to letter size.
2. Transform data into good print quality without rekeyboarding.
3. Print on both sides of paper.
4. Change type styles on a page.

[4] *Advanced Office Concepts,* March 1982.

5. Use customized printing formats.
6. Merge text and data.
7. Serve as a convenience copier.

Several other vendors offer products that integrate various functions—for example, the Wang Laser Printing System Model LPS-12 and the Xerox 5700 Electronic Printing System (see Figures 14 and 15).

Another related phenomena that can be expected in the electronic office is the increased use of both *nonimpact printers* and *electronic proofs*. Nonimpact printer and laser printer sales are expected to grow by as much as 50 percent annually, because of the speed and cost effectiveness of these systems. Early objections to these printers were based on low quality and lack of ability to make carbon copies. However, quality has improved to the point of public acceptance, and as organizations increase the amount of information in data-base storage, paper copies are no longer necessary, since information can be recalled and reconstructed by electronic means.

Figure 13　IBM 6670 utilizing laser beam technology. (Courtesy of IBM Corporation)

Figure 14 Wang Laser Printing System—Model LPS-12. (Courtesy of Wang Laboratories, Incorporated)

That old standby, the hard-copy proof, is giving way to the electronic proof. Instead of printing out paper proofs and galleys for printing and other communications, more and more proofing will be done by viewing copy and editing it right at the visual display terminal—hence the term *electronic proof*.

Much talk abounds about the paperless office in the future. With a well-organized effort, some organizations may reduce their consumption of

Figure 15 XEROX 5700 Electronic Printing System. (Courtesy of Xerox Corporation)

paper, but most experts agree that significant decreases in the use of paper in the office are still decades away. While paper will lose some of its share of the market to electronic mail and digital or image storage in the 1980s, the actual volume of paper used in communications is likely to grow. To dispense with paper requires such an extensive integration of functions and communications networks that it is nearly an impossibility. Every sender and receiver would require compatible equipment. Although business mail volume is growing, accounting for over 82 percent of all mail, one must consider that 55 percent of that figure is business-to-household, a type of mail that remains relatively impervious to electronic diversion. From this, one can readily realize that the paperless office is indeed many years away. Traditional mail for distributing information will continue to be an important part of the information processing flow.

MAIL SERVICES

Because of soaring budgets for postage and personnel, many organizations have displayed a new interest in professional mailroom management. However, the availability of experienced managers with the knowledge of the mailroom operation is extremely limited. For many years the mailing operation was literally and figuratively "in the basement." Although this location reflected the pragmatic needs for easy street-level access to trucks depositing and carrying mail, it also represented the overall view of most management that the mailroom required little administrative attention.

The mailroom supervisor has seldom been a member of a planning team or been consulted as to projects under way. Yet, users have felt the mailroom did not render adequate service.

Often the mailroom supervisors were not consulted or notified when a large mailing was to be prepared, and they would find themselves backlogged when their staff was required to meet a short deadline, without the advantage of advance planning to reschedule other work.

Mailrooms have seldom been equipped with modern furniture and technology. Most of the furniture found in mailrooms has been discarded from other areas of the organization and mailroom equipment usually has not been replaced for many years. Quite often, mailroom hiring involves entry-level individuals who are expected to work temporarily in the mailroom before moving up in the organization to better jobs. A transient and inexperienced staff is usually too limited to get the job done. Since they are hired as transient or lowest-skill workers, mailroom employees are seldom motivated.

The general attitude toward mailing services contends there is little that can be done to improve the mailroom operation. Therefore, little attention is given to constructive suggestions and/or recommendations for improving the operation. Finally, many organizations view the mailroom function as an overhead item that cannot be controlled, and it thus is not regarded as an opportunity for improving productivity or providing a cost-effective service.

With office automation, a great deal of attention is now focused on increased and improved productivity. In spite of the introduction of facsimile, intelligent copier transmission, and graphics communications through word and data processing, the basic fact is that the amount of paper handled by American business continues to grow. Moving it efficiently and economically within an organization and between organizations has become a major challenge for mailroom operations managers and office services administrators.

With high technology such as computers, in-house printing, word processing, and electronic mail replicating and distributing information, it becomes even more critical that mailroom administrators become knowledgeable and assume an active role in the controlling of communication costs.

MAILROOM EQUIPMENT AND LAYOUT The number and types of mailroom equipment found in various organizations varies according to the size of an organization. Postage meters, scales, sorting bins, workstations, and mail carts are fairly basic items.

Very large organizations may use automatic envelope openers (which may actually be placed in individual departments), folders, inserters, electronic mail-weighing systems, computer output mailing, postage accounting, and electronic remote postage metering and resetting systems.

Postage meters are now standard equipment for almost all businesses. It is too expensive to use labor to purchase stamps and manually affix them. Postage meters are available to meet the needs of all sizes of organizations, The selection of available postage meters is limited to United States Postal Service (USPS)-licensed vendors. The USPS has licensed only a few vendors to lease postage meters. The metering machine may be purchased or leased; however, the meter itself must be leased. A variety of meters are available through the designated vendors—meters that can be connected to mail processing devices that seal and stack the mail, or to folders, inserters, and sorters—thus automating a major portion of the outgoing mail operation (see Figure 16).

The advantages of the newer electronic postage meters are ease of operation, less chance of error, and electronic speed through the use of microprocessor controls, digital displays, and automatic prompting.

A dramatic step forward in the handling of postage is represented by the remote meter resetting systems that eliminate trips to the post office for postage meter setting. A postage meter user can predeposit funds in a trustee bank account by mail or through electronic funds transfer. To reset a meter, the user places a call to a data center, exchanges certain information with the center's computer, and is given a code number to reset the meter.

A mailroom that installs sorting bins and workstations should select designs that are modular in nature, allowing an increase in size of the work area as well as within individual bins used for sorting.

Ergonomic considerations in setting up the equipment and workstations for mailroom personnel should include the height of the bins, the level of the work surface, and color coding for ease of geographical location sorting. The bins should be compactly arranged to occupy minimal floor space. By reducing the steps that mailroom personnel must take while sorting mail and preparing for delivery, the fatigue and stress on an employee can be reduced, thereby increasing productivity.

Proper physical layout of the mailroom can have so much effect on the productivity of mailroom employees that it should not be ignored. Help is available. The USPS and postage mailroom equipment vendors are very eager to assist in designing and laying out mailroom operations (see Figure 17).

Electronic mail-weighing systems or electronic scales are available for all sizes of mailroom. These systems assist in eliminating human error in the calculating of postage and shipping, and can be used to make automatic cost calculations among various modes of delivery, such as first class, parcel post, and UPS. They also can be interfaced with postage meters to imprint envelopes or dispense meter tapes automatically, and can be interfaced with a microcomputer system for managing a charge-back postage system in a large organization.

Computer output mailing systems allow computer-printed continuous forms to be fed into equipment that automatically bursts the forms, inserts them into envelopes, designates zip code breaks, and meter-stamps the envelopes for mailing.

Figure 16 Note the variety of equipment available to improve productivity in a mail room. (Photo, Courtesy of Pitney Bowes)

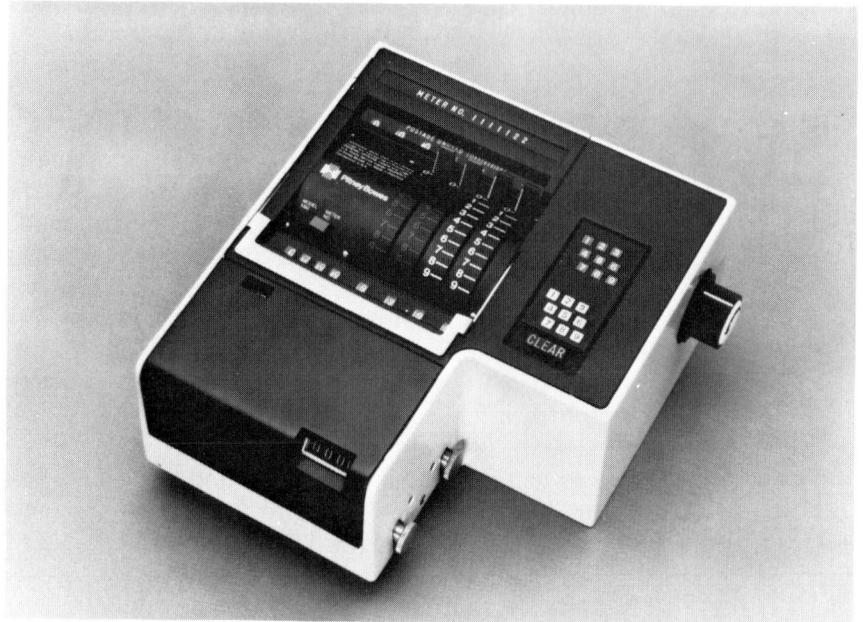

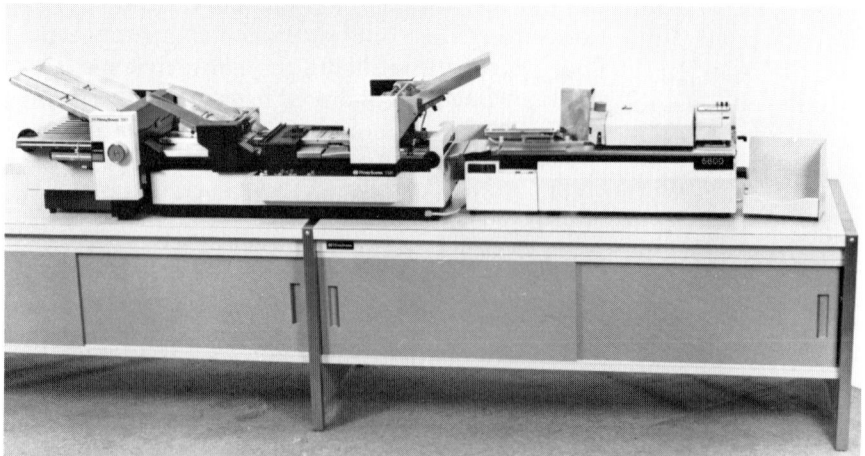

Figure 16 *(Continued)*

Postage accounting systems eliminate the manual keeping of postage records and simplify the accurate and automatic charging back of postage to departments.

INTERNAL MAIL DELIVERY

To the average user, the most visible part of a mailroom operation is the messenger or mail delivery service. Internal mail deliveries can be categorized into two main modes—manual and mechanized.

Manual Mail Delivery

Manual mail delivery is characterized by a well-organized courier/messenger service coupled with established routes and schedules. Frequent, regular pickups and deliveries and courteous personnel are essential to a successful manual delivery system. This service should be structured according to the volume of mail, the number of couriers available, and the length of the route over which they must travel. If the heaviest volumes of mail occur early in the morning and late in the afternoon, then an attempt should be made to schedule more-frequent pickups and deliveries at these times of the day.

Definite routes for couriers should be established and tested to determine how long it will take to cover the route. Following this determination, a schedule of pickup and delivery times should be created and published for all employees, so that users of the service know when to expect pickup and delivery of mail. Many organizations have attained

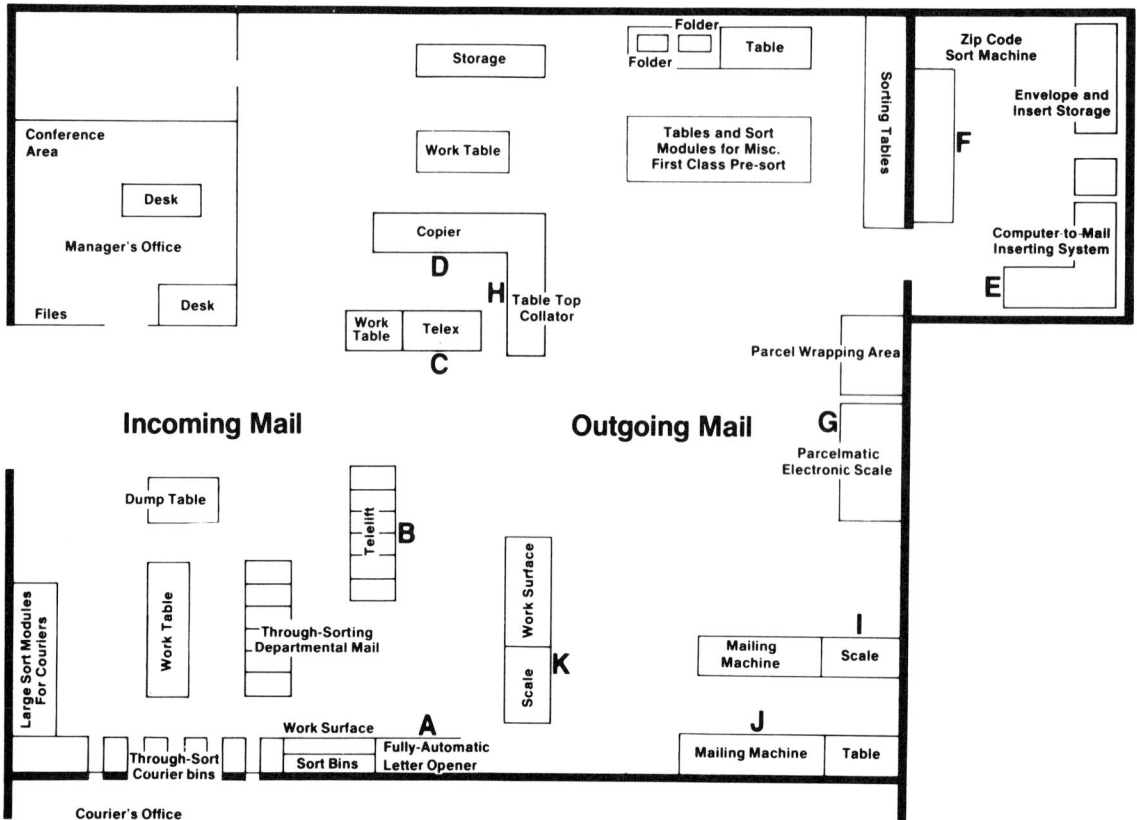

Figure 17 Mailroom layout. (Courtesy of Pitney Bowes).

improved productivity through the use of drop-off points within a given department or of key individuals in each department to receive that department's mail, so that overall sorting, time on the route, and distribution time are reduced. When the number of employees receiving mail is reduced, fewer couriers are required, training time within the Mail Department is reduced, turnaround time of mail delivery is increased, and a more proceduralized approach can be taken for control of the delivery process.

The various departments that receive the mail delivery open the mail, sort it by departmental addressee, and deliver it to responsible secretaries (who may in fact respond to some of the mail immediately), improving overall productivity by removing routine or mundane mail handling from the managers.

A manual delivery system requires messengers to have mail carts with bins or file slots for each delivery stop, as well as a bin for external mail. As messengers stop at the drop-off point, they pick up the outgoing mail, sort it, and put it into appropriate bins in the cart before proceeding to the next stop. This system speeds the delivery of interdepartmental mail and reduces the time spent within the Mail Department. For example, if the Personnel Department stop is before the Communications Department stop, then Personnel's letters to Communications will be picked up and delivered on the same trip. Communications mail to Personnel would be held on the cart until the next delivery, unless otherwise specified by procedure. A consistently heavy volume from one department to another is a factor to consider when determining routes.

MECHANIZED MAIL DELIVERY

Some large organizations have converted to mechanized delivery systems that permit more-frequent and faster deliveries. They are expensive to install and may sometimes require building modifications. One must also be concerned with the maintenance of such systems, since any mechanical device is susceptible to breakdowns.

There are several different mechanized systems available—vertical tray-lift systems for multistory buildings; conveyor belt systems that function horizontally on one or two floors; and pneumatic tube systems, which historically have been used as an automated type of mail delivery. These systems have most frequently been used by large, paper-intensive organizations such as insurance companies. The most recent development is a driverless vehicle called the Mailmobile, marketed by Automated Systems Division of Bell & Howell. It is especially beneficial when there are many mail deliveries and pickups on the same floor (see Figure 18).

All of these mechanized systems depend on a user for certain basic functions—for example, removing the mail from the driverless vehicle or pneumatic tube or conveyor belt carrier—and therefore, a certain amount of user resistance has been encountered. However, as the office continues to automate, acceptance of such devices as the Mailmobile as internal means of delivering communications has improved.

Mailmobiles are cost-effective, since the cost of the Mailmobile is comparable to the salary of one messenger. A messenger is paid year after year, so assuming the cost of the Mailmobile is the same as salary and benefits for one year, there would be a one-year payback on the purchase of the Mailmobile.

Since Mailmobiles are mechanized, they repeat the identical route without error, following an invisible chemical pathway, (see Figure 19), and they can increase the number of pickups and deliveries because they do not stop to talk.

Cost-avoidance factors that justify the purchase of a Mailmobile include the elimination of employee time spent running errands to a central mail department and/or to other departments. Employees are free to concentrate on more productive work and workflow is made smoother. The

Figure 18 The mailmobile. (Courtesy of Automated Systems Division, Bell & Howell)

scheduled timing of the mechanized mail delivery vehicle provides time savings and productivity gains throughout an organization, because the mail delivery is planned for and scheduled, and the driverless vehicle is met on time.

Safety features built into these vehicles allow them to detect obstacles, signal humans audibly that they are arriving, flash lights so that people do not run into them, and immediately brake when the pathway is interrupted. The Mailmobile has sensor devices that prevent the vehicle from running over small, low objects. The programming of the vehicle is equipped with manual override, to allow human intervention.

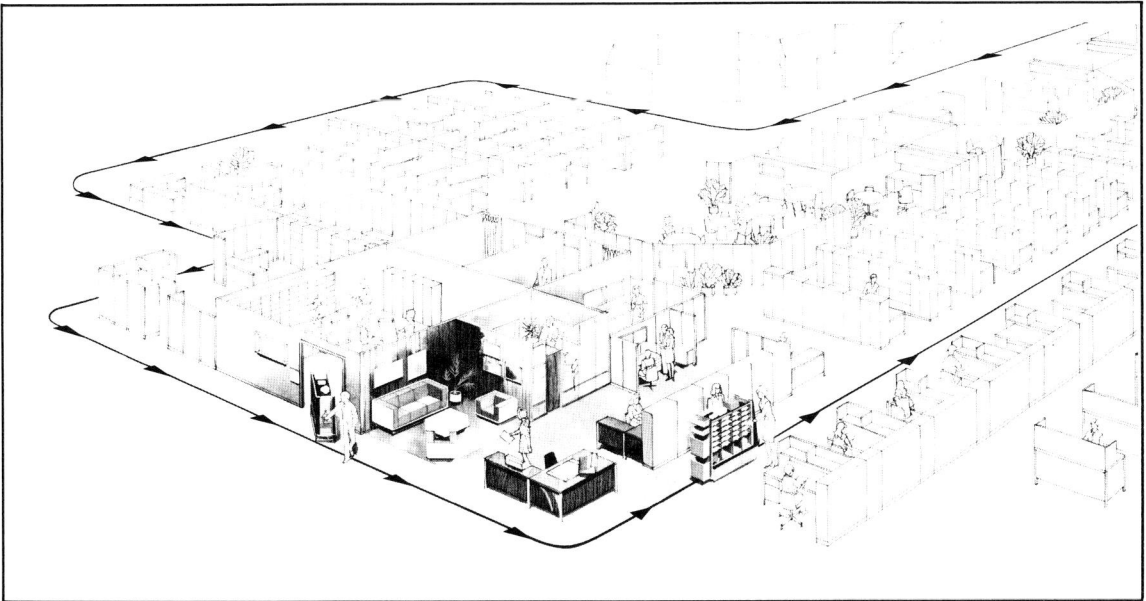

Figure 19 Mailmobile route for delivering mail, paper work, and supplies to designated locations along its invisible guide path. (Courtesy of Automated Systems Division, Bell & Howell)

Whether deliveries are manual or mechanical (as opposed to electronic), paper is a part of the mail distribution process. Therefore, all ways to move paper more effectively and efficiently are part of management's responsibility.

Small changes in procedures can often lead to definite benefits. For example, cost-avoidance benefits can be realized through the reduction in the number of envelopes used for interdepartmental mail, particularly nonreusable envelopes. Grouping and batching departmental mail and delivering to one location and using routing slips or reusable envelopes can contribute to improved productivity as well as to more economical operations.

EXTERNAL MAIL DELIVERY

External mail is defined as that mail which comes into an organization from outside that organization. Mail addressed to specific addressees is often sorted and delivered unopened. Mail addressed to departments may be opened, stamped with a date, and scanned to determine who should receive it.

The overall objective with incoming external mail is to make a quick, accurate determination of who should receive the mail with a minimal investigation of its contents. Whatever method of scanning incoming mail is required by management, a given set of procedures should be established. These procedures allow more accurate handling of mail—meaning that the mail arrives at its destination without "floating around the company" for a while. Procedures also provide easier training of new employees, which in turn improves their morale and productivity.

OUTGOING MAIL   The procedure for mail going outside the organization may seem somewhat simple; however, with the many options available for improved cost savings, it becomes critical to establish a set of procedures that will guide an employee through the proper handling of outgoing mail. To achieve the goal of moving information quickly, frequently scheduled trips should be made to the post office after consulting with the postal officials to determine their regular dispatch times.

Part of mailroom cost-reduction efforts should include taking advantage of the presorted mail offered by the USPS. Presorted first-class mail qualifies for a discounted rate of three cents per piece for mail presorted by zip code. To obtain the special bulk-rate advantages of third-class mail, presorting is required. The costs savings to be attained are sizable, but one must recognize that the presorting requires additional expenditures for labor and/or equipment.

Presorted first-class mail is handled by the post office in the same way as regular first-class mail, with the exception of its preparation requirements and its lower postage rates. Mail qualifying for the presort rate is afforded the same priority handling given to first-class mail. Mail that is undeliverable as addressed is forwarded or returned to the sender at no additional postage. Certified registered and return-receipt service can be used with presort mailings, provided the special fee is paid for all pieces.

Organizations with sufficient volumes of mail to warrant computerized sorting equipment can realize a 16 to 50 percent savings on postage by presorting mail based on the class of mail (see Figure 20). Those who presort by carrier routes gain as much as 50 percent. The USPS will provide, free of charge, materials required to presort.

Generally, computers are used to sort descriptive types of mail such as statements listing transactions, envelopes for advertising, and medium- to large-size mailings with computerized address records. There are presorting service bureaus that will pick up mail from a variety of customers, comingle it into one mailing, and presort it as prescribed by the USPS.

Should the volume of mail be large enough for an organization to benefit from the postage reduction, computerized mailing should be considered by the mailroom administrator.

The handling of foreign mail should involve a specific set of procedures; following these procedures will help cut costs. The Mail Department should investigate the unwritten regulations from field or district offices in various countries in order to understand foreign procedures. An

Figure 20   Computerized mail sorting equipment. (Courtesy of Pitney Bowes)

international postal scale that computes foreign postal rates can save employees from having to look up rates in books. The time it takes to look up rates and the mistakes that may result are significant productivity losses.

The knowledge of postal costs for different ways to send mail to a foreign country can save an organization as much as 80 percent of costs. For example, a three-pound package sent to London via air mail might cost $28.20. The same package, if qualified, can be sent as air mail printed matter for only $11.80.

In addition, detailed procedures should be established, because of the cost variances for using special mailing services. For example, the use of delivery services such as UPS or overnight delivery such as Federal Express or Purolator, instead of USPS priority or express mail, can sometimes lead to major savings in handling external mail.

Valuable sources to aid in the operations of a mail department are *The Postal Service Manual* and *The Postal Bulletin*, as well as any other USPS publications that are relevant to an organization's particular mailing requirements.

When large amounts of external mail are handled, certain management policies and guidelines should be established to cover the handling of an employee's personal mail or correspondence, even when it is prestamped. Sorting of these additional pieces of mail consumes mailroom staff time (particularly during the holidays) and if letters are not delivered, an employee may well place the fault on the company mailroom instead of on the post office. If management decides these personal mailing services will be provided, these services should be recognized as an employee benefit and an assessment of time required to perform these activities should be made.

Improved productivity with external mail handling should be an ongoing objective of the supervisor or administrator of the mailroom. Inaccurate scales, for example, can increase postage costs as much as 10 percent. Or, if a scale is not level, it may not weigh accurately. Economies and quality should be looked for when using outside mailing services. In most cases, certified mail can be used instead of the more expensive registered mail for instances when proof of delivery is required.

An organization should attempt to avoid special-delivery mailings. Special-delivery handling is expensive and often the mail will wait in an addressee's mailroom instead of being immediately delivered.

Cost savings can also be achieved by annually updating mailing lists. Needed information can be obtained by sending post-paid business reply cards to the names on the mailing lists to find out if names and addresses are correct and if addressees want to continue to be on the list. Nonrespondents should automatically be dropped, One can also request the Post Office to verify the accuracy of each address and request notification of changes (which they will do for a fee), or use the USPS address-correction-requested service periodically.

ELECTRONIC MAIL

The foregoing methods of mail handling focus on traditional handling of paper mail. Communication by mail, however, is undergoing an electronic revolution, as are other areas of office services operations. Electronic mail is becoming more available, less costly, and more refined. Electronic mail is a system for delivering messages electronically to the recipient, who receives either a hard copy or a visually displayed message on a CRT screen. Electronic mail can take a variety of forms, as listed below.

WESTERN UNION   Western Union Mailgram is a form of electronic communication. Western Union Electronic Mail, Incorporated, provides a processing and transmission service for business people who prefer to send their correspondence via the E-COM system. Access to the Western Union Electronic Mail facility comes in many forms and can even accommodate an organization's communicating terminal or word processor. Common carriers include ITT World Communications, Incorporated; TRT Telecommunications Corporation; Network Incorporated; and Typan Industries. Western Union offers the service through its existing electronic mail facilities.

FACSIMILE   Facsimile has been around since the early 1930s, yet today it is recognized as a form of electronic mail. Facsimile machines scan documents and convert black or white areas to electrical signals that, when transmitted to a remote receiver, determine whether a black mark is or is not reproduced on the paper at the receiving end. Systems can be configured with separate transmitters and receivers or with transceivers that perform both functions. Some transceivers can even send and receive simultaneously. Some have automatic send and receive capabilities, white space skipping, and encryption (a coding process for security purposes).

Facsimile (fax) combines the replication and distribution functions, since it duplicates exact copies of graphs, pictures, and other documents and transmits them to other locations (see Figure 21).

Facsimile systems are especially useful when an exact copy of the original hard copy is needed. For those who want to transmit a signature on a

Figure 21 Facsimile facilitates low cost transmission of graphs, picture, and text. (Photo, Courtesy of Xerox Corporation)

document, facsimile can provide it. Facsimile can be defined as a distribution method, because it provides a means for distributing text, graphics, data, and photographs. If we adhere to the definition of electronic mail as being any communication delivered wholly or in part by electronic means, then facsimile falls into the electronic mail category.

Facsimile does have advantages: (1) low cost compared with other electronic mail methods, (2) speed, (3) no rekeyboarding and thus no introduction of new errors, (4) easily sent graphic images, (5) high transmission accuracy, (6) minimal operator training, and (7) fairly portable machines.

A disadvantage lies in the fact that a facsimile has a rather loosely structured bit orientation. It is not coded, which makes it difficult to include fax in the scheme of an automated office system.

Most manufacturers or vendors use different compression ratios to send their signals. Since fax cannot receive signals it does not understand, incompatibility between brands is a barrier; however, that problem is being resolved. Another problem is the variance in speed. If a facsimile sender is set at a three-minutes-per-page speed and the receiver is at a six-minutes-per-page speed, either the receiver will get no message at all or the receiver will get all of the information on the transmitted page squeezed into a 5-1/2-inch-long space.

Recent improvements have boosted fax from a $45 million market, according to an International Resource Development, Inc., study, to approximately $1 billion for terminals, supplies, and communication lines.

Some organizations have implemented facsimile to speed up turn-around time on messages because they have encountered problems with the USPS mail handling services. Continuing demand for enhanced communications will cause greater technological advancements in facsimile. In the future, facsimile capabilities will be as much a feature of high-speed, high-volume copiers as are collators. Facsimile may also be an integral part of the CRT workstations in the electronic office.

ELECTRONIC MAILBOX

Computer-based message systems operate on the "electronic mailbox" principle. Each user is assigned an electronic mailbox and messages are left there until the user makes an inquiry. Users make inquiries by punching their special code into the system, which prompts the computer to display the message on the video display screen.

COMMUNICATING WORD PROCESSORS

Communicating word-processing machines combine text editing and high-quality output with communications capability. They can operate over most communication networks. A complete communicating word-processing system can eliminate the need to send hard-copy letters by traditional mail, since all messages are transmitted electronically and appear on video display terminals at their destination. If a hard copy is required, it can be printed at the destination. Although use of communicating word processors has spread slowly, decreasing equipment costs and increasing implementation of network systems in offices will prompt a significantly increased use of communicating word processing equipment.

Electronic mail will at some point in our office evolution be less expensive than first-class mail. The surrounding benefits of speed of message, the convenience of being able to respond to mail at any time by accessing one's own electronic mailbox, the ability to communicate to many places at one time, and the ability to forward data to supplement teleconferencing will all be major advantages that will justify the implementation of electronic mail systems.

What electronic mail basically offers is the capability to get the right information to the right people on a timely basis. The integration of data and word processing ensures that both the data and textual function can be dealt with. Electronic mail illustrates the potential to link all office communications through integration of data and word processing networks with other office communication functions.

Although traditionally the replication function precedes the distribution function, as the costs of distribution increase, more and more organizations will turn to communications or distribution first and replication at the end site. For example, wire or satellite transmission of data from an editorial/composition department to a printer strategically located to minimize distribution costs will be more common.

As the totally integrated support system becomes a reality, both replication and distribution will assume even greater importance, and organizations will no longer consider them low-priority areas.

CHAPTER 8

RECORDS MANAGEMENT

OBJECTIVES

In this chapter you will learn about
1. The role of records management in the automated office.
2. The various types of information needs in the office.
3. The relationship between the life span of a record and the information processing cycle.
4. The objectives of a records management program.
5. Establishing a records management system.
6. Systems design considerations.
7. The role of automation in records management.
8. Records management personnel.

THE NEED FOR RECORDS MANAGEMENT

Information has little value unless it is properly recorded and its storage managed so effectively that it is available to users in a timely manner. Without proper records management and controls, it is easy to lose needed information, overall effectiveness and productivity go down, and costs increase. All organizations need records management. What does this involve?

ARMA (the Association of Records Managers and Administrators, Inc.) defines records management as the science of managing records and information from their creation to final disposition. With this view of records management, the close relationship to the information flow becomes obvious (see Figure 1). However, records are more than individual pieces of paper; they represent units of information that fit into a total information system.

TYPES OF RECORDS

Business managers and executives require many different kinds of information. The following groupings and classifications[1] may be helpful in understanding these requirements:

1. Record and nonrecord.
2. Action and nonaction.
3. Recurring and nonrecurring.
4. Internal and external.
5. Active and inactive.
6. Historical and future.
7. Documentary and nondocumentary.

A *record* is an official document of the organization that furnishes information on organization, function, policy, procedure, operation, or other activities. A *nonrecord* is a convenience copy that assists in the operation of the company; it is normally discarded when no longer needed—for example, one copy of a purchase order would be designated the record copy, and all other copies would be considered nonrecords.

Action information requires the recipient to respond in some way. Examples may include billings that require immediate attention or monthly reports that are demanded at set intervals. Conversely, there is *nonaction*

---

[1] Wilmer O. Maedke, Mary F. Robek, and Gerald F. Brown, *Information and Records Management*, (Encino, Cal.: Glencoe, 1981), pp. 2–4, 72, and 82.

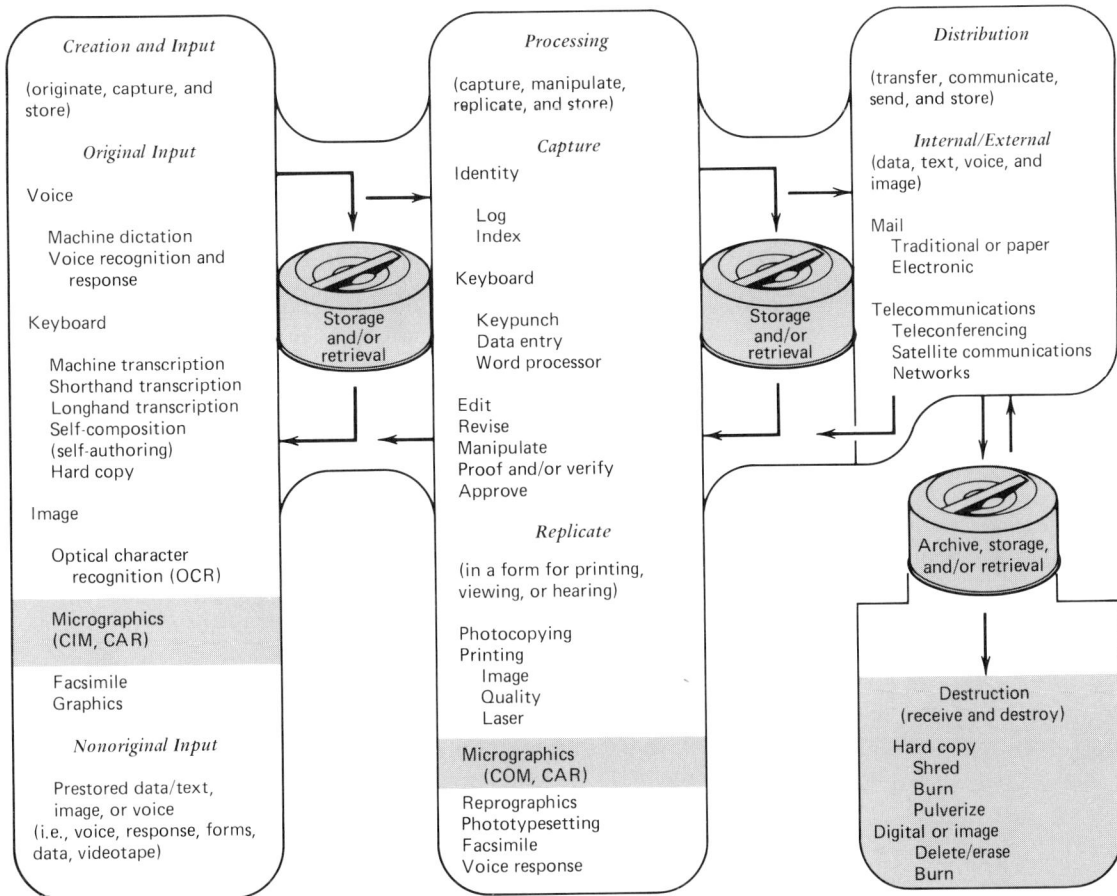

Figure 1 Cycle of information. Note the points of storage and retrieval.

information, on which no action is required: for example, a notice that a shipment of materials has been received. There is also *recurring* information, which is information that regularly recurs in the organization, such as sales, inventory, and production reports. Then there is *nonrecurring* information, or information that is reported and used in an organization once in its lifetime. An example would be planning specifications for a new project.

Some of the most crucial kinds of information are *internal* information, or information generated within the organization, such as production schedules, payrolls, policy manuals, and organizational directives. There is also *external* information, or data from other organizations, such as information concerning products and services of competitors. *Active records* are those consulted in the performance of current administrative work, or records in working files. Records transferred to a records center or other storage area are usually called *inactive*, because the records need not be frequently referred to.

Historical information involves the recording of past events. It is helpful for management decision making and projecting future plans. Such information comes from both internal and external sources. Planning requires information about likely trends of the *future*. For example, anticipated sales of a new product or expected cost savings from installing new equipment.

Documentary information is that which is recorded in some kind of permanent form, such as written or printed materials, computer printouts, punched cards, or microfilm. *Nondocumentary* information is not recorded; it is usually obtained through word of mouth and/or personal observation.

Some managers consider another means of categorizing significant information—transaction documents or reference documents. *Transaction* documents are those that record individual day-to-day transactions of an organization. These documents usually consist of business forms such as requisitions, purchase orders, invoices, statements, vouchers, checks, receipts, contracts, and so on, and are the largest and most common category of records. *Reference* documents contain or communicate information needed to carry on the business. These include records referred to for decisions that have been made in the past, price quotations, opinions expressed, and plans established. Reference documents, the second largest category of records, include business correspondence (letters and memos), reports and studies (formal and informal), printed materials (catalogs, pamphlets, brochures), and technical items (engineering and construction specifications, galley proofs, and advertising copy).

Office automation has added another dimension to the classifying of information. The word *data* is often used to describe information in digital form, within some type of computer or word processor or some form of electronic memory. Information in digital form is *alterable:* that is, it can regularly undergo deletions, additions, and revisions and is ever-changing. On the other hand, hard copy (paper), microfilm, microfiche, and other image storage such as current optical disks provide a *fixed* form of storage that is unalterable in time and format. If it is altered, the alteration itself is also fixed in time and format. All of these different types of business information needs must be recognized and addressed within a records management program, and they become even more meaningful when automation is introduced.

Today's records and information may be found in many forms—papers, photographs, computer printouts, punched cards, magnetic tapes, floppy disks, hard disks, voice recordings, microforms, videotapes, optical disks, and many more. All of these require planned management.

THE LIFE SPAN OF A RECORD

Review Figure 1, which shows the steps in the information processing cycle. Figure 2 indicates similar steps or stages in the life span of a record. Note that each record or piece of information has its own cycle, yet each is a part of the total information processing cycle.

Although records managers most likely will be responsible for storage, retrieval, archiving, and purging or destruction, a need exists for records to be managed throughout the entire information processing cycle. Because of the many similarities between the records cycle and the information processing cycle, the records manager should be included as a member of an office automation study team.

Each record has a point of origin, where it is *created*. Creation is the first step in the life cycle of the record. Created documents (records) may take various forms—letters, memos, reports, and forms. Input of the created record may be made by a variety of methods (described in an earlier chapter.) Preferably, all similar records or documents are *processed* according to an established format and procedure. For example, in one Midwest consulting office, all letters are typed in the Gothic type, do not use a salutation at the beginning of the letter, and eliminate unnecessary marks of punctuation. This is an established format used by all employees and characterizes the firm.

Records are *stored* in different types of arrangements for retention periods determined by Federal and state statutes, and by administrative determination in cases of records not specified under law. Records must be stored so that any user requiring the information can *retrieve* it quickly and easily. In an automated office, retrieval can be by hard copy or by display if only reference is needed. Once they are no longer essential for day-to-day operations, records can be either permanently *retained* or

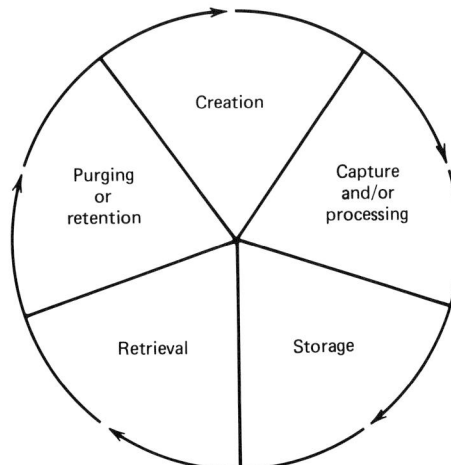

Figure 2 Life span of an office record.

purged through an established destruction schedule. At each stage of activity, some form of controls, (including appropriate standards, necessary policies, and procedures) is mandatory.

OBJECTIVES OF A RECORDS MANAGEMENT PROGRAM

A well-managed records program can develop into a significant part of office automation. However, an organization's information needs must be carefully surveyed and evaluated to design an effective system—manual or automated.

A records management system should include these major objectives.

1. To furnish accurate and complete information when and where it is required for managing and operating the organization effectively.
2. To process and handle recorded information as efficiently as possible.
3. To provide information and records at the lowest possible cost.
4. To render maximum service to the customer (user of the records).

Records management objectives are based primarily upon (1) service, (2) cost/profit, and (3) social responsibilities. Service is important because others need information in order to perform their work most effectively.

The objectives for records management may be specific or general, written or nonwritten, long- or short-term, temporary or permanent, and applicable to the total program or only to segments of the program. Objectives should be established, for without them records management becomes a nebulous activity with no satisfactory basis for evaluating effectiveness.

ESTABLISHING A RECORDS MANAGEMENT SYSTEM

Installing an automated filing system without a previously established records management program is likely to be unsatisfactory, because management and organization policy and procedures must come first. Jesse Clark,[2] a records management consultant, says that any company with a justifiable volume of records and reference activity that implements a manual records management program today is going backward. He explains that while the initial cost for developing a computerized system may be more than a manual program, the ongoing operations, mainte-

[2] Jesse Clark, "An Interview with Jesse Clark, President of the Records Management Group," *Information and Records Management*, September, 1980, p. 22.

nance, and updating cost could be cut in half. This is a significant consideration. But that is only the financial benefit; accountability, control, availability of data, and fast retrieval of information should also be considered.

Where does one start? To establish a records management system where none previously existed or to evaluate the current one in order to determine how to improve it, these major steps should be undertaken.

1. Identify major categories of records.
2. Conduct a records inventory or survey of present activity and volume of each.
3. Establish records processing and filing procedures, if none exist.
4. Establish a records retention and disposition schedule.
5. Establish valid system requirements and select appropriate technology.
6. Conduct education and training and prepare a records management procedures manual.

CONDUCTING AN INVENTORY OR SURVEY

The most critical element is collecting the facts. Some experts advocate conducting a records inventory. Others believe an inventory, because it sounds quantitative and all-encompassing, is likely to overdocument and overcontrol by counting every piece of paper. Therefore they regard as sufficient a survey that provides the means to gain a perspective of user needs, the identification of records, and the answers to certain prescribed questions.

Usually, a survey should include a complete listing of all records used in an organization by record series, together with necessary supporting information. A records series is a group of identical or related records that are normally used and filed as a unit and that permit evaluation as a unit for retention scheduling purposes. The records survey should collect *all* the necessary data at one time, to determine what records exist by volume; to update requirements, frequency, type, and priorities of user demands; to establish points of creation as well as retention requirements; to permit daily use or activity; to identify records, nonrecords, or convenience copies; and to evaluate filing requirements and current operations and equipment.

Such a records survey provides the facts upon which an analysis is based. Duplication of records can be detected, the useful life of files can be assessed, and the legal retention requirements can be appraised.

Documenting the creation, flow, and processing of information is essential to determining how information flows through a firm. Integration is a key concept, because the entire purpose of records management is to unify information storage and retrieval into a standardized system, and sometimes to establish a data base.

The systems study identifies all the parts and provides a picture of the whole. Any study of the paperwork activities of a firm should be carried out throughout the entire firm, rather than in only one department. Systems have seven different characteristics that must be analyzed: (1) function (what a particular unit does and what records it uses); (2) input (who brings information into a unit); (3) output (where information produced in the unit goes); (4) sequence (how information is processed); (5) environment (where the information is produced, and by whom); (6) equipment (what technology is used to produce the information); and (7) procedures (the rules by which information is produced).

IDENTIFYING MAJOR CATEGORIES OF RECORDS

Generally, close attention to the major types of records (forms, correspondence, and reports) is of considerable importance. Appropriate management and control must be directed to them, together with planning for automation to tie them into the total information process.

Forms Management and Control

Underlying most successful records management programs is a strong forms control program with authority to approve or reject all forms reproduced or purchased by the organization. Traditionally a form is defined as a piece of paper with written fixed data but on which spaces are systematically arranged for the entry of variable data. Forms are used to facilitate the handling of recurring but variable data.

Automated systems cast a somewhat different light on forms. It is no longer appropriate to confine the definition of a form to paper; rather, forms must be considered in automation as record formats. These formats still need to be designed to meet requirements of paper systems, micrographics, and computerized systems for COM (computer output microfilm) and CAR (computer-assisted retrieval).

Three out of four of the documents in office records will be business forms. Almost three-fourths of all government records and half of all government reports are forms. They serve as the chief means of capturing, storing, and communicating information in a standardized, repetitive manner.

Correspondence Management

Correspondence makes up a major portion of an organization's records, ranking second only to forms. The correspondence function involves dictating, transcribing, and transmitting information upon which major management decisions are made. Because most letters and memos are personally composed or dictated, considerable cost is involved in their preparation.

Reports Management and Control

Reports convey information and intelligence for management or operational purposes and furnish other departments or offices in an organization with the information needed to carry out their work. A business report is usually the final result of an information processing function, because it represents a summary of data previously collected and processed; often a report will also contain a conclusion and recommended action.

Reports are necessary to control performance, effectiveness of policies, and accomplishment of objectives. They provide information to make effective decisions. They must be clear, precise, and brief. Most important, the cost of the report must be worth the value received from it.

Reports are often the most expensive documents produced in an organization. As an organization grows and the sophistication of management increases, controls are added in the forms of reports. Reports common to most established organizations include accounting statements, credit reports, data processing workload schedules, personnel directives, and so on.

The favorable outcome of many business activities may depend on the quality of written reports. For this reason, prudent management must be able to know the difference between essential and nonessential or ineffective reporting.

ESTABLISHING A RETENTION AND DISPOSITION SCHEDULE

Based upon an orderly study and appraisal of an organization's records, properly developed retention and disposition schedules can lead to substantially reduced record-keeping costs (see Figure 3).

A sampling of organizations indicated that the establishment and utilization of records retention schedules resulted in significant reduction in records kept in the active files, thereby saving space and reducing time spent in handling large numbers of inactive files:

- ▶ 43.6% of the records remained in the active (current, daily) files.
- ▶ 32.3% of the records were transferred to inactive (waiting disposition) storage areas.
- ▶ 24.1% of the records were disposed of as waste paper.

Once a company knows exactly what records it has, it can then determine the retention schedule; that schedule also authorizes and provides for the periodic transfer (from active to inactive, from hard copy to microfiche) and destruction of all the organization's records. Such a schedule assures permanent protection of vital records, as well as the discarding of records that have outlived their usefulness. Most record retention schedules try to preserve records of historical value to the firm without overloading the storage space. Often companies attempt to restrict filing equipment and space to housing active records only. Ultimately a record is either judged vital to an organization and preserved or judged useless and destroyed.

Form No. 4076 5/81

RECORDS RETENTION SCHEDULE   MINNESOTA POWER

DEPARTMENT						SCHEDULE NO.	PAGE OF

ITEM	RECORD SERIES TITLE	RETENTION PERIOD				OFFICE OF RECORD
		OFFICE	STORAGE	TOTAL	NOTE/SOURCE	

All documents not listed in this schedule, but retained in your files are for reference purposes only and should be maintained for a maximum of 2 years. All records listed shall follow the corporate policy designated. Additions to the schedule can be made through Records Administration.

		REVIEWED BY				
DEPARTMENT	DATE	LEGAL	DATE	TAX	DATE

Figure 3 Retention schedule. (Courtesy of Minnesota Power & Light Company, Duluth, Minnesota)

When the time comes to destroy a record, a company may opt for one of several methods: shredding, pulverizing, burning, or selling or salvaging the paper. If information is confidential, a company may invest in a shredder or pulverizer; both machines effectively destroy records by reducing the records to unrecognizable particles or pieces. Some firms use maceration—chemical pulverizers that soften the paper and obliterate the writing. Others use federally authorized incinerators to burn the paper.

Determining whether files are active, vital, inactive, or archival is especially important when applying office equipment to the records processing cycle.

Active Files   Active records are one of the most critical areas in a records management system. Active records are those used frequently and must be very accessible. Such records consist of current information required in day-to-day operations. Active records are generally a prime candidate for automation—perhaps as part of a data base of critical information available through terminals throughout a firm.

Of all the service activities of an organization, the storage and retrieval of business records are the greatest consumers of space, salaries, and equipment. Time, effort, and money are wasted unless records can be produced when they are required. Active records must be systematically arranged according to some storage plan that will make immediate retrieval possible. Few executives give much attention to this phase of office operation until a lost file points to the need for a better system.

An effective files management program must include a sound records-classification-and-filing system, the best physical location of active records for easy access, a designation of official file stations, standards for record equipment, and standards for record supplies.

Vital Records   The term *vital records* is synonymous with essential records. Vital records contain information needed to establish or continue an organization in the event of disaster: that is, those necessary to recreate the company's legal and financial position; and those necessary to preserve the rights of the company and its employees, customers, and stockholders. The loss of vital records could result in the dissolution of an organization, because insurance or accounts receivable could not be collected, contracts could not be enforced, or designs for products that took years to develop could be lost.[3] They are records that could be needed immediately, should be stored in an easily accessible but protected place, and should preferably be in original form.

The cost and complexity of ensuring the availability of every document that might be needed would be prohibitive. Generally, the cost of protection must be weighed in relation to cost of reconstruction. The procedures for ensuring that vital records are maintained and the definition of what constitutes a vital record is essential and must be followed routinely.

Protecting Vital Records.   The protection of the vital records of the firm is one of the most important jobs of a records management program. Safeguarding vital records includes protecting them from such dangers as fire, flood, water damage, mildew, insects, acids, fumes, light, and rodents. They must also be protected against theft and loss and disasters such as earthquakes, windstorms, explosions, and nuclear destruction.

---

[3] Maedke, *et al., Information and Records Management,* p. 92.

The protection program may include duplication of records and the establishing of backup files, stored either in a different location within the organization or off-premises. As automation becomes more common, the method of protection is likely to involve the scheduled and periodic transfer of centralized master files and data bases to auxiliary storage, such as tapes or COM-generated microforms stored in secure off-site facilities.

Inactive Files   Only records that are currently useful should be kept in active files or on-line. Noncurrent records, such as dead files or inactive files (files that need to be retained according to federal guidelines or are awaiting destruction based on a company's "retention schedule") should be stored off-line or in a low-cost, high-volume storage area.

Areas established for the storage and servicing of inactive or semiactive records are generally known as records centers. Such centers may be located either in low-cost space within the firm or off-site, perhaps at a commercial center. The major objective of a records center is to remove noncurrent records from high-cost space and filing equipment into low-cost storage areas as rapidly as possible. When records are declared inactive and moved, a uniform filing system must be followed so that the records can be found again if needed.

Archival Records   Archival records are records that were once considered current files but are now semiactive or inactive and are retained for legal, fiscal, administrative, or historical reasons. When an organization's records are reduced, care must be taken to retain those that have archival value. In the carrying out of such work, there is no substitute for careful analysis.

An archival system must define the criteria for retaining a record, must keep a constant inventory of what is filed and where, must always strive to maintain a balance between too few and too many records, and must determine the most effective and economical means for protection of the organization's records that possess archival value.

The primary difference between a records center and an archives repository is that the archive is established to preserve records for the benefit of the scholar and posterity, whereas the records center is established to preserve records for administrative and operating purposes. When these administrative or operating purposes have been served, the records manager may assign the records for destruction, or, with the advice of an archivist, assign them to an archive.[4]

---

[4] Maedke, et al., Information and Records Management, p. 343.

SYSTEM REQUIREMENTS AND THE SELECTION OF TECHNOLOGY

The price for maintaining paper mode collections is high. A recent Dartnell Institute study revealed a total cost exceeding $1150 per file cabinet, and the cost is rising. Paper documents involve bulk and require space that frequently is located in high-cost office areas that are in constant demand for other activities. The information explosion requires more filing and retrieval actions—which, when accomplished with manual sequentially-arranged paper systems, means constantly escalating clerical costs. Under ideal circumstances with such systems, filing/finding actions average 50 to 55 per clerk per hour. Since misfiles and missing files plague most organizations, lower productivity and delays in meeting user demands result. Management is faced with a need to automate merely to maintain a status quo in costs and timeliness in obtaining information.

Fact-finding activities provide information that is crucial to decision making concerning systems requirements and selection of equipment. Criteria for the selection of technology presented in an earlier chapter apply, but the astute executive will ensure that certain questions are raised with all potential vendors before the final decision is reached. The list shown in Figure 4 provides a logical basis for equitable consideration to alternatives; however, it should be adapted to an individual organization's particular situation.[5]

TRAINING SESSIONS AND PROCEDURES MANUALS

From the outset, all concerned personnel and managers must receive training in records management and control. The scope of the total program should be made clear and separate sessions about specific technologies (such as a computer data base or microfilming) are important. Sessions that explain how to use equipment are important; but most importantly, it must be clearly understood that technology is a user's tool.

Presented in a logical, well-ordered manner, a procedures manual that can be updated easily is a valuable resource for all personnel. By consulting the manual, employees can quickly find solutions by reviewing the policies, procedures, and sample forms. The manual's purpose is to save time for users by providing a ready reference and answers to the situations and problems that are most likely to arise. It is also the best means to keep uniformity in the organization, by communicating the same information to everyone.

The manual should inform all personnel of services that the records management program provides. It should provide instruction and reference for the personnel responsible for creating, preparing, processing, storing, and disposing of records.

[5] Col. (ret.) Leonard Lee, CRM, "Establishing Valid Systems Requirements," *Impact*, November 1981, p. 9.

WHAT TO ASK A RECORDS VENDOR

A multitude of questions should be raised in seeking and evaluating storage/retrieval equipment. The following list offers some of the most important ones.

1. What is the total capacity of the device?
2. How fast does it operate on a sustained basis?
3. Does it permit random filing and retrieval?
4. Is it proven, reliable, dependable, and production-line produced?
5. Does it have a successful, sustained track record among current user installations, and how many devices are currently in operation?
6. Will the vendor provide a list of users so that prospective customers can observe the equipment under actual operational conditions?
7. What is its downtime record?
8. Does the device accommodate mixed-mode media or only one unique format?
9. Does it require that special tabs, holders, or strips be attached to each of the records for coding/retrieval, and are they reusable?
10. If coding is accomplished directly on the media, is there a danger of defacing or damaging the media or its contents?
11. Can more than one record be placed in the carrier or holder?
12. What special features are provided to preclude misfiles and permit rapid audit of contents to detect misfiles or missing files?
13. Does it permit alphabetical, numerical, or both filing techniques?
14. Will it accomplish individual, group, or both categories of retrieval simultaneously?
15. Is the equipment flexible and modular, to allow for future records expansion?
16. How much space is required to house the device?
17. In the event one portion of the system is not functioning, will the remainder continue to operate?

Figure 4   Questions to consider when evaluating equipment. *Source:* Col. (Ret.) Leonard Lee, CRM, "Establishing Requirements," *Impact*, November, 1981, p. 10.

Relationships between the Records Management Department and other departments should be described in the manual. The manual should explain the importance of cooperation among all personnel, to assure the success of the records management program. Effective use of the manual by all employees will guide the staff in such a way that the system will be more effective.

The information included in a manual depends upon the organization. As a general rule, a manual contains these major subjects.

1. Objectives and responsibilities.
2. Vital records.
3. Records retention schedules.
4. Sample forms.
5. Disposal procedures.
6. Organization chart.
7. Automated storage/retrieval systems (if used)
8. Filing systems and equipment.
9. Records center operations.

Separate operating procedures manuals on "how to use" technology may be helpful.

Although the preceding steps for establishing a records management system are closely related to traditional records management, many aspects are also related to the step-by-step approach to office automation.

BARRIERS TO IMPLEMENTATION

The following four barriers or pitfalls are especially important to understand before an automated records management program is implemented:

▶ Integrated approach.
▶ Management commitment.
▶ Organizational standards.
▶ Proper structure.

A carefully planned and properly organized program of information processing must *integrate* all the various elements of records management and information control under a strong leader who is accountable for the entire program. Most records management programs today attempt to be comprehensive; however, in the actual implementation, there are often gaps that can create significant problems. When implementing, one should prevent gaps by creating a properly prepared manual or a well-designed retention schedule.

Often, top management is not aware of how records in an organization interrelate with other activities. They see things in terms of their own corner of the office. By identifying the types of information and kinds of records, and then organizing them, a firm can achieve successful records management.

Management commitment is essential for any records management program to be effective. Unless management understands, approves, and supports proposed changes in the records system, no significant change in actual office practice is likely to happen. Managers who are reluctant or resistant may refuse to abide by a new system and continue to use their own system. A records manager involved in implementation must anticipate this attitude. In selling management, point out that effective records management helps top managers by enabling them to get information in less time and effort—not to mention with less paperwork. Well-organized records management programs assure them that needed records are accessible and available on demand.

Lack of *organizational standards* is another barrier to implementation. Many companies today still have not taken the time and effort to develop standards of quality and quantity in records processing. They regard such standards as oriented toward "manual labor." However, there is an absolute necessity to have working standards of quality, production, and cost in place before any new records management program takes shape.

A final hurdle is the lack of a proper *organizational structure*. It must be clear how records management and the people charged with managing the system fit into the overall organization. They need to have a clear directive or mandate from top management for their job descriptions and authority.

SYSTEMS DESIGN CONSIDERATIONS

Several basic aspects must be studied and analyzed before you try to design a records system. Although they are presented here as separate considerations, to provide you with a clear perspective, none can be determined separately; each must be considered and finally determined in relation to the others.

Quantitative Considerations

Sheer numbers—the quantity or volume of records—will influence the choice of a system. Basic quantitative questions to be addressed are listed in Figure 5.

Qualitative Considerations

Information has a qualitative content—a useful value that relates to decision and policy making. See Figure 6 for a list of some qualitative factors.

Forms of Storage

Today's information storage and retrieval systems take any of three basic forms.

1. Paper.
2. Image (microfilm or optical disk).
3. Digital (electronic).

Bonnie Canning, a records automation columnist for *Office Administration and Automation* (formerly known as *Administrative Management*), suggests that "effective information management depends on integrating paper, microform, and digital documents—maximizing the advantages of

---

QUANTITATIVE SYSTEMS DESIGN FACTORS

Volume. How many records are involved? How large is each? What growth is projected?

Distribution. How many users are there, and how many copies do they need? What does our distribution network look like? Is it wholly in-house? Do users have access to microfilm readers or computer terminals?

Time value. What turnaround time do users require? How critical are the deadlines? Do users need immediate on-line updates, or is the mail fast enough?

Activity. How active are the records? Is the information static, or does it change? How long does it remain current?

Retention value. What are the active and inactive retention periods? Is the information a vital record?

Cost. What is the unit record cost to the organization? (Ultimately, this must be considered in terms of performance, as well as of dollars).

Figure 5   Factors to consider when designing a records system. *Source:* Katherine Aschner, "How Technology is Changing Records Management," *Information and Records Management*, August, 1981, p. 26.

each, while minimizing their limitations."[6] She further suggests that how and in what medium we store our information directly affects our ability to retrieve it. Except for archival requirements, the only reason we store information is because we plan to retrieve it for future use. Methods we choose to store information must be directly compatible with retrieval requirements.

Figure 6   Factors to consider regarding quality of records, when designing a records system. *Source:* Katherine Aschner, "How Technology is Changing Records Management," *Information and Records Management*, August, 1981, p. 26.

QUALITATIVE SYSTEMS DESIGN FACTORS

Contents. What do the records contain? How is the information arranged?

Function. What is the purpose of the information? How is it used?

Format. Is it narrative or tabular? Are graphics involved? Is the format constant or variable?

Image. How important is output quality?

Flexibility. Are the requirements likely to change? How should this be planned for?

---

[6] Bonnie Canning, "Records Automation," *Administrative Management*, April 1982, pp. 84–85.

Paper has the advantage of being traditional and familiar. However, it requires a great deal of space to store and labor to maintain, and (unless multiple copies are filed under various descriptors for cross referencing) it can usually only be retrieved by knowing the one term by which it has been indexed and filed. It is also difficult to automate the retrieval of paper-based documents.

If *microforms* are used as the storage and retrieval medium, there are over 30 retrieval systems on the market that automate some or all of the steps involved in storing, retrieving, displaying, and refiling a wide variety of types of documents. However, microforms have the disadvantage of requiring special equipment to film the image and to display it. Another major factor to consider is the cost and time required to convert a paper record to microfilm and index it. Until the introduction of updatable microfiche, it was difficult to maintain active files in microfilm.

Storing documents in *digital form* in computers or word processors and retrieving them electronically is becoming viable because more information than ever before is being created electronically. Also, the cost of electronic memory is declining, and better and less expensive search-and-retrieval software is being developed. However, much of the information an office must store and retrieve comes into the office from outside sources. They come in a variety of type fonts and layouts, graphics, photos, color, handwriting, and other variable features that presently make wholesale digitization impractical. Adding disk drives or thousands of floppy disks is no more a solution than the continued proliferation of file cabinets and file folders.

The solution may lie in the hybrid that makes the most of all three media. Individual organizations must develop their own generic plans to integrate all components, functions, and resources currently available to input, process, output, replicate, distribute, store, and retrieve (display) both internally and externally produced information.

Centralized vs. Decentralized Filing

The decision to centralize or decentralize has always been a basic concern of management, whether applied to facilities or to records. The location of vital sources of information, or files, is an important issue associated with the interrelationships of information. Firms can use either centralized filing or decentralized filing. In centralized filing, records of common interest or value to many employees are placed under the control of one supervisor in one location. Central location is advantageous because responsibility for managing the files rests with one manager. There is less duplication of personnel, equipment, supplies, and space, and there is greater utilization of filed data. In addition, all related data are kept together and uniform service is available to all users.

With a centralized system, one major problem always arises—to determine what is and is not confidential or personal, and whether to allow "personal" items to remain outside the organizational memory or to place them in the system and establish various security procedures. This problem is especially likely to arise when an organizationwide data base with many points of access is established.

In decentralized filing, records are made, stored, and maintained at the point of origin. Highly specialized data and information that will only be of use to a limited number of people is frequently organized in this manner. The advantage of decentralized filing is that information remains close to the originator, where it is most likely to be used again and referred to frequently.

Some firms combine the two concepts and have certain files in a central location and other files throughout the departments. This is feasible in larger firms and can be used effectively with a well organized central-file control system under a manager.

TECHNOLOGY AND RECORDS

The benefits of automating records management depend on management commitment, on clearly written procedures, and on how well operating personnel perform their jobs. An overview of automated records management systems follows. Keep in mind that planning of such a system depends on a knowledge of the basic principles presented earlier. There are systems for automating paper, images, or digital information. In certain environments, hybrid systems may provide the best course of action. It is important to remember that the benefits of automation depend upon the application of the concepts presented earlier.

Technology can be viewed as it impacts the three major forms of storage available currently—paper, image, and digital. However, keep in mind that a hybrid system is undoubtedly the best manner by which to phase in technology (see Figure 7).

PAPER-BASED SYSTEMS

Organizations of all sizes will find that paper-based filing systems consume costly space. Many have turned from older, conventional vertical-drawer file cabinets to lateral files. Basically a lateral file is a drawer file turned sideways, with the side opening to the front (see Figures 8 and 9). Such files make more efficient use of office space by allowing more records to be held per shelf or drawer. Open shelves speed filing and retrieval, since drawer pulling is eliminated; lateral file drawers require less space to pull out.

Mobile storage systems that put files on tracks have also provided space savings by eliminating aisles for each set of files and providing a single, movable aisle. Vendors of such mobile systems as that shown in Figure 10 claim that 100 percent more storage capacity can be obtained within the

Figure 7   Note the contrast in various forms of storage. (Courtesy of Tab Products, Incorporated)

same area, or that 50 percent of existing space can become available for other purposes.

Because such systems usually also extend higher, additional savings are often possible because they permit storage in more cubic area. For example, standard five-drawer files with fixed aisles would require 178 square feet of floor space to handle 3360 filing inches of hard copy, whereas a mobile system can provide the same number of filing inches in only 74 square feet.

Mechanically driven filing systems, also called conveyors or motorized shelf files, allow an operator to remain seated at a control panel and instruct the record to be brought to the operator (see Figure 11).

Both vertical and horizontal conveyor files store large quantities of paper records or banks of information with obvious space and labor savings.

IMAGE-BASED SYSTEMS

Image-based systems are increasing in use because of both the space savings resulting from image reductions and the recent improvement of such technologies. Micrographics is a familiar technology; videodisk systems are still new.

Figure 7 (Continued)

Figure 8 Lateral files make more efficient use of space. (Courtesy of Tab Products, Incorporated)

Figure 9 Open files allow easy accessibility to files. (Courtesy of Tab Products, Incorporated)

Figure 10 Mobile storage files on tracks allow more files per cubic foot to be stored. (Courtesy of Tab Products, Incorporated)

Micrographics Micrographics is the process of recording and reducing paper documents or computer-generated information on film, and providing a system to store and retrieve that information. Micrographics is the most common image-based system in use today. A reduction ratio is the size of the film image compared with the original document. Microforms may contain from a few to several hundred images in reduction ratios of 18 to 48 times.

Figure 11   Motorized systems allow flexibility for the operator. (Courtesy of LeFebure, Division of Kidd, Incorporated)

Ultrafiche contains images reduced more than 90 times, thus permitting thousands of images per fiche.

This "mini" record storage is achieved through microforms that contain microimages; these include reels or cartridges, aperture cards, microfilm jackets (plastic carriers holding strips of film), and microfiche. The actual transfer of the image is recorded by rotary cameras, continuous form microfilmers, or planetary cameras. All of these systems can quickly and efficiently reduce original documents to a fraction of their original size.

When a firm implements a micrographics system, it must invest in the equipment necessary to make the microimages readable. Readers and reader/printers enable an operator to magnify a microfilm on a viewing screen so the document can be read by the naked eye. Readers may be portable, desktop, or used in combination with microcomputers to assist retrieval. If hard copies of the microimages are required, a printer can produce a copy on a standard-size page. The key to using micrographics is to ensure that all parts of the system—the microimages, readers, and output devices—are available to users so that information may be retrieved quickly and in the form needed.

In deciding whether to implement a micrographics system, a company must perform a feasibility study to determine (1) if microfilming is technically feasible for the company, (2) if microfilm is economically feasible for the firm, and (3) how to devise an effective micrographics system design.

Technical feasibility depends upon the quality and condition of the documents to be microfilmed. Economic feasibility depends on a comparison of the cost of the present system with the cost of a micrographic system or an alternative system. To devise an effective micrographics system, a firm must ensure that it has considered and understood all interrelationships of a complete information system. Figures 12, 13, and 14 show examples of excellent tools to assist with fact finding and cost comparisons.

In the data collection and analysis phase of the feasibility study, a firm needs to examine such factors as (1) the purpose of the record being studied, (2) the user and procedural considerations, (3) the retention periods and legal requirements, (4) the characteristics of the documents, and (5) the space and equipment savings.

A microfilm feasibility study consists of gathering all pertinent facts surrounding the system in use; analyzing those facts to determine costs and needs; and designing a microfilm system to meet those needs at less cost.

Once the study is completed, a test should be made, using the proposed microfilm equipment, to see if it will meet company needs before final purchase is made.

Merging the best elements of different technologies is becoming increasingly viable. COM (computer output microfilm) is produced at the high speed of computer display but delivers output in microform form, with the benefits that microforms imply. Dry-processing laser printers now combine laser and photographic technology to transform digitized information directly into microimages on fiche or roll film without first being printed out (see Figure 15).

The advantages of COM include the ability to pack huge masses of information into easily managed, standardized formats that take up less than 5 percent of the space required by paper. One cabinet of fiche equals 50 cabinets of output paper. One 100-foot roll of 16mm film can hold 4000 images. COM saves time as well as space—both of which translate into solid dollar savings. Fifty minutes of impact printing can be compressed into five minutes of COM printing. Five minutes of COM and the duplication of five copies replaces a half-hour of high-speed nonimpact printing. The paper cost alone can be reduced by 30:1 ratio.[7]

Although paper is convenient (it can be written upon, carried anywhere, and read without supplemental equipment), it is not the most economical medium for printouts. Where impact printers operate at a practical level of 900 lines per minute, the microfilm laser printer produces 10,000 lines per minute onto the microfilm. More and more data processing centers are turning to COM to record computer-generated data.

[7] Mitchell Badler, "COM: A Records Medium for the '80s," *Information and Records Management*, September 1980, p. 23.

MICROFILM FEASIBILITY FACT FINDING WORKSHEET — Side 1

NAME OF RECORD:					Date:
DEPARTMENT:			Contact:		Phone:
RETENTION:	Office	Record Center	Total Years	ICC Code	ICC Requirement

Can original be destroyed if microfilmed?　☐ Yes　☐ No

FUNCTION OF RECORD

Narrative: _____

_____

Does a record unit consist of:　☐ One document　☐ More than one document (File)
Period of file build up: _____ Additions to file per day/month/year _____

VOLUME, SIZE AND CHARACTERISTICS (Office)

Total Page* Volume	Page* Volume Per: Year___ Month___ Day___	Books _____ Per Year Boxes _____ Per Year
Total Cubic Feet	Cubic Feet Per: Year___ Month___ Day___	Drawers _____ Per Year Files _____ Per Year ☐ Loose　☐ Fastened

Page Size Color And Data	Size___ Color___ Volume___ ☐ Horizontal ☐ Vertical ☐ One Side ☐ Both Sides	Size___ Color___ Volume___ ☐ Horizontal ☐ Vertical ☐ One Side ☐ Both Sides	Size___ Color___ Volume___ ☐ Horizontal ☐ Vertical ☐ One Side ☐ Both Sides

Describe type and condition of paper and quality of print on reverse of this form.

REFERENCE AND RETRIEVALS

Office Reference	Per Day	Per Month	Per Year	Reference activity begins _____ hours/days after receipt of record
Retrieval and Refiling Time Per Reference**		Reference Time Per Search***		Wage Rates Per Hour
Reference ___ Persons @ ___ Searches Each Per Day				Cost Per Retrieval And Refile
Distribution ___ Persons @ ___ Searches Each Per Day				
Record Center References	Per Day	Per Month	Per Year	Wage Rates Per Hour
Retrieval And Refiling Time Per Reference**		Cost Per Retrieval And Refile		$_____
TOTAL Office Retrieval Time	Per Day	Per Month	Per Year	TOTAL Rec Cen Retrieval Time	Per Day	Per Month	Per Year

ACCESSIONS AND DISPOSALS

Office:
　Storage Preparation Costs:_____　Manhours @ $_____ Per Hour　$_____
　Annual Disposal Costs:_____　Manhours @ $_____ Per Hour　$_____
Record Center:
　Annual Accessioning Costs:_____　Manhours @ $_____ Per Hour　$_____
　Annual Disposal Costs:_____　Manhours @ $_____ Per Hour　$_____

*If data is on both sides of the page, count as one page.
**Include index referral time and travel time to and from file but exclude reference.
***Include only time document is used.

Figures 12 and 13 Microfilm feasibility fact finding worksheet. *Source: Wilmer Maedke, Mary Robek, and Gerald Brown, Information and Records Management, (2nd Ed.) Glencoe Publishing Co., Encino, California, 1981.*

MICROFILM FEASIBILITY FACT FINDING WORKSHEET — Side 2

SORTING, FILING AND BINDING

1st Sort: Page Volume _____	Manhours _____	Persons _____
2nd Sort: Page Volume _____	Manhours _____	Persons _____
3rd Sort: Page Volume _____	Manhours _____	Persons _____

Sorting Techniques:

1st Sort By: _____

2nd Sort By: _____

3rd Sort By: _____

Filing: Volume _____	Manhours _____	Persons _____

Filing Techniques: By _____

Wage Rates And Costs: (Annual)

Sorters _____ hours @ $ _____ $ _____

Filers _____ hours @ $ _____ $ _____

Material Costs .... $ _____

TOTAL FILING AND SORTING COSTS .... $ _____

Binding Method: ☐ Nylon Post   ☐ Permanent   ☐ _____

Binding Costs: (Annual)

Material: _____ Books @ $ _____ Per Book $ _____

Labor: _____ Books @ $ _____ Per Book $ _____

TOTAL ANNUAL: _____ Books @ $ _____ Per Book $ _____

SPACE (Include aisle space in office if dedicated)

Office Space: _____ Square Foot	Record Center: _____ Cubic Foot
Office	Record Center
Space Costs: $ _____ Per Square Foot	$ _____ Per Cubic Foot

EQUIPMENT VALUE

Sorting: _____ @ _____ $ _____

Filing: _____ @ _____ $ _____

Binding: _____ @ _____ $ _____

TOTAL EQUIPMENT VALUE .... $ _____

HARD COPY REQUIREMENTS

Are documents annotated?   ☐ Yes   ☐ No   How _____

Would paper prints be required if microfilmed?   ☐ Yes   ☐ No _____

If so, how many per: Day _____ Month _____ Year _____

Would reduced size prints suffice?   ☐ Yes   ☐ No

COMPUTER GENERATED REPORTS

Computer Generated Report   ☐ Yes   ☐ No   (If yes, complete the following)

Frequency: _____ Pages per report: _____

Total copies: _____ Paper size: _____ Form: ☐ Yes   ☐ No

Computer printing costs: _____ hours @ $ _____ per hour $ _____

Decollating and bursting: _____ hours @ $ _____ per hour $ _____

Computer print paper: _____ pages of _____ part @ $ _____ per M $ _____

Mailing costs .... $ _____

TOTAL COMPUTER COSTS — Per Run .... $ _____

Figure 13

MICROGRAPHICS FEASIBILITY STUDY
COST COMPARISON SUMMARY

EXISTING SYSTEM:

PROPOSED SYSTEM:

COST FACTORS (Annual)	EXISTING SYSTEM		PROPOSED SYSTEM	
	Cost	Explanation or Reference Notation	Cost	Explanation or Reference Notation
LABOR	$		$	
Sorting				
Staple Removal				
Coding				
Filing/Refiling				
Retrievals				
Filming				
Processing				
Splicing				
Indexing				
TOTAL LABOR				
MATERIALS				
Folders				
Film and Processing				
Cartridges				
Jackets/Cards				
Print Paper				
TOTAL MATERIALS				
EQUIPMENT AND SPACE				
Cameras				
Readers				
Reader-Printers				
Processor				
Housing/Filing				
Equipment Maintenance				
Floor Space				
TOTAL EQUIPMENT AND SPACE				
TOTAL ANNUAL COSTS	$		$	

Figure 14 Micrographics summary of cost comparisons. *Source:* Wilmer Maedke, Mary Robek, and Gerald Brown, *Information and Records Management,* (2nd Ed.) Glencoe Publishing Company, Encino, California, 1981.

Figure 15 Kodak Komstar. (Courtesy of Eastman Kodak Company)

Figure 16 compares computer production of 12 copies of a 3600-page run by the two techniques.

The integration of COM with word processing and various forms of computer graphics (charts, graphs, and diagrams) is rapidly escalating as more of these applications are performed on computer or communicated to computers for output to microfilm.

In today's world, COM also is closely related to document distribution, for it provides an economical way to produce large operational manuals that must be updated and sent to branches or other people in the field. Consider the following: 269 pages of paper will cost at least 10 times as

COMPARISON FOR 12 COPIES OF 3600 PAGE RUN		
	Paper-Mode Impact Printer	Computer-Output Microfilm
Number of pieces	43,200 pages	168 fiche
Stock costs	$300	Under $7
Shipping weight	720 pounds	Under 2 pounds
Cost to mail coast-to-coast	$200	Under $5
Printing time	5 hours	Under 25 minutes

Figure 16 Comparative cost of paper vs. microfilm. *Source:* Col. (Ret.) Leonard Lee, CRM, "The Computer-Record Connection," *Impact*, August, 1982, p. 11.

Figures 17 and 18 Computer Assisted Retrieval (CAR) is a very effective and rapid form of retrieval. (Courtesy of 3M File Systems Division)

much as mailing a four-by-six-inch microfiche containing the same number of pages.

Older methods of manually cranking through a roll of microfilm to find a particular image or fingering through a drawer of microfiche are being replaced by far better means of retrieval. Various indexing systems that provide the addresses of specific images are the key. For especially effective retrieval, the indexing is computerized, thus providing computer-assisted retrieval (CAR) (see Figures 17 and 18).

A computer address might include a year, month, day, and document number. For example, a letter dated December 15, 1983, would be found

Figure 18

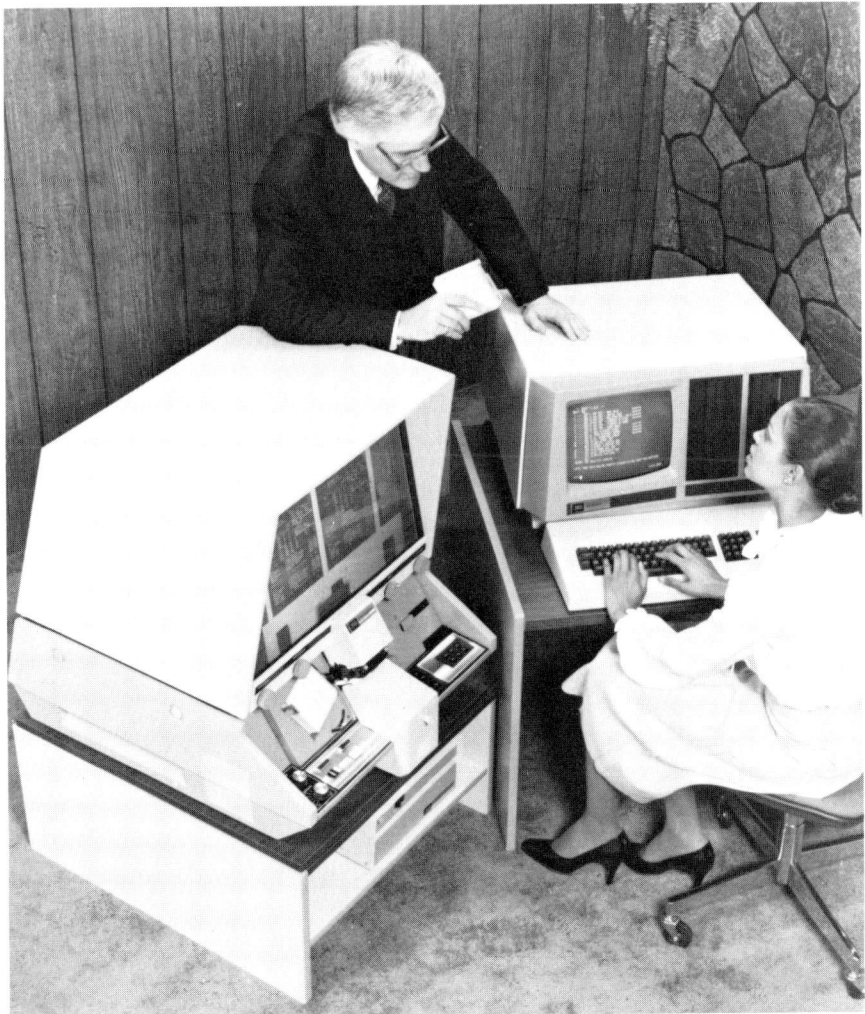

on: #83 (year) #12 (month) #15 (day) and #20 (item—the 20th document microfilmed on a given day).

CAR systems may be put together with a mainframe, a minicomputer, or even a microcomputer. Essentially, computer-assisted retrieval of micro-film is a two-part process. The microfilm is used to store and display data-base information, and the computer is used as an interactive logical search processor to provide fast and accurate storage and retrieval. Another approach is to store the search parameters in the computer along with the location of the microform. Figure 19 shows how a combination of technologies may be used to improve productivity and more efficiently handle information.

The growth outlook for CAR with other integrated information systems is very good. It is expected that future CAR systems will be modular, so that word processing and electronic mail can be added.

Optical Disk

Optical disk storage technology is still being developed. Optical disks use laser technology to provide high-density storage of either data or image information (see Figure 20).

Optical disks can be a better medium for storage of images, since such disks have quicker frame-by-frame retrieval than microfilm, because of their rapid random-access potential and the large number of images that can be stored on each disk. Presently, a four-by-six-inch microfiche will hold only 420 images, according to federal standard, whereas one type of optical disk holds about 80,000 images per side. Optical disks also have considerable potential for high-density storage of digital information. For example, some optical disks can accept the equivalent of about 40 reels of magnetic tape storage. Figure 21 compares storage media costs.

Optical disks still have several disadvantages. An optical disk is not easily alterable and an entire disk must be purged at one time. The cost is high and archival life and error rate are still somewhat unproven. The potential is, however, great, and optical disks are likely to provide another important form of storage in the future.

DIGITAL-BASED SYSTEMS

Many users are attracted by the ease of storage of information in digital form—whether it be on word processing or computer, floppy disks or hard disks. The convenience of using a CRT to retrieve data from a disk is equally attractive. Digital data may be stored externally off-line or on-line (which is presently more costly, but the cost is regularly decreasing with new technology).

Digital-based storage that is shared and accessed by means of electronic devices (such as word processors and computer terminals, and CAR systems) is often referred to as an electronic file—an important component of the office of the future.

Electronic filing and retrieval has many advantages. The most obvious are

1. Faster access to information.
2. Reduction in misfiling.
3. Reduction in amount of office floor space.
4. Storage efficiency through shared access.
5. Portability of files.
6. Time transparency for access.
7. Geographic transparency for access.
8. Limited dependence on human knowledge of filing techniques.

The only limitations of electronic filing and retrieval are that the user must have access to a terminal, and that unless a user is already on-line, it takes a few seconds to dial up a computer system and log on.[8]

It is here that records management performs a key function in determining the needed use of the information. If information to be stored consists of active and dynamic records that constantly are updated or altered (such as airline reservations), on-line storage is required. On the other hand, if the information is document-based and retrieved for reference purposes, it is a good candidate for a CAR system, in which a host computer drives an on-line index and on-line reader. In these systems, the display is electronically interfaced to the film retrieval terminal, which allows the computer to direct the retrieval of microfilmed images.

Data Base "Data base" has yet to achieve a widely accepted standard meaning. Although it is sometimes used to describe any centralized collection or file or material, it most generally refers to storage of computer-based data and content of material thoroughly cross-referenced for ease of retrieval. To accomplish this, the data base must be stored on direct-access storage devices, in order for the computer to be able to utilize the cross-reference capability. A data-base management system (DBMS) is the software that handles the storage and retrieval of the records in this data base and is what users actually work with.

A major advantage of a data-base system is that once a data item has been entered correctly, it need not be entered again to be usable for a number of programs. This is an important cost consideration and emphasizes the correct inputting of front-end data entry. Each step performed on data before they finally enter the computer for processing introduces the possibility of error. Studies have shown that of all the errors detected in data, only about 15 percent actually existed in source data. The remaining 85 percent were introduced during data transcription. The salaries of personnel involved in error correction can account for as much as 80 percent of the total cost of data preparation.[9]

[8] David Barcomb, *Office Automation: A Survey of Tools and Technology*, (Bedford, Mass.: Digital Press, 1981).
[9] Robert J. Kalthoff and Leonard S. Lee, *Productivity and Records Automation*, (Englewood Cliffs, N.J.: Prentice-Hall, 1981), pp. 179–180.

THE OFFICE OF THE NEAR FUTURE

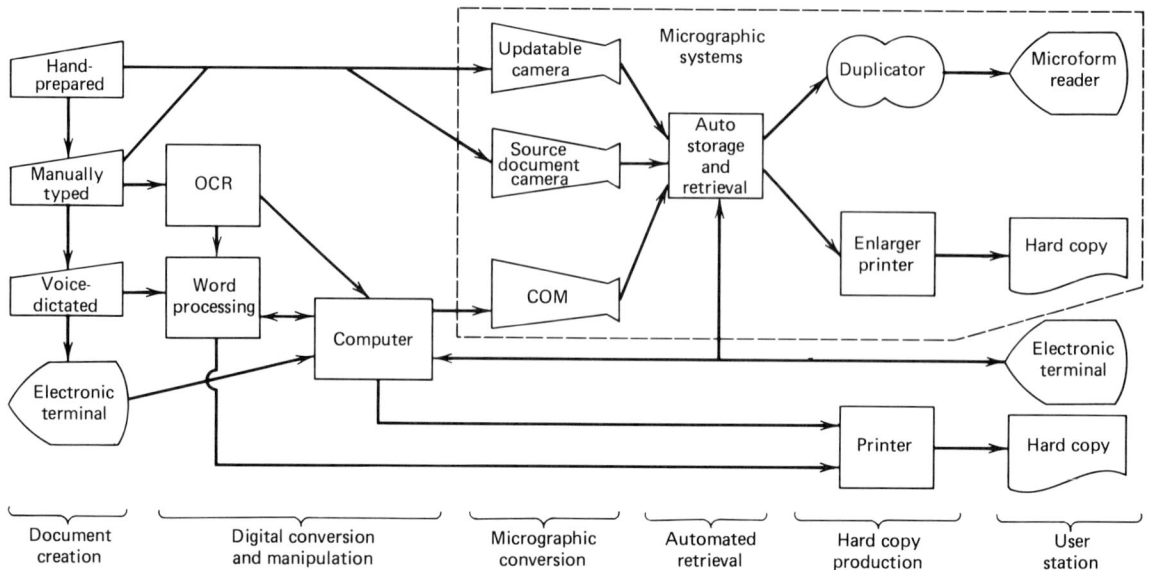

Figure 19 A look at future information retrieval. *Source:* Don M. Avedon, Executive Director, IMC, "Micrographics in the Office of the Future," *Information and Records Management*, May, 1981, p. 11.

Front-end data entry has many obvious advantages for later reference and retrieval. However, a basic problem is the volume of incoming documents (created externally) acquired by every firm. Again, this situation points out that most organizations require several forms of storage for the best solution of their needs.

VOICE-BASED SYSTEMS At present, there are three major forms of information storage: (1) paper, (2) image, and (3) digital. There is a fourth potential media, voice. We already use voice with dictating devices and telephone answering equipment; both provide records that must be managed, including establishing of purging and destruction schedules. Many additional voice storage systems are coming into use and provision for their proper use and management should be made as a part of any ongoing records management program.

RECORDS MANAGEMENT PERSONNEL

Whether a system is manual, automated, or computer-based, people are the most important part of its operations. People create information or records; they process the information; they also store and retrieve it; and people have the final say—they are the decision makers as to whether to

Figure 20 Optical disk technology is rapidly advancing. The rapid speed in retrieving information will significantly improve productivity. (Courtesy of Eastman Kodak Company)

Figure 21 Comparative costs of various storage media. *Source:* "A Brash New Competitor," *Administrative Management*, April, 1982, p. 51.

HOW VARIOUS STORAGE MEDIA COMPARE IN COST		
Types of Media	Quantity Needed Based on Storing 10^{11} Bits	Cost of Media
Magnetic disc	80 200MB disc packs	$40,000
Computer-compatible Tape	90 tapes (2400 feet, 6250 BPI, 8-track)	1350
High-density	2400 feet of 2-inch tape	100
Optical disc	One 12-inch disc	10^a

[a]Projected

purge or retain information. Records would have no life span without people. Even with automation the functions remain the same, only the tools used by people to perform them are changed.

Therefore the total organizational and personnel structure, job tasks, and job descriptions in records management are of immense significance—for they provide the basis for a smooth flow of information.

The success of any records management program depends on the quality of the personnel employed. Not everyone is skilled enough to manage a records management program. Unfortunately most management people believe that anyone can establish a system; this is one of the great fallacies in the modern office.

Generally, records management personnel may be classified on the following three levels:

1. Managers or administrative.
2. Supervisory.
3. Operating.

In addition, there are staff positions for analysts. A records management analyst studies existing systems and procedures used in creating, processing, and distributing records and recommends department filing systems, procedures, and equipment for economical and efficient procedures and utilization. Specialized positions for reports and forms analysts are not uncommon.

To be effective, all personnel should be fully aware of the following concepts, regardless of the nature and scope of the tasks that they perform:[10]

▶ The important role of information and recorded data in serving as the memory of an organization.

▶ The attrition of efficiency and performance when a company's records are poorly managed and accurate information is not readily available when needed.

▶ The need to organize and manage the large and increasing volume of all types of recorded information.

▶ The stages of development through which various types of records pass during their life spans.

▶ The procedures, equipment, and supplies to be used in organizing, systematizing, maintaining, and controlling records.

▶ The role of teamwork in managing records efficiently.

Some observers suggest that "records" still connotes hard-copy paper files. In order to emphasize the importance of total information, the term

---

[10] Maedke, et al., *Information and Records Management*, p. 47.

information resource management has been adopted by many organizations.

Records managers and/or information resource directors or managers play an extremely important role in attaining objectives of good records management. Their organizational functions, relationships, and responsibilities are shown in Figure 22.

The educational background of prospective records managers should

Figure 22 Generic job outline for a Records Manager. *Source:* Wilmer O. Maedke, Mary Robek, and Gerald Brown, *Information & Records Management,* (2nd Ed.) Glencoe Publishing, Encino, California, 1981, p. 48.

Functions
Develop, install, and administer the company records management program in accordance with established policies, including the retention, protection, and disposition of reports, forms, correspondence, and other records.

Organizational Relationships
Reports to: vice-president, administrative services.

Supervises: assistant records manager (1), records control supervisor (1), records center supervisor (1), central records clerk (4), records center clerks (2), microfilm technicians (2), forms clerk (1), keypunch operators (2), clerk typists (3).

Internal: systems and procedures department, legal department, accounting department, department heads

External: Internal Revenue Service, vendors, consultants.

Responsibilities
Company:
1. Establish procedures for retention and destruction of all classes of records on a departmental and company-wide basis.
2. Design and revise forms and procedures pertaining to interdepartmental and intradepartmental projects.
3. Coordinate problems concerning records, files, messenger service, and incoming mail.

Departmental:
1. Plan, develop, improve, and modernize record availability and service capabilities.
2. Maintain and control all records, including files, index cards, business registers, policy samples, microfilm and items stored by other departments.
3. Delegate authority through supervisors or directly to specialized personnel for specific projects.
4. Prepare department and company-wide manuals.

CAREERS IN RECORDS MANAGEMENT

Job Title*	Duties and Responsibilities	Personal Attributes	Qualifications	Career Mobility
RECORDS MANAGEMENT DIRECTOR	responsible for development & implementation of all company records management policies and practices maintains Records Management Manual which details the policies and procedures of the program directs & coordinates personnel and resources	must relate well to people successful supervisor and consultant effective in selling concepts of records management thoroughly versed in the profession of records & information management	ED — minimum of Bachelor's Degree or intensive course work in areas such as business law, accounting, data processing, systems analysis, personnel, records management. Advanced degrees helpful. EXP — 5 years senior records management experience as supervisor or consultant.	higher level staff position such as Manager of Office Services
RECORDS MANAGEMENT ANALYST	surveys, analyzes, recommends department filing systems, procedures, equipment for economic and efficient procedures & utilization reviews, evaluates, recommends changes of retention schedules conducts periodic department inventories participates in training personnel	must relate well to people effective in selling concepts of records management thoroughly versed in the profession of records & information management	ED — minimum of Bachelor's Degree or intensive course work in areas related to records management EXP — 2 years experience as junior records analyst or records center clerk	functional area supervisor or Assistant Director
RECORDS MANAGEMENT COORDINATOR	coordinates with corporate records management staff the various facets of the records management program responsible for maintenance & operation of divisional or subsidiary company level records management program in cooperation with corporate director for records management	must relate well to people successful supervisor and consultant effective in selling concepts of records management thoroughly versed in profession of records & information management	ED — minimum of Bachelor's Degree or intensive course work in areas related to records management EXP — 2-5 years records management experience in any advanced phase	Corporate Records Manager
REPORTS MANAGER	responsible for development & implementation of all company reports management policies and practices develop & implement efficient techniques to assist department and line management in identifying, reviewing, & establishing controls on reports	has high aptitude for identifying problem must relate well to people must be firm, flexible, aggressive, & determined should be self-disciplined & career motivated	ED — college graduate EXP — 5 years experience, preferably in paperwork management & work simplication	supervisory position higher level line or staff position
FORMS MANAGER	plans, implements, coordinates forms control program throughout company provides technical assistance regarding design, use, specifications, cost, procurement of forms prepares & maintains control records for company standardized forms	high aptitude for identifying problem communicates effectively knowledge of hardware and software standards in the records management field knowledge of principles of standard office practices knowledge of forms design	ED — college graduate EXP — 5 years experience, preferably as forms analyst in forms control section of a systems administration, Industrial engineering organization	supervisory position higher level line or staff position

Position	Duties	Skills/Qualities	Education/Experience	Advancement
RECORDS CENTER SUPERVISOR	operates and maintains a corporate records center; selects & supervises records center clerks and support staff; responsible for vital records protection, storage, disposal	work effectively with all levels of personnel; able to supervise effectively; able to coordinate resources available for an effective program; good organizer & decision maker; has an analytical mind	ED — minimum 2 years of college or vocational training in business or related areas; EXP — 2-5 years in records center operations	Records Management Analyst; Assistant Records Management Director; Records Management Director
REPORTS ANALYST	provides on company-wide basis, most efficient methods of reports creation, improvement & control through review of reports procedures & systems; designs and formats reports to obtain maximum information required at minimum cost; participates in training personnel	possess report writing skills; relate well to people and be able to make suggestions without antagonizing them; creative; self-motivated	ED — minimum 2 years of college; EXP — 3 years experience as report writer, preferably in one of the functional departments of a company	Reports Manager; higher level line or staff supervisory position
FORMS ANALYST	investigates and analyzes forms requirements; designs, drafts, & prepares finished art work masters; analyzes, revises & consolidates existing forms; maintains records required to document and control all company forms	relate well to people & make suggestions without antagonizing them; ability to establish priorities of work; broad background in all types of forms design, office equipment, and printing services	ED — minimum 2 years of college; EXP — 5 years experience, preferably in general business functions & management methods, graphic arts, duplicating, or other related fields	Forms Manager
RECORDS TECHNICIAN	operate, control, maintain technical files center of a reasonably complex nature; organizes & maintains file in conformance with system & standards developed by corporate records management; oversees disposal of unneeded records at the proper time	analytical mind; ability to grasp difficult question and derive answers using records at hand; decision maker; good planner and organizer	ED — high school diploma and advanced work in office procedures; EXP — 2-5 years file or records experience in difficult records area; NOT AN ENTRY-LEVEL POSITION	Divisional Records Coordinator
MICROGRAPHICS SERVICES SUPERVISOR	operates a central micrographics program; works closely with records analyst & other corporate members in development of micrographic applications; trains micrographics technicians	mechanical aptitude to maintain equipment; ability to translate micrographics systems specifications into work procedures to prepare film requirements; good organizer and planner; decision maker; analytical mind	ED — high school plus additional training in micrographics; EXP — 3 years experience as micrographics technician (may substitute vocational training for experience)	Micrographics Services Supervisor
MICROGRAPHICS TECHNICIAN	operates various types of cameras; operates film processor; tests developed film for overall quality; operates microform preparation equipment; conforms to production standards	good mechanical aptitude; handle confidential data with utmost discretion; make sound judgments; ability to analyze problems; ability to plan and organize work	ED — high school plus technical training in microfilming; EXP — previous records experience helpful but not necessary	Records Center Supervisor; higher level line or staff position
RECORDS CENTER CLERK	assists in accessioning, reference, retrieval, & disposal activities of center; assists with vital records; searches, sorts, & files records as requested by users	relate well to people; mechanical aptitude; ability to analyze data for answers to questions with discretion; analytical mind	ED — high school where some training in records management and office procedures received; May be an ENTRY-LEVEL POSITION	Records Center Supervisor; Records Technician
RECORDS CLERK (File Clerk 1) (File Clerk 2)	sorts, indexes, files, and retrieves all types of records; may enter data on records; may search & investigate information in files; classifies materials & records; transfers records & disposes of records according to retention schedule	relate well to people; mechanical aptitude; ability to analyze data for answers to questions with discretion; handle confidential requests with discretion; analytical mind	ED — high school where some training in records management, filing, and office procedures received; ENTRY-LEVEL POSITION	Records Technician; Records Supervisor

JUNIOR/COMMUNITY COLLEGE   HIGH SCHOOL

Figure 23 Available careers in records management depending on educational levels achieved. (Courtesy of the American Records Management Association).

include courses in finance, economics, statistics, accounting, business law, psychology, and English as well as courses in principles of management, records management, basic computer concepts, and systems and procedures.

Records administrators should be educated in the methods of selecting personnel for records management work and in the training of new employees. Those who possess knowledge of records procedures and systems and the relationship between the management of records and the management of the organization as a whole will be best qualified for the position of records administrator.

The CRM (Certified Records Manager) designation indicates that the individual holding the title has at least three years of full-time experience in records management and brings a broad background of education and understanding to the field. Interested individuals can obtain more information by writing the Institute of Certified Records Managers, P.O. Box 89, Washington, D.C., 20044.

There are many different types of supervisory positions in records management. As volume and information demands increase, new positions will be created. New technology will also create other positions at both the supervisory and operating levels—for example, in relation to COM and CAR systems as well as data-base management. Figure 23 illustrates the scope and breadth of the career opportunities in this growing field.

Operating personnel are the "nuts and bolts" people in records management. The exact nature of their work depends on the need and an organization's structure. Without competent, interested people in these jobs (and they are becoming more difficult to find) a records management or information resources program will not achieve its potential, with or without automation. The personnel in records management all share one thing in common: their job is to ensure that information is kept in an orderly, organized, and efficient manner. Efficiency is key to building employer and management confidence in the records system, whether it is simple or complex in form.

CHAPTER 9

ADMINISTRATIVE FUNCTIONS

OBJECTIVES

In this chapter you will learn about

1. The need for improved white-collar productivity—management, professional, and clerical.
2. How professionals, executives, and managers spend their time and how automation and other techniques can improve their productivity.
3. How administrative support contributes to increased productivity.
4. Where administrative support fits into the total organizational structure.
5. The uses of multifunctional terminals, managerial workstations, and personal computers to perform administrative functions.
6. The types of software available to assist executives, managers, and professionals to perform their administrative activities.
7. Considerations when implementing office automation for managerial/professional employees.

THE NEED FOR INCREASED
WHITE-COLLAR PRODUCTIVITY

In the early years of office automation, considerable emphasis was placed on the improvement of secretarial/clerical productivity with word processing. This was understandable in the late 1960s and early 1970s, when secretaries earned $6000 a year and a word processor cost $10,000. Today, all office salaries have increased. At the same time, office systems have been steadily decreasing in price.

When white-collar labor costs are analyzed, it becomes apparent that the secretarial/clerical portion originally targeted for word processing represents only a very slight part of the whole. Figure 1 shows that the typing part, representing $4.4 billion of a $375 billion total, is only about 1 percent of the total, and other secretarial aspects account for $17.6 billion, or about 5 percent.

The other major segment of the total white-collar work force comprises the executive and managerial group at $100 billion (or 27 percent) and professional and technical at $150 billion (or 40 percent). Control of these high labor costs has prompted continued studies of office productivity to focus increased attention on executive/managerial and professional/technical productivity. Office automation also is increasingly being applied to more office support needs than just word processing.

HOW PROFESSIONALS, EXECUTIVES, AND MANAGERS SPEND THEIR TIME

Booz, Allen & Hamilton, management and technology consultants, recently performed an in-depth study[1] of 300 knowledge workers (defined as professionals, executives, and managers) that provided almost 90,000 self-recorded activity samples to show how these workers spent their time. Figure 2 pictures the average of all time samples.

Although the exact percentages might vary with any given group, it is very likely that the basic categories concerning use of time would be the same. They provide a good basis for study of the needs of management and professionals.

Use of Technology

Where does automation fit in? Booz, Allen estimated that close to 15 percent of the managerial and knowledge worker's time can be saved through the application of technologies expected to be fully developed and in place by 1985. These time savings, translated into dollars, can contribute to profit. For large companies, potential savings can run into millions of dollars. The impact may be even greater when the "ripple" effect takes place. Kalthoff and Lee[2] have suggested that productivity improvement of the professional and managerial personnel is particularly

---

[1] "Why Office Automation," *Infosystems*, June 1982, p. 9.

[2] Robert J. Kalthoff and Leonard S. Lee, *Productivity and Records Management*, (Englewood Cliffs, N.J.: Prentice-Hall, 1981), p. 30.

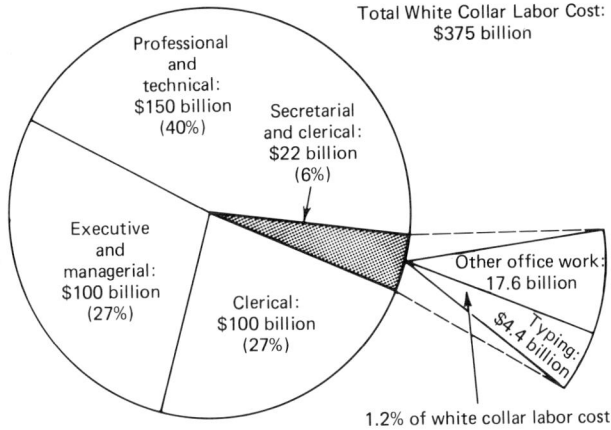

Figure 1 High managerial technical and professional costs are focusing attention on better tools to assist people to improve productivity. *Source: Electronics*, March 10, 1981, p. 160.

important because the quality of their work performance ripples out to affect that of others inside and outside the organization.

Areas of productivity improvement among managers resulting from automation include

▶ Conferencing.

▶ Information transfer.

▶ Information retrieval.

▶ Personal processing.

▶ Project management.

These applications have been covered in previous chapters. Other administrative activities will be addressed in this chapter.

Figure 2 How knowledge workers spend their time. *Source:* "Why Office Automation," *Infosystems*, June, 1982, p. 9.

Booz, Allen identified nine of the "less productive" activities. They are:

1. Seeking information.
2. Waiting/idle time.
3. Organizing work.
4. Streamlining the workflow.
5. Telephoning.
6. Scheduling.
7. Filing.
8. Copying.
9. Transcribing.

Because the above activities can be automated easily, they are the first targets for the time-saving efforts. About half of the 15 percent estimated time savings from automating comes from this category.

Seeking information accounts for more than 30 percent of all "less productive" time. It has the highest productivity improvement potential. The tools to achieve that improvement include automated retrieval systems and some forms of information transfer (the ability to send or receive information through networks without the traditional paper requirements). These help save about 40 percent of "seeking information" time.

Waiting/idle time relates mostly to internal or external business travel when extensive idleness, in a sense, is unavoidable, such as when waiting for a plane or a cab. Office automation tools such as information transfer, audio and video conferencing, and information retrieval could save about 28 percent of "waiting/idle" time by eliminating the need for people to move from one place to another.

Organizing work for more productive activities varies in importance among professionals, managers, and executives. Managers find this activity particularly important because their responsibilities include organizing work time for others and for themselves. About 24 percent of organizing work time can be saved through the use of automatic tickler files, information tracking systems, and word processing. The last-named frees more secretarial time, which can be devoted to assisting those whom secretaries support.

Streamlining the work flow can achieve a 30 percent time savings through automatic tickler files that prompt follow-ups; information tracking systems that monitor responses to requests, and/or reports on the status of work-in-process; and delegation of routine managerial work to secretaries.

The *"telephone tag"* game—trying to contact someone to receive or relay information—ranks among the most frustrating wastes of time for most office workers. Booz, Allen claims time spent in wasted phone calls can be cut by about 26 percent through automated information retrieval and transfer. The implementation of word processing can also free secretarial time to permit more delegation of telephoning activities; when secretaries can delegate typing duties to word processing specialists, they have more uninterrupted time for handling messages.

Scheduling, filing, copying, and *transcribing* account for almost 4 percent of the knowledge worker's time. But these activities offer the potential for a 51 percent (of the 4 percent) productivity improvement through such tools as information retrieval, automated calendars, and word processing.

Managerial workers spend about 75 percent of their time on the four "more productive" categories.

1. Meetings—46 percent.
2. Document creating—13 percent.
3. Analyzing—8 percent.
4. Reading—8 percent.

Time spent here is not so easily automated, because of behaviorial factors such as work habits and the perceived value of these activities. These four activities have an estimated 10 percent reduction potential.

Meetings and related travel are the largest but most elusive targets. Major aids are teleconferencing and those nontechnology aspects of office automation that result in better-structured meetings. These aspects include better communications about the need, purpose, and agenda for the meeting; better vehicles for describing meeting results; and tracking assignments after the meeting.

Teleconferencing (in which participants can see, hear, and exchange documents between remote sites) can reduce meeting-related travel and can increase meeting efficiency. Generally, such meetings tend to be more task-oriented, better-structured, and shorter. Attendees are more likely to show up on time, because of on-the-air scheduling interdependence.

Document creating includes composing, dictating, editing, and drawing/designing. Its potential for productivity improvement is somewhat uncertain, because knowledge workers place high value on this activity. Word processing is the most effective improvement tool in this area, but its direct benefits have yet to be realized by upper management. Professionals are more heavily involved in creating documents than are managers and executives. The most valuable benefits include reduction in editing time and reduction in the number of cycles required in preparation. Business graphics is a fast-developing tool that is eventually likely to benefit this activity.

Analyzing represents a fairly good opportunity for productivity improvement, especially where the work involves manipulation of numbers. Knowledge workers generally regard this activity as an important use of time. At present, personal calculators are the most suitable tools to reduce this time. Managerial workstations and personal computers are likely to replace calculators soon, saving an estimated 27 percent of the time a person now spends analyzing.

Reading and related annotating activities offer little opportunity for productivity improvement. Speed reading courses come to mind as a tool, but the information retrieval features of office automation technology also can contribute; they can save as much as 14 percent of the time associated with seeking *specific* information. As more internal and external data bases become directly accessible to professionals, more time can be saved by selecting information on specific areas of interest.

METHODS FOR INCREASING MANAGERIAL/PROFESSIONAL PRODUCTIVITY

Specifically, how does one go about increasing executive/management and professional/technical productivity? Several possibilities exist. Again, it is likely that no one method is the solution. A combination of various methods put together according to the needs of individual organizations promises to be the best approach. Management will need to consider the many ways in which the administrative function can be improved. Along with the technical aspect, not the least of these is the human aspect.

Increased executive/professional productivity will likely require both new technology and restructuring. Changes are most likely in one or more of these areas.

1. Administrative support.
2. Office automation systems.
3. Office automation tools for professionals.

ADMINISTRATIVE SUPPORT

Administrative support (AS) is a term used to describe the job function of assisting management in carrying out the administrative routines of the office. AS is generally a nontyping, nontechnical function, geared largely to the performance of clerical, conceptual, and administrative office tasks. It is also a complement to the typing function in the office known as word processing (WP). More of the corporate dollar is spent on nontyping office functions than on the typing tasks in the office. (Refer to Figure 3.) The administrative support function may include such tasks as filing, message taking, telephoning, researching, document drafting, proofreading, preparing reports, maintaining schedules, preparing committee meeting minutes, handling special projects, and other management-delegated tasks. The responsibilities of this job range from the simple to the highly complex; they require personnel with skill levels commensurate with the responsibilities involved, and the personnel will work closely with management.

With the bulk of typing removed from administrative support personnel, work specialization can be introduced into the secretarial ranks. Administrative secretaries' time can be concentrated on their particular duties without the constant interruptions of typing. Through this specialization, increased productivity and improved quality of work can be achieved.

Here, too, opportunity exists for executives, managers, and professionals to delegate more of their work. A recent study of 20 companies found that only about 39 percent of the managers' time was spent managing; the rest was spent "doing workers' work or making work."[3] Managers must delegate to others what others are better prepared to do, and managers must manage if their productivity is to be increased.

Also, the administrative support staff then has the time to take on more of the paperwork and quasi-clerical duties currently handled by management. Many of the delegated tasks are the type that most administrative support people find challenging and interesting. With proper organization, the team approach to secretarial work makes the office even more effective, because of cross training and backup support in cases of absenteeism, vacations, and so on. In addition, supervision of the restructured support and established procedures provides greater workflow concentration, coordination, and equitable workload distribution thus resulting in improved productivity.

Along with increased productivity, there are other advantages to administrative support. There is a higher quality of work, from both management and support staff, because everyone is concentrating on a specialized function. In addition, work specialization ensures that all the employees and managers have clearly defined responsibilities. This detailed description allows employees and managers to know what is expected of them.

Studies have shown that substantial cost savings can be gained by delegating clerical duties to entry-level clerical support personnel while delegating more complex paraprofessional duties to administrative assistants.

Through organized support, there is more equitable distribution of workload, as well as increased support provided to management at all levels. Individual members of an administrative support team find that they experience a sense of personal growth and are aware of the opportunity for career advancement. Overall, the company often experiences an increased sense of teamwork, as well as increased efficiency and cost savings.

[3] Alan G. Rockhold, "White Collar Productivity: Top Management Doesn't Know What It Wants," *Infosystems*, April 1982, p. 58.

In the implementation stage of administrative support there is a need to keep in mind the positive goals of economy, efficiency, and career advancement. However, the most important aspect of the entire project is that the office is now viewed as a professional environment where skilled people perform functions vital to the smooth operation of an organization. Each person is contributing that which he or she is prepared to do best.

Administrative Support and the Organization

Administrative support personnel can serve as the vital link between the word processing or correspondence center in an office and the principals or managers of an office (see Figure 3). By serving as that link, administrative support staff can aid overall efficiency in the office.

Administrative support secretaries can specifically help principals and word processing specialists by proofing all final documents and letters, leaving word processing specialists free to concentrate on the production of correspondence and reports. They also can aid the word processing center by helping to draft, prepare, and distribute correspondence throughout the office. By bridging the gap between executives who create work and the word processing center personnel who process the work, administrative support personnel assure that the office is more smoothly run.

Figure 3   In providing a liaison between principals and word processing operations, administrative secretaries relieve executives of routine tasks and help word processing operators prepare and distribute correspondence. *Source: Word Processing Systems*, March, 1980, p. 14.

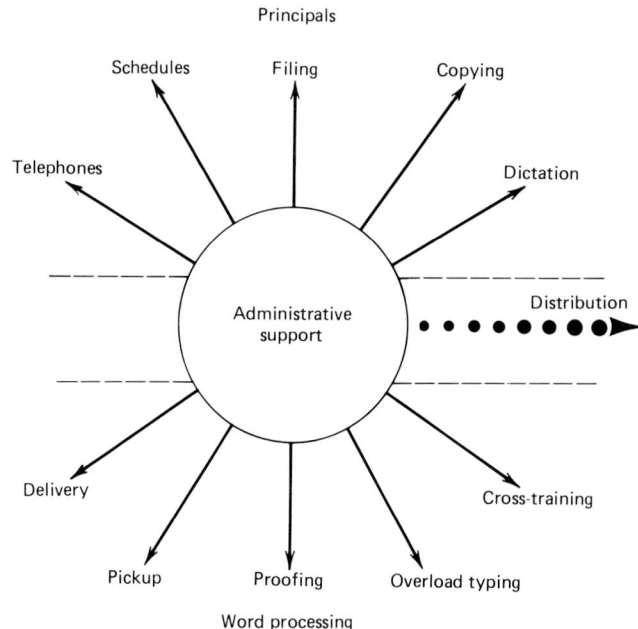

By freeing administrative support staff from typing, a particular organization can realize other significant advantages. Administrative support secretaries can set up meetings, draft meeting notices, and facilitate communications with many groups. On the telephone, instead of asking "Who is calling?" or "Can I take a message?" administrative support people will be in a position and have time to say "How can I help you?" Studies have shown that effective administrative support programs help principals reduce telephone time because properly trained AS secretaries handle requests on the first call and calling parties receive immediate help. Figure 4 depicts the administrative support structure.

Usually, administrative support functions best if it is grouped within a functional area of an organization—perhaps within a vice-presidential area or a department. The administration of the AS group falls on a supervisor in a middle-management position. The supervisor reports directly to

Figure 4 Administrative support structure. Note work specialization for greater control.

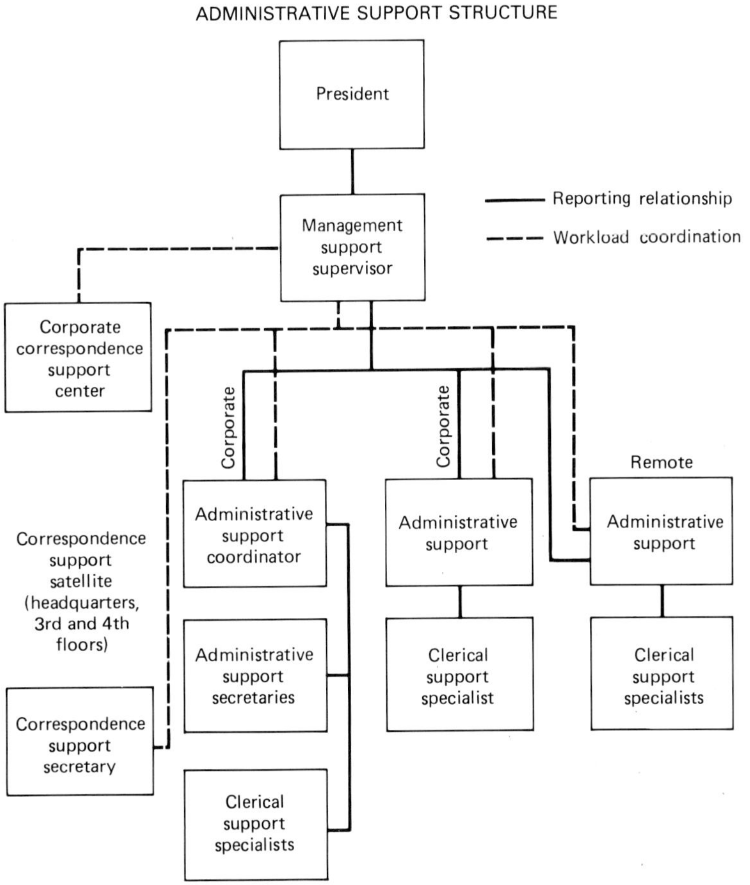

ADMINISTRATIVE SUPPORT STRUCTURE

the departmental executive. The supervisor also coordinates all activity with the word processing or correspondence center. The top supervisor may have several administrative support coordinators reporting to him or her from the various departments in the company. These coordinators in turn organize and manage the administrative support secretaries and clerical workers in their departments. Communications flow vertically in this organizational chart, but there is also horizontal coordination between the various administrative support departments and cooperation to ensure equitable workload distribution. This horizontal link also assures that all departments can aid each other in handling rush work or forming a team to complete a project.

Figure 5 shows how administrative support coordinates with the word processing group and the entire organization. There is constant communication between the word processing and administrative support person-

Figure 5 Organizational and workflow structure. The workflow is represented by the dotted lines, and supervision and control are represented by the solid lines.

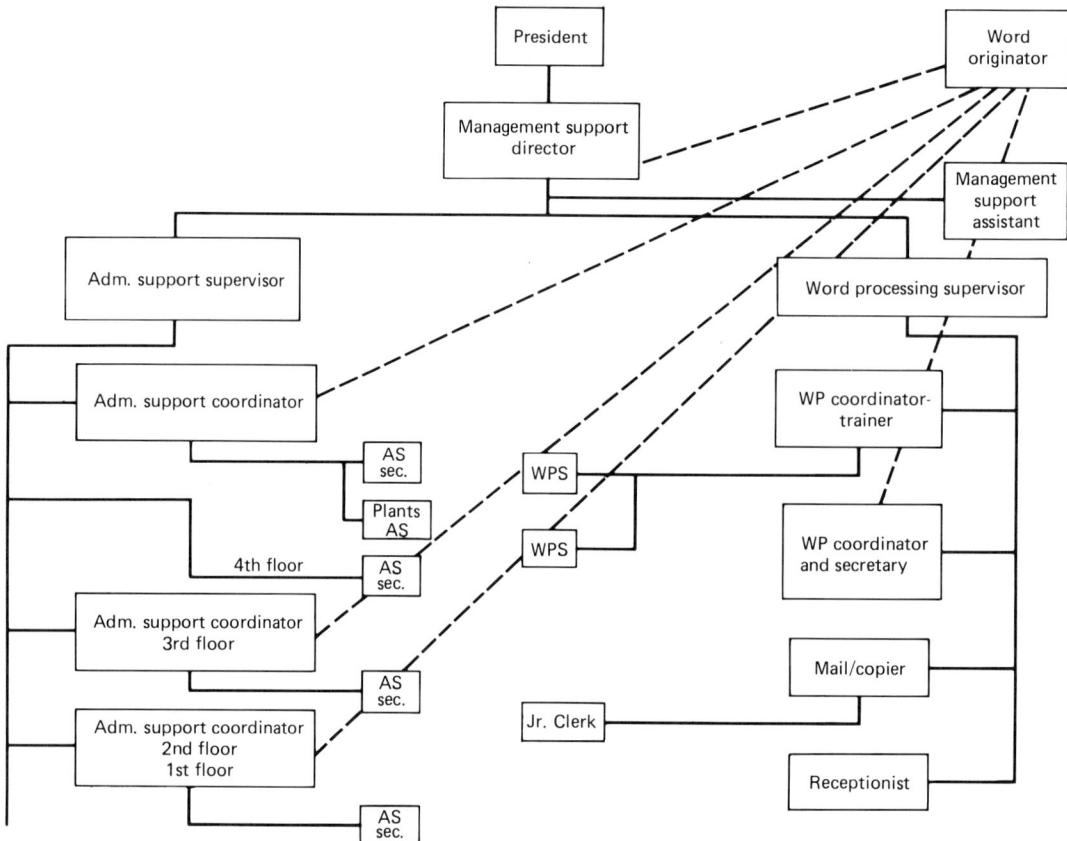

nel as well as communication with the executive levels. Usually, companies try to coordinate both the administrative support and word processing functions under a single supervisor, to ensure communication between the two groups.

Levels of Administrative Support

There are three levels of administrative support—lower-, intermediate-, and upper-level administrative secretaries. All three levels can lead up a career ladder to a management position in charge of both administrative support and word processing. Advancement up this ladder can be attained through mastering the skills required at each level and demonstrating ability to deal with people.

The *lower level* is the entry-level position in administrative support and is often referred to as clerical. Responsibilities at the lower level are very task-oriented and do not provide much opportunity for creativity or personal initiative. It is regarded as a place to learn the ropes about a company and the business world in general. The tasks performed are routine and usually require minimal training. Most skills for these jobs are acquired from on-the-job training or orientation sessions prior to beginning employment. These jobs require no prior knowledge of the organization and are strictly supervised. Most tasks are delegated from someone higher up the ladder. Tasks include processing incoming/outgoing mail, filing, copying, and perhaps receptionist duties.

The *intermediate level* of administrative support is also task-oriented, but more room is provided for initiative here than at the entry level. There is more opportunity for providing support to management and making suggestions on workflow. The intermediate-level employee should have advanced typing skills, knowledge of office procedures, ability to handle the telephone efficiently and professionally, and ability to file and retrieve materials quickly. In addition, employees should have experience in exercising judgment in scheduling and in dealing with management. A full understanding of the department in which the individual works as well as an overall basic understanding of the entire company is usually demanded. Duties for an intermediate-level employee might include preparing expense accounts, maintaining calendars, performing basic research (retrieving information), proofreading, and arranging travel for management.

An *upper-level* administrative support person is required to be less task-oriented and more goal-oriented. Persons in these positions should be creative, interpretive, intelligent, and ambitious. They should expect to assume increasing responsibilities. Duties at this level include drafting and dictating nontechnical correspondence, editing and revising management correspondence, researching management projects, and supervising others in the group. Upper-level staff often handle confidential matters for their managers. They often act as extensions of management in matters delegated by the managers to them, by exercising their own judgment in decision-making with minimal supervision. Effective upper-level admin-istrative assistance requires knowledge of the specifics of the organization and departments. Such individuals often handle detailed and important projects and may well research and draft an entire report for a manager. To reach this level, a support person usually needs to have a proven record as a middle-level administrative secretary. The person must be well accepted by the principals and other members of the administrative support team.

In an organized administrative support structure, exact job duties de-pend almost entirely upon how they are described by the company for the support individual's level within the organization. However, these levels

Figure 6 Sample list of duties of administrative support personnel.

The routine duties that an administrative support person would be expected to handle include

▶ Telephone answering.
▶ Message handling.
▶ Filing.
▶ Opening and sorting mail.
▶ Proofreading.
▶ Distributed typing material.
▶ Copying.
▶ Maintaining of calendars.
▶ Making appointments.
▶ Arranging meetings.
▶ Greeting visitors.

In addition, those administrative support persons who achieve higher positions in an organization would be expected to perform the following types of duties.

▶ Assisting in planning workload, assigning and supervising work.
▶ Processing forms, preparing important and difficult reports.
▶ Dictating communications.
▶ Performing work involving responsible original decisions.
▶ Maintaining principals' accounts.
▶ Preparing budget requests.
▶ Maintaining departmental records.
▶ Requisitioning and maintaining adequate supplies and equipment.
▶ Writing reports and informational materials.
▶ Performing assigned research.
▶ Developing operational procedures.
▶ Establishing priorities within the administrative support center.

are achieved by proven competency. See Figure 6 for a sample list of duties as they might be differentiated for position level.

The final level in administrative support is the supervisory/management level. At this level, people have full responsibility for the operation of an administrative support activity. At the management level, they often are charged with coordinating both the word processing and the administrative support activities. Supervisors/managers have control over the budget and are directly responsible to top management for performance. They are charged with planning and updating the administrative support system for the company. They are also regarded as the direct representatives of top management in the work environment. Usually, one progresses up the career ladder in administrative support by proving competency at each level (see Figure 7).

Figures 8, 9, 10, and 11 show actual job descriptions for different levels of administrative support, including a manager of that function. Note the increasing levels of responsibility and more complex duties as one moves up the ladder. In addition, salaries increase commensurate with position level, as indicated in Figure 12.

The status of the secretary within an organization has undergone drastic changes in the past 60 years. The advancement of a secretary was formerly dependent on her boss and his position progression and influence within the company. In contrast, the administrative support concept is based on viewing the secretary as an independent professional whose pay is dependent on her or his skills and performance. Job descriptions must ensure that secretaries know that job enrichment is possible and that career progression rests on their own initiatives, rather than on a boss's promotion.

In formulating job descriptions, job titles used to describe administrative support positions include "support clerk," "administrative secretary," "administrative assistant," and "paraprofessional assistant."

Preparation Prior to Implementation   As with every other functional area of the organization, once management commitment is gained, a systems study of support activities should be conducted. This study should cover all the duties of a secretary, both

Figure 7   Levels of administrative support personnel. Note the opportunity for upward mobility.

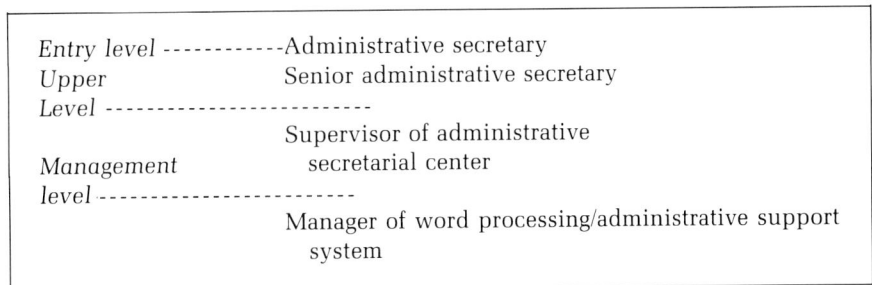

```
Entry level ------------Administrative secretary
Upper                   Senior administrative secretary
Level -------------------------
                        Supervisor of administrative
Management                secretarial center
level -------------------------
                        Manager of word processing/administrative support
                          system
```

Performs a variety of clerical tasks, such as collating specific information and completing reports, copying, filing, collating, backing up the telephone, and various other clerical assignments requiring limited knowledge of the organization, its operating procedures, and its personnel.

Collects information from previously established sources and completes reports requiring simple tabulation or transposing of information.

Acts as backup for answering the telephone, transfers calls to the appropriate party, and takes messages as necessary.

Updates telephone lists; puts together candidate lists; bursts and distributes computer listings.

Obtains photocopies, files, office supplies, and other miscellaneous materials upon request.

Performs filing, retrieval, and refiling activities for the functions served; initiates new files as needed, assigning the appropriate indexing code; and purges files according to a predetermined schedule.

Maintains various manuals by extracting outdated pages and inserting new pages.

Collates, staples, binds, and distributes a wide variety of reports and general correspondence.

Assures compliance with principal's priority and confidentiality.

Performs other miscellaneous activities as assigned by supervisor(s).

Figure 8   Functional outline of entry level of administrative secretary.

typing and nontyping. Figures 13 and 14 provide samples of study forms to obtain the needed information.

In addition, the study should include questionnaires for principals and secretaries to assist in verifying information (see Figure 15).

Once the results of this study are received, an analysis of the results and formulation of recommendations to management should be completed.

When final approval is gained to proceed with an administrative support system, several things should occur simultaneously over the next few months. First, a word processing center should be developed. In this process, a manager should be selected, equipment should be evaluated and selected, a procedures manual should be created, job descriptions and salary ranges agreed upon, and training should take place. At the same time, the administrative support system should be implemented. Managers and supervisors need to be selected, and there should be a reorganization schedule similar to that directing the conversion to word processing. Ideally, secretaries should participate in the planning and creation process. Finally, training programs, including those for management, should be completed so that managers, too, will know how to use the new equipment and understand the new workflow in the office. Once

Performs a variety of secretarial tasks, such as collecting information and completing reports, sorting incoming mail according to principal and subject, reviewing departmental correspondence and reports, making travel arrangements, composing correspondence, scheduling meetings and appointments, and numerous other assignments requiring a basic understanding of the department served.

Collects information from a variety of sources and completes reports requiring a basic understanding of the information being used and the ability to recognize source information that is in error.

Sorts incoming mail according to principal and subject, works through appropriate personnel to obtain any information the principals require to deal with the correspondence, and collects information from principals' mailboxes and performs any action indicated.

Composes a variety of correspondence to request or provide information related to various departmental functions.

Schedules meetings and appointments, reserves conference rooms and obtains any necessary materials or equipment, and keeps the principals alerted to their commitments.

Proofs departmental correspondence and reports to identify and correct errors that require a basic knowledge of the subject matter contained in the correspondence.

Makes the necessary arrangements in conjunction with Corporate Travel Services for domestic travel and international travel, including reserving flights, hotels, and rental cars; obtains the necessary travel funds; and prepares the itinerary.

Organizes and assists in maintenance of departmental files and manuals arranged in a system that requires limited interpretive classification and cross-indexing.

Works with Satellite Word Processing Center to comply with principals' priority. Assures compliance with principals' confidentiality.

Assists administrative secretary with the preparation of speeches and presentations by compiling any specific information needed, drafting a speech from an outline, and developing ideas for visual aids and acting as liaison with the Visual Aids Department to have them produced and ready for use.

Answers incoming telephone calls, responds to inquiries on routine departmental matters and refers specific inquiries of a technical nature to the appropriate administrative secretary and/or principal.

Performs other miscellaneous activities as assigned by supervisor.

Figure 9 Functional outline of intermediate level of administrative secretary.

Performs a variety of administrative tasks, such as collecting information and completing departmental reports, screening incoming mail, and initiating action as necessary, reviewing departmental correspondence and reports, making travel arrangements, composing correspondence, assisting in preparation of speeches and presentations, scheduling meetings and appointments, and numerous other administrative activities requiring an in-depth knowledge of the organization, available information sources, and extensive interdepartmental and outside contacts.

Selects information from a variety of source materials and prepares records or reports involving a variety of steps to complete. Possesses a familiarity with the source material necessary to recognize readily questionable information.

Screens incoming mail, obtains files and/or other information related to the correspondence, and forwards to the principals. Initiates action either personally or through the choice of an appropriate alternate in management during the principals' absence.

Composes a variety of correspondence to request or provide information related to various departmental functions.

Assists the principals with the preparation of speeches and presentations by compiling any specific information needed, drafting a speech from an outline; developing ideas for visual aids and acting as liaison with the Visual Aids Department to have them produced and ready for use.

Schedules meetings and appointments, reserves conference rooms, obtains any necessary materials or equipment, and keeps principals alerted to their commitments.

Makes all necessary arrangements in conjunction with Corporate Travel Services for the principals' business travels, including scheduling flights, hotels, and rental cars; obtaining the necessary travel funds; preparing the itinerary and completing expense statements.

Answers incoming telephone calls, responds to inquiries on routine departmental matters, and refers specific inquiries of a technical nature to the appropriate principal.

Reviews detailed departmental correspondence and reports to identify and correct errors that require a specific knowledge of the subject matter contained in the correspondence.

Works with Satellite Word Processing Center to comply with principals' priority. Assures compliance with principals' confidentiality.

Accomplishes projects and reports on time with little direction from principals.

Organizes and assists in maintenance of departmental files and manuals arranged in a system that requires limited interpretative classification and cross-indexing.

Performs other miscellaneous activities as assigned by supervisor.

Figure 10 Functional outline of upper level of administrative secretary.

OBJECTIVE
To supervise and coordinate the activities of the Corporate Office.

FUNCTIONS

Employment and Training

▶ Final interviewer of all Management Support applicants. Analyzes test results and determines adaptability of personnel.

▶ Prepares an office manual of procedures.

▶ Responsible for supervision of training of Management Support employees, including dictation training.

▶ Reports to president.

Operation

▶ Acts as liaison to Corporate Office and related staffs.

▶ Directly responsible for major job functions being carried out according to procedures. Coordinates activities of corporate office to serve the company. Handles majority of problems independently, making recommendations to immediate supervisor where necessary.

▶ Controls all office equipment purchasing.

Employee Relations

▶ Directly responsible for promoting good interdepartmental personnel relations. Is directly involved in all matters relating to word originators and management of departments served.

▶ Responsible for counseling and assisting corporate office personnel with problems they may have; acts as liaison between originating departments and production area. Requires a quality and quantity consciousness and the ability to instill this trait in personnel under supervision.

Public Relations

▶ Almost constantly in public relations position, and must have the ability to handle people effectively. High-quality relationship with all company personnel is essential in this "service" position.

▶ Evaluates communications with employees and public.

Analyzing

▶ Must analyze incoming work to determine priority; analysis of available work force's competency to complete successfully all assignments is essential. Must be able to determine causes of major slowdowns and/ or problems—evaluate possible solutions and decide upon the most practical and effective one. Should be able to foresee possible problem areas and prevent them from arising.

Initiating

▶ Must have initiative and creativity. Must exercise independent judgement in setting up procedures to handle word activity that does not follow a definable pattern. Must be able to augment procedures where necessary to maintain effectively an orderly workflow.

Figure 11   Functional responsibility of administrative support manager.

Position	Number Reported	Average	High	Low
Administrative secretary	3686	$277.52	$575.00	$107.00
Senior administrative secretary	1505	$308.96	$900.00	$175.00
Supervisor, administrative center	194	$379.96	$750.00	$142.00
Manager, administrative/WP	170	$467.23	$1001.00	$237.00

Figure 12 Salary chart. (Courtesy of International Information/Word Processing Association.)

all of these steps have been completed, the word processing/administrative support system can begin serving the needs of an organization.

If, as frequently happens, word processing has been implemented first, an organized administrative support system can still be implemented to achieve additional productivity gains from both the secretarial/clerical personnel and management/professionals. It is never too late to implement administrative support. The major requirement, however, continues to be management commitment.

Implementing Administrative Support

For an administrative support system to be implemented successfully, a strong management commitment to such a program must be present at all management levels.

An administrative support system cannot work if the supervisor in charge of implementation does not believe in it or does not understand its concept, functions, and benefits. The result: a supervisor who cannot communicate, motivate, educate, and perform. Such a person views implementation as a "job to get done" and not an opportunity to provide the benefits of a restructured, integrated office environment.

In addition, the administrative support staff members must be responsive to end users' needs. During implementation, the supervisor should closely audit performance in terms of quantity, quality, and ability to complete tasks. Interviews should be conducted with principals about the service and work of administrative support personnel.

Predicting exactly how an administrative support system will work out in an individual office is difficult. Because of this uncertainty, the most crucial person in this process is the supervisor who implements the system. An even workflow throughout the new office arrangement will help the initial phase-in period to go smoothly. The supervisor should watch closely to see that the staff adheres to the division of administrative support and typing (word processing) duties and that personnel do not slip

Multipurpose Nontyping Summary					Organization element		Dates From To		
Identifier	Tasks (report in minutes)								
	Shorthand	Copy Duplicating	Mail	Filing Retrieval	Telephone	Receptionist Duties	Composing Material	Proofreading	Research	Miscel-laneous
TOTALS										

*For daily weekly summaries, use secretary's name as identifier. For consolidated summary, use organizational element as identifier.

Secretarial Daily Time Sheet

Name: _____ Date: _____

Please use the following code numbers to describe what you did:

10 Calendaring
11 Errands and deliveries
12 Looking for misplaced files
13 Filing
14 Locating someone
15 Off work (vacation, sick, etc.)
16 Mail
17 Personal time (banking, coffee, etc.)
18 Photocopying/collating
19 Proofreading
20 Reception work

21 Receive or give instructions
22 Taking shorthand
23 Telephone
24 Travel arrangements
25 Waiting for work
26 Other (specify)
27 Recordkeeping, (posting, bookkeeping)
28 Statistics (computations)
29 Keyboarding (computer terminal, keypunch)
30 Typing (regular typewriter)
31 Typing (word processing machine)

Time		Code number	Description	(Optional)
Hrs.	Tenths			
			Total	

6 minutes = 0.1 hour	36 minutes = 0.6 hour
12 minutes = 0.2 hour	42 minutes = 0.7 hour
18 minutes = 0.3 hour	48 minutes = 0.8 hour
24 minutes = 0.4 hour	54 minutes = 0.9 hour
30 minutes = 0.5 hour	60 minutes = 1.0 hour

Figure 13 Sample study forms used to identify functions performed by support staff persons.

back into old habits. The supervisor should monitor and measure quality of work and, in a gradual and positive way, assign jobs to the persons who can do them best.

Several different approaches can be used to implement an administrative support system. The findings of the feasibility study will usually indicate which one is most suitable, because the study identifies the

Category		Explanation
10	Calendaring	Posting activities to your calendar and principal's calendar
11	Errands and deliveries	Performing errands of a business nature within your organization or outside of your organization
12	Looking for misplaced files	Within your area or for another area
13	Filing	Filing done by you including time used to set up new files
14	Locating someone	Time spent physically or by phone locating someone
15	Mail	Sorting, dating, and delivering
16	Off work	Vacation, sick, etc.
17	Personal time	Banking, coffee, etc. while at work
18	Photocopying/collating	Time spent by you copying and collating
19	Proofreading	Any proofreading done by you
20	Reception work	Greeting visitors, giving directions, etc.
21	Receive or give instructions	Any instructions you give or receive during work hours
22	Taking shorthand	By phone or principal
23	Telephone	Placing calls, taking messages, and directing calls
24	Travel arrangements	For principals or yourself regarding business
25	Waiting for work	Time spent waiting for work after you have caught up in all areas
26	Other	Any time you cannot fit in any other category. (Please specify.)
27	Recordkeeping	Posting, bookkeeping
28	Statistics	Gathering information of a statistical nature and computing either by hand or calculator
29	Keyboarding	Computer terminal, keypunch, etc.
30	Typing (electric typewriter)	Any typing done on regular typewriter
31	Typing (word processing)	Typing on word processing equipment

Figure 14 Sample study time form category definitions.

1. What would you estimate the workload in your office to be?
2. How effectively is the work in your office being completed?
3. What situations would you like to see altered in your support area?
4. What jobs being completed by your support staff are administrative in nature?
5. If you could, what administrative jobs would you have assigned to the support staff?
6. Do you have a private secretary?
7. Does your secretary perform many tasks that are nontyping in nature?
8. Does your secretary perform many tasks that are nonsecretarial in nature?
9. If your secretary is absent from the office for the day, who takes his or her place?

1. What jobs do you specifically perform that are nontyping in nature?
2. What activities do you specifically perform?
3. What jobs do you perform that are of an administrative nature?
4. What aspects of your job do you enjoy the most? The least?
5. If you could, how would you change your job?
6. What administrative duties do you think you could perform that you are not responsible for now?
7. How many principals do you report to?
8. Is it personally important for you to identify with your principal?
9. What situations arise that interrupt your own duties?

Figure 15 Sample interview questions for principals and support staff.

needs and nature of the work. During the designing of the administrative support system, several basic questions should be answered in every situation.[4]

▶ Should secretaries be located outside the offices of the principals they support or should they be grouped in a support center?

▶ Should typing and administrative support be processed in the same or in different environments?

▶ To what degree should administrative support activities be specialized?

▶ Should one secretary provide all support for one or a few principals or provide only certain services for all principals in the group?

[4] Arnold Rosen and Rosemary Fielden, *Word Processing*, (Englewood Cliffs, N.J.: Prentice-Hall, 1982), pp. 344–46.

► Should administrative support personnel report to the principals they support, to an office manager, or to a secretarial supervisor?

► If an administrative support supervisor is chosen, does this person report to the function supported or to a WP systems manager who serves all functional areas?

These factors influence the system design in a number of ways. A secretary located directly outside a principal's office will provide immediate, responsible service for that one principal. This setup facilitates communication and fosters a close working relationship. However, it does not effectively utilize the secretary's time and efforts. Consolidated support services permit even distribution of workloads and build a cooperative spirit among secretaries. In the consolidation of support services, it is important to make them accessible both in distance and in communication if the principal is to make use of the system. Should it become inconvenient for principals to obtain or use support, they will often choose to do the work themselves, thus defeating the purpose. With these requirements in mind, a review of the various approaches to implementing an administrative support system should help in the selection of the right one.

The first approach is known as the *principal-secretary* approach. It is basically similar to the traditional boss-secretary relationship, except that secretaries now attempt to "share the workload" voluntarily with one another. This approach does not materially change the workflow or the structure in the office. In this approach, teamwork and group spirit among the secretarial support staff are difficult to encourage.

The second approach is called the *team support* approach. Grouping administrative secretaries in a support cluster brings together two or three secretaries responsible for providing service to eight to twelve principals whom they are designated to support. Each AS secretary is usually responsible directly for half of the principals supported by the team and has secondary responsibility for the other half. By assisting each other and involving themselves in the needed work of as many principals as possible, the secretaries gain an overall awareness of the work being done by each member of the team and are better able to provide secretarial support during travel, vacations, sick leave, and so on. The group is located close to the principals they serve, to facilitate the flow of communication and work. See Figure 16 for an example of how teams may be placed.

A third approach is called the *administrative support center*. It is organized along the same lines as the word processing center, with all administrative secretaries located in a central area. The administrative secretary is assigned to a designated number of principals, as well as being part of the center. In order to have work done, principals come to the coordinator of the center and explain what they want, and the coordinator assigns the work to the designated person (see Figure 17). This type of organization is

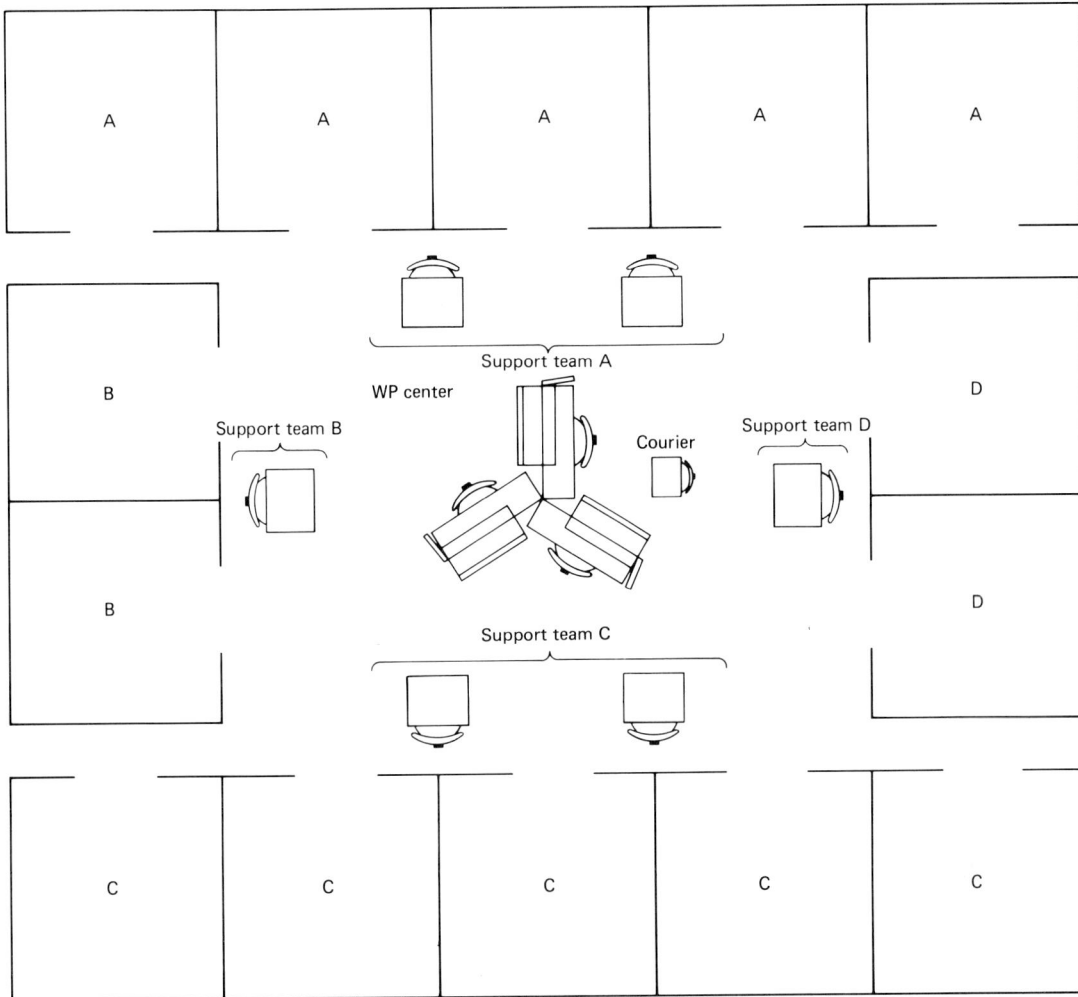

Figure 16 Support team organization shows a generic layout of a support team structure. Note central production area with administrative secretaries located close to users.

feasible only in small organizations—perhaps in a legal environment—where principals have need for support close at hand.

The fourth approach is presently the most popular method. In it, one administrative secretary works with from one to three principals, depending on the work volumes of the principals. This system guarantees the responsiveness of the secretary to the principals' needs. When this approach is used, the administrative secretary must be located close to the principals to work most effectively.

Although the administrative support personnel are assigned to certain principals, they report to and are directly accountable through a separate

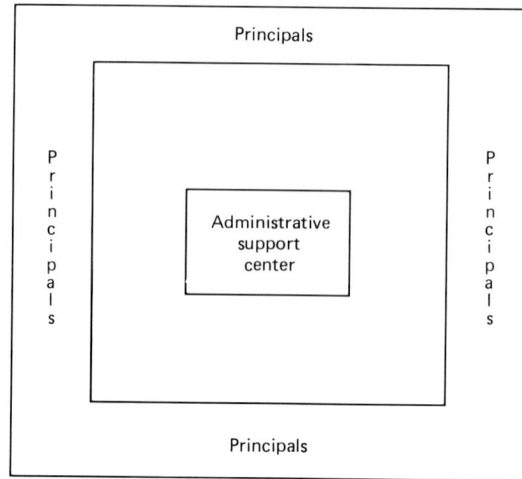

Figure 17 Adminis-
trative support cen-
ter approach.

structure. The word processing/administrative support coordinator provides independent, objective evaluation of performance and intercedes in
event of principal-staff disagreement or work overload.

Whichever method an organization chooses, the most important point
to remember is that the system must be workable within each organization's needs. The feasibility study outlines what needs have highest priority. Whoever implements the system must assure that these needs are met
with minimum disruption and maximum service.

**Administrative
Support and the
Electronic Office**
In the continuing flow of new product introductions, there are an increas-
ing number of systems that can perform some standard administrative
support functions such as message taking, filing, drafting, and so on.
Eventually, every administrative support person should have access to
these electronic devices.

**OFFICE
AUTOMATION
SYSTEMS**
Another means of improving managerial/professional productivity involves office automation systems. Office automation systems offer word
processing as part of a bundle of office functions, including (but not limited to) electronic mail and message distribution, administrative functions (such as calendaring, scheduling, and tickler files), electronic filing,
data access, and data processing.

**Multifunction
Terminals**
Recently several organizations established their own systems designed to
assist managers and professionals. Usually these systems are based on
mainframe computers or minicomputers with special software that provides specific services on computer terminals. Because these terminals
are generally used for many functions, they are called multifunctional

terminals. Executive use of terminals is likely to be governed by their familiarity with computers and terminals and the amount of training they have received. Executives may utilize office automation tools most effectively by providing them to the administrative support staff, thereby again freeing management time through the delegation process. Administrative support personnel also use these tools frequently, to provide needed assistance to those they support.

The effectiveness of these systems depends upon how well they are designed and implemented. Their success or failure is especially dependent upon how well they meet users' needs and how "user-friendly" they are. Success frequently comes as a result of user participation in both the original design and again in refining or improving the system. These systems are usually companywide (or at least wide enough to be helpful to a group of users).

Consider the following applications, presented in earlier chapters. They are all capable of being incorporated into an office automation system.

Centralized dictation systems, whereby users can create documents (by dictation) at any time of day or from any place in the world, thereby assuring immediate input of a document to the organization's information processing system.

Word processing systems, whereby only changes and revisions need be proofread, thereby saving originator's time. Such systems also can be used to check arithmetic and perform sort and selective-retrieval functions from small local data bases, thereby providing immediate response and saving manual labor.

Electronic mail, whereby documents may be distributed quickly and made available for immediate decision making.

Voice store-and-forward systems (electronic mailboxes), whereby decisions can be communicated more quickly and telephone tag can be eliminated.

Teleconferencing, whereby travel can be reduced and additional people may participate in the communications and decision-making process.

Information storage and retrieval, whereby through electronic files and data bases (of microimages or digital storage), information is immediately available for viewing and reference; and through the use of keyword and full-text abstract indexing systems, time in research and retrieval may be saved.

Middle management and professionals who often do not have support immediately available can use multifunctional terminals more heavily than can executives. Figure 18 illustrates a general system with various capabilities to assist users as they perform their regular activities. Note the functions available with the system software: word processing and advanced text management, electronic mail, electronic filing, activity management (sometimes also called personal management), and personal computing. Note also the specific tasks that can be performed by each of the types of software.

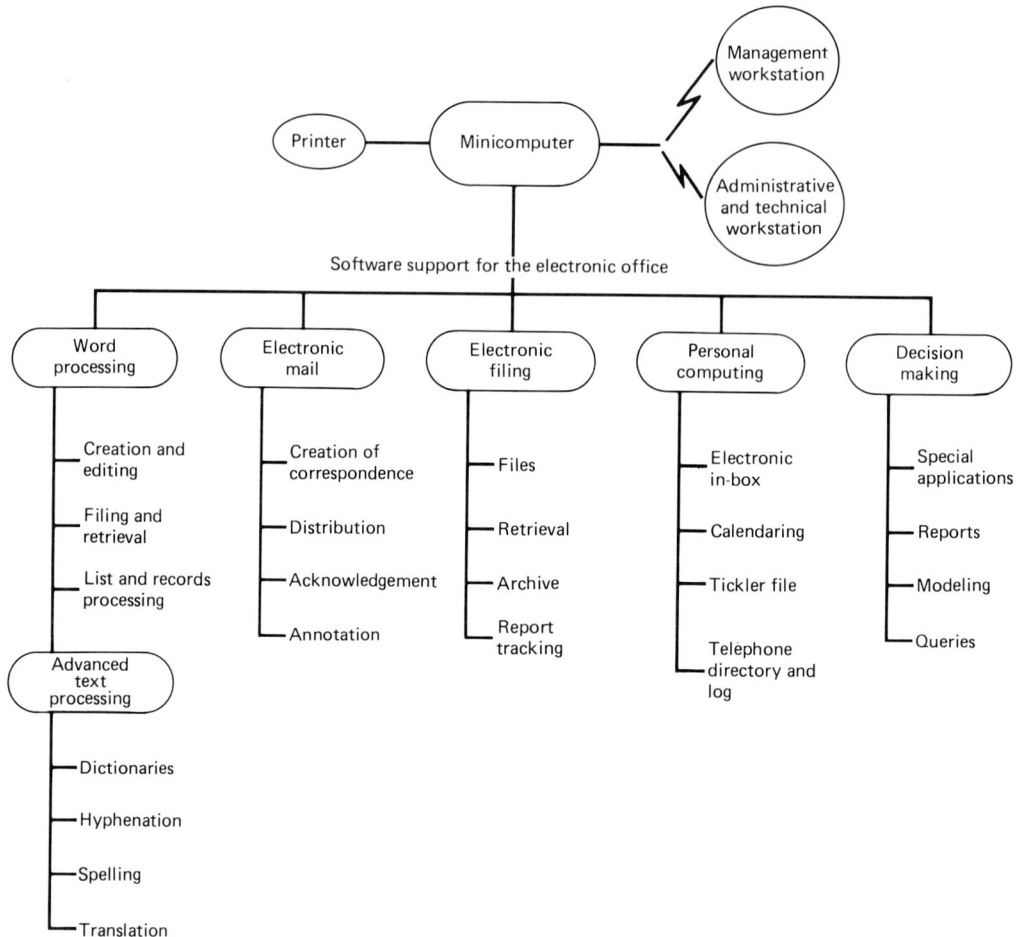

Figure 18   Office automation software support for knowledge workers.

Software capabilities have been designed by individual companies to meet their users' needs. One company put the firm's cafeteria menu, complete with calories, on its mainframe, to be accessed through its multifunctional terminals. The justification was that greater efficiency could be achieved in moving people through the cafeteria when they knew what they wanted to get to eat.

Fleet maintenance is another application that lends itself to computerization. In addition to keeping track of when company vehicles should be serviced, a running total per vehicle of miles driven, problems, and repairs can be kept to determine those due for early trade. Scheduling of vehicles may also be put on the system, for better utilization and pooling.

Many firms have projected expanded use of multifunction terminals as part of their overall office automation plan. Aetna Life and Casualty Co. of

Hartford, Connecticut, the nation's largest diversified financial organization, by November 1981 had installed over 7000 terminals for its 38,000 employees (approximately a 1:5 ratio). The company indicated it expected to boost that ratio to 1:2 by 1985.[5]

OFFICE AUTOMATION TOOLS FOR THE PROFESSIONAL

Professional office automation tools fall into one of three categories. *Multifunction terminals* attached to large systems—as discussed in the previous section, on general office automation systems—comprise one type. The others are especially designed *managerial workstations* and *personal business computers*. All have a number of similarities but also some distinctive qualities.

All are software-based and hence have a variety of capabilities. The differences lie primarily in their storage capacities and communications capabilities for accessing mainframe data bases.

Managerial Workstations

Helpful office machines have had a place in the office world since the first typewriter and telephone. Generally, the "tools" of office automation are provided for the use of support personnel; and managers have been limited to a telephone, personal calculator, dictating machine, and occasionally their own typewriter or terminal. Along with increased attention to managerial/professional productivity, however, has come a new tool called the managerial workstation. The Xerox 8010 Star Information System, introduced in 1981, was a pioneer because both the machine and its software were designed specifically for the professional knowledge worker (see Figure 19).

Managers and professionals often do not have touch-typing or keying skills, which they consider to be clerical skills. To get around typing's image problem, Xerox designed the Star so that the user moves a pointer (the "mouse") on the screen to the symbol representing the desired function. For example, to file a report, the user points to a picture of a folder and then to one of a filing cabinet. These pictures or symbols are called icons (see Figure 20).

The Star is designed to tie into Ethernet, a local area network system, which provides electronic mail capabilities. Incoming mail is depicted on the incoming mail icon while outgoing mail can be sent to any workstation attached to the Ethernet.

Since the announcement of the Star, other office automation vendors have developed their own versions of management workstations. The makers of Apple computers have developed the LISA which is an acronym for local integrated software architecture. The LISA has many similarities to the Star, such as using a mouse for cursor movement and point-

---

[5] "Fighting the Paper Chase," *Time*, November 23, 1981, pp. 66–67.

Figure 19 Xerox 8010 Star designed specifically for the knowledge office worker. (Courtesy of Xerox Corporation.)

ing to images on the CRT screen. Through integrated software, users can move information easily from one file to another. Whether these products are likely to be helpful depends largely on what the user wants to do. Some of the features available on such equipment include

1. *Time-management controls:* calendars, schedules, and the ability to schedule use of meeting facilities.
2. *Text-editing features:* letter/memo/forms/form-letters creation, office dictionary used to correct spelling errors, page layout, printing and typesetting capabilities, and the ability to change the typeface.
3. *Electronic mail capabilities:* the ability to send and receive electronic mail; also, distribution lists, annotation of received mail, confidentiality flags on mail.
4. *Files processing:* records processing, index record, retrieving on- or offline documents from data bases.
5. *Miscellaneous features:* communications with other terminals, arith-

Figure 20 Icons used for user's selection of functions. (Courtesy of Xerox Corporation.)

metic computations, graphics, recording telephone messages and indexing them, client billing, and the creating of voice documents.

A close look at what is offered on these workstations reveals why they are attractive to management. Whether they can be installed on a cost-justified basis may be a problem, for they are the newest form of status symbol. When they are used by support staff or professionals whose work products are quantifiable, they may be easily justified. When *and if* they enhance decision making is another question—one better decision made in a more timely manner could justify the installation of a roomful. Certainly, managerial workstations bring with them a host of new questions and considerations for managers of office automation.

Personal Computers

Personal computers have moved into the business environment in large numbers, especially for use by managers and professionals (see Figure 21). Optimum use requires hands-on experience and the studying of manuals to become thoroughly familiar with the computer's capabilities— something executives may or may not be willing to do. A certain amount of continued use is also necessary to retain familiarity with a system. The personal computer provides freedom and flexibility to experiment, and the advantage of being immediately at hand. Some people predict that personal computers will soon be on every desk and as unobtrusive and reliable as today's telephone. Portable computers are providing convenience for managers and professionals who find it advantageous to work at home or when they travel (see Figures 22 and 23).

Unless personal computer users have considerable programming experience, they must be willing to work within the limitations of off-the-shelf applications packages sold by the computer vendor or by separate software outlets.

Limited amounts of main memory and data storage on floppy disks pose

Figure 21 Personal computers are gaining widespread acceptance as a management tool. (Courtesy of IBM Corporation.)

Figure 22 Portable computers provide flexibility to the traveling business person. (Courtesy of Grid Systems Corporation and Sony Corporation.)

Figure 23

serious limitations for larger business applications, but new market offerings are steadily overcoming these shortcomings.

Communications capability is also an important concern. Managers frequently need access to mainframe data bases, to track corporate data. Difficulties with compatibility of formats, the merging of mainframe data and personal computer data, and the security of corporate information are all problems that require coordination with the Data Processing Department of the organization. Other concerns about interfacing personal and large-scale systems focus on electronic mail, high-speed printing, and access to local and remote networks.

For the present, the greatest benefits of personal computers are likely to be achieved by those individual employees whose applications are personally or departmentally critical but do not require corporatewide information or communications.

SOFTWARE

All of the new systems designed for managerial/professional usage are software-based. Many software applications packages are available. These packages range from PROFS (the IBM mainframe software for professionals) to the thousands available for personal computers. Depending upon the users' needs and the hardware, programmers can write specialized software programs or packaged software can be purchased for immediate use.

Software sales for personal computers are expected to amount to billions of dollars. Generally, those most frequently sold for business usage are for financial modeling, data management, and personal management. Visicalc™, one of the best known, is an electronic worksheet that helps professionals plan budgets, create forecasts, and develop pricing strategies. Personal management packages usually offer a means of managing time and appointments through calendaring. They assist managers in managing by organizing information and keeping track of priorities and expenses. Word processing software provides a means for managers and professionals to input text as they create it. For best use of their time, however, the support staff edits and formats the material into final form.

Top executives frequently need financial data to assist them in decision making. Much of this information already has been stored in outside data bases and can be purchased today in several forms from information vendors. For competitive financial data, for example, one common source is Standard & Poor's Compustat tape, which provides 10 years of data on 130 business variables for more than 3500 companies. Dow Jones News/Retrieval (the publishers of the *Wall Street Journal*) is a subscription news service that provides current business news, quotes, and stock market indicators. To access it requires a personal computer, terminal, or word processor equipped with communications capabilities. Access is also available to a variety of data bases ranging from corporate earnings and economic forecasts to sports updates and nationwide weather conditions.

Business graphics software is growing in importance. Through graphics software packages, visual representations transform raw data and statistics into easily understood line graphs and pie and bar charts. On some workstations the data appears on the screen in color, to enhance meaning even more. Output of graphics may also be produced in color.

A recent Wharton School of Business study on graphics showed that managers can cut 28 percent of business meeting time and make decisions 11 percent faster by using graphics-supported presentations. In terms of revenues, the graphics industry is conservatively clocked at an annual compound growth rate of about 35 percent.[6]

Graphics, however, are not an automatic panacea for managers who desire more and better information. What is unstated and frequently misinterpreted in a manager's desire for graphic data representation is not the need for graphs per se but a dissatisfaction with the content and usefulness of existing information sources. A crucial consideration in the acquisition of management graphics systems is the purpose of the data base and whether it meets interpretive needs. For example, information kept for totaling and accounting purposes may be so voluminous and stored in such a manner that it is impossible to create historical data that can provide relative figures for comparisons of trends. Graphs are really at their most useful if they can demonstrate the relationships between several sets of data. Achievement of this goal would require the ability to retrieve information from a centralized data base, or to request that the large quantities of data in the mainframe be converted to graphics and then sent to computers. Hence, the individual workstation must have the capacity to accept this type of information.

Business graphics software is available for use on all types of managerial workstations, from multifunctional terminals tied to mainframe computers to stand-alone managerial workstations and personal computers. The key is well-chosen software and the availability of the right information so that managers or professionals can use the system themselves easily and effectively.

CONSIDERATIONS FOR IMPLEMENTATION

Many of the criteria for selection of any type of technology apply to managerial/professional workstations. However, several points probably require more attention and consideration.

---

[6] "Worth a Thousand Words," editorial, *Computerworld*, July 19, 1982, p. 30.

Many of today's options are more problem-oriented solutions than "total-system" solutions. If an organization is attempting to put together a total integrated support system, priority consideration must be given to compatibility with a mainframe. Most professional terminals will be used as decision support systems at least part of the time and therefore will require mainframe compatibility. Communications networking options are important because electronic mail is a viable application, as is information retrieval from outside data bases.

User friendliness is another essential requirement. As more and more nondata processing executives begin using terminals and workstations, vendors who provide the easiest-to-use programs and equipment (plus fast, effective, painless, and nonthreatening training) will probably sell the most equipment. In addition, attractive devices that look more like a status symbol than a low-status typewriter are likely to be more readily accepted.

The providing of more tools for the managerial/professional knowledge worker, whether multifunction terminals, managerial workstations, or personal computers, eventually could prove counterproductive. How could having such equipment possibly be counterproductive? An interesting phenomenon is described in Figure 24.

While all of these tools are fascinating, it may be very time consuming to learn about and work with them. Innumerable tasks can be performed with such equipment, but considerable personal time can be expended at a computer to perform the tasks.

Figure 24   Will personal computers create executive stress? *Source:* Ronald N. Ashkenas and Robert H. Schaffer, "Managers Can Avoid Wasting Time," *Harvard Business Review*, May–June, 1982, pp. 98–104. Copyright ©, May–June, 1982 in *Harvard Business Review* by the President & Fellows of Harvard College; all rights reserved.

Although many executives may rationally acknowledge that they do not use their time as well as they should, they cannot change how they spend it. Why? Our observation is that, to a significant extent, managers spend time performing nonproductive, time-wasting activities to avoid or escape from job-related anxiety. All managers experience stress on the job and they have a variety of ways of dealing with it. The most common outlet is busyness: the escape into time-consuming activities that managers find less threatening to perform than the tough aspects of their job. Busyness may take such forms as spending excessive time on routine paperwork; setting up new, unnecessary procedures; reading company reports that do not really apply to the manager's job; writing routine correspondence that secretaries could handle; or bantering with peers. The irony is that busyness involves neglecting important tasks, eventually clutters a manager's schedule and results in more stress—which in turn results in more busyness. It's a vicious circle.

The concept of providing support personnel to provide assistance to executives, managers, and professionals is a sound one. Management should make sure that providing computer terminals or personal computers does not result in transferring clerical functions back to professionals and executives. It is not beneficial to have $50-an-hour professionals spending substantial amounts of their time performing $15-an-hour clerical work.

Whether the goal is increased clerical or managerial productivity, technology is only a tool. If an integrated system is the goal, care must be taken to prevent the proliferation of incompatible equipment that will occur if the requirements of the entire organization are not studied and analyzed beforehand.

PART THREE

ISSUES OF OFFICE AUTOMATION

CHAPTER 10

CHANGE AND THE CHALLENGES OF CHANGE

OBJECTIVES

In this chapter you will learn about
1. The effects of change.
2. The causes of change.
3. The areas of change.
4. The *don'ts* of implementing change.
5. The *do's* of implementing change.

THE EFFECTS OF CHANGE IN THE OFFICE

Individuals who accept and understand the process and rate of change will become more effective managers and workers and be able to progress in the integrated electronic office. The continuing evolution of electronic technology and related software will force ongoing changes in every part of the office—in management philosophy and attitude, organizational structure, job titles and descriptions, work habits, physical and psychological environment, training programs, systems design, methods and procedures, and equipment.

Job success in the changing electronic office will depend on an understanding of what causes change, how to plan for change, and the benefits of change. People need to be flexible in order to respond to new opportunities. Some find it difficult to adjust while others welcome or even take a lead in implementing change. Those who actively participate in implementing change are happier, more fulfilled persons, and more valuable employees.

Change is only good if it is based on planned, sound reasoning. To maintain the status quo in office and information systems without auditing their effectiveness can be tantamount to functioning in an obsolete environment, and may actually mean moving backward as the competition progresses. Changes in the electronic office have impacted the areas of equipment/systems, organization structures, job duties, and management.

Equipment and systems changes have ranged from the implementation of word processing and automation of the secretarial environment to the establishment of managerial electronic workstations for improving time utilization and managerial productivity. To understand the obstacles and problems likely to arise in implemention of the integrated electronic office, it will be helpful to explore the causes of change, needed areas of change, and the necessary factors for successful introduction of change.

THE CAUSES OF CHANGE

MANAGEMENT DETERMINATION

The need for change must be recognized before it can be planned and implemented. Management is ultimately responsible for recognizing the need for change. If it has established goals and continuously measured performance, it can determine if changes are needed. Generally, management establishes goals in terms of productivity, costs, schedules, sales, quality, accuracy, turnaround, and other areas. Therefore, evaluative information about these goals is the main indicator for any change. Management should review and determine if the goals are appropriate. When actual performance varies substantially from the established goals, the organization should prepare to change. Although management is responsible for implementing change, the need for change is often first recognized at the worker level. Sensitive and alert managers should be aware of the conditions and problems of their subordinates.

Sometimes the causes of problems are easy to identify. But identification of real problems and the exact steps required to rectify them often necessitate further fact gathering to document and prove the point conclusively.

For example, personnel reports reflect direct costs such as salaries and fringe benefits. Indirect costs such as employee absences and employee turnover rates may be reported periodically. This data can be easily compared with a company standard to evaluate performance. Differences can be noted and disparities explored. However, indicators such as employee productivity in the office are not so easily recognized or measured. The length of time needed to produce information and the number of people who had to drop everything else to produce this information are not conveniently measured in the traditional office environment. Employee happiness or low morale is nonquantifiable but is reflected in other ways, such as absenteeism or low productivity. Unfortunately, by the time these problems surface, their impact has been magnified and then brought to the attention of top management. An effective supervisor not only measures and evaluates the performance of employees, but also is alert to those intangible factors that can cause problems. In other words, the supervisory level is the best place for an early warning system concerning problems.

UNPLANNED AND INFORMAL CHANGES

When the need for change is not measured or formally recognized, the change may not improve performance. For example, in the mid 1960s, management in a Midwest engineering firm saw a need to improve the response time to typing requests and invested in word processing equipment. No evaluation was made to determine performance improvement. In the mid 1970s, management perceived an additional need, and more equipment was purchased and installed. Again, no evaluation was made. By 1978, however, operating costs were so high that a study was commissioned to evaluate the installed equipment. The results of the study (which covered the firm's total support structure) revealed that equipment was not being fully utilized, functions to be performed had not been defined, and procedures had not been written to ensure best equipment usage. Employees had recognized the need for new job outlines and had taken it upon themselves to define their own job responsibilities. As a result of this lack of central supervision and planning, there was duplication of effort, downtime on word processing equipment, and additional cost to the firm.

This example shows how unplanned and informal changes can occur gradually, without benefiting managers or employees. Employees implemented spotty changes to combat discontent caused by inequitable workloads. But these changes took place in the absence of total organizational goals and were separate from managerial control. In order for managers to be aware of the need for change, they must go beyond reading monthly reports. They must be aware of and appreciate their employees and provide opportunities for effective communication with them on an ongoing basis. One technique used today is the use of regular information-sharing meetings. An informal means of showing appreciation is planned social events for employees and their families.

Although poor response to work requests, lack of appropriate communication, low-quality work, idle time on the part of the secretaries, and ineffective use of management time are indicators of problems, they do not necessarily define the problem. Further investigation of each of the problems will indicate the true need for change and the appropriate action avenues.

EXTERNAL CAUSES

External causes of change may revolve around the need for technology in order to (1) communicate with remote offices or plants; (2) communicate with customers, such as in the case of banking institutions; (3) communicate with outside information sources, such as a large memory of legally precedented cases in a law office; or (4) communicate with other agencies, as in the case of government. These external causes of change may be more obvious than internal needs, but care must be taken here, too, to ensure that actions are appropriate and problems are resolved in the best possible manner.

New laws and government regulations cause many changes and may even require restructuring of employee tasks, creation of specialists in various activities, and department reorganization. New regulations stipulate the dates on which they become effective, and management often has to act quickly to conform. Often federal regulations require conformance that results in pressure on organizations to modify their reporting procedures. In some cases, additional staff or equipment are necessary to meet the increased reporting requirements. For example, organizations now must develop affirmative action programs and maintain ongoing Equal Employment Opportunity (EEO) reports.

Information processing systems are available to produce these reports on a monthly basis with a minimal time expenditure by the support staff, as compared with creating the reports manually from daily logs of personnel records. To meet EEO Affirmative Action Program requirements, some firms have created a new department, with a new reporting relationship and a new set of assigned tasks; further, the organization must acquire technology with the capabilities to get these tasks done. Information processing equipment with records processing ability makes it possible to keep information at hand, and an appropriate sort may be made quickly and easily, as needed. This information then can be easily incorporated into a final report in time to meet a specified deadline. There are obvious advantages over tedious and slow manual methods. Without technology, when special reports are due many workers are often pressed into service at high labor costs.

INTERNAL CAUSES Within an organization, the president or top administrator may require managers to produce reports that will justify the work output of their specific departments. Historically, the manager's belief that his or her staff was hardworking provided sufficient justification. However, with the national emphasis on improved productivity, white-collar managers are obliged to document their departments' productivity with facts and figures. To obtain sufficient justification or documentation often results in establishing productivity goals, creating positions for specialized staff members, and measuring performance against established goals.

In addition, internal pressures from executive-level management to complete routine and additional tasks with the same number of or fewer support staff members often result in a need for change. Another major internal cause for change may be the continual secretarial backlog of day-to-day work demands (correspondence, filing, report drafting, and so on). When management realizes the work is not getting done on time, it seeks an explanation and a solution. The solution may mean additional workers, new equipment, or changing the way of doing the work altogether.

The economic pressures of a recession, lower profit margins, or changes in customer demands sometimes create serious overload problems in support staffs or traditional secretary ranks. For example, a metals company whose income was reduced because of obsolete production techniques decided to diversify, to bolster its profit margins. As diversification proceeded, mergers and acquisitions caused great increases in paperwork and correspondence and overloaded the support staff. There was an immediate need to increase staff size or implement an alternate method. In this case, improvement and productivity were gained through organizing a word processing and administrative support staff and implementing the appropriate electronics in the office. Typing time was reduced in the word processing center, and the traditional secretary was placed in an administrative support mode to absorb more of the routine functions of management. The result: an increase in the efficiency and productivity of the office without changing the number of people.

THE AREAS OF CHANGE

Managers should recognize that changes can be implemented in one or more areas: (1) technology, (2) organizational structure, (3) employee behavior, and/or (4) management styles, techniques, and organizational culture.

TECHNOLOGY   Technological change is most widely seen in the form of computers that address office functions ranging from typing to management decision making.

The computer population grew from approximately 15 in the early 1950s to 6500 in the 1960s. International Data Corporation has estimated that by 1986 there will be over 8 million computers installed in the United States, over 17 million terminals, and over 5 million word processing/electronic typing workstations—more than three times the number of keyboards in place today.

The degree to which an organization maintains its competitive advantage is often determined by how well it adopts technological innovation. Because word processing got its start in the 1960s and grew slowly, there is little information about dollar investment at that time. However, it was minimal.

New methods of creating and typing communications, storing messages, teleconferencing, communication-link networks, worldwide satellite communications, records processing, and management forecasting will all be a routine part of the integrated electronic office of the future. Evidence of this trend is reflected in the 1981-82 Buying Influence/Penetration Study conducted by Modern Office Procedures (see Figure 1).

ORGANIZATIONAL STRUCTURE   Most organizations planning for new technology in the office find that changing the organizational framework (the jobs, tasks, and reporting relationships within the support staff stucture) is a key part of the introduction.

The main reasons for redesigning jobs in the electronic office environment are to improve the quality and quantity of work and to reduce the cost of performing it. Also, the planners and managers who make changes must create a working atmosphere that encourages motivation and job satisfaction.

Feasibility studies often reveal that work specialization among the clerical and secretarial staff is needed and that certain job functions should be eliminated, some jobs simplified, job advancement patterns charted, and supervision responsibilities modified.

The American Management Association estimates that large corporations now undergo at least one major reorganization every two years, for a variety of reasons: diversification of products, expansion of internal operations, acquisition of other businesses, or introduction of technology into the office.

EMPLOYEE BEHAVIOR   Planning organizational change at all levels of management has become a part of business life. Within the administrative ranks, the rate of change has accelerated in recent years, because of the need for new career opportunities and the need for internal training programs for support staff

Office Automation Item	Projected Total Expenditure
Word processing equipment	$2,783,597,488
Word processing peripherals	1,177,118,624
Dictation equipment	261,282,180
WP, dictation, magnetic media and related supplies	223,675,376
Interconnect phone systems	2,618,081,076
Micrographics equipment	538,656,895
Micrographics supplies	363,214,344
Filing equipment—hard copy only	295,969,835
Filing supplies	261,493,420
Conventional office furniture	2,172,049,353
Open-plan furniture/partition systems	2,274,325,186
Electronic typewriters	616,808,118
Convenience copiers	1,244,617,002
High-speed copiers/duplicators	1,517,260,185
Copier/duplicator supplies	921,651,780
Paper handling equipment	178,414,925
Mailroom equipment	515,706,772
Personal computers	488,539,856
Small business computers	2,646,741,435
Programmable calculators	158,369,840
Computer peripherals	4,510,808,981
EDP software	1,437,203,265
EDP magnetic media/related supplies	373,114,272
EDP filing	365,997,780

Figure 1   Buying influence/penetration study. *Source:* Modern Office Procedures Survey, 1982.

within the automated office. Change probably has the most impact on employee behavior. Almost all changes, technological or organizational, result in changes in employees' attitudes or behavior patterns. When technology creates jobs with higher skill requirements, traditional occupations are changed, upgraded, modified, and eliminated.

Managers are now using behavioral science techniques to improve motivation and employee productivity. More and more emphasis is being put on the importance of human needs in daily operations. The need to provide career opportunity and career progression for the support staff (heretofore a rather stable group of employees) has caused management to study the effects of behavioral techniques for implementing attitudinal changes. The steps involved in introducing change will be discussed later in this chapter.

When managers make changes that affect employee attitude or behavior, the success or failure of the change may well depend on whether workers perceive personal rewards or benefits stemming from the change, whether they have the capability to learn new skills, and whether they in fact *want* to learn them. The scope of communication and quality of orientation and training play an important role in successful changes.

The success of the behavioral change that takes place in any organization depends to a large degree upon management's attitude toward its organizational culture. The way that management communicates organization goals and the way employees perceive them determine that culture, which includes values, attitudes, degree of competitiveness, commitment, and top management's approach to decision making (see Figure 2).

MANAGEMENT STYLES, TECHNIQUES, AND ORGANIZATIONAL CULTURE

Top managers from major companies such as IBM, ITT, Digital Equipment Corporation, Delta Airlines, and Atlantic Richfield have said that change can only be effective if it has the unqualified backing of top and middle management.

Top management always sets the style and example in an organization—by its standards and values, by its conservatism or liberalism in attitudes, by the way it solves problems, and by the way it treats others. Its attitudes and techniques quickly filter downward. Lower management levels will most likely follow those patterns, because they perceive them

Figure 2   Behavorial change is often difficult to accept and is usually very obvious.

to be what their superiors want. In other words, if there is unilateral and arbitrary decision making, management by intimidation, or corporate infighting at the top, chances are that the same characteristics will be found at all levels. The more strained and unstable the psychological atmosphere at the lower levels, the greater the difficulty in implementing truly effective changes.

A critical factor in the process of change is a phased-in introduction, so that those involved have an opportunity to participate, understand, provide input, and adjust to the change without being pushed too quickly. The implementation of change by edict or by force often results in employee fear of loss of status or job.

People usually resist when change is first introduced. How well they ultimately accept change depends on how well they understand the need for it and how it affects them.

THE *DON'TS* OF IMPLEMENTING CHANGE

The following example identifies the *don'ts* of change and shows what can happen if a new system fails to receive the unqualified support of top management and how lack of communication can dissipate the benefits.

In 1972, the management of a large insurance company decided to implement word processing, administrative support, and centralized filing. The decision was based solely on a proposal made by one vendor of word processing equipment. Management authorized the purchase without assigning someone to be responsible for implementing the system.

Three years later the secretarial staff was discontented, morale had dipped to an all-time low, productivity was down, turnaround of typing was slow, and the quality of the documents was unacceptable. Management wondered what had gone wrong and sought assistance from an outside consultant.

An initial study by the vendor was performed, but there were no standards against which to measure productivity or to determine areas of needed improvement. Three years had passed without the collection of productivity information. First, benchmarks had to be established for the purpose of measuring existing systems. Work specialization among the staff was implemented, procedures were established, and the supervisor was upgraded.

Once more, management said to go ahead, but still did not follow the consultant's recommendation to throw unequivocal support to the new system and delegate the responsibility and authority for implementing it. Management did not actively participate in the implementation—an indication of its partial commitment.

Within two more years, clerical productivity had increased as determined by benchmark (standards within the industry) figures, cost savings had been realized, and support staff morale had improved somewhat. But the system had still not fulfilled its management productivity potential. Upon entering the company, new managers did not perceive the support of top management. They did not feel compelled to modify their methods of working to fit into the existing system. Consequently, additional secretarial staff was added, operations were decentralized, and word processing/administrative support as a concept was disbanded. Additional costs in equipment and staff resulted from a lack of management coordination and commitment.

UNSUCCESSFUL ATTEMPTS AT CHANGE

Unsuccessful attempts at change are characterized by the following patterns:

1. There is a lack of central control and change begins from a variety of starting points and occurs to varying degrees. Managers and staff are allowed to accept and utilize only those aspects of any recommended system that they desire to use. Therefore, inequitable treatment of staff soon becomes apparent to those within the system.

2. Politics are allowed to interfere. Lengthy decision-making and study processes are characterized in the group approach to investigation. Although the committee or task force provides broader participation of personnel, it may create political situations that are not in the best interests of the total organization.

3. The implementation of change does not follow rational sequential steps. One implementation phase does not logically follow or overlap with another. For example, procedures may be prepared but not well communicated; moreover, management may not be sufficiently committed to carrying out procedures or to undertaking training in new methods such as dictation, use of secretaries, time management, and the art of delegation.

4. The introduction of change appears to come via dictate or mandate, as opposed to management's seeking the participation of support staff in the joint preparation of procedures that are acceptable and workable to all members of the group.

This example identifies more *don'ts* for implementing change. The project manager in charge of implementation in the example did not accept the accuracy of a study that recommended word processing and new procedures. He failed to communicate to the staff, refused to learn tasks performed by the people on the support staff, and did not become familiar with their functions. He saw the project only as a job that had to get done, and not an opportunity to gain the benefits of a restructured integrated office environment. Inequitable workloads, lack of procedures, and low morale resulted.

THE *DO'S* OF IMPLEMENTING CHANGE

Compare the foregoing unsuccessful scenario with that of a company that approached change in a positive and committed manner. This latter illustrates the *do's* of change.

The management of a major financial firm saw the need for change. Executives determined that the company did not have internal talent or the time to satisfactorily study its own operation. An outside consultant was engaged, a study was performed, a detailed analysis was completed, and potential cost justification was projected. Opportunities for productivity improvements and for improved morale were identified. However, to realize the benefits, management had to make a basic commitment to change its way of working with the support staff. First, management established objectives for (1) improving employee morale; (2) assigning specialized tasks to the persons with the appropriate skill level; (3) training support staff and managers in time-saving techniques; and (4) establishing guidelines to measure improvements in the operation.

Having determined these goals, management appointed a supervisor to implement recommendations and to be responsible for meeting the objectives. Not only did the firm meet its objectives, but it also established upward mobility and career opportunity for the support staff, because of the creation of new supervisory and management positions.

Forced austerity programs or identified performance problems are conditions that cause top management to enforce successful change. In identifying these types of problems, management becomes aware that solutions are not simple.

Another requirement for productive change is that executive or top management understand technology and the potential benefits that it offers. An appointed individual within the organization (or a consultant) must explore and examine recognized problems, working with top management and deriving authority from that level. Once the individual has been appointed, employees should be informed in advance that their procedures and their duties will be analyzed in hopes of improving work flow.

All levels of management must support this feasibility study. The study should involve all levels within the organization in the fact-finding process, interviews, brainstorming sessions, and data collection, in order to identify a need for improvement.

Based upon results of the study, the designated leader presents to top management recommendations for solutions through either structural change, technological change, or modification of procedures. These opportunities for improvement are discussed with top management. The following steps are necessary to implement successfully any new program:

1. Setting up implementation steps in a logical order of progression.
2. Getting top management to commit to and support every step in the program.
3. Organizing and scheduling orientation and training sessions for all people involved in the changes.
4. Establishing methods of measuring performance, to determine productivity increases and other forms of improvement.

FACTORS FOR SUCCESSFUL INTRODUCTION OF CHANGE

It is important to introduce change in an appropriate manner, to assure successful implementation.

The improvement of productivity should be the key reason for change. *Productivity* measures the ratio of work done to the time spent doing it. Managers and consultants traditionally thought that clerical productivity was the key area. In 1965, when word processing was first announced, it was felt that this was the alternate panacea to improved clerical productivity, in relation to those tasks performed by clerks, clerk typists, stenographers, and secretaries. Further gains in productivity were followed from the introduction of specialization of activities via administrative assistants, administrative support personnel, clerical support, and various expansions of secretarial roles.

Cost

Today the emphasis is also on management productivity, since greater cost savings can be achieved in that area. A number of experts at industry conferences have suggested a productivity improvement for office employees as follows:

Management, 10 to 15 percent.
Secretarial, 20 to 30 percent.
Clerical, 35 to 40 percent.

Actual dollar benefits will of course be higher with increased management productivity, because of the higher salaries paid at that level.

Now the process of changing to a total electronic office is beginning to take place, and in the eighties more emphasis will be placed on this evolution than ever before.

Organization

Too often the electronic office is designed on the basis of advanced technology alone. However, the human aspects of office automation will become critically important to effective managers. In the process of introducing change, technology alone is not the solution to improved productivity. Change must be introduced with a combination of improved technology and modified management styles, philosophies, and techniques.

Objectives   The reasons for change should be clearly outlined and specific objectives defined and agreed upon in order to facilitate change. These objectives can be clearly identified. To improve morale or equity in workload, procedures must be established and the organizational structure modified. To improve clerical productivity, work specialization and technology are necessary. To improve management productivity, work delegation to the appropriate level of competency and the infusion of technology should be implemented. To provide more information more quickly for management forecasting aimed at gaining a competitive advantage, quick information-gathering techniques and information processing technology should be utilized.

Involvement   Another critical element of office change is involvement of all appropriate levels of management support staff and utilization of their expertise and talent (executive decision-making personnel, human resource staff, analytical staff, and/or technical consultants, and so on). The purpose of involving the executive decision-making level is to monitor progress and maintain control and to review the likely impact of the various steps throughout the entire organizations. The purpose of involving the human resources staff (personnel) is to provide the expertise to redevelop, redesign, and/or restructure job descriptions and appropriate reporting relationships. The purpose of involving the analytical groups is to collect information and data and to analyze and define what is revealed by that data—both statistical data and subjective collection of feelings and thoughts. Technological assistants or equipment analysts also may be involved, to evaluate and assess appropriate technology in order to find the most effective cost/benefit ratio.

Communication   Following the decision to implement change, extensive orientation and communication about the process of change must be given to those individuals and departments involved, so that they will begin to accept their changing functional roles and reporting relationships. This process also provides management with the opportunity to evaluate how satisfactorily acceptance is growing and the ability to make a final determination of the extent of change to be achieved and the results to be expected. Specifics about this orientation and communications process are provided in later chapters.

Education   Another essential step is recognition that change takes place only through a learning process. That learning process is referred to as the learning curve—the period of time from the introduction of any specific change to the time when savings result from that change. The learning process means that the transition from operating one method to operation of another requires an investment of money at the outset. The length of time required depends on the degree of change and the size of the organization

Figure 3 Commitment to change and forward-thinking management are essential to successful implementation of change.

in which change takes place. A general rule for training costs in a changing environment is that 25 percent of the system's costs should be devoted to the education and training required to implement a new approach.

Flexibility   The design of any office system should be flexible enough to respond to users' needs and requests. Traditionally the office environment has been responsive to users and has undergone change quickly to meet needs, and it will continue to do so. This flexibility should be a recognized factor for success in implementing change.

Successful change is a dynamic process, and one that should be accepted as an ongoing management challenge. At the same time, change provides an opportunity for staff members to modify and improve their career plans and progress.

In summary, management of change requires that executives commit to change, set clear objectives, and establish the right organizational culture or climate. They must follow up and control the change. They must be aware of technology as it relates to their organization. They must recognize the need for education and training, as well as behavioral modification (see Figure 3).

Although these steps may not guarantee success, they will improve its likelihood, and at the same time reduce the number of problems confronting a manager who implements change.

CHAPTER 11

MANAGEMENT'S ROLE

OBJECTIVES

In this chapter you will learn about
1. The importance of management commitment.
2. The real costs of office labor.
3. The benefits of a total support structure, including office automation.
4. The steps necessary to achieve the integrated office.
5. The issues related to the change process.
6. The scope of the roles and commitment of various levels of management.

Change can be successfully implemented only when the management of an organization commits itself to the need for innovation and is involved in the process of change. *Commitment* may be defined as pledging one's support and displaying one's belief in a process through involvement. *Involvement* may be defined as taking part in, or being included. Commitment and involvement are major factors in successful organizational change.

Management should be highly visible in the change process and make sure that others do not wonder where it stands. The organizational culture, or the attitudes and perceptions of others, will be greatly influenced by management's role. Management's leadership, or lack of leadership, directly relates to whether the change is accepted or rejected by others.

What management is willing or not willing to do affects what can be done and how those who implement it can proceed.

This chapter will explore the process of acquiring management's commitment, the extent of management's involvement, and the roles of the various levels of management in the implementation of office automation. A change in policy is shown in the way an organization handles certain issues when converting to the integrated office, since the change process involves human, structural, procedural, and technological issues.

ACQUIRING MANAGEMENT COMMITMENT

Management's commitment is essential whether change is implemented at the introductory level or at advanced levels.

The process of involving management in a program of change and guiding it smoothly through evolutionary or developmental levels requires the following: (1) understanding the traditional office versus the office of the future as to how they relate to office functions and productivity, (2) selling management on the benefits of total integration of the various system and equipment components and functions, (3) providing the facts to support the benefits that will warrant management's commitment to automating the office, and (4) determining the steps needed to achieve an integrated office, as shown in Figure 1.

Understanding the Traditional Office versus the Office of the Future

Management was content with the traditional office until escalating costs and inefficiencies started to attract attention. Frequently, management personnel are neither aware of the benefits of office technology nor sufficiently knowledgeable about the concept to commit to its application.

Surveys of management decision makers have revealed some interesting perceptions and attitudes about the electronic office.[1]

---

[1] *"Word Processing, A Survey of Perceptions and Attitudes of Top Management,"* a study conducted by Starch Inra Hooper, Inc., for *Newsweek*, 1977, pp. 2–3.

1. They have a superficial understanding of new concepts (such as word processing).
2. They have hazy notions of how technology might be integrated and used on an organizationwide basis.
3. They believe that the problems outweigh the advantages.
4. They presume there will be negative personnel reactions that will disrupt work flow.
5. They express a lack of confidence in obtaining accurate cost/benefit analysis.
6. They need to know how to implement a system.
7. They are concerned that equipment cannot be used productively without intensive education and persuasion.
8. They believe that each system must be custom-designed to meet the needs of a specific organization.

Some of the above attitudes are myths and misconceptions; others are accurate. Sometimes their validity is based on whether systems are intro-

Figure 1 Achieving successful office integration requires the evaluation through various levels of communication and acceptance.

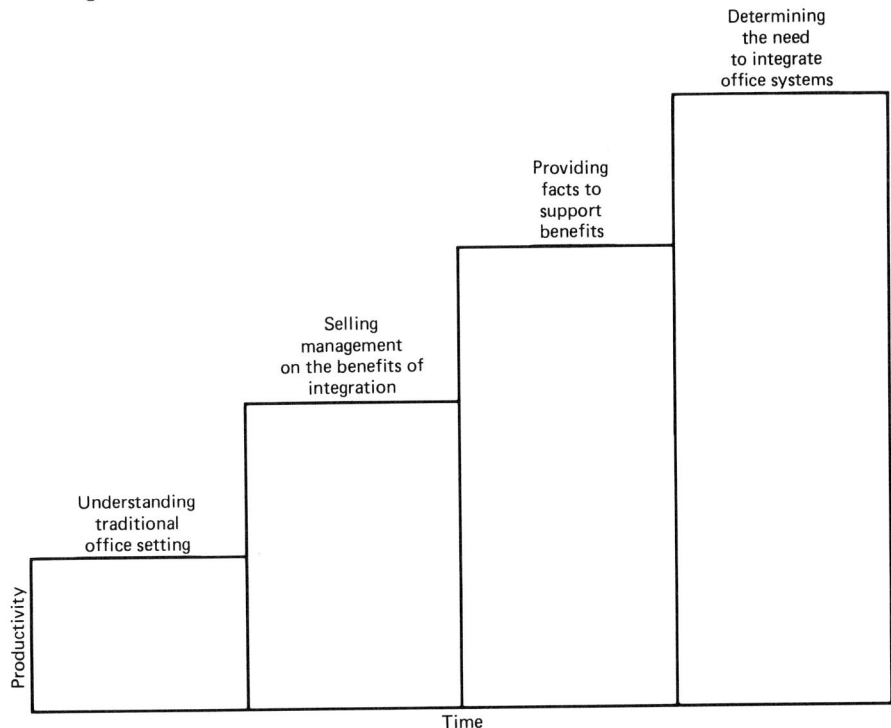

duced because of solid organizational requirements and whether they are implemented in a proper manner.

In the past, top management has seldom been concerned with office productivity and costs. But as white-collar workers have become the largest part of the work force and labor costs have escalated, a new consciousness about office productivity and costs has been developing. Payroll costs alone, however, do not comprise the entire cost of labor. The national average cost of fringe benefits is now about 37 percent of payroll costs, with some businesses providing benefits at a 50 to 60 percent level. Because of the lack of supervision and controls, poor workload distribution, and idle time, office workers make effective use of only 40 to 60 percent of their worktime, according to observers. Figure 2 provides a view of the total real costs of office labor. When one recognizes that these probable real costs are stated at conservative levels, they are startling.

Now that the real cost and productivity aspects of the office have greater bearing on overall organizational effectiveness and competitiveness, it is important for decision makers to gain a more thorough understanding of office functions in their organizations. With more in-depth knowledge, they will recognize that the advantages of office technology outweigh any problems. If personnel recognize the benefits both to the organization and to themselves, negative reactions may be avoided and disruptions in workflow will be minimal.

To dispel the myths and misconceptions surrounding office automation, intensive education and persuasion is necessary at all levels. Annual budgets for education and training will not only improve skill levels but also reduce resistance. It is important that management commit to the education and training of all office employees.

Education of top management personnel has helped speed the acceptance of the concepts of office automation. Current articles and other

Figure 2 Probable real costs of office labor are significantly higher than actual salary.

Annual Salary	Salary Plus 37% Fringe Benefit Average	Real Salary Cost for 60% Productivity
$7,000	$9,590	$15,983
$10,000	$13,700	$22,833
$13,000	$17,810	$29,683
$18,000	$24,660	$41,100
$24,000	$32,880	$54,800
$30,000	$41,100	$68,500
$35,000	$47,950	$79,917
$40,000	$54,800	$91,333

literature contain frequent references to the infusion of technology. Vendors are certainly impressing upon top management the need for technology. Many seminars and conferences are being held on the subject of the changing office, and it is a frequent subject of discussion among the managers of various organizations.

The Office Technology Research Group, established to educate and help senior managers and employers from various disciplines, also provides a forum through which they exchange viewpoints and information. John J. Connell, the executive director, emphasizes the need for education as follows:

> Management must understand that the office of the future is not a variety of unrelated technologies, but a variety of methods of moving information which must be connected together in compatible networks. Senior management must be taught to think of all the technologies, not just computers. . . . Managers resist technology. That resistance must be broken down by accommodation, not by fighting them. Education is the key. Senior management, fellow managers, employees, vendors and academicians must all be told of the real needs of the office of the future.

SELLING MANAGEMENT ON THE BENEFITS The major benefit of a total support structure, including office automation, is its demonstrated ability to improve productivity, or output per hour, within the office environment. Improved office productivity has become one of the important results of implementing word processing, the initial step to integrating the total office.

The original emphasis on improving office productivity focused on secretarial/clerical activity. Word processing and administrative support systems have proved their worth in improving productivity in those activities. Executive and professional productivity also should be a major target of office automation.

The labor costs of managers and professionals (also called knowledge workers) are usually two to four times greater than those for secretaries and other office support people. This fact has been ignored too often. When the ratio of professionals or managers to support personnel becomes too high or is not appropriate to the nature of the work, office support personnel cannot deliver work according to schedules or in the quantity or quality needed. The result is that a highly paid knowledge worker will spend valuable time performing clerical activities, such as running photocopies, which could be performed by a support clerk earning far less—perhaps half the salary of the manager. Research shows that managers and professionals spend much of their time on clerical tasks and are not as productive in their own specialized activities as they should be. Office automation, by one estimate, can save an average of 15 percent of a manager's time in the near future.[2]

The introduction of office automation with too much emphasis on clerical productivity may actually produce a negative impact on professionals and managers. For example, in one firm the supervisor's goal of improved clerical productivity led to the requirement that all work brought to word processing should be in a form ready for keyboarding. The result was that knowledge workers were observed laboriously copying in longhand certain aspects of computer printout that they wanted included in tables. Also, word processing personnel did not make additional copies on a copier; presumably, these were to be run by administrative support personnel. All too often, managers and professionals were observed standing in line at convenience copiers to obtain needed copies. It is little wonder that word processing was poorly received.

Any office automation system should offer clearly visible benefits to all. Human nature is such that all people tend to view anything from a "what's in it for me" perspective. Individuals are likely to view potential improvements in office productivity from a personal viewpoint. A market research survey of executives from Fortune 500 companies revealed the reactions reported in Figure 3. Note the high level of agreement about overall office productivity, compared with the much lower level of agreement where personal relationships and convenience are threatened. Whether those affected are top- or middle-management personnel or sup-

Figure 3　Executive responses to office productivity questions. *Source:* "Management Attitudes Toward Office Productivity and Equipment Suppliers," a survey designed and conducted by Belknap Marketing Services for *Fortune Market Research*, February, 1976, p. 15.

Questions Directed to Management	*Total Agree*
Office productivity is just as important as factory productivity	96%
Office productivity in my company could be greatly improved	89%
The costs of the most modern office machines are more than offset by their greater productivity.	73%
Traditional boss-secretary relationships are a luxury in these days of heavy pressure on costs.	48%
I would be willing to give up my personal secretary if my typing could be done faster and more efficiently.	29%

[2] "Productivity and Information Systems for Tomorrow's Office," special advertising section, *Fortune*, September 22, 1980, p. 46.

port staff, all levels need to be shown sufficient personal benefits to win commitment and willingness to change.

There are many additional specific benefits of a total support system, such as better communication at a faster rate of speed, work specialization for greater efficiency, flexibility to fulfill changing needs, and improved direction and control of office employees and workload.

These changes improve productivity at the management level. In addition, organizations will gain these advantages: (1) visible career progressions for employees, (2) control of equipment purchases, (3) decreased personnel requirements, (4) better quality work, (5) increased support to management, (6) decreased operation costs, and (7) increased net profit.

The process of convincing management of the benefits of office automation is easier and more effective with clear identification and conversion to profit figures. Improved productivity equates to dollar savings, and dollar savings mean an increased chance of management commitment.

PROVIDING THE FACTS   Such benefits were apparent in the case of a Midwest manufacturing corporation that discovered that secretaries had unequal workloads and that priorities were handled on an individual basis rather than on an established priority basis. Some executive secretaries were overloaded with document preparation or chart preparation; others had to create work or had considerable idle time, especially when their superiors were out of town.

Peak workloads differed among departments and were not coordinated in terms of effectively utilizing idle or nonproductive secretaries and other clerical personnel across departmental boundaries. While some departments were inundated and worked overtime, others had excess time available. Comparison of the seasonal and peak work activity of several departments indicated that cross-staffing exchanges between departments could compensate for peaks and valleys. At that time there was no plan for interchanging trained personnel for similar jobs in several departments.

The keyboarding rate of individual administrative personnel ranged from 18 to 83 lines per hour. The rate for all secretarial/stenographic personnel averaged 50 lines per hour. Industrywide statistics show that personnel in a word processing center using stand-alone equipment are capable of keyboarding, at the very least, 150 finished lines per hour.

As a result of the findings, a need for change was established. Conditions indicated that benefits could be attained from specialization of function or division of work into document preparation and administrative support teams; in this way, peaks and valleys could be minimized and balanced workloads achieved. Further study indicated a variety of uses as well as duplicate keyboarding of data base information. All of these findings led to identification of the need for full office automation. Consequently, the integrated office approach was implemented and a network was developed among subsidiary offices and customers consisting of compatible communicating word processing units, computers, and electronic mail systems.

Even though an 83 percent increase in the number of managers requiring support was experienced, existing support staff members were able to achieve a 98 percent increase in their productivity and were able to handle the increased growth in management head count. As a result of this increased productivity, management was able to see the benefits of the total support approach.

Along with the specific productivity benefits described above, there are personal benefits to the people in organizations that implement a total integrated support system, including satisfaction resulting from personal achievement, personal growth, orchestration of a successful system, use of teamwork, and opportunities for career progression.

TAKING STEPS TOWARD THE INTEGRATED OFFICE

The need for increased office productivity and the use of electronic technology are two factors that most experts agree will be major influences on the office of the future. However, those who want change still must learn how to establish and achieve their goals, if they are to make the office of the future a reality.

The goals of any office automation effort are classic management objectives: to increase productivity, to reduce costs, to save time and money, to improve quality, to shorten the production cycle, and so on. The important thing to remember here is that goals should not be defined in terms of hardware, systems, or organization structures—they are the means to achieve the goals.

Goals of office systems change. Building the system is evolutionary. If business volume increases, the type of business activity changes, and so must the organization structure, jobs, workloads, and equipment mix.

Organizations that start out to build an office system should look upon the entire project as a climb up a ladder. The first rung may represent the installation of word processing equipment designed to improve the clerical/secretarial activity. The second rung may be the interfacing of the WP equipment with a phototypesetter. The third rung may be the adding of communications to link up with a computer system or a remote location, and so on (see Figure 4).

A successful step from one stage to the next depends on the strong base of the first. In other words, managers must measure and prove the performance against the goals set for the first stage before embarking on the second. If the word processing system is not operating effectively in the secretarial environment, it is not likely to function well for phototypesetting.

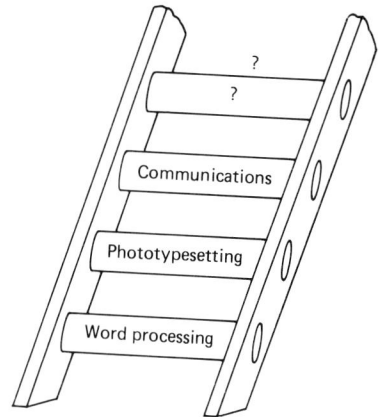

Figure 4 Office systems hierarchy requires phasing in one step at a time.

The proper organizational structure for management of both the functions and the human resources is the basis for increased productivity and better utilization of management time. There are many aspects to be considered: people, procedures, equipment, attitudes, perceptions, and involvement, as well as commitment.

In making the transition, management should provide time to develop the new office structure in logical steps. Simplistic approaches to implementing office automation are being replaced with strategic plans that include the entire organization. An example of an implementation schedule listing areas of planning is shown in Figure 5.

Special attention should be exercised to avoid the stress, resistance, confusion, and delays that often result from the introduction of new procedures and new machines. Dramatic changes affect employees' morale and sense of security, at all levels. Without a complete and satisfactory explanation of how changes will benefit them, employees may fear demotions or job loss, or finding themselves with obsolete skills or losing authority. These fears could result in negative attitudes, resistance to learning, power struggles, and a tense working atmosphere.

During this evolutionary process, all levels of management should be evaluating, in relation to long-range goals, the benefits of the various functions to be integrated: word processing, data processing, reprographics, micrographics, telecommunications, phototypesetting, voice transmission, teleconferencing, electronic mail, and overall communications.

IMPLEMENTATION ISSUES

The implementation process for the integrated office requires that management take an active role in addressing issues related to (1) adding technology to existing environments, (2) changing the way people work,

MANAGEMENT SUPPORT IMPLEMENTATION

EVENT SCHEDULES

WEEK OF

FUNCTION

Management Support Study,
Analyze Needs, Recommendation
of Equipment

Management Presentation
& Commitment to Program

Ordering Equipment

Selection of Manager

Selection of Personnel

Restructuring of Reporting
Relationships

Preparing Job Descriptions
Drafting Procedures

Installation of Equipment

Train: Secretaries & Principals

On—Line Implementation

Ongoing Design of
Stored Documents

Ongoing Updating of
Procedures

Management Reports
Prepared Regularly

PHASE 1

PHASE 2

PHASE 3

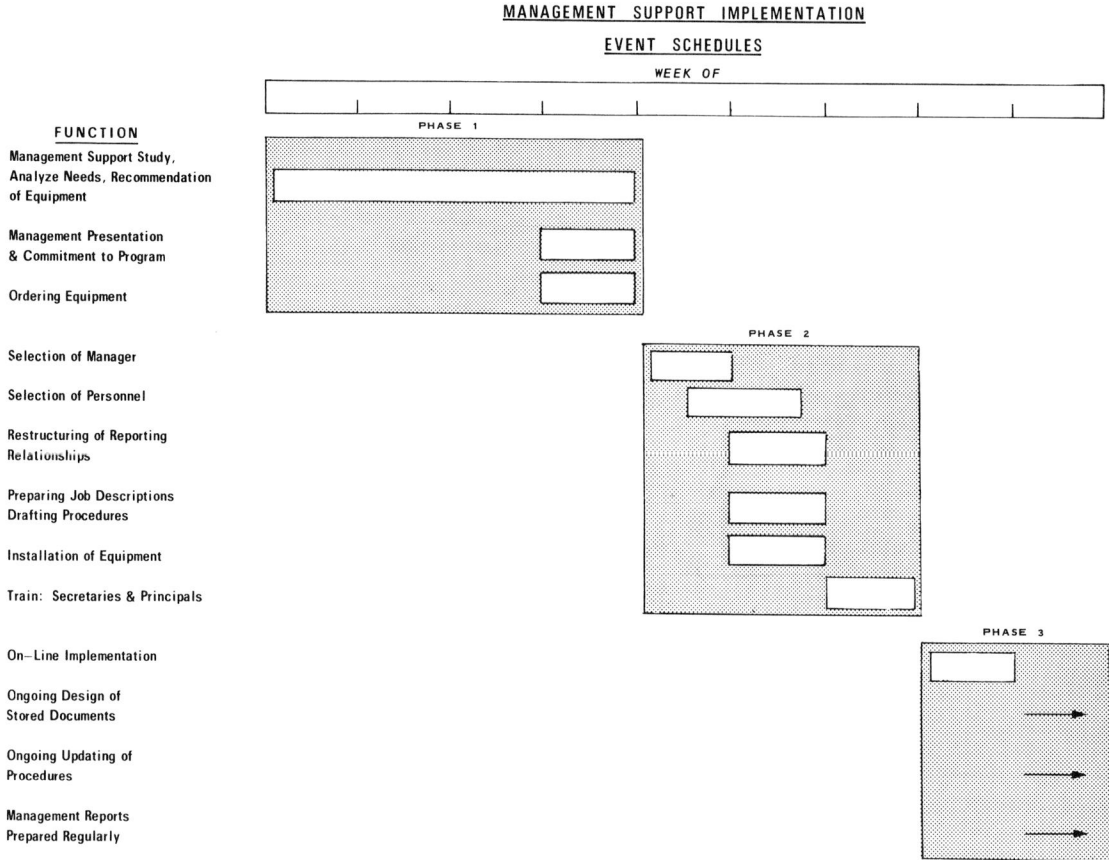

Figure 5   Implementation schedule for the electronic office.

(3) dealing with the stress and fatigue factors that accompany increased demands, (4) preparing procedures for a smooth transition from traditional operations to automation, and (5) addressing the concerns relating to networking and technology. These issues can be placed into four categories: (1) human, (2) structural, (3) procedural, and (4) technological.

HUMAN ISSUES   Human issues encompass the perception and reaction of office staff to office automation. When people are fearful of what they do not understand, stress and fatigue play an important role in their resistance to change. Lack of understanding will also cause adverse reactions such as resistance to change and employee turnover. Therefore, communication to employees about management planning processes is important. Issues to be addressed are

1. *Continuing education.* Will the organization provide ongoing training on new equipment and procedures?

2. *Health hazards.* Will the organization provide the right physical environment and working conditions to reduce stress and fatigue with the introduction of new office tools?

3. *Work measurement.* Why is it necessary to measure staff? What is expected of staff? How does work measurement aid planning?

4. *Isolationism.* If there is work specialization, how will it affect the employees?

STRUCTURAL ISSUES

Management must take an aggressive, positive approach. The "wait and see what will happen" perspective in relation to office automation is not appropriate. This modification to historical patterns of management thinking revolves around such issues as

1. *Management of office automation.* Who will manage the development of a system? Who is responsible for control of costs?

2. *Implementation approach.* Will office automation be phased in or will it be a project in total?

3. *Centralization versus decentralization.* Will equipment be placed by application needs? Will the structure be established for central support services? Will there be special user applications at a variety of locations? Who will supervise the various aspects of technology?

4. *Organizational impact.* How will office automation change traditional employee roles? What type of management structure will be used? Who will develop the functional descriptions?

PROCEDURAL ISSUES

Converting the traditional office to an electronic office must be accompanied by the setting of rules. In the office setting, these rules are generally termed operating procedures or guidelines. Procedural issues to be addressed are

1. *Preparation of procedures.* Who is responsible for drafting working guidelines for an office that has been relatively unstructured? What aspects of the office will have written procedures? Who will receive training and orientation on those procedures?

2. *Batch information or interactive information.* Will the system be set up to batch information for a period of time before it is communicated to another point? Is there a need for interactive communications? What technology will address these requirements?

3. *Security/privacy.* Are guidelines for security of information necessary? Should there be a policy for privacy of the content of messages that go into a system? Who will determine this policy?

4. *Training.* What kind of training will be provided? Will it be ongoing? What level in the organization will receive equipment training? Procedures training? Supervisory training?

5. *Standards.* What areas of the organization require productivity guidelines? Will there be ongoing measurement or periodic audit? How often will the organization want reports on productivity? What justification will be required?

6. *Data base.* Who will handle the fragmented data-base environment so that adequate and meaningful information can be provided?

TECHNOLOGICAL ISSUES The technological issues center around the degree of systems integration required to meet the needs of an organization. Issues include

1. *Total system versus phase-in.* Are monies available to implement totally integrated networks of information? Will there be a phased-in, budgeted approach with specific objectives?

2. *Stand-alone workstations versus shared systems.* Are stand-alone systems cost-effective? Will a shared system better meet the needs? Is there a need for personal computers?

3. *Networks.* Does the company need a network? Will it require satellite communications? Does the organization have the talent to implement a network?

4. *Vendor selection.* Is the proposed vendor reliable, stable, financially sound, and progressive? Does it have a track record for prompt service? Will it provide training?

5. *Legal concerns.* Are there safeguards against security leaks? Is there provision for confidentiality of individual information? Is there an audit system to prevent computer theft? Are there software liability issues involved?

6. *System requirements.* How are user needs translated into an integrated system in order to take advantage of existing resources as well as new developments?

7. *Multinational considerations.* What are the issues for multinational companies, particularly transborder data flow? Is the merging of text, data, graphics, and voice really required?

MANAGEMENT'S INVOLVEMENT

Achievement of the goals established for a totally integrated support system demands management's commitment, involvement, and leadership. Management must play a role in implementation by changing the organi-

1. The ability to manage and work with a diverse group of people.
2. A general management perspective.
3. An understanding of organizational relationships.
4. A systems perspective—the ability to recognize the need to be conversant with all levels of management and support and with all technologies.
5. A successful track record in managing projects with the ability to develop short- and long-term plans.
6. An understanding of technology.

Figure 6 Qualities of the electronic office manager. Note the importance of the people aspect of management.

zational culture, for it is through the culture that others are given a sense of how to behave and what they should be doing. Because an organization's culture is so pervasive, changing it becomes one of the most difficult tasks that any chief executive can undertake.[3]

All levels of management must actively participate in the process and possess the ability to manage technology and understand the concepts. The qualities needed in a manager are shown in Figure 6. Managers must be able to manage information *and* people. In a large organization, each level of management has to be involved and have a role to play. In a smaller organization, the same responsibilities may be assigned somewhat fewer managers, but all responsibilities must be assumed and fulfilled.

The basic functions of management are planning, organizing, directing, and controlling. All apply in the changing office. Top management is responsible for conceptualizing for the total organization, middle management for implementing and coordinating details in a given area, and first-line management for maintaining and supervising the ongoing operations at the departmental level. Each level of management has its own level of decision making. Top management is concerned with strategic, long-range decisions, with implications more than 90 days hence. Middle management is more concerned with tactical short-range decisions, with implications from 1 to 30 days hence. The supervisory level must make immediate operational decisions that cannot wait another day. Management involvement and functions at the different levels can be broken down as follows:

TOP MANAGEMENT LEVEL

1. Establish proper long-term organizational goals and objectives to be achieved through an integrated electronic office.

[3] Howard M. Schwartz, "Corporate Culture", *Business Week*, October 27, 1980, p. 149.

2. Establish proper short-term organizational goals and objectives to be achieved through an integrated electronic office.

3. Organize structure and personnel staffing to provide support as needed; make use of technology and specialization of functions.

4. Establish and support policy for achieving the organizational goals for an integrated electronic office.

5. Lead the way by adopting new practices such as machine dictation rather than writing out materials in longhand.

6. Demonstrate and maintain a consistent and positive attitude toward the necessary changes.

7. Maintain communication flow with various areas and departments.

8. Motivate employees to want to achieve goals and objectives.

9. Be aware of problems encountered.

10. Track productivity and cost savings.

11. Delegate the authority to design systems and develop action plans.

12. Evaluate the performance of middle management.

13. Designate appropriate funds for expenditures related to the office.

MIDDLE MANAGEMENT LEVEL

1. Communicate to decision makers the appropriate recommendations concerning conceptual change and its timing.

2. Delegate sufficient authority to enable lower management to make necessary on-the-spot decisions and effectively carry out day-to-day operations.

3. Set up procedures for its areas in harmony with goals and objectives established in the conceptual plan of top management.

4. Assign first-line management the responsibility to prepare and carry out day-to-day procedures.

5. Act as liaison and maintain information flow to both top- and first-line management.

6. Monitor environmental factors affecting the organization.

7. Evaluate the performance of first-line management.

8. Demonstrate and maintain a consistent and positive attitude toward the necessary changes.

9. Be aware of the problems encountered.

10. Track productivity and cost savings.

11. Encourage recommendations or suggestions from personnel who are actively involved in carrying out the functions of the area.

FIRST-LINE SUPERVISORY LEVEL

1. Communicate specific objectives to all those within its span of responsibility, so that employees understand their roles clearly.
2. Meet continually with users and potential users to discuss requirements and needs, identify new applications, resolve any problems, and obtain recommendations on how to serve them better.
3. Encourage recommendations or suggestions from personnel who are actively involved in carrying out the functions of the department.
4. Evaluate the performance of staff.
5. Maintain production records.
6. Maintain communication flow with middle management in its area.
7. Supervise day-to-day operations in a manner consistent with organizational goals and objectives.
8. Track productivity and cost savings.

SUMMARY

Decision making at all levels should be based on information. The procedures for collecting and establishing this base of information will be presented in the next chapter. Effective managers will use this base of information as a tool, however, and will not allow it to constrain them from reaching goals and objectives. The uncertainties of change require management to be flexible, open-minded, and, most important, to be aware of and responsive to human needs.

CHAPTER 12

OFFICE SUPPORT SYSTEMS STUDY

OBJECTIVES

In this chapter you will learn about
1. Feasibility studies, and why they provide a major planning tool.
2. The areas of the automated office in which feasibility studies might be conducted.
3. Why a feasibility study is needed.
4. The need for top management commitment.
5. Possible purposes of the study.
6. The types of information that a feasibility study should reveal.
7. Who should conduct the feasibility study and what preparations should be made before the study.
8. The steps for conducting a study.
9. Various methods for collecting data.

Planning for both short- and long-range goals must be a managed process. The feasibility study is a major planning tool. It focuses on the present and clarifies what the present office is providing and how it is operating. A feasibility study (1) provides benchmarks against which to measure the success of implementation, (2) provides the information necessary to establish work standards of productivity in various areas of the office, and (3) allows management to set objectives based on identified need.

Usually management can easily establish objectives of a general nature—improvement of office employee productivity, for example. However, more precise objectives concerned with improving productivity are far more complex—implementation of an electronic mail system between the home office and branch A by the first of next year, for example.

The question of how employee productivity can be improved can only be answered when there are sound quantitative and qualitative methods of measurement. The feasibility study is the means that management uses to determine if it is presently getting the best possible results or if an investment in new systems and/or office organization will improve efficiency.

In order to make this decision, one must be acquainted with the mechanical, electronic, or manual methods presently employed by the support staff in accomplishing assigned job functions, as well as the procedures used to provide the flow of information to management. One way to determine these methods is to perform a feasibility study.

WHAT IS A FEASIBILITY STUDY?

A feasibility study is a survey of all support functions presently being performed by both management and the support employees of a given area. The purpose of a feasibility study is to determine if a change in present methods is necessary or desirable. The findings also provide a basis for the direction management planning should take. The areas to be studied usually encompass the typing, dictating, administrative, and related office functions, such as the use of information from other departments (data processing, telecommunications, and copy or printing centers, etc.). Analysis of collected information generally results in recommendations concerning any or all of the following necessary functions:

1. Administrative support.
2. Calendaring.
3. Data access.
4. Data entry.
5. Data processing.
6. Dictation.

7. Document distribution.
8. Electronic filing.
9. Electronic mail.
10. Records processing.
11. Regular mail.
12. Scheduling.
13. Self-authored text.
14. Telephone log.
15. Tickler files.
16. Word processing.

The approaches to a study of the feasibility of automation vary according to the size of the organization. For a small office (1-20 employees), the study may involve the completion of questionnaires and the preparation of guesstimates of workload (both discussed later in the chapter).

For a larger organization (more than 20 employees), the methodology may incorporate the overview approach, but generally more detail is required and an in-depth study is performed using work measurement, time sheets (for management and staff), interviews, questionnaires (for management and staff), and detailed charting and analysis. (This methodology is also discussed below, and in the next chapter.)

DETERMINING THE NEED FOR A FEASIBILITY STUDY

A support systems feasibility study is generally prompted by one of the following occurrences:

1. Management perceives a need for improved employee productivity per staff dollar expended.
2. A need is identified for more immediate information, to retain a competitive edge in the decision-making process.
3. An inequity of workload distribution among support staff personnel is causing low morale.
4. A need arises for improved control of capital expenditures for equipment proliferating in the office environment.
5. A lack of compatibility among technologies within the office is defined as a detriment to advanced planning for future technological communications developments.
6. Creation of new structures within the organization results in the need for new or different systems to meet the demands of the new structure.
7. A determination is made that coordinated workflows, restructuring of staff, and the design of organizational policies for equipment purchases are needed.

8. As a result of education about the office of the future and new technology, management perceives a need for greater internal emphasis to be placed on the use of technology and the control of its power.

Once it has been determined that there is a need, management usually decides that a study should be undertaken. Any of the above needs or a combination of needs could cause management to decide to perform a support systems feasibility study.

TOP MANAGEMENT COMMITMENT

Management may be aware that costs in certain areas are excessive but may be reluctant to conduct a study, because it could disrupt the overall routine of the organization. Although management can expect that conducting a study will cost money, the cost of a feasibility study will be recouped on a continuing basis as a result of (1) improved employee productivity, (2) improved configuration of support staff, and (3) improved use of equipment.

Conversely, however, management may be interested in the feasibility of using more technology for instant access to information and may, therefore, cause a study to be undertaken to provide justification for the expenditure of money for equipment.

The decision to initiate a support systems feasibility study must be accompanied by certain understandings.

1. Top management will support the study wholeheartedly.
2. During the study, all people involved should show willingness to accept change and to expect disruption to routine workflow.
3. Management will delegate sufficient authority to the group involved in the study in order to assure that information collected will be valid.

SPECIFIC STUDY PURPOSES

Management and the study team must agree upon both the purposes and the extent of the study to be undertaken.

A costly but very important part of the study is the time invested in overcoming resistance to participating in a study that is perceived as a threatening change. Employees often fear that recommendations will result in structural changes, preparation of new procedures, and implementation of a new approach to the support staff environment that may cost them their jobs. Therefore, they resist the study process.

The overall feasibility study usually should involve these aspects: technological, structural, operational, procedural, and economic feasibility.

Technological feasibility involves examination of specific applications and whether technology is available to meet these applications, together with a review of the direction of likely future technological advancements and their relationship to the specific areas studied. Technological feasibility is concerned with both hardware and software benefits and reliability. Specific applications of individual areas have to be defined and the appropriate technology recommended.

Structural, operational, and procedural feasibility involves determining the degree of change in the structure necessary to implement any proposed technology, as well as determination of appropriate operating procedures. The acceptance level of support and management personnel who must adapt to a new system must also be determined.

Economic feasibility involves determining whether there will be an adequate return on investment of dollars for equipment and training to convert to a modified or restructured system, and an estimate of ongoing savings in the area studied.

One part of economic feasibility that must be understood is that information gathered during the feasibility study provides the data for comparison of "before" implementation with that available "after" implementation. True return on investment can only be determined by the comparison of "before" and "after" performance data.

When an economic feasibility study is evaluated, some subjective estimates of the improved productivity must be provided. These subjective estimates are often reported in terms of an intangible "soft-dollar" justification that is difficult to measure accurately. Examples of soft-dollar benefits are management time savings, improved efficiency on the part of support staff, and instant access to information.

UNDERSTANDING THE STUDY

Because a feasibility study affects the day-to-day working lives of individual support and management personnel, it is extremely important to go beyond the purely quantitative analyses of information. To be effective, the feasibility study requires an understanding by all involved of terms such as *objectivity, subjectivity, quantitative, and qualitative.*

Objectivity is the tendency to deal with things rather than thoughts or feeling; a numerically measurable item.

Subjectivity is the tendency to view things through personal values and interpretations (an individual's feelings are considered a criteron of values); a nonnumerically measurable attribute.

Quantitative denotes the testing of something to find out what the components of the work are, as well as how much of a component there is; that which can be counted or measured.

Qualitative denotes the quality or qualities of components such as the intangible specialties that make up systems; applying to any distinctive or characteristic feature that usually is immeasurable.

The qualitative and subjective information and data collected during a support systems feasibility study directly reflects the employees' perception of how and why things are done within the system. For example, this information directly relates to such factors as employee attitude, morale, and dedication to organizational goals.

On the other hand, quantitative and objective information directly relates to such measurable items as the quantity of work being accomplished, the type of information required by management, and the time it takes to produce this information. Whenever people are being studied, both qualititative and quantitative input are necessary for sound recommendations based upon the results of the feasibility study.

PREPARING FOR A FEASIBILITY STUDY

Several approaches to the feasibility study are available: (1) the use of an in-house study team, with or without advice and counsel from outside experts (consultants); (2) the use of a consultant, with in-house assistance from an assigned staff member; and (3) the use of a study team provided by a vendor, with or without assistance from an assigned in-house member.

Each of the alternatives has advantages and disadvantages. Consultants can provide more objectivity, since they do not work for the firm; and they have technical expertise based upon knowledge and experience of a wide range of companies and philosophies, which can be extremely helpful to an organization. However, the hiring of an outside consultant may involve a high upfront cost.

The choice between hiring an outside consultant and using internal personnel to perform the study may depend on several important considerations, such as

▶ Do in-house personnel have the experience to knowledgeably conduct the study?
▶ Do in-house personnel have the time available, or are they completely tied up on projects already in progress?
▶ What are the budget constraints?
▶ What is the estimated time required and estimated labor cost for in-house personnel to conduct the study?

Vendors usually do not charge to conduct initial studies, since they expect to recover their costs by selling equipment. But such studies can lack objectivity—that is, both the study and resulting recommendations will be slanted toward the vendor's equipment and its capabilities.

An in-house study team with representatives from key office areas—data processing, word processing, records management, reprographics, telecommunications, and so on—can bring to the study an invaluable perspective about the entire organization and what is being done in individual areas. Such team members may already be aware of many of the likely areas of people problems and resistance to change and hence provide guidance in how to avoid certain barriers or problems.

Using personnel from within the organization may pose problems, too. They may lack expertise in the skills needed to conduct a study and lack depth of understanding of the various aspects of total systems support. They may also lack a broad perspective about the total organization and/or about technology and office automation. When final recommendations are made, they may favor those that are more beneficial to the areas they represent. If in-house personnel are selected, they must have the complete backing of management and must be provided the necessary time and training to conduct the feasibility study properly.

The selection of qualified team personnel is a critical part of the feasibility study preparation process. Personnel involved in the feasibility study report should be knowledgeable about data collection techniques, the structure and operational aspects of the organization, and the office support functions. They should also understand the sensitivities of people, in order to incorporate properly the qualitative findings of the study with the quantitative results. Figure 1 illustrates team members for both small and large organizations.

In smaller organizations, it is often practical to have only a secretary and a manager familiar with administrative services serve on the study team. In such cases, an outside consultant probably should be employed to provide guidance on how and what to study, and especially to analyze results and recommend appropriate technology.

In larger organizations, the study team should have a representative of the secretarial staff who is familiar with office functions; a representative from administrative services who is familiar with word processing, phototypesetting, micrographics, and communications; a member of the data processing group; a representative from telecommunications or electronic mail; a member from the methods and procedures group who has knowledge of how to design operating procedures properly; and a member of the

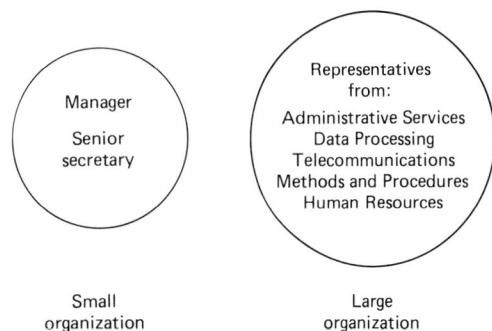

Figure 1 Study team members for large and small organization. Note the involvement of various departments in the large and small organization.

Manager
Senior secretary

Small organization

Representatives from:
Administrative Services
Data Processing
Telecommunications
Methods and Procedures
Human Resources

Large organization

personnel or human resources area who is familiar with testing, preparing job descriptions, and restructuring for organizational development.

If the past education and experience of study team members has not provided them with up-to-date knowledge of the automated environment, it may be helpful to provide outside orientation and briefing. Management should encourage attendance at night classes at universities, colleges, or technical vocational schools; participation in industry seminars; viewing of vendor demonstrations of various equipment options; and subscriptions to trade journals related to the automated office industry.

In preparation for the study, it is important that the study group (1) be familiar with company policy (for example, when the office opens and closes, the traditional privileges regarding coffee breaks and lunch hours, overtime); (2) determine the essential information (and avoid collecting mundane trivia); (3) set up status report periods within the study time frame, in order to maintain the scheduled completion of the study; (4) determine if there are existing logs or reports that can provide quantitative information and save time during the data collection process; and (5) consider how the final data will be presented in the study report for guidance as how information should be collected.

CONDUCTING THE STUDY

Conducting the feasibility study requires following prescribed methods for collecting information. Specific data collection techniques may vary from company to company or within different areas of the same company. However, the generic set of collection and analysis techniques suggested here should apply to most office automation and administrative functions. A determination must be made as to the appropriate forms to be used to collect the required data, in order to make sound recommendations to management. In most organizations these eight steps are recommended.

1. Tour the facility, giving particular attention to the area or unit being studied.
2. Conduct orientation sessions with management personnel.
3. Conduct orientation sessions with all support staff personnel who will be involved in the study.
4. Conduct personal interviews with support staff employees and management individuals.
5. Collect and coordinate information pertaining to the existing organizational structure.
6. Analyze all collected statistics and information and verify the results with the management of a particular department.

7. Prepare a detailed written report.

8. Present the results of the study to management decision makers.

An explanation of each of these steps follows in this and the next chapter.

TOUR OF A tour should be conducted for the consultant and/or members of the
FACILITY study team during work hours by an executive or supervisor who knows
the area being studied and who can explain the functions being performed
at the various locations. A tour of the target area after working hours is
also helpful in determining the degree of efficiency being exercised at the
various workstations based on how they are left at the end of the day. This
is an example of a subjective and qualitative form of measurement.

In addition, the study team and/or consultant can observe the area being
studied, to learn about the construction of the building and walls to determine the possibilities for making layout changes. The use of movable
partitions and modular furniture (also referred to as open-plan, landscape, or systems furnishings) can aid in the effective use of office space,
often placing more people and equipment in the same area than traditional layouts could accommodate and thus permitting sharing resources
(staff and equipment). These steps are illustrated in Figure 2.

Figure 2 Steps in conducting a feasibility study.

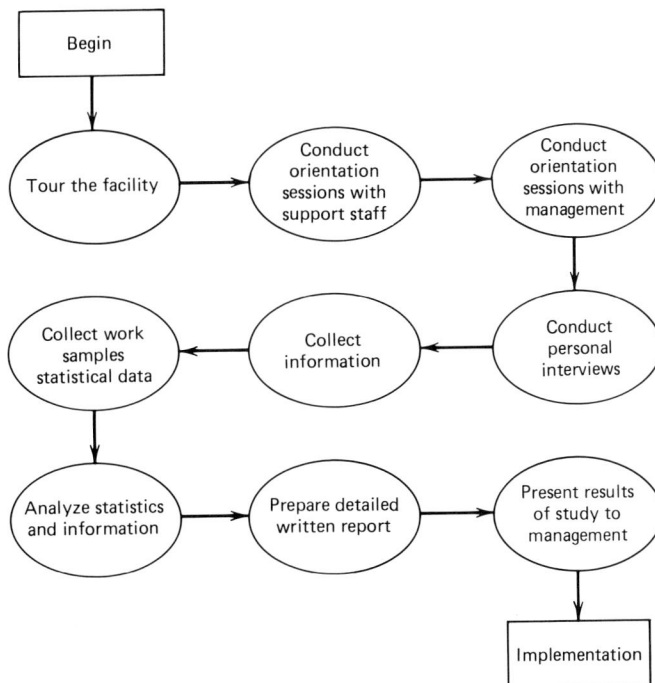

MANAGEMENT ORIENTATION SESSIONS

Although some part of management has determined the need for the study and established a team to carry out the study, many other members of management need to be informed about what is to occur. Depending upon the size of the department or group to be studied, more than one orientation session may be necessary, as groups should consist of 10 to 12 participants.

These sessions are intended to inform all involved management and supervisory personnel of the purpose of the study, and to assure them that the project has the backing of top management. These sessions also provide the opportunity to communicate fully the goals and purposes of the study and how extensive the study will be. A management orientation session provides the opportunity to explain the potential benefits of any modified system that may result from the feasibility study. Potential quantitative benefits such as controlled equipment purchases and hard-dollar savings from elimination of overtime, as well as qualitative benefits such as more equitable workload distribution and career progressions for support staff, may be presented. This session should be viewed as an opportunity for educating management in the process of change.

SUPPORT STAFF ORIENTATION SESSIONS

During these sessions, study forms are distributed to all employees who will be collecting data. The project leader or other study team member should explain the purpose of the form and how to fill it out, and should answer all questions concerning its use in the orientation session. These sessions provide the opportunity for quelling rumors that sometimes float among the support staff concerning the intentions of the study, and apprehension over the presence of the study team and/or consultant in the department or unit. If these rumors and concerns are addressed in a group session, all employees will receive the same explanations, communicated by the people directly responsible for conducting the feasibility study. The study team members and/or the consultant should stress that the feasibility study does not involve evaluation of individual employees.

PERSONAL INTERVIEWS

Interviews with members of management and with support staff individuals provide an excellent means of obtaining and verifying quantitative information or data. If objections arise or resistance is apparent, the interviewer (study team member and/or consultant) should reassure support employees that a proposed new system will not jeopardize their job security. Their cooperation and participation in the feasibility study is necessary to ensure the validity of data collected. Interviews should be scheduled in advance, so that the individuals being interviewed can plan their time accordingly and minimize disruption of their normal work. Scheduling also gives employees an opportunity to preplan and note specific ideas or problems relating to existing operations.

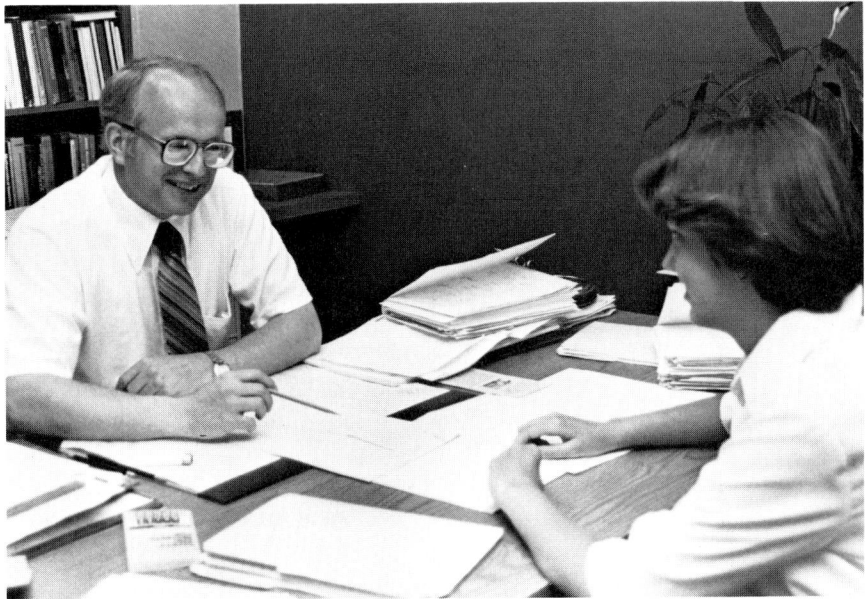

Figure 3 Individualized personal interview requires that the interviewer be sensitive to the staff person's needs.

Study leaders should obtain clearance from supervisors before interviewing support staff individuals, and explain to the supervisor about the results expected from the interviews. Although supervisors may want to accompany the interviewer during the interviews, this practice should be discouraged, because it often inhibits conversations and may result in important information being withheld. Qualitative results are usually obtained from interviews in which there are few people and little interference in the time allotted (see Figure 3). At certain times during the study, it may be beneficial for the study team to have additional meetings with members of the support staff; however, attendance at these meetings normally should be limited to no more than six people, to ensure better communication during the meeting.

Interviewers must be flexible and sensitive to the personality of the individual being interviewed. An interview usually begins with the interviewer indicating the information desired and removing any misconceptions about the scope of the study. The interviewer should clearly explain that study objectives usually are to streamline workflow, improve employee productivity, provide better controls and supervision, and minimize the routine tasks involved with the secretarial/clerical environment.

The objectivity of the interviewer is extremely important. Information gained during the management interviews may not duplicate information gathered from support staff personnel. Supervisors and managers are often not aware of what their support staffs are doing outside of work that they directly request of the staff. Very often, support personnel must complete their regular duties by working overtime or working through lunch hours. This situation may never come to their supervisor's attention. This absence of awareness on the part of management generally stems from the fact that traditionally they had no methods of controlling and measuring office work, or failed to utilize them if they had them.

During the course of interviews, the interviewers should usually take handwritten notes; however, the practice of using dictating equipment and tape recorders is becoming more acceptable. Whatever method is used, it is important to tell people being interviewed that their ideas are valuable enough to be noted.

At the conclusion of each interview, if the interviewer has not taken sufficient notes, an immediate review and a summarization of topics discussed should be made by the interviewer, so that the notes are accurate and complete enough to be used for further reference during the report preparation. Figure 4 provides guidelines for the interview process.

COLLECTING INFORMATION ABOUT THE PRESENT ORGANIZATION

The data collection process should attempt to include complete information pertaining to the present organization, such as numbers of support staff and management, salaries, operating costs, and the overall organizational structure. Normally, some of this information may come from organization charts showing existing staffing for each organization unit. Pay levels and pay ranges, together with percentages of fringe benefits to be added onto salaries, are useful when the cost justification is computed. Special efforts must be made to maintain the confidence of individual salaries, and therefore it is often important to use average salaries in the cost justification calculations. In addition, future personnel requirements should be projected for the organization or the department involved in the study.

The study team and/or consultant must consider the *management philosophy* of the organization. For example, if it has been stated that no employee will lose a job as a result of recommendations made based on

Figure 4 Interview guidelines emphasize the need for objectivity and patience.

Be thorough.
Stress to individual that interviews are essential to the study.
Be tactful and objective.
Be patient.
Do not dispute differences of opinion.
Be prepared.
Be prompt.

the results of the feasibility study, this philosophy should be considered by the study team when preparing recommendations. However, if the organization will commit itself to not replacing individuals as attrition takes place, so that replacement costs may be avoided, that, too, is a management philosophy that should be known to the study team and/or consultant. Another important aspect of data collection is consideration of future workloads that cannot be measured during the study.

A review of present and proposed organizational charts is necessary to determine potential workloads. Mergers or acquisitions often require structural changes in both personnel and reporting relationships that may add functions and workload. Both available personnel and the physical environment often determine the area eventually responsible for any automated or electronic approach to future office evolution; thus, there may be an increased workload in some areas and not others.

Further identification of workloads must be made by collecting information about internal and external needs for communications capabilities within the various functions of the office environments or with branch offices. For example, needs should be identified for capabilities such as phototypesetting, data processing, or electronic mail. Data collected should include the cost of outside services for such functions presently being expended on an annual basis, so as to provide a benchmark against which to measure the improved effectiveness and cost justification of bringing these types of services in-house.

All of this information provides a useful overview of the current operation, as well as a benchmark against which to measure the project recommendations.

Work Samples and Volume Counts

Part of the data collection process involves collecting sample materials for quantitative measurement by size, nature of the material, and required format. The collection of work samples is usually handled by instructing the staff to make a copy of each document prepared and noting thereon origination of document, volume in lines, and method of creation. Copies of work are collected for a fixed period, usually for 10 workdays, unless work in a particular organization is cyclical, which would require several work samplings. Once data is collected, the study team and/or consultant counts the work by volumes: quarter, half, or full pages, or by line. The best method of counting typing volumes is usually by line, since standards of productivity are frequently presented in lines (see Figure 5) and it therefore will be easier to compare the information and use it for configuring equipment. The study team and/or consultant may also want to note the workflow patterns from authors to typists and through a given department or organization.

Another part of the data collection process is the evaluation of existing productivity records (if they are being maintained) or instructions to secretaries to complete a log sheet listing pertinent information about each

DAILY LINE COUNT

Typist's Name _____ Date _____

Typist For _____ Equipment _____

Daily Typing Volume (check one): Average _____ Above Average _____ Below Average _____

INSTRUCTIONS: Complete the following summary. TOTAL LINES UNDER TYPE OF DOCUMENT *MUST EQUAL* TOTAL LINES UNDER METHOD OF INPUT. Envelopes, labels, and forms should be counted under "self-composition" where appropriate.

TYPE OF DOCUMENT	ORIGINAL INPUT # of Lines	REVISION TYPING Author Rev. # Lines	REVISION TYPING Sec'y Rev. # Lines	PLAYBACK # of Lines	TOTAL # Lines	# of Documents		TOT. # OF DOCUMENTS
Narrative (3 or more pages)								
Letters (1 or 2 pages)								
Statistical								
Outlines								
Labels/Envelopes								
Forms								
DAILY TOTALS								

←————Must Agree————

METHOD OF INPUT	STORED DOC. (SD)	LONGHAND (LH)	SHORTHAND (SH)	SELF-COMPOSED (SC)	MACHINE DICTATION (MD)	HARD COPY (HC)	TOTAL # Lines
# Lines							

Figure 5 Daily line count forms should collect information on type of document, method of origination, and revision cycles.

⬡ ROCHE				WORK LOG SHEET					
Job Compl.	No.	Date Received	Author	Job Description	Operator	Deadline		Date Completed
						Date Required	Revised Date	

Courtesy of Hoffman-LaRoche Limited, Vaudreuil, Quebec, Canada

Figure 6 Work log sheet provide ongoing statistics for continued control and justification. (Courtesy of Hoffmann LaRoche Limited, Vaudreuil, Quebec, Canada.)

document typed (see Figures 6 and 7). Some organizations have computer programs that can be used to process the information gathered on log sheets. In such a case, the log sheet becomes the source document fed into the computer.

Timekeeping Methods   A variety of methods of keeping time can provide the necessary data for the support systems feasibility study. Whatever data collection process is used, the data should be supplemented with the qualitative interview process to gain an impression of employee attitudes and the work sample collection process, so that peak and valley situations that occur outside the study period can be charted—for example, those workloads that occur on a monthly, quarterly, or annual basis.

Time Ladder. This approach, displayed in Figure 8, provides the opportunity for each individual involved in collecting data to list the functions performed and then to color in the block of any 10-minute increment during which those functions are performed. This is generally a very time-consuming process. Although it requires a great deal of time devoted to analysis and charting to summarize the information, it is a more detailed method. The overall results will not deviate more than 4 to 6 percent from other, easier methods used to keep time.

Time and Motion. A time-and-motion study is the most traditional approach to determining opportunities for improved efficiencies in the office environment. In the automated office feasibility study approach, however, this method is rarely used, because it is a time-consuming and therefore a costly approach to gathering data for recommending systems for the automated office.

Time-and-motion studies are performed by having a study team member and/or consultant sit at the support staff person's workstation with a stopwatch, timing each motion or activity performed by the individual being studied. Subsequently the information obtained is fed into a computerized program and/or summarized at the individual workstation or by statisticians.

Best Guesstimate. This method of collecting data is an estimation of workload and time expended, based on input from the support staff individuals being studied (see Figure 9). When analyzing estimated workload data, remember that what is involved is only an estimate that may be less quantitative than is desired for configuring systems for recommended approaches. This is a rapid way to gather information when time does not permit an in-depth study. It has also proved effective in the small-office environment.

ROCHE

WEEKLY LINE LOG SHEET

DEPARTMENT: ______________________

NAME: ______________________ WEEK OF: ______________________ 198-

Docu-ment	Origi-nator	No. of Pages	Fr.	Eng.	Machine Dicta-tion	Long Hand	Copy Type	Lines Re-turned	Lines Re-keyed	Pre-Recorded	Tables Set-up	Statistics & Programs
TOTALS												

Courtesy of Hoffman-LaRoche Limited, Vaudreuil, Quebec, Canada

Figure 7 Weekly log sheet for compilation of needed information. (Courtesy of Hoffmann LaRoche Limited, Vaudreuil, Quebec, Canada.)

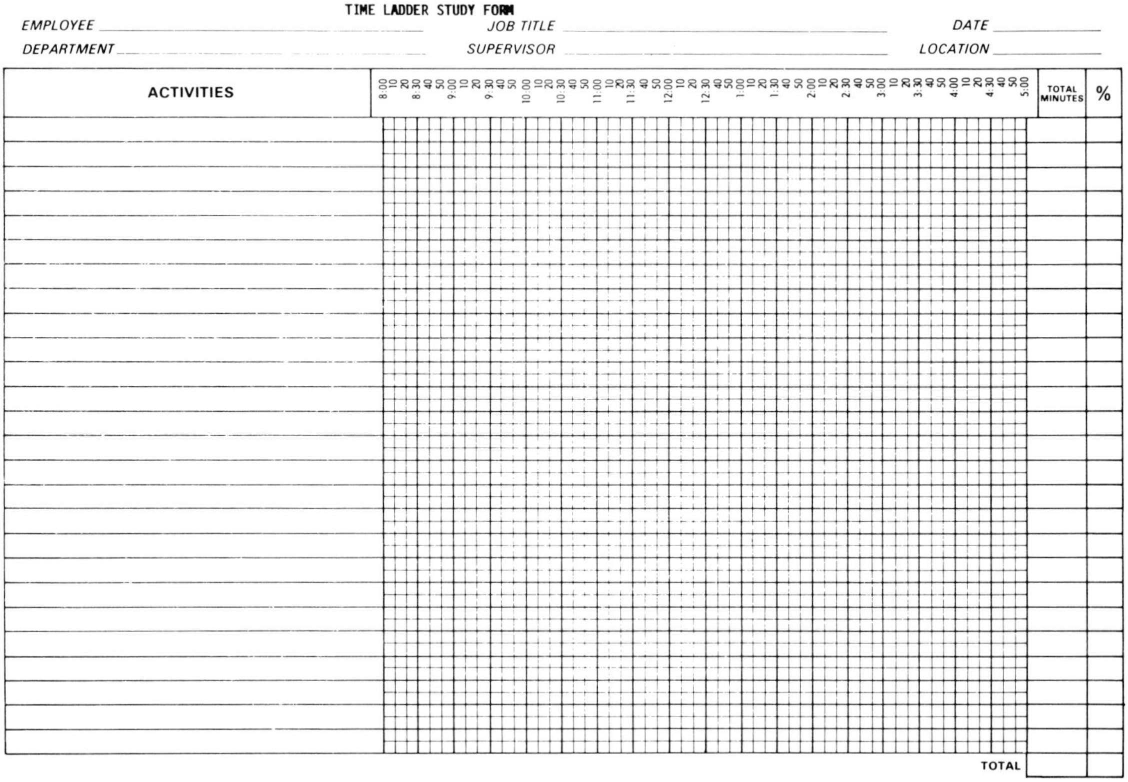
TIME LADDER STUDY FORM

EMPLOYEE ____ JOB TITLE ____ DATE ____

DEPARTMENT ____ SUPERVISOR ____ LOCATION ____

ACTIVITIES | 8:00 10 20 8:30 40 50 9:00 10 20 9:30 40 50 10:00 10 20 10:30 40 50 11:00 10 20 11:30 40 50 12:00 10 20 12:30 40 50 1:00 10 20 1:30 40 50 2:00 10 20 2:30 40 50 3:00 10 20 3:30 40 50 4:00 10 20 4:30 40 50 5:00 | TOTAL MINUTES | %

TOTAL

Figure 8 Time ladder form gathers information in ten-minute increments.

Time Sheet. This method is popular, since it allows the support staff individuals and management personnel involved in the study to maintain time sheets on a daily basis without the assistance of, or interference from, a study team member and/or consultant. This sheet allows the individuals keeping time to put their workloads into a quantitative form (see Figure 10.) This is the approach commonly used in large organizations.

ANALYZING COLLECTED STATISTICS AND INFORMATION

Once all data has been collected, it must be arranged into a logical format. Statistics must be summarized and charted, showing percentages of total time and volume; the validity of the collected information must be checked and verified; and careful attention must be given to the meaning of the information collected. Because the feasibility study is a major planning tool, care must be taken to assure that the information obtained clarifies what support the present system is providing and how the present system is operating.

Whichever data collection method is used, the following guidelines should be used in analyzing collected data:

Tools of Survey
Sample Task List

Name	Position	Tenure
Department	Section	
Supervisor	Date	

Task	Description	Quantity	Hrs./ Week

Administrative
  Shorthand
  Filing
  Mail
  Telephone
  Copy Machine
  Posting
  Special
  Miscellaneous
    Proofreading
    Collating
    Calculating
    Receptionist
    Requests
    Errands
    Other

Typing
  Memos and letters (1-page)
  Memos and letters (2-page)
  Reports—narrative
  Outline
  Statistical
  Forms
  Miscellaneous
    Envelopes
    Labels
    Other

Seasonal task

Unusual factors in workload

Peakload weeks

Suggestions

Overtime

Figure 9 Best guesstimate form provides a tool for estimating amount of time spent on various tasks.

SECRETARIAL DAILY TIME SHEET

Name: _____ Date: _____

PLEASE USE THE FOLLOWING CODE NUMBERS TO DESCRIBE WHAT YOU DID:

10 CALENDARING	21 Receive or give
11 ERRANDS and deliveries	INSTRUCTIONS
12 Looking for MISPLACED	22 Taking SHORTHAND
FILES	23 TELEPHONE
13 FILING	24 TRAVEL ARRANGEMENTS
14 LOCATING Someone	25 WAITING FOR WORK
15 MAIL	26 OTHER (specify)
16 OFF WORK (vacation,	27 RECORDKEEPING,
sick, etc.)	(posting, bookkeeping)
17 PERSONAL TIME (banking,	28 STATISTICS (computations)
coffee, etc.)	29 KEYBOARDING (computer
18 PHOTOCOPYING/	terminal, keypunch)
COLLATING	30 TYPING (regular typewriter)
19 PROOFREADING	31 TYPING (word processing
20 RECEPTION work	machine)

Time		Code Number	DESCRIPTION (Optional)
hrs.	tenths		
		TOTAL	

6 minutes = .1 hour	36 minutes = .6 hour
12 minutes = .2 hour	42 minutes = .7 hour
18 minutes = .3 hour	48 minutes = .8 hour

Figure 10 Time sheet is a tool utilized to gather statistics to the closest tenth of an hour time on all functions performed by staff members.

1. Is the collected data uniform, so that similar jobs or tasks can be compared and performance and costs easily tabulated?
2. Are the findings expressed in measurable terms, such as volumes, time, number of personnel, throughput, or money?
3. Are these findings about costs and/or performance measurable against valid standards or goals, to evaluate the present efficiency?
4. Can proposed methods and procedures be easily compared with present performance?
5. Is the result cost-effective? Is the proposed change cost-justified?
6. What benefits are there for management, staff, and the organization?
7. The desired end result of a feasibility study is to obtain the right information to assess needs properly.

Sometimes a feasibility study is called a needs assessment study. The goal, by either name, is to gain an overall perspective of the organization and a basis for planning. Needs to be identified and evaluated must include but not necessarily be limited to the following:

Applications.

Equipment selection or modification.

Organizational structure or restructure.

Land facilities.

Personnel requirements.

Space requirements.

The next chapter will present details on steps 7 and 8 of the total study process—preparing a written report and presenting the study results to top management.

CHAPTER 13

PRESENTING STUDY RESULTS TO MANAGEMENT

OBJECTIVES

In this chapter you will learn about
1. The importance of communicating study results to top decision makers.
2. Different methods of presenting study findings to decision-making management.
3. Which method of presentation is best, according to the circumstances.
4. Guidelines for preparing the written report.
5. The parts of a feasibility study report.

THE IMPORTANCE OF THE PRESENTATION

A thorough, well-organized study gives management the information it must have in order to make sound decisions and take action. A sound action, however, depends on the study results being communicated clearly and effectively to management. Members of the study team and/or the consultant all have a responsibility to communicate the study results and their recommendations to top management. Findings must be as factual and objective as possible (regardless of politics). The team should be able to assure executive management that it can proceed with the decision-making process, based on the present findings.

METHODS OF PRESENTING AND INTERPRETING INFORMATION

What techniques are most effective in summarizing and interpreting the study results? Any or all of the following techniques have benefits under certain circumstances, and hence should be weighed in relation to the particular type of information to be communicated.

1. Narrative or text.
2. Tables.
3. Graphics.
4. Charts.
5. Layouts.

NARRATIVE OR TEXT

Narrative is necessary in all reporting of study results. Top management has selected a study team and/or consultant to conduct the study because management needs not only facts but also interpretation of the meaning of the facts. This is especially true in regard to the office, because top management usually has time only to keep up with the general aspects of changing office technology and philosophy.

Narrative is the means for communicating all concerns that are of critical importance to decision makers. The personal and political aspects often are those that make or break an implementation of change. At the management level, the choice of the right approach to gain acceptance based on organization cultures is often critical. At the staff level, it is essential to consider the "people concerns" (for job enrichment and career advancement) to gain acceptance of change.

TABLES

Tables communicate some information better and more clearly and briefly than text, and some information can be presented effectively only in tables. In reporting study results, tables are necessary to present certain facts in a numerical form, such as statistics related to volume and production counts by each employee. Reporting the information in text would take at least three times as much space and would not make a point as clearly or quickly. Tables are the preferred means to present exact representation. Tables usually should be supplemented with text that provides interpretations and draws conclusions, as well as verifies the formulas used to arrive at conclusions. Figure 1 illustrates a compilation of volume data on method of input statistics.

GRAPHS Graphs present numerical data in a visual form and therefore are often more easily and quickly analyzed and remembered. Business graphics is becoming an increasingly important part of information processing and a frequent management tool. Graphs are statistical pictures.

While graphs are useful in presenting information pictorially, they have weaknesses and limitations. The number of facts is usually limited to four or five; it is best to use a table when more items are involved. Only approximate values and comparisons such as percentages can be illustrated, and attempts at exact mathematical accuracy are time consuming and should be evaluated as such in deciding between the use of tables or graphs.

Line graphs Line graphs are most effective in showing fluctuations in a value or quantity over a period of time—for example, the quantity of documents or lines produced over a period of months. The line graph is also an effective method of depicting a comparison of trends over a period of time (see Figure 2).

Bar graphs Bar graphs present quantities by means of horizontal or vertical bars. Variations in quantity are indicated by the length of the bars. Such graphs are most effectively used to compare a limited number of values, generally not more than four or five. A bar graph would be an effective means to compare the amount of typing or copying in each of several departments (see Figure 3).

Circle or Pie Chart The circle or pie chart is a form of graph that is used to show the manner in which a given quantity is divided into parts, preferably in percentage quantities—for example, how a group of secretaries' time is divided among various duties. The complete area of the circle represents the whole quantity or time, whereas the divisions within the circle represent the parts or various duties (see Figure 4).

Section 1	Etchison	Faucett	(12 other participants)	TOTAL
Administrative				
Shorthand	5.0	5.5		27.5
Filing	1.0			20.5
Mail	5.0	13.5	"	67.0
Telephone	7.5	2.5		91.5
Copy	1.5	2.5		28.0
Miscellaneous	5.0	1.0	"	54.5
Personal	1.0	2.5		7.5
Order placing				3.0
Reports			"	13.0
Errands		1.0		4.0
Machine dictation			"	
Proofreading				12.5
Posting			"	14.5
Invoices				1.5
Time locks			"	29.0
Collating		5.0		10.0
Import recap			"	17.0
Research problems				2.5
Record keeping			"	5.0
Depositing checks				2.0
Licenses			"	6.5
Subtotal	26.0	33.5	"	417.0
Typing			"	
Memos (1 page)	5.0	9.5	"	59.0
Memos (2 page)	2.0	.5		10.5
Reports/narrative	2.0		"	37.0
Statistical	.5			2.0
Forms	2.0		"	14.0
Letters				22.5
Weekly bulletins			"	13.5
Dictaphone				4.0
Notes			"	1.0
Seasonal package				4.0
Cards/envelopes			"	1.0
Outlines				.5
Miscellaneous			"	2.5
Training				10.0
Speeches			"	5.0
Licenses				2.5
Subtotal	11.5	10.0		189.0
Total	37.5	43.5		606.0

Figure 1 Compilation of volume data can best be presented in chart form.

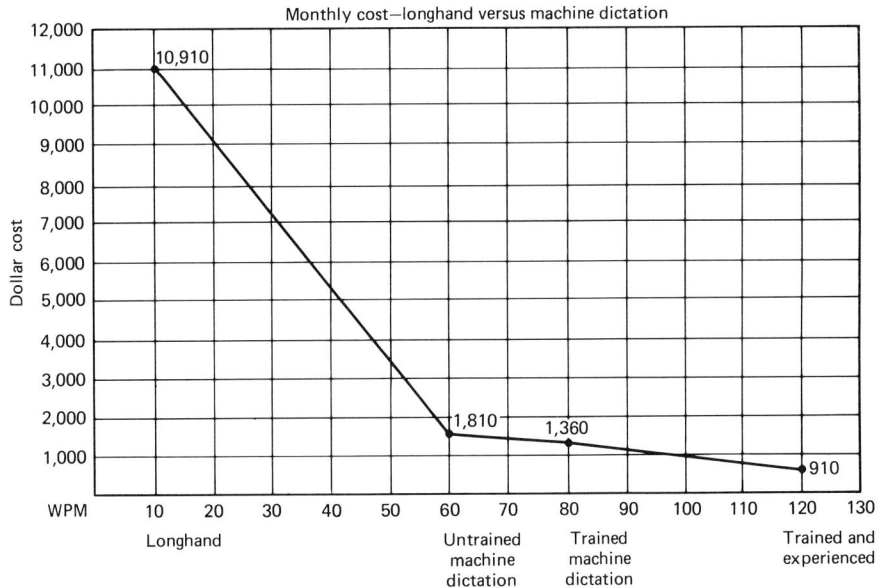

Figure 2   Line graphs reflect fluctuations in a dramatic way.

CHARTS
Flowcharts or Process Charts, and Organization Charts

Flowcharts or process charts, as well as organization charts, most likely will be used in presenting study results to management. Flowcharts are useful in picturing the process of work and paper as they flow through the office. Unnecessary steps and duplication in the past flow of activity are more obvious when pictured and compared with recommended flow (see Figure 5).

An organization chart is a graphic presentation of the organizational structure of the business; it points out responsibility relationships. An organization chart provides visual answers to two basic questions: (1) Who reports to whom? and (2) Who is responsible for what? (see Figure 6)

Layouts or Floorplans

Layouts or floorplans provide a means of pointing out graphically how an area should be physically arranged—that is, the placement of furniture and equipment and the spatial relationships of individuals. By means of arrows on a floorplan, the physical movement of people or the flow of work may be easily seen. Duplication of effort and backtracking become readily apparent.

SUMMARY

All of the above-mentioned tools are useful because they simplify and speed understanding. They also provide a means to compare old methods with recommended new ones. They may be used to supplement narrative;

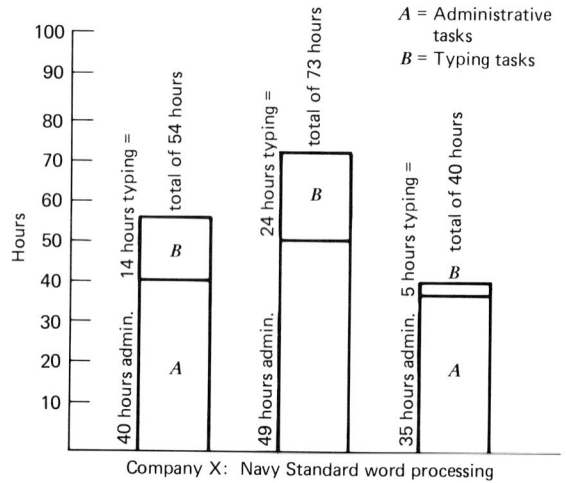

Figure 3 Bar graphs effectively present a limited number of values.

or text may be used in conjunction with tables, graphs, charts, and layouts to interpret advantageously or provide justification for recommended change.

Further, all of these forms of presentation are essential for understanding when recommendations for an automated office network are presented.

PREPARING THE WRITTEN REPORT

Because the people who collect study data are so familiar with it, it is important to remember that the management team that hears the presentation can only truly understand it if the important details are spelled out in an understandable fashion. The report must be presented in a logical

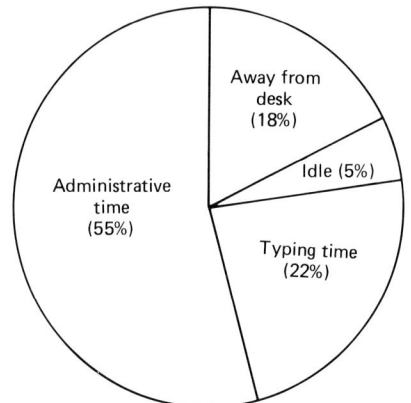

Figure 4 Pie chart.

manner to provide the managers who will be making decisions the opportunity to progress through the same evolutionary and educational process through which the study team and/or consultant has moved.

The first step is to prepare an outline that will also form the substance of a table of contents for the report, such as shown in Figure 7.

I INTRODUCTION This page of the report should provide the name(s) of the individual(s) who authorized the study, and the names of the project leader and study team members and/or the consultant. This information is provided so that any new management individuals or managers who subsequently are promoted into decision-making positions will not only be able to review the background and purpose of the support systems feasibility study but also will know the names of the members of the study team and/or the name of the consultant involved. A sample introduction follows:

> The support systems feasibility study was authorized by John Jones, president of ABC Corporation. The study began on January 1. The study project leader was James Smith, office automation analyst; primary study coordinators were Marilyn Brown, personnel supervisor, and Mary Johnson, office services supervisor.

II SCOPE AND PURPOSE The part describing the scope and purpose of the study should detail the parameters, the areas or departments involved, and the objectives of the study. One portion of this description of scope may include the study organization and a listing of names of employees participating in the data collection process and/or the interview process. In the case of particularly large studies, however, it will be easier to read if the study organization is listed separately. In this event, the scope of the study might read

> The study was conducted on the Personnel Department. Those individuals who participated in the study are listed in the Study Organization section of this report. The purpose of the study was to (1) determine the feasibility of automation, (2) assure the opportunity for upward mobility for support staff personnel, (3) provide for control and supervision of support staff workload, (4) eliminate a two-week correspondence-processing backlog, and (5) stop a 50 percent increase in secretarial costs.

III STUDY ORGANIZATION This section of the report lists the individuals who participated in the study, and it should be shown to correspond with the staffing breakdowns used in the summary statistical charts. This listing may be broken out by

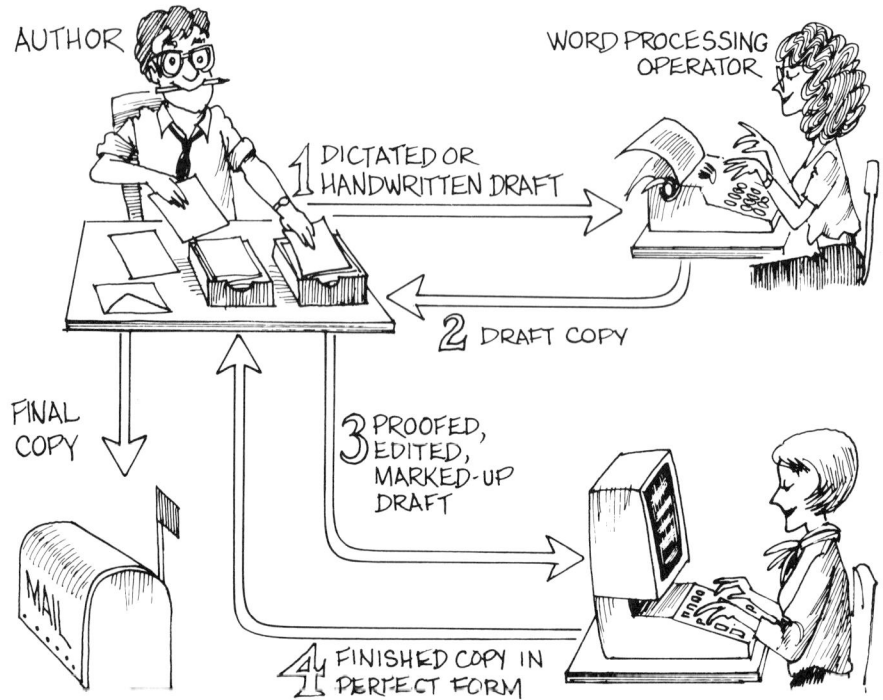

Figure 5   A workflow chart illustrating word processing flow from creation through distribution.

floor of the building, or by department or area studied, or by reporting relationships (for example, all employees who report to a specific corporate vice-president or director). A sample study organization section follows:

> It was determined that the study would be conducted in sections, because of the large number of employees involved in the collection of data, as well as the number of locations. The sections as shown in all statistical charts are as follows:
>
> Section I—Building A—4th Floor
> Section II—Building B—3rd Floor etc.

IV METHODOLOGY OF THE STUDY   The methodology section describes the techniques used during the study process to collect statistical data and qualitative information. For example,

The Management Review Committee approved a two-week study of office support activities on June 1. The study took place from June 15 to 29 in three departments: Sales Administration, Engineering, and Technical Publications. It included all personnel, including the three section heads, nine supervisors, 40 technical and professional workers, and 23 secretarial, clerical, and other support personnel.

Methods employed to gather data were

1. Personal interviews, to determine job responsibilities, workflow, and attitudes and to detect existing or potential personnel problems.
2. Copies of typed work, to determine secretarial output.
3. Time sheets, to measure the diversity of clerical and secretarial activity.
4. Management interviews, to determine purposes and goals of department activity and to identify existing standards of departments and individual performances.

V OBSERVATIONS AND COMMENTS

To validate the qualitative information gathered during interviews, a summary should be provided; it should briefly point out concerns expressed by employees. Observations made by the study team and/or consultant throughout the study process should be included, to add objectivity to these expressed employee concerns. Care should be taken to protect the confidentiality of the *source* of the information provided during personal interviews. Therefore, an observations-and-comments section might be written as follows:

▶ Employees expressed concern about waiting in line to use the photocopier.

▶ Managers expressed concern about slow turnaround on their typed documents.

▶ Observations revealed duplicative effort in reports from various departments.

VI STATISTICAL DATA SUMMARY

Each chart, as shown in Figure 8, should be summarized within the report, together with an introductory paragraph and analysis of the data shown on the chart.

This chart reveals that 68 percent of the work produced during the study was done in longhand. If the method of origination is converted to machine dictation, an improved productivity gain of at least 60 percent could be realized.

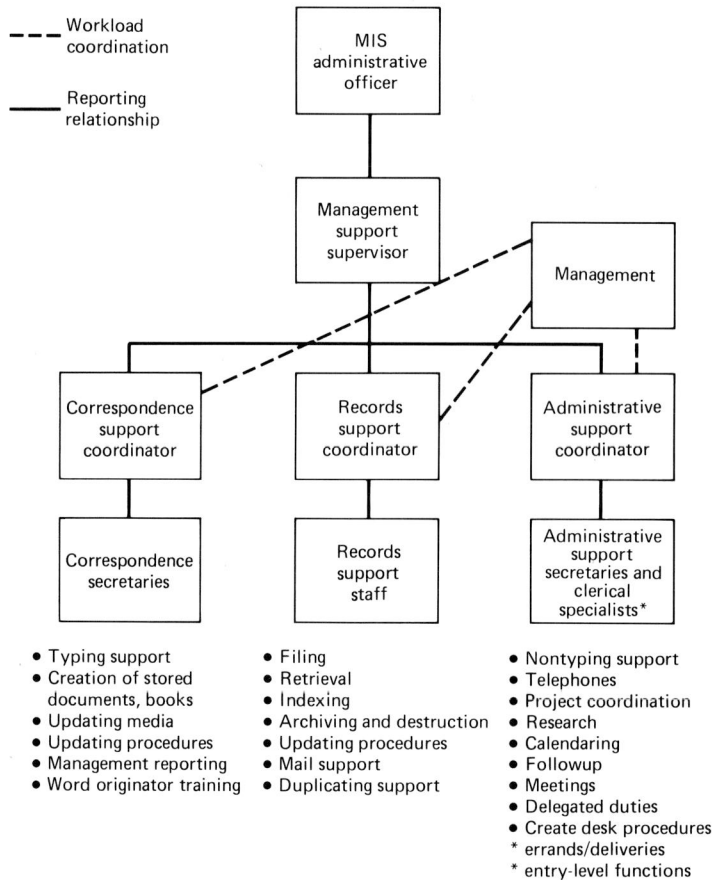

Figure 6   Support staff organizational chart graphically depicts reporting relations.

Supporting proof provided by other charts should be included for all production measured, such as

Log sheets of word processing centers.
Typing productivity of secretaries.
Daily time by staff.

VII RECOM-MENDATIONS

The Recommendations section is the heart of the report. Recommendations should be presented in a logical sequence, clearly stated, with supporting charts or graphs whenever graphics will aid in clarifying the overall picture. Broad recommendations can be described in an introductory paragraph, which should list the recommendations and the overall cost-

Table of Contents

I. Introduction
II. Scope and Purpose of the Study
III. Study Organization
IV. Methodology of the Study
V. Observations and Comments
VI. Statistical Data Summary
VII. Recommendations
  A. Staffing
  B. Equipment
  C. Space
  D. Networking
VIII. Justification
IX. Procedures
X. Training
XI. Implementation
XII. Summary
XIII. Appendices

Figure 7 Sample report table of contents is the first step in preparing an outline for management presentation.

Figure 8 Summary of document origination as shown should be accompanied by narrative explanation.

SUMMARY OF DOCUMENT ORIGINATION IN LINES BY SECTION

Method of Input	Sec. I	Sec. II	Sec. III	Sec. IV	Sec. V	Sec. VI	Total	Percentage
Stored document		15.0					15.0	0.1
Longhand	630.0	4,536.0	3,364.0	968.0	4,251.0	534.0	14,283.0	67.9
Shorthand	1.0					27.0	28.0	0.1
Self-composed	19.0	263.0	128.0	100.0	604.0	550.0	1,664.0	8.0
Machine dictation	390.0						390.0	1.8
Hard copy	619.0	727.0	1,341.0	631.0	1,073.0	265.0	4,656.0	22.1
Total (ten days)	1,659.0	5,541.0	4,833.0	1,699.0	5,928.0	1,376.0	21,036.0	100.0
Average daily total	165.9	554.1	483.3	169.9	592.8	137.6	2,103.6	

justification considerations, with detailed recommendations following by subsection. For example,

> This report provides data and cost justification totaling $102,600 annual savings in secretarial and report preparation activities in locations A, B, and C. To achieve these savings, we recommend that management implement word processing systems, install central dictation, establish communication between WP and inside and outside phototypesetting and the data processing division, install an electronic mail network, restructure job descriptions, and create procedures manuals.
>
> Details of and justification for these recommendations are shown in the following sections of this report.

Staffing   The staffing portion of Recommendations is developed from the collected statistics and presented to management in an organizational chart such as the one shown in Figure 9.

Personnel selection is discussed in depth in a later chapter. Staff savings based on reduction of staff or attrition are shown in the Justification section of this chapter.

Equipment   Configuration should be based on the application of productivity standards to production counts collected during the study and presented as a hard-dollar cost in the Justification section of the report.

Space   Certain guidelines are available for use when creating new environments for automated workstations. Recommendations and costs are presented in the Justification section of the report. Ergonomic considerations are presented in a later chapter.

Networking   Networking involves bringing many technologies together with a variety of different machine languages and operating techniques. With the current emphasis on networking in the automated office, it is essential to present the concept properly to management and to consider the impact of interconnecting technologies in the recommendations presented to management.

Networking considerations are presented to management in the Recommendations section of the report. Networking is discussed in another chapter.

Cover Summary   Some top managers prefer that feasibility reports be preceded by a cover letter or cover page. This page contains a highly condensed summary that tells management (1) the nature of the problems, (2) recommended solu-

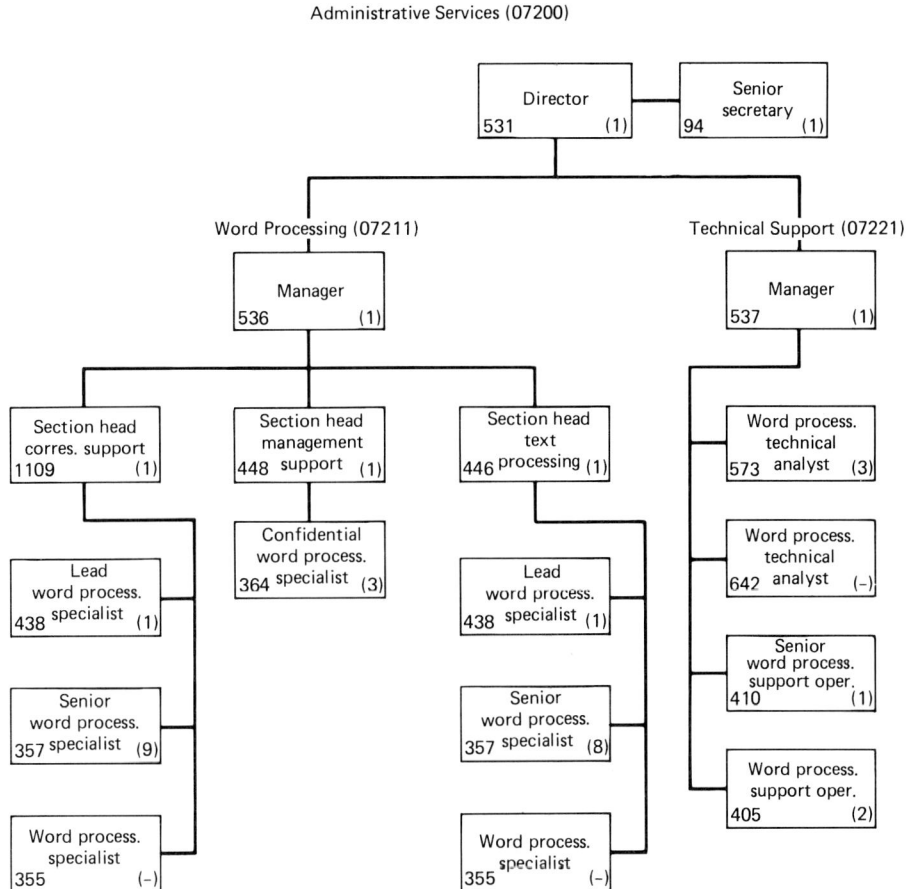

Figure 9 One company's organizational chart showing reporting relationships. (Courtesy of Western-Southern Life.)

tions, and (3) the benefits of the proposed solution. The page serves as a quick orientation and refresher for executives who have many priorities competing for their attention.

VIII JUSTIFICATION Management is intensely interested in hard-dollar (quantitative) savings, and valid soft- or intangible dollar (qualitative) savings. Presenting this section of the report in an outline or table form is more effective than presenting it in narrative form. Items to include are savings realized from reduction of staff, reorganization reduction through attrition (the normal level of those leaving their positions via resignation, promotion, etc.), improved productivity, cost avoidance, and reduced costs of temporary help and overtime. For example,

Hard-dollar savings are those savings realized by reduction of staff.	
2 staff persons @ $15,000 per year =	$30,000
Soft-dollar savings include savings resulting from improved productivity in all employees by converting from longhand to machine dictation and by delegating duties presently performed by management.	
2000 hrs per year @ $30/hr =	60,000
Cost avoidance of eliminated or reduced costs such as temporary help and overtime and not having to add budgeted personnel.	
2100 hrs per year @ $6/hr =	12,600
Overall annual savings =	$102,600
Less first-year equipment cost =	−50,000
First-year savings =	$ 72,600

IX PROCEDURES

Emphasis should be given to developing new procedures, or modifying existing ones, should the decision be made to implement all or even part of the recommendations. In the case of the study team approach, a representative from Methods and Procedures can be extremely helpful in ensuring these valuable tools are created or modified wherever necessary. If a consultant performed the study, the consultant's experience in developing procedures can assure the preparation of appropriate procedures.

The Procedures section of the report should emphasize the absolute need for procedures and should present ideas on what would be included in any procedures manual developed for the modified support system. For example,

Procedures are the heart of any management support system. A procedures manual should be developed, printed, and distributed to all staff members. It can be used as a guidebook to the entire operation of the system, as a training aid for new employees, and as a user guidebook to service. The management support staff should develop a procedures manual to include, but not be limited to

▶ Established turnaround requirements.
▶ Letter formatting for entire department.
▶ Policy on personal work in correspondence support areas.

> ▶ Feedback policy and forms for feedback.
> ▶ Guidelines for administrative support typewriter placement and usage.

X TRAINING A new support system can be implemented effectively only if employees are involved. Employee productivity and effectiveness is dependent upon proper training—not only training in the use of new technology, but training in using newly developed procedures and techniques for working with peers, supervisors, and/or subordinates. This section of the report should provide suggested training topics for management, for new supervisory positions resulting from the recommendations, and for the support staff. For example,

> Sessions should be conducted with management as soon as the executive decision to implement is made. Suggested topics are
>
> **1.** Restructuring orientation.
> **2.** Departmental implementation.
> **3.** Procedures familiarization.
> **4.** Dictation skills training.
> **5.** The art of delegation instructions.
>
> A new supervisor should be provided training and assistance by the consultant and/or members of the study team throughout implementation in areas such as
>
> **1.** Personnel selection.
> **2.** Career progression planning.
> **3.** Management support staff training.
> **4.** Report-forms design for management communication.
> **5.** Productivity measurement.
> **6.** Procedures development.
> **7.** Initial phase-in of implementation.
>
> In addition to the on-the-job training provided throughout the implementation phases of change, ongoing training opportunities through seminar and class attendance on the subjects of interpersonal skills, communication skills, and advances in telecommunications and data processing should be provided.
> During the phase-in implementation process, training sessions for all of the support staff should be conducted, covering the following types of topics:
>
> **1.** Telephone etiquette.
> **2.** Conference planning.

   3. Problem solving.
   4. Work organization.
   5. Desk organization.
   6. Time management.
   7. Priority setting.
   8. Scheduling.
   9. Work measurement.
  10. Decision making.
  11. Communications.
  12. Professionalism.

XI IMPLEMENTATION In order to put the recommendations into perspective so that management can see how they will work internally, this section of the report should provide a schedule of events that outlines Day One of implementation and takes the reader through to on-line implementation. For example,

Based on our experience, the entire conversion process will require approximately 4-6 months. Special note should be made that evaluation should not be attempted until this period of time has elapsed. We recommend the following approach:

Week 1—Report presentation to management.
Week 2—Report presentation to staff.
Week 3—Order equipment.
Weeks 4 & 5—Commence selection of staff.
Week 6—Begin development of procedures and schedule training.
Week 7—Start accumulation of information for data base storage.
Week 8—Commence training of managers.
Week 9—Commence training of support staff.
Week 10—Continue training and procedures development.
Week 11—Start word processing center and debug equipment.
Week 12—Phase in first department into new system.
Week 13—Phase in second department. etc.

XII SUMMARY This section provides the opportunity to compliment the management of the organization on their forward-thinking approach to alternatives to existing ways of operating. The summary paragraphs should be dynamic, so that the reader will be motivated to give the new system a try, while at the same time they should remind the reader of the many benefits that will be accorded the organization as a whole and the management and support staff employees individually. For example,

> Although we are suggesting a reduction in staff, this will take place only through normal attrition. Implementation of our recommendations will provide improved employee productivity, improved morale, faster turnaround time for work products, improved quality, greater communication capabilities, faster access to the flow of information, and time savings to the originator.
>
> The management of ABC Company are to be complimented on their open-minded approach to change and progress into the information age. We have enjoyed working with the staff at ABC.

XIII APPENDICES Whenever possible, provide additional tools for understanding and graphics in the appendices, so that the report is succinct and logical in sequence. Although summary statistical charts should be included in the body of the report, detailed charts showing statistics for each person in the study can be provided in an appendix, thereby minimizing the number of pages that have to be shuffled back and forth as the recommendations are being reviewed. Materials furnished in an appendix can be read at leisure, without the reader's losing the main theme of the report. Appendixed materials might include

▶ Glossary of terms used in report.
▶ Recommended training session agendas, or contract letter or commitment memo to perform study.
▶ Formulas used to calculate savings.
▶ Proposed job descriptions.

REPORT CHECKLIST

After analyzing and drafting the results of a support systems feasibility study, you must determine whether all information is ready for presentation to decision-making management. A checklist to review follows.

1. Is the data collection process complete?
2. Have the objectives or the original study purpose been met?
3. Should any areas identified outside the original scope of the study be recommended for further study?
4. Have feasible alternative approaches been defined for improvements to the present operation?

5. Are the cost savings resulting from the recommended approach sufficient to warrant the process of change, and do they provide the ongoing savings to justify capital expenditures?

6. Have there been changes in the organization that have taken place during the course of the study or since data collection was completed that will significantly impact the recommendations being made?

7. Might any of the areas studied show dramatic resistance to change and impede or interfere with the recommended implementation process? If so, have these areas been so noted?

PRESENTING THE REPORT TO MANAGEMENT

When the study team and/or consultant are satisfied that all of these questions have been answered, a meeting should be scheduled with the level of management involved in decision making, to review the report, determine if this group is totally committed, assure successful implementation, and respond to any questions. It should be remembered that the study team and/or consultant are intimately familiar with the project at this point and may well have overlooked explaining certain intricacies that would make it easier for management to accept the recommendations and to commit itself to change.

In most instances, a feasibility study for a potentially automated office will show the need for change and restructuring. Such automation will touch the working lives of everyone in the office. Unlike its predecessor, data processing, which could be implemented and changed in a relatively independent and isolated area, automating the office environment means changing the work habits, styles, traditions, and modes of operation of *every* member of management and of the support staff.

TECHNIQUES FOR MANAGEMENT PRESENTATIONS

Having prepared a report in its final form, the study team and/or consultant must now choose the most effective way to present its findings and recommendations. During the course of the study, the study team and/or consultant should have assessed which types of management presentations are preferred and well received. For example, some teams make management reports using 35mm slides or colored charts. If this is what is preferred and the equipment is readily available, then slides and/or colored charts should be part of the presentation method. However, an office automation feasibility report is usually large and requires a great deal of time for presentation of all the information. Management may also want the lights on so that notes can be taken; in such cases, visual overhead transparencies are a satisfactory method of report presentation.

Transparencies should be prepared to illustrate the need for improved productivity, greater supervision, workload distribution, and the economic benefits accruing to the entire organization, as well as the qualitative and subjective benefits for management.

THE REPORT PRESENTATION MEETING Individuals present at the report presentation meeting should be decision makers within the organization. The presentation should be controlled by use of an agenda with specific time frames.

An agenda might include the presentation of the report and pertinent data, a review of the report structure and explanation of the visuals, and coordination of the answering of questions by various team members.

An example of such an agenda is shown in Figure 10. Note how it is self-explanatory. It identifies *who* will be presenting each section; *what* that individual will be discussing; *how* long it will take; and, finally, what time the meeting can be adjourned. It should provide the information necessary for the decision makers to plan their time and formulate their questions, and it should impress them with the organization and detail of the study group, to lend credibility to the report.

Coordination permits those team members who participated in special areas of the study to respond effectively to questions pertaining to that area. (For example: "How long will it take to write procedures?" The representative from Methods and Procedures can respond intelligently on the basis of past experience within the organization in developing or

Figure 10 Automated office report agenda illustrating times and person responsible for each segment of presentation.

July 17, 1985			
9:00 A.M.	Introduction of study	Chairman, study team	15 minutes
9:15 A.M.	Review study approach and organization	Chairman, study team	5 minutes
9:20 A.M.	Discuss statistical data	Statistician	20 minutes
9:40 A.M.	Present recommendations and cost effectiveness	Consultant	45 minutes
10:25 A.M.	Review benefits of recommendations	Chairman of study team	20 minutes
10:45 A.M.	Answer questions	Consultant and study team	15 minutes
11:00 A.M.	Adjourn meeting		

modifying procedures). If consultants performed the study, they respond to the questions by management, for they can draw on experience, present analagous situations, and "bite the bullet."

A set agenda moves the presentation along in a logical manner and keeps the study team leader and/or consultant from letting the meeting lapse into mundane conversation (which often can be a problem in a large group of management decision makers). It also allows presentation of the entire report, with time for answering specific questions.

If and when the study recommendations are approved, management must also commit itself to the transformation of potential benefits into reality with all the ensuing consideration required to implement technology and change.

Information about how to implement the study recommendations is presented in the following chapter.

CHAPTER 14

IMPLEMENTING THE RECOMMENDED CHANGES

OBJECTIVES

In this chapter you will learn about
1. Planning for implementing the changes and for informing management and staff.
2. The differences between the traditional and the automated office environment.
3. The individuals responsible for various parts of the implementation process.
4. Various implementation tools and guidelines.
5. A total approach to implementation.

Implementation is simply the process of carrying out the approved recommendations. Because the traditional office has long been viewed as a place where only the handling of paperwork occurs, many aspects of the office have been taken for granted. Recently, management has recognized that information is a critically important business resource. The office as an entity requires management, so many executives find it difficult to grasp the dramatic changes necessary to implement a new type of office support system that will service them for many years in the future. Their readiness to commit themselves to change is affected by many factors explained in previous chapters.

Some executives will be ready to implement change immediately after the initial presentation of the study results; others may need time to study and ponder the information provided them. A series of additional meetings may be needed to answer their questions and continue to "sell" the benefits to be obtained through change.

Management cannot be expected to decide upon a drastic change unless it thoroughly understands the benefits. Automation of office functions provides a buffer against inflation, improves productivity through the appropriate training and delegating processes, and provides a support system more consistent with management desires in meeting company goals. Management needs to be thoroughly convinced that the benefits derived from the investments in technology, training time, and staff resources can be dramatic. It must be clearly understood that the evolutionary or revolutionary (depending upon how one views it) change process cannot take place in a short period of time.

TYPES OF PLANNING FOR AUTOMATION

There are two major approaches to the implementation of office automation. One is the interim or short-term approach, referred to as *transitional*. The other is the longer-range strategy that implements extensive electronic integration, referred to as *office automation*. Management principles of short- and long-term planning for the budgeting, controlling, and directing of the traditional office are slightly modified in the transitional approach, the electronic integration approach, and implement revolutionary changes in the office.

The primary difference between the transitional and the automated-office process lies in the interconnection of the various electronic and/or technological components. A transitional approach at a later time can phase into a network of information for the integrated electronic phase. Further, the integrated phase brings onto the network more administrative work terminals and management workstations. Therefore, implementation planning requires a firm management commitment and both a short- and long-range planning process.

RECEIVING MANAGEMENT COMMITMENT TO IMPLEMENTATION

Cost benefits are of major importance to management. It may be necessary periodically to reemphasize cost benefits in order to receive management's commitment to support the implementation process. One change with great impact is the restructuring of the office organization. The most effective way to convince some members of management may be to point out the cost benefits to be obtained.

Cost Benefits

One of the costs benefits can be stated in *hard dollars,* or those dollars saved through the reduction of the support staff necessary for the principals involved in the proposed structure. The recommended changes and benefits can be identified as a result of the feasibility study described in detail in a previous chapter. Once they have been identified, they can be effectively illustrated to management through a summary table (see Figure 1). Note that Figure 1 shows all secretaries in the present support system to be at a similar salary level, without evidence of work specialization or career opportunities. In the proposed system, work specialization and different levels of positions are apparent.

In addition to the hard-dollar savings, efficiency gains in other areas should be emphasized. For example,

1. Eliminating rekeystroking of typed text.
2. Transmitting messages electronically versus delivering them physically within an organization or department.
3. Eliminating double proofreading of correctly keystroked information.
4. Delegating to entry-level clerks the task of standing in line waiting to use photocopiers, compared with the real costs of management performing this function.

Figure 1 Dollar comparison of present and proposed systems. A summary table such as this shows at a glance past and future costs of a project.

Present Support System	
32 secretaries/clerical staff @ $18,000/yr.	$544,000
32% fringe benefits	174,080
Annual cost—present system	$718,080
Proposed Support System	
21 secretaries/clerical (including working coordinators, administrative assistants) @ 18,000/yr.	$378,000
3 correspondence secretaries @ 18,000/yr.	54,000
3 clerical support center @ 14,000/yr.	42,000
27 secretaries/clerical staff	$474,000
32% fringe benefits	151,880
Annual salary—proposed system	$625,880
Savings achieved through proposed system	$ 92,200

All of these benefits can be identified as potential *productivity gains* or *cost avoidance* areas and, based upon information learned through the feasibility study, can have a dollar savings placed upon them. They also can be a part of the summary table of cost benefits.

Additional benefits to be realized are in the *soft-dollars* area—through the potential savings of time from improvements in the work habits of managers and support staff. These costs can also be identified as a result of the feasibility study and should he included in the cost benefits table. The total of these potential savings less the cost of technology will provide management with a better picture of the different sources of potential cost benefits (see Figure 2).

In a table such as Figure 2, it is important that the areas of benefit be defined for the *transitional* (short-term) as well as the *integrated electronic* or office automation (long-term) phases.

Item #1, the hard-dollar savings, can be projected: $36,552 × 5 years = $182,760 (cost savings to be applied to the integrated environment).

Item #2, improved productivity and cost avoidance, is a less easily measured item and should be shown in a less quantifiable manner for the integrated electronic phase, since it will need auditing during the transitional period. Estimates can be made based on the first year. $142,308 × 5 years = an estimated potential for five-year savings of $711,540.

Item #3, soft-dollar savings, are directly related to the ability of managers to create work faster through work organization and electronic dictation rather than by longhand. The hours used to compute soft-dollar savings are taken from the statistics relating to Method of Document Origination gathered during the study.

After the time savings potential is calculated, it is presumed that all managers will not achieve 100 percent proficiency in the art of using

Figure 2 Cost benefits table shows short- and long-term benefits.

	Transitional, First Year	Integrated Electronic, Fifth Year
1. Hard-dollar savings	$ 36,552	$182,760
2. Improved productivity or cost avoidance	142,308	
3. Soft dollars (80%)	$ 83,776	
4. Estimated potential annual savings	262,636	
5. Less approximate cost of technology (first year)	38,460	
Net estimated potential savings	$224,276	

dictation equipment; therefore, a conservative estimate of 80 percent efficiency improvement is projected. $83,776 x 5 years = a conservative estimate of $418,890.

The summarization of the foregoing type of material is important in helping management realize the worthwhile nature of investing in changes and committing itself to a plan for implementation both in the transitional office and in preparation for electronics.

Proposed Structure

When an organization's lines of authority and reporting structures are changed, those changes must be communicated to all affected, so that there should be no misunderstanding about functional and reporting relationships. Organization charts can show present and proposed structures and are useful in clarifying differences. Structure and reporting relationships generally comprise one of the most discussed areas of any management report, because recommendations for change affect traditional secretarial/management relationships and the way people interact with the automated areas of the support environment. A number of alternative structures are possible; and as a result of the feasibility study, the most desirable alternative for any given area will become apparent. Sample organizational charts for one aspect of a support structure are shown for a large organization in Figure 3 and for a small organization in Figure 4. A sample future or integrated approach is illustrated in Figure 5. Graphic presentations to management are essential in the process of receiving commitment to implementation.

Proposed Implementation Plan

A proposed plan or outline should be developed to keep management aware that implementation cannot take place overnight and that considerable *time* is involved in the process.

One such plan, called an event schedule, is shown in Figure 6. This approach gives management an overview of implementation scheduling and the functions to be performed. Note the week-by-week detailing and the use of a phase approach. This approach is helpful in informing management.

A more specific plan, shown in Figure 7, is a Gantt chart. The Gantt chart, created by Henry L. Gantt, visualizes a plan and schedule of work to be accomplished. The vertical scale shows the functions to be implemented and the horizontal scale shows the estimated time required for each function. Note the overlaps in time of various functions.

The Gantt chart identifies the major implementation tasks, which usually consist of

▶ Management support study, analysis of needs, recommendation of equipment.

▶ Management presentation and commitment to program.

▶ Ordering equipment.

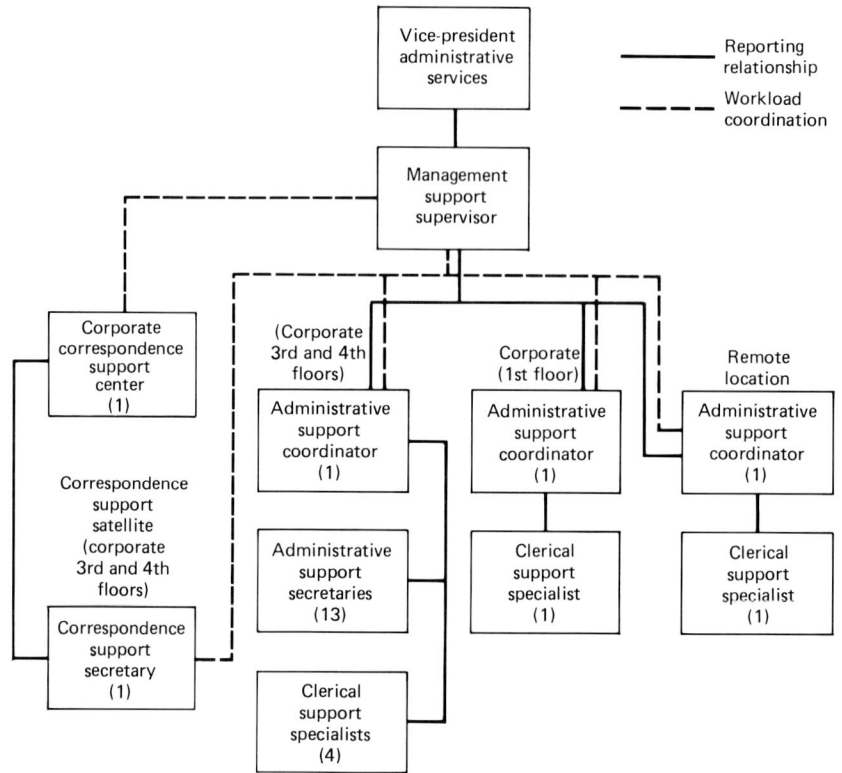

Figure 3 Support structure for a large organization may be complex but illustrates specialization.

Figure 4 Support structure for a small organization, though simple, clearly shows specialized responsibilities.

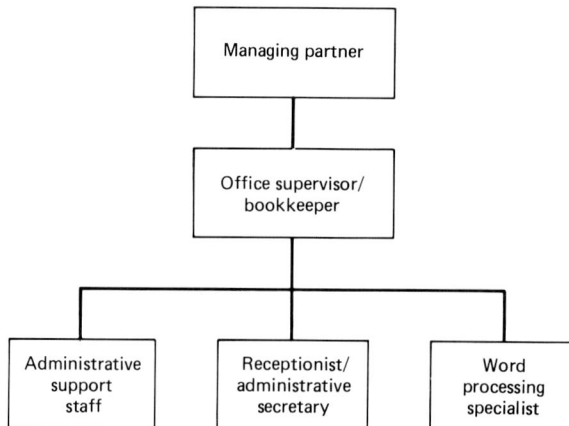

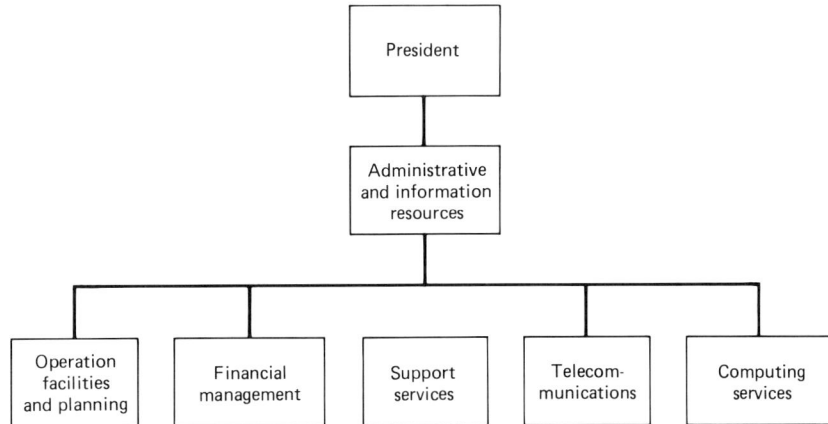

Figure 5 Integrated office organizational structure depicts overall proposed management structure.

- ▶ Selection of manager.
- ▶ Selection of personnel.
- ▶ Restructuring of reporting relationships.
- ▶ Preparing job descriptions.
- ▶ Drafting procedures.
- ▶ Installation of equipment.
- ▶ Train: secretaries and principals.
- ▶ On-line implementation.
- ▶ Ongoing design of stored documents.
- ▶ Ongoing updating of procedures.
- ▶ Management reports prepared regularly.

Too many interrelated activities are involved to identify precisely the day-to-day steps in the implementation process. Many of these activities may be carried on in parallel; yet they must mesh. The Gantt chart provides the means for illustrating the important decisions on implementation.

IMPLEMENTATION REQUIREMENTS

BELIEVING IN THE SYSTEM   Successful implementation depends upon top management commitment and a positive approach to, and objective viewpoint of, potential improvements in a support structure on the part of the supervisory individual in charge of implementation.

Week 1	Management approval through the budgeting process.
Week 2	Presentation to all departments of results of the study and of management's commitment to implementation.
Week 3	Develop and mail RFPs to word processing and voice vendors.
Week 4	Begin developing revised job descriptions and salary structure for management support positions.
Week 5	Continue developing job descriptions for management support staff.
Week 6	Begin selection process of management support staff.
Week 7	Evaluate response to RFPs; order equipment.
Week 8	Begin development of written procedures and scheduling of training sessions.
Week 9	Continue development of procedures and scheduling training sessions.
Week 10	Begin accumulation of documents for storage, from area(s) to be implemented first.
Week 11	Begin training secretaries, managers, and professionals of area(s) to be implemented first.
Week 12	Continue training sessions and procedures development for the area(s) to be implemented first.
Week 13	Proceed with on-line implementation of interim support until sophisticated equipment is delivered (e.g., use existing stand-alone units with newly-developed procedures and revised staffing configuration).
Week 14	Continue interim implementation by department.
Week 15	Shared/distributed system is delivered. Begin operator training.
Week 16	Begin storing documents collected from first area to be implemented.
Week 17	Begin implementing OPTIMUM on-line support, by area, until all departments within the organization have been reconfigured under office automation.

Figure 6 Event schedule depicts detail of project and anticipated time for completion of activities.

Conversely, such a system will have a traumatic beginning if the supervisor in charge of implementation

▶ Disbelieves the accuracy of a feasibility study.

▶ Fails to communicate.

▶ Is not knowledgeable about the functions being performed by the individual staff persons and/or does not educate himself or herself about those functions.

Recommended Time Schedule for Implementation

Weeks	1	2	3	4	5	6	7	8	9	10	11	12	13	14	15	16
Management support study: analyze needs, recommend equipment	███	███	███	███	███											
Management presentation and commitment to program					███											
Order equipment					███											
Select manager						███										
Select personnel						███	███									
Restructure reporting relationships						███	███	███								
Prepare job descriptions, draft procedures						███	███	███								
Install equipment									███							
Train: secretaries and principals									███	███	███	███	███	███	███	███
On-line implementation									███	███	███	███	███	███	███	███
Design of stored documents											███					
Update procedures									███	███	███	███	███	███	███	███
Prepare management reports ongoing																███

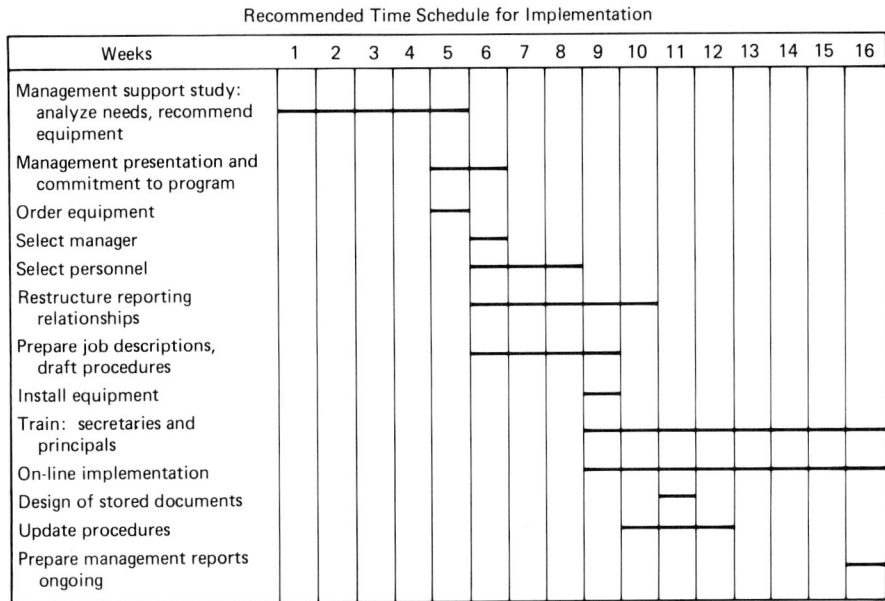

Figure 7 Recommended time schedule shows expected completion of project steps using a Gantt Chart. Note overlap of times.

▶ Views the implementation project as a "job to get done" and not as an opportunity to provide the benefits of a restructured, integrated office environment.

MANAGEMENT COMMITMENT

Experience has shown that implementation of office support systems without the total support of top and middle management ends in disorganized failure. This concern underscores the steadfast need for a positive attitude and an objective, open-minded approach to implementing study recommendations and defining potentials for future improvements as modifications to the initial design become apparent and as the transition to electronic integration reaches fruition.

Support staff members must be responsive to users' needs, positive in their attitudes toward a new secretarial structure, and willing to accept new responsibilities and new challenges. With this open-minded approach, great opportunities exist for increased job satisfaction, for upward mobility (if desired), and for evaluations of performance based upon one's own merit (and not dependent upon an immediate supervisor's position in the organization).

Presentations to management must take a confident, forthright approach in illustrating that the benefits will far outweigh any disturbances to the normal course of business during the process of implementation.

IMPLEMENTATION RESPONSIBILITY CHART

Implementation Function	Space Planner	Management Support Supervisor	Personnel Department	Equipment Vendor	Central Services Coordinators	Mary M Ruprecht, Inc.
Departmental feedback*						*
Develop RFPs		X				*
Order equipment		X		X		
Select coordinators		X	X			*
Restructure reporting relationships		X	X			*
Modify job descriptions		X	X			*
Develop procedures		X			X	*
Design office layout space; order furniture and supplies	X	X		X	*	*
Install equipment		X		X		
Training on word processing equipment		X		X	X	
Train secretaries, managers, and professionals on dictation equipment		X		X	X	
Store documents from phase-in areas		X		*	X	
Implement on-line phase-in		X			X	*
Ongoing updating of procedures		X			X	
Management reports		X			X	
Training sessions for management support staff (desk organization, time management, professionalism, telephone etiquette, etc.)		X				X

* As needed.

Figure 8 Implementation responsibility chart clearly illustrates who is accountable for completion of each phase.

ESTABLISHING IMPLEMENTATION RESPONSIBILITIES

With the support and commitment of management to the implementation process, the next step involves appointing an individual to be responsible for overall implementation; whatever the title (implementation manager, manager of support systems, etc.), such a person is necessary. The implementation of a total support system cannot be accomplished in a piecemeal fashion. Many people will be involved, but one person must be delegated the responsibility and authority to orchestrate the total effort. Without such a coordinator there is little likelihood of achieving the desired short-range goals—let alone the long-range goals.

An excellent implementation tool is the implementation responsibility chart. It helps to establish the functions or tasks to be performed and designates who is responsible for each task (see Figure 8).

Implementation of a restructured system offers the company an opportunity to classify work, upgrade skill levels through training (in some instances), and provide career progressions; therefore, a personnel planning chart should be prepared. This work would involve the person in charge of personnel or human resources. At the same time, the preparation of the responsibility chart identifies the individuals involved in change. The level of staff to be affected is determined by the study results as well as by the implementation steps listed in the planning process. Usually, persons involved in the activities shown in Figure 8 will be a part of the implementation process and will have responsibilities commensurate with their job functions. For example, purchasing people will be involved with the acquisition of equipment; space planners will be involved with the redefining and remodeling of workstations, as necessary; personnel and training people will be responsible for the reclassification of jobs, testing, and possibly training; and methods-and-procedures people will be involved in the drafting of procedures for the new operating system.

All these activities and the departments involved in the implementation need to be coordinated by the manager in charge of support systems. That individual (project manager) would in fact have a direct reporting relationship to the executives who have committed themselves to change.

PURCHASING EQUIPMENT

The acquisition of equipment will follow a series of planned steps. Decisions to buy, rent, or lease are seldom made by one person, unless the organization is very small or the purchase is routine, such as a replacement. Usually a team of people participates; all are involved in the procedures or system in which the equipment will be used.

The process usually takes a pattern that closely follows the following steps:

1. Realize the need or problem exists.
2. Get agreement to look into equipment to meet needs.
3. Survey present work and procedures, and future needs.
4. Survey present equipment, and estimate future requirements.
5. Learn about equipment and its capability to do your work.
6. Narrow selection down to the models that appear to fulfill your requirements and specifications.
7. Attend equipment demonstrations. Ask vendors to perform work samples.
8. Make final selection.
9. Include recommendations in management report if acquisition is part of the feasibility study.
10. Present recommendations to approving committee.
11. Receive budget approval and purchase authorization.
12. Request purchasing to issue purchase order.
13. Inform all involved people of decision.
14. Set up training and orientation schedules.
15. Inform all involved of space changes, furniture needs, special installation requirements, and scheduled installation date.

SPACE PLANNING Concurrent with the purchase, the allocation of space and modifications of that space for work areas more consistent with time management and work specialization must be designed and construction begun. This function is coordinated by the manager of support systems, however, with the specific responsibility delegated to the office services or space planning personnel. Ergonomic considerations will be covered in a later chapter.

PROCEDURES DEVELOPMENT Procedures are the heart of any system. A procedures manual should be a guidebook to the entire operation of the support system, a training manual for new employees and a user guidebook to service.

A well-outlined procedures manual should be developed *prior to implementation* of a support system, and printed and distributed to all staff members. It can then be used in training and orientation sessions during the implementation phase.

User Manual An introductory section of the manual should include procedures on all typing and nontyping activities, including telephone coverage, vacation and illness backup, priorities, and delegation.

A general section of the manual would provide tips on English skills (including punctuation, grammar and effective writing, proofreading, and letter writing), unusual formats required by the user staff, and sample forms for requesting work from the support staff and centers. Items such as those shown below should be included.

1. Typing—how to get work into and out of the center.
2. Dictation—how administrative secretaries can dictate handwritten documents.
3. Proofreading (proofreader's marks).
4. Nontyping—list of tasks assumed by Administrative Support.
5. Telephone coverage.
6. Travel/meeting arrangements.
7. Composing and dictating routine correspondence.
8. Vacation/illness backup.
9. Setting priorities.
10. Role of administrative supervisor.

The section on word processing services would describe the operation of the center and provide instructions on how to work with the center, as shown below.

1. Hours.
2. Pickup and delivery.
3. Turnaround—regular input and special projects.
4. Priorities—rush, revisions, routine.
5. Input—dictated, handwritten, portables.
6. Types of information processed in center—original dictation, stored material, special requests (unusual formats, terms).
7. Information *not* processed in the center.
8. Stationery.
9. Standard formats (letters, memos, proposals, speeches, etc.).
10. Carbon copies (number and carbon copy notations).
11. Revisions.
12. Drafts.
13. Mailing and enclosures.
14. Envelopes/labels.
15. Media—regular, hold, stored.
16. Printed materials.
17. Proofreading.
18. Technical terms.
19. Computer language.
20. Signature—letter and memos.

21. Inserted information.
22. Unusual format.
23. Abnormal workload.
24. Stored document book.
25. Frequently used addresses.
26. Postal state abbreviations.

Word Processing Manual Manuals for the word processing operators should also include equipment instructions and would consist of the following:

1. Media procedures (handling, filing, retention).
2. Margins, tabs, and so on (keyboard features).
3. Applications (paragraph assembly, variables, etc.).
4. Equipment and supplies care and storage (media, print wheels, ribbons, etc.).
5. Record keeping procedures.
6. Personnel practices of the center (backup, lunch, breaks, etc.).
7. Training manuals and/or self-paced training packages from manufacturers.

Continual review and updating of the procedures manual will ensure a current, effective tool for both management and support staff use.

Desk Manual A desk manual, often referred to as a workstation manual, is a working tool and training guide for any employee who is a part of the office support system. It is not a manual that travels with employees as they change jobs. It is a guidebook for particular duties and tasks and it remains with the job and workstation for which it was written.

Developing a Desk Manual.   During the implementation process, a desk manual should be created according to the following guidelines:

1. List daily functions in detail.
2. Divide functions into morning duties and afternoon duties.
3. Itemize peak periods on an annual basis.
4. List unusual or periodic duties by week, month, quarter, etc.
5. Categorize each function.
6. Detail step-by-step procedures to perform each function.
7. Prepare a detailed table of contents.
8. Index clearly, with tab dividers, by function and time frame for performance.
9. Review with secretary and principal.

Sample procedures for calendaring and handling expense accounts might read as follows:

Calendaring

1. Schedule meetings for principals, as instructed, and put on secretary's calendar (located on top of desk).
2. Record these meetings on principals' office calendars.
3. Periodically check principals' calendars to determine whether they have scheduled meetings without notifying secretary.
4. Enter meetings they have scheduled onto secretary's calendar also.

Expense Accounts

When received from principals:

1. Verify figures and completeness of form.
2. Obtain approval from principal's immediate supervisor.
3. When approved, take expense account to Accounting Department for processing.

PERSONNEL CONSIDERATIONS DURING IMPLEMENTATION

The most important part of the implementation process is the challenge of successfully adapting people to the new environment, policies, procedures, and equipment. Personnel at all levels require preparation and orientation. Separate orientation programs should be designed and scheduled for executives, middle managers and other principals (users of the system), support supervisors, and support staff. There should be periodic follow-up sessions to assure that day-to-day operation moves smoothly. Project leaders should emphasize the importance of teamwork and of how interrelated activities affect each other. This awareness of what goes on around one's own job will increase the degree of cooperation among personnel.

THE CONVERSION

Conversion to a new support system is generally a phased-in process even when it is a pilot or prototype installation. It consists of installing new equipment and converting the work from old to new equipment, changing to new procedures, relocating personnel to new or different workstations, and communicating these moves on a daily basis. Careful planning and open communications can prevent complications and make the conversion a less disruptive experience. There are generally four methods of converting.

1. Converting an entire group or company on one given date to all new methods, procedures, and technologies. This is usually not recom-

mended, because of the size of the task, the traumatic disruption to the daily activities, and the length of time it takes to convert activities and prepare backup procedures manuals.

2. Phasing in all departments of an organization by one type of work at a time: for example, converting the clerical activities to the support staff, then preparing procedures and converting the typing activity to a word processing environment, then restructuring administrative support secretaries by groups of specialization, then commencing implementation of a new records support system, then beginning interface with outside electronics (such as typesetting or electronic mail).

3. Phasing in by work specialization in one given area or department, such as commencing with clerical support, then moving on to word processing, administrative support, and records support, and finally completing implementation by interfacing with other technologies such as mainframe computers, typesetting, and electronic mail. The department-at-a-time approach is usually the most desirable, since it allows a conversion over an activity that is small enough to be closely supervised and controlled. It also provides a better opportunity to make changes.

4. Another method of implementing is to establish a prototype or pilot installation: that is, to set up a test situation of the type of installation that is being considered for wider use in the company. Some advocates of prototypes believe they can take the place of the traditional feasibility study. However, information about volumes and performance before installation is needed to provide a basis for a "before and after" comparison.

Prototypes also require consideration of the human factors. Top management commitment is necessary here, as well as careful attention to communication with employees.

Prototypes have both advantages and disadvantages that must be carefully considered by managers in relation to the organization's financial situation and general management philosophy. A pilot study or prototype requires the investment of hard dollars and personnel time, both of which can become costly unless realistic limits are established and the prototype is well managed. Unrealistic limits can prevent the prototype from being sufficiently measurable to make an intelligent buying decision.

CONCLUSIONS

Practical implementation requires a management commitment to restructuring and a philosophical decision to change through division of work, work specialization, and crossing of departmental lines. The implementation process itself deals with carrying out all of the steps previously described in this chapter. The important considerations listed below will be explored in greater depth in other chapters.

1. Reporting relationships.
2. Restructured and revised job descriptions.
3. Human engineering and personnel fit of the proper person and the proper job.
4. The communication leadership and training of the process of restructuring.
5. Designing the space to fit the needs of the new structure.
6. Preparing the procedures.

The implementation process should be flexible, dynamic, and easily modifiable. Implementation is usually a complex activity that requires careful planning, control, and coordination of all resources in the planning process. After the change has taken place, ongoing day-to-day evaluation of a new system must be undertaken by the manager in charge of the program. It should be periodically audited to determine if it meets the original objectives and the ongoing cost benefits, and if the procedures and policies still coincide with management's objectives.

A system is only beneficial when it meets objectives. A system may need reevaluation when the office becomes too crowded, equipment is out of date, and procedures are no longer relevant. At this point, a total audit or feasibility study of the existing system should be performed, and a new system cycle may start again.

CHAPTER 15

THE ERGONOMICS OF THE AUTOMATED OFFICE

OBJECTIVES

In this chapter you will learn about
1. The science of ergonomics as it relates to the electronic office.
2. Specific ergonomic considerations for the automated office, including the recognition of the importance of environmental factors (such as acoustics, lighting, and temperature) in the worker's environment.
3. Environmental effects on productivity.
4. Possible health hazards related to inappropriate workstation design.
5. A clear-cut action plan for determining environmental factors.
6. Study guidelines used in the automated office.
7. Various approaches to office layout (including the open plan and the traditional office plan).

Ergonomics is a relatively young science; its growth has been spurred by the arrival of electronic hardware in the office workplace. Introduced to the white-collar design community in 1973, it was first described as follows:

> Ergonomics, in the simplest sense, is the science of interfacing all the essential factors to create satisfying and productive work environments.[1]

Typical factors include systems and job analysis, time and work study, the selection of tools and hardware for housing and equipping the worker, the physiology of the worker, the behavioral responses of workers to their work environments, and the external factors that physically and psychologically affect workers (such as light, temperature, sound, color, texture, shape, and appearance). Ergonomics also includes the interface of man and machine. Many aspects of equipment such as keyboard arrangement, functional keys, printer location, and type of screen affect productivity and people satisfaction.

In summary, all the elements that profoundly affect workers' attitudes and performance at the workstation and within the office are a part of ergonomics.

Ergonomics has come of age because planners and designers of offices have realized, in the course of studying and developing each of these factors separately, that considering all factors together at the outset of planning results in well-designed offices. The proper application of ergonomic principles pays off in

▶ An organization that successfully projects the organization's objectives and personality.

▶ An office layout strategically planned for the most efficient flow and handling of information.

▶ Offices that can quickly, easily, and economically adapt to the changing needs of an organization.

▶ Surroundings that are comfortable and satisfying to workers.

▶ Workstations configured for maximum worker productivity.

These considerations are basic for both transitional (short-range) and integrated electronic (long-range) office planning.

Management is faced with no small challenge when attempting to provide a work environment that takes into consideration not only employees' needs but cost factors as well. At the same time, management needs to consider long-range goals as well as those established for the short-run or

---

[1] John B. Dykeman, "Ergonomics, a Path to a Productive and Satisfying Work Environment," *Modern Office Procedures*, September 1973, p. 8.

transitional office. To meet the challenge and achieve established goals certainly requires a managed, planned approach, for without proper attention, expensive chaos can easily result.

THE ENVIRONMENTAL INFLUENCE ON PRODUCTIVITY

With the infusion of electronic technology into the office environment, it becomes necessary for management to study the planning and managing of the office environment, to assure a setting conducive to productivity. According to John B. Dykeman, associate publisher of *Modern Office Procedures*, the "responsibility to create productive and pleasant environments is just as important as it is for making business equipment decisions. In fact, the two areas are becoming more interrelated."[2] More and more, the influence of office environment on worker productivity is being recognized.

A Steelcase-sponsored survey conducted by Louis Harris Associates showed that a 57 percent majority of the office workers felt that there was a great deal of connection between being satisfied with office surroundings and doing a job well.[3] Also, while workers believe that pay is the strongest stimulus to productivity, more comfortable heat, air conditioning, and ventilation are second in importance to them.

Other aspects of their offices that workers feel are important in relation to their job performance are the ability to concentrate without noise and distraction; access to tools, equipment, and materials; and conversational privacy[4] (see Figure 1).

An earlier Steelcase study on the effect of environment on office workers' productivity revealed a 7.8 percent increase in workers' productivity after a new, modern, ergonomically sound office landscape was implemented.[5] Various sources have revealed a 20 to 30 percent improvement in productivity from implementing appropriate office designs that took into account important factors such as human considerations, workflow patterns, territorial concerns, teamwork, location, improved morale concerns, and continuing ability to modify the office layout.

Both the transitional and the integrated electronic office promise increased productivity, but this promise can be realized only by complete planning of every aspect of the physical environment, too.

---

[2] John B. Dykeman, *Modern Office Procedures*, July 1978, p. 8.

[3] *The Steelcase National Study of Office Environments*, No. II, "Comfort and Productivity in the Office of the 80s," conducted by Louis Harris and Associates, Inc., 1980, p. 2.

[4] *Ibid.*, p. 7.

[5] G. F. Tyson, project director of Steelcase, "The Effect of Environment on Office Worker Productivity," *Tests Results in Steelcase Word Processing Center*, August 1974, p. 10.

Figure 1 A workstation that allows an individual to concentrate without distraction, having access to tools, equipment, materials, and conversational privacy. (Courtesy of Steelcase, Inc. Illustrates Steelcase Ultronic 9000® Systems Furniture.)

ERGONOMICS FACTORS

For a better understanding of ergonomics, one must understand all of the various factors and how they must be effectively integrated.

ANATOMY The anatomical considerations involve analysis of the individual's body structure, body dimension, and the physical movement demanded in the work area. Designers in office planning are concerned with *anthropometry*, or the study of human body measurements for the correct scaling of sizes, heights, and shapes of furniture and equipment to the dimensions of the workers (see Figure 2). Adjustable furniture is the most effective and economical way for a company to achieve this end (see Figure 3).

Biomechanics is the study of the musculoskeletal effort of human beings. Biomechanical factors help a designer to plan work spaces and layouts that will minimize the strain of physical work and therefore increase efficiency and reduce error. For example, where will supplies or the tele-

How to Make the Workstation Work for You

1. Adjust the height of the seat to a position where the feet are flat on the ground, and the thigh is on a slight upward angle.

2. Adjust the back of the chair to catch the lumbar concavity.

3. Now that you are seated properly and comfortably, adjust the work surface or equipment height to allow the arm to be parallel or at a slight downward angle.

4. Adjust the light source to remove direct or reflected glare, and then apply a comfortable intensity.

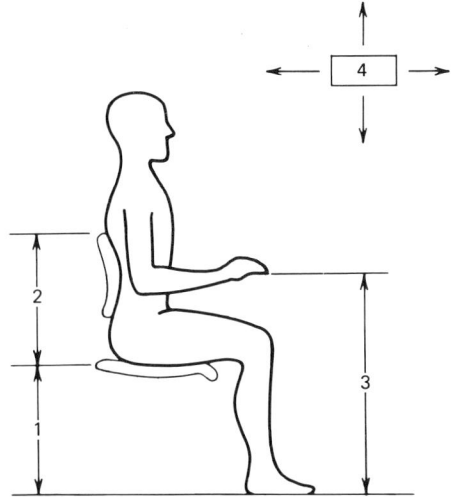

Figure 2 Anatomical considerations. (Courtesy of Modern Office Procedures, June 1980, p. 140.)

phone be placed at the workstation? Are they conveniently located and easily reached, or is the worker required to bend and stretch so frequently and in such a way that a severe strain is placed on the musculoskeletal system?

Another factor that can contribute to muscular strain is the positioning of hands and wrists on the keyboard without the ability to rest them. Wrist

Figure 3 Adjustable terminal base designed to accommodate anatomical considerations. (Courtesy: IBM Corporate Health and Safety Department.)

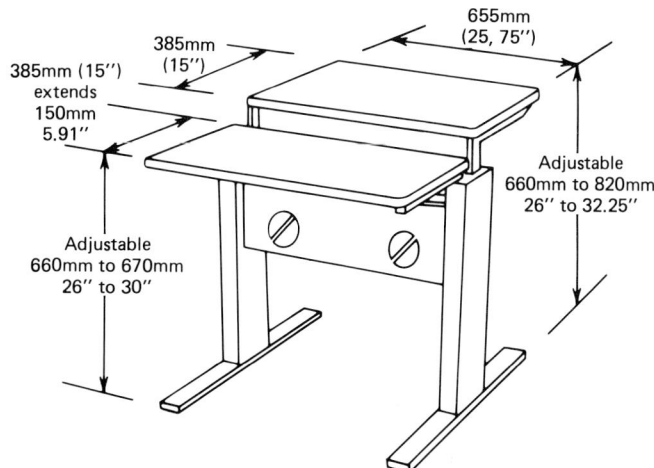

655mm
(25, 75")

385mm
(15")

385mm (15")
extends
150mm
5.91"

Adjustable
660mm to 820mm
26" to 32.25"

Adjustable
660mm to 670mm
26" to 30"

rests placed adjacent to a keyboard provide support to the wrists which reduces muscular stress and fatigue (see Figure 4).

In addition, swivel-base terminal stands, like the one shown in Figure 5, allow the operator to rotate the terminal base 360 degrees. This flexibility reduces screen reflection, permits screen access by numerous people, and allows a 7 percent tilt forward and backward which reduces fatigue, stress, strain, and frustration.

PHYSIOLOGY   Physiological considerations involve environmental factors such as light, color, sound, and heat. These factors may have both physical and psychological impact on workers. For example, excessive noise may damage hearing; but, likelier in the office environment, noise can contribute to stress also. The principles of ergonomics require that designers attempt to

Figure 4   Wrist support is designed for operator comfort at the keyboard. By supporting the wrists, it reduces strain on the upper arms that often leads to operator fatigue and keystroke error. (Courtesy of Wright Line, Worcester, Mass.)

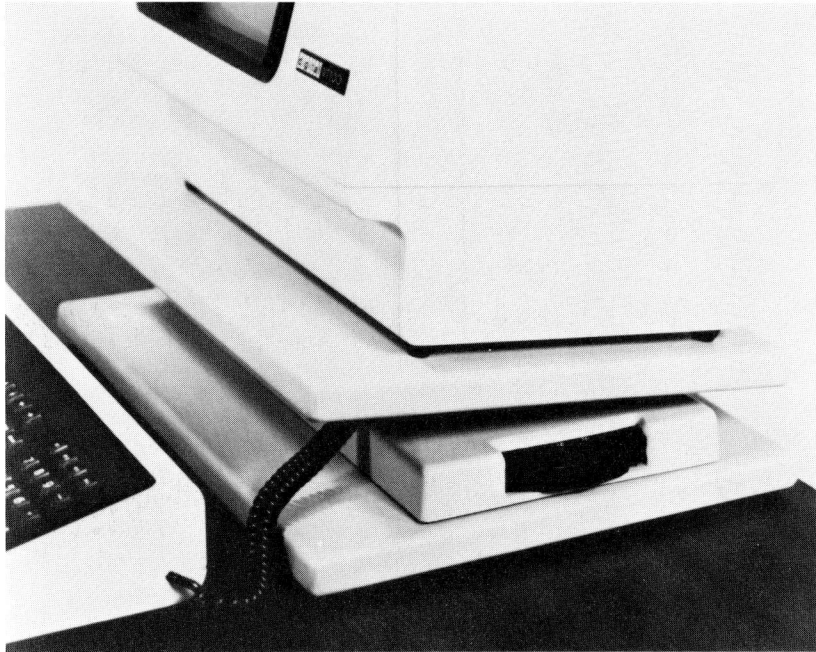

Figure 5   Swivel tilt bases allow any VDT user to adjust the terminal for comfortable, glare-free viewing. Tilt adjustments are made by turning a single, finger-tip control wheel. (Courtesy of Wright Line, Worcester, Mass.)

minimize noise and ensure that the equipment and workstations are designed to accommodate human biomechanical and sensory capabilities.

PSYCHOLOGY   Psychological considerations involve the factors in the work environment that affect the behavior and attitudes of workers. Workstations need to be designed to meet the social needs of the worker and minimize the causes of stress and disruptions. Yet, the workspace must also provide a conducive atmosphere for productive work output. Psychological considerations often determine whether workers have positive or negative attitudes toward their work. Too often the workplace is not designed to meet the psychological needs of the worker: for example, the provision of sufficient privacy and quiet to a worker whose job requires freedom from disruption. Frequently, little attention has been directed to this question. One of the least recognized drawbacks to proper workstation and layout planning has been overemphasis on style and appearance, to the extent that the workers' efficiency and comfort have been penalized.

SOCIAL IMPACT   Along with the anatomical, physiological, and psychological factors, the ergonomic planner must think of the social impact of an office layout. A need for territoriality, or boundaries for one's workspace and personal use, is inherent. At the same time, people need to feel a part of a social group, and this social communication must be facilitated by office design.

Robert Propst, the president of Herman Miller Research Corporation, has done considerable in-depth research and analysis of the office. He explains the privacy-versus-involvement conflict as follows:

> *Safety, security, protection of territory is a universal legitimate concern for every man. It is not at all surprising therefore that given a choice of the kind of office one wants, everyone wants "a private office." The logical idea, a natural instinct, is for "a safe, protected, assured place . . . your own, identified, marked, secure."*

But is privacy the only answer to what we need in offices? Certainly not. We need involvement. We cannot exist without a full and healthy exchange with others. Involvement is an essential need, a good idea . . . to be part of, visible, wanted, needed, recognized, part of the family of activity.[6]

The quandary in human desire may be expressed by "an office should neither closed nor open be."[7] Propst suggests that the reconciliation of privacy and social needs requires a new language of enclosure and access.

To meet both closed and open needs or enclosure and access needs, Propst suggests moderating both needs and desires in a so-called compromise answer. One way to achieve compromise is through the use of modular panels of differing heights and through consideration of the principle of operation concerning enclosure and access, as illustrated in Figure 6.

PHYSICAL LAYOUT Attention to workstation design is especially important when restructuring of the office organization suddenly places workers in new jobs, new locations, and new reporting relationships.

These changes often will be less traumatic if workers can see the possibility of status improvement in the new work. For example, if traditional secretaries become correspondence (word processing) typists or administrative secretaries in a new support structure, a well-designed modular workstation would prove to be a big advantage in making the change a pleasing one—in addition to making more effective use of space.

People also need to have access to areas such as lunchrooms, lounges, and other facilities that support their social needs. Finally, the physical environment must help to interface the employee with the technology of the modern office. As technology present in the office environment increases, the potential for alienating people increases, because their self-

---

[6] Robert Propst, *The Office-A Facility Based on Change* (Zeeland, Mich.: Herman Miller, Inc., 1968), p. 25.

[7] *Ibid.*, p. 42.

The classical human search for environmental support has imbued us with very discreet feelings about space and enclosure.

We are uncomfortable in open space without a back-up element.

1. Bad

A back-up element provides us with great psychological comfort. We now have a personal reference point. We can face the world and invite involvement or we can turn away and limit involvement.

2. Good

If the back-up can give us some enclosure, we are even better off . . . now we have a way to express relative exposure and gain a greater degree of privacy.

3. Better

Three sides with a slightly widened opening appears to be the best enclosure of all as a generality. There is good definition of territory, privacy is well expressed and the ability to survey or participate is well maintained.

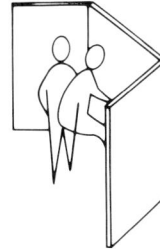

4. Best

Four sided enclosure is bad for the wide awake and activity-oriented man. He is isolated, insulated, and remote. His ability to be part of an organizational family is diminished.

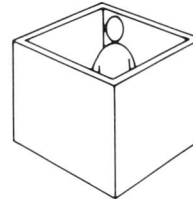

5. Bad

Figure 6 Principles of Operation: Enclosure and Access (Courtesy of Herman Miller, Inc., Zeeland, Mich., Robert Propst, "The Office, A Facility Based on Change;" 1968, p. 43.

confidence decreases. The employees in an average word processing center will spend 85 percent of their time working with one or more of the word processing systems. Everything possible must be done in both the machine and nonmachine portion of their physical environment to overcome any real or potential employee morale and motivation problems. For example, as part of person-machine compatibility, such things as being sure that the individual work surface heights make the hardware as easy to use as possible are important. Proper acoustical treatments to reduce noise levels, the proper use of color, and nonregimented furniture layout are examples of important nonmachine aspects to be considered when interfacing people with technology.

Ergonomics must take all of these factors into account. First, the office layout must provide the proper task-oriented components (such as work surfaces, seats, files, storage, screens, lighting, pin-up surfaces, reference shelves, and specific equipment). Second, the layout must facilitate direct visual and physical access to members of the same work group and related groups. By combining the personal privacy needs of workers with their needs for social interaction, the designer can create a positive working atmosphere and develop a smoothly integrated workflow in the office.

Along with all of the employee needs, the organization has certain needs that must be served. A coordinated office workflow requires both face-to-face communications and electronic communications. The flow of paper documents and materials from management to workstation must be smooth. There must be control of internal and external paper traffic, and the physical grouping of the employees must match their activities and tasks.

ORGANIZATIONAL, TASK PERFORMANCE, AND BEHAVIORAL CONSIDERATIONS

Ideally, the design of a workstation for optimum performance capabilities should take into account the spectrum of organizational, task performance, and behavioral needs.

Organizational Needs

Organizational needs include the requirements for face-to-face as well as electronic communications; the flow of paper documents and materials; the grouping and positioning of workstations in accordance with team and departmental activities and tasks; control of internal traffic, with external visitor traffic channeled to bypass work areas so that it does not interfere with individual and group tasks (by use of restrictive zones); the placement of common files, equipment, and services so as to serve participating groups of individuals.

Task Performance Needs

Task performance considerations include provisions for acoustical privacy for those tasks that require confidentiality and security, freedom from interruption in concentrative and creative work, security from having people walk or stand directly behind a worker, privacy of information and documents both on or within the workplace, and protection from intrusive noise and interruptions.

Behavioral Needs

Behavioral and social needs include the need for territoriality, the sense of belonging enhanced by proper grouping of workstations; the realization of status expectation commensurate with title; the need to alter, adjust, and personalize the work area, to create a feeling of involvement, participation, and control; and amenities to support social needs (lounges, lunchrooms, and other communual facilities).[8]

The decrease in dependence on others and the wedding of the operator to the terminal may have negative effects on socialization and tend to isolate the operator. If there is no day-to-day contact with others in business, the fundamental need for social interaction may not be fulfilled. Isolation represents to some individuals a serious degradation in the "quality of worklife" and could lessen motivation, pride, and other factors that affect productivity.

TEMPERATURE, HUMIDITY, AND VENTILATION

As indicated in the Steelcase survey, workers believe that comfortable heat, air conditioning, and ventilation affect their job performance. Conditions that allow an office to be "too hot" or "too cold" can lead to reduced concentration, unproductive or costly errors, and increased absenteeism among employees.

Therefore, comfort control is important in management planning. Many considerations are involved in creating and maintaining the desired temperature conditions—for example, the size and shape of the area, the number of people normally working in the area (there is a heat buildup created by body heat), the kind and amount of equipment (equipment also generates heat). Humidity is important, along with temperature; the two cannot be separated in considering comfort.

Although the Steelcase study found that office workers generally supported the need for uniform temperature control, such as that found in the Carter administration's energy regulations, many found the restrictions of no more than 65 degrees in winter and no less than 78 degrees in summer to be uncomfortable.[9] Individual preferences and needs will differ, so it is nearly impossible to satisfy all people. However, the temperature and relative humidity guide shown in Figure 7 indicates those combinations that satisfy various percentages of people. For example, most people are comfortable when the temperature is 75 degrees and the relative humidity is 30 percent.[10] This table is based on the ASHRAE American Society of Heating, Refrigerating and Air Conditioning Engineers Comfort Chart, which applies to inhabitants of the United States only.

People may adapt to temperature levels with such measures as wearing heavier or different clothes; but temperature, humidity, and air distribution also affect equipment performance. If relative humidity falls below

[8] Archie Kaplan, "Ergonomics of the Open Plan Workstation," *Modern Office Procedures*, April 1978, p. 49H.
[9] *The Steelcase National Study of Office Environments*, No. II, p. 111.
[10] *Planning the Office for Word Processing*, IBM, 1972, p. 14.

TEMPERATURE AND RELATIVE HUMIDITY GUIDE			
Season	Temperature (Fahrenheit)	Relative Humidity	Percentage of People Feeling Comfortable
Summer	80°	15%	
	75°	30%	95%
	72°	50%	
	77°	15%	80%
	75°	35%	
	75°	15%	50%
	72°	40%	
Winter	76°	20%	97%
	75°	30%	
	74°	10%	90%
	70°	45%	
	73°	10%	85%
	70°	37%	

Figure 7 (Courtesy of Walter Kleinschrod, Leonard B. Kruk, and Hilda J. Turner, "Word Processing Operations, Applications and Administration," Bobbs Merrill Co., Inc.)

25 percent, static buildup may occur and affect some equipment. Although antistatic mats may be purchased, the need for them can be avoided. Maintenance of a stable climate is a key factor in overall office planning.

SPACE Space is the basic resource the planner starts with. Attention must be given to how much space is currently used and how effectively it meets current needs; how much space is available; and what space will be required for changes, in both the short and long run. Flexibility must be a primary concern. Space planning and office layout should be based upon

1. Providing a smooth flow of paperwork and communications.
2. Balancing the territorial and social needs of workers.
3. Providing adequate access to electrical and communications circuits.
4. Giving attention to proper lighting, climate, acoustics, and other environmental factors.

There are many advantages to effective space utilization. Space standards in offices can save a company planning time and future modifica-

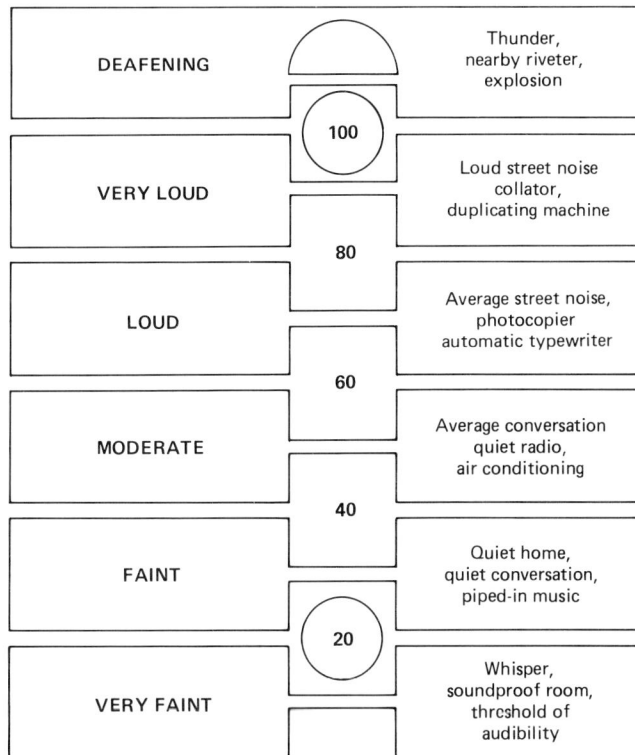

Figure 8   Decibel level chart. The noise level of an average office is 50 decibels.

tion expense, and avoid employee complaints concerning favoritism. A Davis Associates of Chicago report suggested that other benefits are increased predictability in planning, improved management control of cost factors, reduction in time and cost of implementation, and increased mobility of personnel within an organization.[11]

ACOUSTICS Noise reduction has become a major concern in the modern office. Noise affects the human nervous system and worker productivity. Studies show that workers in a noisy environment require almost 20 percent more time to complete a given amount of work than do those in a quiet place. Noise can also inhibit decision making and produce medical problems. Long exposure to noises over 70 decibels can permanently impair hearing. The noise level at the average office is about 50 decibels. A noisy office ranges from 60 to 80 decibels, equivalent to an average factory (see Figure 8). In a roomful of word processing equipment with no acoustical treatment, the

[11] Helen Parvis, "Planning for the Total Word Processing Center," *Modern Office Procedures*, February 1981, p. 69.

level could climb as high as 100 decibels. Proper ergonomic planning can significantly decrease the impact of noise in the modern office.

There are two principal methods of controlling noise: by engineering and by architecture. Engineering controls significantly reduce noise levels at a given position. An example of an engineering control is an acoustical hood enclosure, which significantly reduces the noise level at the output station or printer. The effectiveness is, however, governed by the operator and whether the hood is used or left up for convenience in inserting paper. Architectural methods involve treating hard surfaces such as ceilings, floors, and walls with sound-absorbing materials and designing office layout effectively. Acoustical wall panels can dull noise traveling laterally. Screens and dividers can be placed around the workstation both to absorb noise and to guarantee work privacy. Wall coverings (especially linen or carpet) as well as draperies can effectively mask noise. Flame-resistant and static-controlled carpeting may be effectively utilized in the modern office. Masking sounds (i.e., "white noise" such as waves or crackling leaves) and music systems can also help. Solving sound control problems often requires a combination of techniques.

SEATING Many tasks in the modern office involve long periods of sitting. This can potentially result in fatigue and discomfort if chairs are not properly fitted. A chair can be considered a prosthetic device to counteract the force of gravity acting on the body in a seated position.[12] Reasonably good seating can be achieved by proper dimensions, construction, and flexibility of a chair. Anatomical considerations (both anthropometric and biomechanical) are paramount in proper seating. Chairs should be designed for comfort, freedom of movement, and for minimization of fatigue. Growing evidence shows that uncomfortable chairs cause fatigue and, conversely, that comfortable ones contribute to higher energy and productivity.

Chairs should be adjustable, to provide for human body differences such as those shown in Figures 9 and 10. Each chair should fit the individual it will serve by providing anatomical support. It should be flexible in movement, to allow stretching and reaching as well as to fit the activity of the job. For example, a clerical worker usually operates in a tighter workspace than a manager. Clerical workers move from side to side and around in the chair. They would need chairs with both flexibility and support.

Work surfaces should also be adjustable, to meet the needs of workers of differing heights. Work requirements often differ in workspace required. The workspace height and size often must change to accommodate keyboards, CRTs, and printers rather than typewriters.

---

[12] Archie Kaplan, "Sitting Ergonomically," *Modern Office Procedures*, June 1980, p. 142.

Head not excessively
bent over, inward
curve at neck.

Outward curve of the
spine in the thorax.

About a 90° angle
between the upper and
lower arms, upper arm
near vertical.

Inward curve of the
spine in the lumbar
region.

No pressure against the
lower back of the thigh.

Feet flat on the floor
or footrest.

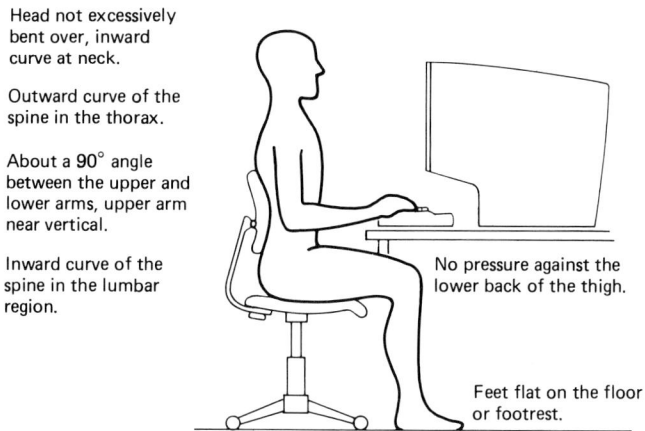

Figure 9 Ergonomically designed chair. (Courtesy of IBM Corporation.)

One should not underestimate the importance of ensuring that the office furnishings are comfortable and flexible to both individual worker and organizational needs, now and in the future. Already we are seeing more and more provision for electronically wired furniture to accommodate electronic office components, since the workstation of the future is likely to become more of a communications console than a writing surface.

COLOR/DECOR The creation of a comfortable, pleasing atmosphere is a goal of ergonomics, and skillful use of color and decor can help to achieve desired goals. Greens and blues are soothing, cool colors; reds, yellows, oranges, and browns are warm, vibrant colors that tend to be stimulating. Color theory is built around color contrast, the relation of color to color as well as the relationship of areas of color and color to background. Archie Kaplan, the president of Environment Planning, Inc., suggests that "the realities of electronic hardware, CRTs, and keyboard devices should be offset and balanced by a richer environment." The new color schemes appear to

Figure 10 Synergetix® chair. (Courtesy of IBM Corporation.)

reflect an increased need for peace and tranquility in the office environment. Hence, the pleasing earth tones have increased in popularity. Dark colors can make an area seem small and closed in; light colors can make it seem more spacious. Kaplan also suggests that "color as a catalyst can affect mood, productivity, and creativity in the chemistry of the human psyche." Choice of color should be based on the space involved, the type of work performed, the period of time spent in the area, the furnishings, and the equipment. Carpet, draperies, plants, and pictures can also aid in the decorative effort and provide personal territory for the worker. Colors, textures, and patterns of ceilings, walls, floors, draperies, and other furnishings should all harmonize.

LIGHTING   The problem of efficient yet effective office illumination has plagued office planning for years. It is a recognized fact that better illumination is directly related to an increase in effort and office productivity (see Figure 11). A sufficient quantity of light is important for the accurate performance of a task. Further, poor lighting can cause visual problems and decrease employee morale. It is also important to note that lighting consumes the most energy of all interior planning elements.

To meet individual needs and reduce energy costs, a trend toward use of task and ambient lighting has emerged. Task lighting is lighting that is required for an employee to perform a specific task. It is usually provided

Figure 11 Workers' reaction to increase in illumination. Note that improved lighting directly relates to improved productivity.

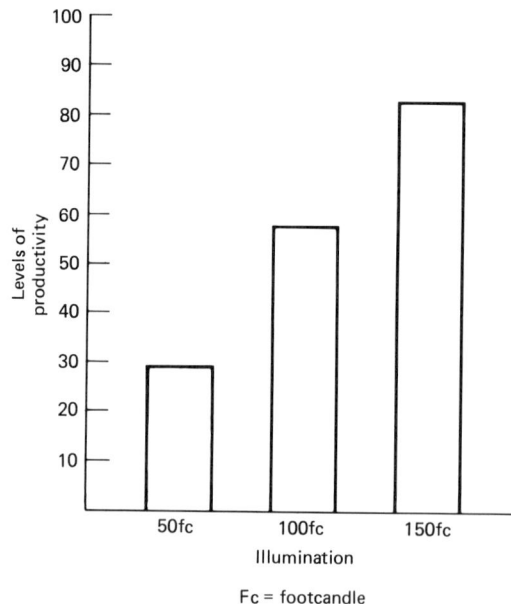

Fc = footcandle

by light fixtures built into the furniture. Ambient lighting is the background lighting. It is used to complement task lighting.

Two basic sources of light are used in most offices: incandescent (the familiar light bulb) and fluorescent (the principal light source in most businesses, which can provide an approximation of daylight). Modern offices generally rely on fluorescent lighting combinations, since they provide nearly shadowless lighting, generate less heat than incandescent lighting, and use less electricity.

Several types of physical problems caused by office lighting have been recognized. A veiling reflection (when light bounces off the task or workstation surface into a worker's eyes) can create the effect of a thin, gauzy veil between the task and the observer. Glare is another quality concern, since it can cause eye fatigue, headaches, and decreased productivity. A good lighting system can significantly improve employee morale, enhance the safety and security of a building, and improve office appearance and image.

Over the next 20 years, soaring energy costs will force offices to attempt to use low-cost lighting to illuminate office space. Greater use of CRTs and microfilm viewers may "self-illuminate" certain tasks and the adoption of indirect lighting will decrease overall lighting levels. One can expect lower light levels in offices in the future.

HEALTH HAZARDS

An increase in white-collar productivity is of great importance to our national economy. The gains in office productivity resulting from the use of video display terminals (VDTs) are significant. However, with the increased utilization of these devices in the modern office comes the increased fear of major health hazards resulting from the equipment.

In a report issued by the National Institute for Occupational Safety and Health (NIOSH), three areas of concern with video display terminals were studied: eye fatigue, muscle fatigue, and job stress. In this study, 250 VDT operators in California were compared with a control group of 250 people doing comparable office jobs without using VDT equipment. The study concluded that implementation of the following guidelines could significantly minimize problems with eyes and muscle fatigue and with job stress.[13]

▶ Flexibility in work.
▶ Control over job tasks.
▶ Challenge in work tasks.

---

[13] Marvin J. Dainoff, National Institute of Occupational Safety and Health, "Occupational Stress Factors in Secretarial/Clerical Workers," 1979, p. 26.

▶ Completion of a total job.

▶ Appropriate workstation design (ergonomics).

A 1981 study by the FDA on radiation emitted from VDT units included that "the consensus appears to be that machines emit little or no harmful radiation under normal operating conditions and the emissions that are detectable are well below any national and international standards. Compared to some common sources of radiation, VDT's present a much lower risk. Fluorescent lamps emit more visible and ultraviolet light."[14] Thus, VDT units, used by an estimated 7 million Americans, were given a clean bill of health by the FDA.

The glare produced by the VDT screens is another key area of concern. A study done at the Loughborough University of Technology (London) found that the perceived increase in visual defects in VDT operators resulted not from the screen glare but rather from uncorrected vision defects in the operator. The researchers indicated that between 20 percent and 30 percent of the population have uncorrected visual defects. When these people use a CRT screen (VDT unit), the screen causes discomfort. The use of such equipment simply accentuates the visual defect.

STUDY AND IMPLEMENTATION: SPACE DESIGN

Creating a new office environment requires an implementation process as thorough as one for a new system or organization structure. Warren Chol, vice-president of Environetics, Inc., suggests the following process:

Step One: Target schedule.
Step Two: Fact finding.
Step Three: Space analysis/data collection.
Step Four: Space planning design.
Step Five: Budget control.

Whatever the size of the organization, the steps are standard and should be followed. In a large organization the facilities design department may assist in implementation, or in a small office the project leader may direct implementation. Design consultants may also provide valuable, objective assistance to any sized group.

STEP ONE: TARGET SCHEDULE   The time required to execute the necessary steps to complete a new office (whether it involves an entire building, remodeling, or a departmental layout) should be scheduled at the outset. Adequate time for data collec-

---

[14] FDA Study, Associated Press release, April 25, 1981.

tion, management approval, purchasing (including the bid process, if used), and implementation should be allowed (see Figure 12).

**STEP TWO:
FACT FINDING**

This step includes a series of studies. The following information should be gathered: a study of traffic patterns in the office; an inventory of existing furniture and an appraisal of its condition, to determine whether to reuse, reassign, or discard it; and an accounting of available floor space.

**STEP THREE:
SPACE
ANALYSIS/DATA
COLLECTION**

This step involves development of space requirements based on people, machine, and facilities. To arrive at the proper amount of space needed for a new environment, a planner must take a head count of present personnel; be familiar with each job description; record the individual requirements of each job for machines, work surfaces, storage, interpersonal activities (meetings), and privacy; estimate the rate and types of projected growth and range; and understand the workflow, materials, and procedures of the group being studied. Additional information about the machines should include the type and number of machines to be used and

Figure 12 Sample time schedule. Time to complete a new office setup should be scheduled at the outset of planning.

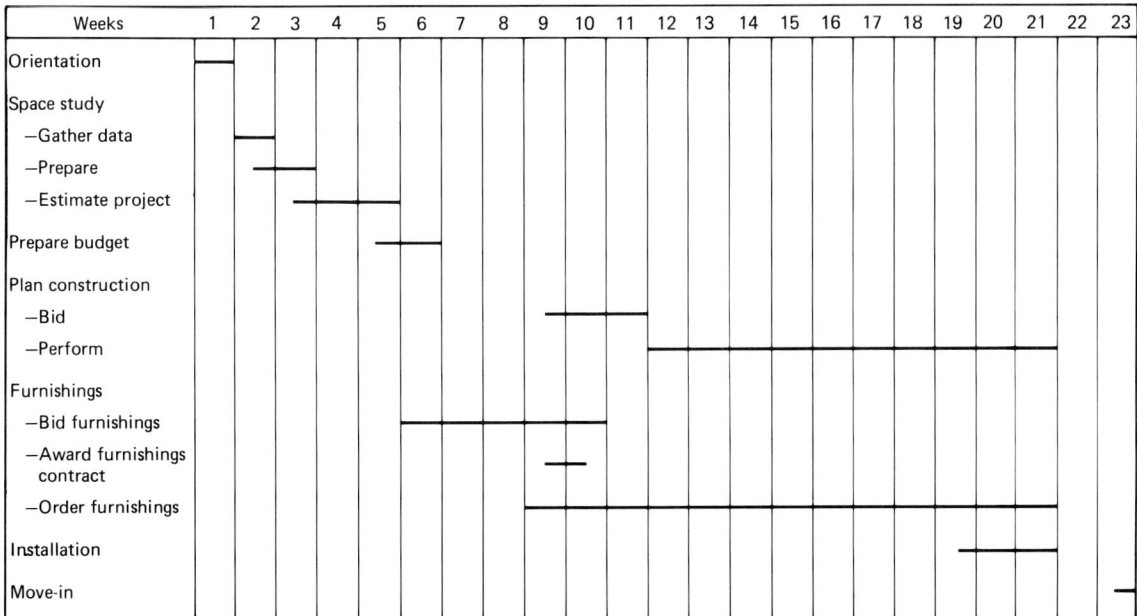

Sample Time Schedule

(15,000 – 50,000 square feet of office space)

the equipment requirements in terms of energy, space, and so on. Equipment specification sheets available from vendors for each product model are good sources of this type of information.

The following types of facility conditions must be known: size of space to be occupied, location of the space in the building, energy and power sources, acoustical controls, and traffic flow.

STEP FOUR: SPACE PLANNING/DESIGN

Space planning and design involves the development of the actual design based on square-footage requirements. Minimum square-footage requirements by station are a good starting base. For example, the following table is suggested by Herman Miller, manufacturers of Action Office "systems furniture," as a guide:

Secretarial station: 30-50 square feet.

Supervisor/coordinator/manager station: 50-100 square feet.

General manager: 100-150 square feet.

Dictating booth: 20 square feet.

Systems analyst/proofreading/training: 50-80 square feet.

Storage: 48 square feet.

Break area/lounge/coat room: 16-80 square feet.

Files: 8-16 square feet.

Copy machine area: 50-100 square feet.

These figures do not include circulation space, which can be estimated at 10 to 15 percent of the total square footage.[15] Once standards have been established, an expansion report, or plans for future office development, should also be considered.

Although preestablished space standards are useful as a guide to the planner, it would be unwise to accept them without questions. In the final stages, space allocation for each office workstation must be made on the aggregate basis of actual requirements of each job, and provisions for expansion or change. Space planning based on too loose an estimate could result in either too much or too little space.

At this point, an actual physical drawing of the new workstations or office layout should be made. It should include all environmental factors (noise control devices, furnishings, lighting, etc.). A full-scale model should be developed for the management presentation.

STEP FIVE: BUDGET CONTROL

The coordinator of the office design project should ensure adequate budget control and authority before purchasing begins.

---

[15] *Herman Miller Word Processing Resource Manual*, Herman Miller, Inc., p. 111.

The space planning, budgeting, and purchasing functions are closely interrelated. A complete and accurate budget paves the way for a smooth purchasing process. A good budget relies on the accurate results of the space planning and analysis function.

A complete budget will list every item involved in a new office environment. The costs of reconstruction or remodeling (including electrical and communications work) are available from contractors' or architects' quotations or proposals. The budget should list *all* furnishings, item-by-item, to go into the new offices; that item listing should mention product description (or preferred brand, part number, style, color, and other pertinent information). Applicable discount or bid information should appear in the budget. If delivery and installation charges are not included with the product, they should be reported separately. The budget should also take into account trade-in or salvage values of present furnishings.

OPEN OFFICE PLANNING VERSUS CONVENTIONAL PLANNING

An increasingly popular method of office planning is "open planning" or design without walls. According to one estimate, more than 10,000 offices have gone "open" in the last five years. Approximately $5.2 billion was spent in the seventies for open-plan systems.[16] By 1981, open plan furnishings surpassed those of conventional or traditional office furniture in the United States.

The traditional office-plan floor layout usually consists of continuous rows of one-windowed offices reserved for senior management. Parallel rows of smaller interior offices are reserved for junior staffers and the "bull pen" or "secretarial pool" for the support staff. Corner offices, with larger windows and more space, are reserved for top executives.

There are two types of open plan. In both, the entire staff intermingles in an open area with no permanent dividing walls. Each area has some exposure to the building exterior. The planning revolves around function versus order of command. The first approach to office planning was developed in Germany in the 1950s and was called "office landscaping." This plan uses free-form clusters of furniture throughout a floor, with screens or plants placed to prevent eye contact.

The other plan is the modular approach, in which freestanding partitions are set up on the floor with components attached to or hanging from the partitions. This approach is more detailed and expensive. The American plan is an adaptation of both plans in an attempt to use wide space areas and yet maintain certain levels of privacy for some positions.

[16] "Open Plan Systems Work for the Offices of the 1980's," *Modern Office Procedures*, January 1980, p. 60.

Alternative aids in utilizing space efficiently and flexibly include purchasing modular and panel-hung furniture and clustering workstations. Panel-hung storage areas allow expansion vertically instead of horizontally, by the use of air space above a workstation rather than floor space beside it. Blue Cross-Blue Shield of Indiana found the use of modular workstations resulted in a 30 percent increase in space. In addition, supplies stored in panel-hung bins were more convenient for employees and contributed to increases in productivity.

Without a doubt, there are definite advantages to the open-plan system. Communication is facilitated, flexibility in personnel and equipment movement is maximized, and productivity has been found to increase as much as 30 percent. The system, if properly designed, is more tailored to individual needs. Floor space is better utilized and egalitarian office relationships are introduced.

Perhaps the most important benefits to cost-conscious management are the ease and economy of making workstation and layout changes. With modular or open-plan furnishings, single workstations or entire departments can be arranged overnight or over a weekend, without reconstruction. An office maintenance staff can make almost all changes.

Since the components are all part of one system, they can be removed from one workstation and added to another. Additional cost-benefit data appears in the "cost of change" section later in this chapter.

Although it offers great advantages, the open plan is not appropriate for every office environment. Most employees are used to working in an existing environment, and any change is bound to meet with resistance at first. Not all firms can have the open system, because of confidentiality and privacy considerations. Existing walls and other physical constraints sometimes cannot be changed in present facilities. Compromise between the open and conventional plans is always a possibility. The best way to determine if an office needs an open or a conventional plan is to examine the situation, purpose, and activities of the organization (as shown in the space planning analysis) and then determine if open planning would yield more benefits than disadvantages.

PROBLEMS AND SOLUTIONS IN IMPLEMENTATION

PEOPLE Several aspects of human behavior must be considered when office change is planned. Human nature is such that it is important that change provide improvement in the workplace and not be made merely for the sake of change. Otherwise, quite naturally the worker will perceive the change as bad.

According to the Steelcase survey, a small percentage of office workers perceive that employees now have a say in planning new offices and selecting office equipment. Moreover, they believe that their recommendations could lead to increases in productivity and greater efficiency. Design professionals also feel that they have too little contact with the employees who will ultimately use the facilities. Planning committees with representation and input from the office workers could benefit both the planning of and communication about change.

ENERGY   Energy concerns are paramount today. In ergonomic planning, business needs to implement systems that conserve energy. The AMS Committee of 500 survey in 1980 indicated that most businesses have already taken these concerns into account. Over 55.3 percent of the companies have a formal energy savings program in effect. Some 54.1 percent have conducted official energy audits and surveys, and 86.9 percent of those have implemented the results of those surveys in their energy goals.[17]

Companies are also reducing energy consumption for heating, lighting, and air conditioning. Over 75 percent of the companies have decreased air conditioning and heating during nonworking hours and have adjusted temperature standards during working hours. Some more recently constructed buildings are designed to capture the heat generated by lighting and recirculate it as a part of the total heating system.

Conservation attempts focused on lighting and electricity are also being pursued. Universal lighting systems can provide initial energy savings of between 10 and 20 percent. With a coordinated task/ambient lighting approach, the total number and energy output of overhead lights can be reduced. The world famous GEW Building in Cologne, West Germany, revolutionized modern office planning by making lighting conservation, as well as overall energy conservation, a top priority and achieving energy consumption levels about 50 to 60 percent below those in older office buildings.[18]

COST   The need to change an office environment can place tremendous pressure on an organization. New equipment requirements, the desirability of adequate equipment testing before installation, expansion of space needs, and personnel adjustments are all pressures to be faced. In addition, changing a traditional office facility is time consuming, costly, and often just plain irritating. Yet the organization faces a dilemma: either change to meet changing conditions or remain stationary and face even bigger renovation pressures and costs later. Office space costs are continually rising.

---

[17] Edward Thomas, CAM, *Management World*, March 1981, p. 15.
[18] Victoria Jackson, "Energy Efficient Office Provides an Example to the World," *Modern Office Procedures*, March 1981, p. 86.

In 1981, office space costs ran at a national average of $16 a square foot, or double that of 1975.[19]

Some people claim that changing to a modern office layout (i.e., open plan) can yield enough rewards to justify a costly change. For one thing, the cost of changing a modern open office format is 50 to 75 cents per square foot, as compared with $10 to $20 per square foot to change a traditional office facility. Thus, if an organization changes only a third of its space in five years time, the cost of change in a conventional 10,000 square-foot facility would be $60,000. The same change in a modern open office would cost $2500 or less.

Initial construction costs for a conventional office versus an open office also show the open office to have cost advantages. Comparisons of the initial construction costs for each type of office clearly indicate that open office construction is significantly *less expensive* than conventional office design.

Proponents of the conventional plan claim that the cost of the office furniture is too high for the open office plan. Though the open office is far from cheap in terms of furniture—prices range up to $2500 for a single workstation—it looks much more economical when thought of as walls-plus furniture. The open plan allows far more flexibility than a fixed-wall setup, because a few workers with hammers and wrenches can change the layout of a sizable office area overnight.[20] Any evaluation of costs should include not only the outright furniture cost but also the interrelated aspects of the costs of change and preparation for continuing change.

The greatest advantage to a modern office layout is savings in time and labor. In an office with movable furniture (flexible furnishings and panels), one man can move and make significant office changes overnight. The cost of change should not be a significant deterrent to office renovation, for changing now to the modern open office provides preparation for the transition to and the proper basis for moving into the integrated electronic office.

[19] "Office Space in Demand," *The Office*, July 1981, p. 206.
[20] Ann M. Morrison, "Action Is What Makes Herman Miller Climb," *Fortune*, June 15, 1981, p. 168.

CHAPTER 16

SELECTING THE SYSTEM

OBJECTIVES

In this chapter you will learn about
1. General considerations for selecting hardware and software.
2. What to know about present office operation before you try to determine office equipment needs.
3. What to learn from an equipment demonstration.
4. Criteria for selecting vendors and equipment.
5. What you should know about software.
6. Methods of financing equipment.

AN OVERALL VIEW

Among the most important decisions made by management are those concerned with selecting the hardware and software to meet productivity goals. With the current technological explosion in office hardware and software, the decision about what to buy and which vendor to select is a major one and demands a great deal of study, comparison, analysis, and justification (see Figure 1).

It is important to remember during the selection process to choose equipment that best suits the needs of the individual office, and not necessarily that which represents the most recent technological breakthrough. Many executives are susceptible to the "keep-up-with-the-Joneses"syndrome and end up overbuying and paying too much for equipment that is too sophisticated or powerful for immediate needs. On the other hand, underbuying, buying on a piecemeal basis, or giving too little consideration to long-range planning is equally harmful.

Specific considerations depend upon the situation and are usually identified for the particular situation by the feasibility study.

There are, however, a number of important considerations that must be taken into account before any office technology is selected, ranging from specific equipment design to the general goals of management. The following list shows the major areas to consider:

1. Objectives of the organization.
2. Total information needs of the organization, including interfacing systems.
3. Volume and nature of the work and methods of creation, processing, distribution, and destruction of information in the organization.
4. Requirements in terms of time, personnel, skills, and costs necessary to process business information.
5. Configuration needs or number of pieces of equipment that will be needed.
6. Upgradability and compatibility between current and new equipment.
7. Available physical space.
8. Information storage requirements of an organization.
9. Access time requirements.

Each of these considerations merits close attention, because the findings will guide the executive toward an office automation system most appropriate for an organization.

MANAGEMENT OBJECTIVES

First to be considered are the management objectives of the organization. It is important to determine exactly what management expects to gain from an office automation system. For example, management's goal may

"DO YOU HAVE ONE THAT LISTS CRITERIA FOR TECHNOLOGY SELECTION?"

Figure 1 Selecting equipment requires more than shopping at the local store. It requires analysis and research.

be to decrease costs and/or to provide increased service to its customers. Which is the primary goal and which is secondary? Perhaps both are of equal importance. In addition, it must be determined exactly how much management is prepared to budget for new equipment, as well as management's expectations of the new system. However, that figure will be affected by the strength and accuracy of the proposal placed before management. Knowing what management expects will help the persons presenting the final equipment proposal to know what to stress in their presentation.

INFORMATION NEEDS

The second consideration is to explore the exact needs of a total support system in an organization. The typing function is the most recognized support function in nearly every organization, but there are other support functions that are using more and more technology to increase efficiency and productivity. Studies should be done to determine the need for photocomposition units, OCR units, telecommunications and dictation equipment, or the automation of other functions such as records processing, handling mail, and message taking.

For the purchase of equipment, a systems approach should be used—this involves an awareness of how one component of an equipment system interfaces or links up with other components in the office. For example, does the dictation equipment feed directly into the word processing or typing equipment, or is an intermediate step needed?

THE NATURE OF THE WORK

The third consideration is an accurate tally of the volume and nature of the work being performed in the office. When the volume of work is determined, specific figures and statistics should be recorded to find out how much capacity will be required from new equipment. In addition, a record should be kept to indicate the heavy and light times of workflow and if there are periods when volume is consistent or widely fluctuating.

For volume determination, statistics should be gathered by the type of work being performed. For example, most offices require typing; however, the typing requirements of some departments may primarily involve correspondence, whereas others may produce reports exclusively or compile charts and graphs. Is the work highly repetitive? How much of it is revised, and how often? Must the work be performed in only one location or could it be batched (sent in a group) to a central location? Who will be performing the initial keyboarding—professional or office staff? Answers to these questions help to determine equipment needs. The exact type of work required of a piece of equipment is an important factor in the deci sion as to which type or model will best meet office needs.

The specific hardware or equipment needs of an organization should surface as the result of a study. For example, the study should determine what input, output, copying, mailing, and communication methods are used in the office. By taking an accurate survey of current procedures, personnel, and equipment, the person(s) responsible can better evaluate systems, and more closely match the hardware to the work.

STAFFING REQUIREMENTS

Staffing requirements and costs required to process information in the automated office must also be considered. When the traditional functions and procedures are changed, staffing and equipment requirements change. An identification of the skill levels necessary, the cost justification for such change, and identified time savings for improved productivity are necessary to determine the requirements of personnel and investment needed.

EQUIPMENT NEEDS

A fifth consideration focuses on the configuration or number of pieces of equipment that will be needed. The statistics already gathered about workflow and work volume will go a long way in helping the manager in the equipment selection.

PRESENT EQUIPMENT

A sixth consideration is a determination of the upgradability of present equipment and any equipment under consideration. For example, take a firm that currently has a Qyx Intelligent Typewriter in its office. The manager is contemplating the addition of new functions to increase productivity. In this case the five add-on features provided by the current equipment, the Intelligent Typewriter, should be investigated first. By utilizing the maximum capacities of present equipment, the organization can often increase its efficiency and productivity more than it could if it bought an entirely new system.

Many modular systems on the market now can be totally upgraded simply by new software or by additional hardware components, such as disk drives or memory. Whenever new equipment is being considered, the organization should determine how adaptable that equipment will be in future years. Projections of future workload and work type are necessary for effective planning.

Another major consideration is compatibility—how any new equipment can interface, or communicate, with current equipment. Different brands of word and data processing equipment employ a variety of operating systems, code structures, and application software. The differences can make it difficult or impossible to exchange information unless interface devices are available.

PHYSICAL SPACE

A seventh consideration is how much physical space is available for new equipment. A new system that requires 60 square feet of space would be useless if the space available is only 30 square feet. An inventory of floor space must be conducted early, because equipment sizes and configurations vary widely.

In addition to determining the work needs of the office, a study should investigate the physical structure requirements for equipment purchase and expansion. For example, one may want to determine the soundproofing needs that will be required by a new system. Some of the new systems make noise when generating or processing work, and building soundproofed areas into the office design will minimize the noise pollution in the office. In addition, this is the time to determine where new equipment will be placed in the office. Deciding on the location of new equipment also will help to determine the space allowance. Space dividers should be investigated, and projections made as to whether there will be adequate growth room for future expansion and development for equipment capability. One should ensure adequate electrical availability and adequate storage for media. All of these physical structure requirements are related to purchasing equipment for the modern office.

STORAGE REQUIREMENTS

Another consideration involves the storage needs of an organization. By law, some offices need to store large amounts of documents and sources for long periods of time. Other offices can discard information quickly. For example, if an organization must retain information, it may want to invest in equipment that uses floppy disks or mag cards for easy external storage. Conversely, if it can discard information quickly, it may be able to invest in electronic typewriters with limited internal storage. Determination of the storage demands will help to determine what kind of processing equipment a company should invest in.

ACCESS TIME REQUIREMENTS   The ninth consideration is time required to retrieve information. Some organizations demand that information be available immediately, whereas others may prefer to archive (store) it. If an organization needs information instantaneously, it may want to invest in an on-line system, in order to recall the information within a matter of seconds. If time is not critical in retrieving stored material, an organization may prefer to remove stored material from the system (through the use of floppy disks, for example) that may be stored in a separate place.

Of course, the most important consideration when choosing equipment is to assure that the needs of the office are adequately met. There are several ways to determine these needs.

DETERMINING EQUIPMENT NEEDS

The best way to determine equipment needs is to perform a systems study (described in an earlier chapter). This study should identify the workflow of the office, the volume and type of work produced, the attitudes of the employees toward new technology, the proficiency of the present employees with new technology, and the total cost of new equipment. This study should also determine where to apply the networking approach, or the linking of different types of equipment together into an integrated system.

The selection process should include an investigation of a system's capabilities to accommodate—to a reasonable degree—future improvements. One of the greatest concerns among buyers is the fear of obsolescence. Evaluation of the future potential of an office automation system calls for a thorough judgment, because new developments and enhancements appear at a rapid rate.

Because a system must remain flexible for years to come, the buyer should look out for the possibility of hardware or software obsolescence. When equipment will be used in a multifunction mode (word processing and accounting, for example), the choice of software packages is important. Hardware that is not software-based would be justified only if the application is highly dedicated and rapidly cost-justified. Software obsolescence is becoming an important consideration in automated systems that may start small but grow. Users of some 8-bit systems find that vendors will offer them the ability to run their 8-bit programs on larger, 16-bit systems they may need later. This kind of software protection gives users the best of the old and the new.

An organization wants to be sure that the equipment selected meets its specific needs, with room for addition or expansion to respond to changing conditions.

A survey by the Association of Information Systems Professionals (formerly known as International Information/Word Processing Association) revealed interesting trends in the types of equipment being purchased. The most popular feature that users selected in their equipment was a display screen. Although screen equipment was originally considered necessary to assist learning and for revision work, most operators have come to believe it is necessary and/or desirable in all applications. Users also wanted equipment that had communication capabilities and high-speed quality printers.

There are several useful ways to assist the prospective buyer in selecting equipment. One study indicated that most buyers (81 percent) attended equipment exhibits at trade shows and conventions. These exhibits are frequently held during annual conventions or meetings sponsored by professional associations. Shows provide an excellent means of obtaining an overview of what equipment is available and of keeping up with enhancements or new product announcements. Other popular methods used in evaluation and selection include talking to other users, performing feasibility studies within the buyer's organization, reading reports in word processing publications, and reviewing the manufacturer's literature. Most respondents use several evaluation techniques.

Of all feasibility studies used to guide the evaluation of equipment, over 70 percent are performed by the users on their own behalf; about 20 percent are performed by manufacturers, and another 12 percent by consultants. Over 84 percent of those responding to the study used feasibility studies at some phase of the new-equipment buying process.

VENDOR AND EQUIPMENT CHECKLIST

In the selection of new equipment, the most important step in the process is evaluation of the vendor and the vendor's equipment. Reliability is the single most valuable asset a vendor can offer. These steps can help the buyer to evaluate vendors.

1. Determine equipment requirements and available alternatives.
2. Determine the quality of local maintenance.
3. Determine exact costs and cost variables.
4. Determine the extent of installation support provided.
5. Determine the extent of training provided.
6. Evaluate equipment by means of an equipment demonstration.
7. Evaluate carefully the "user friendliness" of equipment.

8. Evaluate the expansion capabilities of the equipment.

9. Determine the reputation of the manufacturer.

10. Determine the level of vendor assistance with installation.

These steps can be accomplished more easily with the use of a checklist as shown in Figure 2.

ORGANIZATIONAL EQUIPMENT REQUIREMENTS

First, as already outlined, the organization should review its own equipment requirements (i.e., workflow, work volume, type of work, and space requirements). During this phase of investigation, it should also determine what equipment alternatives are available—either by collecting information from different vendors or by attending a vendor show.

SELECTING A VENDOR

Second, when selecting a vendor, the buyer should find out the level of equipment that is available locally. Chances are that quite a bit of service will be needed during the installation period, and periodically during the life of the equipment. The buyer should check references and other local users concerning the reliability and competence of the maintenance personnel. When encountering equipment problems, the last thing a user needs is to have an incompetent vendor or one that is a thousand miles away.

PRICE VARIANCE

Third, the buyer should compare the total costs of the equipment purchase. Prices for equipment may vary, depending upon the vendor, customer, and supply and demand. Most vendors offer special governmental and educational pricing. Many vendors offer volume discounts. Large national firms usually can negotiate a national contract that offers standardized pricing regardless of location. The buyer should also find out if support, systems design, and software are priced separately or are included, in whole or in part, in the purchase price. Usually initial training is included for a specified number of operators, but there may be a charge for additional or new ones.

VENDOR SUPPORT

Fourth, an organization should investigate the amount of vendor installation support provided. The most critical time is when equipment is first installed; this can be a very confusing and tense period. It is essential for the vendor to be present during the transition period. Ask the vendors what they will do during installation, and how much time they plan to spend.

WORKSHEET FOR EVALUATING WORD PROCESSING EQUIPMENT

Vendor _____ Equipment _____

Scoring: excellent-10, good-8, average-5, poor-2, unacceptable-0

NOTE: Numbers in parens ( ) indicate maximum possible points

Evaluation Criteria		Value × Weight = Score	
1. VENDOR FIRM			
1A Financial/Organizational Stability		3.5	
1B Quality of Proposal/Caliber of Local Staff		1.5	
1C Experience with Similar Applications		1.0	
1D References		1.0	
1E Maintenance/Service		3.0	
1E1 availability	(2)		
1E2 response time	(2)		
1E3 equipment reliability	(3)		
1E4 warranties provided	(3)		
	Vendor Firm Total Score	_____	
2. EQUIPMENT CHARACTERISTICS			
2A Configuration Flexibility		3.0	
2B CRT Unit		2.0	
2B1 characters per line displayed	(3)		
2B2 lines displayed	(3)		
2B3 zoom capability	(1)		
2B4 reverse image capability	(1)		
2B5 brightness/contrast control	(2)		
2C Mag Media Employed		2.0	
2C1 tape	(1)		
2C2 card	(2)		
2C3 floppy disk	(3)		
2C4 hard disk	(4)		
2D Output Units		2.0	
2D1 carriage widths	(1)		
2D2 speeds	(1)		
2D3 continuous forms feeder	(1)		
2D4 single sheet feeder	(1)		
2D5 variable type styles	(2)		
2D6 variable pitch	(2)		
2D7 print quality	(2)		
2E Miscellaneous		1.0	
2E1 communications capability	(1)		
2E2 shared logic	(2)		
2E3 software based	(3)		
dual station input unit	(4)		
	Equipment Characteristics Total Score	_____	

Figure 2 Worksheet for evaluating equipment. (Courtesy of International Information/Word Processing Association.)

Evaluation Criteria	Value × Weight = Score		
3. OPERATING CHARACTERISTICS			
3A Concurrent Input/Output		4.0	
3B Sorting Capability		1.0	
3C Format Capability		2.0	
3C1 forms mode	(1)		
3C2 auto tab memory	(2)		
3C3 automatic underline	(2)		
3C4 automatic centering	(2)		
3C5 automatic margin adjust	(3)		
3D Input/Editing Capability		2.0	
3D1 automatic hyphenation	(1)		
3D2 automatic pagination	(1)		
3D3 glossary feature	(1)		
3D4 horizontal scroll	(1)		
3D5 word wrap around	(3)		
3D6 global search and replace	(3)		
3E Automatic Logging System		1.0	
Operating Characteristics Total Score			_____
4. TRAINING PROGRAMS			
4A Operator Training Program		3.0	
4B Supervisor Training Program		3.0	
4C Reference Materials Provided		2.0	
4D Supplementary Training Available		1.0	
4E Self-Instruction Program Available		1.0	
Training Programs Total Score			_____
5. COSTS			
5A Equipment		3.0	
5B Delivery/Installation		1.0	
5C Maintenance		2.5	
5D Mag Media/Supplies		2.5	
5E Training Programs/Reference Materials		1.0	
Costs Total Score			_____
RATING SCORE			
1. VENDOR FIRM		2.0	
2. EQUIPMENT CHARACTERISTICS		2.0	
3. OPERATING CHARACTERISTICS		2.5	
4. TRAINING PROGRAMS		2.5	
5. COSTS		1.0	
FINAL RATING SCORE			

Figure 2 (Continued)

VENDOR TRAINING

Fifth, along with installation, an organization should determine the type and extent of training a vendor provides with new equipment. The amount of time that training will continue will often influence the selection of a vendor. The longer the training period and the more training options offered, the more satisfactory is likely to be the outcome. Another important consideration: Does the vendor provide orientation and training both to the operators *and* to the management and supervisors working with them? Both kinds of training usually contribute to a more effective installation.

As more and more low-end stand-alone text processors and personal computers are sold through retail outlets, and prices become lower, many vendors will offer only an instruction manual and a phone number to call if the user encounters difficulty. A call for a personal visit from the vendor's customer support representative most likely will involve a per-hour charge.

Consideration should be given not only to the training at the time of the installation of equipment but also to needs as attrition and turnover occur. Most vendors initially train two persons per machine and then charge a flat rate per person for each additional trainee.

Also, carefully evaluate any materials that are provided with the equipment. Some are excellent; some are poorly written and essentially are only operator reference manuals, rather than training materials that reinforce learning.

VENDOR DEMONSTRATION

Sixth, once the number of possible vendors has been narrowed down, the user should arrange for an equipment demonstration in the user's office. This demonstration should be based upon the type of work the system is expected to produce. A good technique is to develop a demo package of your own applications, so that you can see exactly how your work would be accomplished. Such a demo package ensures that all systems you see will be evaluated according to the same criteria and, most important, your actual needs rather than what a vendor wants to show you. The purpose of the demonstration is to evaluate the hardware of the machine (keyboard, video, printer, storage, etc.), extra features and functions, the ease of operation, options and peripherals (additional hardware such as paper feeders), the software available, and media and supplies required.

The evaluation of word processing systems through demonstrations is summarized in Figure 3. The process should be similar for all forms of technology.

EASE OF USE

Seventh, the user should evaluate carefully the "user friendliness" of the equipment: that is, how easy or complicated it is to use the system. It is important that the demonstration package not be preprogrammed, so that

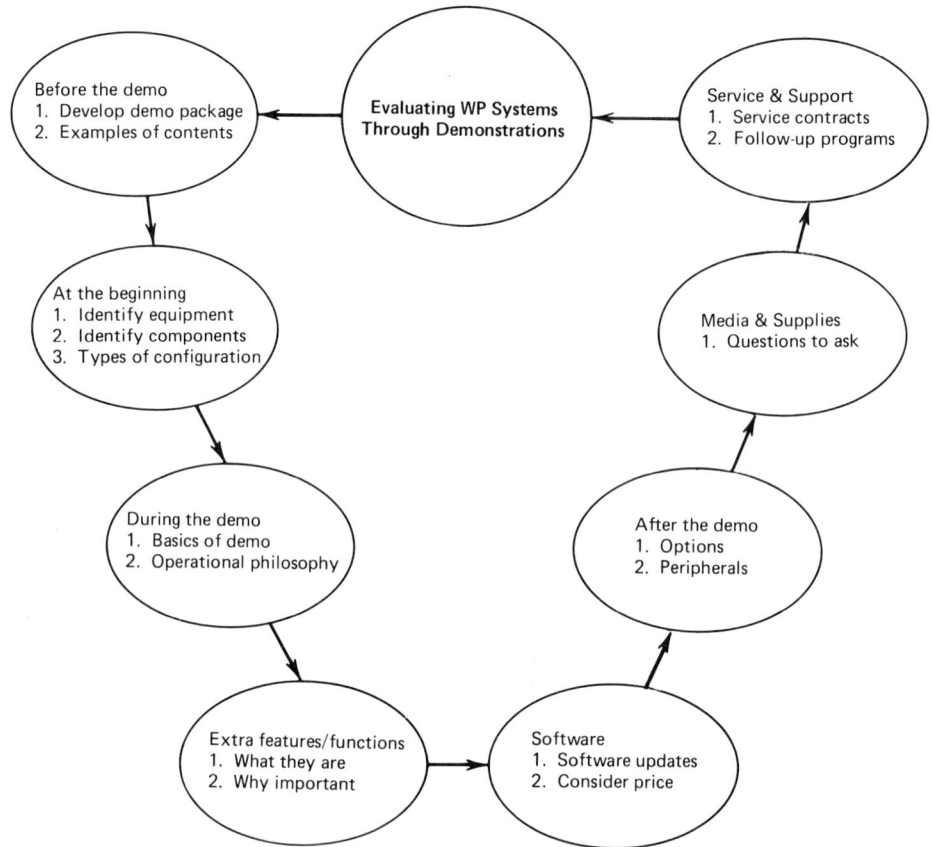

Figure 3 Evaluating systems through demonstrations. (Source: D. Martin, "How to Get the Most from a WP Demonstration," of Modern Office Procedures, June 1980, p. 8)

you can determine the number of steps and time required to accomplish a task from beginning to end (throughput). If an organization has considerable turnover, the ease of learning to operate the equipment is important. If turnover is minimal, however, the extent to which programming of steps and format can be stored (which may be somewhat more complicated) is of major importance, because of the potential for even greater increases in productivity.

MACHINE EXPANSION Eighth, as already mentioned, the user must examine the expansion capabilities of the equipment. Is the equipment upgradable through purchase of additional software, or must an entirely new unit be purchased? Expansion capabilities are a "must" in new equipment.

VENDOR'S REPUTATION

Ninth, an organization should determine the reputation of the manufacturer. If a manufacturer has been in business for a long time, that generally proves some degree of reliability and financial stability. The extent of the vendor's commitment to a range of office automation products is helpful if an organization's long-range goals involve networking or integrating office systems. It is generally easier to work with one or a few vendors, rather than with many. One should consider whether the manufacturer has a widespread marketing and service-and-support organization.

Some manufacturers do not service their own products. Instead, they contract with other companies known as third-party maintenance firms. There are several national and international third-party firms that offer several levels of service, accessed through a toll-free self-help WATS line, and guarantee response times within hours of receiving a service call. Some third-party firms have built outstanding reputations. Not only do third-party firms represent specific manufacturers, but some firms will also contract with the end user to perform all service on all the customer's equipment.

One should discover whether the vendor has acquired widespread acceptance among other local users and further, if the firm will continue to provide service and support for long periods of time.

INSTALLATION ASSISTANCE

Tenth and finally, the user should determine how the vendor will install equipment. What assistance will be provided and for how long? Will you be on your own concerning certain aspects of installation, such as electrical requirements, space requirements, humidity and static considerations, storage, and lighting?

A comfortable relationship with the vendor can help a smooth installation, as well as pave the way for service and support for years to come.

SOFTWARE CONSIDERATIONS

In the past, most office equipment was designed to perform certain functions and special features were either resident in the machine or could not be added during the life cycle of the equipment. In today's world of electronics and microprocessors, software packages are creating a new and different situation.

Many products having one set of features and capabilities can be upgraded by modification of the original software or the addition of new or additional software packages that increase the power and capability. Some vendors provide software upgrades automatically; some do so without charge to their customers. This, of course, is an added support expense for the vendor, because it involves high labor costs to create better software. Many vendors are beginning to package software into separate programs and charge for it. This follows the pattern of how data processing software is made available. Some vendors charge for each software package and each upgrade; others charge only for those that are markedly different or add entirely new capabilities to the equipment (such as records processing or math); while still others offer full trade-in value for old software as customers upgrade to improved software. Every organization wants to be able to improve its office systems continually. Important considerations in product selection include the method a vendor uses to handle software upgrades and its record concerning the frequency and quality of software upgrades.

The same types of microprocessors are being used on both word processing equipment and small computers. Hence, another development has been the creation of some standard operating-systems software (CP/M, Unix, etc.). Many vendors have made CP/M (control program for microprocessors) available on their systems (both word and data processors). Both Xerox and IBM also can use the CP/M operating system software on their personal computers. All types of applications software written for CP/M operating systems are now available for use on many different pieces of equipment. It is very important to know the difference between operating and applications software.

Operating-systems software tells the computer or microprocessor how to act. A machine is literally inoperable without operating-systems software (example: CP/M).

Applications software tells the computer how to do the specific job you want it to do (examples: payroll, word processing).

The applications software market is huge and covers many types of business operations and every conceivable office task. The breadth of the software market is shown in Figure 4. In addition to these types of applications, software, special software packages for spelling verification and correction, proofreading, and grammar are also available.

Considerable differences exist in the marketing of software. Reputable vendors will often demonstrate the software, allow customers to visit a showroom to try it and/or to study manuals and documentation, and sometimes offer a trial period or guarantee. Others, who market by mail, provide little or no opportunity to evaluate the software product, but the cost may be less. The old adage of *caveat emptor* or "let the buyer beware" applies.

Software evaluation will become more important than hardware evaluation in the transition to the automated office. Important factors in the selection of software include compatibility with the operating system, how much working memory capacity is required on the equipment, the completeness of manuals or amount of documentation, user friendliness (ease of use and the number of special codes and commands to be learned), and, of course, price. Ultimately, however, one must focus on

APPLICATIONS SOFTWARE

Manufacturing/Industrial Control

Inventory control   CAD/CAM
MRP   Manpower planning
Project costing   Purchase orders

General Accounting

General ledger   Accounts receivable
Accounts payable

Financial

Fixed assets   Forecasting
Capital budgeting   Modeling

Human Resources

Payroll   Benefits
Personnel

Sales/Marketing Distribution

Order entry   Sales analysis
Billing/invoicing   Distribution account

Decision Support Systems

Word Processing

Graphics

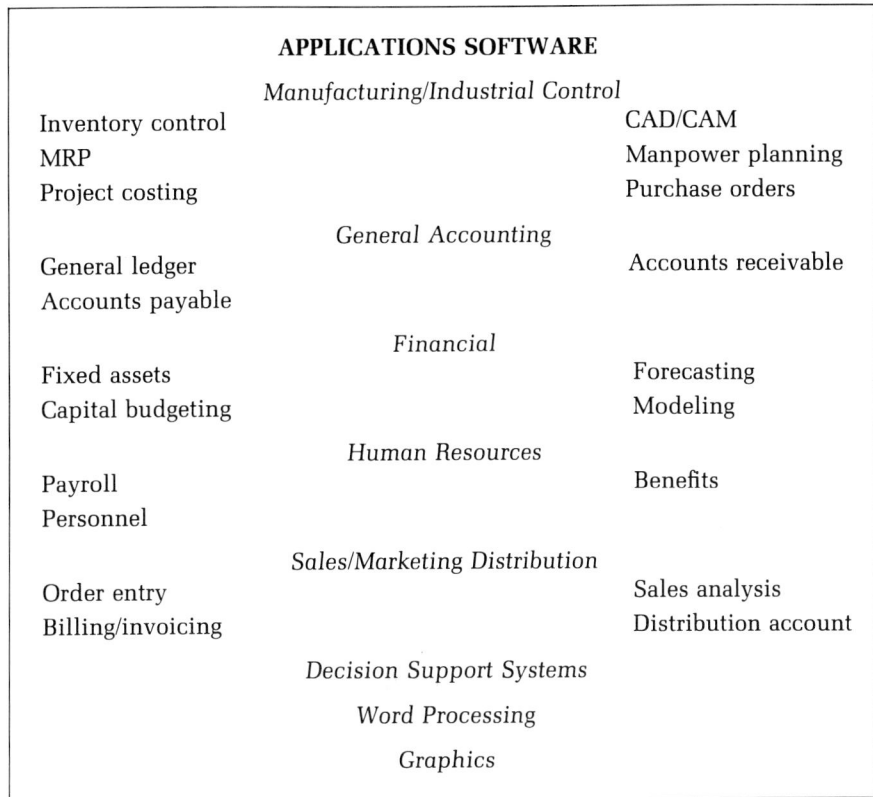

Figure 4 The software market covers many types of business operations.
Source: "How MIS Management sees the Software Market," *MIS Week*, 1982.

whether the particular software, just as it is, helps to perform the tasks to be accomplished.

FINANCING

Both the technology and the cost of equipment have changed substantially in the past several years. Technological advancements require greater sophistication in measuring benefits and costs when evaluating various types of equipment. Decisions also must be made in light of total-organization considerations and financial status. This section presents the various advantages and disadvantages associated with alternative methods of financing acquisitions of new equipment.

RENTING Renting is the most viable option when a company intends to use equipment for a short period of time or when it is unsure if the equipment will meet the needs of the company in the future. Renting does not involve financial commitments over an extended period of time, as does leasing or outright purchase. It also allows the user to change to new equipment if the needs of the company indicate that is necessary. Rented equipment is also easier to upgrade quickly. Renting guarantees maximum vendor support, since the equipment still belongs to the vendor. There are some tax advantages in renting of equipment, because rental is a business expense and equipment is not capitalized. Maintenance costs are often included in rentals, so there are no unexpected expenditures for repairs or upkeep. For many of these reasons, renting may be easier to justify to top management.

The flexibility provided by renting, however, does have its price. Rental payments are generally higher than lease payments for similar time periods. If the monthly rent figure does not include maintenance, that will be an additional expense. Also, the company should always find out if a portion of rental payments can be applied to the purchase of the machine at some time in the future.

LEASING   When leasing equipment, the lessee usually commits itself to the equipment for a longer period of time than it would when renting. Equipment can be leased from the manufacturer or from a third party who has purchased the equipment and in turn leases it to customers.

Two kinds of leases are available: an operating lease and a financial lease. With an operating lease (sometimes referred to as a service lease), the equipment is leased for a fixed sum each month; the lessor does not normally recover the full cost of the equipment over the period of the lease. When the lease expires, therefore, the lessor must either find another lessee in order to recover the cost, or sell it to the original lessee for a price that recovers the remaining cost and conforms to tax regulations. A financial lease allows the lessor to recover the full cost of the equipment, plus expenses and a profit. The lessee, therefore, may receive title to the equipment at the end of the lease period.

Leases have many of the same advantages and disadvantages of renting. There is added flexibility over purchasing in terms of changing equipment, but the tax allowances are less favorable.

BUYING   Outright purchase offers significant advantages. The buyer benefits in the reduction of taxes from investment credits and depreciation. When purchasing equipment, a company is obtaining assets that benefit the entire company. There is usually trade or resale value on the equipment if the company decides to make a change. However, purchase decisions should be made in relation to the organization's cash position: that is, how much is in the bank. Finally, when a company purchases equipment, there is a proven management commitment to the new system.

Buying has the disadvantage of committing a company to a certain type of equipment, thus reducing flexibility to change. Of course, if during the selection process a company attempts to plan for further expansion and modular additions of equipment and software, this is not a problem. Purchasing also forces upkeep costs on the company.

Government and educational institutions that receive funding from taxes are faced with somewhat different situations and legal restrictions. Laws vary as to the type and extent of financial commitment allowed, and some funding is in the form of specific one-time grants. Often, different regulations cover hardware and software. Those involved in the acquisition of equipment and software for such organizations must learn about the regulations and restrictions within which they must make their decisions.

Whichever method an organization uses to acquire equipment and software, the most important thing to remember is the need for a strong management commitment to making the new system work. Change in the office is always difficult; and without full management support and backing, organizations are likely to abandon a new system during the frustration of implementation and training. Only through clear, strong management commitment to improvement can an organization realize the full benefits of the automated office.

PART FOUR

OFFICE AUTOMATION MANAGEMENT CONSIDERATIONS

CHAPTER 17

STRATEGIES FOR ACTUATING THE INTEGRATED ELECTRONIC OFFICE

OBJECTIVES

In this chapter you will learn about

1. The requirements and considerations involved in actuating the electronic office.
2. The issues involved in designing the electronic office.
3. Additional administrative operations to be considered in planning and implementing a totally integrated office system.
4. The short- and long-term planning processes to meet integration objectives.
5. The responsibilities and realities to be faced in actuating an integrated office system.
6. Alternative approaches to implementation.
7. A plan for a step-by-step or phase-in approach to integration.
8. The necessary coordination and control to ensure the success of implementation.

Electronic office systems implementation covers a broad spectrum of technologies and raises many human, structural, procedural, and technological issues. The initiative to plan the automated office environment will generally come from the top management level, where the need exists or is perceived to exist. However, the change affects the lives of executive management, middle management, professional and technical staffs, and clerical/secretarial staffs. The multidimensional aspects of office systems evolve through a number of phases before reaching a mature level of integration. No phase can be avoided; in each phase there must be a planned, objective, budgeted, and controlled process implemented by responsible managers who are accountable for actuating the integration process.

To actuate (start a process) an electronic office, management must assign a person and/or task force made up of individuals who will be responsible for

1. Understanding the organizational structure, the corporate culture, and the philosophy of the organization.
2. Establishing benchmarks against which to measure progress in the actuating process.
3. Developing the organization's objectives of office automation.
4. Identifying the issues involved from a human, structural, procedural, and technological perspective.
5. Exploring the alternate structures available to the organization.
6. Developing a strategic plan.
7. Identifying other related considerations to the total support approach in the electronic office.
8. Determining the technological components (equipment—hardware and/or software) to be implemented and ultimately integrated.

Automating the office requires an understanding of the flow of information and the need for communication in the office environment (see Figure 1). Remember that information is not instantaneous—there is a float period from the time information leaves its source until it reaches its destination.

Office automation consists of multiple technologies, including those that provide the communication of information through voice, image, data, or text supporting a variety of equipment applications—data processing, word processing, phototypesetting, telecommunications, and so on—that supplement the human mental and physical processes. From a planning perspective, these technologies and applications provide a foundation for integration within the office. Therefore, attention must be focused specifically on analyzing the organization; structuring for future potential; assigning priorities to the human, structural, procedural, and

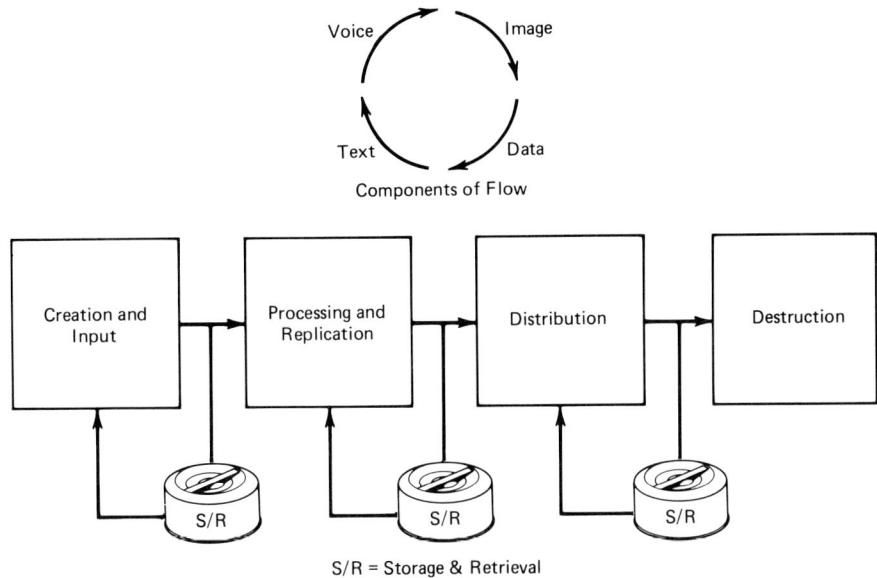

Figure 1 Flow of communication. Automating and managing the components of the communication flow are the challenges of information managers.

technological issues; and defining budgeted resources with which to acquire available technologies.

Attention to all of these factors is necessary to obtain the maximum benefit with the least amount of confusion and trauma in the workplace. This attention will help to ensure later success, as the integrated system reaches maturity.

Further understanding of the concept includes knowledge of the existing organization's management philosophy and culture. This knowledge provides a special and philosophical profile of the business, and of the existing internal administrative demands in terms of costs, resources, and existing equipment. Familiarity with the basics of planning for office automation can be gained in the following ways:

1. Joining one or more professional organizations that focus on some aspect of office systems.
2. Subscribing to office automation or research periodicals, newsletters, and special reports.
3. Attending conferences at which advanced technology is displayed, promotional material is available, and continuing education seminars are held.
4. Taking classes at educational institutions that offer courses about office automation.
5. Contacting office automation consultants to obtain firsthand knowl-

edge of the integrated electronic office environment and its requirements.

6. Meeting with vendors whose products and services include word processing, micrographics, reprographics, electronic mail, communications, and data processing equipment.

7. Meeting with other organizations to determine their approaches to and plans for actuating an electronic office.

ISSUES IN THE ELECTRONIC OFFICE

Actuation of the electronic office requires attention to issues that can generally be categorized as human, structural, procedural, and technological.

HUMAN ISSUES The nontechnical issues must be addressed if office systems are to effectively operate within the society of the organization. Preparation and planning as it relates to the human issues should cover the following areas:

Ergonomic or Environmental Increased attention must be given to the facilities planning, the esthetics of the workstation, the surrounding space, and appropriate privacy depending upon the functions performed. Appropriate levels of temperature, noise, and humidity must be maintained, together with the right use of color to ensure human comfort and enhance productivity. Ergonomic considerations are detailed in earlier chapters.

Health and Safety Attention must also be focused on postural, visual, auditory, and other human factors, as detailed in an earlier chapter.

Social Responsibility For those employees, at whatever level, who are displaced by technology, expected to use technology effectively, or required to assume a variety of duties for which they have not been trained, an organization must plan for both continuing education and retraining programs. These programs are part of the organization's social responsibility. In addition, continuing education and communication must take place in order to reduce the resistance to change. A positive approach both to the unknown and to job security must be taken by the managers in charge of implementation.

Unionization Concern for the well-being of employees involved in automating an office environment and open communication can go a long way to reducing the effects of unionization. Open communications must be maintained, to assure the staff that career opportunities and career progression will be as good as or better than they have been in the past organization.

Cottage Labor   An organization that pursues office automation may well open up opportunities for part-time help working at home on electronic equipment. If this option has potential for an organization, it must be addressed as an alternative to the present work environment, and thereby will affect full-time employees. Figure 2 indicates some of the considerations, along with their many implications, that must be taken into account in designing a system that will integrate this alternative.

STRUCTURAL   The structure selected by an organization directly relates to the degree of
ISSUES   control that management wishes to maintain, ranging from total centralization to a loosely structured decentralized approach. Control depends upon factors such as formal organizational policy and responsibility, the degree of management's desire for centralization or decentralization, the degree of geographic dispersement, the level of budgetary processes, and approval of funding.

A combination of centralized and decentralized organizational characteristics is known as a *matrix management*. Although different management philosophies dictate the alternative selected, most organizations find the matrix or combination the most practical and realistic alternative, because it

1. Provides coordinated guidance and direction while encouraging decentralized operating responsibilities.
2. Reduces duplication of effort and resources over a fully decentralized environment, yet provides a certain degree of control over the outcome of various endeavors.
3. Ensures that the appropriate administrative methods, cost controls, authorizations, standards, and guidelines are in place and consistent from one area to another.
4. Provides corporate expertise, guidance, and advice in applying state-of-the-art concepts.
5. Shares research, prototype, and actual experiences as well as the cost of development, while simultaneously spreading the risks.
6. Stimulates communications, backup, and other interrelationships between semiautonomous business units in a corporate structure.

In small businesses, the matrix type of management is often portrayed by providing the availability of management resources to individual project groups and/or profit centers. Examples are illustrated in Figures 3 and 4.

PROCEDURAL   Procedural issues are vital not only to implementations but also to ongo-
ISSUES   ing operations. In any successful new plan, there are standard operating procedures. A policy statement about management of the information and

WORKING HOME

Tomorrow's office worker will work at least part-time at home. The network approach to technology supports that method of operation, since its underlying premise is that all information and technological capabilities available in the downtown office location are equally available wherever one can tie into the network. Further, the benefits to the employee, in terms of avoiding the trauma and costs of rush-hour commuting, of being able to work in a time frame that fits one's personal requirements, and of being able to concentrate on work without interruption, are powerful incentives to pursue the work-at-home idea. In fact, studies to date show a substantial increase in productivity for employees in such programs.

However, the existence of a technological capability and the possibility of benefits accruing from its use are not sufficient incentives to embark on alternate work location programs without examination of the consequences in some detail. Companies that have tested such programs, including work-at-home as well as work in various combinations of downtown and suburban locations, verify the benefits from both the company's and the employee's point-of-view.

At the same time, they have identified problem areas that should be recognized and addressed.

▶ The attitude of the supervisor toward the new work arrangement is a key factor in its success. The belief that "out of sight" means "on the golf course" quickly undermines the employee/supervisor relationship.

▶ Certain assignments—those with clearly defined tasks requiring minimal group interaction—are good candidates for work-at-home programs. But many assignments do not have those characteristics, and the choice has to be made carefully, lest the charge be leveled of inequitable treatment of employees.

▶ There are legal implications associated with work-at-home programs, such as restrictions on working hours and the constraints of local zoning ordinances; insurance considerations involving liability for accidents and damage to equipment; tax, security, and safety questions; and a variety of other factors that must be taken into account because today's laws and work rules are based on a central office approach to work location.

▶ Serious attention has to be paid to formal training for work-at-home employees, their participation in periodic group activities must be encouraged, and assurances must be given that they will receive equal consideration with central office employees for career advancement opportunities.

▶ Attention must also be paid to family considerations. The wife at home, who says she married her husband "for better or for worse but not for lunch," and the wife who admits she works in order to get away from the house are voices that demand to be heard in selecting candidates for a work-at-home program.

Overall, whether by working at home, participating in videoconferences, or responding to one's mail on a tube, human behavior will be affected by new office technologies in diverse ways. Any successful use of the technologies must anticipate and allow for behavioral change.

Figure 2   Management considerations for use of cottage labor. (Courtesy of Modern Office Procedures, March, 1982, p. 62.)

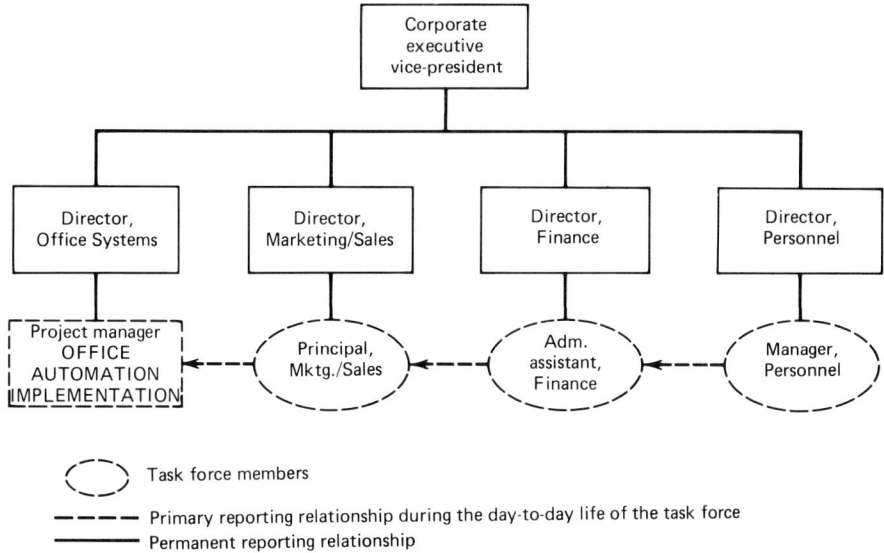

Figure 3 Office automation project structure—matrix relationship.

Figure 4 Support structure matrix relationship. Note the dual relationships: day-to-day workflow and reporting structure.

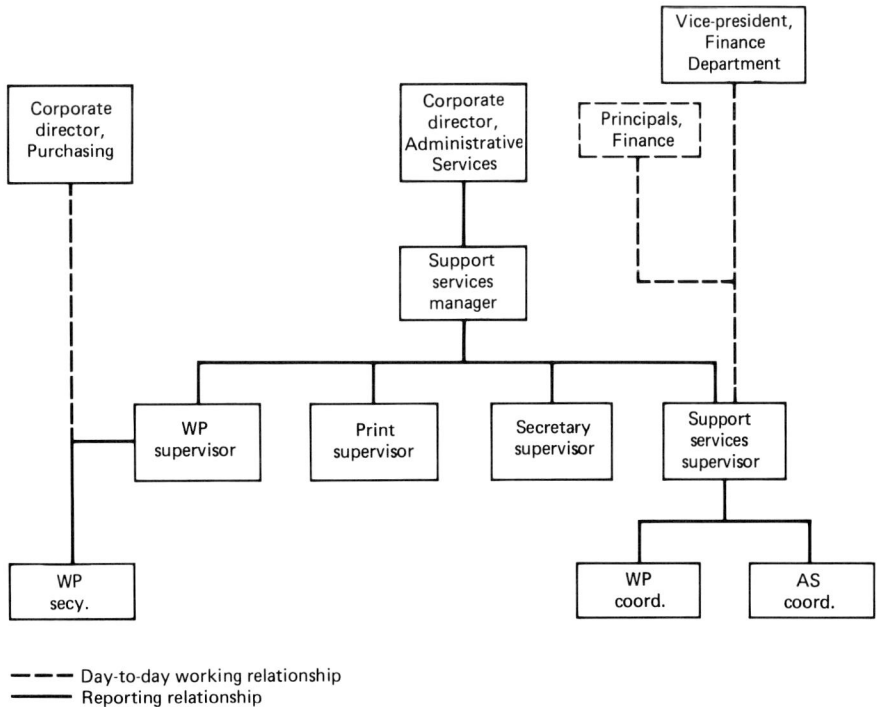

the individuals responsible for it should be clearly stated in an operating procedures manual. Policies and procedures must be developed for

1. The operation of each of the work-specialized systems (for example, word processing, reprographics, micrographics).
2. The security of information of a confidential and sensitive nature and privacy in terms of what actually goes into an information flow system.
3. Training and continuing education.
4. Standards against which to measure productivity gains and that can be used for further cost justification of technology.
5. Followup and feedback, in order to modify and improve the implemented system.

TECHNOLOGICAL ISSUES   The issues surrounding technology directly relate to the planning, control, and development of the appropriate system. Many of these issues have been discussed in earlier chapters. Alternative approaches and a logical phase-in plan are detailed in this chapter.

ADDITIONAL ADMINISTRATIVE OPERATIONS

Additional areas to be addressed in planning a total support system involve the procedures and methods of handling other traditional administrative activities indirectly related to technology. Some of these activities are cafeteria control, fleet maintenance, supplies purchasing, and energy control. Each of these operations requires timely and reliable information. Hence, they often are candidates for inclusion in a totally integrated office system.

CAFETERIA CONTROL   In those organizations large enough to have an internal cafeteria, the budgeting process for that cafeteria, for employee work schedules, menus, and purchasing supplies, or for monitoring of the outside catering service involves information that can be processed as a part of the total information processing system.

FLEET MAINTENANCE   Many organizations keep records pertaining to company-owned cars on computer-based equipment. Since this computer usage is a specialized application, stand-alone microcomputers are often used. Serial numbers, depreciation schedules, locations, usage patterns of various vehicles, and maintenance schedules comprise the kind of information and applications that must be considered in the total approach to office automation.

SUPPLIES PURCHASING Control of the purchasing of office supplies is needed. The cost of supplies is a significant factor that is often overlooked by many organizations. Standardization of equipment allows quantity purchasing and significantly simplifies the allocation of supplies and the maintenance of inventories. Because office operations have been fragmented, supplies have frequently been purchased by individual secretaries. As a result, any efforts at control and at folding this process into the total system must be recognized as major changes, and handled accordingly. Supplies purchasing is a special application that must be part of a totally integrated system.

ENERGY CONTROL Energy control consists of two basic parts. One is the actual reduction in the amount of energy required to operate the office environment, and the second is the monitoring of that environment. A computerized control system requires communication lines to the various energy control devices. Energy control may be either a separate system or a part of a company-wide information system.

The emerging and interrelated areas of data processing, telecommunications, and office systems have in many instances already created overlap among traditional organizational functions. The need for integrated planning and coordination cannot be ignored and requires effective leaders, change agents, and motivators.

DEVELOPING A STRATEGIC PLAN

The development of a strategic plan requires a thorough study of the organization and of both its short- and long-term information needs. Strategic planning may involve the hiring of outside consultants to provide direction and overview support and to assure the best possible results from such a study. A structured planning process involves top management. During the planning, management input is most critical, and management reactions should be carefully noted. Management's approval of a plan is one of the required steps in obtaining commitment to the program. The plan should be

1. Based on business functions. The technological requirements and the extent of change necessary to allow business functions to be performed more rapidly must be identified. Also, the goals and extent of communications improvement to be achieved must be established.

2. Supportive of the business goals and objectives. The overall objective of integrating the electronic office should always be to improve productivity from the standpoint of both effectiveness and efficiency of the office and the administrative environment. To accomplish this objective, short- and long-term goals such as the following might be iden-

tified: improve decision making; improve external relations; increase management, professional, and support-staff productivity; provide support-staff job enrichment; increase profitability for the organization; reduce overhead expenses; attain a competitive advantage; enhance the quality of the work environment of all levels of employees; provide more technology and tools for better and more timely analysis and synthesis; and establish a phased-in foundation for effective information/communication integration.

3. Responsive to management concerns. The world is ever-changing, and outside forces may create a need to redirect a firm's plans. For example, EEO (equal employment opportunity) legislation has caused a redirection in hiring practices and a recession may slow many firms' expansions. No one can foresee all aspects of the future; hence, a plan must be flexible and responsible to management concerns.

ACTUATING THE ELECTRONIC OFFICE

RESPONSIBILITIES OF THE PROJECT ADMINISTRATOR

A successful implementation program requires that the administrator responsible for the project or program possess the skills of people management and financial management, as well as knowledge of the importance of methods and procedures. This individual must have complete responsibility for all aspects of the implementation project and should approach the actuation through a planned, budgeted, and committed perspective.

Implementation is extremely complex and technical and should be approached carefully and methodically, with a detailed project schedule and implementation checklist accompanied by responsibility charts.

Benchmarks or milestones to be achieved must be clearly defined, to avoid delays in the implementation process that might push the project beyond the original funding. The manager responsible for implementation must above all achieve user satisfaction while remaining constantly aware of the bottom-line payback on the process of change. If the project suffers from significant time delays and increases in the expenditure of dollars, the process must be reevaluated.

DEVELOPMENTS IN TECHNOLOGY

Management's philosophy of and commitment to integrating technologies across departmental and functional lines will have a significant effect on the rate and degree of progress likely to be achieved toward a totally integrated system. Although some new technologies will come about only when the office is fully integrated, the majority of integration opportunities for immediate payback on investment monies will come from the combining of existing stand-alone technologies into cost-effective and capable hybrid systems. Note the following examples:

1. Laser printers that act as high-speed word processing and data processing printers as well as quasi-typesetters can be acquired from a number of vendors and interfaced by communications or by the movement of floppy disks from one system to another.

2. Microfilm systems can be directly related to mainframe computers for computer output microfilm (COM). Microfilm can also be stored and indexed, to gain the advantages of the computer-aided search and retrieval (CAR) of individual documents.

3. An advanced generation of telephone exchange allows for the easy connection of terminals and other devices using existing telephone lines.

4. Communicating word processors can communicate with other word processors or with computers—minis, micros, and mainframes.

5. Typesetters can be linked to word processors.

6. Voice message systems can share disk storage and processing power with distributed word-processing systems.

7. Teleconferencing facilities can directly link to on-line data bases for instant information display in meetings.

As the phases of implementation develop, all of these functions are being tied together more and more through network and telecommunications technology that permits various disparate technologies to share communications facilities, thereby allowing information to be transferred to and from similar as well as incompatible devices. Therefore, it is not necessarily the merger of word and data processing that should be planned in the implementation program, but rather the integration or the convergence of independent office technologies into the communications network.

Developments in office automation have blurred the distinctions between the specialized departments in the traditional office. Thus, the separateness of the various technologies no longer has a valid technological base and cannot be defended as in the past. The equipment in the electronic office is and will become more multifunctional; the link to real multifunction is telecommunications.

During implementation, the project manager must be aware of all possibilities for utilizing office automation to the fullest. For example, if it is determined that electronic mail would be beneficial to an organization and if that process is targeted to be implemented externally as well as internally, it is important to identify who has electronic mail equipment external to the company. Aside from TWX and telex systems, there are no public directories of equipped electronic mail locations. This is also true in the case of facsimile—there are no public directories of facsimile equipment installed in large companies or at central points of communication. Therefore, each organization must determine not only who or what firms it communicates with most frequently, but also what type of communications equipment those firms use.

Although this particular determination must be made by the implementing manager, it is not a major drawback. It is, however, a consideration that must be addressed in determining which phase of implementation should involve electronic mail—in other words, at what point in the total process of implementation electronic mail will begin to provide the greatest benefits and be most cost-effective.

ALTERNATIVE APPROACHES TO IMPLEMENTATION

There are two basic approaches to automation of the electronic office.

The Total-Project Approach

One approach is to employ management commitment and budgeting to implement the totally integrated office. Generally, this total-project approach is taken with one specific department or area, then another, and so on. The financial procedure (if any) often is to consider the undertaking as a research and development (R&D) project. Such an approach usually presumes there are no individual technologies already successfully installed (or ignores them), and implementation begins from a base of zero.

The other option is planning for immediate payback and phasing into integration through a budgeted building-block approach. The technological considerations are essentially the same with each approach, because no one vendor offers all technologies. With both approaches, the capabilities of a variety of vendors and software houses still will have to be merged to get all the necessary systems.

The total-project approach, however, provides the opportunity to plan for and implement immediately those areas that impact management productivity. Because of the ripple effect of improved management productivity, this approach has greater potential for increased productivity throughout the organization and from all levels of employees. The total-project approach also allows project management more latitude, since it has greater flexibility in planning and is not tied to existing systems.

The Phase-in Approach

The most common approach, usually because of financial constraints, is the building-block approach—phasing into integration through careful planning and budgeting. Each phase requires identification of needs and a plan for the most rapid payback possible on initial investment.

Here the 80/20 rule can be applied effectively. Users and project development personnel sometimes get carried away with the potential of a new system. Everyone, however, should be aware that the 80/20 rule is applicable—that is, that 80 percent of the applications can be impacted with 20 percent of the effort required to realize the full potential of the system. In other words, the implementation of a system at the highest level of sophistication would require five times the effort of simply attending to the most critical 80 percent. The planning strategy is gradually to get all critical systems operational, then gradually attend to higher and higher levels of sophistication as the availability of time and resource permits. The 80/20 rule is illustrated in Figure 5.

The management philosophy, the competitive requirements, the level of technical maturity and education, the economics of the organization, and the staff's maturity are all important considerations in the planning process. Integration phases are as follows:

Phase 1   Planning for applications that meet the most critical needs or that handle big-volume applications that promise the biggest savings and paybacks.

Phase 2   Planning for applications that expand the capabilities of administrative functions.

Phase 3   Implementing applications that improve management productivity.

Phase 4   Implementing decision support systems.

Phase 5   Implementing the network.

Phase 1.   Research into the user environment and establishment of a planned and coordinated program to meet the most critical needs for immediate payback are initial steps in this phase (see Figure 6). Usually the needs study begins with the support staff areas, since word processing

Figure 5   The 80/20 Rule: "*80% of the necessary information can be obtained with only 20% of the effort expended to realize the full potential of the system.*"

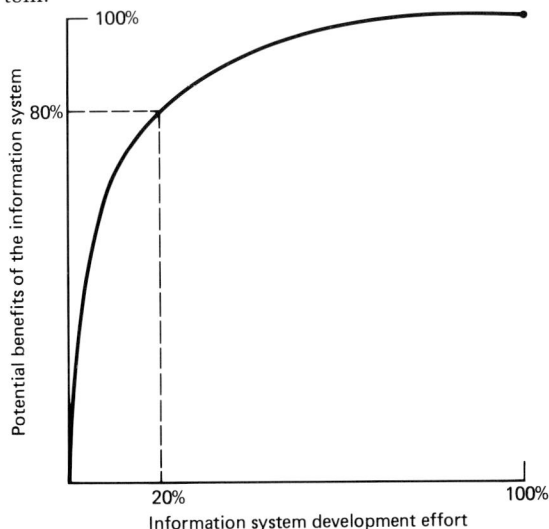

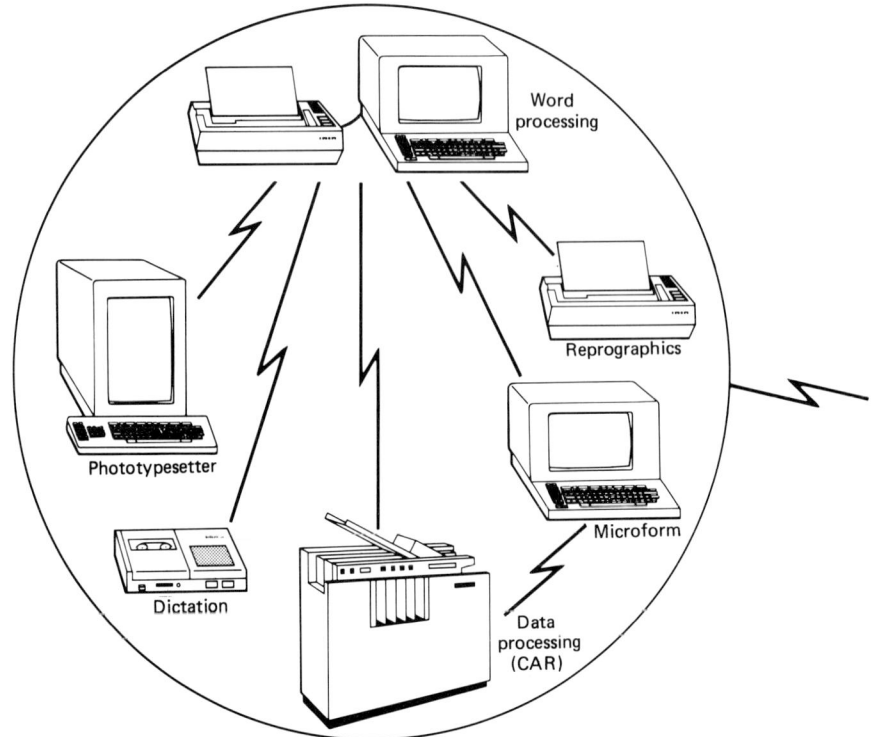

Figure 6   Phase one. Planning for applications that meet the most needs.

and dictation requirements are made relatively easy to identify by the wide range of equipment available and the availability of productivity standards against which to measure.

Further integration in this phase can be accomplished by setting up communication between word processors and phototypesetters, thereby communicating captured keystrokes and eliminating rekeying. The user-needs study should define the need for reprographics, laser intelligent copiers, and/or printers as part of the replication cycle. In addition, micrographics can be integrated into replication in phase one. Through the communication of information from the word processor to the computer, computer output microfilm (COM) can become a part of the information cycle. Micrographics also leads to the consideration of computer-aided retrieval (CAR) capabilities for information stored on microfilm.

One of the eventual goals of a totally integrated system will be implementation of an organization-wide data base of most-used information. To attain this goal, planning toward it must occur from the very beginning. For example, phase one, which includes word processing, is the logical place to begin a system of text management. Since generalized access to machine-sorted information will eventually be provided to managers and professionals over an information network, the information (text) must be organized to facilitate such access.

Many organizations simply carry paper-based systems of filing over to data processing and word processing. The traditional system for indexing correspondence has been alphabetical by name of the person to whom a letter is addressed, perhaps with some cross-referencing by subject. In practice, relatively little cross-referencing has occurred, because of the time and file space it consumes. Because machines can scan information so quickly and correspondence can be retrieved by name, date, key words, or other criteria, the labor time and effort associated with paper filing is not necessary. To achieve the benefits, however, of a good data-base management system requires planning that can evolve into the desired end result. It will not automatically come about.

Phase 2.   In this phase you should gain management acceptance to expand the use of technology to other administrative functions (see Figure 7). These functions could include incorporating distribution of the

Figure 7   Phase two. Planning for applications that expand administrative capability.

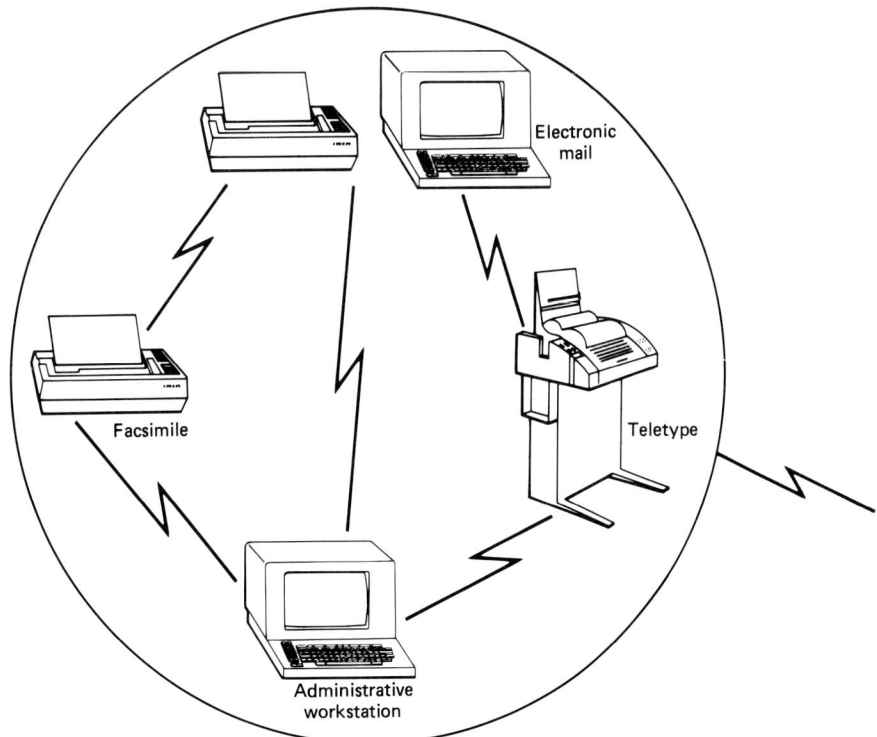

prepared word processing text and communicating it to other locations, both internal and external, in the form of electronic mail. Facsimile and other forms of electronic mail might be implemented, too. Also included in this phase is the automating of administrative functions that presently reside at a secretary's desk. With records processing and records management software, functions such as calendaring, ticklering, come-up systems, and file indexing can be performed at the secretarial workstation. Continuing study and emphasis must be placed on telecommunications throughout this phase of implementation, because it is telecommunications or networking that will eventually tie all parts of the whole together.

Phase 3.   This phase will impact management productivity; it is probably one of the more critical phases in terms of potential dollars saved for the organization (see Figure 8).

The assignment of delegatable administrative functions to the most appropriate level of competency and the provision of administrative software and procedures for the electronic workstation facilitate the perfor-

Figure 8   Phase three. Implementing applications that improve management productivity.

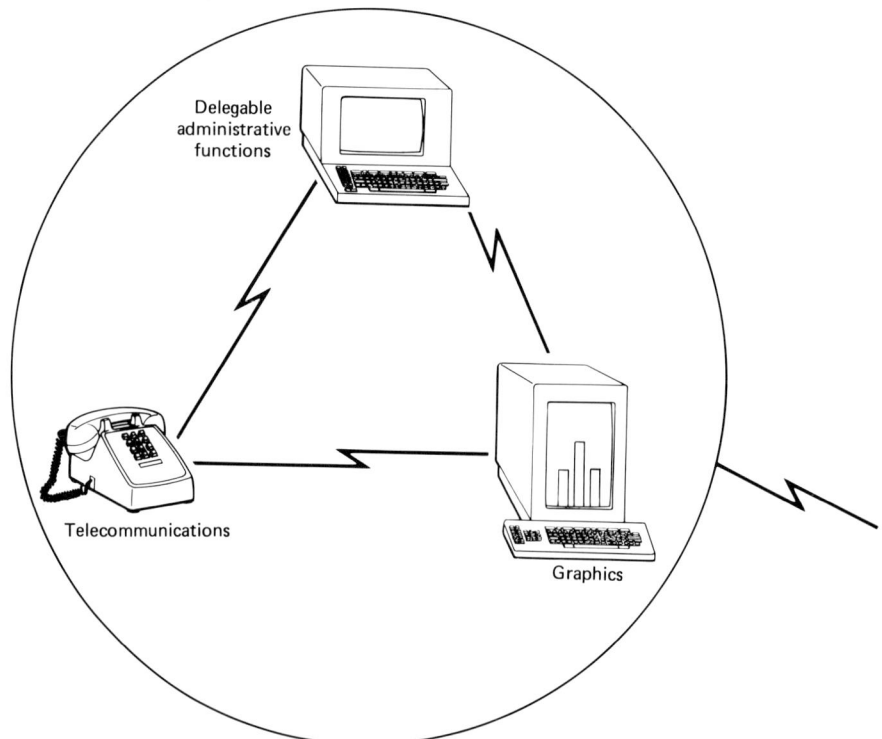

mance of such tasks as keeping track of the managers' calendars, maintaining local files of information and telephone lists, indexing, meeting arrangements, travel arrangements, and a variety of other activities that consume valuable managerial time.

As administrative duties are automated and delegated to the secretarial staff, consideration should be given to the integration of graphics. The ability to retrieve information from machine storage and convert it to visual presentations, such as bar charts, pie charts, curves, and other visual displays, can be productive. Graphics applications allow data to be extracted from a computer file and converted on screen to a multidimensional color display. Graphics can expose the hidden relationships that exist in the data and at the same time present management with an overview from a new perspective. This puts the actual process of creating the drafts into an automated mode and allows the manager to concentrate on decision making.

Note that telecommunications systems and networks should be implemented during this phase, in order to allow smooth movement into additional phases.

Phase 4. The fourth phase provides management and professional staffs with executive workstations and decision support systems. These systems provide the ability to minimize the time needed for business decisions and to project results from pursuing one course of action versus another. Decision support systems are based upon special software that provides significant aids for financial planning, portfolio analysis, tax planning, and market analysis, and for projecting business situations that require mathematical formula calculations.

The next step in this phase is consideration of computer conferencing or teleconferencing, which allows managers to conduct ongoing meetings with personnel in various geographical locations. Effective conferencing utilizes the integrated capabilities of facsimile, electronic message systems, and electronic blackboards and allows management the opportunity to access internal data bases. Such a data base provides management with the ability to access information stored in the company's central computer, retrieve it as is, or selectively structure and manipulate it as desired. Data-base warehouses of information available from external sources should also be accessible. Telecommunications is required for the interaction of these needed functions (see Figure 9).

Phase 5. Phase five involves the implementation of the final network design for the integration of all technologies to actuate the electronic office into a mature office system incorporating the convergence of telecommunications, information systems, and administrative services (see Figure 10).

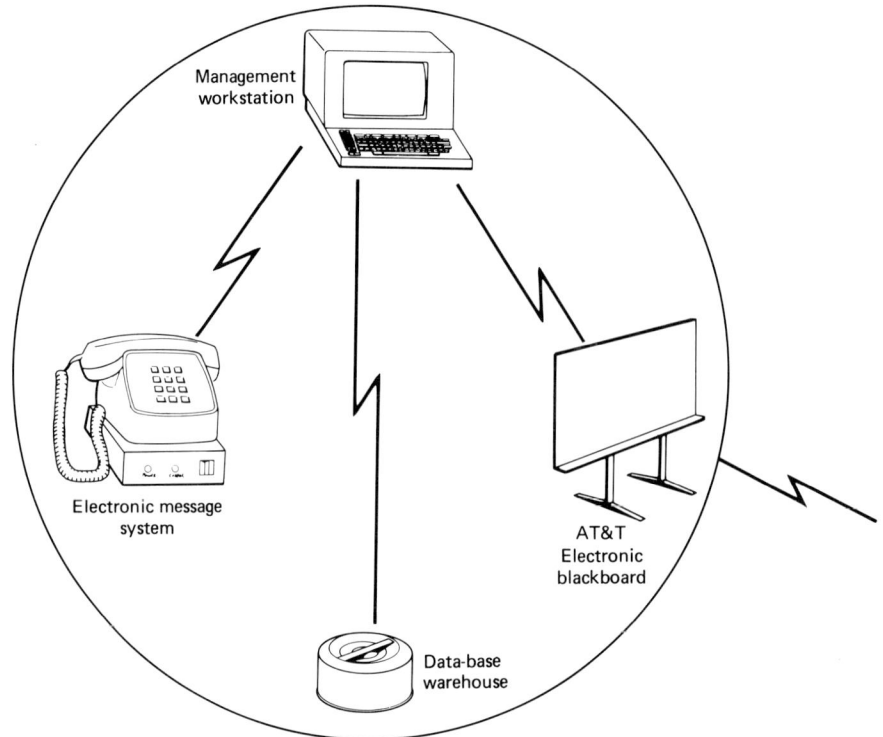

Figure 9 Phase four. Implementing decision support system.

Phase five is the point at which all critical systems are operational and higher and higher levels of sophistication are implemented as time and resources permit (see Figure 11).

It is important to reiterate the need for attention to aspects of the office other than the technological. In the stages of early development (1965-70) of office automation, attention was given to rapid return on investment of equipment. The emphasis on word processing and dictation, however, yielded less opportunity for improved productivity than is available in the current decade.

Figure 12 shows the percentage of productivity improvement in support and managerial functions in three time frames from 1965 to 1985. The 1965-70 figures show the percent improvement achieved primarily by implementation of word processing and dictation systems. The 1970-82 figures show the percentage of productivity improvement made possible by work specialization in the office (resulting from the restructuring of staff and supervisory duties), delegation of management duties to appropriate lower levels, and improved utilization of hardware. The 1982-85 time frame shows the greatest potential for productivity improvement through implementation of multifunction administrative support work-

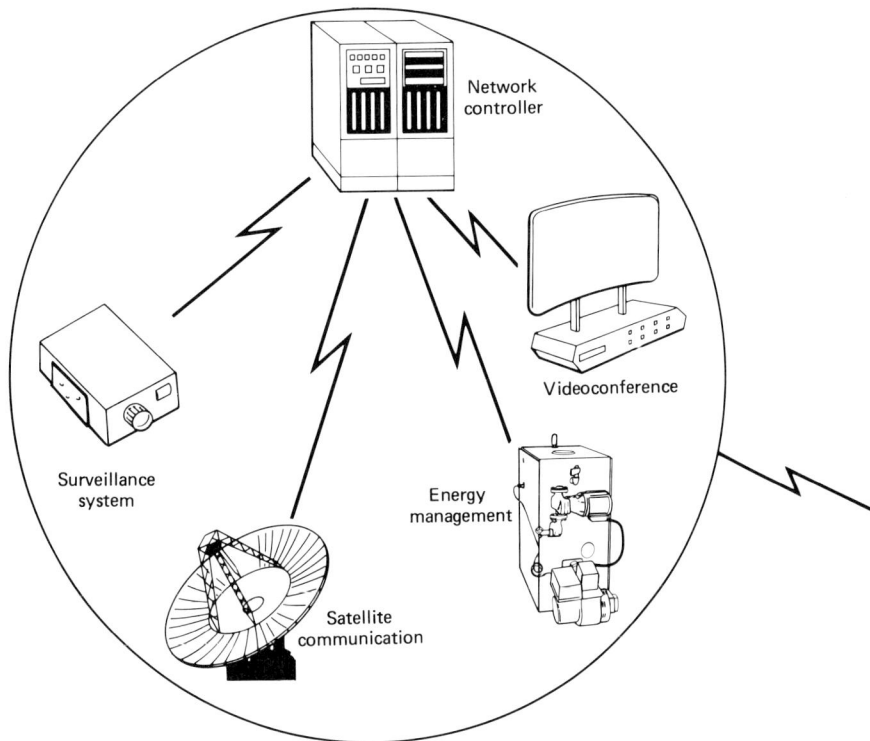

Figure 10 Phase five. Implementing the network.

stations, management decision-making systems, electronic mail, communications networks and conferencing, and the reduction of clerical labor requirements.

Continuing opportunities for improved productivity will be available through the 1990s. Management practices, attitudes, and operating procedures will improve office organization and motivation, and stimulate employees. Performance and productivity will be improved by job enrichment and quality-of-life expectations; however, this criterion is immeasurable at this time.

All technologies are supplemented by the appropriate human, structural, and procedural changes required to bring the electronic office into a cohesive information communication system for the entire organization.

REQUIREMENTS FOR CONTINUING SUCCESS

The implementation process is dynamic and continuous—new products that should be considered and implemented enter the market, needs are not static (indeed, users' perceptions of needs change as they become

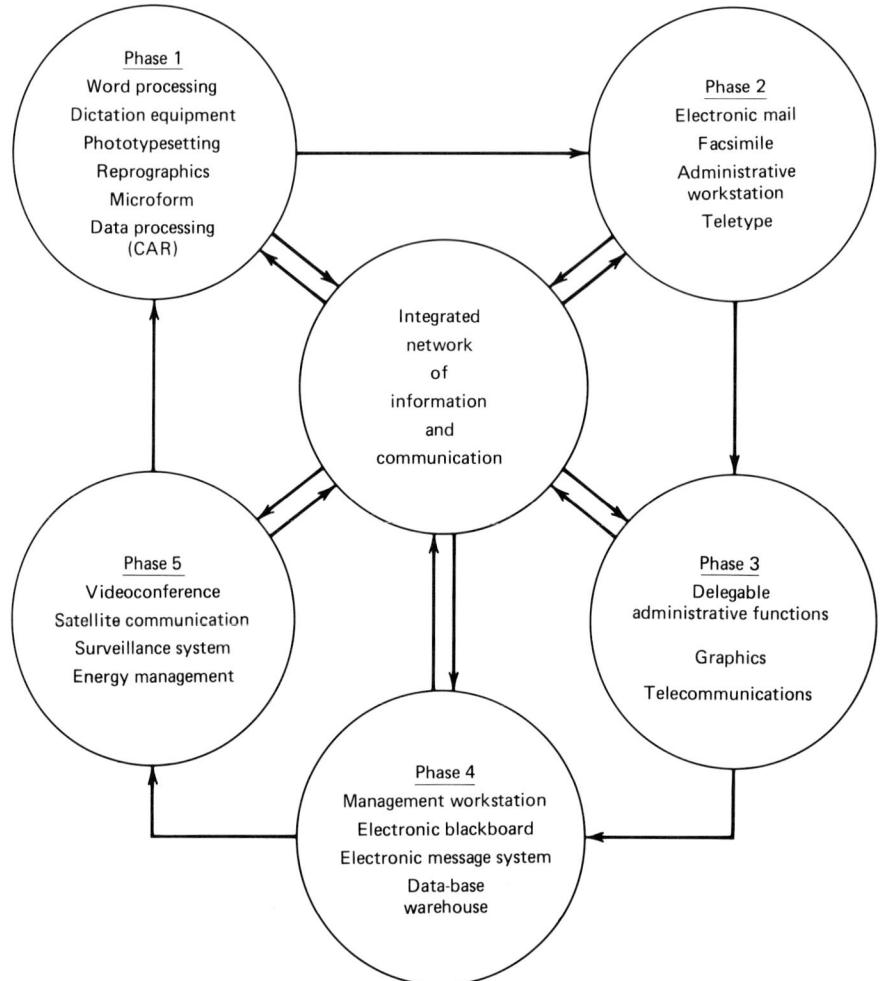

Figure 11 Integrated network of information and communication.

more knowledgeable and begin to experiment with technology), and people enter and leave an organization, bringing with them (or taking away) notions of what ought to be done. To achieve continuing success, two additional steps are necessary.

CONTINUING EDUCATION AND TRAINING

An overlay to the entire actuating process must be continuing communication, education, and training during all phases of an implementation program. A preinstallation training or orientation process must include concepts on equipment training, system performance, on-line plans, and scheduling. This orientation process allows users to ask questions or raise

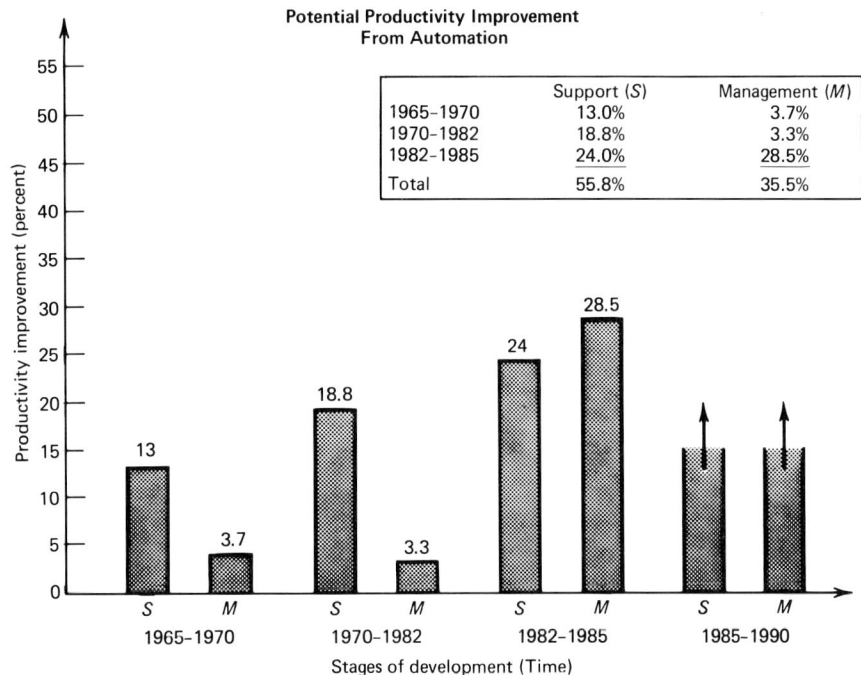

Figure 12   Potential productivity improvement from automation. *Source:* Mary M. Ruprecht & Associates, Incorporated, *Productivity Standards,* and Multi-client Information; and Ronald P. Uhlig, David J. Farber, and James H. Bair, "Monograph Series of the National Council for Computer Communications," *The Office of the Future,* North Holland Publishing Company, Amsterdam, New York, Oxford, 1980, p. 368.

issues and to begin understanding what the electronic office is all about, and helps to avoid problems, concerns, and fear of change. The orientation process enhances the users' awareness and directly involves employees in the implementation process.

Installation training provides orientation on the equipment to the specialists who will operate the equipment and to the users who will be retrieving information from it. From the training, users of the system will be able to use all advanced features, which, in turn, will improve their productivity.

Following implementation, it is important to keep educating users on additional functions to be automated and new technologies and features in software as they become available. Regular information-sharing sessions should be conducted, to optimize usage of the system and to continually enhance user skills.

Additional educational support can take the form of newsletters, external seminars on the use and applications of office systems, and internal staff meetings.

USER FEEDBACK AND EVALUATION

After the initial feedback on user satisfaction has been obtained, and problems in the operation have been corrected, an annual audit or study of the plan will ensure its continuing success and provide information to the manager for continuing enhancements of the system.

Successful implementation requires that the manager and/or team of people, with the advice and counsel of external experts, possess the skills of attention to detail, use of checklists, excellent human relations, outstanding negotiation skills, budgeting, scheduling, education, and communication.

> The point in implementation is that while alert information processing executives should be planning future systems, their plans should be built in manageable steps with a system that will grow up modularly, according to John B. Dykeman, in his August 1982 editorial in Modern Office Procedures. Dykeman goes on to say, don't run away and ignore office automation or networking. . . . After all, the point at which and how you cross over the threshhold between multifunctional office systems and advanced office automation is really academic, The bottom line is still how much more effective, economical, and productive the system, regardless of its name, makes your office, and reaching that objective is a continuous process.

Improving the productivity of the office will change the white-collar sector of the enterprise from being merely an overhead item to a contributor to corporate or organizational success. The effective management of information will provide management with the tools necessary to compete in the business environment. Those who work in offices will find themselves challenged to improve their performance, thereby helping to improve productivity while expanding their human potential. In addition, they will discover that the very quality of work life will be improved.

CHAPTER 18

PERSONNEL SELECTION, EVALUATION, AND COMPENSATION

OBJECTIVES

In this chapter you will learn about

1. The role and importance of people in an electronic office.
2. Management concepts and purposes regarding support staff and work specialization.
3. The need for forecasting and restructuring of staffing needs.
4. The purpose of a job study program.
5. The purpose of job analysis, job descriptions, and job specifications.
6. The purpose of job evaluation and the relationship of classification systems and salary administration.
7. The importance of job fit.
8. Steps in the selection process.
9. Government regulations and their effect on the selection process.
10. Technical advances that enable increasing numbers of handicapped employees to become productive employees.

Regardless of the degree of automation, the efficiency of an office ultimately depends on how well the people perform. That performance, in turn, depends on the quality of their training, and before that, on the process of selecting the right person with the right qualifications for the right job.

The selection of personnel for office support activities requires the matching of skills and aptitudes to diverse functions, including word processing, administrative support, records management, reprographics, data processing, telecommunications, and other functions discussed in earlier chapters of this text.

Each of these functions is carried out in all organizations, whether they be large, medium, or small. But the structure established and the job descriptions vary with the type and size of organization and quantity of paperwork. In larger offices, there will likely be more than one person responsible for secretarial functions of an administrative (or nontyping) nature, for word processing specialists who perform typing, for receptionists (who may also be file clerks, depending on the size of the office), and for clerical staff who perform other functions.

STRUCTURE

An integrated electronic office cannot succeed without careful attention to organizational structure and the selection of qualified, dedicated personnel to manage and staff it. The total systems approach requires creating a structure consistent with the management philosophy and with established productivity goals. Two basic principles should be followed when determining job assignments: (1) work specialization, or division of labor; and (2) delegation of responsibility and authority to the appropriate level of competency. Both principles lead to improved productivity and greater efficiency.

WORK SPECIALIZATION In the traditional office, every staff person was to some extent a generalist, or a person whose job description contained several different duties. For example, a secretary would be charged with transcription, typing, proofreading, filing, greeting visitors, running errands, and so on. There was little specialization. Most typewriters were used about 20 percent of the time, and machine transcription equipment even less. Interruptions were constant, and little time or opportunity was available to concentrate on being efficient or productive. Work specialization is more necessary in the automated office. The cost of electronic equipment requires that it be well utilized and not allowed to sit idle (see Figure 1).

The operation of electronic equipment requires that competent specialists know the equipment inside and out—know how to use it and make

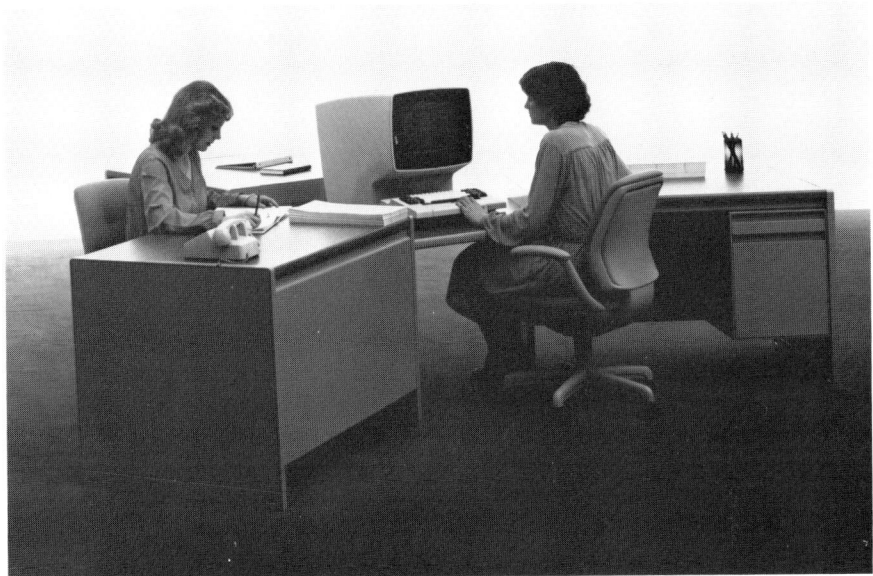

Figure 1 Work specialization is economical in the automated office. It provides for full utilization of equipment. (Courtesy of Steelcase, Incorporated.)

full use of all its capabilities. Specialists have the added advantage of working with fewer interruptions. They can concentrate on their assigned tasks and are able to achieve higher productivity levels.

DELEGATION TO THE APPROPRIATE LEVEL

Delegation to the appropriate level means that nonmanagement tasks should be assigned to administrative or clerical support personnel, depending on the nature of the task. For example, making copies or deliveries would be given to clerical-level people; and research and report preparation would fall to administrative support personnel, whose work is of a paraprofessional nature. The objective of delegating is to allow the managerial levels to devote maximum attention to management functions. Delegation is something that managers or professionals must always be conscious of; they must resist their personal tendencies or compulsions to "do it myself because then I'll know the job is done and done right."

Substantially improved management productivity can result from redistribution of work. Participants in the Booz, Allen, and Hamilton, Inc., study of managerial and professional productivity felt that 18 to 30 percent of their time was spent on nonproductive or lower-level work.[1]

---

[1] John J. Connell, "Management Productivity—Three Major Studies," *Impact*, September 1980, p. 4.

Delegation can provide managers with the time to be more productive and to perform true managerial-level tasks. At the same time, there are costs benefits to be attained from seemingly small items. For example, if a manager, paid about $36,000 a year, needs only one copy of an item but spends five minutes to walk to the copier, make the copy, and settle back to work, that copy costs $1.44. If the task is delegated to a clerical support person, paid about $9000 a year, that single copy costs only 36 cents.

The act of delegation requires forethought and patience on the part of the delegator. He or she must be sure to convey all the instructions that the delegatee needs to carry out the task. Often, delegators do not give clear instructions, in haste or impatience, and simple tasks do not get done.

During the selection process it is important to look for support staff personnel with the ability to understand delegated tasks quickly and to recognize complete instructions at the beginning.

Delegation to the appropriate level also means technology will be utilized in an appropriate fashion: for example, mailings will be sent to the mailroom, where such tasks as folding, inserting, and sealing can be performed most efficiently with the right kind of equipment.

Many benefits can be achieved with the proper organizational structure and job designs. Wasted labor charges can be prevented and higher levels of service achieved. Intelligent assignment of personnel also provides increased job satisfaction and more highly motivated employees.

HUMAN RESOURCES STAFFING

In many traditional offices, little planning or forecasting of personnel needs took place. Often people (also called human resources) were hired only when a vacancy occurred or when the work piled up to the point where another person was needed. Occasionally, when additional management or professional positions were created, additional office support positions were also added. The pattern has been to hire today for today's needs.

The planning or forecasting of staffing requires balancing the work force, with careful attention paid to peaks and valleys in workloads and to overstaffing or understaffing. Understaffing can cause an organization to get behind in its work and give employees the feeling of being hopelessly overworked; it does not provide much flexibility, either. Overstaffing however, is just as costly, because idle people are given makework jobs. Effective use of additional personnel so that time is provided for systems study, writing of procedures, and/or for all to be better trained can enhance the transition to the automated office. Ultimately this process will allow the organization to reap greater productivity gains in a shorter period of time.

One way to minimize overstaffing or understaffing *and* provide flexibility is to develop specialized teams in which members work together to perform the right quantity and quality of support required by their managers and principals.

Another worthwhile step in human resource staffing is future workforce planning, which is related to the timing or phasing-in of various parts of the information network. Such planning leads to the identification of qualifications for yet-to-be developed jobs. Through attention to the screening and selection process, discussed later in this chapter, competent and qualified employees will be on hand when needed.

Before we proceed with human resource staffing, some preliminary questions need to be asked.

1. Is the present workload distribution equitable? Are priorities balanced in the organization? What is the current work turnaround time?
2. Is the support team administratively flexible?
3. Is the support team trained to respond in emergencies? Is there a cross-training program? What are the backup positions?
4. To what extent is automation currently used, and for what purposes? What are the organization's future plans in regard to updating automation?
5. Is the employee turnover rate high in the organization? Why? Turnover is the rate at which employees leave an organization. For ease of comparison, the rate of turnover is expressed as a percentage. The U.S. Department of Labor suggests that it should be calculated on the total number of separations (those quitting, dismissed, dying, or leaving for whatever reason) divided by the average number of employees on the payroll during a particular period. Turnover rate (annually, semiannually, etc.) may be figured for an entire organization, an office, or a particular group of employees such as those in word processing or data processing.
6. What is the age of the support staff? What does a cross section of the total support staff look like?
7. Is there a need to develop new positions? Or can we begin with a redesign of present ones?
8. How receptive to change are the originators? The support staff?
9. Where do we start?

This type of information provides important background and a basis for decision making on restructure and job design.

JOB STUDY PROGRAMS

Once these questions and considerations are answered (usually by a complete study such as that described in an earlier chapter), management should proceed to a thorough job study program. The elements of a job study program are job analysis, job design, job description, job specification, and job evaluation.

Job analysis is the process of studying the duties and operations to be performed in a specific job, the conditions of each job, and the qualifications necessary to perform the job.

Job design is the process of dividing all the work into units that individuals will be assigned to carry out; it defines what a job should be.

Job description is the written, organized presentation of the information learned from the job analysis.

Job specification is the designation of minimum job requirements (such as a typing skill level of 40 wpm).

Job evaluation is a formal procedure for appraising, classifying, and weighting a set of jobs or positions in relation to other jobs and with respect to their worth to the employing organization.

JOB ANALYSIS

Traditionally, job analysis pertained to the study of existing jobs, usually as a basis for job evaluation. It involved compiling information on the duties and operations performed on each job, the conditions of the job, and the qualifications to perform the job. Good personnel administrators have periodically reviewed jobs, because as conditions and/or supervisors change, specific job duties may change. However, as an organization becomes actively involved in the implementation of change and the transitional process, a new approach becomes advisable. In addition to the study of *what is* (often a part of the feasibility study), job analysis should include a study of what *should be*. Then a plan for reshaping the existing personnel structure and jobs should be developed.

JOB DESIGN (OR REDESIGN)

Job design or redesign results from the job study or analysis. Keeping an eye on both short-range and long-range goals for a total support system and automated office, management must divide the total office/group function into parts that individuals will carry out; management must define what each of those jobs should be.

There are two elements in designing a job: to fit the *process* and to fit the *people* who must perform the job. Both must be used in effective job design.

In the office environment, the process-centered approach is required where technology and the information flow are concerned—jobs must be designed to utilize technology and to facilitate the information flow and processing of paperwork. On the other hand, the people-centered approach is equally important. Thought must be given to the person or persons who will be performing the jobs. Work specialization requires attention to questions such as the following: Is the job more challenging and more interesting if one person carries a single project through to completion (for example, the keyboarding and revising of an entire sales manual)? Would it be too fatiguing and take too long for one person to perform the entire job cycle? Would more centralization and the team approach work better?

Job designers—supervisors and personnel specialists—must seek the best possible balance between organizational and procedural needs and the needs of the people involved. A pragmatic, or practical, approach is required. The entire personnel structure and job design will be affected by the differing support requirements of departments and individuals, short- and long-range goals, and so on.

Job analysis and design should include the following steps:

1. Study carefully the information learned in the feasibility study to determine *what is*—the personnel structure, the job descriptions, present levels of productivity, quality, turnover, and morale.

2. Study carefully what the function of each job *should be* and what duties the person *should* perform (relative to total goals and planning for the electronic office).

3. Determine how present jobs should be restructured and what new jobs may be necessary.

4. Review your plans with others who are knowledgeable about the changing office and technology—consultants or those in other companies who are at more advanced stages in the transitional process.

5. Establish the plan of jobs for your organization based upon your study and review, with consideration given to both process and people.

6. Follow up and evaluate regularly—make changes as needed. Do not allow the same job designs to remain as change continues—they will no longer be appropriate.

JOB DESCRIPTION Good job descriptions result from a thoughtful determination of the most important job information to be presented in written form. Job description formats differ somewhat from company to company, but they are usually prepared by the Personnel or Human Resources Department. Essential details usually include the heading (which may include title, grade or classification level, whether the position is exempt or nonexempt,[2] names

---

[2] *Nonexempt* refers to positions covered by the Fair Labor Standards Act (FLSA) that must be paid the applicable minimum wage and overtime for all hours worked beyond a certain number, and so forth. *Exempt* refers to positions (such as managers and professionals) that are exempt from the requirements of the FLSA.

of persons who have written and approved the description, the date, etc.), the job objective or purpose, duties and responsibilities, and the job specifications or requirements. It is also helpful to provide information on whom the position reports to, by title and area of responsibility. Every job description should carry, *without fail*, the data of preparation. Note the sample job descriptions here and in pertinent chapters throughout the text (see Figures 2 and 3).

Usually a job description should describe the job *as it now is*, not what it ought to be.

Many different titles and descriptions apply to positions for the office of the future. The important thing, according to Jack Kaplan, vice-president of Jon Harvey Associates, is that job descriptions should be relevant work-

Figure 2 Note the various parts of this job description. (Courtesy of Western-Southern Life, Cincinnati, Ohio.)

(SSA) Western-Southern Life		JOB DESCRIPTION	
JOB TITLE Confidential Word Processing Specialist		JOB NUMBER	364
DEPARTMENT Administrative Services	DIVISION Word Processing	GROUP	

REPORTS TO (JOB TITLE)
Section Head, Management Support

JOB SUMMARY, DUTIES AND RESPONSIBILITIES, JOB REQUIREMENTS

JOB SUMMARY

Provides typing support for management people in our user departments throughout the Home Office. Has access to confidential information. Confidential Word Processing Specialist must set the pace in excellence of quality, time service, and good judgement. Deals directly with management personnel and their secretaries.

DUTIES AND RESPONSIBILITIES

1. Types routine letters, memos and reports from management personnel, using advanced dictation and typing equipment.
2. Types confidential information which includes Employee Salary Reviews, Counseling and Exit Interviews, new product characteristic memos, etc.
3. Proofreads work for accuracy and neatness.
4. Types special assignments requiring experience and excellence.
5. Substitutes for secretarial people on vacation in any user department and in the Executive Suite.
6. Performs any other duties assigned by manager by following oral or written instructions to accomplish desired results.

JOB REQUIREMENTS

1. Thorough knowledge of Business English in a Western-Southern environment.
2. Excellent typing accuracy and speed.
3. Practical knowledge of equipment and procedures in department.
4. Ability to work under pressure.
5. Ability to deal effectively with people.

POSITION DESCRIPTION

Position Title		Level	Job No.	Date		F
Senior Typesetter				1/1/83		x
						J
Div/Dept/Section		Reports to				
Graphic Arts/Word Systems		Administrator – Graphic Arts/Word Systems				
Previous Title		Level	Job No.	Date		
Sr. Typesetter						

Major Purpose

Keyboards and formats various company projects. May consult with client on less complex projects when special typographic discretion is required. Assists in the training and development of Typesetter.

Requirements

Typing ability of 55–60 WPM and 85% accuracy. Good knowledge of math and English grammar. Typographic skills as could be gained from a minimum of one year typesetting experience. Good interpersonal skills needed to communicate well with all levels of employees, as well as assisting in the training and development of the Typesetter. Must have well-organized working habits, and be able to work under pressure of deadlines.

2nd level of 3 step progression

Forced Progression: Yes _____ No _X_   Progression Leads To: Advanced Typesetter

Titles of Immediate Subordinates	Scope Data
	Average number of monthly projects produced by a typesetter: 37

Primary Functions	%
1. Evaluates job to determine basic framework and interpret goals of project. May consult with client for further clarification. Uses technical knowledge and aesthetic judgment to select appropriate previously-established format, or use client's suggested specifications with modifications if necessary. Creates appropriate format by establishing basic typographic parameters (type styles, sizes, leading, measure) and any special functions needed (such as: indents, runarounds, tabs, outline format, rules, letterspacing, positioning, etc.).	45
Keyboards copy from manuscript (making formatting alterations where needed), inserting appropriate typesetting codes to determine visual arrangement within given space. Records information and electronically communicates it to photo-composition equipment. Processes typeset galleys and proofreads or delivers to proofreader. After proofreading, recalls stored information to typesetting terminal and makes any needed corrections. Checks accuracy of corrections and delivers final galleys to art department for paste-up.	50
2. Maintains consistent quality of typesetting production by assisting in training and development of Typesetter, and by assisting in evaluating and training on initial new projects, of a more complex nature. Informs Advanced Typesetter of any equipment problems, or supply shortages, and by assisting in the maintenance of equipment.	5
Progression: Typesetter Sr. Typesetter Advanced Typesetter	100%

Form 16353 5-80

Figure 3 Note the various parts of this dated job description.

ing documents that accurately describe the positions and their responsibilities, but have enough flexibility to provide for unforeseen situations. They must be detailed and specific enough to allow for accurate ranking and effective recruiting. The qualifications demanded by a job description should be meaningful and relevant. Yet, the job description must be able to respond to changing office conditions. Job descriptions are usually developed after an intensive organizational study to answer the questions and examine the considerations outlined above. Once that process is completed, specific wording can take place.

It is necessary, however, to monitor the descriptions as change takes place, to assure that the actual functions and duties do not differ greatly from the description; if they do differ, each description and job should be checked carefully for the cause of discrepancy. Is the job itself no longer as designed because of other developments in the total system? Or has the individual filling the position influenced the functions and duties performed? If so, why? Was the description inappropriate for evolving needs? Is the job too big for one person to handle, so some tasks are done by others? Is the job too small, so other tasks have been picked up? Did the individual filling the position lack needed qualifications? Could others with better qualifications be found? Or is too much expected for the grade or classification level assigned to the job? Solutions may be based on job redesign and/or reevaluation of the position, or even on personnel reassignment. Only by seeking and finding the cause of differences can management determine how to rectify them.

Management should not be concerned that differences occur—that is the sign of a healthy, dynamic organization that is undergoing the transition to the automated office. If there are no differences, it is likely that progress is not satisfactory.

JOB SPECIFICATIONS

Job specifications, sometimes called placement criteria, serve several purposes. They stipulate the minimum requirements in skills, knowledge, education, experience, and special requirements (such as working hours). They are frequently used as a basis for rating the job in the process of job evaluation.

Job specification information, however, is also very useful in the employment, selection, training, and counseling of workers, because such information actually identifies the qualifications a person should possess to qualify for a particular position. Such information also helps management establish training and development programs and employees establish personal and career goals.

JOB EVALUATION

Job analysis and job design, job descriptions, and job specifications or requirements are all prerequisites to job evaluation. They provide the basis for objective evaluation of the worth of each job in relation to other jobs and to the organization. They help to make sure that it is the job that is rated, not the person on the job.

The steps required to complete a job evaluation process (which also relates to an equitable salary policy) are as follows:

1. A careful analysis of each job description should be undertaken. Studying and talking to current employees doing the same or similar work is an important verification step. If no current position is available for comparison in yet-to-be implemented areas, then a proposed job description should be created and used for evaluation purposes.

2. Each job is then evaluated with respect to its worth to the organization. The several methods available for this purpose are discussed on the following pages. The jobs are then rated and assigned job grades.

3. Once this type of data has been collected and analyzed, and job grades assigned, the results provide an objective basis for a salary administration program.

Methods of Rating There are four principal methods of rating for job evaluation purposes: (1) by ranking, (2) by job classification, (3) by factor comparison, and (4) by points. The larger the organization, the more necessary it becomes to evaluate office jobs in a systematic manner.

Ranking. In this method, all jobs in the area are ranked from top to bottom (most important to least important) with respect to their worth or value to the firm. Ranking is the simplest and oldest form of job evaluation. Ranking is often performed by the "boss" in a small organization or it may be performed by a committee to obtain a consensus ranking.

Job Classification. The job classification method, also known as a job grouping grading structure, utilizes predetermined classes or groups. Jobs with the same and/or similar tasks and other requirements can be grouped into general job classes or occupational groupings. For organizations with EEO compliance requirements, "Job Groups" and "EEO Categories" have become familiar terms. Most of the data from the U.S. Bureau of Labor Statistics and state employment services are categorized according to job groups or occupational groups—clerical, stenographic, and so on. Groupings such as administrative, managerial, and technical are also used. In larger organizations with larger number of employees in specialized areas, groupings such as accounting, data processing, or word processing may be appropriate: for example, Figure 4 lists all of the positions within a word processing grouping.

The most common example of the job classification method is the General Schedule used by the federal government, which covers all its jobs and positions (professional, scientific, clerical, administrative, and custodial). The General Schedule is composed of 18 job classes (GS-1 through GS-18). The less difficult the job, the lower the job class number; the greater the responsibilities and qualifications needed to fill the job, the higher the job class number.

Factor Comparison. The factor-comparison method begins with a set of factors on which to base evaluation. Usually four to seven factors are chosen. Job factors might include education, experience, mental requirements, skill requirements, physical requirements, responsibility, and

Utility clerk
Operator
Technician
Copy editor
Specialist
Instructor
Backup supervisor
Unit supervisor
Analyst trainee
Analyst
Section supervisor
Coordinator
Division manager

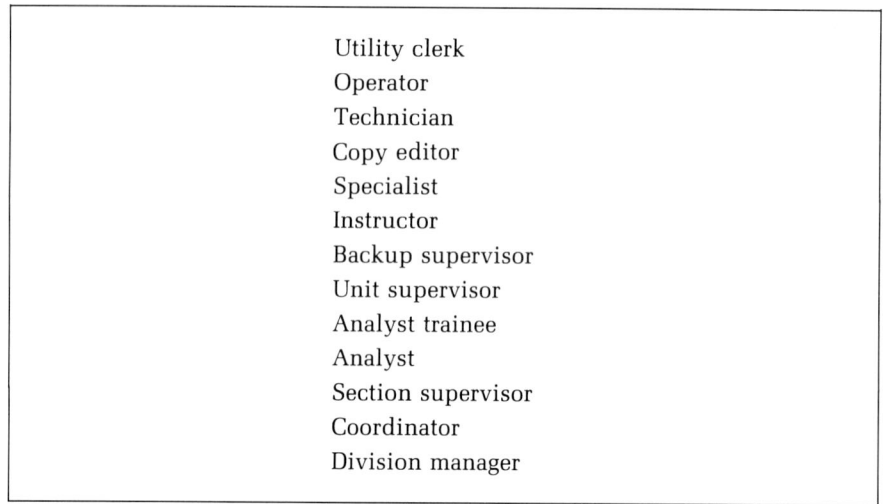

Figure 4   One large firm's information processing groupings showing various job functions.

working conditions. This method is also called the "job-to-money" method, because job factors are related to money. For example, education might be valued at up to $50 and experience up to $75. The total salary would be based upon the total of all the factors; each factor represents a portion of the total salary.

To establish a factor-comparison system, the evaluator must establish a set of benchmark jobs, or jobs upon which a consensus exists as to worth and value. These benchmark jobs are then ranked according to worth, and a value judgment is made regarding the contribution of each of the factors to the total worth of the job. For example, if secretaries are paid $200 per week, a comparison can be made of the worth of two positions. The salary of each position is broken down into factors. For example, suppose that for secretaries, $80 derives from skill, $70 from responsibility, and $50 from mental requirements. With this basic breakdown, each secretarial position in the firm can be compared to the benchmark position to arrive at a final rating and ranking. If a messenger is established as a benchmark job, the same method would be applied, although the total salary might be $130 and the job factors and their portion of the total would differ. Clearly, this method is usually cumbersome; it is rather difficult to explain and communicate to workers. It also is inflexible in regard to prevailing salary rates outside the firm, which are caused by supply and demand. Its major advantage lies in its fair degree of accuracy, since each job is compared against a benchmark or key job and by factor against factor.

Point Methods.   Finally, point methods can be utilized. Point plans are the most popular method currently in use. Under the point method, a set of common factors is chosen for consideration (education, skill, responsibility, effort, etc.) A scale or range of points is devised for each compensable factor, representing increasing levels of worth up to a maximum for the factor. Each level is assigned a given number of points; it is common to rate each factor for each job according to the degree of demand for that factor on the particular job being evaluated. All jobs are ranked and classified according to the set standard.

Once evaluation points have been determined and totaled for each job, the jobs can be priced. The point method provides a consistent internal basis (that is, the rates paid within the enterprise should be directly associated with the evaluation) for determining what the rate of pay should be for each job. Figure 5 illustrates factors and levels of degree used in a point method.

The point factor is probably less subjective and provides more consistency than any other rating method, because each factor is defined by level, with further definitions by degrees or points. Although the method is relatively uncomplicated to perform, the point system does require a great deal of time to develop. Personnel must be trained to administer the plan. Also, employees must be educated about the plan. A company using the plan must take care to comply with the Equal Pay Act, which requires equal pay based on actual job requirements and performance. Job requirements and job performance are not necessarily assigned equal points under a point plan.

SALARY PLANS   Effective salary plans involve many other considerations. Salaries account for 75 to 80 percent of total office costs and therefore represent the single largest cost item. When implementing an integrated electronic office, management should establish a sound, well-planned program that will allow the organization to implement change smoothly yet consider the entire organization and its ability to pay. In this era of inflationary pressures and shortages of competent office workers, this task is not easy. Other criteria to be considered include the productivity of the employee, the job requirements, the expectations of office employees, governmental regulations, and salaries paid by other companies.

One of the newer ways to establish salaries is the *guideline method*, a technique for interpreting and reflecting the value of jobs in the labor marketplace. Job rates change according to the forces of supply and demand, and a realistic salary plan takes this into account.

To utilize the guideline method, a substantial list of key jobs or benchmark jobs is selected. The key or benchmark jobs are those that are easily identified in the marketplace by a large number of firms through salary surveys. The Administrative Management Society uses capsule job de-

KEY EVALUATION FACTORS FOR CLERICAL JOBS

The following examples indicate that there is little difference in the factors taken into consideration when performing job evaluation. Whatever system is in effect in your organization, you can achieve positive results when establishing job outlines.

CLERICAL JOB EVALUATION TECHNIQUE

Clerical Job Difficulty Catalog:
Prerequisite Skills: A B C D E F
  Mental Skill
  Manual Skill
  Associated Experience
Responsibility:
  Judgement
  Error Repercussion
  Structured Assistance
Interaction:
  Communication
  Coordination
  Human Relation Skills

FACTOR DEFINITIONS FOR THE FACTOR EVALUATION SYSTEM USED TO CLASSIFY POSITIONS IN THE GENERAL SCHEDULE (U.S. CIVIL SERVICE COMMISSION — 1977)

Factors: Levels & Points:
Knowledge Required by Position
Supervisory Controls
Guidelines
Complexity
Scope & Effect
Personal Contacts
Purpose of Contacts
Physical Demands
Work Environment

MIDWEST INDUSTRIAL MANAGEMENT ASSOCIATION (MIMA) JOB EVALUATION PLAN FOR OFFICE JOBS

Job Factors: 1st-7th Degrees:
Education
Experience
Complexity of Duties
Supervision Necessary
Effect of Errors
Contact with Others
Confidential Data
Mental and/or Visual Demand
Working Conditions

For Supervisory Positions Only:
Type of Supervision
Extent of Supervision

CO-OPERATIVE WAGE STUDY (CWS): A JOINT UNION-MANAGEMENT STEEL INDUSTRY PLAN FOR HOURLY RATED NON-CONFIDENTIAL CLERICAL JOBS

Factors: 1-32 Levels
Pre-employment Training (3)
Employment Training & exp. (9)
Mental Skill (6)
Manual Skill (5)
Responsibility for Material (32)
Responsibility for Equipment (16)
Responsibility for Operations (8)
Responsibility for Safety of Others (5)
Mental Effort (5)
Physical Effort (5)
Surroundings (5)
Hazard (5)

Figure 5   The use of factors, levels, and degrees in the point method.

scriptions for a number of office positions and annually collects salary information about them. Data is provided for the United States and Canada and for some cities (see Figure 6). The Association of Information Systems Professionals (formerly known as The International Information/ Word Processing Association) performs a similar service for some more-specialized positions (see Figure 7). Other organizations perform similar services, as do some magazines such as *Datamation* and *Infosystems*, which annually conduct surveys concerning both data processing and word processing.

All key jobs should be reviewed and evaluated in light of salary surveys, and any inequities should be corrected.

Effective salary administration may have considerable effect on motivation of employees. This point will be discussed at greater length in a later chapter.

BASIC TERMS

Certain terms, used widely in both the job study program and the selection of employees, need to be defined for use within an organization, to assure consistency and preciseness. Proper use of these terms by management and supervisory personnel will facilitate communication with the Personnel or Human Resources Department. Figure 8 presents some of the most basic terms.

SELECTION OF EMPLOYEES

Selection of the right employees is always of major importance—particularly so when an organization is in the midst of the transition from the traditional office to the integrated electronic office based upon the total support system. Careful selection will be reflected in lower employee turnover, saving both time and money. Studies have shown an average cost of $1200 to train a new employee and develop him or her to normal productivity. Where use of sophisticated equipment is involved, costs are even higher. Inadequate support provided to managers and professionals during a new employee's learning period, although an intangible cost, is also an added expense. Hiring costs (possible agency fees, screening, testing, interviewing, checking references, etc.) add other expenses. Hence, careful selection to prevent turnover is essential. The process involved in finding the right employee for a job is called job fit or job match.

JOB FIT In determining whether there is a "good match" between an individual worker and a given job, management should examine three factors: skill,

JOB TITLES AND DESCRIPTIONS

A WORD PROCESSING TRAINEE

Entry level position with 0-12 months' experience. Performs routine transcription and manipulation of text from various types of source information (dictation, handwritten, etc.). Proofreads own work. May perform light secretarial duties.

B WORD PROCESSING OPERATOR

Uses word processing equipment to input, edit, customize, and deliver medium-to-complex typed documents with established quality and time standards. Proofreads and edits own work. Incumbent is familiar with department terminology and company practices. Equipment includes the use of microprocessor-based, standalone, or shared-logic word processing systems utilizing a CRT screen. I.E., Xerox 850-86, Wang, Lanier, Vydec, Redactron, etc. May also perform general secretarial duties.

C LEAD WORD PROCESSING OPERATOR

Utilizes full scope of equipment capabilities to produce and revise complicated documents, such as lengthy technical and statistical reports, from complex source information, including the retrieval of text and data. Leads the activities of lower-level operators.

D COMPUTER OPERATOR

Operates computer utilizing established programs or programs under development. Oversees loading of computer and manipulation of controls. Determines the nature of errors or equipment failure and takes corrective action following established procedures. May instruct or give limited direction to less experienced operators.

E DATA ENTRY OPERATOR

Operates alpha/numeric data entry equipment to record and/or verify detailed or non-coded data, using key to tape or key to disk. Corrects errors, usually follows standardized procedures, and may handle exceptions and special non-standard procedures requiring close attention to detail. Keypunch operators recording key to card may be included.

F PROGRAMMER

Under general supervision, using Cobol, participates in the analysis, program design, coding and other applications/programming tasks needed to produce reports and mathematical computations on an established system. Prepares all elements of program documentation, test data and organization of program testing schedule. Debugs programs, and designs conversion procedures. Trains and prepares training material for operators and users of the program.

G PROGRAMMER/ANALYST

Under general supervision, using Cobol, participates in the analysis, program design, coding and other applications/programming tasks needed to produce reports and mathematical computations or to maintain existing information files. Projects are of an intermediate complexity level. Interfaces with user as necessary. Defines the applications problem, determines system specifications, recommends equipment changes, designs data processing procedures and block diagrams. May prepare machine-logic flow charts and codes. Devises data verification methods and standard systems procedures. Trains and prepares training material for operators and users of the system.

H ACCOUNTING CLERK B

Checks, verifies and posts journal vouchers, accounts payable vouchers, payroll, or other simple accounting data of a recurring or standard nature.

I ACCOUNTING CLERK A

Maintains a complete set of accounting records in a small office, or handles one phase of accounting in a larger unit which requires the accounting training needed to determine proper accounting entries; reconciles entries, prepares accounting reports, analyzes accounting records to determine causes of results shown, etc. May direct work of junior clerks or bookkeepers (excludes supervisors). May include accounts payable clerk, payroll clerk, etc.

J SECRETARY - LEVEL B

Performs a limited range of secretarial duties in a small company or for a supervisor in a larger firm. May take dictation and transcribe from notes and dictaphone with speed and accuracy. Screens calls, makes appointments, handles travel arrangements, answers routine correspondence and maintains filing systems.

K SECRETARY - LEVEL A

Performs an unlimited range of secretarial duties for middle management personnel or more than one individual. Composes and/or takes and transcribes correspondence of a complex and confidential nature. Position requires a knowledge of company policy, procedure and above-average secretarial and administrative skills.

L EXECUTIVE SECRETARY/ADMINISTRATIVE ASSISTANT

Performs a full range of secretarial and administrative duties for high-level member of executive staff. Handles project-oriented duties and may be held accountable for the timely completion of these tasks. Relieves executive of routine administrative detail. Position requires an in-depth knowledge of company practice, structure and a high degree of technical skills.

M LEGAL SECRETARY

Performs an unlimited range of secretarial duties for one or more members of the firm, usually a junior, senior, or managing partner. Takes and transcribes dictation with a high degree of speed and accuracy. Position requires knowledge of the specific legal terminology within the attorney's areas of specialization; i.e., litigation, probate, corporate, etc. May utilize word processing equipment.

N FILE CLERK

Performs general alphabetical and numeric filing, sorting and cross referencing. Locates and removes material upon request and keeps records of its disposition. Maintains and updates files according to an established system. May deliver files, copy material from files, and purge out-dated materials.

O CLERK B

Performs basic office or clerical duties on short assignments and tasks which are highly structured in accordance with established procedures. This is a higher-level position than a file clerk involving a variety of routine and semi-routine duties.

P CLERK A

Performs diverse clerical tasks requiring some analysis, judgment and a detailed knowledge of department and/or company policies and procedures dealing with the incumbent's area of responsibility, such as claims operations, shipping and receiving, etc. Duties may require proficiency with one or more types of operational office equipment, such as CRT. Minimum supervision required.

Q SWITCHBOARD OPERATOR/RECEPTIONIST

Operates a call-director type telephone system, greets visitors, screens incoming calls and performs basic clerical tasks. May operate a multiple position console and keep records of calls and toll charges.

R CLERK TYPIST

Produces draft and/or finished typed copies of documents from a variety of originators. Form and content usually follow standard guidelines. May perform other clerical duties of minimum difficulty.

S CUSTOMER SERVICE REPRESENTATIVE

Provides guidance and assistance to customers in oral or written form regarding problems with accounts or merchandise. May use CRT to verify information. Duties include records search, investigating problems/complaints, policy interpretation, response preparation and adjustment, or correction of records. May also open new accounts or provide general information.

T PHOTOCOPY MACHINE OPERATOR

Operates and maintains photocopier (i.e. Xerox 9200), loads blank paper, inserts handwritten or typed originals and determines the proper selection of controls to obtain desired copies. Maintenance includes cleaning and performing minor repairs. Contacts service representative for major malfunctions.

TOTAL UNITED STATES

TOTAL ALL TYPES OF BUSINESS	JOB CATEGORY																			
	A	B	C	D	E	F	G	H	I	J	K	L	M	N	O	P	Q	R	S	T
AVERAGE	208	246	282	288	226	367	439	228	270	246	276	323	286	182	208	239	224	213	260	220
FIRST QUARTILE	178	211	241	241	191	316	388	191	231	211	241	281	241	158	173	201	191	183	211	201
MEDIAN	201	241	281	281	221	363	426	221	261	241	271	316	281	173	201	231	221	211	241	211
THIRD QUARTILE	231	271	316	316	251	426	501	251	301	271	316	363	338	201	231	261	251	241	291	241
NO. COMPANIES	552	1543	897	2606	2832	1604	1606	3124	3486	2941	3554	3416	617	1817	2602	3091	3524	2041	1715	841
NO. EMPLOYEES	2739	7297	2740	8930	19600	8887	10551	18712	18737	43034	42976	19763	3934	14427	45382	49311	8022	25556	15966	2725

CANADA

TOTAL ALL TYPES OF BUSINESS	JOB CATEGORY																			
	A	B	C	D	E	F	G	H	I	J	K	L	M	N	O	P	Q	R	S	T
AVERAGE	258	297	355	340	284	397	459	272	339	292	321	367	300	239	260	304	264	254	317	234
FIRST QUARTILE	221	251	316	271	251	338	426	231	281	251	281	316	241	201	221	261	231	221	261	191
MEDIAN	241	281	388	338	271	426	476	261	338	281	316	363	301	231	251	301	261	241	338	241
THIRD QUARTILE	291	338	388	388	338	476	501	301	388	316	363	426	338	271	291	338	291	281	338	251
NO. COMPANIES	30	101	73	185	219	126	117	265	322	225	290	224	36	161	219	265	320	206	119	79
NO. EMPLOYEES	67	348	219	450	975	370	426	1152	1279	1917	1985	754	90	803	2065	2499	528	1305	587	166

Figure 6 Variety of job titles and descriptions shows opportunities available in the automated office. (Courtesy of the Administrative Management Society, Willow Grove, Pennsylvania.)

motivation, and growth/development need. Skills include all aspects required to perform the job. Motivational considerations revolve around the question of whether the applicant will *do* the job. The growth/development concerns focus on the applicant's need for career progression and growth. For the most effective job fit, all of the above factors should be met by the job. During evaluation of an applicant, questions should be asked to uncover potential problems in any area that could prevent an applicant from being happy or satisfied on the job. If most of the applicant's personality traits match the key functional requirements of the job and none is so different that it guarantees failure, there is probably an applicant-job

Figure 7 Generic job titles and descriptions and relative salary levels. (Courtesy of the International Information/Word Processing Association, Willow Grove, Pennsylvania.)

JOB TITLES AND DESCRIPTIONS FOR WORD PROCESSING PERSONNEL

NOTE: All positions are non-exempt (hourly wage) except where noted.

A. WORD PROCESSING TRAINEE

Entry level position for those having 0-12 months word processing experience. Must have adequate typing skills, good knowledge of grammar, punctuation, spelling and formatting, the ability to use dictionaries, handbooks and other reference materials, and be oriented toward teamwork and the use of machines. A trainee's functions include routine transcription and manipulation of text from various types of source information (dictation, handwritten, etc.). Maintains own production records and may be required to proofread own work.

B. WORD PROCESSING OPERATOR

The next level up from Word Processing Trainee for those having 6-24 months word processing experience. In addition to having all the qualifications and functions of position A, a Word Processing Operator handles special documents, meets established quality standards, uses all of a machine's text editing functions and is familiar with department terminology and company practices.

C. WORD PROCESSING SPECIALIST I

A Word Processing Operator with a minimum of 18 months experience who can format, produce and revise complicated documents, such as lengthy technical and statistical reports, from complex source information, including the retrieval of text and data from electronic files. Exercises independent action when interpreting instructions to produce a quality document, understands proofreader marks, and assumes full responsibility for document accuracy and completeness. Has a thorough knowledge of center procedures and maintenance of records. May operate word processing equipment in the telecommunications mode.

D. WORD PROCESSING SPECIALIST II/ASSISTANT SUPERVISOR

A person at this level exercises all of the competencies of position C and may act as Assistant Supervisor. A Word Processing Specialist II is able to operate all the information processing equipment within the installation. Responsibilities include coordinating and assigning work, analyzing requirements for specific projects, communicating with users, compiling production statistics, and recommending changes in center procedures. May also assist in training personnel.

E. PHOTOTYPESETTING SPECIALIST

A Word Processing Operator who enters special codes while keyboarding and revising text that is to be output on a photocomposition system. Has knowledge of points, picas, typefaces, leading, format requirements, production techniques, and other aspects of typesetting and printing.

F. WORD PROCESSING TRAINER

Someone with a minimum of 24 months experience operating word processing systems who spends the majority of time training new operators. May also be responsible for instructing users in dictation methods and other procedures to ensure maximum utilization of a wp center. Should make recommendations to management concerning new equipment purchases from the standpoint of ease of use.

G. PROOFREADER

Proofreads typed copy for text content, spelling, punctuation, grammar, and typographical errors. May be responsible for setting grammar and format standards, guidance and/or training of secretaries and principals.

H. WORD PROCESSING SUPERVISOR

With all the competencies of a Word Processing Specialist II, a Supervisor is responsible for the operation of a center (or section within a large center). Schedules and coordinates workflow, assists word processing personnel in document production and in establishing and maintaining quality standards. Also analyzes production data and procedures, identifies potential improvements and may be responsible partially for budgets and equipment recommendations. Reports to Word Processing Manager.

I. WORD PROCESSING MANAGER

Exempt (salaried). Responsible for the overall operation of a word processing center, including the guidance of supervisors, personnel administration, staff requirements, user liaison and evaluation, design and implementation of future word processing systems. Also is responsible for budgets, overall production reports and coordination of services with administrative support. May also manage the operation of photocopying, printing, mailing or graphics services. In larger organizations, the Word Processing Manager reports to Information Systems Manager.

AA. ADMINISTRATIVE SECRETARY

Someone who works with a group of principals as part of a team under the direction of an Administrative Support Supervisor or Manager. Responsibilities include such support functions as filing, photocopying, maintaining calendars, records and lists, and providing special secretarial services, etc.

BB. SENIOR ADMINISTRATIVE SECRETARY

Has a record of exceptional performance. At times may act as assistant to supervisor of an administrative team and is qualified to compose and edit documents for principals, provide research support and perform other para-professional duties. Handles special projects and is fully aware of company standards and practices.

CC. ADMINISTRATIVE SUPPORT SUPERVISOR

May have the responsibilities of position BB in addition to scheduling and administering workflow to a team of administrative secretaries. Responsible for liaison with and training of users who benefit from administrative support. Evaluates staffing requirements, prepares management reports and recommends new methods of handling administrative secretaries. Reports to Administrative Support Manager.

DD. ADMINISTRATIVE SUPPORT MANAGER

Exempt (salaried). Has full responsibility for developing, maintaining and evaluating all services under administrative support within an organization, such as filing, telephone, mail, and para professional support. Monitors the success of the administrative support group and is familiar with the company's goals and objectives. Works closely with the Word Processing Manager to ensure cooperation of the two functions. May manage other major administrative duties such as records and retention, microfilm, print shop, purchasing, etc. Reports to Information Systems Manager (in large organizations).

EE. STAFF ANALYST

Exempt (salaried). Responsible for consulting and assisting Word Processing and Administrative Support Supervisors and Managers. Conducts studies, reviews operations and determines and recommends appropriate staffing, procedures and equipment. Reports to Information Systems Manager or Word Processing Manager or Administrative Support Manager.

J. INFORMATION MANAGER

Exempt (salaried). May be Vice President or Assistant to Vice President in some organizations. **Has total responsibility for all aspects of an organization's office systems, including word processing, administrative support and other information processing functions.** Ensures the collaboration of all support functions. Reports to a chief executive officer.

Figure 7 *(Continued)*

TOTAL UNITED STATES

		NO. COMPANIES	NO. EMPLOYEES	AVERAGE	HIGH	LOW	MEDIAN	MODE
A	WORD PROCESSING TRAINEE	337	1,716	212.90	462.00	107.00	212.00	212.00
B	WORD PROCESSING OPERATOR	466	4,237	256.26	525.00	107.00	237.00	237.00
C	WORD PROCESSING SPECIALIST I	461	3,179	277.58	525.00	132.00	262.00	262.00
D	WORD PROCESSING SPECIALIST II/ASSISTANT SUPERVISOR	378	1,357	300.86	575.00	107.00	287.00	262.00
E	PHOTOTYPESETTING SPECIALIST	118	258	280.52	525.00	165.00	262.00	262.00
F	WORD PROCESSING TRAINER	112	169	324.89	650.00	107.00	312.00	312.00
G	PROOFREADER	163	428	262.36,	487.00	117.00	262.00	262.00
H	WORD PROCESSING SUPERVISOR	431	1,171	363.61	1,001.00	107.00	362.00	362.00
I	WORD PROCESSING MANAGER	522	656	442.68	1,001.00	185.00	437.00	525.00
AA	ADMINISTRATIVE SECRETARY	201	3,868	277.52	575.00	107.00	262.00	237.00
BB	SENIOR ADMINISTRATIVE SECRETARY	161	1,505	308.96	900.00	175.00	287.00	262.00
CC	ADMINISTRATIVE SUPPORT SUPERVISOR	64	194	379.96	750.00	142.00	362.00	412.00
DD	ADMINISTRATIVE SUPPORT MANAGER	113	170	467.23	1,001.00	237.00	437.00	387.00
EE	STAFF ANALYST	94	198	474.24	1,001.00	165.00	462.00	387.00
J	INFORMATION MANAGER	220	297	602.00	1,001.00	237.00	575.00	650.00
	AVERAGE HRS/WK	38.7						
	COMPANIES RESPONDING	1,747						

*Small samples produce less significant data.
MEDIAN: Middle occurrence
MODE: Most frequent occurrence

Figure 7 (Continued)

Task. An action or series of actions taken by a person to produce a result. A task may be either mental or physical and may involve thought processes or manual work or a combination of both; or interpersonal communications between two or more people. *Example:* to transcribe from dictation.

Skill. The proficient, manual, verbal, or mental manipulation of data, people, or things. Skill embodies observable, quantifiable, and measurable performance parameters. *Example:* skill in typing at 50 wpm with no more than three errors (or corrections) per page.

Knowledge. An organized body of information, usually of a factual or procedural nature, which, *if* applied, makes adequate performance of the job possible. *Example:* knowledge of English language, spelling, punctuation, grammar; knowledge of the capabilities of equipment.

Aptitude. A potential for performing an activity. *Example:* mechanical aptitude—a potential for working with equipment.

Ability. The power to perform an activity at the present time (also implies a lack of barriers, either physical or mental, to performing the activity). Abilities emerge when aptitude is combined with knowledge. *Example:* ability to format business documents of all types.

Figure 8 Basic terms chart defining terms used in developing good job descriptions.

match. Herbert and Jeanne Greenberg reported in *Harvard Business Review*[3] that persons who had been deliberately matched with their jobs outperformed to a statistically significant degree those who had not been matched.

HOW TO FIND THE RIGHT PERSONNEL

Preliminary Data Collection and Standard Setting

Before any organization can find specific people to fill specific jobs, the organization must complete an internal job analysis process to determine its needs and identify the specific tasks to be performed. This job analysis can be done by internal personnel or outside consultants. Following the job analysis, specific job descriptions and job specifications should be prepared, so that personnel needs are clearly identified.

Once the specific job descriptions are agreed upon, the organization needs to set specifications for job requirements, or basic attributes they are looking for in applicants. These attributes can include specific skills (e.g., a certain typing proficiency), communication and English-language skills, knowledge of the organization, or general behavioral characteristics (such as a positive, businesslike attitude, pride in appearance and work, a ma-

---

[3] Herbert M. and Jeanne Greenberg, "Job Matching for Better Sales Performance," *Harvard Business Review*, September/October 1980, pp. 132–133.

chine orientation, flexibility, the ability to be a team worker, and dependability). A specific salary range should also be established (see the section on Job Evaluation). Only by thoughtful identification of specific job requirements can the right job fit or match be made.

Locating Applicants

There are several ways to locate applicants for a given position. These include (1) internal advertising, (2) external advertising, (3) employment agencies, (4) industry contacts, (5) professional associations, and (6) schools/colleges.

Advertising within the Organization.   There are many advantages to internal hiring that should not be ignored. First, applicants know the organization. Second, they have a commitment to the organization and their future in the group. Third, internal hiring helps to build good rapport with the support staff; it demonstrates a career progression possibility.

Classified Ads in Newspapers.   This method will announce a vacancy to a large number of people. It can be called the shotgun approach. Good composition and layout of the ad will contribute greatly to high readership levels. Clear and well-written copy (text) will go far in attracting good qualified candidates and eliminating many unqualified and undesirable candidates. Sunday editions in most newspapers are usually the best read.

There are four types of help-wanted ads. *Closed ads* are those where the applicant is asked to apply to an anonymous box number. Note the closed ad example in Figure 9. These are the least effective, since applicants are normally hesitant to provide detailed personal information to an unknown source.

The second type of ad states the identity and address of the employer and invites interested applicants to visit or call. This approach works well if the firm has sufficient staff and space to accommodate a large group of applicants (see Figure 10).

The third type of ad lists the type of business, general location, the name of a contact person, and a phone number. This approach allows the firm to carry out preliminary screening over the phone, thus saving both applicant and firm time (see Figure 11).

Figure 9   Closed advertisement depicting anonymous box number.

LEGAL TYPIST

Fully experienced, good shorthand, for busy office.
Box 735, AITKIN INDEPENDENT URGE

> Medium size, downtown firm wants an experienced typist to a senior partner. Prior experience and shorthand skills required. Write to Wagrecht and Associates, 123 Happiness Lane, Pleasure, USA 56469.

Figure 10   Ad stating the identity and address of the employer.

> *Administrator.* Midwest law firm seeking administrator. Responsibilities include supervision of nonlawyer personnel, financial supervision, procedural development, file management, and facilities and equipment maintenance supervision. Minimum three years supervisory office management, experience necessary, college degree desirable. Send resume with salary requirements, and inquiry to Wagrecht & Associates, 123 Happiness Lane, Pleasure, USA 56469, telephone 218-727-5150.

Figure 11   Specific ad allowing for prescreening through telephone interviews.

Some advertisements sell a position rather than simply announce a job opening (see Figure 12). Such an ad must be distinctive in size and layout, and must explain (1) the job and its requirements, (2) the employer, and (3) how to apply. The ad must appeal to the psychological as well as the economic needs of an applicant.

Employment Agencies.   Employment agencies can prescreen and match qualifications to jobs, thus saving the firm time. Agencies can be either

Figure 12   Ad selling a position.

> ### TYPIST—LEGAL WANTED
>
> Mr. Hansen, our senior estate lawyer, needs an expert typist to assist him in preparing legal documents such as deeds, bills of sales, contracts, probates, etc. Excellent typing skills and a good vocabulary and grammar are important. No shorthand required. Many promotional opportunities within the firm.
>
> Location in downtown area in modern, open-plan surroundings. Near RR, bus and taxi. All benefits, excellent salary.
>
> Apply in phone or in person to Mr. Pouset, Personnel Department.
>
> HANSEN, WILLIAMS & ASSOCIATES
> 1756 Ridgeway Drive
> Riverton, Wyoming
> 307-856-3585

public or private. There are even specialized agencies (e.g., Jon Harvey Associates, which specializes in office automation personnel). When using an employment agency, the firm must develop a good working relationship with the agency, so that both the firm's general philosophy and exact position needs are known. The agency can then perform the screening and "fitting" process.

One prestigious law firm that had been using a private employment agency service for some time decided to use an open classified advertisement to attract more applicants. The ad resulted in over 100 telephone calls and about 80 walk-in applicants. The reception area was so crowded with applicants that there were no seats for clients. Many of the applicants were not suited for the position. The time it took to obtain just basic information, let alone to screen and interview, was so great that the personnel director concluded that never again would the firm use an open ad. The fees paid the agency were worth it. Although the agency normally sent over only three or four applicants for a position, it was effectively screening and matching applicants to the firm's needs.

Contacts with Other Companies.   Many major cities have a severe shortage of office automation personnel, and often employers must entice the slim pool of competent people to switch jobs with handsome salary offers.

Professional Associations.   Annual conventions provide the opportunity for employers and job seekers to make valuable contacts with potential management and technical positions. Professional groups such as the Association of Information Systems Professionals (formerly known as International Information/Word Processing Association), Office Technology Management Association, Inc., (formerly known as Word Processing Society, Inc.), and Professional Secretaries, International (formerly known as National Secretaries Association) all provide potential hiring grounds.

Schools/Colleges.   Word processing and management courses are offered in a number of schools (vocational-technical, community colleges, and universities) across the nation. Often the training provided in schooling requires additional on-the-job training for the applicant. Potential applicants can be found through college interview programs and the establishment of a strong summer employment program for interested students.

The shortage of qualified office personnel is expected to become more acute as the years go by. One possible solution to this problem would be to attract more men into support positions in the office of the future. Accordingly, the image of the office assistant must be defeminized, and the salaries must be on a par with those of computer technicians and programmers.

Preparing for Personal Interviews/ Application Forms

Application forms can be used to screen candidates effectively. A well-prepared application form can reduce the number of qualified interviewees to about 10 percent of the total applications received (see Figure 13).

Also, the application form can reveal much about a potential candidate concerning attention to detail, carefulness or carelessness, completeness, and language skills such as spelling. By adding questions requiring narrative answers, the interviewer will be able to evaluate an applicant's proficiency in grammar, punctuation, sentence structure, and so on.

Interviewers can prepare for personal interviews by reviewing applications and resumes (if available) of applicants and having them on hand for discussion with each applicant. The interviewer should prepare a list of *job-related* questions to ask and avoid any questions that could appear discriminatory. See the section of this chapter on Government Regulations for information about questions to avoid. The interviewer should also check references to obtain information about the applicant's work performance and absentee record. Also, the interviewer should have available for discussion a copy of the job description, together with the determined salary range.

Interviewing

The interview is the basic tool of hiring. Interviews have two key functions: (1) to provide the applicant with an orderly presentation of facts about the organization and a description of the position open and (2) to enable the interviewer to obtain facts and impressions concerning the applicant. The interviewer must create the most friendly and relaxed environment possible for the interviewee. A great deal of information must be discovered in less than 30 minutes, so adequate preparation is necessary. Interviewers should keep in mind the following guidelines:

1. Hold the interview where you will not be interrupted.
2. Be friendly; speak quietly, conversationally, to encourage the applicant to talk.
3. After an initial warm-up period—two to three minutes—let the applicant do the talking.
4. Do not overreact to the applicant's comments and do not argue.
5. Ask open-ended questions (what, who, how, why); avoid yes/no questions.
6. Be an attentive listener. Let applicants finish their answers, don't rush them. Look attentive, nod, and appear interested.

During the course of the interview, the interviewer should do the following:

1. Request that the applicant complete any gaps in the application form.
2. Give facts to the applicant about the firm.

APPLICATION FOR EMPLOYMENT
(PRE-EMPLOYMENT QUESTIONNAIRE)   (AN EQUAL OPPORTUNITY EMPLOYER)

PERSONAL INFORMATION

DATE _____

NAME _____
LAST   FIRST   MIDDLE

SOCIAL SECURITY
NUMBER _____

PRESENT ADDRESS _____
STREET   CITY   STATE

PERMANENT ADDRESS _____
STREET   CITY   STATE

PHONE NO. _____   ARE YOU 18 YEARS OR OLDER   Yes ☐   No ☐

SPECIAL QUESTIONS

DO NOT ANSWER **ANY** OF THE QUESTIONS IN THIS FRAMED AREA UNLESS THE EMPLOYER HAS **CHECKED** A **BOX PRECEDING** A QUESTION, THEREBY INDICATING THAT THE INFORMATION IS REQUIRED FOR A BONA FIDE OCCUPATIONAL QUALIFICATION, OR DICTATED BY NATIONAL SECURITY LAWS, OR IS NEEDED FOR OTHER LEGALLY PERMISSIBLE REASONS.

☐ Height _____ feet _____ inches   ☐ Citizen of U.S. ____ Yes ____ No

☐ Weight _____ lbs.   ☐ Date of Birth* _____

☐ What Foreign Languages do you speak fluently? _____ Read _____ Write _____

☐ _____

*The Age Discrimination in Employment Act of 1967 prohibits discrimination on the basis of age with respect to individuals who are at least 40 but less than 70 years of age.

EMPLOYMENT DESIRED

POSITION _____   DATE YOU CAN START _____   SALARY DESIRED _____

ARE YOU EMPLOYED NOW? _____   IF SO MAY WE INQUIRE OF YOUR PRESENT EMPLOYER? _____

EVER APPLIED TO THIS COMPANY BEFORE? _____   WHERE? _____   WHEN? _____

EDUCATION	NAME AND LOCATION OF SCHOOL	*NO. OF YEARS ATTENDED	*DID YOU GRADUATE?	SUBJECTS STUDIED
GRAMMAR SCHOOL				
HIGH SCHOOL				
COLLEGE				
TRADE, BUSINESS OR CORRESPONDENCE SCHOOL				

*The Age Discrimination in Employment Act of 1967 prohibits discrimination on the basis of age with respect to individuals who are at least 40 but less than 70 years of age.

GENERAL

SUBJECTS OF SPECIAL STUDY OR RESEARCH WORK _____

U.S. MILITARY OR NAVAL SERVICE _____   RANK _____   PRESENT MEMBERSHIP IN NATIONAL GUARD OR RESERVES _____

TOPS FORM 3285 (REVISED)   (CONTINUED ON OTHER SIDE)   LITHO IN U.S.A.

Figure 13 Application form for employment can reveal a lot about an applicant such as attention to detail.

FORMER EMPLOYERS [LIST BELOW LAST FOUR EMPLOYERS, STARTING WITH LAST ONE FIRST].

DATE MONTH AND YEAR	NAME AND ADDRESS OF EMPLOYER	SALARY	POSITION	REASON FOR LEAVING
FROM				
TO				
FROM				
TO				
FROM				
TO				
FROM				
TO				

REFERENCES: GIVE THE NAMES OF THREE PERSONS NOT RELATED TO YOU, WHOM YOU HAVE KNOWN AT LEAST ONE YEAR.

	NAME	ADDRESS	BUSINESS	YEARS ACQUAINTED
1				
2				
3				

PHYSICAL RECORD:

DO YOU HAVE ANY PHYSICAL LIMITATIONS THAT PRECLUDE YOU FROM PERFORMING ANY WORK FOR WHICH YOU ARE BEING CONSIDERED? ☐ Yes ☐ No

PLEASE DESCRIBE:

IN CASE OF EMERGENCY NOTIFY

NAME   ADDRESS   PHONE NO.

"I CERTIFY THAT THE FACTS CONTAINED IN THIS APPLICATION ARE TRUE AND COMPLETE TO THE BEST OF MY KNOWLEDGE AND UNDERSTAND THAT, IF EMPLOYED, FALSIFIED STATEMENTS ON THIS APPLICATION SHALL BE GROUNDS FOR DISMISSAL.

I AUTHORIZE INVESTIGATION OF ALL STATEMENTS CONTAINED HEREIN AND THE REFERENCES LISTED ABOVE TO GIVE YOU ANY AND ALL INFORMATION CONCERNING MY PREVIOUS EMPLOYMENT AND ANY PERTINENT INFORMATION THEY MAY HAVE, PERSONAL OR OTHERWISE, AND RELEASE ALL PARTIES FROM ALL LIABILITY FOR ANY DAMAGE THAT MAY RESULT FROM FURNISHING SAME TO YOU.

I UNDERSTAND AND AGREE THAT, IF HIRED, MY EMPLOYMENT IS FOR NO DEFINITE PERIOD AND MAY, REGARDLESS OF THE DATE OF PAYMENT OF MY WAGES AND SALARY, BE TERMINATED AT ANY TIME WITHOUT ANY PRIOR NOTICE."

DATE   SIGNATURE

===== DO NOT WRITE BELOW THIS LINE =====

INTERVIEWED BY   DATE

HIRED: ☐ Yes ☐ No   POSITION   DEPT.

SALARY/WAGE   DATE REPORTING TO WORK

APPROVED: 1.   2.   3.

EMPLOYMENT MANAGER   DEPT. HEAD   GENERAL MANAGER

This form has been designed to strictly comply with State and Federal fair employment practice laws prohibiting employment discrimination. This Application for Employment Form is sold for general use throughout the United States. TOPS assumes no responsibility for the inclusion in said form of any questions which, when asked by the Employer of the Job Applicant, may violate State and/or Federal Law.

Figure 13   (Continued)

3. Give a brief description of the open position and how it relates to the rest of the firm.

4. Show office manual and procedures.

5. Indicate career ladders available in the firm.

6. Review the firm's written personnel policy with the applicant. Read the major headings and give a brief description of each.

7. Discuss the hourly rate of compensation or salary figure.

8. Question the applicant and make brief notations on the application regarding previous employment, school subjects preferred, school or other activites pursued, and starting salary requested by applicant.

When closing the interview, reiterate the tasks and responsibilities involved with the position, the salary and the benefits, and the office policies and procedures of the firm. Be sure to tell applicants when you will be notifying them of the firm's decision. All applicants, chosen or not, should be notified of the firm's decision.

Checking References After the interview, call the applicant's last employer and/or a teacher for a reference. All possible references related to performance should be checked. Personal references, however, are usually not worth checking. No one is going to supply the name of someone who is likely to say something bad about him or her.

Testing Testing can be a helpful tool in the selection process. Preemployment tests are generally considered to be measurements of work-related capabilities and characteristics of applicants. Performance tests, or "can-do" tests, are widely used. For office employment, most firms use obvious job-related tests such as tests for typing, basic math, and clerical skills. Such tests help determine what applicants can do, not what they will do on the job.

Government rulings and regulations require that tests (1) directly relate to the job's content and (2) not discriminate unfairly against the person taking them. Consequently, any tests to be selected must be carefully evaluated before use. In other words, it would not be right to require a typist or word processing specialist to take a test that requires a shorthand competency.

Companies may develop their own tests that are directly related to the jobs to be filled, but that can be time consuming and costly. Therefore, many companies purchase ready-made tests from specialized test publishers. All tests, however, must be fully validated and their reliability proved before they can meet governmental requirements. *Validity* means that the test really measures what it is intended to measure. *Reliability* means that the test consistently measures what it is intended to measure: that is, if an applicant were to take the test several times, the score would be the same.

GOVERNMENT REGULATIONS

When hiring, one must be cautious about meeting fair employment standards. Discrimination is prohibited, under various laws, because of race, color, religion, national origin, sex, age, or physical handicap. *Title VII of the Civil Rights Act of 1964* stipulates that it is unlawful for an employer to discriminate against any individual in employment, promotion, or retention because of the individual's race, color, religion, sex, or national origin. Title VII is administered by the Equal Employment Opportunity Commission.

In addition to Title VII, it is generally considered unlawful to obtain certain, possible discriminatory information from an applicant prior to employment. Currently, the EEO advises employers not to ask the following types of questions:

1. The applicant's maiden name, marital status, and ages and number of children. These questions tend to have differing effects on women applicants.
2. Questions about height or weight. These questions screen out disproportionate numbers of women and certain ethnic groups. In order to ask these questions, the employer must establish a relationship between the questions and the job.
3. Arrest and conviction information.
4. Questions about owning a car. Since minorities have less wealth than other groups, the question tends to be discriminatory. Car ownership must be demonstrated to be essential to the job.
5. Citizenship questions.
6. Health questions. Questions about pregnancy should be omitted.
7. Garnishment questions. Any policy that excludes applicants because of poor credit ratings must be justified on the basis of business necessity.
8. Questions on whether any relatives work with the firm. This question would potentially show favoritism toward or discrimination against applicants who are relatives of current employees.
9. Requests for photographs during the prehiring stage.

The 1971 U.S. Supreme Court decision in the *Griggs vs. Duke Power* case has had an important effect on the use of employment tests, which now are permitted only if the tests are job-related. The word *test* is interpreted broadly to include any paper-and-pencil or performance measure that is used in an employment decision. Hence, included in this interpretation are not only traditional tests but also scored application forms, scored interviews, and interviewers' rating scales—even though such measurements may be intended to be objective rather than subjective.

The *Age Discrimination in Employment Act of 1967* and similar state laws promote the employment of the older worker based on ability rather than age. They also prohibit arbitrary age discrimination against employees and applicants between the ages of 40 and 70 and help employers and employees find ways to meet problems arising from the impact of age on employment. It is against the law for an employer to

1. Fail to hire, discharge, or in any way discriminate against any individual as to compensation, terms, conditions or privileges of employment.
2. Limit, segregate, or classify employees by age.
3. Reduce the wage rate of any employee in order to comply with the act.

PHYSICALLY HANDICAPPED WORKERS

The *Rehabilitation Act of 1973* and similar state laws impose upon employers substantial obligations not only to prevent discrimination against handicapped individuals but also to take affirmative action to hire and advance the handicapped, if the person is able to perform the job with a reasonable accommodation. The handicap laws do not require employers to hire persons who are incapable of performing the job for which they apply.

There are, however, many openings for special employment groups in the office of the future. People with hearing impairments can use many of the new word processing machines without difficulty and function as well as other employees. The National Institute for the Deaf in Rochester, New York, was one of the first schools in the country to provide word processing training. Some examples of tasks the deaf can perform are copy typing, operating photocomposition equipment, proofreading, opening and screening incoming mail, and establishing files.

The visually impaired or blind can also find fruitful employment in the automated office. Technology is playing a major role in assisting these individuals to become productive employees. Some examples of innovative developments for this purpose follow. The OPTACON is a machine that permits direct access to printed material for the blind. A hand-held calculator that talks is called the SPEECH + the LPVT (Large Print Video Terminal). DOTTRAN is a computer program that allows a computer to translate its output into braille. Others are the Talking CRT, the Talking Telephone Directory, the Talking Information Management System, and the Talking Word Processor.

Robin McFarland, a blind telephone operator at the University of Kentucky, handled 85 calls per hour using the Talking Telephone Directory, while her sighted counterparts, using conventional methods of retrieval handled 50 to 55 calls per hour.[4]

---

[4] Flyer on systems for the blind, Maryland Computer Services, Inc., 502 Rock Spring Avenue, Bel Air, Maryland.

Figure 14 A braille typewriter, a typewriter key showing braille, and a page of braille output. (Courtesy of IBM Corporation.)

Several different types of voice synthesizers now on the market enable visually impaired individuals to interact with computers or word processors.

The IBM Audio Typing Unit monitors the host typewriter and through the technology of voice synthesis produces electronic speech. This speech corresponds to the typewriter keybuttons the operator has depressed, or to previously typed text stored in the host typewriter's memory. The audio responses take the form of characters, words, or sentences and includes all punctuation. In addition to verbalizing the words being typed, the Audio Typing Unit is capable of verbalizing over 200 audio responses. For example, it will tell the typist the typewriter is out of ribbon, whether it is set in 10 or 12 pitch, and other things.

Some companies have also developed braille devices that emboss (raise) information on a page so that a blind typist can proofread her or his work.

Figure 14 (Continued)

Figure 15 A quadriplegic operating dictation equipment. (Courtesy of Sony Corporation, Business Products Division.)

Special computer terminals have also been developed for individuals with extensive motor impairment, such as cerebral palsy victims and quadriplegics. Although these individuals may be slower than others, experience has shown they are far more careful and conscientious, and employers usually find them to be top-notch employees.

Telecommunications also contributes to opportunities for the handicapped. Terminals placed in the home can be interfaced through a telephone with the computer of the employing firm. Consequently, the handicapped do not have to be concerned with transportation problems.

The electronic office and technical advances are enhancing opportunities for not only the handicapped office support employees but also professionals. With microprocessors and small computers, it has become possible to tailor equipment to individual needs at less cost; consequently, a source of previously untapped capable employees is available (see Figures 14, 15, and 16).

Figure 16   The Audio Typing Unit (ATU). (Courtesy of IBM Corporation.)

SALARY   Adequate salary is one way of attracting quality personnel. During interviews for job candidates, the *salary range*, or minimum/maximum salary for a given position, should be stated. Periodic salary review should be guaranteed (usually after the first six months, and thereafter annually). Potential tangible rewards such as salary increases and promotion should be communicated. To lure executives away from another company where they are happy usually requires a base salary increase of 20 percent or more. However, candidates are still primarily interested in better opportunities and the chance to make greater use of their abilities; money is not necessarily the major motivator. A later chapter will discuss more fully management techniques for motivation of employees.

CHAPTER 19

TRAINING

OBJECTIVES

In this chapter you will learn about
1. The purpose, objectives, and benefits of training.
2. Management's role in establishing training plans.
3. Alternative types of training and a basis for deciding which type to use under which circumstances.
4. Identifying who needs training, and why.
5. Necessary training content and topics.
6. Alternative instructional methods and a basis for evaluating which is appropriate.
7. A variety of effective training techniques, and when to use them.
8. Considerations in designing training sessions.
9. A basis for evaluation and follow-up of training.

THE PURPOSE AND OBJECTIVES OF TRAINING

Training provides the means to achieve desired learning goals. Learning takes place whether training has occurred or not; however, without planned training, learning may be hit-and-miss, may be inadequate, and may lead to major problems. It is far better to assure that learning is planned and guided to achieve what is needed and desired.

Time spent on training will provide both direct and indirect benefits. Direct benefits result from the smooth implementation and operation of office automation and the total support system. Indirect benefits come from a properly operating system that does not require considerable management time to handle problems that training could have prevented. Training should be both general and specific and planned for day-in-and-day-out implementation.

Through a variety of types of training sessions, involved personnel can be helped to understand change and to learn how they may become a part of it. Understanding and participation lead to acceptance of—and indeed, sometimes to the welcoming of—change.

MANAGEMENT'S ROLE

Establishment of the framework and objectives for training is a managerial function. The broad organizational objectives should be established by top management. Specific operational objectives for a department or area should be established by middle managers, while the specific operational objectives for individual employees should be established by their immediate supervisors. Continuing training programs are essential. Too often, excellent training occurs when change is first implemented, but as time passes and new employees take over existing jobs or job details change, training does not continue at the original high level. New employees may lack understanding and the solid foundation gained through training. Without training, performance gradually crumbles away and small problems begin to build into major problems.

Regardless of the size of the organization, training should be provided; for without it, the wrong type of learning may easily occur. Small businesses normally do not have facilities for formal training, but management should give thought to goals and objectives, and take time to communicate those objectives. In the rush and press of business activities, supervisors and managers often neglect to take sufficient time to train. However, in no area of business operations will a little time spent provide a greater return in time saved in the future.

The larger the company, the harder it is for white-collar employees to see the broad picture and understand how they and their work fit into the total picture. In small companies, where employees are more frequently on their own, they may be able to gain broad perspective but still need assistance with specifics. Technology, even in small offices, requires specific training as never before, to assure that equipment is used effectively and that cost benefits are achieved.

Management has no real choice. It needs to provide for training in its strategic planning and must assume the responsibility to assure that effective training takes place.

TYPES OF TRAINING

There are many choices to be made concerning types and sources of training. Among the choices to be considered are

1. Preemployment training.
2. Employee orientation or induction training.
3. On-the-job training.
4. Training of specialists.
5. Vendor training.
6. Education programs—high school and college.

Management must weigh each of these choices in terms of how it satisfies overall training objectives and company policy. Different alternatives may be appropriate at different times and under different circumstances—and in fact, also with different employees.

PREEMPLOYMENT TRAINING

Preemployment training by itself is usually not sufficient for new employees. Some specifics may have been learned if an individual was previously employed in another organization in a similar job. Basic skills are transferable.

Preemployment training also includes that obtained at high school, business college, vocational school, or college or university. This type of training is best for the basics such as typing or keyboarding skills, basic formatting, and language skills. This type of training may provide a sound basis for understanding, but it requires reinforcement in the particular business organization in which the specific tasks are to be performed. As schools begin to teach more word processing and office automation, preemployment training will prove of greater value to business.

EMPLOYEE ORIENTATION

Orientation or induction training acquaints new employees with company history, philosophy, policy, practices, and procedures (office rules and regulations, employee benefits, etc.). It is very basic. As the office environment has grown, it has become popular to provide orientation information about support services available, such as copying, in-house printing, mail distribution and pickup.

This training takes place in-house and should include wherever possible a tour to point out facilities and their location. Depending upon the size and structure of the organization, orientation may be provided by training specialists and/or by representatives of involved departments, such as Personnel or Human Resources.

Steno Services of McDonnell Douglas[1] provides its new employees with a week of orientation that includes:

1. Review of company benefits.
2. Equal-opportunity counseling.
3. Duplicating procedures.
4. Telephone procedures.
5. Travel procedures.
6. Security procedures.
7. Formatting of different types of documents (memos, letters etc.).
8. Career path counseling.

During orientation, "actual time" typing exercises are also included, to become better acquainted with an employee and to gain a picture of each employee's capabilities.

ON-THE-JOB TRAINING

On-the-job training is—as the words express—training on the premises of an employer for those who are employees of the organization.

Workstation Training

Most frequently, this type of training consists of the supervisor or an experienced worker describing and/or showing new employees the responsibilities or tasks to be performed. Usually, this type of training is performed right at the workstation and the worker learns the new tasks by actually performing them. The trainer first explains the simpler jobs and gradually moves on to those of a more complex nture. Care should be taken to prevent supervisors or workers serving as trainers from hurriedly explaining all of the responsibilities and tasks at once. New employees find it difficult to absorb too much at one time. If workstation training is to be effective, trainers need to have sufficient time to assist new employees in an unhurried manner.

Procedures manuals for specific workstations are important aids in training; they provide a checklist of those tasks and responsibilities that are part of the job. They help avoid hit-and-miss training in which items a new employee should learn are omitted.

[1] Presentation by Jackie Oughton, Southern Illinois University, Edwardsville, Ill., June 18, 1981.

The major advantage of workstation training is that the employee learns the actual job to be performed in the environment in which he or she will perform it. The supervisor responsible for the employee can observe progress (see Figure 1). Even when a supervisor has another worker do the actual training, the supervisor can feel a greater responsibility for the new employee, maintaining better communications and a closer relationship with him or her than would be the case if someone outside the work group were in charge of training and it occurred away from the work environment.

On-the-job training does not require additional training staff or the purchase of extra equipment; it therefore may appear to be the most economical form of training. On the other hand, the time spent by a worker or supervisor must be considered, as well as the cost in terms of lower productivity. Also, the personnel who perform this type of training may be ineffective teachers, and improper training can result. For these reasons, and if two or three people are trained at one time, the organization may choose to implement a vestibule or classroom training program.

Figure 1 Individualized training being provided at a workstation.

Vestibule Training   Vestibule or classroom training is training that takes place away from the workstation but on the premises, usually in a classroom setting. Specialists usually perform this training. They are persons who spend most of their time training and usually are more effective teachers. In a vestibule or classroom training situation, the learner is not subject to the pressures of the real job. The learner and trainer are not likely to be interrupted, and training can progress rapidly (see Figure 2).

Although such training has advantages, there are also several disadvantages. Cost is a major consideration. The salary and benefits for the trainer must be considered, together with the space required for training and, in the case of training operators, additional office equipment is required. Also, trainees do not contribute to productivity, as they might with on-the-job training at the workstation. Supervisor and trainer must work closely together to assure that the training is meaningful and, in the case of equipment, that the training applies to the particular work.

TRAINING SPECIALISTS   Many organizations find that it is beneficial to have training departments and full-time training specialists. With so much change in office technol-

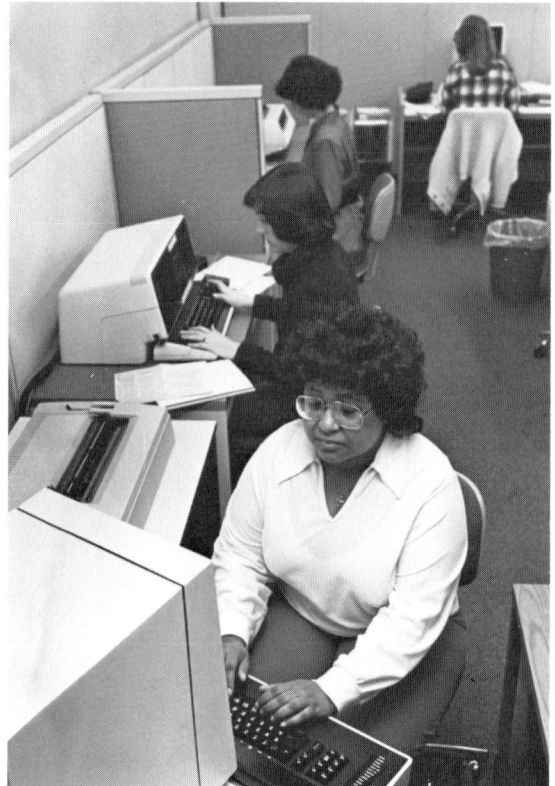

Figure 2 Classroom training.

ogy, organizations often find the need to train their training specialists. This can be accomplished by sending in-house training specialists to seminars and workshops, to fully acquaint them with the total planning and implementation process. Some organizations find it advantageous to bring in independent consultants who have the benefit of experience and may serve as models for an organization's own training specialists or can assist them in their new roles.

Educators may also be brought in for specific types of needed training. Both consultants and educators, however, should be checked for references and evidence of ability to perform effectively and meet organizational needs.

TRAINING BY VENDORS
Initial training for specialized areas such as data processing and word processing traditionally has been provided by vendors, because no other source was available. However, as the industry matures and competition within the industry increases, vendors have "unbundled" their training—meaning that the vendor provides certain services at a charge to their customers. Training is frequently a part of unbundling, because of the high costs involved. The *Training and Development Journal* stated in November 1980 that

> A 1979 industry survey places the average cost of a stand-alone word processing system in the $12,000 range. Classroom training costs about $900, but the manufacturer is usually able to charge $300 for training (and this usually only after two operators have been trained free of charge). The turnover rate for a word processing operator is 2.7 per year per machine. The picture is grim. In order to keep up with operating training, each machine costs the manufacturer $1,900 per year, and the training must be offered regardless of the machine's age.[2]

In addition to the expense of basic training and of providing applications and systems support, increasingly complex software and equipment adds to the cost a vendor charges for training, because of the high salaries for skilled marketing support personnel. As a result, vendors are shifting more of the responsibility for training to the customer.

When IBM's Office Products Division announced the Displaywriter in June 1980, it also announced that there would be no operator training on the Displaywriter on IBM premises. Instead, a self-paced manual would accompany the system, allowing operators to train themselves at their own speed, in their own time, and in their own office environment. Other vendors have followed IBM and have indicated they will no longer provide individualized operator training. Some are providing training pack-

[2] *Training and Development Journal*, November 1980, p. 8.

ages with equipment. Others are providing specialized training materials at an additional cost. Still other vendors continue to provide on-premise training and support for their equipment; because of high costs, however, even these vendors have often reverted to audio self-paced training in their training classrooms and are decreasing or eliminating individualized attention to operator training.

Some vendors provide a phone-in support center, with someone on hand to answer questions. A number of vendors also provide follow-up seminars that operators are encouraged to attend, to upgrade their skills and learn new applications.

One of the criteria in selecting equipment should be the type of training and support available. Whether training packages are available or whether an operator is merely expected to learn from an operator's reference manual is an important consideration. Training materials should be designed for learning, whereas operators' manuals are often designed as reference tools only.

In addition to equipment training, some vendors also provide supervisor and/or management seminars. An important benefit here is the knowledge that comes from associating with supervisors from other organizations and from the sharing of ideas. Figure 3 illustrates an agenda of a user seminar.

EDUCATION PROGRAMS

For some types of training, it may be best to send employees to business schools or colleges. For example, there are many benefits to be obtained by sending supervisors to take courses in management techniques or to attend special workshops and seminars on specific topics such as appraising performance, motivating employees, or disciplining employees. Many organizations provide tuition assistance or refunds for approved educational courses. Company tuition-assistance programs usually mean that the employing firm reimburses full or partial tuition when an employee satisfactorily completes an approved course. Usually, the courses will be held at the educational institution, although occasionally, if there are enough employees for a course, arrangements can be made to send the teacher to the organization's premises.

School training is especially effective for development of human, technical, and conceptual skills and for learning the theory and practical application of supervisory techniques. Group instruction off-premises provides the advantage of objective analysis of situations in which a supervisor may be involved. The supervisor's role is a lonely one, and sharing experiences and problems with others is often helpful. Sometimes discussion is more inhibited with classes on an organization's premises, even though company personnel may develop cooperative relationships that benefit the overall organization.

In addition to regular course work, schools and other groups, such as

---

DICTAPHONE CORPORATION

Cordially invites you to attend a

Special Free Seminar on

**"New Developments in Word Processing
and
Records Processing for the Legal Profession"**

**at the STATLER HOTEL, 107 Delaware Avenue, Buffalo, NY
Parlor B — Mezzanine Level**

YOU WILL HEAR:

Experts on applications of new <u>Word Processing Concepts</u> for the Legal Profession.

YOU WILL SEE: <u>Legal — Word & Information Management Systems</u>

The only Information Processing system with two interactive displays and full-function word and records processing (billing/docket control) for the law office.

YOU WILL RECEIVE:

A 50-page guidebook on the newest applications of Word Processing in Law Offices.

Reserve your place for one of the following sessions by returning the enclosed card.

Tuesday, April 6th, 1982

Session 1	10:30 AM — 12:00 Noon
Session 2	2:30 PM — 4:00 PM
Session 3	5:30 PM — 7:00 PM

Wednesday, April 7th, 1982

Session 1	10:30 AM — 12:00 Noon
Session 2	2:30 PM — 4:00 PM
Session 3	5:30 PM — 7:00 PM

Or, call (Mary Beth Faherty) at our office (634-7322) <u>NOW</u> to reserve your space.

Refreshments served

Figure 3 User program sample seminar agenda. (Courtesy of Dictaphone Corporation.)

ANNOUNCING
HOW TO MANAGE
WORD PROCESSING/MANAGEMENT SUPPORT
FOR IMPROVED
EMPLOYEE PRODUCTIVITY

An intensive in-depth course on the management of personnel, procedures and modern equipment for effective management support services through word processing/management support systems with emphasis on increasing productivity. Maintaining the proper psychological environment and employee attitudes through motivation are part of the agenda.

Bulk Rate
U.S. Postage
PAID
Duluth, MN 55806
Permit No. 276

MAY 4-5, 1981 ATLANTA
MAY 12-13, 1981 CHICAGO

sponsored by

Mary M. Ruprecht
& Associates, Inc.

Word Processing & Management Consultants

FOR: WP/AS Managers, Administrators, Directors, Supervisors, Executives, Lawyers, Educators/Training Directors, Systems Analysts and others interested in using word processing/administrative and management support systems in their business.

Chairperson: Mary M. Ruprecht, CMC

Figure 4 Two-day management seminar designed for continuing management education. (Courtesy of Mary M. Ruprecht & Associates, Incorporated.)

PROGRAM

First Day

I. PLANNING FOR SUCCESS

How to
- Determine whether WP is right for your organization
- Prepare management and personnel for word processing
- Set objectives for your WP/AS installation
- Secure a management commitment for support
- Sell the management support concept to employees
- Prepare cost justification data
- Structure the organization of a WP/AS group
- Budget and audit management support systems
- Set up the proper reporting structure for your company

II. PERFORMING WORK MEASUREMENT FOR JUSTIFICATION

How to
- Evaluate technology in today's market place
- Establish standards for measurement
- Prepare cost justification data
- Prepare meaningful production reports for management
- Set up a continual cost justification system
- Maintain data which will enable you to evaluate the upgrading or changing of equipment

III. MOTIVATING FOR CHANGE

How to
- Maintain support staff morale and motivation
- Get user cooperation and enthusiasm
- Create an ongoing training and evaluation program
- Select the right administrative support and WP specialist personnel
- Choose the right supervisor
- Maintain a communicative liaison between support staff and users
- Motivate for increased productivity

Second day

IV. IMPROVING PRODUCTIVITY THROUGH TRAINING & PROCEDURES

How to
- Train WP specialists and supervisors
- Train administrative support staff
- Develop English and proofreading skills in employees
- Create systems and procedures manuals to ensure quality control
- Provide support staff with a motivational physical environment.
- Train for working within management support systems

V. COMMUNICATING TO TODAY'S OFFICE

How to
- Select modern communications technology
- Communicate on an ongoing basis with employees
- Recognize a morale problem
- Enhance employee satisfaction through effective communications

VI. SOLVING PROBLEMS WORKSHOPS

- Real-live case studies and/or problems will be explored, discussed, and resolved during the workshops.

SPECIAL FEATURES

★★You will receive a comprehensive set of charts and forms to assist you in your daily work of creating, supervising or managing a management support system.

★★An informal "meet the speakers" reception will be held after the opening day's session.

★★All attendees will receive certificates of completion.

★★You will leave with a personal ACTION PLAN to start implementing your own Management Support System.

Figure 4 (Continued)

Datapro and the American Management Association (AMA), offer short courses for two or three days designed for a variety of special needs in office training. Figures 4 and 5 illustrate examples of special-needs seminars.

Seminars with such titles as "Planning for Office Automation," "Integration of Word Processing and Electronic Data Processing Systems," "Introduction to Telecommunications," "Word Processing: Effective Operations Management," and "Records Retention and Files Management" are frequent offerings and can be extremely helpful to firms embarking on the

Figure 5   Specialized area of continuing education. (Courtesy of Office Automation Seminars.)

road to a total support system and integrated electronic office. Fees may be high, but they are often paid by the employer.

WHO NEEDS TRAINING?

For a smooth transition to the integrated electronic office, a full training program is essential. Training cannot be limited to one group (such as the secretaries); training should be provided for all involved white-collar personnel within the office environment. These personnel fall into three major groups: support personnel, supervisors, and originators.

SUPPORT PERSONNEL
Former secretaries and clerks need training to help them understand the difference between the old and the new office structures and the purpose of the restructuring. Effective training of these persons will often determine if they will accept or resist the change. Orientation sessions should concern restructure and change; longer and more-formal training programs should be established to train these people to perform their daily operational tasks.

SUPERVISORS
The education and training of office supervisors has often been ignored in the past. Some supervisors have had supervisory training. But more often in the word processing environment, those promoted to supervisory positions have risen from the ranks of secretaries or other office positions. They often have neither the experience nor the training to meet many of the problems they face. A national Delta Pi Epsilon study found that barely 50 percent of the word processing supervisors had had any supervisory training before assuming their positions.[3]

Particular attention should be given to the training of first-line office supervisors. They must thoroughly understand the goals of a total support system in an electronic office. They need not only the broad perspective but also a clear understanding of what they are to do. Since they will oversee the operation of the system, they must learn how it should operate. These first-line supervisors are the people closest to the many changes in operations that occur, and they are crucial to obtaining acceptance of change from their subordinates.

ORIGINATORS
Originators (or users) primarily consist of the executives and professionals for whom support is being provided. Administrative support person-

[3] Jolene D. Scriven, Jeanne L. Holley, Kathleen P. Wagoner, Richard D. Brown, *National Study of Word Processing Installations in Selected Business Organizations*, (St. Peter, Minn., 1981), p. 64.

nel, such as top-level administrative secretaries or administrative assistants, may serve as intermediaries in the support process and should be provided the same type of training as their principals are given. Users, whatever their positions, need to understand the benefits of the new structure and what it will provide them.

TRAINING CONTENT AND TOPICS

Because different groups of people will interface with the new support systems and technology in different ways, the training content and topics covered with these different groups should be somewhat adjusted to the interests and needs of each audience. However, all involved should receive, prior to implementation, a general orientation on the changes and on the specifics of the restructuring.

GENERAL ORIENTATION Orientation training is important to smooth acceptance and inclusion into the organization. When an organization is restructured, another form of orientation training is necessary to assure acceptance of change and smooth implementation. These sessions should develop the conceptual understanding of the total support system and the integrated electronic office. Here is an important opportunity to stress all the benefits that people will personally gain from the new system. Questions to be answered concerning restructure and change include the *why*, the *what*, and the *how*. If management has established long-range objectives and expects to phase in additional changes from time to time, employees should be informed of what is coming.

For example, some basic reorganization of methods, even those used in manual systems, is necessary and must be accepted and used effectively at the manual level before it becomes feasible to consider implementation of more sophisticated systems that use technology. For instance, a uniform classification system for all files throughout an organization is necessary before the implementation of CAR or sophisticated micrographics systems. Employees at all levels must be trained to use and accept the classification system; so-called bugs should be removed, and the system should be refined to assure effective use before any attempt is made to carry it over to higher-technology uses. All persons involved are likely to accept it better, however, if they understand how the system fits into the long-range goals established by management and why such a system is needed to implement technology.

DEVELOPMENT OF SPECIFIC SKILLS AND PROCEDURES In addition to orientation to the conceptual base for the changing office, training in specific skills and procedures is needed for each of the involved groups of personnel. Each group has a different type of need and training should be planned and organized to meet these needs. Generally, operational personnel will have an intense interest in the new skills and procedures they need to develop. The interest and reaction of management or professional personnel is likely to be affected by how they view the benefits to themselves—the "what's in it for me" syndrome.

Ideas concerning specific content and topics for the various involved groups are presented in the following pages. Note how each group has very specific content that pertains to its personnel alone. It is important, however, that this content be presented in relation to the total system. In this way, personnel will be given direction for their jobs and a perspective that will reduce the likelihood of blunders.

Word Processing In the case of word processing, involved employees should receive information about the people they will work with and support, and about policies and procedures for the center or for their work area. After the background on relationships and functions has been provided, the specific operational procedures should be presented, including

1. Operation of the specific equipment.
2. Information concerning what is expected of each operator and what assistance they will be provided.
3. The formats used within the firm.
4. Editing procedures.
5. Proofreading techniques.
6. Language arts, including
   (a) Abbreviations
   (b) Capitalization
   (c) Expressing numbers
   (d) Grammar
   (e) Hyphenation
   (f) Punctuation
   (g) Spelling
   (h) Syllabication
   (i) Vocabulary

When other tasks and responsibilities are performed within a specific area, special training should also be provided: for example, instructions for machine transcription, instructions for special features on word processing equipment such as files-processing, communication, and so on.

Administrative Support All administrative support personnel—whether clerical or administrative secretary, or paraprofessional—should receive orientation on the purposes of an administrative support structure and on the policies and procedures for their work group and their individual positions. Whenever equipment use is part of their responsibilities, complete training on the particular equipment should be provided: for example, in proper use of copying equipment, facsimile, OCR, and telephone handling techniques.

When managerial workstations or terminals are introduced, training for administrative support personnel is necessary. They, too, will use the calendaring and message capabilities of the equipment to support and/or back up management and professional users.

A review of basics might include such areas as language arts, proofreading techniques, listening skills, and filing rules. Specific policies and procedures for interfacing with word processing and other office systems should also be included. When administrative support personnel are responsible for tasks such as researching information, composing letters, arranging for travel, or preparing charts and graphs, they should be provided with the appropriate company policies and procedures. Because administrative support is a recent concept, additional help in the development of administrative assistants and/or paraprofessionals should be given in such areas as

1. Development and use of visual presentations.
2. Effective persuasion techniques.
3. Basic negotiating skills.
4. Problem solving, planning, and organizing.
5. Performance planning systems and techniques.
6. Prioritizing, budgeting, and workflow planning.
7. Decision making, flowcharting, and procedure writing.
8. Time management.
9. Understanding the industry or firm and its future development.
10. Nonverbal and written communication skills, body language, and listening.

It is likely that continued training will be needed to encourage administrative support personnel to assume more tasks normally performed by originators.

Records Management

Training for records management personnel should include basic orientation to records management goals for the organization and operating policies and procedures. Where microfilming or computer storage and retrieval are involved, specific training concerning operating techniques for the microfilm system or computer system should be given. A review of basic filing systems (such as alphabetic, numeric, subject-based, or geographic), should also be covered, together with such basic filing rules as indexing, cross reference, and charge-out methods. Other task-related topics should cover the protection of vital records and methods, records inventory and appraisal, and retention and disposal systems.

Other Aspects   A review of the suggested topics for word processing, administrative support, and records management shows that training should be organized around four major aspects. The same four aspects provide a framework for organization of training topics and materials for all other areas of the integrated electronic office.

1. Orientation to the purposes of the area and explanation of how the area fits into the total system.
2. Equipment training, where pertinent.
3. Review of basics related to the area.
4. Specific tasks and information to assist employees in performing these tasks.

Supervisors   Special emphasis should be given to the orientation and training of management. Often, supervisors are hesitant to suggest and stress specific aspects to higher-level management.

Because supervisors are in charge at the operating level—the level at which things happen—they especially need an orientation to management's philosophy and plans for change. They need to learn and understand how and where their departments fit into the whole system and the role they must play to make the system work. At the same time, they need training in areas that will assist them in day-to-day performance of their functions.

General orientation topics include functions of management, basic steps in planning, organization of work, nature of controlling, among others.

Research has shown that supervisors spend more of their time on the directing function (dealing with people and people problems) than on any other. Also, most office supervisors have little background or previous training in this area. Human relations topics most likely to be helpful are

1. The art of leadership.
2. Giving instructions and orders.
3. Appraising employee performance.
4. How and when to discipline.
5. Understanding personality and behavior.
6. Improving three-way communications.
7. Handling complaints and grievances.
8. Guiding and developing employees.
9. Building job satisfaction and morale.

Other topics to be covered might include

1. Figuring and controlling costs.
2. Writing procedures.

3. Preparing reports for management.

4. Effective memo writing.

5. Preparing position descriptions.

Nearly three-fourths of the supervisors participating in the national Delta Pi Epsilon research study expressed the need for ongoing training beyond that provided at the time of implementation. Participants also mentioned several needs, ranked in the following order:[4]

1. Management information systems (including the interfacing of word processing and data processing).

2. Methods and techniques of supervising people.

3. Development and implementation of goals and objectives.

4. Budgeting and accounting skills.

Originators Originators, too, need to be oriented to the concepts and benefits of the total support system and the electronic office environment. Periodic re-emphasis of the personal benefits serve to sell the originators and keep them sold. Training for first-time users in operation of equipment is absolutely necessary; this should include, for example,

1. Use of machine dictation equipment—and the related procedures and organizational skills that are necessary to produce effective communications.

2. Use of new telephone equipment—with attention to special features, such as call forwarding and call waiting, that will assist them in day-to-day operations.

3. Use of terminals and/or special executive or managerial workstations—with appropriate related instruction in keyboarding, calendaring for appointments, conferences and meetings, electronic mail, making travel arrangements, and so on (see Figure 6).

The purpose of training originators and users at managerial and professional levels is to help them increase their productivity. Other basic topics appropriate for this purpose are time management and prioritizing of work, use of computer graphics to enhance presentations, and delegation of tasks to administrative assistants and paraprofessionals or clerks (whichever the nature of the work would suggest). Several of the topics—especially delegation—should be reinforced through continued training.

INSTRUCTIONAL METHODS

There are many training methods. Each has its strengths and weaknesses, and most often the effective trainer will use a combination of methods

---

[4] Scriven *et al.*, *National Study of Word Processing Installations*, p. 67.

Figure 6 "Gentlemen, we are here to learn production planning using the new R-180—*not* how many ways to destroy the invading asteroids from Planet Zendor." Management training is an essential part of the implementation of change in the office environment.

rather than only one. A variety of techniques adds spice to instruction and helps to hold attention. The content to be presented and the level of the learner will help determine which methods are appropriate.

INDIVIDUALIZED VERSUS GROUP INSTRUCTION

The first decision a trainer must make is whether to teach in groups or through individualized instruction. Specific job skills or operation of equipment should usually be individualized; the availability of equipment will also influence this decision. Individualized instruction does not always mean that instruction will be provided on a one-on-one basis. With individualized instruction, the learner works through a planned program of materials at his or her own rate; this is known as self-paced instruction. Personalized or individualized training is more expensive and time consuming than training in groups. But for many purposes, group instruction is just as effective. For example, for explaining the concepts of a new support system and of the electronic office, a group session is likely to be most effective. Group instruction assures that all employees in a particular area receive the same information and orientation. Group sessions also offer a good opportunity to deliver first presentations and explanations of procedures manuals developed for an area.

The *conference method* of group instruction, as differentiated from the *lecture method* (in which the instructor does all the talking), permits trainees to express themselves orally and to exchange and compare ideas. By allowing trainees to express themselves, instructors can judge the trainees' understanding and acceptance of the subject material. Figures 7 and 8 illustrate the conference and the lecture methods of training.

Role playing can be an especially effective technique in presenting situations involving employee relations. This method permits trainees not only to participate but also to gain insight into their own behavior and that of others, and to view a situation more objectively.

EQUIPMENT TRAINING   Equipment training requires the development of specialized training and instructional materials. It is rare for employees to apply themselves to a

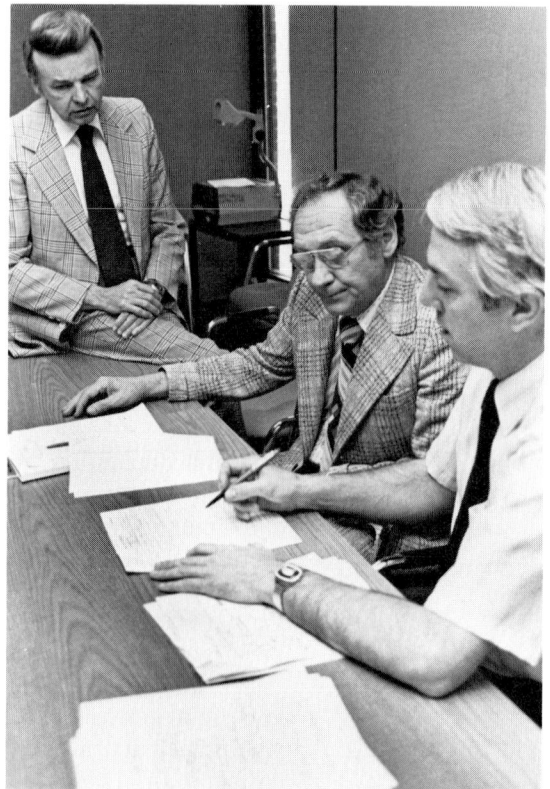

Figure 7 Conference method of training

Figure 8   Lecture method of training.

manual to learn how to operate equipment. Operating manuals are valuable training aids, but they are no substitute for instruction.

Equipment training should begin with a demonstration of equipment capabilities. Vendor training packages tend to be very specific and based on the step-by-step approach ("push this button, then this one," etc.). Vendors who produce the product also must produce training materials for it. Some vendors consider the operations manual provided to be enough and do not prepare specific training manuals. Often, their writers are not familiar with the value of such educational principles as repetition and reinforcement; as a result, trainees receive only an introduction and need more practice in order to develop competence and confidence.

Although many kinds of word processing equipment have been on the market over the past 20 years, only recently have conceptually based training systems provided information that can apply to many different brands of equipment.

One form of individualized instruction is *computer-assisted instruction (CAI)*, which utilizes electronic equipment itself as a training tool. Instructions, questions, and guiding statements are displayed on the screen as the learner progresses through the training program (see Figure 9). These visual display instructional programs have the advantage of allowing the trainee to proceed at his or her own pace and to learn immediately whether a right or wrong answer has been given. However, CAI appears to work best when an instructor is present to answer questions and help prevent trainee frustration when progress is not smooth.

Programmed instruction, another self-instruction method, utilizes a systematic presentation of information to the trainee. Material is presented one step or frame at a time, so that it may be easily understood. The

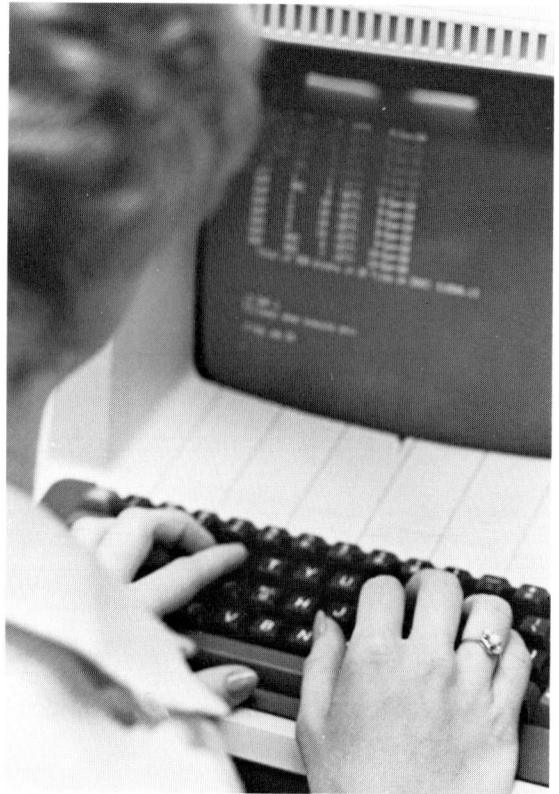

Figure 9 Computer-assisted instruction (CAI).

trainees advance gradually from the simple to the complex aspects of the material, at their own individual pace.

In-basket techniques realistically simulate actual office conditions; they are a form of a business game. Trainees are given assorted business papers and told to perform the necessary operations involving those papers and to prioritize the handling of the problems and situations represented by the papers. This technique is effective in the development of decision-making skills. The *incident process* involves the presentation of an incident or a problem situation in only a few sentences. Trainees are expected to ask careful questions in order to obtain additional necessary and pertinent facts. This technique effectively stimulates thinking and develops insight and problem-solving skills.

TRAINING TOOLS AND AIDS

A variety of tools may be used to enhance training. Experienced educators and trainers are well aware that different people learn in different ways;

therefore, as part of planning for either individual or group instruction, provision should be made for use of materials that are (1) visual, yet self-paced; or (2) audio and self-paced; or (3) a combination of audio and visual. Each of the tools or aids has its own advantages and disadvantages, and the choice should be based upon the nature of the material to be presented and the group or audience involved. Figure 10 lists the tools, the types of material for which they are most advantageous, and the training situations.

DESIGNING TRAINING SESSIONS

Careful planning and designing of training sessions will pay off. Such factors as when the meetings are held and other details concerning the learning environment often have a psychological effect on the learner.

How We Learn
3% smell
3% taste
6% touch
13% hearing
75% sight

SETTING TIMES

The orientation sessions should be scheduled carefully. If they are scheduled too soon in the implementation process, trainees will not recall much of the information when it is needed. On the other hand, they can be scheduled too late, in the sense that the grapevine is likely to operate and uncertainties can build into resistance to change.

Other time factors to be considered are the time of day and the day of the week. What time is best for the most people? What time will have the least effect on continued necessary operations? Also, if possible, it is important to consider what time of day learners are most likely to learn best. The best times for each group are likely to be different, so the work schedules and habits of the involved personnel should be considered carefully. The time most appropriate for the originators or users is of greatest importance and, if scheduling conflicts occur, should be given priority.

SETTING THE TONE

The first training sessions should always focus on orientation to the change, for they are the most critical. These sessions often set the tone for acceptance or resistance. It is difficult to alter habits by changing procedures and structures, and the groundwork to gain acceptance must be carefully laid. The tone of the meeting should be explanatory and helpful without being dictatorial or authoritarian. The leader must make every

Tools	Advantages	Limitations
Slides	Require only filming, with processing and mounting by film laboratory. Result in colorful, realistic reproductions of original subjects. Easily revised and updated. Easily handled, stored, and rearranged for various uses. Increased usefulness with tray storage and automatic projection. Can be combined with taped narration for greater effectiveness. May be adapted to group or individual use.	Can get out of sequence, be turned upside down, and be projected incorrectly if slides are handled individually. Best in a darkened room, which limits note taking.
Films	May consist of complete films or short film clips. Are particularly useful in describing motion, showing relationships, and giving impact to topic. Are useful with groups of all sizes and with individuals. Ensure a consistency in presentation of material.	May be expensive to prepare in terms of time, equipment, materials, and services. Best in darkened room, which limits note taking. Require careful planning and some production skills.
Videotapes Videodisks	Require some planning and production skills commensurate with quality desired. Permit showing of action, relationships, and otherwise unavailable scenes. Almost immediately available after production. Playback capability of video recording permits analysis of on-the-spot action.	Sound and action must be planned to occur effectively at the same time. Space must allow technical requirements of production and showing. Require relatively expensive equipment
Cassettes	Easy to prepare with regular tape recorders. Can provide applications in most subject areas. Equipment for use is compact, portable, easy to operate. Flexible and adaptable as either individual method of training or in conjunction with slides and other programmed materials. Duplication is easy and economical.	Subject to a tendency to overuse. Fixed rate of information flow.
Manuals: Operations Procedures	Easy to prepare with the use of copying machines. Step-by-step sequence can be provided for operations or procedures. Can be carried around for use anywhere, including study at home. Act of putting in print often brings care and clarity.	Require user to be a good reader. Can be overused.
Overhead transparencies	Can present information in systematic, developmental, or step-by-step sequence. Uses simple-to-operate projector with presentation rate controlled by instructor. Require only limited planning. Can be prepared easily by variety of simple, inexpensive methods. Particularly useful with large groups.	Require special equipment, facilities, and skills for more advanced. preparation methods. Type must be large enough to be read. Are large and can present storage problem.

Figure 10 A variety of training tools and aids are available. The most appropriate one should be carefully selected.

effort to maintain open communications and to handle questions and objections as they arise. Sensitivity to individual differences and needs is important. Emphasize ease, enjoyment, and benefits—a positive tone is the basis for acceptance.

THE COMPOSITION OF GROUPS
Even group size is important. For both convenience and expense, groups should be as large as feasible; however, it is usually easier to maintain open communications within groups of 12 to 15 than within larger groups. The right combination of individuals and departments also merits attention. It is also best to avoid putting individuals in the same group when known personality conflicts exist.

When personnel from several departments are combined, consideration must be given to whether their needs and applications are sufficiently similar to warrant combining them into one group. Boredom and misunderstandings may result if needs of one part are overlooked, downplayed, or ignored.

EVALUATION AND FOLLOW-UP OF TRAINING

Training programs must have provisions for follow-up and evaluation. After employees complete their training and return to their jobs, follow-up studies should be conducted to measure the effectiveness of the training experience. Both performance and attitude should be assessed. It is imperative that, when separate training facilities exist, trainers and supervisors communicate fully and work together for uniform ways to assure that the training process will be positive and beneficial for the organization. If resistance and low performance is prevalent, the training program (or lack of it) may be one of the causes, and immediate steps for improvement should be determined. Follow-up within each area should be made

Figure 11 Learning retention rates illustrate how quickly we lose learning if it is not regularly used.

Time Interval Since Learning	Percent Forgotten	Percent Retained
$\frac{1}{3}$ hour	42	58
1 hour	56	44
$8\frac{3}{4}$ hour	64	36
1 day	66	34
2 days	72	28
6 days	75	25

periodically, to assure that all new involved employees, whether they be new hires or transfers, receive the required orientation and training.

The data appearing in Figure 11, compiled by the Research Institute of America, reveal how fast our learning disappears.

If what is taught is not used, all the time and effort devoted to training will be wasted. You must follow up to be sure that training is used.

BENEFITS OF EFFECTIVE TRAINING PROGRAMS

Many benefits flow from an effective training program. Some of the most important are

1. *More positive work environment.* Effective training builds confidence in management and in its plans. An understanding of goals leads to smoother implementation. An understanding of the interdependence of jobs improves communication and leads to a better spirit of cooperation.

2. *Improved quality of work life.* Effective training motivates and stimulates employees; it builds employee self-confidence and morale. Job satisfaction increases and employees are more fulfilled.

3. *Improvement in the quality of work.* Effective training assists employees to know what to do and how to do it, and therefore to make fewer mistakes. Knowing the *why* of the company's policies and procedures helps them to perform more intelligently and avoid errors.

4. *Increased productivity.* Effective training leads to increased productivity. The best methods can be standardized and taught to all employees. Skilled employees do a more intelligent job, are more self-reliant and less hesitant. The need for detailed, close supervision is reduced, and the levels of support for managers and professionals are increased, so that they too become more productive. Increased productivity leads to reduced costs.

5. *Improvement of competitive position (or enhanced service posture).* Creation of a more positive environment, improvement in the quality of work life and the quality of work, and increased productivity all lead to improvement of a business's competitive position. Or if the organization provides services, more can be offered to the public it serves.

CHAPTER 20

SUPERVISORY/ MANAGEMENT TECHNIQUES AND HUMAN RELATIONS

OBJECTIVES

In this chapter you will learn about

1. Supervisory/management requirements.
2. Various leadership styles.
3. When the various styles of leadership are appropriate.
4. The influences that affect an individual's ability to lead effectively.
5. Relevant human needs and motivational theories.
6. A means of self-appraisal.
7. The basic traits and personal skills of an effective administrator.
8. Guidelines for giving instructions.
9. The handling of disciplinary steps.
10. Motivational techniques to stimulate productivity.

In the integrated electronic office, the effective management and motivation of people becomes more important than ever before. The flow of information and integration of office functions requires greater interaction among all personnel. Key considerations to successful "management of people" are communications, human relations, motivation, and employee development. In this chapter, techniques to achieve these ends will be explored, including leadership styles, management skills, and application of motivational theory.

LEADERSHIP STYLES

Leadership is a complex concept that eludes easy explanation. No single leadership pattern is all-inclusive. Dictionary definitions include terms such as *show* the way; *guide* in direction or course; *cause* conduct; *influence* or *induce, command* or *direct*. Lester Bittel's definition expresses it succinctly: "Leadership is the knack of getting other people to follow you and do willingly the things you want them to do."[1] Note that there are two major parts of leadership—accomplishing the task and satisfying the people needs. Figure 1 illustrates some of the considerations in each of these aspects. Successful leaders produce results *and* build good working relationships.

Figure 1   There are two major parts of leadership: accomplishing the task and satisfying people's needs.

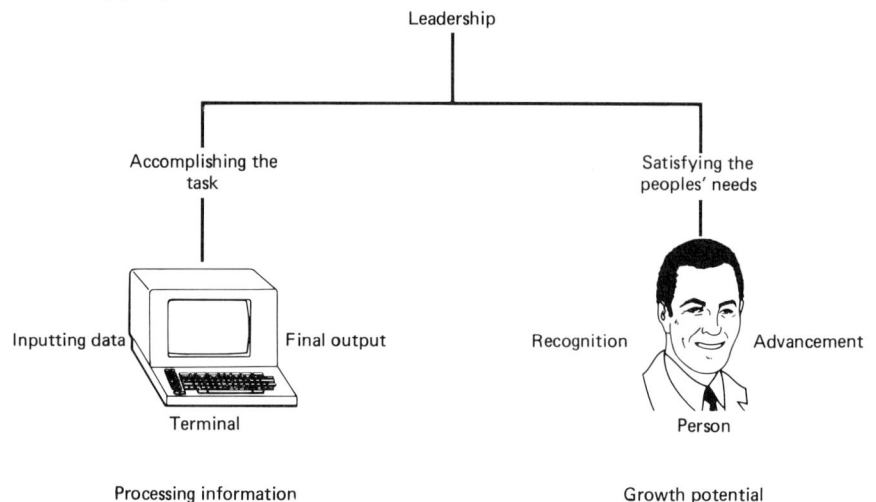

[1] Lester R. Bittel, *What Every Supervisor Should Know* (New York: McGraw-Hill, 1980), p. 82.

The "how to" part of leadership is difficult to explain. Some individuals may be born leaders, but most people become good leaders because they have worked hard at it. To improve leadership abilities, one should learn more about leadership styles, traits of successful leaders, and approaches to leadership. In so doing, those who aspire to leadership come to know what it involves.

Much research has been conducted on the leadership styles associated with getting the job done and on their effect on employee morale and performance. There are three principal styles of leadership: autocratic, democratic, and laissez-faire. In practice, these styles are seldom found in their pure forms, because most leaders intermingle them to fit their own personalities and the situation.

AUTOCRATIC LEADERSHIP

The autocratic leader seeks obedience from subordinates, makes all major decisions, and determines the activities of all others. Autocratic leaders range from the dictatorial to the benevolent. The dictatorial leader is highly critical of others and has a negative relationship with subordinates. Employees are expected to perform or they will be punished or replaced.

Benevolent autocrats are leaders who let others rely on them. This type of leader assumes a fatherly or paternalistic role. Subordinates are dependent on this leader, who makes all decisions. As a result, work deteriorates or stops when the leader is absent, and there is little innovation on the part of followers. Such followers usually do not become leaders themselves. This style is often found in small companies or in small law offices or doctor's offices.

DEMOCRATIC LEADERSHIP

Democratic leaders encourage worker participation in the decision-making process. They prefer to involve employees in planning and organizing and to obtain their ideas through discussion or consultation. However, the democratic leader retains the ultimate authority and responsibility for the decision, even though a group process has been involved in arriving at it. Generally, a cooperative spirit exists and there is mutual respect between the supervised and the supervisor.

LAISSEZ-FAIRE LEADERSHIP

The style of leadership known as *laissez-faire* is also called free-rein leadership. Laissez-faire leaders serve as information givers to members of the group but delegate responsibility for all decisions to employees, allowing them to establish their own goals and make their own decisions.

This method or style is the most permissive of all, and some critics consider those who use it to be weak leaders who hesitate to accept responsibility. Leaders or managers who do not take active roles may be abdicating their authority and responsibility. Leadership is necessary to ensure that work is not done haphazardly or improperly. The laissez-faire technique is quite effective when employees are working on projects that require individual skills and creativity; this group includes researchers, scientists, engineers, and technicians. The leader exercises minimal control and depends upon the employees' sense of responsibility and good judgment to get things done. For the supervision of systems analysts, programmers, and others who are at the forefront of implementing office change, the laissez-faire method is often applicable.

COMBINED STYLES

Classification of leaders into these three types primarily helps the learner to understand characteristics of each. The effective leader usually will use a combination of styles. The skill of leadership lies in knowing when to use which method, according to the conditions or the situation and the people involved, both the leader and followers (see Figure 2).

Within the changing office, different situations require handling in different ways. It would be entirely possible and perhaps even appropriate for a top management that has committed itself to the implementation of new systems autocractically to *direct* middle managers or supervisors to study and learn about office systems. However, for final planning and organizing purposes, top management may choose democratic leadership and *consult* with the various managers or supervisors about how to restructure and interface or integrate the technology. In a large and complex organization the laissez-faire style would be necessary, for it is unlikely top managers will have either the time or the expertise to become highly involved in the process of changing the office. Therefore, they would tend to *suggest* to middle management and to implementation teams that it would be beneficial to the organization to restructure and/or develop new procedures to achieve desired results.

Figure 2   The effective leader knows the skills required to motivate employees and breed enthusiasm.

Are You a Boss or a Leader?

1. A boss creates FEAR—a leader creates CONFIDENCE.
2. "Bossism" breeds RESENTMENT—leadership breeds ENTHUSIASM.
3. A boss says "I"—a leader says "WE."
4. A boss fixes BLAME—a leader fixes MISTAKES.
5. A boss KNOWS how—a leader SHOWS how.
6. "Bossism" makes work DRUDGERY—leadership makes work INTERESTING.
7. A boss relies on AUTHORITY—a leader relies on COOPERATION.
8. A boss DRIVES—a leader LEADS.

CONTINUUM OF LEADERSHIP BEHAVIOR

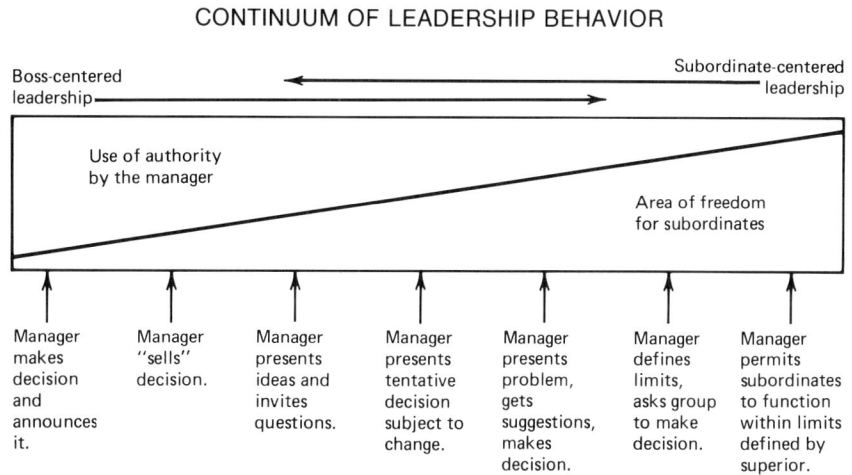

Figure 3

Reprinted by permission of the Harvard Business Review. An exhibit from "How to Choose A Leadership Pattern" by Robert Tannenbaum and Warren H. Schmidt (May/June 1973). Copyright © 1973 by the President and Fellows of Harvard College; all rights reserved.

Figure 3 illustrates a continuum of leadership behavior that applies to the process of change. The proportions of authority and freedom differ at various points. Management might begin implementation at any one of the behavior points. On the other hand, in a lengthy and involved process such as the long journey to the office of the future, during which employees learn and develop, management may gradually move almost from point to point—from boss-centered leadership to subordinate-centered leadership.

To assure the completion of a specific task such as the input of information, it would be appropriate to *direct* a word processing specialist to keyboard the contents of a procedures manual. However, the actual content of the manual would probably best be achieved by first allowing someone (perhaps a systems analyst or programmer) to use individual capabilities in creating (figuring out) the best procedures (on a step-by-step level) to be used to perform a given task. Evaluation and effective communication of the procedures, however, may well be achieved through the *group process on a consulting basis*. Other external influences, such as governmental regulations, unionization or threat of unionization, and other societal influences, may also help to determine the leadership style to be used in a given situation.

Besides analyzing a situation, an effective leader attempts to understand the personalities involved, and how they may interact with his or her own personality. How to choose the leadership style required? There is scarcely a single characteristic that does not influence choice; some of the more obvious are age, background, and experience. A mature person may generally be provided more opportunity for participation or free rein, whereas someone young or inexperienced will function best under a more autocratic approach. The more familiar the employee is with the job or assignment, the more likely that democratic or free-rein leadership may be used to the satisfaction of both the leader and follower.

Certain personality types, as indicated by their behavior, also may provide clues as to what type of leadership to use. The dependent person requires a more authoritative style than the independent person, for a dependent person needs firm guidance and reassurance. Such a person will usually function well under the democratic method, especially if the individual is group-minded and enjoys teamwork. Individualists, who are competent and know their field, will usually do their best work on their own.

Individual behavior is always influenced by the group to which an individual belongs. Standards, performance, motivation, and morale will settle to a low level if the group lacks proper leadership. Leaders must be assertive and positive in setting standards, objectives, and policies if their group is to function smoothly and effectively. Group objectives or purposes provide more indication of the group character and attitude. Only through close communication with the group can a leader learn how the group reacts and how to work with the group.

In recent years, two additional approaches to leadership have become popular—contingency and results-centered leadership.

CONTINGENCY OR SITUATIONAL LEADERSHIP

The contingency theory, developed by Fred Fiedler,[2] maintains that leaders will be successful in a situation only if three factors are in balance. These three situational factors—leader-member relations, task structure, and position power—determine how effective the leader is. Fiedler says together they determine whether a more democratic or more autocratic leadership style is called for.

Leader-member relations covers the extent to which leaders get along with their subordinates and the extent to which subordinates are committed or are loyal to their leaders. If leaders have a good relationship with their subordinates, the leaders' power and influence is willingly and quickly accepted. This is the most important variable in Fiedler's model.

Task structure refers to how routine and predictable the work group's task is. Tasks or jobs that are highly structured, spelled out, or programmed give the leader more influence than tasks that are vague or nebulous. A leader's power is harder to question when the job is spelled out than when job or project assignments are stated in general terms.

Position power is the degree to which the job itself enables leaders to get their group members to comply with their wishes. If leaders have control

[2] Fred Fiedler, *A Theory of Leadership Effectiveness* (New York: McGraw-Hill, 1967).

over hiring, firing, promotion, and discipline, their influence over followers' actions will be considerably greater than if they merely oversee work on a certain project.

RESULTS-CENTERED LEADERSHIP   Results-centered leadership is connected either to the "work itself" approach to motivation or to productivity and management by objectives, discussed in the next chapter.

FACTORS THAT AFFECT LEADERSHIP

Consideration of leadership styles and approaches alone does not give us the full picture of successful leadership. Robert M. Fulmer suggests that the following influences often affect an individual's ability to lead effectively:[3]

1. *The size of the organization* in which the leader must operate plays a definite role in success as a leader.
2. *The amount of interaction* taking place within an organization also encourages or inhibits the growth of leadership talents.
3. *The personalities of the leader and group members* make up the third factor influencing leadership functions.
4. *The level on which decision making is encouraged* constitutes another factor affecting leadership skills.
5. *The organization's health* has much to do with the amount and strength of organizational leadership.

Obviously, leaders who wish to achieve the best possible results must be attuned to their situations and be very people-oriented, for results come from people, not technology alone. Certain basic leadership traits are essential (see Figure 4).

Peter F. Drucker, a well-known management authority, suggests that all individuals can perform better as managers by improving their performance of basic activities.[4] He suggests five formal, basic work categories of the manager: (1) setting objectives, (2) organizing, (3) motivating and communicating, (4) measuring, and (5) developing people (including the leader himself).

Drucker believes that being able to perform these operations does not make a person a manager, but that without them the person cannot be an adequate manager. Setting objectives, organizing, measuring, and devel-

---

[3] Robert M. Fulmer, *Supervision: Principles of Professional Management* (Beverly Hills, Calif.: Glencoe Press), 1976, pp. 284–87.

[4] Peter F. Drucker, *Management: Tasks, Responsibilities, Practices* (New York: Harper & Row, 1974), pp. 400–401.

A good leader must

► Be trustworthy (i.e., have integrity).
► Have initiative.
► Have good judgement.
► Act with authority.
► Support subordinates.
► Think in terms of objectives, not objections.
► Never compromise basic principles.
► Be optimistic.
► Lead by example.

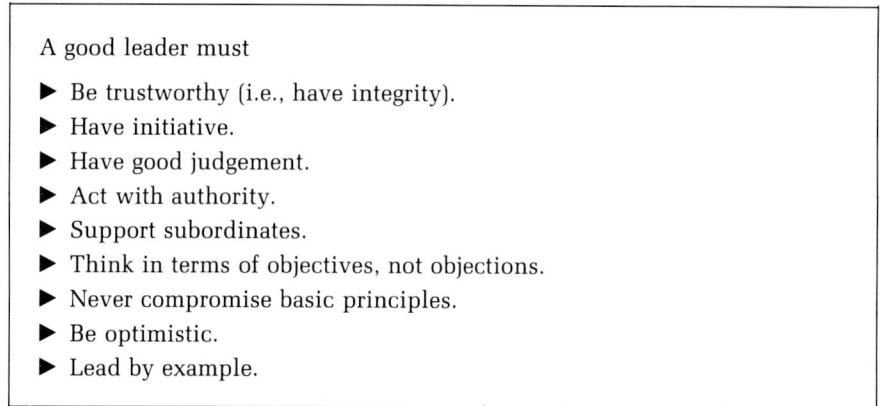

Figure 4 Results-oriented leaders possess certain basic leadership traits.

oping people are discussed in more specific detail in other pertinent chapters in this book. This chapter provides perspectives on motivation and communication.

MOTIVATIONAL THEORY

What do all of us want from life? How does what we want relate to our work? Several psychologists have focused their work on human needs and motivation, and their theories have relevance to these questions.

MASLOW'S NEEDS HIERARCHY

Abraham Maslow is well known for what he called the five basic categories of needs[5] (see Figure 5). He said these needs are organized in a series of levels—a hierarchy of importance—and that each level becomes active or aroused only when the need level immediately below it is reasonably satisfied.

Physiological Needs

The first level is the physiological, which includes such basic physical and biological needs as food, water, air, rest, exercise, shelter, and protection from the elements. Only when these needs are reasonably satisfied do the needs at the next level begin to become important—to motivate.

Safety or Security Needs

The second level of need is for safety, including physical and psychological security. Safety needs are the needs for protection against danger, threat, deprivation. People want to feel safe from accident or pain and from an uncertain future—to feel secure.

[5] Abraham Maslow, *Motivation and Personality* (New York: Harper & Row, 1954), p. 97.

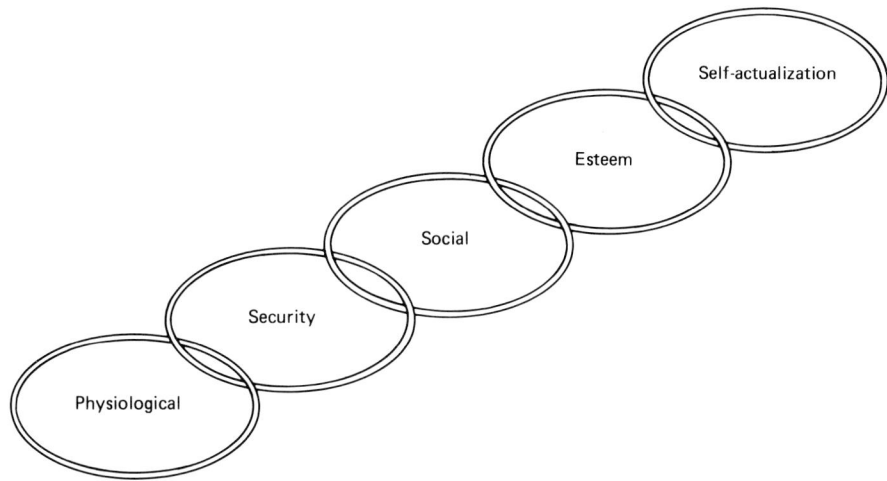

Figure 5 Maslow's hierarchy of needs.

Social Needs Once physiological and safety needs are adequately met, they no longer motivate behavior, and social needs emerge. These are needs for belonging, for affiliation or association, for acceptance by others, and for giving and receiving friendship, affection, and love. A tightly knit, cohesive work group may be very effective in achieving such goals—it may motivate positive behavior. If management attempts to break up the group and thus thwart social needs (and perhaps safety needs), employees are likely to become resistant and uncooperative.

Ego or Self-Esteem Needs Next in the hierarchy are the ego needs, those that relate to one's self esteem—needs for self-respect, self-confidence, independence, achievement, recognition, status, prestige, and for the deserved respect of one's fellows. Unlike the lower needs, these are rarely satisfied. They do not appear in any significant way until all the lower needs are reasonably satisfied; then individuals seek indefinitely for more satisfaction of ego needs. These needs are of greatest significance to management, for this is the level to which job design and organization structure should be directed, so as to provide workers with opportunities to obtain the respect of others for outstanding performance on the job. It is at this level that the drive for recognition, if not adequately met, may lead to behaviors that may be generally unacceptable to the organization and to other employees.

Self-Fulfillment Needs Finally, as a capstone to the hierarchy, come the self-fulfillment needs, also called self-realization or self-actualization needs. These are the needs for the realization of one's own potentialities, for continued self-development, and for being creative in the broadest sense of that term. Employees need to do work they like and in which they find an opportunity for expression. Those who like their work often become wrapped up in it; otherwise, they turn to hobbies and other outside interests.

The human needs motivate individuals to achieve a goal or objective. The process of satisfying needs is continuous. If, however, an individual's needs are blocked, the result may be frustration, conflict, aggression, escape, or avoidance. However, management can only provide the conditions that provide opportunities and encourage the fulfillment of needs. It cannot provide an individual with self-respect or the respect of others. Herein lies the challenge of human relations in the business environment—to understand people for fulfillment of needs and to provide opportunities.

HERZBERG'S MOTIVATION-HYGIENE THEORY

Frederick Herzberg,[6] another motivational expert, studied thousands of workers to learn what caused them satisfaction and dissatisfaction on the job. He expected that poor working conditions or poor company policies always would give dissatisfaction and that good working conditions and good company policies always would give satisfaction, but he discovered this was not the case.

He found a distinction between motivators—achievement, recognition of achievement, the work itself, responsibility and growth or advancement—and dissatisfaction avoidance or hygiene factors—company policy and administration, supervision, interpersonal relationships, working conditions, salary, status, and security. See Figure 6 for a chart showing the factors that are involved in causing job satisfaction and job dissatisfaction. Note that the factors that can lead to job dissatisfaction are extrinsic—they come from "outside" the person. They can prevent dissatisfaction when they are adequate. The motivator factors are intrinsic—they come from "inside" the person. They lead to motivation when you build them into the way you manage.

Motivators or achievement needs are long-term and bring about a sense of commitment and job satisfaction. On the other hand, hygiene factors (also called maintenance factors) are short-term, but are the prerequisites for motivation even if they do not motivate in and of themselves.

Herzberg learned that when working conditions are bad, they create dissatisfaction; but when they are good, they do not create satisfaction—they simply fade from consciousness. This parallels Maslow's view that people who are deprived of water will be very thirsty and concerned with getting a drink, but that once people have a supply of water, their attention turns to other needs (see Figure 7).

[6] Frederick Herzberg, "One More Time: How Do You Motivate Employees," *HBR Business Classics*, 1975, pp. 16–17.

FACTORS AFFECTING JOB ATTITUDES AS REPORTED IN 12 INVESTIGATIONS

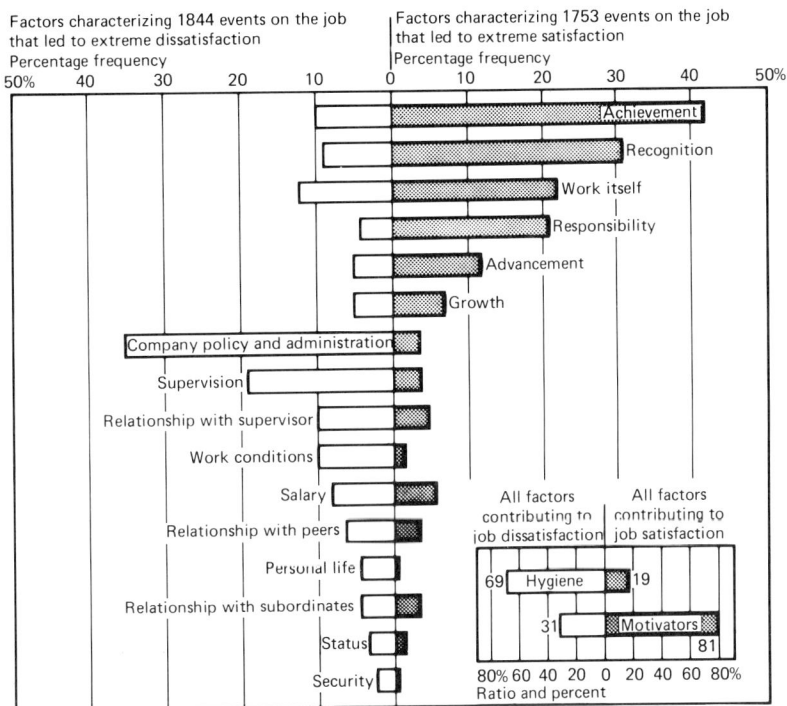

Figure 6
Reprinted by permission of the Harvard Business Review. An exhibit from "One More Time: How Do You Motivate Employees" by Frederick Herzberg (January/February 1968). Copyright © by the President and Fellows of Harvard College; all rights reserved.

Figure 7 Note the parallel comparison of needs between Maslow and Herzberg. (Courtesy of Macmillan Publishing Company Incorporated, from the New Management by Robert M. Fulmer, 1974).

Comparison of Maslow and Herzberg Models

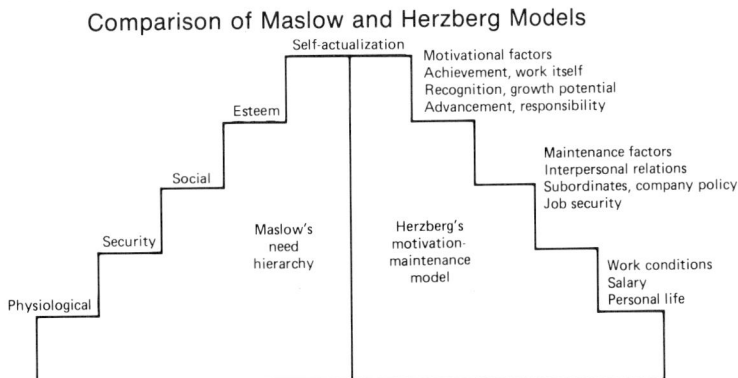

Reprinted by permission of Macmillan Publishing Company, Inc., from The New Management by Robert M. Fulmer © 1974 by Robert M. Fulmer

---

Theory X is based upon three propositions.

1. Management is responsible for organizing the elements of productive enterprise—money, materials, equipment, people—in the interest of economic ends.

2. With respect to people, this is a process of directing their efforts, motivating them, controlling their actions, modifying their behavior to fit the needs of the organization.

3. Without this active intervention by management, people would be passive—even resistant—to organizational needs. They must therefore be persuaded, rewarded, punished, controlled—their activities must be directed. This is management's task—in managing subordinate managers or workers. We often sum it up by saying that management consists of getting things done through other people.

McGregor's Theory Y policy suggests that

1. Management is responsible for organizing the elements of productive enterprise—money, materials, equipment, people—in the interest of economic ends.

2. People are *not* by nature passive or resistant to organizational needs. They have become so as a result of experience in organizations.

3. Their motivation, the potential for development, the capacity for assuming responsibility, the readiness to direct behavior toward organizational goals are all present in people. Management does not put them there. It is a responsibility of management to make it possible for people to recognize and develop these human characteristics for themselves.

4. The essential task of management is to arrange organizational conditions and methods of operation so that people can achieve their own goals best by directing their own efforts toward organizational objectives.

Figure 8   Theories X and Y describe two very different management approaches. Theory X is an autocratic approach, while Theory Y is a participative approach. *Source:* Douglas McGregor, *Leadership and Motivation*, MIT Press, 1966, pp. 5 and 15.

MCGREGOR'S THEORY X AND THEORY Y

Douglas McGregor is known for his work on Theory X and Theory Y management. Theory X stands for an autocratic approach to management, Theory Y for more participative management styles. Note the difference in management's approach in Theory X and Theory Y shown in Figure 8.

The assumptions underlying Theory X[7] include

▶ The average man is by nature indolent—he works as little as possible.

▶ He lacks ambition, dislikes responsibility, prefers to be led.

---

[7] Douglas McGregor, *Leadership and Motivation* (Cambridge, Mass.: M.I.T. Press, 1966), p. 6.

▶ He is inherently self-centered, indifferent to organization needs.

▶ He is by nature resistant to change.

▶ He is gullible and not very bright, the ready dupe of the charlatan and the demagogue.

McGregor suggested that the conventional approach of Theory X is based on mistaken notions of what is cause and what is effect. The wrong assumptions and a philosophy of management by direction and control may be a self-fulfilling prophecy, and people may indeed be like those described.

Theory Y is a process primarily of creating opportunities, releasing potential, removing obstacles, encouraging growth, providing guidance. McGregor subscribed to Maslow's theory and proposed Theory Y based on what he considered more adequate assumptions about human nature and human motivation. Theory Y relates to management by objectives.

Theory X places exclusive reliance upon external control of human behavior, whereas Theory Y relies heavily on self-control and self-direction.

A combination of Theory X and Theory Y is needed in performing daily supervisory functions. Sometimes Theory Y will be more appropriate, sometimes Theory X. Management should be prepared to use either approach, depending on the situation and types of people involved.

LIKERT'S PRINCIPLE OF SUPPORTIVE RELATIONSHIPS   Professor Rensis Likert[8] has developed a different leadership principle. He studied employees in hundreds of companies and concluded that there is a "principle of supportive relationships." The managers who are most successful are those who treat their people with a sense of individual attention and understanding rather than an impersonal attitude that they are only people who must get a job done. These managers are perceived by their subordinates as being supportive, friendly, and helpful rather than domineering and hostile. Supportive leaders manage to be kind but firm, do not threaten, and appear to be genuinely interested in their subordinates' development and happiness. They express confidence in their employees' abilities and talents. They manage to walk the line between authoritarianism and democratic leadership.

OUCHI'S THEORY Z   William Ouchi's Theory Z is a comprehensive management and/or company philosophy. In this theory, interpersonal skills are central. Because Z companies are less rigidly structured—formal reporting relationships, job assignments, and divisions between departments are less precise and often unclear—leaders must recognize the potential for problems and be prepared to deal with them.

[8] Rensis Likert and Jane Likert, *New Ways of Managing Conflict* (New York: McGraw-Hill, 1976), pp. 108–109.

Ouchi suggests that the skills required may be thought of as basically of two types, and that with practice these skills can be learned. The first skill is that of *recognizing patterns of interaction* in decision-making and problem-solving groups. Examples of this skill include

1. Learning to see when a group moves too quickly to a solution in order to avoid discussing the real problem.
2. Learning to observe how some members interfere in subtle ways with an open discussion.
3. Learning to note when the group drifts off.

The second skill is that of *providing leadership* in such a group so that the group can quickly identify the important issues, get to the bottom of conflicts, and arrive at high-quality, creative solutions that have everyone's support.[9]

SELF-UNDERSTANDING

The adage "Know thyself" applies to everyone. Whether we aspire to leadership or not, we will be dealing with others throughout our lifetimes; to understand others, we must also understand ourselves, our individual attitudes and motivations.

Recall the leadership styles and motivational theories presented earlier in this chapter. How do you react? What are your needs? Your interpersonal skills? What do you want from your life? Your job?

In order to best improve leadership skills, managers should constantly evaluate themselves in terms of a variety of skills. The self-appraisal test given in Figure 9 provides one example of such an evaluation. Note the three major areas for evaluation. Which ones can you answer positively now? All can serve as goals for the future either as they are written or as ideas to adapt for whatever supervisory position you hold. Prepare yourself through attention to the technical, supervisory, and personal aspects.

TRAITS OF AN EFFECTIVE ADMINISTRATOR

There are many different skills demanded in a given job and an administrator must be proficient in many of them. An administrator must adapt to changing environments, respond to situation factors, and support the human needs of his employees. A study by Professor Edwin Ghiselli examined over 300 managers from 90 different businesses in the United States.[10] All subjects were middle managers from firms in the transporta-

[9] William Ouchi, "Going From A to Z—the Steps," *Management Digest*, May 1981, pp. 12–13.

[10] Gary Dessler, *Human Behavior: Improving Performance at Work* (Reston, Va.: Reston Publishing Company, 1979), pp. 237–38.

Technical	Yes	No	Score		Yes	No	Score
Have I established ongoing training programs for secretaries under my supervision?	+10	−10	____	Do I delegate authority commensurate with responsibility?	+10	−10	____
Do I monitor equipment to ensure the most suitable and cost-effective combination for the applications processed?	+10	−10	____	Have I established a cross-training program to meet peaks and valleys of workload fluctuations?	+10	−10	____
Do I provide up-to-date operating guidelines and job descriptions to those under my supervision?	+10	−10	____	Within my area of authority, have I structured a career path for those under my supervision?	+10	−10	____
Do I provide a method for accurate performance measurement for those under my supervision?	+10	−10	____	Have I established short- and long-term results-oriented goals?	+10	−10	____
Have I established checkpoints within my area of responsibility to assure quality results?	+10	−10	____	Have I communicated those goals to my staff and asked for their ideas and suggestions?	+10	−10	____
Have I considered, studied, and implemented a fast, accurate method of dictation input to the word processing system?	+10	−10	____	Have I made every effort to match the skills of my staff to the jobs required?	+10	−10	____
Do I continuously monitor cost-benefit ratio for methods and equipment and look for improvements?	+10	−10	____	*Personal* Have I established short- and long-term goals for myself: ____ in business life?	+5	−5	____
Supervisory				____ in my personal life?	+5	−5	____
Am I open to new ideas and suggestions?	+10	−10	____	Do I have a plan to continue my formal education in my area of responsibility?	+10	−10	____
Do I give credit to those who offer good ideas and suggestions?	+10	−10	____	Do I actively participate in professional organizations?	+10	−10	____
				Do I study books, magazines, bulletins, and other literature related to my supervisory position?	+10	−10	____
				Do I get along well with others, and if not, am I taking action to improve?	+10	+10	____
				TOTAL			____

Figure 9 Self-appraisal is an important aspect of a supervisor's growth. One method is illustrated here. *Source:* Betty Primrose, *Modern Office Procedures,* "Self Appraisal for Word Processing Supervisors," 1979, p. 38.

tion, finance, insurance, manufacturing, utilities, and communications industries.

Ghiselli found that several traits characterize effective managers in a wide range of companies. The most significant trait is *supervisory ability*, or the capacity to direct the work of others and to organize and integrate their activities so that the goal of the work group can be attained. Next in importance was a cluster of traits. Effective managers were more *intelligent* and *decisive* than less-effective managers, as well as more *self-assured*. Effective managers were also more *achievement-oriented*, in that they desired to attain high-level positions within their own company. Finally, more-effective administrators had a high need for *self-actualization*, for they seemed to need and seek the opportunity to utilize their talents to the fullest extent possible. Possession of these traits does not assure that an individual will be an effective leader. Yet a manager who possesses them has a higher chance of being effective than one who does not.

The ingredients for good leadership have been described by Lester R. Bittel as shown in Figure 10. Men and women who prove to be successful leaders are characterized by these qualities.

A word of caution, however: the "trait" approach to leadership can be misleading. Some natural leaders display few of these desirable character-

Figure 10 Leadership ingredients. *Source:* Lester R. Bittel, *What Every Supervisor Should Know*, McGraw-Hill, 1980, pp. 83–84.

Sense of mission. This is a belief in your own ability to lead, a love for the work of leadership itself, and a devotion to the people and the organization you serve.

Self-denial. This essential of leadership is too often played down. It means a willingness to forgo self-indulgence (such as blowing your stack) and the ability to beat the headaches the job entails.

High character. Few persons become successful leaders who are not honest with themselves and with others, who cannot face hard facts and unpleasant situations with courage, who fear criticism or their own mistakes, who are insincere or undependable.

Job competence. There's been too much talk about the significance of technical job skill to the supervisor. A person who knows the job that is being supervised has one of the best foundations for building good leadership.

Good judgment. Common sense, the ability to separate the important from the unimportant, tact, and the wisdom to look into the future and plan for it are ingredients that make the best leaders.

Energy. Leadership at any level means rising early and working late. It leaves little time for relaxation or escape from problems. Good health, good nerves, and boundless energy make this touch job easier.

---

istics. You have only to consider Hitler, Mussolini, and General George Patton to find notable examples in which some of these traits are missing.

Peter Drucker has suggested that *integrity* is one absolute requirement of a manager, the one quality that he has to bring with him and cannot be expected to acquire later on. He further states that "the men with whom a man works, and especially his subordinates, know in a few weeks whether he has integrity or not. They may forgive a man a great deal: incompetence, ignorance, insecurity, or bad manners. But they will not forgive his lack of integrity."[11]

BASIC PERSONAL SKILLS

Robert L. Katz identified three basic personal skills required for an effective administrator: *technical, human, and conceptual* skills. Administrators need (1) sufficient *technical* skill to accomplish the mechanics of the particular jobs for which they are responsible, (2) sufficient *human* skill in working with others to be effective group members and to be able to build cooperative effort within the teams they lead, and (3) sufficient *conceptual* skill to recognize the interrelationships of the various factors involved in their situations, which will lead them to take those actions likely to achieve the maximum good for the total organization.[12]

He further amplifies his explanation of *human skill* by dividing it into (1) leadership ability within the manager's own unit and (2) skill in intergroup relationships. He suggests that having both skills is rarely possible. Consequently, he considers internal intragroup skills to be essential in lower and middle management roles and that intergroup skills become increasingly important in successively higher levels of management.[13]

Without a doubt, the most critical skill is the human skill. It is critical at all levels of management. As John D. Rockefeller once said, "I will pay more for the ability to deal with people than any other ability under the sun." According to a report by the American Management Association, an overwhelming majority of the 200 managers who participated in one survey agreed that the most important single skill of an executive is his or her ability to get along with people.

GENERAL SUPERVISORY/MANAGEMENT SKILLS

COMMUNICATION   Communication skills are essential to effective leadership. Communication may be direct or implied. A leader must be able to understand hidden messages. Hidden messages that have a considerable effect on manager/

---

[11] Drucker, *Management*, pp. 456–462.

[12] Robert L. Katz, "Skills of an Effective Administrator," *HBR Business Classics*, 1975, p. 33.

[13] Katz, "Skills," p. 34.

group perception and interaction may be classified as verbal, physical, and nonverbal.[14] Each type is important, in its own way, to the overall effectiveness of an administrator.

Verbal Messages   The ways in which persons use words and create images can reveal much about their working style. When you pay close attention to the words other people use, you notice that most people draw characteristic verbal pictures of themselves and the world around them. The imagery and metaphors that a person most frequently uses can often provide a clue to understanding that person's world. Vocabulary shows what is valued, what is feared, and what the speaker's behavioral traits are.

Often verbal communication is difficult, because two people assume that they are using the same words to mean the same things. Communication becomes a problem when people fail to recognize the personally distinctive ways in which others use words. As Fritz Roethlisberger observed, "We fail to notice the differences and we read into our experiences similarities where differences exist."[15]

Keeping these differences in mind, one can try listening to conversations with a more attuned ear. For example, one might listen for the following three characteristics of a speaker:

▶ Does the person use concrete or abstract words? Different people are comfortable with different levels of abstraction. Some people use vivid, concrete expressions; others favor -ism and -ion words that describe states and conditions. A listener expecting to hear concrete terms often rejects what others who talk at an abstract level say and will not even bother to listen.

▶ Does the person joke and kid a lot? Joking is a way some managers use to make risky statements and avoid immediate detection.

▶ Does the person often say "I" or "we"? With whom does the person identify? For what groups are they willing to say, "We need to. . . ." Speakers who use the royal or editorial "we" to refer to actions they have obviously performed alone can sound pompous or may be unwilling to accept sole responsibility for their actions.

The way in which a person handles questions is another aspect of the verbal environment. Questions often contain assumptions that not only frame the problem in a certain way but also tend to force its resolution to conform to the implicit assumption. People often feel obliged to answer a question, even if it is poorly framed. A good question is posed at the right time and requires that a person be willing to answer it. As an exercise, listen to the questions that are asked in your environment. See how many

[14] Michael McCaskey, "The Hidden Messages Managers Send," *Harvard Business Review,* November/December 1979, pp. 135–36.

[15] McCaskey, "Hidden Messages," p. 136.

of the questions are really statements. Questions are not as easy to decipher as they seem.

The ability to ask the right questions is a valuable leadership asset. Some managers have an outstanding ability to get right to the heart of a problem by asking only a handful of simple questions, whereas others find themselves laboriously conducting an inquisition over the same problem. When trying to find answers to technical or procedural problems, effective managers state questions in ways that elicit definitive answers—questions that directly identify problems and causes are best. If a situation involves personality differences, questions should be phrased to encourage the parties to first reveal their feelings and motivations. In either situation, questions should elicit answers that in most cases go beyond simple "yes" or "no" replies.

Physical Messages   The physical environment that surrounds a person reflects and conveys much about his or her character. People use physical space in different ways. A thoughtful and observant manager can better read what people are saying through their use of space. Managers can also examine their own space to see what it is saying to others.

Physical workspace represents personal territory. The importance of territory shows up in the office. When a manager and subordinate meet, whose office do they use? If the manager is sensitive to place as territory, the purpose of the meeting will decide the question. To conduct an adversary discussion, the manager will probably hold the meeting in his or her office. If, however, the manager wants to reach out to the subordinate, he or she might consider traveling to the subordinate's office or space.

Other than territoriality, managers can use their office space to influence the character of transactions that take place there. For instance, many managers set up their offices with two separate areas—a desk-centered area and a conversational area. The desk arrangement, in which a manager talks to a guest across the desk, emphasizes the manager's authority and position. In the second area, a guest would feel like a welcome visitor and equal. With chairs at right angles, one can more easily move into another's personal space. As a result of furniture arrangements, then, people can and do become more friendly or more distant.

Most individuals set up their offices to encourage a certain type of transaction. Consciously or unconsciously, they send strong messages about themselves. A person's office can reveal much about what is important to that person. Notice how an office has been personalized with photos, pictures, plants, and so on.

In addition, notice the textures. If the person had a choice, did he or she use tactile fabrics, long-haired rugs, coverings that invite a visitor to touch them? This person may be signaling a desire to "be in touch" with what is going on. On the other hand, are the surfaces neat and clean and polished? This might mean that the person prefers orderliness, cleanliness, and distance. Without a doubt, how people utilize their space can communicate a lot about their personality and leadership aims.

Nonverbal Messages

Nonverbal messages also provide a key to understanding a person's behavior. Body language and paralinguistics convey important messages that color, support, or contradict the words people use. Paralinguistics takes into account tone of voice, pacing, and other extralinguistic features that surround talking. Messages that are important but cannot be communicated verbally for some reason are sent through these channels. Because nonverbal messages are often subtle and ambiguous, if one senses disapproval of listeners by body language (such as facial expressions and body postures), one can quickly reinterpret or even change the message. This type of nonverbal communication and adjustment occurs every day in business.

For many people, the most important communicator of an idea is the face. Some research indicates that over 90 percent of the communication between two people is done through facial expression. Reading the faces of speakers can provide vital clues to their real meaning and intent.

Eye-to-eye contact is one of the most direct and powerful ways for people to communicate nonverbally. In the United States, social rules suggest that in most situations, eye-to-eye contact for a short period of time is appropriate. Prolonged eye contact is usually viewed as threatening or highly romantic. Skillful use of eye contact can improve a speaker-listener communication. For example, most managers consciously look directly at members of the audience during a speech, to establish rapport. However, few listeners are aware of the importance of looking at a speaker to maintain contact during a conversation. Eye contact from listener to speaker makes the listener an active participant in a speech. A lack of eye contact may indicate that the speaker is losing the listener's attention.

Silences and pauses also convey powerful messages. Silences can have a whole range of meaning. At one extreme, some people use them as a weapon to force the other party to become so disconcerted that they give in. Used in a positive way, a pause or silence can allow individuals to gather their thoughts and feelings.

One special type of pause is the "filled pause," in which a speaker uses sounds such as *uhhhhh* to fill the space between words. Filled pauses are used to provide continuity, to show that the speaker is still in the business of completing a reply even though he or she cannot immediately muster up the right words to accomplish this task.

Conclusions

Two ultimate lessons emerge from this examination of different types of communication. First, it is very difficult to mask the real intent of a speaker. Intents "leak out" one way or the other. Trying to suppress or censor what you feel will only confuse the messages and signals more. Second, body language and paralinguistics are always part of an interaction. Managers who can increase their skill at reading and interpreting these subtle signals can markedly increase their ability to work with others. Effective communication is basic to many aspects of supervision.

GIVING INSTRUCTIONS

How many times have you failed to follow through on an assignment because you did not understand the instructions? Why? Think about all the reasons.

More often than not, employees do not perform properly because instructions are not specific or complete or because those that are provided are poor. Remember, too, that words do not mean the same thing to everyone. Assumptions become involved. Supervisors assume employees understand and know what to do; employees have different perceptions of what is expected.

Lester R. Bittel, who has assisted thousands of supervisors to become more effective, suggested that there are no assurances that employees will not get hung up about a particular assignment, but there are guidelines to minimize trouble. Study the guidelines presented in Figure 11.

DELEGATION

Another necessary managerial skill is the ability to delegate tasks. Proper delegation fosters a feeling of confidence in subordinates and is taken as evidence of management's confidence in them. It gives them an opportunity for creativity, individual expression, and independence and is an important factor in building self-esteem and human potential. Frequently, it is difficult for managers to delegate, even though they may recognize that delegation is a vital key to motivation and effective leadership. Studies have revealed that the principal reason behind managerial failure often is an inability or unwillingness to delegate to subordinates.

To delegate more effectively, follow these steps.

▶ Pursue vigorously the training and development of skills in your subordinates. They will be unable to effectively assume authority unless they are capable and skilled.

▶ Delegate to your subordinates in terms of goals to be obtained. Do this in a step-by-step method, so that they understand all that is important to success in completing the job.

▶ Develop a communications feedback to recognize subordinates' successes and areas of management that need improvement. This activity will help them progress on the job.

▶ Emphasize the importance of results obtained rather than methodology and other details contributing toward accomplishment.

▶ Set up control points in the work process, so that it is possible as to prevent any action that might seriously jeopardize successful attainment of the objectives.[16]

[16] Charles Dillon, "Delegation of Authority Is Key to Success," *In-Plant Printer*, 1979, p. 28.

Guidelines for Directing, Ordering, Assigning, or Instructing

1. *Don't make it a struggle for power.* If you approach too many order-giving situations in an "I'll-show-you-who's-boss" frame of mind, you'll soon be fighting the whole department. Try to focus your attention—and the worker's—on the goal that must be met. The idea to project is that it is the situation that demands the order, not the whim of the supervisor.

2. *Avoid an offhand manner.* If you want employees to take instructions seriously, then deliver them that way. It's all right to have fun, but be firm about those matters that are important.

3. *Watch out for your words.* As you have seen, words can be unreliable messengers of your thoughts. Watch the tone of your voice, too. Few people like to feel that they are being taken for granted or pushed around. Most employees accept the fact that it is the supervisor's job to hand out orders and instructions. Their quarrel is more likely to be with the way orders are given.

4. *Don't assume that the worker understands.* Give the employee a chance to ask questions and to raise objections. Have the employee confirm an understanding by repeating what you have said than afterward.

5. *Be sure to get feedback right away.* Give the employee who wishes to complain about the assignment a chance to do so at the time. It is better to iron out resistance and misunderstanding before the job begins.

6. *Don't give too many orders.* This is an area where a communications overload will be self-defeating. Be selective in issuing instructions. Keep them brief and to the point. Wait until an employee has finished one job before asking that another be started.

7. *Provide just enough detail.* Some jobs require more information than less complex ones do. Some workers need more detailed instruction than others do. Think about the information needs of the person you are speaking to. For an old hand, there is nothing more tiresome than having to listen to familiar details.

8. *Watch out for conflicting instructions.* Check to make sure that you're not telling your employee one thing while supervisors in adjoining departments are telling their people another.

9. *Don't choose only the willing worker.* Some people are naturally cooperative. Others make it difficult for you to ask them to do anything. Be sure that you do not overwork the willing person. Make sure the hard-to-handle people get their share of the rough jobs, too.

10. *Try not to pick on anyone.* It is a temptation to punish a person by handing out an unpleasant assignment. Resist this temptation if you can. Employees have the right to expect the work to be distributed fairly. So if you have a grudge against an employee, don't use a dirty job assignment to get even.

11. *Above all, don't play the big shot.* New supervisors are sometimes guilty of flaunting their authority. Older supervisors feel more confident. They know that you don't have to crack the whip to gain employees' cooperation and respect.

Figure 11 Delegating is a component for successful management and an art. Note the need for good communication. *Source: Lester R. Bittel, What Every Supervisor Should Know, McGraw-Hill, 1980, pp. 83–84.*

Proper delegation of authority will result in increased morale, increased productivity, and less pressure on management. Although managers can delegate authority to accomplish a given project, they cannot delegate responsibility. The ultimate responsibility for any project rests with the management level at which it originated. It is important that managers remember this when they are delegating authority for a project.

DISCIPLINE IN THE OFFICE
One of the key problems in the modern office is how to deal with employees who fail to carry out their assignments, resist doing them, or just outright refuse to do them. Years ago, a manager could simply fire an employee without warning, notice, or formal procedures. There was little chance for repercussions. In today's office, one needs to handle insubordination very carefully, to avoid violating employment regulations and to minimize the disruption to the office. A manager must be able to determine when a subordinate is unable to develop further and when that person can no longer adjust and respond to policies and assignments. The manager must then be able to justify the termination of that person.

Usually, a five-step process can effectively deal with this problem:

1. Document the problem.
2. Meet and notify the employee.
3. Monitor continued performance.
4. Prepare a memo for the employee and the file.
5. Send a notice of termination.

When there are problems within the office between a manager and staffer, the manager should first *document the problem*. Documentation can be provided by a memo describing the incident, the individuals involved, the witnesses, date, and time, and the supervisor's signature. When problems do arise in the office environment, it is always best to attempt to resolve them through informal discussions between the employee involved and the appropriate management or supervisory level. However, if the manager wants to handle the incident, documentation is essential.

Along with documenting the problem, the manager must meet with and/or notify the employee that his or her behavior is being monitored and recorded for future action. This notification often can be enough to straighten out the subordinate. The notification should be delivered in a firm and yet unemotional manner. The supervisor should not appear negative toward the employee, but merely indicate that the behavior has been noticed and is being recorded in the individual's personnel file.

The supervisor then will *monitor continued performance and prepare a memo* to the employee and place a copy in the employee's file.

When it is clear that the situation is serious, the supervisor meets with the employee to attempt to discover what the problem is. At this meeting, the employee should also be warned that unless improvement is shown, the employee will be terminated.

A situation that is serious enough to warrant termination should have been documented for an extended length of time. The *notice of termination*, including written documentation, should be presented to the employee and to pertinent persons within the organization. The manager should announce the termination to the employee in a firm, straightforward, and well-timed manner. Then, the manager should notify fellow staffers or whatever groups need to know of the termination, in order to minimize gossip, innuendo, and anxiety. No good manager wants to rely on termination as a key tool. But termination should always be used when continued employment of the problem employee jeopardizes the work unit's effectiveness or when all other avenues of redress have failed.

The key to handling insubordination within the office is to be fair and firm without getting personal with the employee in question. Most incidents of insubordination are one-time affairs. However, in the rare case of serious insubordination, it is essential that the manager documents the employee's behavior and then has the courage to carry out disciplinary action.

One of the best ways to maintain peace in the office is to develop a system that can identify complaints early and then respond to them. However, when an incident cannot be resolved through established channels, it may be a good idea to submit the issue to outside arbitration. The arbitration system assures an objective decision and a hearing in private for all those involved.

A recent study carried out by the University of Michigan Survey Research Center under a U.S. Labor Department grant indicated a growing number of cases in which American workers were unwilling to accept decisions of supervisors that they considered unreasonable or illegal. Cautious management should be prepared for such occasions with sound detection systems for identifying and documenting problems.

One way to minimize or eliminate performance problems is to manage the office by example. Managers must be able to demonstrate that they can manage themselves. Today's manager must deal with employees on equal terms and gain their respect through the quality of the manager's performance. An effective manager projects an aura of ability and competence.

If a manager has a high level of self-confidence, employees will have confidence in the manager as a leader and will respect him or her. As a manager, you can gain the confidence and respect of your staff if you do the following:[17]

▶ Display ability as a manager.

▶ Believe in yourself and in the company and its products or services.

---

[17] From Troy Bussey, "Casting a Credible Shadow for Employees to Follow," *Modern Office Procedures*, March 1981, p. 73.

▶ Show that you are trying to meet employee needs.

▶ Deal with employees in an honest, straightforward manner—on their terms.

Note how the topics discussed in this chapter tie in with the list of employee expectations given in Figure 12.

The actions of individual supervisors are closely related to employee job satisfaction. Research has determined that supervision is the variable which most dramatically affects the level of job satisfaction of word processing specialists. Supervisory style, supervisory intensity, and supervisory personality are directly related to job satisfaction. Supervisory policies and practices are indirectly related to job satisfaction. The three most frequently noted suggestions for the improvement of word processing supervision were the following:[18]

1. Consistency in applying rules and policies.

Figure 12 Employees have certain expectations of their supervisors. Note how their expectations relate to meeting established goals.

The following list shows the top 15 expectations (not in order of importance) employees have of their supervisors and/or employers.

▶ Confident leadership—an example they can respect and follow.

▶ Clear direction—knowing what is expected of them.

▶ Recognition—feedback about their behavior and performance.

▶ Fair and consistent supervision.

▶ Recognition as being part of a "team," involved in the decision-making process and contributing to the firm's success.

▶ Maximization of their abilities and talents, with an opportunity to learn new skills.

▶ Opportunity to achieve objectives toward career goals.

▶ Sympathy or understanding of their problems—both on- and off-the-job.

▶ Interesting and worthwhile work.

▶ Organization and flexibility within the firm.

▶ Adequate pay.

▶ Security—personal and economic.

▶ Open communication.

▶ Freedom of expression, including the opportunity to voice suggestions and complaints.

▶ Consideration of their families and private lives.

---

[18] Robert B. Mitchell, "An Investigation of Job Satisfaction among Correspondence Secretaries and the Impact of Supervision," *Delta Pi Epsilon Journal*, January 1980, pp. 32–40.

2. Mastering the machines and the procedures of the systems; leading in all aspects of the work.

3. Giving more supervision to new workers and helping all workers advance personally.

This list is not all-inclusive. Many skills are required for a particular job position. However, if managers have the skills discussed above, they will be well on the road to effective leadership.

MOTIVATIONAL SKILLS

The average worker gets only three hours and 45 minutes of production out of an eight-hour work day according to national statistics. If U.S. business and industry could get just 15 minutes more in daily production from each employee—or only four hours' work in an eight-hour day, they'd solve the country's inflation problem.[19]

Motivation, a key to productivity and morale, may be the most vital, yet most subtle factor in production. Motivation is a willingness to act, created by a desire to achieve, attain, or overcome. In order for motivation to be effective in any environment, people must identify the organizational and personal goals. Company needs include higher productivity at lower costs, less absenteeism, fewer errors, and more coordination. Employee needs include increased job satisfaction and more feelings of achievement and contributions, opportunities for personal growth, and a sense of self-esteem, worth, and pride.

Overall, motivation is a continuous, day-by-day process that needs constant care and constant attention. The rewards are worth the price, however, in terms of saved dollars, increased morale, and increased productivity.

Theories of motivation help to explain why people behave as they do. How managers can effectively motivate others, however, is a question that needs to be addressed in more detail.

There appear to be at least four key ingredients[20] necessary for a productive motivational process and direction. The first key is *commitment*. Those in positions of responsibility must be committed to growth and change. They must be willing to undergo whatever personal or professional changes are necessary so that they can carry out their responsibilities. Each person must acknowledge the fact that "motivation begins with me." This is another way of managing by example.

The second key is *modeling*. Those in positions of leadership must be willing and able to act as well as to talk about motivation. They must

---

[19] Bussey, "Casting a Credible Shadow," p. 72.

[20] From John W. Arnu, Jr., Gail Long, and Ben Strickland, "Giving Employees A Boost," *Modern Office Procedures*, April 1980, p. 168.

provide effective models of leadership and motivation for others to follow. Each person must acknowledge the fact that "I must be able to demonstrate to others what I expect of them." To put it another way, managers
cannot expect anything of an employee that they do not expect of themselves.

The third key is *continuity*. Those in positions of responsibility must
provide continuing rather than occasional support if the motivational
process is to have any continuity. Inconsistent support generates frustration or apathy rather than motivation for productivity. Without continuity, the motivational process cannot be a functional part of the organization, and people can only hope it will happen on its own.

Each person must acknowledge the fact that "individual support is the
oxygen of motivation—you either have it or you don't."

The final key to motivation is *skill development*. Those in positions of
responsibility must provide for the necessary skill development and
maintenance. Continual assessments must be made as to the level of existing skill development, the level needed for desired productivity, and the
most effective plan for attainment of production goals. Skill development
must be continuous. Each person must acknowledge the fact that developing skills "is like swimming upstream—if you don't stay with it, you can
get behind very easily."

These four keys tell the manager what kind of example to set for employees. In addition, managers should develop three important attitudes
about motivation.[21] First, *managers should think people rather than products*. In the midst of declining productivity, it is hard to focus attention on
people (producers) instead of on products; but it is important for managers to do so, because the producers determine productivity.

Second, *managers should think internal rather than external*. When
self-generated, motivation is usually accompanied by a feeling of responsibility that stimulates individual initiative. When motivation is generated from outside, a person tends to expect others to assume responsibility and merely reacts to situations rather than to demonstrate initiative.
Motivation persists only as long as its source persists.

Finally, *managers should think process rather than event*. Decreasing
productivity or morale creates panic among managers and supervisors,
who respond to it with high-visibility gimmicks. The impact of such
gimmicks is usually temporary. Continuity is essential in any plan of
action for motivation. It generates trust and dependability, and it reas-
sures people that they are of continuing importance to the organization.

---

[21] From Arnu *et al.,* "Giving Employees a Boost," p. 169.

CHAPTER 21

CONTINUING DEVELOPMENT AND GROWTH

OBJECTIVES

In this chapter you will learn about
1. The means for continuing the development and growth of employees while improving productivity.
2. Job enrichment and its relationship to job redesign.
3. The management-by-objective (MBO) theory and its importance in planning for continuing development and growth.
4. Quality of work life (QWL) and its role in continuing development and growth, and the quality circle (QC) approach to employee participation and growth.
5. Upward mobility and career progression.
6. The relationship between organizational goals and employee goals.
7. The theory of group behavior and how it relates to the modern office.
8. The importance of constructive employee evaluation in consistent job performance.
9. The role of employee self-evaluation.

People comprise the most important part of any system, and the solution of "people problems" is the most critical aspect of implementing the automated office. Implementation of the electronic office requires a substantial commitment on the part of management. It takes much more time and effort to build a system around people than it does to build a system around machines.

Greater job satisfaction may be one of the key employee benefits of the modern office. Satisfaction can stem from job enrichment and career opportunity. These are based, in turn, on job descriptions organized into career paths, with standards for each level of achievement and objectives for every workstation. Awareness of the overall goals and objectives, the career opportunities, the standards for each step on the ladder, and how well one meets these standards can create challenge. It is the role of these growth factors—job enrichment, career progression, evaluation, and continuing education—and their effect upon productivity that this chapter will explore, along with the increasing importance of the role of groups and teamwork in the automated office.

IMPROVING PRODUCTIVITY

One way to improve productivity and develop employees is through participation. The more involved people are in the challenges of production, the more productive they will be. Four major techniques involve participation (see Figure 1).

1. Job enrichment/redesign.
2. Management by objectives.
3. Quality of work life.
4. Quality circles.

JOB ENRICHMENT/ REDESIGN   According to Frederick Herzberg, "Job enrichment seeks to improve both task efficiency and human satisfaction by means of building into people's jobs, quite specifically, greater scope for personal achievement and its recognition, more challenging and responsible work, and more opportunity for individual advancement and growth. It is concerned only incidentally with matters such as pay and working conditions, organizational structure, communications, and training, important and necessary though these may be in their own right."[1] Job enrichment, when properly implemented, can lead to greater employee satisfaction and increased productivity.

[1] William J. Paul, Jr., Keith B. Robertson, and Frederick Herzberg, "Job Enrichment Pays Off," *Harvard Business Review*, April/March 1969; *HBR Classics*, p. 141.

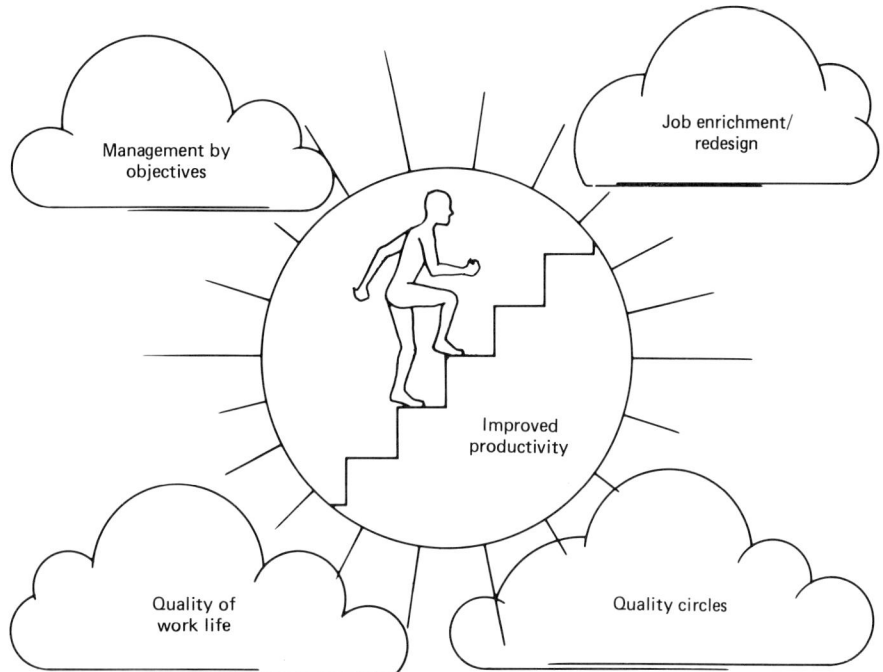

Figure 1 Motivating techniques to improve productivity.

Individual reaction to job enrichment is as difficult to forecast in terms of attitudes as it is in terms of performance. Those already genuinely interested in their work develop real enthusiasm. Not all people welcome having their jobs enriched, but so long as the changes present opportunities rather than demands, there is no reason to fear an adverse reaction from employees. If people prefer to keep things the way they are, they can simply continue referring things to their supervisors. In attitudes as well as in performance, the existence of individual differences should not prevent you from investigating the possibilities of job enrichment.[2]

The application of job enrichment principles to a specific job is illustrated below, for a word processing operator (listed in an Air Force Word Processing Administrator's handbook).[3]

▶ Locate equipment and operators in the working areas they support.
▶ Have operators set goals for their jobs.
▶ Provide operators with feedback, both positive and negative, from users.

[2] Paul *et al.*, "Job Enrichment," p. 155.
[3] "WP Job Enrichment," *Word Processing Systems*, August 1980, p. 42.

▶ Publish "peaks" and "valleys" of work week.

▶ Arrange flextime within the center to cover peak periods.

▶ Publicize turnaround times and priority systems.

▶ Involve center personnel in negotiating work priority systems.

▶ Allow operators to give informal briefings at staff meetings in the centers.

▶ Educate users on what the word processing center can and cannot do, and on the capabilities of the equipment.

▶ Delete work that should be done on nonword processing center type-writers.

▶ Have brainstorming sessions between word processing personnel and users, to generate better service arrangements.

Mouton and Blake suggest that job redesign is the same as job enrichment. The idea is that a person who is involved in rethinking his or her job and what it contains is very likely to want to expand it by taking on more horizontal and vertical activities and being responsible for them. This tends to increase the complexity of work in both directions. Once complexity is increased, the job requires more thought and involvement; therefore, one person is contributing more output under the redesigned job than previously.[4]

Job enrichment offers motivation to employees through the growth opportunities and the excitement of participating in job redesign in the changing environment.

MANAGEMENT BY OBJECTIVES

Management by objectives (MBO) is a systematic way of incorporating into a more effective framework the things that people do, or should be doing. Stated more formally, MBO offers a way to practice the basic management functions—planning, organizing, staffing or leading, and controlling. In other words, management by objectives is a way of managing. It is not just a part of, nor is it something in addition to, the manager's job. It is not a secondary program or procedure attached to some other process or function. It is a results-oriented management system. The idea is that when a person sets objectives, that person becomes involved in demonstrating an ability to accomplish these objectives. The result, of course, is greater productivity.[5]

MBO is a process by which the members of an organization jointly establish organizational goals. Individuals, with the assistance of their bosses, first define their areas of responsibility. They set objectives that

[4] Robert Blake and Jane Srygley Mouton, *Productivity: The Human Side* (New York: AMA-COM, 1980), p. 5.

[5] Blake and Mouton, *Productivity*.

clearly state the results expected of the individual or group. They then develop performance measures that can be used as guides for determining whether goals are met and for evaluating individual contributions to the organization.

There are four basic components to the MBO system: (1) setting objectives, (2) developing action plans, (3) conducting periodic reviews and (4) annual performance appraisal.

There are four classes of objectives that need to be addressed in the MBO process. First are the *regular or routine objectives*. These are the necessary statements of objectives for any organization and are definitions or the regular, ordinary requirements that are necessary for the survival of the firm. For example, regular objectives might include that machine operators must produce at standard rates of output or that accountants must produce a monthly report. Performance is measured by comparing what has been done to predetermined standards or by exception.

In *problem-solving objectives*, problems are identified and clearly defined, the causes of the variance from the standards determined, and solutions developed and applied. Performance is measured by time and solutions. Examples would include the uncovering of the causes of defective work or the causes behind a decline in the market.

Innovative or creative objectives start with the assumption that even the successful completion of routine objectives is not good enough, and that problem solving is merely a necessary step in maintaining the status quo. Innovative objectives constitute the highest order of objectives—they are ones that make things happen. Examples would include goals to make your company bigger than your largest competitor by the end of the fiscal year or to capture 25 percent of the market share by a given year. Performance is measured by productive changes achieved on time.

Personal development objectives are concerned with the acquisition of additional knowledge, skills, and experiences that will allow the individual to improve his job performance and will stand him in good stead whether he is promoted or stays in his present position. Examples might include the completion of course work required for a graduate degree by a given year or subscription to two professional journals. Performance is measured by improvements in job performance.

Management by objectives is an effective concept for a number of reasons. First, work expectations are better understood, because objectives are visible to all concerned. In addition, the "political atmosphere" of the office is minimized, because there is no need to try to give the boss what he wants in an attempt to please him. Communications are improved, because objectives provide a common framework for employers and employees to relate to. Feedback is provided, so the subordinate knows how he is doing. Teamwork is promoted and innovation in problem solving is encouraged. Challenges are provided to all those participating and planning is more precise and useful to all those implementing.

MBO has many benefits. First, there is improved performance. Individuals will more likely achieve what they set out to achieve, because of increased motivation and commitment. Second, improved planning results. Managers will no longer think in terms of work, but rather in terms of results. There is also improved control, and yet flexibility. There is a shift from control over people to control over operations. More immediate response to deviations from the standards are achieved by anticipating potential obstacles to goal achievement and the use of contingency planning. Further, there are improved employer-employee relationships. The chances of personal development are maximized and overall there is an increased ability of the organization to adapt to changing conditions.

However, MBO also has its limitations and drawbacks. Sometimes managers and top executives expect too much of the system. They expect the plans to work just as originally conceived. That, of course, does not always happen. In addition, too much sometimes is attempted at once. MBO is not a cure-all; it is merely a way to approach planning. Sometimes management and subordinates fail to operate within the plan that was formulated. Once group cohesiveness breaks down, MBO will break down also. MBO is only as good as the people who use it.

If the results meet the objectives, this should not be ignored. Management should praise the employee and encourage continued development. If the results do not meet the objectives, management should determine the reasons for failure and aid the employee in planning a corrective approach.

The concept of *flexibility* makes the MBO approach work for support staff as well as for management. Flexibility involves the ability to adjust to changing conditions in the office environment and to demands without a concrete plan in operation. Rigidity in past office practices cannot work successfully in the automated office. Responses to changing conditions have to be flexible, in order to balance technology's rigid discipline.

MBO is indeed a process that provides a way to measure the extent to which both company goals and individual goals have been achieved.

RECENT APPROACHES TO IMPROVING PRODUCTIVITY

Improving productivity within the office is of major importance. How to motivate people to achieve increased productivity is, of course, the primary question. People can make or break any system. It is therefore not surprising that two approaches to improving productivity that have received attention in recent years are quality of work life (QWL) and quality circles (QC). The major difference between them and participatory management is that they involve rank-and-file employees in the process of suggesting changes as well as in implementing them. Improved quality as well as quantity is the goal of these approaches.

QUALITY OF WORK LIFE

The Quality of Work Life (QWL) program is based on the belief that people are the organization's greatest assets. As one company's written statement of the philosophy explains, "We believe in the dignity of each human being and place a high value on human life. Thus, quality of work life is a continuous, upgrading and on-going process which enriches, encourages, and provides the opportunity to each individual for freedom of expression and participation in factors affecting one's environment, regardless of job assignment, race, color, age, physical, emotional or mental limitations, religion, sex, or national origin." The company's statement goes on to say that as the people succeed, so will the company. "In succeeding, however, we recognize that one individual does not have all of the solutions or answers to a very complex environment. Therefore, our quality of work life theme proclaims that individually we do not have it all together, but together we have it all. People do not only make the difference, but people are the difference to a successful Quality of Work Life program."[6]

This approach to improved productivity through worker participation has been emerging in the past few years. If workers are involved more directly in the challenges of production, they will respond with ideas and efforts that improve productivity. This is "direct" participation, often with the formal supervisory system replaced by QWL specialists who lead discussions, act as communications channels to higher levels of management, and so on.[7]

QUALITY CIRCLES

In the quality circle approach, a group or circle of employees meets to discuss how to improve the quantity and quality of work. The underlying principle is that those who do the work have many ideas about how to do it better, and if they are listened to and what they recommend is implemented, improved productivity will result.

Quality circles have been used in this country for some time, but they have received more attention recently because the Japanese have used them in attaining significant increases in productivity. However, all aspects successful in Japan are not practicable in this country. Figure 2 tells of one company's experience with an adaptation of the quality circle approach.

The philosophy behind both the quality of work life and quality circle approaches is logical; but as pointed out by Jane Mouton and Robert

---

[6] "Quality of Work Life," *Muncie Star*, September 6, 1980, Section B, p. 3.

[7] Blake and Mouton, *Productivity*, p. 16.

In March 1980, Cal-Farm Insurance Company of Sacramento, California, implemented a program called Quality Commitment. The voluntary program, based on the quality circles used by the Japanese, provided an environment where employees could meet, on company time, to address problems with workflow and recommend changes to management. The meeting groups were called Total Involvement Teams.

The results were dramatic. An annual savings of $357,500—from a 72 percent increase in productivity—was the direct result. Examples of results from several suggestions:

▶ A team from the Life Department reviewed the eight major workflows of that department. Procedures were developed that reduced the total processing or turnaround time for each of these workflows. In some instances, the reduction was as much as 15 days.

▶ Following a suggestion from one team, most processing units in the firm now receive their first mail delivery from the mailroom two hours earlier than before.

▶ A team from the Cashiering Department made several recommendations that are being incorporated into an extensive revision of Cal-Farm's installment billing system. These proposals include major data processing enhancements, revisions of forms, elimination of some manual record keeping, and several other short-term and long-range procedural changes.

When the results of the Quality Commitment program were thoroughly analyzed after a year's experience, several critical elements were identified. "The managers who did not understand or who did not believe in the approach did not manage the program. Thus the employees in those areas fulfilled their managers' fears and used the team meetings as grievance sessions. Also, the team members did not realize the impact that workflow changes would have on other departments. Nor did they have any knowledge of how difficult implementation of major changes could be. Finally, there was a lack of expertise in the teams concerning simple methods-and-procedures knowledge. Without their manager's support, implementation could not be accomplished."

The first change that resulted from this analysis was to get the manager involved. Quality circles are not imposed on managers; they are offered as tools. When a manager receives an assignment, that person may choose to use the quality circle program for completion of the task. If this approach is chosen, then the manager has a vested interest in making it work. In addition, each team was given an operations analyst to facilitate the team's work. The analysts are trained in the techniques of methods analysis, work simplification, and work measurement in order to guide the group to more effective results.

Figure 2   One company's experience with an adaptation of the quality circle approach. *Source:* "Quality Circles Program Reaps a $350,000 Harvest," *Modern Office Procedures,* August, 1982, pp. 54–58.

The diagram below illustrates how a more formal approach, which everyone understands, is now being used for the study of a particular department's workflows and procedures.

DEPARTMENT MANAGEMENT

1. Makes assignment & establishes schedule

OPERATIONS ANALYST

2. Receives & outlines assignment

6. Accepts, rejects or modifies recommendation

QUALITY CIRCLE

5. Presents recommendation

QUALITY CIRCLE

3. Researches problem & alternative solutions

4. Selects & documents best solution

Source: "Quality Circles Program Reaps A $350,000 Harvest," *Modern Office Procedures,* August, 1982, pp. 54–58.

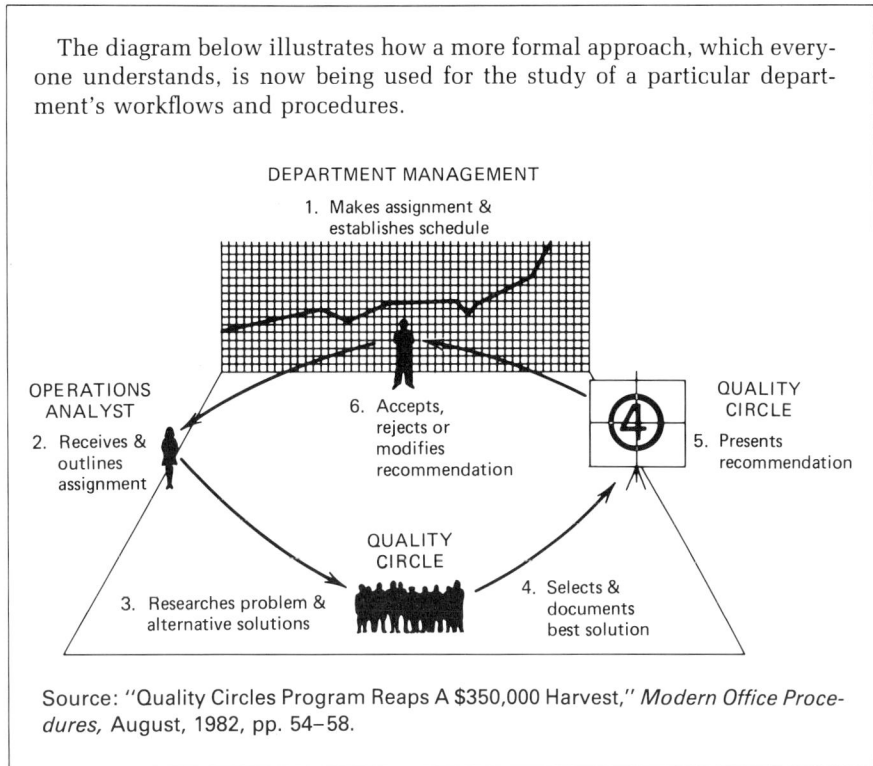

Figure 2 (*Continued*)

Blake, there are many limitations inherent in both approaches, particularly when employees already have a negative attitude toward management and the company. They suggest that "many discussions may be gripe sessions, not sessions in which constructive thinking is done about how to advance productivity." Beyond that, many employees wait for implementation of suggestions that may not be practical, given the cost and the budget available for them. When nothing happens, the old attitudes reappear, often expressed by "See, we told them, but they don't give a damn. Why should we try to be productive when they don't care?" Participative forms of management are inevitable parts of change, but they must be implemented cautiously and wisely. Without question, the key factor in the success or failure of any of the approaches to increasing productivity is the manner in which they are handled by management.

Each of the participative techniques offers employees opportunities for continuing growth and development, but in different ways. Job enrichment affects employees personally on a day-to-day level. The use of MBO provides a means for seeing and evaluating progress made. Both the QWL and QC approaches provide for increased communication, which, as discussed, may be positive or negative, depending upon the circumstances.

CAREER PROGRESSION AND PATHS

Employees will be more highly motivated (especially those who are ambitious) if they can see stepping stones to advancement available to them within the organization. Organizations need to develop well-structured career paths, or ladders of advancement. The ladder is made up of jobs ranging from those that require basic skills to those that require advanced skills. The jobs should be placed on the career path ladder according to the value of the job to the organization.

There are two primary types of career paths: lateral (horizontal) and vertical. Lateral career paths move horizontally, allowing employees who either do not have managerial qualifications or who do not wish to work in managerial positions to move on to jobs that are on the same level as the positions they formerly held. For example, a word processing operator who specializes only in correspondence may move to another correspondence position in another area, such as Personnel or the Legal Department (see Figure 3).

Vertical career paths lead upward to positions of increased responsibility, and on to managerial positions. A vertical career path within an organization may be similar to the one shown in Figure 4. Vertical career paths provide increasing responsibility as the employee moves upward. Usually, vertical career paths also provide for higher pay as one progresses upward.

Career progression is a key factor to individual success. According to one survey, about 80 percent of administrative personnel started their

Figure 3 Horizontal career path allows an employee who does not wish to move upward in an organization to move to similar type work in another area.

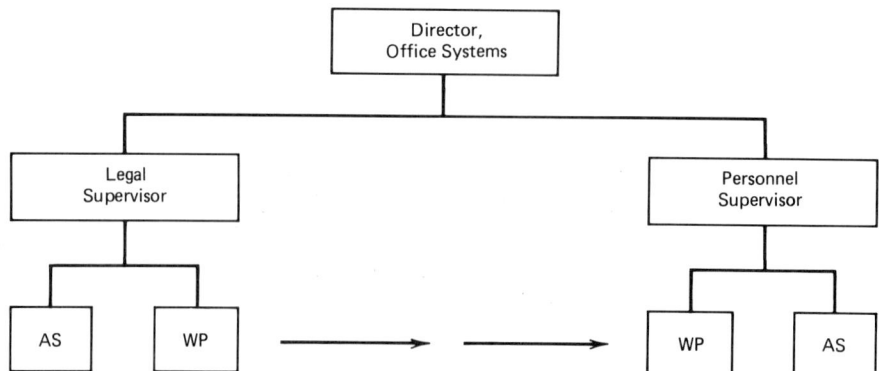

Administrative Services (07200)
(See 7-A)

Director
531 (1)

Senior secretary
94 (1)

Word Processing (07211)

Manager
536 (1)

Technical Support (07221)

Manager
537 (1)

Section head corres. support
1109 (1)

Section head management support
448 (1)

Section head text processing
446 (1)

Word process. technical analyst
573 (3)

Lead word process. specialist
438 (1)

Confidential word process. specialist
364 (3)

Lead word process. specialist
438 (1)

Jr. word process. technical analyst
642 (-)

Senior word process. specialist
357 (9)

Senior word process. specialist
357 (8)

Senior word process. support oper.
410 (1)

Word process. specialist
355 (-)

Word process. specialist
355 (-)

Word process. support oper.
405 (2)

	Jobs	Complement
Admin. services gen.	2	2
Word processing	8	26
Technical support	5	7

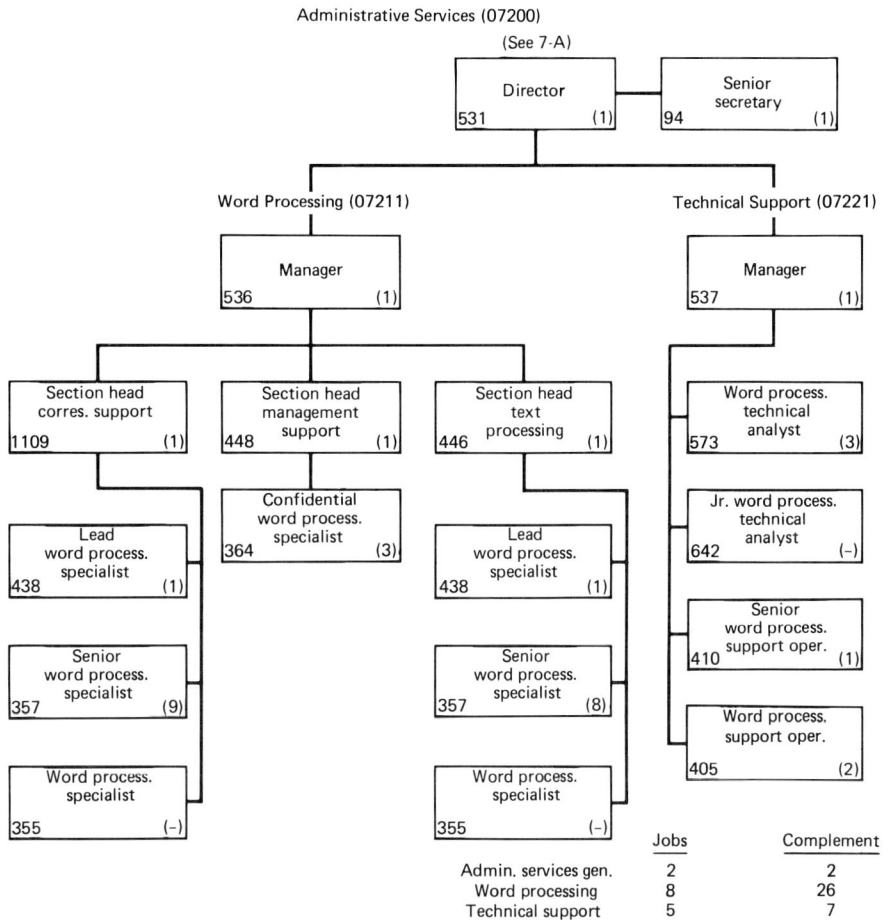

Figure 4 Vertical career path provides an opportunity for upward mobility. (Courtesy of Western-Southern Life, Cincinnati, Ohio.)

careers with their respective companies at a lower level than the supervisory and climbed the ladder to supervisory jobs.[8] A 10-year study done by Alfred Swinyard and Floyd Bond, in attempting to identify the characteristics of this new—and younger—breed of manager, made these observations about people who got promoted.

▶ New entrants into the ranks of U.S. top management are better educated than were their predecessors.

[8] Alfred Swinyard and Floyd Bond, "Who Gets Promoted?," *Harvard Business Review*, September/October 1980, p. 6.

▶ The largest percentage of advanced degrees are held in business administration, with law and engineering the next most prevalent.

▶ Newly promoted executives are not likely to be any younger than their predecessors were when they made the grade.

▶ Those who become president of an organization usually come from a group of vice-presidents. They will probably have been chosen from within the company and will not have spent more than four years at their current position.

▶ Top executives now tend to be more mobile, because of changes in promotional patterns across the country.

A company can be very successful in recruiting and keeping talented people by assuring periodic review and being able to demonstrate an established career progression.

WP and AS structures have provided better career definitions, salary increases, and advancement opportunity. For example, a secretary in the Real Estate Department of a Midwest corporation of 400 employees became a word processing specialist in an automated office implementation plan. After two years, she progressed to word processing supervisor and then to a manager's position in the office structure (see Figure 5). Also, a secretary to a vice-president of a *Fortune 500* company became a coordi-

Figure 5 Many employees are looking for career advancement and upward mobility in the automated office.

nator of a word processing center, then a supervisor of word processing, and presently serves as a word processing consultant in the MIS Department. These examples illustrate the potential benefits of developing and communicating established career progression charts, making periodic evaluations, and meeting competency levels and standards.

THE RELATIONSHIP BETWEEN
ORGANIZATIONAL GOALS AND EMPLOYEE GOALS

In order for any management-training and career-path progression to work, managers must recognize that there must be a link between the organizational goals and the individual's goals. Francis Dinsmore's book *Developing Tomorrow's Managers Today* illustrates this concept[9] by examining the "four *R*s of performance" that must be met in order to guarantee a match-up between the individual and the organization. To combine individual needs with organizational needs, one needs to examine results, responsibilities, resources, and requisites.

Results stem from good performance. For the individual managers, the desired results include moving the business ahead, developing those under them, and advancing themselves up the corporate ladder. The organization, by contrast, desires profit, growth, and perpetuation. Maximization of individual results, in this case, can lead to the attainment of organizational results. With developed, satisfied managers, the organization cannot help but grow and develop itself. The combination of the two concepts' individual results and organizational results is a simple one.

Responsibility, by contrast, is not so easy to integrate. *Responsibilities* comprise the manner in which adequate performance is achieved. The responsibilities that guarantee an organization's survival are leadership, authority, and controls. By contrast, the responsibilities of the individual are initiating, influencing, and administering his or her part of the organization. Clearly, the two responsibility areas can conflict, since executives who are initiating without adequate control or authority may threaten the life or operation of the entire organization. Similarly, if the organization will not delegate authority and control to individuals, it may lose its most qualified people. The way to merge these two areas is to ensure that individual growth and career progression are provided within the organizational structure, without the organization losing total control over its future. The organization needs to realize that only by allowing sufficient

---

[9] Francis W. Dinsmore, *Developing Tomorrow's Managers Today* (New York: AMACOM, 1975), pp. 48–71.

growth and freedom to its managers can it grow. By the same token, the managers cannot abuse the trust that the organization bestows on them. If the goals of the organization can become the goals of the individual (if the individual is "sold" on the organization), then the merger between the two can be successful.

The *resources* of the manager and the organization might be viewed as the basic sources of power for the exercise of responsibilities and the achievement of results. Of the many skills and abilities that fall into this category, the most important are those resources that are directly related to responsibilities and results and that can be expanded and improved. Thus, the most fundamental resources of the manager are knowledge, imagination, and ability to reason. Knowledge includes knowledge of the job, of the business, and of people. Imagination means creative thinking in terms of what is, what can be, and what should be. An ability to reason guarantees a synthesis of ideas and organization.

The basic resources of the organization are the procedures, policies, and principles that have been developed out of experience and that, when properly utilized, can help managers to do a better job. In order to integrate the resources of the manager with those of the organization, the organization has to ensure that its principles include employee growth and development. Procedures and policies also need to be updated to keep up with changing conditions. In addition, managers must be required to use their knowledge, skill, and reason in their work to guarantee advancement. To a great extent, the resources of the organization grow out of the resources of the individual.

Finally, *requisites* are fundamental factors that can be controlled and measured. An individual's requisites would appear to be money, status, and opportunity. The organization's requisites are hiring, firing, and retaining. Individual and organizational requisites are related, since and organization that can hire and fire effectively will guarantee successful managers. Similarly, managers will feel that their position is safe if they are provided adequate pay, security, and status. Integration of the four *R*s into the relationship between individual employees and the organization will go a long way toward guaranteeing a smooth-running operation.

ROLE OF GROUPS IN THE MODERN OFFICE

In *Productivity: The Human Side*, Blake and Mouton outlined the importance of groups in the office environment.[10] Group values are based on norms—that is, on any uniformity of attitude, opinion, feeling, or action

[10] Blake and Mouton, *Productivity*, pp. 18–75.

shared by two or more people. Groups are characterized by the norms that their members share. For all practical purposes, a group cannot be a group if it lacks norms to regulate and coordinate interactions among members; there would be no basis for coordination or cooperation without these norms. If norms were absent, we might refer to the individuals who are physically assembled in the same place as an aggregate rather than a group.

Some of the obvious norms that exist in the workplace are related to how people at various levels dress, when coffee breaks are taken and for how long, and whether managers leave the office with a briefcase. These examples indicate how the term *norm* is being used: to describe regularities in behavior that characterize two or more members of a group. Even though we talk about our personal attitudes fairly freely as we go about our daily activities, we are responding to group-centered norms far more often than we realize.

Norms regulate much of our lives—our personal and familial interactions, our careers, and even our recreation and leisure habits. These kinds of norms, therefore, often regulate our productivity behavior.

Not all norms promote desirable activity. A norm may be effective at an early stage and later become outmoded as a basis for interpreting behavior or interrelating to others. When this process occurs, the norm keeps us engaged in activities that have become irrelevant or even damaging.

For example, a manager may state as a norm, "We will always use one-to-one manager-to-secretary ratios in this office," and explain that norm by saying, "We've always done it that way." But the one-to-one ratio may be an outmoded tradition, as evidenced by the fact that other organizations have changed their organizational structures to take advantage of innovative technology. A more responsive approach to management may necessitate a change in this basic past practice, with the pleasant result of improved productivity in the office. The key to whether a normative system is sound and effective is its ability to meet current requirements for increased turnaround of work product and improved productivity.

The existence of a norm—and the attitude that flows from it—is therefore highly significant. It can lead to heightened productivity or restricted output, to prompt or tortuously slow decision making, to the exploitation or the missing of opportunities, to the stifling or the stimulating of creativity. Because norms are so important, we need to understand how they operate in a group.

The first aspect of group norms is the idea of *convergence*. Convergence occurs whenever there is little or no prior basis for reacting to a phenomenon and expressing reactions to it. Although personal reactions vary widely at first, as experience increases reactions tend to come together—that is, to converge on a common point. Through this process, people come to share a similar perspective. Social reality has been created through this process of convergence; and this coming together around a single set of attitudes, opinions, feelings or actions constitutes a norm.

Convergence plays a significant role in organizational life and thus merits comment. Suppose that two young people at the beginning of their careers join a company, one as a management trainee and the other as a manual worker. Neither knows very much about business, and when it comes to an attitude toward profit and profitability, neither has much of an opinion either way.

As the person who joins management acquires experience, he or she comes to develop a positive attitude toward profit and profitability and can give sound reasons for that attitude, such as "without profit there would be no incentive." If you ask this person where the attitude came from, the response would be, "Well, I more or less thought this thing out by myself." If you ask whether the job as a member of management had anything to do with the person's attitude, he or she likely would respond, "Probably not."

Based on the research presented up to this point, we would surmise that the management trainee has been influenced by his or her managerial colleagues, and that the opinion expressed resulted from the trainee's convergence to the management group norm relating to profitability.

Now, let us track the employee who became a manual worker. In time, the employee joins the union and becomes an officer in it. If we probe his or her attitudes and opinions on the same question, the union officer might say, "Profit is fine, as long as the workers share in it." If we were to ask this person where he or she got this idea, the response would no doubt be, "I came up with it myself."

These two examples indicate the phenomenon of convergence. In each case, the final attitude around which convergence occurs depends on the norms of the group within which the person holds membership. We know less about convergence than we should, because it is a phenomenon that happens quickly when attention is focused elsewhere. Once it has occurred, it seems so natural that people cannot and will not admit to its existence.

A second phenomenon associated with groups is *cohesion*. People tend not to like others whose ideas, attitudes, opinions, feelings, and actions differ significantly from their own. The result is that in everyday life a person comes to spend more time with those who think that same way and to spend less time with people who are significantly different. Voluntary groups form around people who share the same or approximately the same attitudes, opinions, feelings, and actions—and this phenomenon is called cohesion.

Cohesion exerts a powerful influence in organizational life, because, as studies have shown, the more attractive the group is to the individual, the greater the influence the group is able to exert on that person. Recognizing that we like those who agree with us helps us to understand organizational life. For example, in promotion and advancement, bosses tend to like subordinates who share their outlook.

Just as people develop feelings toward one another, they also develop feelings toward the organization; they can either be positive about the organization or negative. Given these opposite feelings, it follows that the person who experiences positive feelings toward the organization accepts the norms and values of the organization and that the converse is true for those who have a negative view toward the organization.

A third phenomenon within a group is *conformity*, the tendency to behave and express opinions consistent with group norms—that is, to comply with group attitudes and expectations. Peer pressure on fellow workers, management pressure on workers, and union pressure on management are all examples of pressure to conform to a given viewpoint.

A final phenomenon that must be discussed in relation to groups is the role of primary and reference groups. *Primary groups* are the face-to-face membership group in which people know the norms that govern the conduct of each member. Primary group members are frequently in contact with one another and stand ready to enforce norms. An example of the primary group is the family.

A *reference group* is any recognizable organization that in itself can be characterized as having norms and standards. A reference group is unlikely to bring all its members together to meet face to face as a single entity, though members may be in contact with one another. All a person needs to be a part of a reference group is a feeling of pull or positive emotions toward the group. One such group would be the student body at a small college.

In organizational terms, most workers see their organization as a reference group. For example, if a company has established a tradition of fair dealings with customers, all its employees are guided by this tradition and will tend to deal fairly with the public. The same is true for organizations known for slippery dealings.

The most important effects introduced above with respect to reference and primary groups include the following phenomena:

1. When two or more people gather and share their thoughts, feelings, attitudes, and actions, their viewpoints tend to converge. Once such convergence occurs, it takes on the character of a norm.

2. When a norm has been established, group members feel the need to conform to it.

3. Any indication that a member is departing from a norm is likely to cause others to exercise pressure to bring that member back into line.

4. The member who persists in deviating from a norm runs the risk of isolation and rejection.

5. Since norms are widespread, they have a significant controlling effect on what people in organizations do and do not do. This influence is exerted independently of what bosses may direct or expect.

6. Even though norms may become outmoded or out of tune with what is needed, they continue to control individuals.

One can see that groups exert a powerful influence within organizations. The way that groups look at continuing development and career progression will help to determine what kind of steps a company must take to ensure both. For example, if a work group is negative toward members going back to school or getting advanced training, the organization may have to provide greater incentives to stimulate interest in continuing growth. By contrast, if a work group encourages individual growth and development, then implementation of a career progression chart or development program will be aided by group efforts.

EMPLOYEE EVALUATION

Performance evaluation of employees used to have a negative connotation attached to it. In the modern office, however, employee evaluations conducted in a positive, constructive manner can help employee performance and spur overall productivity. Employee evaluations are based on a form of measurement for determining the level of employee performance on the job. Measurement tools can include forms, interviews, observation, tests, or supervisory opinions.

One way to evaluate activities is to use a measurement form listing the factors that make up an employee's job along with performance level descriptions such as "excellent," "satisfactory," or "needs improvement." The first factor evaluated should be the basic, operational, functional knowledge of the job itself and of the equipment used.

Then comes evaluation of the employee's proficiency in routine applications and tasks. This step attempts to evaluate how well employees perform routine jobs in their office environment: for example, message taking, photocopying, and receptionist duties, for clerical support positions.

A final factor might be an evaluation of the employee's creativity in developing new concepts and applications within their job descriptions. This area of evaluation is more subjective than the other areas and may involve opinions on the part of supervisors. Nevertheless, the three areas always should be combined for a final evaluation conclusion.

Another way of conducting evaluations of employees is to break a job description down into its various work elements and to evaluate an employee by elements such as quantity of work, quality of work, work compiled on time, relevant creativity, recognition by others for advancement, personal habits (appearance, tardiness, absenteeism, punctuality), and support of the group's effort (teamwork). By being able to break down a given position into its various work demands, an evaluator can set clear and fair objectives to be achieved within a given period of time. In addition, use of this process makes it easier to include the employees in the process of breaking down and setting work performance standards for each work task (that is, in developing objectives and applying the MBO system). As Figures 6 and 7 indicate, each responsibility is described by clear objectives, and then an employee's actual performance is measured on a scale of achievement.

The advantages of using this approach are that employees become constantly aware of their progress, they know their place in the organization, and they can set their personal and professional career plans more easily. It also provides a vehicle to determine the need for further training or education. This concept of employee evaluation is similar to the one employed in MBO theory.

MBO concepts and open evaluations with give and take provide an opportunity for the staff to participate in their organization, as well as for behavioral growth. Growth for some people may mean continuing education; for others, it may mean advanced training; for yet others, it may mean promotion and a consequent redirection of efforts.

Career growth plans vary considerably from company to company according to company philosophy and the perspective of the Personnel or Human Resources Department. Note the differences in the direction established in the two plans illustrated in Figures 8 (traditional structure) and 9 (matrix reporting structure).

SELF-EVALUATION AND SELF-DEVELOPMENT

By encouraging self-evaluation and self-development of employees, a company can help to assure a contented staff and help employees to decide whether a career with that company is what they truly want. Goals are the motivators of action. Without clearly defined goals, the individual will drift and the company may lose a talented employee. To identify and implement a constant formal self-evaluation process and a self-development plan, you must follow several steps. Larry Nelson of Measurable Performance Systems recommends the following 12-step process:[11]

Step One   Ask yourself what you would like to see happen in your life in the next year or so. Write it down. List tangibles and intangibles as well as career and personal items.

[11] Larry Nelsen, "Career and Personal Goal Setting: The Key to Happiness and Success," *The Word*, April 1981, p. 26.

			Level of Achievement				

PERFORMANCE EVALUATION

Name _____

Title _____ Records Clerk _____

1 = unacceptable; on notice
2 = marginal; must improve
3 = acceptable; improvement expected
4 = good
5 = excellent

Responsibility	Objective	Actual Achievements	Level of Achievement				
			1	2	3	4	5
Records maintenance	Sorts, indexes, and files records independently, with minimal instructions; retrieves all types of records; enters data on records as instructed; searches and investigates information in files on request; classifies received materials and records independently whenever possible; transfers records and disposes of records according to printed retention schedules						
Work organization	Organizes own workstation, work method, and work procedures, enabling complete coordination						
Special projects	Accomplish projects and reports on time with little direction from the records center supervisor						
Judgement	Creates original ideas; avoids preconceived ideas; communicates well; makes sound decisions; adapts well to changing situations.						
Personal	Pleasant manner and appearance; good attitude displayed in office; works well with others; accepts guidance						

Summary

1. Employee strengths:

2. Significant accomplishments:

3. Areas of improvement

4. Plan for accomplishing improvement

5. Employee career interests:

6. Employee interview comments:

Interviewer comments:

Review agreed upon _____
            (date)

_____

Signed _____
         (Employee)

_____

Overall rating _____

Figure 6 Performance plan—records clerk. Setting objectives and establishing productivity guidelines are important for full employee understanding of an employer's expectations.

			Level of Achievement				
PERFORMANCE EVALUATION		1 = unacceptable; on notice 2 = marginal; must improve 3 = acceptable; improvement expected 4 = good 5 = excellent					
Name _____ Title _Administrative Secretary_							

Responsibility	Objective	Actual Achievements	1	2	3	4	5
Mail	Distributes promptly and correctly; handles mail to completion without instructions, whenever possible.						
Filing	Files correctly; locates documents rapidly; updates files regularly.						
Telephone	Handles calls correctly and pleasantly; handles calls to completion without instructions, whenever possible.						
Work coordination	Works with WP Center to meet priorities; proofreads for manager(s) signature.						
Work organization	Organizes workstation, work methods, and work procedures, enabling complete coordination with all managers on a timely basis and in an orderly manner.						
Special projects	Accomplishes projects and reports on time, with little direction from manager(s)						
Judgement	Creates original ideas; avoids preconceived ideas; communicates well; makes sound decisions; adapts well to changing situations.						
Personal	Pleasant manner and appearance; good attitude in office; works well with others; good working relationship with manager; accepts guidance; keeps emotional interests from influencing work						

Summary

1. Employee strengths:

2. Significant accomplishments:

3. Areas of improvement

4. Plan for accomplishing improvement

5. Employee career interests:

6. Employee interview comments:

Review agreed upon _____
                              (date)

Signed _____
              (Employee)

Interviewer comments:

_____

_____

_____

Overall rating _____

Figure 7 Performance plan—administrative secretary.

Company ABC

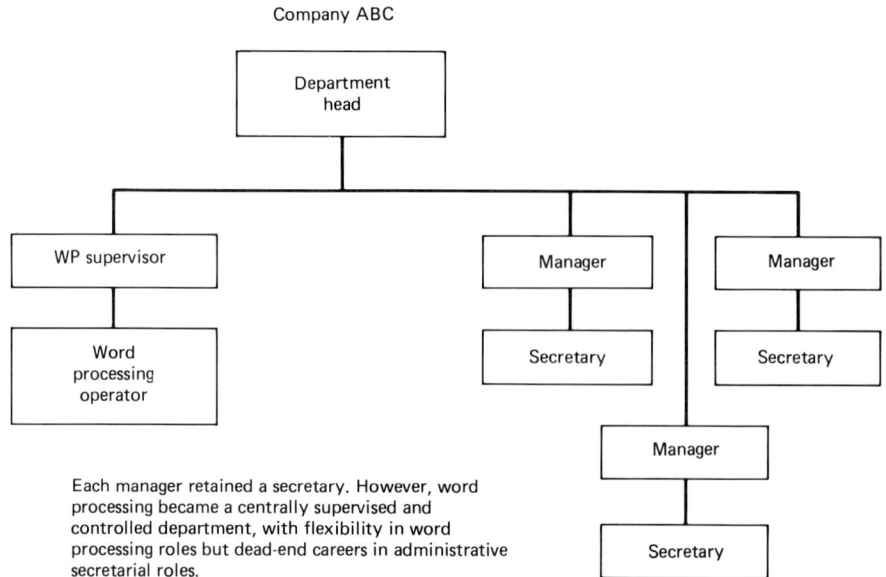

Each manager retained a secretary. However, word
processing became a centrally supervised and
controlled department, with flexibility in word
processing roles but dead-end careers in administrative
secretarial roles.

Figure 8 Traditional structure. Each manager retained a secretary. However,
word processing became a centrally supervised and controlled department with
flexibility within word processing but dead-ended careers in administrative
secretarial roles.

Step Two   Go through your list. Try to picture how you would like
to appear to others and to yourself one year from today.
Expand on the ideas you have written down in step one.
With each idea, ask yourself why. Identify each goal's
importance and explain why it is important to you. Be
totally honest with yourself.

Step Three   As you consider your list again, keep two things in mind.
First, your goals must be in harmony; when you see a
conflict, cross out the less important goal. Second, if you
see a goal that is not within your potential or is not
realistic, cross it out, too. You are the one who can best
gauge your potential. Reach as far as you can without
overstepping.

Step Four   As you study your list again, pick out three to five goals
that you would like to work on in the next year. Two
should be tangible goals and two should be intangible
goals. Keep the remaining list; it will serve as a good
replacement list as you accomplish your other five.

Step Five   Now you are ready to make a positive statement about
yourself, incorporating your goals. Write your goals on a

Company XYZ

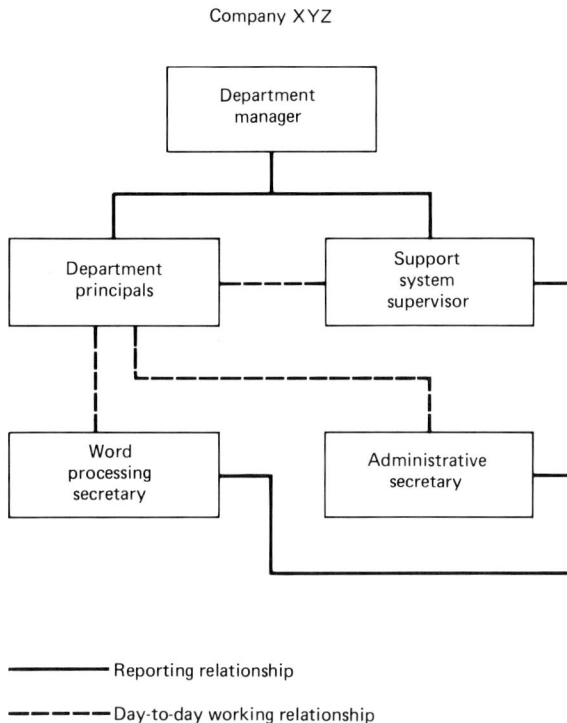

——————— Reporting relationship

— — — — —Day-to-day working relationship

Central control of all support staff for more equity in approach
and more flexibility in career growth.

Figure 9 Matrix structure. Central control of all support staff for more equity in approach and more flexibility in career growth.

	piece of paper in a positive, factual manner. Read this list to yourself first thing each morning and last thing in the evening.
Step Six	Decide when you will accomplish the goal statement—and be specific. Set a realistic date on your calendar.
Step Seven	Now that you have chosen your major goals, make a list of the priorities that will help you accomplish your goals. Then rate each priority in terms of its importance: *A* if it must be done immediately, *B* if it is a near- or short-term priority, and *C* if it is a long-term project.
Step Eight	Decide on the steps you are going to take and develop a plan. In order to achieve even a short-term goal, you must be prepared to give something up, to pay a price for achievement.

Step Nine   Next, develop a timetable. Break your plan down into management stages. Record your plan on your calendar. Then ask yourself, What else can I do? Who else can help me to attain this goal?

Step Ten   This is the time to be realistic. What factors are there that might interfere with the attainment of your goal. Ask yourself which problems you can simply dismiss as of no importance and which others you will have to handle. Plan how you will handle them.

Step Eleven   Follow through with your plan, and begin to do so immediately. If you do not, you will lose steam.

Step Twelve   Most important, establish a small group of two or more friends whose thinking is compatible with your own. Sit down with them regularly to think together and talk.

Informal self-evaluation involves constant review of where one is, where one is going, and how one will get there—in other words, how well self-development is proceeding. The informal self-evaluation method outlined above is less formal and rigid than a measurable performance scale or a system used to evaluate actual performance on the job. However, it is an integral part of an employee's success. Challenging an employee during the evaluation period to pursue self-evaluation and self-correction is an integral part of an employee's success and is the obligation of any good supervisor. A self-development plan should be encouraged by the supervisor. However, employees must understand that the pursuit of a self-development program is each individual's responsibility.

Ongoing education and continuing development can be achieved through industry seminars and trade association meetings as well as college and university courses of a specialized nature. Regardless of the method selected, what is most important is that the automated office should encourage and provide such continuing growth and development to its employees. The result will be improved productivity and morale.

CHAPTER 22

PRODUCTIVITY: MEASURING, REPORTING, AND BUDGETING

OBJECTIVES

In this chapter you will learn about
1. Measuring productivity.
2. Objectives of work measurement.
3. Techniques used in data collection.
4. Applying productivity guidelines and standards to workload.
5. Reporting productivity to management.
6. Budgeting alternatives—traditional and zero-based.

Joseph Quick, retired chairman of Science Management Corporation, suggests that responsibility for the decline in U.S. productivity rests with management, and calls upon management to make the same sort of investment in improving productivity that it has made in marketing and technology.

Productivity can be defined as the power to produce. In office parlance, it is making the best use of an employee's time to produce work with greatest effectiveness and efficiency. In this chapter, we will discuss how to determine productivity through work measurement, apply productivity guidelines and standards to workloads, report productivity to management, and budget for continued productivity.

MEASURING PRODUCTIVITY

Management readily realizes the value of committing the time, effort, and personnel to develop ways to improve productivity of both management and support staff. Investment in technology for the office becomes increasingly important when the productivity gains can be measured in tangible terms such as units produced, time saved, money saved, quality, accuracy, and turnaround time. Therefore, it is necessary to establish benchmarks for measurement and then to measure productivity on a regular basis.

APPLYING PRODUCTIVITY GUIDELINES The increasing use of word processing and data processing has brought about a need for ongoing cost justification and productivity measurement. Those measurements tell management that the system is producing what is expected and that the system continues to deliver savings or other previously projected benefits. Adequate measurement standards help determine how well a system is performing. In addition, *work measurement* determines the extent of progress and improvement in work or a work group by comparing what was done to what should be done. More basically, it compares actual production or effort to a standard.

A *standard* is any agreed-upon rule against which comparison can be made; it is usually determined by management or an authority. Standards include objective units of measure such as quantity, weight, and extent of usage, and subjective factors such as quality. Standards should minimize subjective judgment and provide practical, objective gauges of employee and company performance.

Work activities can be measured in a variety of ways, ranging from a simple observation, such as counting pieces of paper, to complex studies and data collection. The form of measurement used depends on the needs and resources of the organization.[1]

---

[1] The bulk of the information and the sample forms is taken from *Management Support Work Measurement and Standards Manual*, Mary M. Ruprecht and Associates, Inc., 1979.

Other methods of productivity measurement include the logging of time and production counts. To gather this information, one needs to do some type of study.

Electronic counting devices and software programs connected to or installed in equipment provide methods for measurement of production, workload controls, workload distribution, and charge-backs. Some organizations use *line counters*, which count lines, and *keystroke counters*, which count how many keystrokes are produced on input devices. All these methods provide quantitative results for evaluating productivity immediately.

Although their duties are extremely varied, administrative support personnel (secretarial/clerical workers who do not type) should be measured for efficiency of time use. Several types of measurement commonly are used in this area, including "time ladders" the "best estimate" approach, or timekeeping in tenths of hours or minutes, which provides a complete breakdown on how time is spent. These measures indicate how efficiently administrative support personnel use their time.

The collected data provides managers with the facts needed to alter work assignments, redistribute workloads, correct problems, and justify addition or reduction in support personnel. Whatever the selected form, one thing is certain: companies will continue to measure employee productivity. Only with a knowledge of present volumes of work can a firm appropriately plan for the future.

OBJECTIVES OF WORK MEASUREMENT

Consciously or not, most people measure everything they do against some form of standard. In the office, standards are set up for dozens of duties, such as typing words per minute, the time it takes to schedule meetings, the time it takes to proofread a page, and so on. It is important for established standards to be accurate and truly reflect a "fair day's work." Again, the objective of work measurement is to determine the worker's performance by measuring performance against the established standard.

Other objectives of work measurement can include using the results to

1. Plan and schedule work more effectively.
2. Improve the forecasting of manpower requirements.
3. Determine the most economic work methods.
4. Determine proper work assignments.
5. Determine the time and cost of work to be performed and the selection of employees to perform it.
6. Determine an employee's worth to the company.

By accomplishing the above objectives, management gains information with which to make better decisions. Such improved decisions ultimately result in lower costs for word processing or any office operation.

CREATING A WORK MEASUREMENT SYSTEM

The development of an effective work measurement system involves two basic steps: (1) creating standards and (2) creating the techniques to measure productivity against those standards. Two different ways to create these standards are through measurement of time and of work.

TIME STANDARDS   Time standards can come from a source outside the firm, such as a management consultant, or can be developed as a result of internal study. Regardless of how a *standard* is developed, it is defined as the amount of work that should be done under specified conditions and methods. It provides the basis for evaluating performance.

A standard is usually considered to be the amount of production considered fair to both the company and the employee for a specified period of time under specified conditions.

Written instructions found in a procedures manual, outlining the method of performing work, provide a valuable guide in establishing work standards. Such documentation also aids in the changing of standards when methods are revised (e.g., through a change in equipment or in job description). When substandard performance is detected through the use of standards, the reasons can be determined. Changes in procedures should reflect back to the standards, if necessary.

In word processing, a number of standards affect the "allowed time" for performing work, including such factors as the nature, length, and format of text typed; the dictation and typing machine used; the procedures and related tasks required of the employee to complete the job; the quality and nature of input of text; and quality standards for output. Any time the system or operation changes, it is important for the standards to change also. If they do not change, they rapidly become useless.

WORK STANDARDS   Three work measurement approaches are used in the modern office—the subjective, statistical, and engineering approaches. Each has its place, depending on the precision needed and the stage of development of work measurement programs in the company. The subjective approach is less accurate than the statistical and engineering approaches.

The most reliable approach is the statistical approach, which is explored extensively in this chapter. The engineering approach involves more precision and is often considered an extension of the statistical approach.

Subjective Approach   The subjective approach can include rule-of-thumb standards based on the experiences and opinions of individual supervisors. Sometimes such standards are fairly accurate, but supervisors readily admit that production goals developed by this method are not factually supported or justified. Probably the most serious disadvantage of this method is that the judgment of supervisors can vary widely. If a company opts to use the subjective or "guesstimate" approach, it must recognize that actual production records may differ substantially from the rule-of-thumb standards established.

Statistical   The statistical approach can use one or all of three methods: historical
Approach   data, work sampling, and time studies. *Historical data* involves the gathering of information from past records about the time and the amount of work needed for a certain job. Some companies use this information to establish standards, realizing that the results express what was done rather than what should be done. This method does not establish what the production standard should be. Since it is only a tally of current conditions, it only lays the groundwork for setting standards. In setting standards from past data, one must collect an array of average times for a given task (such as typing from hard copy). To arrive at the standard unit time, you can use one of the following approaches: (1) from the entire array of unit time, select the one that in your opinion is most reasonable to attain; (2) select the median time; (3) from the upper quartile of time, select the one you consider most reasonable to attain. Each of these methods involves an attempt to establish the goal for a qualified employee working continuously and consistently at a normal pace.

The second method of collecting data is *work sampling*. This involves observing work at random periods or gathering copies of work to determine the amount of work accomplished in a sample period. This method does not always provide an accurate representation of the conditions affecting work or the methods used to accomplish work. The important thing to remember is that measurement is a process used to determine what is possible to achieve and not what is being done. Lines are the most universal form of measurement in word processing, since pages, words, and forms can be converted to lines. Some equipment offers an option feature that automatically counts words or keystrokes, which can be converted to lines of production.

In the electronic office, automated work-measurement data will be electronically transmitted to a common collection point. Until that time, we must continue to measure in words or lines.

The third method of collecting statistical data is through *time studies*. This is the oldest technique of work measurement. Standards derived from this method are more accurate than the ones derived from historical data and easier to develop than the ones from the engineering approach. Generally, an individual job or operation is analyzed or reduced to individual tasks. These tasks are then timed to determine the average length of time per task.

Engineering   A third approach is the *engineering approach*. Standards established by this method involve greater precision in development of measurements. The engineering approach can be considered an extension of the statistical approach. In many cases, the two approaches complement each other. In the development of engineered standards, an individual job or operation generally is analyzed in detail, to reduce it to its vital parts. The individual work elements or tasks are then identified and studied for possible elimination or combination with others. In addition, equipment, machines, workplace layout, and workflow are standardized. After standardization, additional analyses are made to establish the standard time for the work elements of the job or operation. These times can be determined by using standard elemental times to measure time and motion (MTM) or predetermined times provided by an outside source.

MTM standards are used successfully in many office operations. Basically, predetermined times can be applied to approximately 95 percent of all office work. They are generally administered by experts who apply time measurement units (tmu) to each singular movement or task. A *tmu* is equivalent to 0.00001 hours, or 0.036 seconds. The base times are derived from MTM tables for the work elements. They are then altered to allow for the personal needs of an operator and justifiable work contingencies, to establish the final unit standard.

When can one use these highly refined engineering standards? The answer to that question usually depends upon whether the expense of refined standards is warranted. Although these standards provide closer control of operations to obtain optimum production output per man hour, they usually are not cost-justifiable unless repetitive tasks are performed hundreds of times a day. When it is advisable to develop engineered standards, cost reductions will generally result from increased production.

To make the job of creating standards easier, some basic guidelines should be followed. First, the persons attempting to establish standards should provide a fairly even and consistent flow of work. In addition, they should try to reduce the amount of judgment required in doing a task, by standardizing the method or by presenting the employee with a pattern of choices as to how to accomplish that task. Standards should make it possible for the supervisor to establish priorities and schedule times for the completion of work assigned to employees. Most importantly, persons conducting the work measurement study should make sure that the size, repetitiveness, and volume of a job justify the expense of such a study.

WORK COUNT UNIT STANDARDS   The important facets of work count unit measurement are to define specifically what the work count unit is and then to describe accurately the types of work to be measured. This description should include such variables as the way that input and output of work occurs and the activity performed.

The unit of measurement, or *work count unit*, is a standardized predefined specific quantity such as a character, a line, a page, or a document. For example, the standards shown below define a character as one keystroke on a typewriter (i.e., one letter, number, or punctuation mark).

WORD: 5 characters per word

LINE: 10–12 words per line
56–65 characters per line

PAGE: 8½ × 11 = 30–33 lines double-spaced
8½ × 11 = 55–66 lines single-spaced
8½ × 14 = 45–55 lines double-spaced
8½ × 14 = 75–80 lines single-spaced

A word is defined as five characters. A line is 10 to 12 words with a total of between 56 and 65 characters per line. An 8½-by-11-inch page should contain between 30 and 33 lines double-spaced, and 55 to 66 lines single-spaced. An 8½-by-14-inch page should contain 45 to 55 lines double-spaced and 75 to 80 lines single-spaced.

The most important step in work unit measurement is to make sure that everyone understands exactly what the unit of measurement (e.g., character, line, page) is and how it is to be tabulated. Since a "fair day's work" is what is to be measured when setting up standards, it is important that the unit of measurement selected accurately reflects the variety of tasks performed and can accurately count the amount of work done: for example, an insurance company page may be a letter of 20 lines on 8½-by-11-inch paper; however, a page in the Legal Department of the same company may be a lease of 50 lines on 8½-by-14-inch paper.

Besides comparing production, work counts can also provide valuable information for such things as the establishment of unit costs, determination of the most efficient flow of work in the office, the planning and scheduling of work, and evaluation of alternative methods of performing the job.

When defining a unit of measurement, you should consider such factors as how well management understands the work measurement unit, how much detail management requires, the ease of the total office operation, and how much expenditure the firm is willing to spend in the study. Some managers find it difficult to understand what a work count unit is and how to use it; but such understanding is essential to any study using work count measurement units.

Once the work count unit is defined, a description of the types of office work to be measured needs to be taken. Some common classifications include the following:

1. *Correspondence work.* This category includes both internal and external communications (e.g., letters, memos).
2. *Manuals, guides, and reports.* This category uses a variety of formats

and contains a minor amount of statistical material. It includes legal documents and technical reports.

3. *Statistical work.* This consists of documents that are primarily numeric, in columnar form, with column headings and item descriptions.

4. *Forms "fill-in".* This includes a wide variety of forms that may involve the entry of an X in the box or dates, names, addresses, and descriptive material.

Whatever the work being done, specific classifications need to be established so that the person conducting the study knows what tasks will be included.

COLLECTING THE DATA

Once the work count unit and the categories have been defined, one can begin collecting the data. *Data collection* is the process of gathering information about the office operation in order to formulate standards. There are several aspects to data collection.

Typing production is one of the facets of total office production dealing with the processing of written documents. Typing production data techniques are designed to assist in the collection of data to determine the amount of equipment required to accomplish work production, the features necessary on the equipment to get the job done, and the proper placement of the equipment in the office to ensure efficiency. Most feasibility and benchmark studies in the area of typing production are conducted for a period of 10 working days. The duration of the collection period is agreed upon by the participants of the study and the individual(s) conducting the study.

The method of determining typing production rates is by line counting. This method involves the counting of lines produced within a given period of time. The most important thing in doing a line count is to ensure that all study participants are consistent in their measurement procedures (see Figure 1). The form contained in Figure 2 helps study participants to keep track of lines produced.

In addition to the manual counting process, management control devices (such as Dictaphone's Nucleus and Lanier's Super-Vision) provide current data in lines, which eliminates the need for the same degree of manual counting. Further, keyboard keystroke counters can be converted to lines based on standard line lengths.

The following standard measurements can be used to determine current typing production data via the line-count method:

1. *Narratives/memorandums.* Count each line, no matter how long or short, as one (1) line.

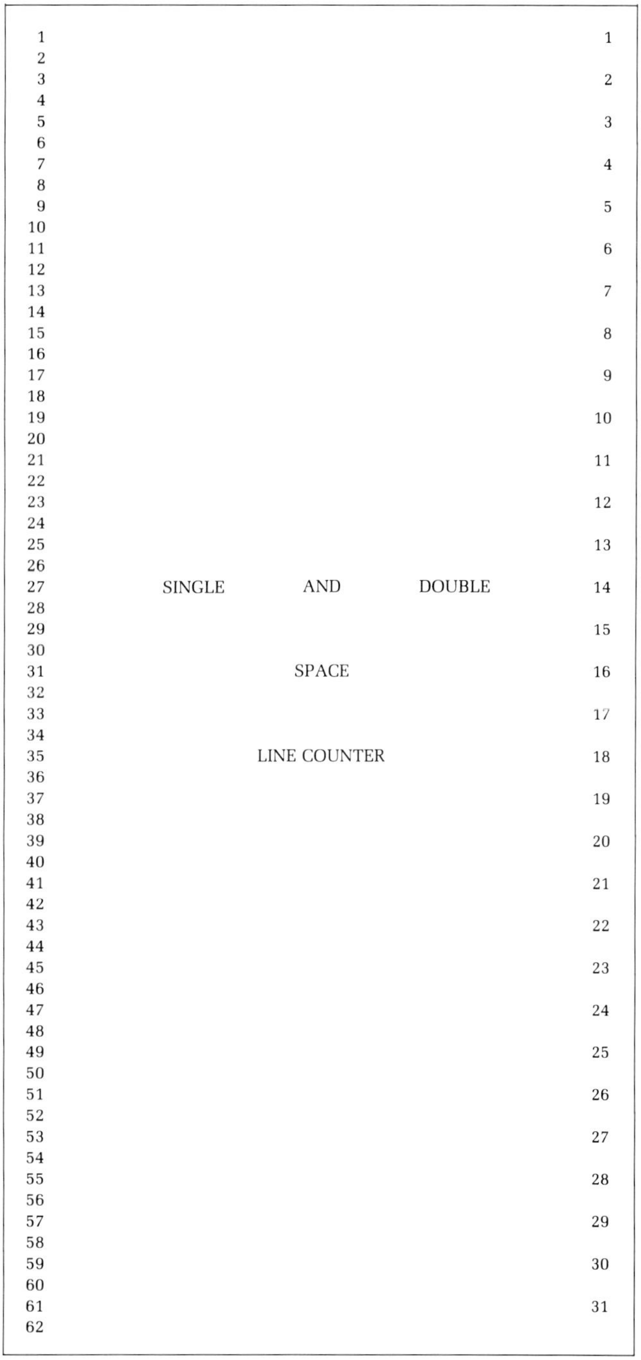

1			1
2			
3			2
4			
5			3
6			
7			4
8			
9			5
10			
11			6
12			
13			7
14			
15			8
16			
17			9
18			
19			10
20			
21			11
22			
23			12
24			
25			13
26			
27	SINGLE	AND	DOUBLE	14
28			
29			15
30			
31		SPACE	16
32			
33			17
34			
35		LINE COUNTER	18
36			
37			19
38			
39			20
40			
41			21
42			
43			22
44			
45			23
46			
47			24
48			
49			25
50			
51			26
52			
53			27
54			
55			28
56			
57			29
58			
59			30
60			
61			31
62			

Figure 1 Line counters provide consistency in measuring and ease in the data collection process.

DAILY LINE COUNT

Typist's Name_____ Date_____

Typist For_____ Equipment_____

Daily Typing Volume (check one):   Average _____   Above Average _____   Below Average _____

INSTRUCTIONS: Complete the following summary. TOTAL LINES UNDER TYPE OF DOCUMENT *MUST EQUAL* TOTAL LINES UNDER METHOD OF INPUT. Envelopes, labels, and forms should be counted under "self-composition" where appropriate.

| TYPE OF DOCUMENT | ORIGINAL INPUT # of Lines | REVISION TYPING | | PLAYBACK # of Lines | TOTAL # Lines | # of Documents | TOT. # OF DOCUMENTS |
		Author Rev. # Lines	Sec'y Rev. # Lines				
Narrative (3 or more pages)							
Letters (1 or 2 pages)							
Statistical							
Outlines							
Labels/Envelopes							
Forms							
DAILY TOTALS							

←————Must Agree————

METHOD OF INPUT	STORED DOC. (SD)	LONGHAND (LH)	SHORTHAND (SH)	SELF-COMPOSED (SC)	MACHINE DICTATION (MD)	HARD COPY (HC)	TOTAL # Lines
# Lines							

Figure 2   Daily line count forms provide a log for study participant to conveniently maintain production counts.

2. *Letters/memos.* The information at the top of the page before the body of the message should be counted as one (1) line. The lines in the body of the message should be counted as one (1) line each, regardless of the length of the line. The closing and all other information at the bottom of the document should be counted as one (1) line.

3. *Statistics.* Count each line as one (1) line, no matter how many columns there may be on 8½-by-11-inch paper. If paper is inserted in the typewriter lengthwise, count two (2) lines for every one (1) line typed.

4. *Outline.* Any line over one-half the width of the page is considered to be one (1) line. In word outline, count one (1) line for every ten (10) words typed.

5. *Envelopes.* Count each envelope as one (1) line.

6. *Forms.* Any line over one-half the width of the page is considered one (1) line. For form fill-ins, count one (1) line for every ten (10) words typed.

By using the above guidelines, an office can quickly and accurately obtain a comparable measure of typing production.

A second method used to determine typing production is the counting of documents. A document is considered to be any letter, report, or envelope. Any typed article as a whole is a document. For example, a 10-page report would be counted as one (1) entire document. At the end of the day, an office using this method should record the total number of documents on the daily line count form (see Figure 2) and the ten-day line count summary (see Figure 3). This method allows a supervisor to discover not only the amount of work production but also the exact type of work taking place.

Production logging is a second aspect of data collection in the modern office. Production logging is a systematic gathering of information about all aspects of a given work project, to develop a profile on what is required to accomplish that job. Production logging should be used in an office that has no historical data base to draw from or an office that has never attempted to formulate work production standards.

Logging procedures should include information on the following aspects of work:

1. The originator and department served at the time of work production.

2. The type of machine used to produce the work.

3. The type and number of documents keyboarded (i.e., were they narrative, memos, letters).

4. The method of input (i.e., the manner in which a typist received information—longhand, shorthand, machine dictation, etc.).

5. The time and date received, completed, and delivered.

TEN DAY LINE COUNT SUMMARY

Typist's Name _____ Date _____

Typist For _____ Equipment _____

Daily Typing Volume (check one):   Average _____   Above Average _____   Below Average _____

INSTRUCTIONS: Complete the following summary. TOTAL LINES UNDER TYPE OF DOCUMENT *MUST EQUAL* TOTAL LINES UNDER METHOD OF INPUT. Envelopes, labels, and forms should be counted under ''self-composition'' where appropriate.

TYPE OF DOCUMENT	ORIGINAL INPUT # of Lines	REVISION TYPING Author Rev. # Lines	Sec'y Rev. # Lines	PLAYBACK # of Lines	TOTAL # Lines	# of Documents	TOT. # OF DOCUMENTS
Narrative (3 or more pages)							
Letters (1 or 2 pages)							
Statistical							
Outlines							
Labels/Envelopes							
Forms							
DAILY TOTALS							

←————Must Agree————

METHOD OF INPUT	STORED DOC. (SD)	LONGHAND (LH)	SHORTHAND (SH)	SELF-COMPOSED (SC)	MACHINE DICTATION (MD)	HARD COPY (HC)	TOTAL # Lines
# Lines							

Figure 3 Summary line count forms provide a summary of data to assist in the analytical process.

6. The secretary doing the work.
7. The number of errors in the work.
8. The number of priorities handled.

The minimum amount of information to prepare an adequate report should be obtained from manual log sheets, as shown in Figures 4 and 5.

A third technique is *carbon copy collection*. Carbon copy collection is designed to develop a duplicate sample of work done during a set time period. For a carbon copy collection, study participants should be instructed to put an extra carbon set in their typewriters and to make an extra copy of everything they type, including letters, memos, reports, documents, messages, revisions, and notes. This carbon should contain any original errors. As each carbon is completed, the study participant should pencil in the following abbreviations in the upper right-hand corner of the carbon copy:

1. Typewriter used: EL (electric office typewriter) or WP (word processing typewriter).
2. Preparation method: OR (original, or first-time typing), RE (retyping, or revision work), or PL (playback of prerecorded material).
3. Source of document: SD (stored documents), MD (machine dictation), HC (typed or printed copy, may be marked up), SH (shorthand notes), LH (longhand draft), or SC (self-composition).
4. Persons requesting the work: the last name or initials of the person for whom the work was done.
5. Lines typed: record the number of lines typed in the document.

For example, under this system, a 20-line document prepared on an electric typewriter for the first time from machine dictation recorded by Mr. Melvin would contain the following information in the upper right-hand corner of the copy: EL/OR/MD/Melvin/20.

The contents of these documents are reviewed confidentially and then destroyed. This review process graphically illustrates the applications that exist within the organization and makes equipment selection much easier by showing exactly the kind of work that must be done. It also provides a means to audit data collection form accuracy.

Once the original logging and description have been completed, one can begin implementing the *timekeeping procedures* of the study. This part of the study involves measuring the time it takes individuals to perform certain tasks, whether typing or nontyping. Simplified secretarial and management daily time sheets are provided in Figures 6 and 7. These charts indicate the categories of work most commonly found in all types of clerical/secretarial positions. Daily time sheets will give an average picture of each workstation studied. The definitions of the categories ap-

LOG SHEET

Disc   #
Cassette #
Mag Card # _____   Operator _____   Date _____

DOCUMENT NO.	ORIGINATOR	REV.	RUSH	DESCRIPTION	DATE		TIME		LINE COUNT
					IN	OUT	IN	OUT	
TOTAL									

LINE COUNT:
Regular   _____
Statistical   _____
Revision   _____
Error   _____
TOTAL   _____

Figure 4 Log sheet provides a supervisor with the minimum amount of information required for management report preparation.

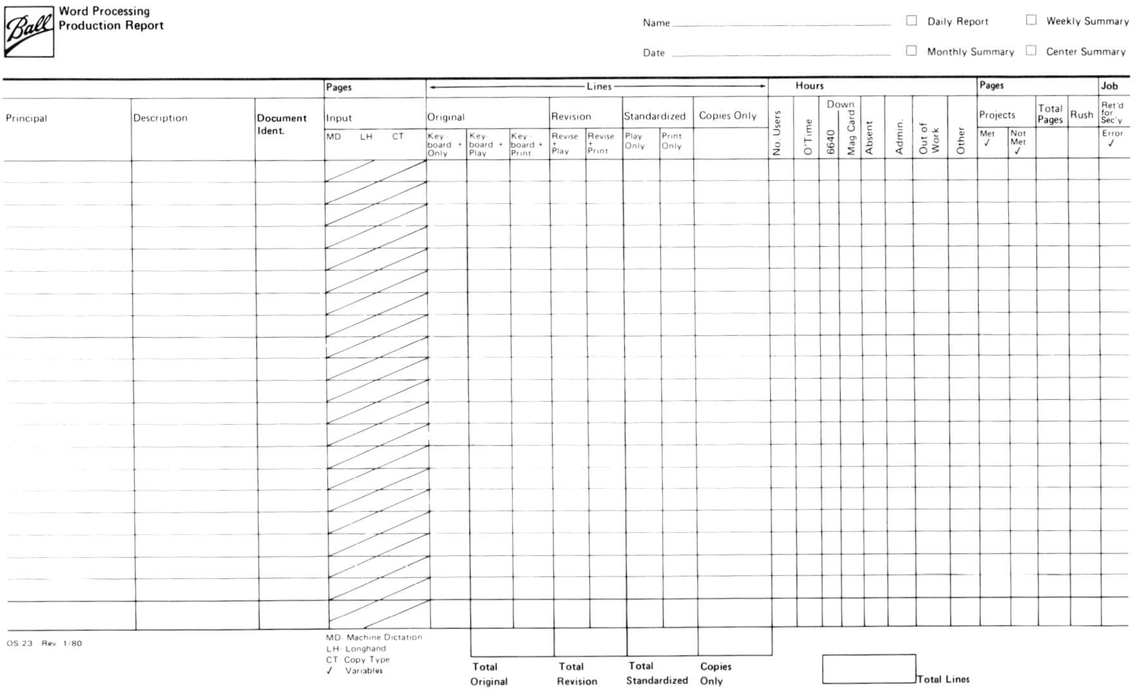
Ball Word Processing Production Report

Name ____ ☐ Daily Report ☐ Weekly Summary

Date ____ ☐ Monthly Summary ☐ Center Summary

Principal | Description | Document Ident. | Pages: Input (MD LH CT) | Lines: Original (Key-board Only; Key-board + Play; Key-board + Print), Revision (Revise + Play; Revise + Print), Standardized (Play Only; Print Only), Copies Only | Hours: No. Users, O'Time, Down (6640, Mag Card), Absent, Admin., Out of Work, Other | Pages: Projects (Met ✓; Not Met ✓), Total Pages, Rush | Job: Ret'd for Sec'y Error ✓

OS 23 Rev. 1/80

MD- Machine Dictation
LH- Longhand
CT- Copy Type
✓ Variables

Total Original | Total Revision | Total Standardized | Copies Only | Total Lines

Figure 5 One company's log sheet. (Courtesy of Ball Corporation, Muncie, Indiana.)

pearing in Figures 6 and 7 can be found in Figures 8 and 9. All time kept for a given period is then transferred to summary sheets.

This procedure provides a clear picture of how employee and management time is being used. It can also show areas in which work can be done more efficiently and employee time and resources utilized better.

A final important part of conducting a work measurement study is the use of *confidential questionnaires* to gather suggestions, concerns, and opinions about those intangible factors that affect both managerial and secretary/clerical productivity. A sample questionnaire that can be used for managers is shown in Figure 10. Suggestions, concerns, and feedback from secretarial/clerical staff are equally important, and a sample survey form is shown in Figure 11.

Questionnaires can be used in several ways. They can be completed by employees and returned in sealed envelopes to the individuals conducting the study. They can be used as an interview tool, should confidential personal interviews be conducted. The balance of the staff should be given the opportunity to input information into the study by completing the questionnaires and returning them in confidential envelopes. This process should be followed whether the study is being conducted by in-

SECRETARIAL DAILY TIME SHEET

Name: _____   Date: _____

PLEASE USE THE FOLLOWING CODE NUMBERS TO DESCRIBE WHAT YOU DID:

10 CALENDARING	21 Receive or give INSTRUCTIONS
11 ERRANDS and deliveries	22 Taking SHORTHAND
12 Looking for MISPLACED FILES	23 TELEPHONE
13 FILING	24 TRAVEL ARRANGEMENTS
14 LOCATING Someone	25 WAITING FOR WORK
15 MAIL	26 OTHER (specify)
16 OFF WORK (vacation, sick, etc.)	27 RECORDKEEPING, (posting, bookkeeping)
17 PERSONAL TIME (banking, coffee, etc.)	28 STATISTICS (computations)
18 PHOTOCOPYING/COLLATING	29 KEYBOARDING (computer terminal, keypunch)
19 PROOFREADING	30 TYPING (regular typewriter)
20 RECEPTION work	31 TYPING (word processing machine)

Time		Code	
hrs.	tenths	Number	DESCRIPTION (Optional)
		TOTAL	

6 minutes = .1 hour		36 minutes = .6 hour	
12 minutes = .2 hour		42 minutes = .7 hour	
18 minutes = .3 hour		48 minutes = .8 hour	
24 minutes = .4 hour		54 minutes = .9 hour	
30 minutes = .5 hour		60 minutes = 1.0 hour	

Figure 6   Support staff time sheet to simplify timekeeping process.

MANAGEMENT
DAILY TIME SHEET

Name:_____   Date:_____

PLEASE USE THE FOLLOWING CODE NUMBERS TO DESCRIBE DELE-
GABLE TASKS:

10 CALENDARING
11 ERRANDS and Deliveries
12 Looking for MISPLACED FILES
13 FILING
14 LOCATING Someone for
   Support
15 MAIL
16 PHOTOCOPYING/COLLATING

17 PROOFREADING
18 Receive or give INSTRUC-
   TIONS to Support Staff
19 TELEPHONE
20 TRAVEL ARRANGEMENTS
21 OTHER Delegable Activities
22 Route Correspondence of a
   responsive nature
23 Special Meetings & Arrangements

| Time | | Code | DESCRIPTION (Optional) |
hrs.	tenths	Number	
			TOTAL

6 minutes = .1 hour	36 minutes = .6 hour
12 minutes = .2 hour	42 minutes = .7 hour
18 minutes = .3 hour	48 minutes = .8 hour
24 minutes = .4 hour	54 minutes = .9 hour
30 minutes = .5 hour	60 minutes = 1.0 hour

Figure 7 Management time sheet to simplify timekeeping process.

Category	Explanation
10 *Calendaring*	Posting activities to your calendar and principal's calendar
11 *Errands & Deliveries*	Performing errands of a business nature within your organization or outside of your organization
12 *Looking for Misplaced Files*	Within your area or for another area
13 *Filing*	Filing done by you including time used to set up new files
14 *Locating Someone*	Time spent physically or by phone locating someone
15 *Mail*	Sorting, dating and delivering
16 *Off Work*	Vacation, sick, etc.
17 *Personal Time*	Bankng, coffee, etc. while at work
18 *Photocopying/Collating*	Time spent by you copying and collating
19 *Proofreading*	Any proofreading done by you
20 *Reception work*	Greeting visitors, giving directions, etc.
21 *Receive or Give Instructions*	Any instructions you give or receive during work hours
22 *Taking Shorthand*	By phone or principal
23 *Telephone*	Placing calls, taking messages and directing calls
24 *Traveling Arrangements*	For principals or yourself regarding business
25 *Waiting for Work*	Time spent waiting for work after you've caught up in all areas
26 *Other*	Any time you cannot fit in any other category. (Please specify)
27 *Recordkeeping*	Posting, bookkeeping
28 *Statistics*	Gathering information of a statistical nature and computing either by hand or calculator
29 *Keyboarding*	Computer terminal, keypunch, etc.
30 *Typing (Electric Typewriter)*	Any typing done on regular typewriter
31 *Typing (Word Processing)*	Typing on word processing equipment

Figure 8 Support staff time sheet category definition.

Category	Explanation
10 *Calendaring*	Posting activities to your calendar such as scheduling meetings
11 *Errands & Deliveries*	
12 *Looking for Misplaced Files*	Within your area or for another area
13 *Filing*	Filing done by you including time used to set up new files
14 *Locating Someone for Support*	Time spent physically or by phone locating someone to provide you with clerical/secretarial services
15 *Mail*	Sorting and opening mail
16 *Photocopying/Collating*	Time spent by you copying and collating papers
17 *Proofreading*	Any proofreading done by you
18 *Receive or Give Instructions to Support Staff*	Any instructions you give to clerical/secretarial staff
19 *Telephone*	Placing calls, taking messages and directing calls
20 *Travel Arrangements*	For yourself regarding business
21 *Other*	Please describe any delegable tasks that do not fit in any other category
22 *Routine Correspondence of a Responsive Nature*	Response to letters requesting routine information; i.e., Meeting dates, travel arrangements, seminar schedules, etc.
23 *Special Meeting Arrangements*	Any special meeting arrangements other than typical one-to-two-hour meetings

Figure 9 Management time sheet category definition.

house personnel or by outside consultants. It is very important to ensure the confidentiality of the information gathered. Information from these confidential surveys can reveal areas in which management can increase work productivity and improve performance.

Once all of the above steps—typing production, production logging, carbon copy collecting, timekeeping procedures, and confidential surveys—have been completed, the person conducting the study must evaluate the information in order to formulate specific productivity standards. Determination of standards is difficult. There are no easy formulas that apply to every firm. The best step is to study the information and formulate working standards that are suited to the individual firm.

CONFIDENTIAL

MANAGEMENT QUESTIONNAIRE

Name_____   TITLE_____

_____

1 Please describe your major responsibilities. List up to five, in order of their importance.

1. _____

_____

_____

2. _____

_____

3. _____

_____

_____

4. _____

_____

_____

5. _____

_____

_____

2 Please list major labor-intensive manual activities that you perform. (For example, recordkeeping, report preparation, calculating, etc).

_____

_____

_____

3 Do you have peak workload periods?   Yes_____   No_____   If yes:

When?   How Long?   What are the reasons?

_____

_____

Figure 10   Management questionnaires provide a tool whereby management can contribute needs information on a one-time basis.

4 Please list any tasks you now perform that could be delegated (other than those identified on the daily time sheet) if more support time were available:

		Identify to whom delegable: —Secretary —Administrative
Delegable tasks	Est. time saved	—Specialist

_____

_____

_____

5 Please indicate the average amount of time (in hours or minutes) you spend each week in each of the following general activities:

_____ Personnel matters that relate to your support staff (interviews, performance reviews, evaluations, counseling, timekeeping, absenteeism, vacation scheduling, etc)

_____ Administrative activities related to support staff workload coordination and/or resolving priority conflicts

_____ Training or orienting support staff employees.

_____ Budgeting equipment and support staff expenditures.

6 Please list documents received that are computer generated:

_____

_____

_____

7 What are some additional applications which you feel can be computerized?

_____

_____

_____

8 What do you feel are the most important aspects of file maintenance and retrieval? (Please mark them from "1" (most important) to "5" (least important):

Accessibility to records	_____
Physical location of files	_____
Pick-up and delivery	_____
Security	_____
Scheduled destruction	_____

9 Please use the rest of this form and the other side if needed to note any suggestions you have for improvements in the systems, procedures, or methods used in your job.

Figure 10 (_Continued_)

CONFIDENTIAL

SECRETARIAL/CLERICAL QUESTIONNAIRE

NAME_____ POSITION_____

DIVISION/DEPARTMENT_____ KIND OF TYPEWRITER_____

REPORTS TO_____ DATE OF HIRE_____

1 How long have you held this particular position?_____

2 What are your primary functions? (i.e. typing, answering phone, making appointments, filing, etc)_____

3 What secondary duties do you have (i.e. filling in for Ms Jones when she is away from her desk, etc)_____

4 What situations tend to hinder your work?_____

5 What changes could be made to give you more satisfaction?_____

6 What is the current turnaround time at your typing station? (2–4 hours, same day, next day, etc)_____

7 Do you have backlogs of work? If so, what are the specific tasks?_____

8 Does your present job fit in with your career goal?_____

9 Please list seasonal tasks and time required for completion_____

10 What are some administrative support duties you feel you could perform for your managers?_____

11 Please use the other of this form to note any suggestions you have for improvements in the systems, procedures, or methods used in your job.

Figure 11 Support staff questionnaire serves as a basis for personal interviews and a suggestion form.

APPLYING PRODUCTIVITY GUIDELINES AND STANDARDS TO WORKLOAD

Productivity standards are valuable only when they are applied to actual operations to prove significant increases in productivity or substantial cost savings. Standards can be used as a basis on which to prove cost justification of new systems or equipment. However, it is important to keep in mind that work standards should never be the *sole* reason for or criterion used in hiring and firing decisions. Rather, standards are primarily designed for determining the need for additional equipment, changing job duties, configuring equipment, and deciding the location of the equipment. They can also be used as productivity data from a word processing operation for management reporting purposes. The proper use of equipment results in management time savings plus the hard-cost savings of greater productivity.

Figure 12 outlines average acceptable standards of production in word processing equipment, which represent the result of 10 years of study by Mary M. Ruprecht and Associates, Inc. They provide a base on which a firm can develop standards of its own. If performance figures are below recognized standards, it is apparent there are productivity problems. One possible way to isolate and identify the problem is to compare the performance figures to the table.

By comparing performance against standards, you can also measure equipment capacity and utilization. Based on a production of 4800 net lines per day, the various categories of equipment can be cost compared in the manner outlined in Figure 13.

Any successful office automation operation must produce continuing and definable cost savings. To determine cost savings, itemize operating costs such as equipment, labor, supplies, and overhead costs; each component of these areas is summarized in Figure 14. Then determine the amount of possible savings achieved through equipment that offers higher productivity performance or capacity.

Figure 12 Guide line standards of productivity provide a benchmark against which to measure production. (Courtesy of Mary M. Ruprecht, CMC, President, Mary M. Ruprecht & Associates, Incorporated.)

Type of Machine	Outstanding	Superior	Acceptable	Unsatisfactory
Standard electric	500 and over	250–500	200–250	Less than 200
Magnetic media	1450 and over	1000–1450	500–1000	Less than 500
Microcomputer	2500 and over	1500–2500	900–1500	Less than 900
Minicomputer	4000 and over	2500–4000	1000–2500	Less than 1000

EQUIPMENT CAPABILITY & COST COMPARISON BASED ON AVERAGE STANDARDS

Based on a production of 4800 net lines per day, the various categories of equipment can be cost compared in the following manner, using equipment and staff costs outlined below.

EQUIPMENT CATEGORY	AVG. LINES PRODUCED PER DAY (1)	NO. OF UNITS REQUIRED	APPROX. LEASE OR RENT COST PER MONTH	MONTHLY EQUIPMENT COST (2)	NO. OF STAFF REQUIRED	MONTHLY SALARY	MONTHLY STAFF COST (3)	TOTAL MONTHLY SYSTEM COST
Electric	375	13	× $ 30/mo. =	$ 390	13	× $1,000/mo. =	$13,000	$13,390
Magnetic Media	1200	4	× $350/mo. =	$1,400	4	× $1,200/mo. =	$ 4,800	$ 6,200
Microcomputer	2000	3	× $550/mo. =	$1,650	3	× $1,200/mo. =	$ 3,600	$ 5,250
Minicomputer (shared/distributed logic) (4)	3250	2	× $450/mo. =	$ 900	2	× $1,200/mo. =	$ 2,400	$ 3,300

(1) Midpoint of "Superior" production from "Average Acceptable Standards in Word Processing" shown on previous page.
(2) Modular expandability allows greater cost reduction, depending on size of installation.
(3) Secretaries with electric typewriters average $1000/mo while electronic equipment justifies and requires highly-skilled operators, at an average of $1200/mo.
(4) Central Processing Unit costs are not included in these figures.

Figure 13 A sample of an equipment cost comparison based on production.

Equipment	Labor
1. Leasing equipment.	Salary, including fringe benefits:
2. Renting equipment.	Insurance programs.
3. Purchasing equipment.	Retirement funds.
4. Maintenance agreements.	Social security.
	Educational programs.
	Etc.
Supplies	Overhead
1. Ribbons.	1. Space.
2. Media.	2. Rent.
3. Paper.	3. Heat.
4. Etc.	4. Light.
	5. Depreciation.
	6. Janitorial.
	7. Maintenance services.

Figure 14 Cost considerations to be analyzed when charting hidden costs involved in implementing office automation are shown above.

In calculating total cost justification, a report should include any or all of the following areas of potential savings:

1. *Hard dollars.* Hard-dollar savings realized from implementation of a total support system are those salaries and fringe benefits that can be saved through the reduction of labor hours required to produce the same volume of work. Reduction in the staff also occurs through normal attrition and through better utilization of staff time, specialization of duties, and controlled, supervised workload coordination.

2. *Soft dollars.* These savings are less tangible than hard-dollar savings, because they are affected more by people's acceptance of or resistance to change, which is difficult to predict. For example, employees using machine dictation will have more time to be productive than those using longhand. However, how effectively they use dictation and what they do with their available time are unmeasurable. Another form of soft-dollar savings is time saved by management when delegating work and utilizing time management techniques.

3. *Cost avoidance.* This area involves factors such as reduction of overtime, reduction of temporary help, reduction of equipment purchases, and the avoidance of current costs that a firm would continue to incur had it not installed a new system (e.g., reduction in the number of projected full-time employees necessary for optimum productivity).

The foregoing data provide a firm with the information to project short-

Hard dollars	$36.550
Soft dollars	83,700
Cost avoidance	2,400
Improved productivity	140,000
Potential annual savings	$262,650

Figure 15   Recap of potential savings available through implementation of office automation.

and long-term savings in dollars or improved management and staff productivity (in hours, which can then be converted to dollars). In the final analysis, improved productivity ultimately means increased profitability. Figure 15 illustrates the opportunity for increased profitability of a Midwest organization.

REPORTING PRODUCTIVITY TO MANAGEMENT

The measurement and assessment of integration of the electronic office requires an understanding of the variables within an organization that go beyond equipment. Variables in any work environment can involve either descriptive or measurable tasks.

Descriptive variables relate to those tasks of a less tangible nature, such as delegation of a job by management to subordinate levels. It is difficult to measure the productivity of work that consists of dozens of varied duties. The term may also be applied to the degree to which employees follow procedures within an organization, which is difficult to measure precisely because of the many variables (e.g., attitude of employees, degrees of proficiency, amount of control).

Even the *measurable* areas are subject to variables. For example, the application of standards to word processing production based on certain kinds of equipment is relatively easy to measure. However, consider the variables of performance, training, and proper procedures, as well as control. The actual measurement of these activities would be ideal if one could control them.

Return on the investment (ROI) in office automation systems can be identified as a result of the measurement process (see Figure 16). When a system automates a manual process, reduces the time for a process, or increases the efficiency of communication within the electronic office, employee productivity and effectiveness are improved. For example,

1. Elimination of duplicate processing of the same information anywhere in the information processing cycle. Traditionally, an idea would be

CASH FLOW INVESTMENTS JUSTIFICATION

I. *AMOUNT OF INVESTMENT* − $64,700

II. *JUSTIFICATION COMPUTATION*

Years	1	2	3	4	5	6	7	8
A. Annual Income*	14,655	15,827	17,094	18,461	19,938	21,533	23,256	
Equipment Trade-in or Salvage Income***							6,470	
Gross Annual Income	14,655	15,827	17,094	18,461	19,938	21,533	29,726	
B. Annual Expense								
1. Maintenance**	2,820	2,989	3,169	3,358	3,560	3,774	4,000	
2. Telephone	100	100	100	100	100	100	100	
Total Annual Expense	2,920	3,089	3,269	3,458	3,660	3,874	4,100	
C. Incoming Cash Flow (inc. less exp.)	11,735	12,738	13,825	15,003	16,278	17,659	25,626	
D. Present Worth Factor								
@20% (new items)	0.8333	0.6944	0.5787	0.4823	0.4019	0.3349	0.2791	0.2326
@15% (repair/replace)	0.8696	0.7561	0.6575	0.5718	0.4972	0.4323	0.3759	0.3269
III. ROI (Return on Investment)	14.157%							

* Wage savings based on elimination of $4,000 per year in outside help and $10,655 per year reduction in shorthand dictation time. Total labor savings $14,655 accelerated at 8% per year.
** Maintenance costs accelerated based on 6% annual increase.
*** Trade-in value at end of 7 years estimated at 10% of purchase price.

Figure 16   Return on Investment (ROI) Chart.

written or dictated to a secretary, typed, retyped, reedited, proofread, put into final form, and subsequently hand-delivered or mailed to its final destination. Depending upon the extent of office automation implemented within an organization, this process could be reduced to voice input to a keyboarding function and to distribution, eliminating the in-between steps, or directly to distribution from a keyboard (e.g., electronic mail).

2. Wasted efforts that do not contribute directly to productivity are reduced (e.g., the make-ready and put-away time in dealing with rough drafted reports, or the handling of multiple carbon copies). Communications to a laser printer would eliminate the handling of carbon copies. Another example is the wasted function of communicating messages over the telephone. A misdialed number, a busy signal, and a call when the recipient is temporarily out of the office are all inherent negative factors that do not directly contribute to productivity. With automatic dialing machines, message forwarding, and message switching systems, much of the time lost can be reduced.

3. Payback on automation is derived directly from the replacement of manual processes with machine processes, eliminating certain labor

steps. If automation does not result in a reduction of labor functions, then time savings are not available and personnel productivity is not improved. Labor reduction measurement is a direct and immediate payback.

4. The actual saving of time through the full utilization of administrative time in the office is a significant payback. According to a Naremco study, average secretarial idle time per day amounted to 18 percent. If controlled supervision reduces the idle time of this high-level support staff employee, then full productivity will be improved at the rate of 18 percent per day.

5. Idle time is reduced and benefits result from supervision, control, work specialization, and proper procedures.

Work measurement can provide the base against which to measure improved productivity. However, the value of a measurement program depends upon the use of that information. For a measurement system to be effective, information must be collected and distributed in a thorough and timely manner and must be more than historical in nature. Decision-making managers need to know the base against which productivity is being measured, the improvements in percentages or dollars, and a projection and a comparative methodology as to what should be happening. A manager must receive the data necessary to compare current operations with projected goals and objectives. Important information for the manager includes deviations from a given plan, the effects of key decisions, and the amount of risk to be taken in achieving the identified goals.

Key performance reports allow managers to pinpoint trouble spots without having to analyze a large volume of paperwork. Managers can compare monthly reports to identified objectives and highlight variances and trends. The key components of an office automation system and their objectives should be identified, benchmarks set for the productivity levels, and a measurement trend established on a monthly basis to be reviewed by management.

REPORT DESIGN Reports to top management should contain only that information which directly bears on the success or failure of office automation operations. This includes information necessary to make informed decisions on adjusting the direction of original objectives. The details in the report for management should be limited to that information that is directly under the electronic office manager's control. Also, any data not needed to understand the final result should be eliminated.

The report should contain actual performance, variance from objectives, and actual costs and percentages over or under budget or targets. The figures used for reporting purposes should not be broken into units smaller than an executive needs to comprehend or control results.

Office automation reports should be written in management language, with clear and precise titles, column headings, item names, and descriptions. Technical jargon of the office automation industry should be avoided. Data of particular significance should be highlighted, and footnotes, appendices, or supplemental reports can serve to point out less-obvious but important facts.

Graphs (as described in a previous chapter) often can be used to illustrate clearly trends that may be difficult to present in words. Graphs can also be used for comparisons: for example, month-to-month comparisons of the total productivity of a word processing center, or of increased images being microfilmed in the new Reprographics Department, or of the growth in volumes of copies produced in a given period of time by use of intelligent copier/printers. Another advantage of graphs is that they can be easily updated by adding the latest month's figure to last month's chart.

Proper design is imperative with graphs. For example, time progression should be illustrated on a horizontal scale. Small changes in the variables being measured on a vertical scale must be clearly evident. In most cases, a broken scale that does not begin with zero can achieve this result without causing confusion as to the meaning of figures identified.

Reports to management are a valuable component of the productivity aspect of the electronic office. However, the basis of much of the information produced in reports to management will be derived from, and compared with, the budgeting process.

BUDGETING FOR CONTINUED PRODUCTIVITY

Budgets are an essential tool in cost control. A budget is a short-term plan for how an organization is going to obtain and use its financial resources. There are two types of budgeting processes: traditional (incremental) and zero-base budgeting.

TRADITIONAL BUDGETING The traditional budget assumes that expenses for the coming year will be based on the preceding year or on some average of preceding years. All existing programs are maintained. This budget can be as simple as a form-filling administrative exercise that merely involves adding an inflationary factor to last year's actual costs and revenues. The disadvantage of such superficiality is that it will not help to control costs or serve as a management decision-making tool. Budgets organize financial information for an entire organization or department, to show actual expenditures and forecasted estimates. Budgets also produce an integrated plan for the coming period. In other words, budgets are an active rather than a passive tool. A major concern in the budgeting process is to address how an organization will maximize returns on investments with the lowest possible risk.

The budgeting process for office automation should consider such aspects as

1. Equipment investment.
2. Physical alterations of office space necessary to accommodate hardware.
3. Personnel requirements, including support staff, supervisors, coordinators, and managers of office automation.
4. Pay scales with fringe benefits.
5. Workflow improvement in terms of cost avoidance of temporary help, overtime, and the hiring of additional staff (e.g., less duplication of effort, faster exchange of information—particularly that internal to an office location as well as that to distant offices—and work specialization through the delegation process to the appropriate level of competency).
6. Costs for service, maintenance, supplies, tax considerations, depreciation, and purchase versus lease.

Each of these considerations would be calculated in the return on investment in the area of soft dollars, hard dollars, improved productivity, and cost avoidance, as detailed earlier in this chapter.

Budgets allow day-to-day decision making within a frame of reference, provide guidance to and a basis for monitoring the costs of office integration, and help management evaluate the efficiency and effectiveness of a department and a company.

A key factor in the budgeting process is accountability. An appropriate budget allows the variance, either lesser or greater, to be traced to the division or department or component responsible for the excess or the lack of meeting projected goals. If conditions warrant deviations from budget, budgets should be analyzed for possible revisions. In order to justify these revisions, accountability is essential. Some important *do's* and *don'ts* in budgeting are shown in Figure 17.

ZERO-BASE BUDGETING

Zero-base budgeting attempts to reevaluate all programs, activities, and expenditures in terms of cost benefit. It is not based on the last year's budget, but on the belief that each year the budget should be rebuilt from a base of zero. It is a method of forcing managers to defend every controllable activity.

The development of zero-base budgeting (ZBB) began in 1964, when it was introduced in the U.S. Department of Agriculture. Then, in 1969, while at Texas Instruments, Peter Pyhrr further developed the concept.

IMPORTANT BUDGETING GUIDELINES

Do's

1. Discuss and come to joint agreement (congruence) about all budgetary decisions with those responsible for the expenditures.

2. Try to relate budget amounts to some level of activity—productivity or sales level, for example. In an administrative setting, this might be the number of invoices, number of people on payroll, number of reports, etc.

3. Coordinate and integrate your budget with the entire organization.

4. Plan ahead; design budget forms and obtain assumptions *before* requesting subordinates to supply initial budget estimates.

5. Remember that budgets are a plan of action and are not "cast in stone." Should economics or assumptions change, the budget should be amended to reflect those changes.

6. Use favorable budget performance as the basis for providing incentives and rewards.

Don'ts

1. Prepare your budget without obtaining senior management's support and advice.

2. Think of all costs as fixed. (Note: they must vary in the long-term with the level of activity.)

3. Base budget estimates on an extension of last year's costs. (It's better to bring new thinking to cost reduction and revenue improvement opportunities during the budgetary process.)

4. Allow "slack"—the universal problem of "padding" budgets by setting higher budget amounts than are actually necessary for maintaining normal operations.

5. Prepare a budget without a system—and without clear lines of responsibility and authority that trace costs, etc. to individual managers responsible for decisions, management, and action. (Note: the opposite approach should be used.)

Figure 17 The do's and don'ts of budgeting should be carefully considered. Note the degree of planning in each positive step outlined in the Important Budgeting Guidelines. *Source:* Stan G. Webb, "Getting a Head Start on Next Year's Budget," *Administrative Management,* August, 1982, p. 60.

Texas Instruments first used it in its Staff and Research divisions and then expanded it to the entire company in the following year.

There are three basic steps in zero-base budgeting: developing a decision package, ranking packages in order of importance, and allocating resources accordingly.

A decision package is a document that identifies and describes a specific activity in such a manner that management can (1) evaluate it and rank it against other activities competing for limited resources and then (2) decide whether to approve or disapprove it.

A decision package can be developed for staff, a program or project, service received or provided, line item of expenditure, cost reduction, or capital expenditure. The contents of the decision package usually include

(1) objective, purpose, or scope; (2) what is to be done and how; (3) consequences of not doing the activity; (4) alternative methods; (5) costs and benefits of recommended activity; (6) resources required.[2]

In preparing decision packages, a manager first defines the unit's objective and purpose. After a description of how the unit currently operates and resources are utilized, the manager then develops workload and performance measurement techniques, considers alternative methods of operation, and performs an incremental analysis. The final decision package will be placed in one of the following three support-level categories: (1) different methods or levels of effort to perform each activity; (2) "business as usual" levels of effort, where no other alternatives or changes are considered; and (3) new activities and programs.

Once the manager has bundled all the mandatory and discretionary activities into a package, a ranking process follows. Usually, the manager ranks all packages in order of decreasing benefit to the company on a cost-benefit basis. This ranking activity begins at the cost center level. A committee is formed by all managers in the cost center. The committee reviews all the packages presented to it and ranks them in importance (by vote). The packages considered most beneficial to the cost center as a whole receive the highest rankings, while the least important receive the lowest. A cutoff point is now established. Given the general amount of funds available in the coming fiscal year, all packages above a given ranking are accepted by the group and all those below a certain point are rejected.

These decisions are then passed up to the next-higher management level. Here the manager reviews the rankings to determine if they fit into the organization's goals and to decide whether the rejected packages offer enough benefits to expand the level of funding. Upper managers briefly examine only a preestablished percentage of the packages, to control volume. This process is repeated until all the accepted activities have filtered up to the top of the organization, where the budget for the entire organization is then created.

ZBB does not supplant the corporate budget. It is not suited to all organizations, or to all activities of an organization. It has little use in budgeting for production costs such as direct labor, direct materials, and direct overhead, which are largely determined by production and sales volume. It is applicable primarily to the service and support areas of an organization that has discretionary costs. In general, the responses show that ZBB is a good process with which to change the total budget level, to reallocate costs and manpower, to learn more about the organization, and to improve efficiency and effectiveness within the organization. Also, it is valuable as a management planning and control system.

---

[2] Peter A. Pyhrr, "Zero-Base Budgeting," *Harvard Business Review*, November/December 1970, p. 112.

ZBB is typically prepared in advance of the annual budget. Because of the tremendous effort required to develop decision packages, it is recommended that after the initial analysis of activities is completed an annual update of the decision packages be made, thus eliminating much of the clerical effort. Each package should be ranked again according to the current priorities of the company.

ZBB is not, and should not be considered, a panacea for management's budgeting problems. The technique should not be built up to promise more than it can realistically provide. In order to apply ZBB successfully, observe the following guidelines carefully:

1. Review the ZBB methodology and determine its appropriateness.
2. Analyze the need of your organization before implementing ZBB; that is, ask, "Is my organization ready for ZBB?"
3. Define the resources required before implementation. This includes obtaining adequate staff for the budgeting department, setting up a top-management steering committee, and appointing local budget coordinators.
4. Sell high-level management on ZBB in advance of its implementation.
5. Make sure that long-range or strategic planning precedes ZBB.
6. Develop a ZBB method, including a review procedure, tailored to your organization's environment.
7. Allow adequate time for training budget personnel and users.
8. Communicate to all levels of management the objectives and goals and provide a clear assignment of responsibility for justifying expenditures and setting priorities.
9. Test ZBB in a single department before implementing it throughout the organization.
10. Link ZBB to existing financial control systems, providing effective and timely management reports.
11. Encourage all levels of management participation, especially top management's cooperation and commitment.[3]

In the initial implementation of a budgeting process, top management should be involved in giving direction and setting objectives and a credible financial accountant should be enlisted to help. It is obvious that budgeting is a detailed, time-consuming, necessary process, particularly for the electronic office. However, budgeting should be approached from a positive, forward-thinking perspective, so as to broaden the knowledge of the person responsible for preparing the budget, maintaining it, monitoring it, and reporting to management.

---

[3] "ZBB Fits DP to a Tee," *Datamation*, September 1980, pp. 177–80.

PART FIVE

A LOOK AHEAD

CHAPTER 23

THE FUTURE OF OFFICE AUTOMATION

OBJECTIVES

In this chapter you will learn about
1. Technological and sociological aspects for the future.
2. Technological developments on the horizon.
3. Fast-growing current technologies to consider in the future.
4. Sociological impact on the office workplace.
5. Human relations needs from the worker perspective.
6. Legal ramifications of the electronic office.

> *The third wave offers us the opportunity to shape that future toward humane and decent ends. It is not merely a once in a lifetime chance, but a once in all history chance. . . .*
>
> *Alvin Toffler*

For the automated office of the future, fresh, creative thinking will be needed to integrate total support systems. In the past, implementation of office automation has been delayed by four general conditions (see Figure 1).

1. *Vendor uncertainty.* Changing trends and marketing techniques have caused a low comfort level for organizations about to spend large amounts of money. Factors involved in this lack of buyer security are the uncertainty of not knowing (a) the stability of the vendor with whom one is dealing, (b) the expansion potential of a particular piece of equipment, (c) the ability to plan for continued growth within an organization, and (d) the modular expandability of the equipment.

2. *Unavailability of experienced information processing personnel.* The lack of experienced, trained personnel to evaluate and implement the integrated office, as well as of qualified personnel to operate the equipment, has been a significant detriment to many organizations. Future success will depend on management's commitment to the use of the skills of the newly educated personnel.

3. *Inability to identify dollar savings accurately.* In many organizations, it has been difficult to show or prove to management the opportunity for time savings and improved productivity, particularly at the top management level. This does not mean that possibilities are not within reach. Many of the benefits that accrue to an organization through management time savings come from delegating activities to an appropriate level, but this delegation process depends entirely upon the willingness of management to carry it out.

4. *Historical management thinking.* Traditional stereotypes of managers and support staff make it difficult to change office structures and practices and to alter management styles. Change is never easy, particularly when it involves adjusting the traditional mindsets of both employees and managers. The key to opening the door to office automation, both

Figure 1 Many myths still prevail in the office. Lack of knowledge rather than resistance to change are some of the deterrents to office automation.

---

1. Vendor uncertainty.
2. Unavailability of experienced personnel.
3. Inability to define cost benefits.
4. Historical management thinking.

---

technologically and sociologically, is first to gain the acceptance and support of the people who will use it.

WHAT IS THE OFFICE OF THE FUTURE?

The office of the future is a combination of functionally related computerized subsystems and skilled people who will perform the functions in the integrated office. The information flow within the office deals with (1) input or creation, (2) processing and replication, (3) storage and retrieval, (4) output and distribution, and (5) archiving and/or destruction. Within each of these phases of the information cycle are systems that deal with specific applications. In this chapter, we will explore the future of these and additional technologies and the impact of electronification on the human element in the office.

The human issues of the future office will include education, energy, laws, human relations, and ergonomics. A critical objective in preparing for the future is to provide a satisfactory man-machine interface with improved productivity while continuing to provide a satisfactory work environment for the employee.

According to Clifford Lindsey, vice-president and director of the word-processing industry service Dataquest, "The automated office will not enslave us in tedium; it will free us from drudgery. When office workers on all levels grasp that truth (and vendors' systems meet that goal), psychological and sociological factors will no longer impede the growth in installation of office systems. Then we can concentrate on solving the very real problems concerning office productivity and the quality of decision-making."[1]

THE TECHNOLOGICAL FUTURE

The technological future of the automated office suggests that we should be making more finite definitions of various terms. The most succinct definitions presented to date are those suggested by Amy Wohl, president of Advanced Office Concepts Corporation:[2]

1. *Integrated systems.* Systems that do not differentiate between word processing and other functions (such as data processing or data access). Such systems permit multiple functions to occur simultaneously and permit the user to combine text and data in a single application with little or no difficulty. Soon we will expand our notion of an integrated system and demand that voice and image also be readily integrated with data and text.

[1] Clifford M. Lindsey and Robert G. Costain, *Modern Office Procedures*, June 1982, white paper, p. 51.

[2] Amy Wohl, *Advanced Office Concepts Newsletter*, April/May 1982, p. 4.

2. *Office automation systems.* Systems that offer word processing as part of a bundle of office functions including (but not limited to) electronic mail and message distribution; administrative functions such as calendaring, scheduling, and using tickler files; electronic filing; data access; and data processing. Such systems are perceived as being directed to a more general business audience than correspondence secretaries—clerical personnel, secretaries, administrative staff, professionals, managers, and executives.

3. *Information processing systems.* Office of the near future scenarios that assume a system in which all kinds of business information (data, text, image, and voice) will be freely accessible to any level of worker, within the necessary security restrictions. Such accessibility assumes new types of interfaces that do not require typing skills or intensive training and unobtrusive systems that will become pervasive throughout all business environments.

The above definitions signify the degrees of technological change that have taken place and that will continue to evolve through the next decade. Future success in the office will depend on the ability of management responsible for planning the electronic office to visualize the direction, growth potential, and related implications of new technologies. Technology will have a significant impact on the entire structure of the office as well as on our society—on the methods we use to work, to travel, and to communicate, in both the office environment and the home environment.

Continued technological advancement and the resultant lower costs will provide enormous opportunities to use automation in aspects of our environments that have never before been considered. The trends toward lowered costs are illustrated in Figure 2, and device penetration is illustrated in Figure 3.

An ever-increasing proliferation of personal computers and microprocessing products is expected to continue. These smaller products will be capable of performing a remarkably broad range of specialized functions at very low cost. We have already begun to witness a trend toward increased functions of personal computing workstations for the office. Management's acceptance of electronic products is being accelerated by user-friendly equipment and the ability to meet individual requirements at the point of use with a variety of software products.

The growing demand for increased communication capability will be a driving force in developing the electronic office. The communication capabilities in networking to transmit voice, data, text, and image information simultaneously will provide opportunities to design newer systems.

The software available is becoming more user friendly as computer languages migrate from traditional languages toward user-oriented, easy-to-use languages.

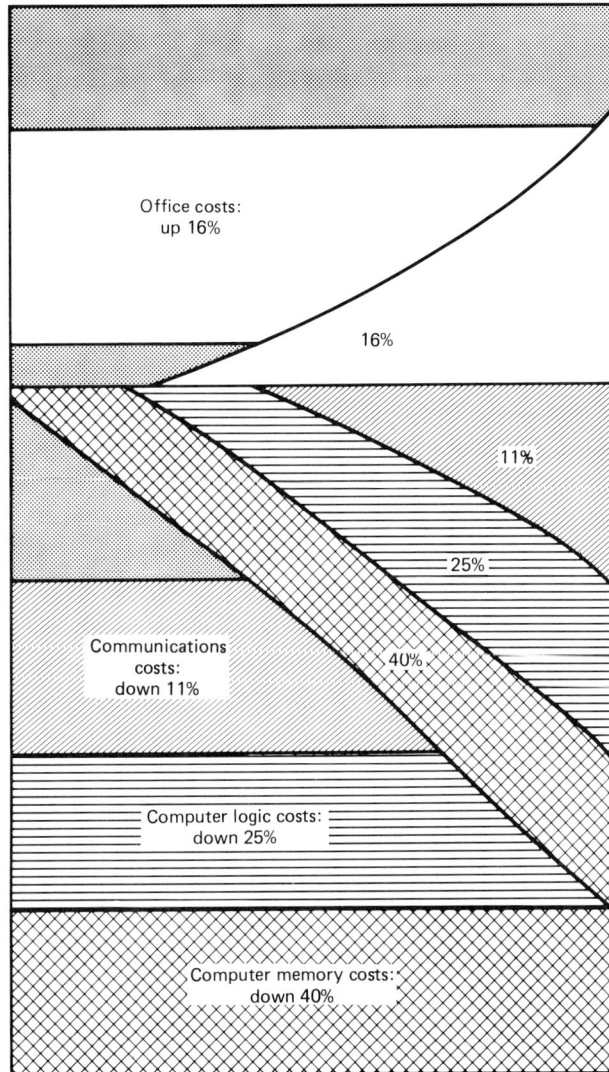

Figure 2 Annual office integration cost trends continue to point to the advantages of technology.

TECHNOLOGICAL ADVANCEMENTS

Input

Voice Recognition and Response. Voice technology has been a much anticipated feature in office automation; to most, it has been an impossible dream or just a theory. In recent times, several large vendors in the information processing industry have been actively researching and developing voice recognition and response technologies. According to George Glaser of George Glaser, Incorporated, of Los Altos, California, in his presentation entitled *The Next Five Years,*

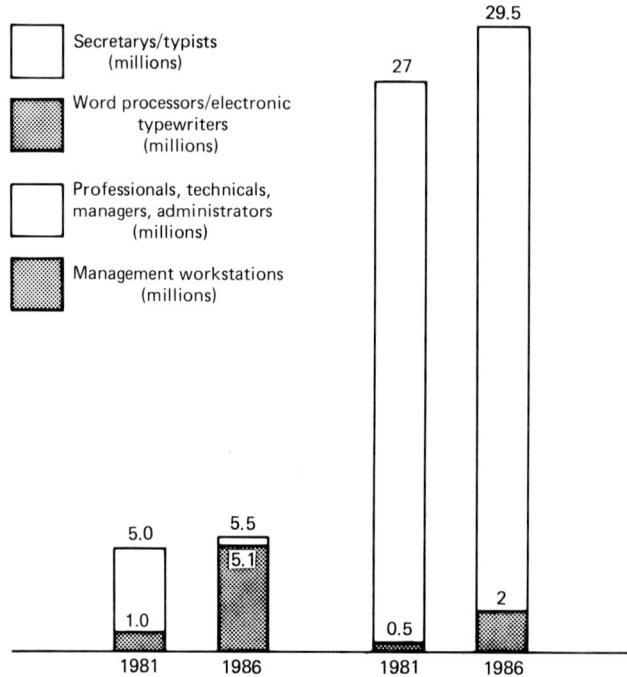

Figure 3 Device penetration. *Source:* International Data Corporation, U.S. Government Statistics, "Trends in Computing Applications for the 80's, *Fortune,* Special Supplement.

> To use one's voice to issue commands to a system—or to request information from it—is very appealing; likewise, to receive verbal responses to our queries and to be given verbal instructions or warnings is also very appealing. Mankind has relied on vocal communications for such activities since primeval days, and as vocal expressions progressed into verbal communications with the development of languages, dependency on voice has become so firmly entrenched that humans are quick to embrace the use of voice as the most effective and most desirable means of communications available.[3]

Six basic kinds of voice-based systems are expected to appear in our office environment within the next decade: (1) voice recognition, (2) voice response, (3) voice identification, (4) voice mail, (5) language training, and (6) language translation. According to Glaser, manufacturers of voice products tend to offer either recognition or response capability; however, it seems inevitable that the combination of technological and market

---

[3] "Voice Recognition and Response—The Next Five Years," presentation by George Glaser, 1981.

forces will move them to develop expertise in and offer both recognition and response technologies.

Voice identification (or speaker verification and/or authentication) is used to verify the identity of a person accessing a system by comparing spoken passwords with computer-stored voice patterns. Voice identification offers a possible method for controlling and accessing secured locations or sensitive data.

Voice mail is the term used to describe systems that store and forward voice messages in much the same way that other communication systems deliver electronic messages.

Electronic language training will someday be an important tool in foreign language education and in the rehabilitation of persons who suffer from speech disabilities. Language translation will provide the capability to translate from one language to another and to translate from the spoken word to text (the ultimate aim of the voice recognition community).[4]

The inability of voice recognition devices to recognize continuous speech has been a barrier to advanced voice-recognition systems. Computer-based voice systems that can recognize the voices of many speakers and many words are still being researched. The handling of tones, accents, and variations in pronunciation and the differentiation of words with the same spelling but different meanings are technological barriers yet to be hurdled.

Future research will be directed toward two major goals.

1. To allow the speaker to speak in a continuous conversational mode without artificial pauses between words, thus allowing technology to recognize complete sentences.
2. To enable recognition of words spoken by speakers who have not previously been trained on the system, with the ultimate goal being to recognize a significant percentage of the general public native to the language.

Voice recognition is one of the least developed unprojected technologies on the horizon.

OCR Technology as an Input Device. Traditionally optical character readers were somewhat limited in their recognition capabilities. However, in the early 1980s, OCR technology has advanced to the point where most page readers can read a broad variety of type styles, including the familiar Courier, Prestige, and Letter Gothic typefaces. The capability to accept a variety of typestyles enables users to capture data from a wider selection of typewriters. Previously, OCR units could recognize only one face, making work from all other typewriters unreadable.

Users of office automation have prompted OCR manufacturers to pro-

[4] Glaser, "Voice Recognition."

duce systems called "convenience scanners." Users want to read anything on paper and input it to word processors, personal computers, phototypesetters, communication devices, and to mainframes containing large data bases. At the same time, users demand that an OCR device be similar to a copying machine in ease of use and friendliness.

Optical character recognition systems are an integral part of today's office. They will continue contributing to the success of information processing systems that increase productivity.

One major alternative to OCR will be voice input systems. As machines become more and more able to understand the human voice and translate it to machine-readable language, OCR will be used less and less for short input documents. It is likely, however, that OCR will remain an important component for capturing lengthy documents, as its unattended mode will allow capture to occur with no labor requirement. The use of OCR systems in connection with professional workstations will play an important role in office automation capabilities in the 1980s. In many instances, the limiting factor to the full use of these workstations is the lack of data bases applicable to a user's workload.

For a number of years to come, as long as we have a paper-based office environment, OCR will play a significant role. As the technology expands to accept typewritten copy, printed copy, statistical data, charts, or drawings, OCR will become the means to input paper-based information into a system. Data-base management systems will allow information to be available instantly to users through their own workstations and terminals. Figure 4 illustrates the flow of paper-based information through OCR into a data base for management access.

The future development of combined OCR and facsimile will allow for the capturing of drawings and charts. These two functions appear to complement each other—both handle data in the form of images recorded on paper. In combination, the natural economies and increased capabilities of the systems can provide the user with increased automation that relates directly to productivity. OCR will continue to provide a means of capturing large amounts of data and transmitting it quickly to a video display for manipulation and/or electronic filing on magnetic media. A new phenomenon will be systems designed to read only areas highlighted with an optical-sensitive marker; this will allow selective capture of text from a typed or printed document. Future OCR devices will be small enough to carry in a briefcase or to be contained in a letter-size desk drawer. These miniature systems will be easily integrated into the professional workstation or carried to the worksite for immediate data capture. As long as a need exists for converting information from printed or typed format to machine-readable language, OCR will make its capabilities felt.[5]

---

[5] Richard D. Barber, "OCR Technology: Where It Is and Where It Is Going", *The Office*, June 1982, p. 56.

Facsimile. For some time to come, the need to communicate paper-based information will continue, even with the advent of local area networks. Because of continued use of paper-based information, there will be a need to integrate facsimile capabilities into such networks. Facsimile, OCR, and other useful peripheral technologies will become part of the total system, mainly through integration into CRT workstations.

As with OCR, miniaturized facsimile machines that can be tucked into a briefcase are under development.

Facsimile is far from a dying technology. However, planners must evaluate facsimile as part of the integrated office network, not just on a point-to-point basis. Planners will need to become accustomed to working with it in combination with other technologies—a process that, if accomplished with imagination, could spawn into some very powerful and capable systems.[6]

Processing, Replication, Storage, and Retrieval

Advancing technology and lowering costs will provide new opportunities in these areas. The demands of users in the office environment will give impetus for continued improvements in large-scale integration technologies. Similar improvements will occur in magnetic storage devices as capacity increases and costs diminish. In the 1960s, it cost about $25 to $30 to store 1 million characters of information. Today, the same amount of information can be stored for less than 40 cents.[7] This trend will continue over the next decade.

With the continuing cost reduction in hardware, the office automation industry will proceed to move toward systems that are smaller, faster, and less expensive (see Figure 5).

A rapid proliferation of personal products began in the very late 1970s. The early 1980s have already witnessed the beginnings of integration of word processing, data processing, communications, and typesetting capabilities.

One of the more dramatic innovations will come in reprographics. Convenience copiers, unlike some other office automation technologies, will not undergo dramatic changes. Most experts in the field believe that it is unlikely that there will be any major technological innovations; instead, we will see refinements in features, such as self-diagnosis, microprocessing, and fiber optics in the smaller plain-paper units. As predicted by an industry executive in the January 1982 issue of *Modern Office Procedures*, a working prototype of a briefcase copier became a reality in 1983.

One of the more promising reprographic products is the dual-application copier, which can be used as a stand-alone copier and as a word processing systems printer. It is expected that the intelligent copier/

[6] "Facsimile Grows to Meet the Future," *Modern Office Procedures*, July 1982, p. 83.
[7] Mark A. Leiberman, Gad J. Selig, and John J. Walsh, *Office Automation* (New York: Wiley Interscience, 1982), p. 211.

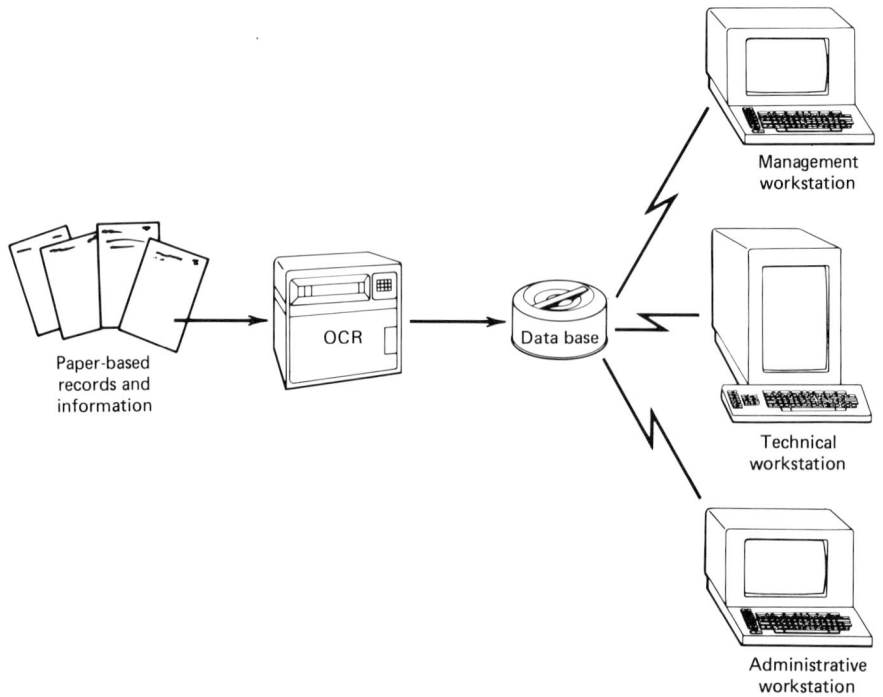

Figure 4   Inputting paper-based information to databases for management access must still be a part of planning as long as we have paper in the office.

Figure 5   *Source: "Backspaces," Word Processing & Information Systems,* August, 1982, p. 46.

printers will have a variety of capabilities, including memory retention and high-quality data scan with printout capabilities. Intelligent copiers that integrate with other equipment, such as small computers, facsimile, and electronic typewriters, will play an important part in the office equipment business. In the next five years, it is expected that the intelligent midrange copiers will have the ability to merge with other office systems, such as word processors and facsimile equipment.

Intelligent copier/printers will continue to have the ability to receive information from electronic sources and create hard-copy output without the need for a hard-copy document. Copier experts do not seem to think that the paperless office will have a large impact on the reprographics industry for many years. It appears that in the near future, no matter how a copy is created on our present and future products, that copy will be replicated, transmitted, or transformed, and end up as hard-paper copy.

Among rapid advances in the micrographics field, electronic photography will provide options to store, recall, transmit, edit, and review images and color. These images will then be positioned to be merged with text and transmitted to printers, digital typesetters, or other devices for printing.

One of the most significant advancements expected in the next decade in storage and retrieval will be the videodisk. Although presently the videodisk is primarily used in home entertainment, continuing research by information processing firms in the United States, Europe, and Japan indicates the development of a new and innovative storage-and-retrieval technique. Indications are that videodisks will have a limited impact on storage and retrieval of digital data in the early 1980s. The technology is expected to have a more dramatic impact late in the decade. According to Mitchell M. Badler, publisher and editor of *Micrographics Newsletter*, videodisk will likely impact COM the most, since it, like direct read-and-write optical disk systems, deals with computer-generated data. Most COM applications seem to be safe, since cost performance criteria are in favor of microforms and will remain so for many years.

The future of videodisk lies in the area of large-storage capacity, fast-access, automatic retrieval systems—an area that microforms have never truly capitalized on. The trend toward digital storage and the superiority of the video process for high-density storage guarantee a place for videodisk in applications for archival storage of digital information. Videodisk technology should appear in 1983-84. Microforms other than COM will also remain as a storage-and-retrieval medium for at least another decade.

Videodisks also offer potential for other fields. Two major vendors, Wang and Eastman Kodak, are working together to solve a mutual problem—effective and economical training of word processing operators. The chosen medium is interactive videodisk, integrated with a Wang workstation, providing computer-aided instruction.

Distribution   Both voice and digital communications are the primary catalysts in expanding the office of the future. In the 1970s, the introduction of clustered word processing systems, shared-logic systems, and communicating word processors set the stage for internal electronic communications. At the same time, the development of information distribution networks between remotely located offices was taking place. Now, satellite communications have become a part of the working world. As communications becomes more accepted in larger organizations, and as educational institutions explain the electronic office as a viable entity, resistance will diminish.

Forward-looking managers are conducting meetings with video conferencing and electronic blackboards in today's offices. These are preliminary concepts that will be integrated into the automated office. They are beginning to cause dramatic changes in the behavioral patterns of personnel within the office environment, in the social structure of workers working in the home, and in the education required for future employees.

Software   The goal of providing information to knowledge workers, secretaries, and all other echelons of management (to allow them to extract, process, and communicate information) will depend entirely on software. It will be necessary to provide software in Englishlike commands, in order to allow users to create their own software to manipulate the information. Access to internal and external data bases will be among the critical applications of the office of the future. Raw data from sources is not enough—managers in automated offices need to understand what that data means. To do so, they must be able to process and compare that data, look for trends, find statistical significances, and compare expected against actual values; hence, software must allow the user to manipulate data.

Traditionally, the development of software took a long time. This trend appears to be changing. Software is available in experienced senior-level programming procedures. Other tools automate the development of large segments of commonly used programs and thus permit junior-level programmers to build a complete program. The bottom line is represented by easy-to-understand common commands that will allow user programming in the automated office.

Maintenance of Office Systems   In the future, users must have systems that have an absolute minimum of downtime. They cannot tolerate a vendor who does not offer reliability. If equipment is leased, the cost of maintaining equipment is usually included in the monthly bill. If a user buys equipment outright, vendors usually provide maintenance agreements for a monthly or annual fee. Either way, the vendor is obliged to support the hardware. Since prompt response to user calls for service has been a serious problem in the past, the evaluation of a vendor's service capability must be a necessary step in the buying process.

Major vendors have put into effect several practices that enable them to offer improved service while holding down cost.

1. Restructuring field support orientation: shifting from offering local service to providing "800"-number telephone service for centralized remote support.

2. Encouraging user self-maintenance: cutting costs by allowing the user to assume some maintenance responsibility, such as initial problem identification and board swapping.

3. Offering disposable products: moving toward the age of "throw-away" circuit boards and replaceable terminals.

4. Offering built-in test equipment for fault detection and isolation: making problem determination easier by building diagnostic test programs into computer systems.

5. Offering remote diagnostics/communications: fully implementing the ability, from a host site, to determine and resolve system problems through communications lines.

6. Building in system and component redundancy: building redundancy into crucial components of computer systems.

7. Offering walk-in repair centers: establishing a network of carry-in depots to which users can bring equipment for repair.

THE SOCIOLOGICAL FUTURE

Technological growth through the next decade will affect people in our society and in our offices. A new set of experiences will result from the increase in knowledge made possible by information processing systems (see Figure 6.) These learning experiences will provide many of the solutions to the structural, behavioral, and personnel changes that will be required to implement the integrated office. The office and the home as we know them will change radically as a result of communications-based technology. Less reliance will be placed on the office as a place of work; information distribution will allow work to be brought *to* the worker. It will change internal procedures as we know them in the office today, as well as travel schedules and arrangements to and from work. This dispersion of workers will cause administrative and personnel managers to restudy the nature of fringe benefits for the worker of tomorrow.

The impact of this information age on aspects other than technological center around (1) human relations (interaction, structure, and isolationism), (2) the work environment (ergonomics), (3) education (to prepare workers for the office of the future), and (4) laws (as they relate to the use of information that is no longer in traditional hard-copy form).

Human Relations

Human relations involve the structure, interaction, and management of people working inside and outside the structured office environment. The structure will change dramatically as more electronic terminals are pro-

"Miss Farber, would you please tell me
what this piece of paper is doing on my desk?"

© DATAMATION

Figure 6   When will there be a truly paperless office? *Source: Datamation,*
March, 1981, p. 120.

vided to personnel. The role of the secretary will become that of a technical specialist. When an employee begins to use a terminal for data and
word processing, storage and retrieval, and communications, job descriptions and objectives change. Not everyone receives technological innovation with enthusiasm.

A great deal of mention is made of managerial workstations. Yet some
managers resist the automation of their functions as strongly as some
secretaries resist the introduction of word processing. This resistance has
challenged vendors to make equipment more user friendly. However, the
challenge to executives and administrators is to explain the benefits of
automation in such a way that it gains the approval and acceptance of
users in management and staff.

As administrative workstations have begun to become accepted, they
have spawned other problems, such as isolationism (i.e., the diminished
contact among employees that reduces the social structure of the office).
In the case of the "cottage industry" worker, it is essential for organizations to establish a plan to reduce the amount of stress caused by working
alone. Conversely, it should be noted that millions of people already
conduct their daily business activities alone, at home, or on the road.
Sales representatives, customer engineers, delivery personnel, and police
officers face these same kinds of sociological circumstances. Many traveling executives find that an office may be a hotel room or a limousine.

There are no simple solutions to the problem of isolationism or the
problem of control of the work force outside the structured office environ-

ment (see Figure 7). This concern will be eliminated, however, when total voice communication becomes available for the delegation of work, providing these remote workers with the human contact on an ongoing basis.

Ergonomics   To alleviate isolationism in the office, many office administrators are paying more attention to the work environment by providing office workers with a pleasing workplace. In addition, environmental considerations such as humidity, heat, appropriate lighting, and convenience are part of the concerns of ergonomics, as explored in an earlier chapter.

Education   Historically, educational institutions have been slow to emphasize new technologies. Many educators continue to teach about the office of yesterday, primarily because the typical office did not change much until the late 1960s. However, the integrated electronic office is not an extension of the past, and future professionals cannot be educated in office practices that have become, or are becoming, obsolete.

The need to increase the productivity of all office workers and the advent of electronic hardware have already altered how the office is organized, managed, and staffed. It is now, more than ever, important that business educators keep up to date by reviewing trade and technical publications, attending seminars and participating in creative study projects, and being active in local and national professional associations.

Business educators must develop their curricula to meet the growing demand for office professionals. It is also important for business educators to continue to form advisory committees composed of local corporate business representatives. Creative business educators today who plan for the continuing growth of technology and expand their own personal hori-

Figure 7 *Source: Infosystems,* February, 1981, p. 116.

zons through continuing education will be the leaders of our educational community.

Educational institutions are sometimes placed in a role that may seem contradictory, because they must provide students with a foundation of traditional skills but at the same time expose them to the opportunities of the information revolution. Business educators should attempt to teach students the flexibility to adapt, since those with flexibility will be more likely to succeed in the office of tomorrow.

LEGAL RAMIFICATIONS The new technology raises a number of legal issues, such as acceptance of video images as legal evidence in courts and the acceptance of teleconferences for important decision-making meetings. Government and regulatory reporting requirements, energy regulations, and the continuing emphasis on equal opportunity within the office environment are all issues that must be of concern to the office automation systems project manager and the executives of those organizations implementing change.

It has taken more than a decade for word processing to progress to its present point. It has taken more than 20 years for data processing to arrive at a point of integration. It has taken people in office environments centuries to reach the point where they are today. Areas for continued concern for human relations include (1) motivation, (2) recognition, (3) self-ego, (4) understanding the nature of work, (5) organizational structures, and (6) management philosophies.

CONCLUSIONS

Today, new products become obsolete quickly—not because they no longer do the job, but because new ideas foster new methods for performing similar jobs better or more easily. It appears that each technological period of development is shorter and shorter in time. Technology has accelerated so rapidly that people must be prepared for the changes it will bring, both technologically and sociologically. Human beings have the power to shape technology, and manufacturers are creating that technology to be more flexible than ever before.

John J. Connell once said, "The office of the future is one in which technology is used to augment human capabilities, not replace, not automate, but augment." Technology and equipment are only tools—acceptance and utilization are what make tools productive. For an effective and painless transition into the integrated electronic office, technological applications and cost-effective benefits must evolve parallel to the needs of the people-oriented environment.

The time has come for the business community to think in global terms and to prepare to do business in those terms. The technology is available, but planning is critical. The way to prepare is to anticipate.

GLOSSARY

ability. The power to perform an activity at the present time.

access time. (1) The time in which a machine is operating and available for use. (2) The time required to receive information once the computer has been signaled.

acoustics. An ergonomic consideration relating to the level of noise within an office and workstation. Noise can be controlled through the engineering and/or the architecture of the space.

action information. Information that requires the recipient to respond in some way.

active files. Records that are used frequently.

active records. Those records consulted in the performance of current administrative work, or records in working files.

actuating. (1) Implementing or starting a process. (2) Putting a process into action.

administrative support. The job function of assisting management in performing tasks of a nontyping nature.

Age Discrimination in Employment Act. A federal statute that prohibits discrimination in hiring on the basis of age.

agenda. A list of topics to be discussed at a meeting, within specific time frames.

alterable information. Information in digital form that can regularly undergo deletions, additions, and revisions, and is everchanging.

analytical staff. Personnel who collect information and data and analyze and define what is revealed by both statistical data and subjective collection of feelings and thoughts.

anatomical considerations. Analysis of the individual's body structure and dimensions and of the physical movement demanded in the work area.

anthropometry. The study of human body measurements for the scaling of sizes, heights, and shapes of furniture and equipment to the dimensions of workers.

applications software. Sets of instructions used to tell the computer how to do a specific job.

aptitude. Potential for performing an activity.

archival record. Records once considered current files that are now semiactive or inactive and are retained for legal, fiscal, administrative, or historical reasons.

archive. To store information.

archives repository. An area established to preserve records for the benefit of posterity.

archiving. The storage of files not currently required but that may be required in the future.

archivist. An individual whose responsibilities include preserving records for the benefit of posterity.

ASCII (American Standard Code for Information Interchange). A character coding system used for transmission.

asynchronous transmission. The mode of transmission between equipment with different protocols, in which a "start" signal precedes and a "stop" signal follows each character to check synchronization, and characters move one at a time along the line.

attrition. Reduction in staff because of resignations, retirement, and so on.

bar graph. A chart that presents information through the use of horizontal or vertical bars.

baseband. A digital pathway ranging from around 1 million bits per second to 50 million bits per second.

batched. Sent in a group; usually refers to the grouping of information and its transmission to an information system.

baud rate. In telecommunications, the rate of signaling speed. The rate of speed expressed in bauds is equal to the number of signaling elements per second.

behavioral change. A type of change that demands the most modification in employee behavior and attitudes.

behavioral modification. A planned approach for attitudinal change, through education and training.

benchmark. A point of reference used in determining a plus or minus accomplishment.

benchmark position. A job which has been measured; performance criteria have been established that provide a determination as to the worth and value of the position.

benevolent autocrat. A leader who lets others rely on him.

best-guesstimate study. A study in which estimates of workloads and time expended are based on input from the support staff individuals being studied.

biomechanical. The study of the musculoskeletal effort of human beings.

black box. An intermediate interpretation device or program used with equipment having different protocols; often called a translator.

body language. Nonverbal messages sent by a person, including paralinguistics (tone of voicing, pacing, etc.).

boilerplate. Presorted documents, such as letters or contracts, to which variable fill-in information can be added via the keyboard.

broadband. Common-cable TV cable that employs modems and allows multiple streams of data to be transmitted simultaneously.

budget. A short-term plan for how an organization is going to obtain and use its financial resources.

bus network. A network that consists of a length of coaxial cable (called a bus) along which individual devices tap into the communications cable. There is no centralized hub—signals from one station move along the bus in both directions to all stations tapped into the cable.

CAI (computer-assisted instruction). The use of electronic equipment as a training tool.

"can-do" tests. Performance tests.

CAR (computer-assisted retrieval). The retrieval of historical information from a company's records through the use of a video-display terminal. Infor-mation can be read from the screen or produced in hard-copy form.

carbon copy collection. The collection of the copies of all typing accomplished during a set time period.

career and life planning. Identifying what it is one wants to do, not only for the present, but also for some steps beyond that.

cassettes. Magnetic tape for recording information.

CAT (computer-aided transcription). The capture of keystrokes onto a magnetic media that is then processed through a computer and printed out.

CBX (computerized branch exchange). A digital communication device.

centralization. The location of one or more functions at a single site with a central support staff organization.

CIM (computer input microfilm). A microform-based information storage and retrieval system.

cohesion. The formation of voluntary groups who share the same or approximately the same attitudes, opinions, feelings, and actions.

cold type. Typesetting on typewriterlike machines or by photocomposition.

color/decor. An ergonomic consideration relating to appropriate office and workstation colors based on space, type of work, time spent in area, and so on.

COM (computer output microfilm). A micrographics form of output whereby microfilm and microfiche are produced directly as computer output, without the intermediate hard-copy and microfilming steps.

commitment. The pledge of one's support of and display of one's belief in a process through involvement. Committed personnel must be willing to undergo whatever personal or professional changes are necessary to carry out their responsibilities.

communications processing. The manipulation and distribution of information through video-display terminal devices.

compaction. A reduction in the number of characters per page achieved by reducing the length of the lines and the size of the characters.

computer graphics. Graph representations produced on the computer.

computer output mailing system. A mailing system that allows computer-printed continuous forms to be fed into equipment that automatically bursts the forms, inserts them into envelopes, designates zip code breaks, and meter-stamps them for mailing.

computer teleconferencing. A telecommunications process in which words, data, facsimile images, and voice are transmitted from one geographical location to another.

conference method. A training session in which trainees are encouraged to express themselves orally and to exchange and compare ideas.

confidential questionnaires. Forms used to gather confidential suggestions, concerns, and opinions about intangible forces that affect both managerial and secretarial/clerical productivity.

conformity. The act of behaving and expressing opinions consistent with group norms.

contingency or situational leadership. Leadership that relies for success on good leader/member relations, a well-defined task structure, and the power of the position.

continuity. Continuing rather than occasional support; equal treatment.

conventional planning. The designing of office space with many enclosed areas divided by permanent walls.

convergence. The act of coming together and uniting in a common interest.

cost avoidance. The elimination or reduction of costs in a budget through elimination of the necessity for temporary help, overtime, or additional budgeted personnel.

cost avoidance factors. Those elements of a budget, such as overtime salaries, temporary help, and budgeted additional employees, that are amenable to cost avoidance procedures.

cost benefit. The hard- and soft-dollar savings achieved by implementation of an automated system.

cost center. The part of a business department that is responsible for costs that pertain to that area.

cost of change. The dollars that must be expended to implement change in an office.

cottage labor. A part-time work force operating at home; may use electronic equipment.

counting-documents method. A method used to determine the amount of typing produced whereby any completed task (letter, report, etc.) is counted as one document and documents are then totaled for over a set time period (a day, a week, etc.).

counting-lines method. A method of determining the amount of typing produced by counting the lines produced within a given period of time.

CPU (central processing unit). The information storage area shared by multiple data or word processing terminals.

CRM (certified records manager). A professional classification granted to records managers who have completed prerequisite training and met the accreditation requirements for certification.

CRT (cathode ray tube). An electronic vacuum tube, similar to a television picture tube, that displays text as it is entered from the keyboard.

data base. The compilation and storage of information consisting of data and/or text for the purposes of access, retrieval, and/or printout.

data-base management. The management of data via machine storage rather than paper files.

data collection. The process of gathering information about office operations.

data processing. The manipulation of numbers through various computations to deliver meaningful totals and create useful statistical information.

data retrieval. The recall of prestored material from a system.

DBMS (data-base management system). A computer software that handles the storage and retrieval of records stored in direct-access computer data bases.

decentralization. The locating of minicomputers and terminals, as well as word processors with stand-alone intelligence, in the various departments of an organization.

decision package. A document that identifies and describes a specific activity in such a manner that management can (1) evaluate it and rank it against other activities competing for limited resources and (2) decide whether to approve or disapprove it.

decision support systems. Special software that provides significant aids for financial planning, portfolio analysis, tax planning, and market analysis, and for projecting business situations that require mathematical formula calculations.

delegation. The assigning of tasks to others.

democratic leadership. A style of leadership in which workers are encouraged to participate in the decision-making process.

desk manual. A guidebook to particular duties and tasks that remains with the job and the workstation for which it was written.

destruction. The shredding, pulverizing, or burning of hard copy; the purging, erasing, or deleting of magnetic media or on-line storage.

determinants of effective leadership. The situational elements that dictate which type of style will be successful in a given situation (e.g., the size of the organization, the amount of interaction, the personalities of leader and group members, the level on which decision making is encouraged, the organization's health).

dictatorial leadership. A style of leadership marked by criticism of others and negative relationships with subordinates.

digital. Data transmission in the form of discrete units; a process that transmits data by translating sound waves into on/off digital pulses.

discipline. Necessary action taken to correct a problem within the office.

distributed system. A system that provides decentralized memory and storage capacity yet allows network connections and communication over dissimilar peripherals.

distribution. The moving of information from one point to another.

documentary information. Information that is recorded in some kind of permanent form, such as in written or printed materials.

documentation. (1) A memo that describes an incident clearly and fairly, and thus permits a problem to be confronted supportively and with just cause. (2) Observation of a machine in operation, to determine its usefulness to an office.

downtime. Time when equipment cannot be used because of malfunction.

DSK (Dvorak simplified keyboard). Developed in 1932, this typewriter keyboard makes it possible for 70 percent of the work to be done on the home row and a majority of the stroking to be done by right hand.

EBCDIC (extended binary coded decimal information code). An eight-bit alphanumeric code used on all IBM computers.

editing. The correction, refinement, or revision of written material.

EEO (equal employment opportunity). A 1966 federal act that provides a nationwide pattern for fair employment practices by prohibiting discrimination in hiring because of race, color, religion, or national origin.

electronic blackboard. A blackboard developed by Bell Laboratories, division of AT&T, that transmits graphics and handwritten communications over telephone lines for viewing on video monitors in distant locations.

electronic data processing. The manipulation of data through the use of electronic computers.

electronic mail. A system of communicating messages electronically to a recipient who receives either a hard copy or a visually-displayed message on a CRT screen. The message may be transmitted electronically by facsimile, communicating word processors, computer-based message systems, public-carrier-based systems, public postal services, or private and public teletypes.

electronic mailbox. A computer-based message system on which messages can be left until the user makes an inquiry.

electronic proof. Data-base storage from which information can be recalled and reconstructed by electronic means. Proofing is accomplished by viewing the copy and editing it right at the visual display terminal.

employee turnover. The leaving and replacement of employees in an organization.

employer evaluations. A form of measurement for determining the level of employee performance on the job. Measurement tools can include forms, interviews, observation, testing, and supervisory opinions.

enclosure and access needs. These space design needs may be determined by type of work performed. Space design must also recognize the need to access areas such as restrooms and lunchrooms, so as not to contribute to a congested traffic pattern.

energy concerns. Ergonomic considerations related to the cost-effective consumption of energy (heating, lighting, water, etc.)

engineering approach. An approach to the analysis of office functions based upon the detailed study of individual jobs, which are broken down into their vital components to see whether they can be eliminated altogether or combined with other jobs.

Equal Pay Act. A federal statute that requires equal pay based on actual job requirements and performance.

ergonomic concerns. Workstation features designed to promote optimum employee performance.

ergonomics. Facilities planning focused on the esthetics of the workstation and its surrounding space (e.g., the needs for privacy, a smooth flow of paperwork and communication, balanced territorial and social concerns, adequate access to electrical and communications circuits, and proper lighting, climate, acoustics, and color/decor.

ergonomics and productivity. The relationship between ergonomics principles and maximum worker productivity.

event schedule. A written timetable of steps to be taken to accomplish a goal (e.g., a step-by-step plan to implement office automation).

evidential-value records. Records that show how an organization came into being, how it developed, how it was organized, what its function has been, and the results of its activities.

evolutionary. The process of gradually implementing change.

exempt positions. Jobs that are not covered by the minimum-wage standards set by the Fair Labor Standards Act.

external information. Data that originate outside an organization, such as information concerning the products and services of competitors.

facsimile (also called fax). A process that involves the transmission of an exact copy over communications lines; facsimile combines replication and distribution functions, since it duplicates exact copies of graphs, pictures, and other materials and transmits them to other locations.

factor comparison. The use of a set of factors (e.g., education, experience) for evaluation.

Fair Labor Standards Act (FLSA). A federal statute that sets minimum wage guidelines.

feasibility concepts. Aspects of the traditional office that must be examined by the feasibility study and what changes are likely to occur.

fiber optics. The technique of converting communication signals to light pulses that are sent over strands of hair-thin glass fibers.

financial lease. A lease arrangement whereby the lessor recovers the full cost of the equipment, plus expenses and a profit. The lessee may receive title to the equipment at the end of the lease period.

first-line supervision. Management of ongoing operations at the department level.

fixed information. Hard copy, microfilm, and other image storage that is unalterable in time and format.

fixed-frame video. A video process in which a new picture is transmitted several times per minute; the monitor displays an image for a number of seconds, until the next frame is received.

fleet maintenance. The process of monitoring the maintenance of a company-owned vehicle and maintaining records on computer-based equipment (serial numbers, depreciation schedules, etc.).

flexibility. The ability to adjust to changing conditions and demands.

floor plan. A graphic portrayal of how an area should be physically arranged. Arrows usually are used to show the flow of work.

flowchart. A diagram that uses symbols to illustrate the flow of work and paper through the office, from origin to completion.

formatting. The process of composing the basic form or style of text.

fringe benefits. Employee compensation outside the basic salary.

full-motion video. A closed-circuit television setup in which all activity is captured and transmitted to another location.

furnishings. Office fixtures (chairs, desks, equipment, pictures, plants, etc.).

Gantt chart. A graphic illustration (developed by Henry L. Gantt) of scheduled work on a vertical scale (function) and horizontal scale (estimated time).

generalist. A person whose job description contains several different duties.

global network. The worldwide integration of many networks.

goals. Something at which effort is directed; end result.

guideline method. A technique for interpreting and reflecting the value of jobs in the marketplace.

half-duplex. A type of transmission in which signals travel in both directions, but only in one direction at a time. Half-duplex is satisfactory for most transmission between computers and terminals.

hard dollars. Those expenditures of money that can be measured and controlled (e.g., the salaries of employees, cost of equipment).

hard-dollar savings. Those salary and fringe benefit costs that can be saved through reduction of staff.

hardware. A basic piece of equipment.

health hazards. Dangers to employee health attributable to the performance of a job (e.g., eye fatigue from constant work with video display screens).

hierarchy of needs. Abraham Maslow identified a hierarchy or ladder of needs and theorized that people can attempt to satisfy a higher-level need only after satisfying at least some of the lower-level needs.

historical data approach. An approach to studying an office that involves gathering information from past records about the time and amount of work associated with a certain job.

historical information. Records of events related to a particular topic, which are retained for purposes of history.

hot type. A form of typesetting in which the form of the letter to be produced is cast in molten metal (e.g., handset and casting).

human resource staff. Employees who redevelop, redesign, and/or restructure job descriptions and appropriate reporting relationships.

human resources. People on staff.

icon. A picture or symbol on a video display screen that depicts or symbolizes a computer function; when a user points to the icon with a "mouse" a pointer displayed on the screen), the computer performs the function depicted.

image copying. The process of replicating images through the use of OCR, laser copiers, or facsimile duplication.

image printing. A printing process in which the entire image is produced in hard-copy form from a stored picture of that image in a cathode ray or an internal source.

improved productivity. An increase in the amount of work performed.

inactive files. Files that must be retained only because of legal guidelines or that are awaiting destruction at a time specified by the company's retention schedule.

inactive records. Records infrequently referred to. Inactive records often are transferred to a records center or other storage area.

in-basket training. A simulation of actual office conditions, often conducted in the form of a business game.

incident process. The presentation of an incident or a problem situation in only a few sentences, designed to force trainees to ask careful questions in order to obtain additional pertinent facts.

incremental budget. A budget in which expenses for the coming year are based on the preceding year or on some average of preceding years.

information management. Supervision and control over a system that creates, gathers, processes, replicates, distributes, stores, and/or destroys the information utilized by an organization.

information processing. An integrated system created by the merger of data processing and word processing. In an information processing system, all forms of business information (data, text, image, and voice) are freely accessible to workers at all levels, within necessary security restrictions.

informational-value records. Records that provide information that should be preserved for future generations.

innovative objectives. Goals that represent a new stage in technology or theory.

in-plant printing. Printing done within an organization rather than by an outside printer.

input. The entering of source data or text into a system for processing.

integrated systems. Systems that permit multiple functions to occur simultaneously and permit the user to combine text and data in a single application with little or no difficulty.

intelligent copiers. Copiers that can electronically store materials such as often-used forms, and thereby eliminate the need for hard-copy storage facilities.

interconnection. That part of the integrated electronic phase in which various electronic and/or technological components are tied together.

interface. The potential for communication between or among different machines in an office.

interim approach. A stop-gap, short-term approach to office automation.

internal information. Information generated within the organization (production schedules, payrolls, policy manuals, organizational directives, etc.).

involvement. Taking part in; being included.

job analysis. The study of the duties and operations to be performed in a specific job.

job classification. The analysis and rating of jobs according to predetermined classes (the same or similar task groupings).

job description. A written, organized presentation of the duties involved in a specific job.

job design. The process of dividing all the work into units.

job enrichment. The process of heightening both task efficiency and human satisfaction by providing greater scope for personal achievement and recognition in jobs, more challenging and responsible work, and more opportunity for individual advancement and growth.

job evaluation. Any formal procedure for appraising, classifying, and weighing a set of functions.

job fit. A successful match between an employee and a job.

job redesign. The rethinking of a job and what it contains, with a view toward expanding the job by including in it more horizontal and vertical activities.

job specifications. The minimum requirements of a job.

keyboarding. The process of logging data into a system and assigning to the data an index designation for future distribution and/or retrieval.

keystroke counters. Electronic counting devices that count the number of keystrokes produced on input devices.

knowledge. An organized body of information, usually of a factual or procedural nature.

knowledge worker. Any management, professional, or clerical worker who processes information for use in decision making.

laissez-faire leadership. Leaders who serve as information givers to the members of the group but delegate responsibility for all decisions to employees, allowing them to establish their own goals and make their own decisions.

LAN (local area network) duplex. An interlinked arrangement of computers (usually microprocessors) that permits a single computer in the network both to operate independently and to access directly other computers in a network over a limited area (1500 feet to three miles).

laser printing. A printing process similar to image printing, except that it operates by laser control rather than direct impact.

lateral career paths. Horizontal career moves that allow employees who either do not have the qualifications to move upward or do not wish to work in a position with increased responsibility to change jobs while remaining at the same level.

lateral file. A drawer file turned sideways, with the side opening to the front.

leader-member-relations task structure. The extent to which leaders get along with their subordinates and subordinates are committed to their leader.

learning curve. A measure of the rate of learning in relation to the length of training.

lecture method. A method of instruction in which the instructor conducts a training session and does all the talking.

life cycle. A system cycle that meets the objectives of the organization. When the office becomes too crowded, equipment is out of date, and procedures are no longer relevant, a new system cycle should be implemented.

life span or cycle of a record. The successive stages undergone by a record (creation, processing, storage, retrieval, and retention or destruction).

lighting. An ergonomic consideration that takes into account the effect of illumination within offices and workstations on the eyes of workers.

line counting. The electronic or manual process of counting typed lines.

line graph. A chart that uses various types of lines to show fluctuations in a value or quantity over a period of time.

logging. The act of putting information onto a log sheet or into a system.

long-range strategy. A long-term plan for implementing the optimum office automation goals.

LSI (large scale integration) circuits. The process of mass-producing electronic circuits by etching up to 10,000 transistors onto silicon chips.

machine dictation. The act of speaking into a microphone and recording ideas on magnetic tape for later transcription onto paper by a secretary or word processing operator.

magnetic media. Any type of magnetically-charged belt, card, disk, or tape used to store, make corrections, erase, or rewrite documents.

Mailgram. Correspondence sent via the E-COM system, an electronic mail facility.

Mailmobile. A driverless vehicle designed for mechanized mail delivery. The cost of a mailmobile is comparable to the annual salary of one messenger.

mainframe. The central processing unit (CPU) that houses the hardware, software, and operating controls of a computer.

make-ready and put-away time. The time spent dealing with roughly drafted reports that can be eliminated through the use of proper equipment.

Management by objective (MBO). A management strategy that focuses on goals.

management effectiveness. The measurement of how productive the managerial staff is.

managerial workstation. A work area designed for the professional knowledge worker. It usually contains a computer terminal with time management controls, text editing features, electronic mail capabilities, files processing capability, and other features.

manipulation. The process of rearranging the format of text and data (e.g., changing the order of the paragraphs) to come up with the most workable form in which to present the information.

matrix management. An organizational setup that combines centralized and decentralized characteristics.

micrographics. The process of recording and reducing paper documents or computer-generated information on film and providing a system to store and retrieve that information.

microprocessor. A miniscule logic circuit on a microchip of silicon that can perform over 1 million calculations per second.

mobile storage system. A storage system in which files are put on tracks in order to eliminate the need for aisles for each set of files.

modeling. That aspect of leadership that involves providing an effective model of efficiency and motivation for others to follow.

modem. A *modulator/demodulator*, which converts digital information to and from analog form.

Motivation-hygiene Theory. A theory (set forth by Frederick Herzberg) that holds that attention to the external as well as the internal factors of an individual will promote job satisfaction or dissatisfaction.

mouse. The electronic pointer on a video-display screen with which a user designates the function he or she wants the computer to perform.

MTM (measure time and motion). The measurement of time by applying time measurement units (tmu) to each singular function or task to determine time and motion standards.

multifunction terminals. Systems based on mainframe computers or minicomputers equipped with special software that provide specific services on computer terminals; such terminals generally are used for many functions.

narrative. A report in text form, as opposed to chart or graph form.

needs assessment study. A study aimed at providing an overall perspective on an organization's needs as a basis for future planning.

network. A system that interconnects a wide assortment of information processing devices through a communications line or data base.

networking. The linking of various information processing devices, such as word processors and data entry units, storage devices, printers, processors, and other peripherals, to send, receive, exchange, store, or reproduce information.

nonaction information. Information on which no action is required.

nondocumentary information. Information that is not recorded. Usually obtained through word of mouth and/or personal observation.

nonexempt positions. Jobs covered by the Fair Labor Standards Act that must pay the applicable minimum and overtime wage scales.

nonimpact printers. Photocomposition printers.

nonoriginal input. That information already existing in a system.

nonrecord. A convenience copy that normally is discarded when no longer needed.

nonrecurring information. Information that is reported and used once in its lifetime.

norm. Any uniformity of attitude, opinion, feeling, or action shared by two or more people.

objective data. Data that deal with things rather than with thoughts or feelings.

objectives. See goals.

OCR (optical character recognition). The process by which a system scans typewritten pages and stores the scanned characters in digital form.

OCR (optical character reader). A machine that can read printed or typed characters and then digitally convert them into input to a data or word processor.

off-the-shelf applications package. Software packages sold by computer vendors or by separate software outlets. Such packages provide freedom and flexibility to experiment, as they can be obtained and used or discarded quickly and easily.

office automation systems. Systems that offer word processing as part of a bundle of office functions that includes electronic mail and message distribution, electronic filing, data access, data processing, and administrative functions such as calendaring, scheduling, and tickler systems.

office services. Support or administrative services provided to employees (e.g., supplies inventorying, printing).

offset printing. A printing process in which copies are made from an original copy produced on either a paper or a metal plate.

open-office planning. Designing office space with minimal enclosed areas, using movable wall panels.

operating lease. A lease arrangement whereby equipment is leased for a fixed sum each month. The lessor does not normally recover the full cost of the equipment over the period of the lease.

operating-systems software. Sets of instructions used to tell the microprocessor how to act.

optical disk. A disk that uses laser technology to provide high-density storage of either data or image information.

organization chart. A graphic presentation of the organizational structure that points out responsibility relationships.

organizational concerns. The human, procedural, and technological concerns involved with automating an organization's office environment.

organizational culture. A company's values, attitudes, and degree of competitiveness and commitment, which reflect top management's approach to decision making.

organizational objectives. Company goals.

organizational structure. The hierarchy of authority, span of control, and areas of responsibility within an organization.

orientation or induction training. Training that acquaints new employees with the company's history, philosophy, policy, practices, and procedures (office rules and regulations, employee benefits, etc.).

original input. Information put into a system for the first time.

originators. Individuals who create information or text.

overhead transparency. A clear plastic sheet that, when placed on a lighted glass surface, projects the image on the sheet in magnified form onto a screen.

overstaffing. The employment of too many people; idle people are given makework jobs.

PBX (private branch exchange). An electromechanical communications device—usually, a manned switchboard.

performance appraisal. A formal evaluation of an employee's job performance.

peripherals. Hardware added onto a basic system (e.g., printers and paper feeders).

personal computer. A computer designed for use by managers and professionals rather than by computer specialists.

personal development objectives. Goals concerned with acquiring additional knowledge, skills, and experience that will improve present job performance and help an individual move upward.

phase-in process. An area-by-area approach to office automation.

phototypesetter. A device that converts text in digital form to printed material.

phototypesetting. A method by which information can be reproduced efficiently through a printing process that prints characters optically by taking pictures of them at high speeds.

physiological considerations. Those factors in the work environment that affect the behavior and attitudes of workers.

pie chart. A circular diagram divided into sections ("slices") that normally is used to present information in percentages.

pilot. A prototype installation.

point method. A method of evaluation in which a range of points is assigned to a set of common factors (e.g., education, skill).

position power. The degree to which the leadership position itself enables leaders to get group members to comply with their wishes.

presorted mail. Mail that is sorted according to zip codes, carrier routes, and so on before mailing.

primary group. A close-knit group whose members know the norms that govern the conduct of each member.

principle of supportive relationships. A theory of manager-employee interaction that holds that the manager should treat employees as individuals who deserve attention and understanding rather than as faceless people who must get a job done.

privacy/involvement conflict. The human conflict between personal desire for a private office and the need for involvement. One way to achieve compromise, according to Robert Propst, is through the use of modular panels of differing heights and through attention to the principle of operation concerning enclosure and access.

problem-oriented solution. The process of identifying and isolating a problem and providing a solution to that one problem.

problem-solving objectives. Goals for identifying a problem and developing a solution.

processing. The manipulation of information that has been input into a system for replication and for distribution in the form of communication.

production logging. A systematic listing of jobs accomplished in a day, a week, and so on.

productivity. Measurement of the ratio of work done to time spent doing it.

productivity gains. Improvements in employee work output.

PROFS. IBM mainframe software for professionals.

programmed instruction. A self-instruction method in which information is systematically presented to the trainee.

protocol. The language in which a message sent from one machine to another is packaged and handled.

prototype. A test situation involving installations or equipment being considered for wider use in the company.

psychological considerations. Environmental factors such as light, color, sound, and heat.

qualitative data. Employee perceptions of how and why things are done within the system.

quality circles (QC). A group or circle of employees that meets to discuss how to improve the quantity and quality of work.

quality of work life (QWL). A factor of work life that can be enriched when employees are involved in decisions affecting their work environment.

quantitative data. Measurable work being accomplished, the type of information required by management, and the time it takes to produce such information.

QWERTY. The left-hand top-row characters on standard typewriters and keyboards. (Originally designed by Christopher Sholes in order to avoid clashing typebars.)

ranking. The sequential listing of all jobs in an organization, from top to bottom, according to their perceived worth to the organization.

real labor costs. All labor costs, including payroll costs.

record. Official document that furnishes information that is stored for future reference.

records center. Areas established for the storage and servicing of inactive or semiactive records.

records format. Formats designed to meet requirements of paper systems, micrographics, and computerized systems.

records management. The systematic handling of documents from creation to destruction, including filing and micrographics, archiving, and destruction.

records series. Identical or related records that are normally used and filed as a unit and that can be evaluated as a unit for purposes of retention or destruction.

recurring information. Information that an organization regularly and frequently uses, such as sales, inventory, and production reports.

reduction ratio. The size ratio between a film image and the original document.

reference documents. Documents that contain or communicate information needed to carry on the business.

reference group. Any recognizable organization that in itself can be characterized as having norms and standards.

regular or routine objectives. Necessary statements of goals that define the regular, ordinary requirements for the survival of the organization.

Rehabilitation Act of 1973. A federal statute that prohibits discrimination in hiring on the basis of physical or other handicaps.

replication. The duplication of information in another form.

report. A compilation of information and intelligence that is furnished to management or other departments or offices in an organization.

reprographics. The various techniques of replicating information with the ultimate objective of distributing it in some form. Replication techniques include printing, phototypesetting, duplicating, and COM (computer output microfilm).

requisites. Fundamental factors that can be controlled and measured.

resources. Basic sources of power for the exercise of responsibilities and the achievement of results.

responsibilities. Something for which one has a moral, legal, or mental accountability.

responsibility chart. A chart indicating who is responsible for each implementation function.

results. Consequences, effects, or solutions.

results-centered leadership. Leadership that is concerned with the "work itself" approach to motivation.

retrieval. The recalling of stored information for reuse.

rigidity. The inability to adapt to changing conditions. Strict adherence to a concrete plan of operation.

ring network. A network in which individual devices are connected in a loop or ring, via a string of signal repeaters. If one device in the ring breaks down or is added to, the entire network is put out of operation.

role playing. Acting out common situations. Trainees participate in role playing to gain insight into their own behavior and that of others, and to view situations more objectively.

satellite communications. Electronic telecommunications via worldwide satellite transmission.

self-evaluation. A review of where one is, where one is going, and how one will get there through a program of self-development.

self-paced instruction. Instruction through individual learning packets that consist of a planned program through which an individual moves at his or her own pace.

shared-logic system. A system in which multiple video-display screens and output devices simultaneously use the memory and processing powers of one computer.

short-range strategy. A short-term plan for implementing office automation.

silicon chip. See microprocessor.

single-element typewriter. A typewriter that uses a type ball containing characters (e.g., Selectric typewriters).

skill. The proficient manual, verbal, or mental manipulation of data, people, or things.

soft dollars. Those expenditures of money that can be estimated but not controlled (e.g., improved productivity through conversion from longhand to machine dictation).

soft-dollar savings. Reductions in expenditures that come about when management employees delegate work and utilize time management techniques.

software. A program that instructs a computer to perform operations it ordinarily cannot perform.

space. Office work area.

specialist. A person whose job description limits the duties for which he or she is responsible.

stand-alone display system. A self-contained word processing unit that uses its own memory and processing powers for keyboarding, storage, text editing, and printing.

standard. Any agreed-upon rule against which comparison can be made. The amount of production considered fair to both the company and the employee for a specified period of time under specified conditions.

star network. A network in which all communications pass through some form of switcher at the hub of the configuration.

statistical approach. An approach to studying an office that uses one or all of the following methods: historical data, work sampling, and time studies.

steps of implementation. Those procedures followed to put something into effect.

storage. The systematic preservation of information within the system in some form.

strike-on composition. Composition in which keys strike paper to make a mark (e.g., typing).

study team. A group of people responsible for conducting a study. The team is usually made up of representatives from key office areas, such as data processing, records management, and reprographics.

subjective approach. An approach to studying an office that focuses on rule-of-thumb standards based on the experiences and opinions of individual supervisors.

subjective data. Data that reflect personal values and interpretations.

support personnel. Those employees who provide assistance to others.

support-systems feasibility study. A study conducted to determine the volume and kind of work done in an office by both management and support employees.

synchronous transmission. The mode of transmission between equipment with different protocols, in which each character must arrive at a predetermined time—which requires synchronization between sender and receiver.

table. A list of facts and figures formatted in columns or blocked paragraphs for easy reading.

task. An action or series of actions taken by a person to produce a result.

task-oriented responsibility. Responsibility without much opportunity for creativity or personal initiative.

telecommunications. (1) The electronic transfer of data or information from one point in an information system to another through a unit that performs the necessary format conversion and controls the rate of transmissions, including transmission from one computer system or station to remotely located devices. (2) The ability to relay messages from one place to another without paper.

telecommunications manager. A person who has total responsibility for the management of the personnel who plan, install, maintain, and create networks of communication and monitor the transmission lines for the communication functions of an organization.

teleconferencing. Simultaneous processing of data messages and visual connections for the purpose of sending pictures and voices through telephone wires to screens and speakers in other locations.

temperature. The degree of hotness or coldness of something; ergonomic factor whereby comfort control and humidity are given consideration when designing office space.

territoriality. The need for personal work space.

text input. The keyboarding of text into an information system.

Theory X and Theory Y. Two theories of management. Theory X assumes that successful management of people requires total control. Theory Y assumes that employee self-control and self-direction, with minimal managerial involvement, will result in successful management. A combination of both theories usually is required to perform daily supervisory functions.

Theory Z. William Ouchi's theory based on the belief that a management and/or company philosophy should be less rigidly structured than Theory X or Y (e.g., formal reporting relationships, job assignments, and divisions between departments are imprecise and unclear).

third-party service. Service obtained from a company other than the equipment manufacturer.

throughput. The volume of typing, including dictation, transcription, and revision.

time and motion study. The timing of each motion or activity performed on a job.

time ladder. A list of functions performed together with colored-in time periods indicating when employees performed each task.

time sheet. A sheet that lists the functions performed each day and the length of time it took to perform them.

time standards. The amount of work that should be done under specified conditions and methods.

time studies approach. An approach to studying an office in which an individual job is analyzed or reduced to individual tasks, which are then timed to determine the average time per task.

timekeeping procedures. Measurements of the time it takes individuals to perform support tasks, both typing and nontyping in nature.

Title VII of the Civil Rights Act. A federal statute that prohibits discrimination in hiring on the basis of race, color, religion, sex, or national origin.

tmu. A time measurement unit equivalent to 0.00001 hours or 0.036 seconds.

topology. The physical and logical configuration of networks; the way in which devices are connected to one another and to a traffic processing system.

total support system. A planned structure for integrating all services formerly considered separate functions into a support staff under centralized supervision and control.

total system solution. A comprehensive, integrated support system in which priority consideration is given to compatibility with a mainframe.

touch-typing. A method of typing that involves memorizing the keyboard and typing while looking at the copy; memorization is facilitated by the use of 10 home-key positions to which the fingers always return.

training specialists. People within the organization who are responsible for instructing others.

transaction documents. Documents that record the individual day-to-day transactions of an organization.

transaction processing. The processing of a specific business action such as a sale, a paycheck, or a change in inventory.

transcribing. The keyboarding of information into a system for future access.

transitional approach. An interim or short-term approach to automation.

transitional office. The conversion of a traditional office into an electronic office through a series of logical steps and strategic plans.

tuition assistance. Refunds for approved educational courses provided by the organization to an employee.

typesetting. Methods of printing, such as handset, casting, typewriter composition, and photocomposition.

typing production. Typing volume measured in lines, pages, documents, or other criteria for a specific period of time.

unbundled services. Services not included in the original purchase of equipment and provided by vendors for a separate charge.

understaffing. The hiring of too few people to meet the demands of the workload.

upgrades. Additions to or replacement of software or hardware that updates existing software or hardware.

upward mobility. The opportunity to move from one (vertical) job level to another; career progression.

user-friendly. The attribute of a system that is easy to use.

user manual. A guidebook for principals describing the services that the support system provides.

vendor. A company that sells technology, furniture, supplies, and services to meet the needs of the automated office.

verbal imagery. The ways in which people use words to create images.

verbal input. The dictation of information into an electronic dictation system or the voice input of information into a voice recognition system.

vertical career paths. Career paths that lead upward to positions of increased responsibility and on to managerial positions.

vertical files. Conventional file cabinets, whose drawers open at the front.

vestibule or classroom training. Training that takes place away from the workstation but on the premises, usually in a classroom setting.

videodisk. A television recording on magnetic disk.

videotape. A television recording on magnetic tape.

Visicalc. An electronic worksheet that helps professionals plan budgets, create forecasts, and develop pricing strategies.

visual display. The process of displaying information on a cathode ray tube (CRT) or video-display terminal (VDT).

vital records. Information needed to establish or continue an organization in the event of a disaster.

VLSI (Very Large-Scale Integration). Circuits that incorporate vast quantities of logic; the compression of more than 10,000 transistors on a single chip.

voice activation. A feature on dictation equipment that activates the tape when a person speaks and deactivates it when there is a pause.

voice mail. The storing of messages in digital form for transmission to a receiving point at a later time.

voice recognition. The process by which systems "recognize" spoken words and convert them to digital signals sent to an attached system or display device.

voice response. The process by which systems "respond" to an inquiry by converting the answer stored digitally in computer memory.

voice synthesis devices. Machines that enable visually-impaired workers to interact with computers or word processors.

word processing. The transcribing of an idea into a document by means of automatic equipment.

work-count unit. A standardized, predefined specific quantity, such as a character, a line, a page, or a document.

workflow. The path or steps that work takes from origination to completion through a given department or organization.

work measurement. A method for determining workload volumes and improvements in work or in work groups by comparing what has been accomplished against a standard.

work sample. A collection of sample materials for quantitative measurement by size, nature of the materials, and required format.

work-sampling approach. An approach to studying an office in which a manager observes work at random periods or gathers copies of work to determine the amount of work accomplished in sample periods.

work standards. Work measurement approaches—subjective, statistical, or engineering.

zero-base budget. A budget that is rebuilt from a base of zero each year.

APPENDICES

A. SAMPLES OF OFFICE AUTOMATION OBJECTIVES
B. OFFICE AUTOMATION FEASIBILITY QUESTIONNAIRE
C. IMPLEMENTATION PLAN
D. JOB DESCRIPTIONS
E. PERFORMANCE GUIDELINES AND MEASUREMENT
F. REQUEST FOR PROPOSAL AND EQUIPMENT EVALUATION CHECKLISTS
G. PROCEDURES AND CONTROL FORMS

APPENDIX A

SAMPLES OF OFFICE AUTOMATION OBJECTIVES

Setting objectives for office automation is the first step in achieving the organization's goal.

Ralston Purina Company

Ralston Purina Company
St. Louis, Missouri

Carol S. Morrison
Senior Staff Consultant, Productivity
Human Resources Division

PRODUCTIVITY IMPROVEMENT DEFINITION

The measurable gain derived from the planned change of policies, methods, procedures, organizations, and/or processes that increase business unit effectiveness with the same or fewer resources, thus adding value to the business unit.

CHARTER

Goal

Provide a human resource framework and direction for effectively managing office productivity.

Scope

Effective human resource management of office productivity encompasses people and organizations, machines and tools, facilities, and information.

Responsibility

The Human Resource Division Productivity function will:

▶ Assist management in setting overall direction for productivity improvement.
▶ Assist in defining and sharing ideas for improvement.
▶ Guide in planning and implementing overall productivity improvement strategy:
  —evaluation and assessment;
  —implementation and tracking;
  —training;
  —audit and analysis.

Objectives

1. Establish measurement target(s) that will show improved office productivity.
2. Streamline information flow in conjunction with workflow.
3. Assist in establishing requirements for automated office technology.
4. Promote increased awareness of human resource office management as a vital responsibility necessary to control and reduce costs and improve productivity.

Exhibit A-1 A sample of the productivity improvement definition indicating a goal and setting objectives (courtesy of Ralston Purina Company, St. Louis, Missouri).

OFFICE SYSTEMS ADVISORY COMMITTEE PURPOSE AND OBJECTIVES

The purpose of the Office Systems Advisory Committee is to assist both the user and Ball State University to achieve the best possible equipment acquisitions. This can best be accomplished following a coordinated approach that recognizes short- and long-range objectives.

The objectives of the committee are:

A. To ensure acquisition of appropriate equipment and services for the requisitioning units.

B. To ensure the adequacy of the proposed system as a solution for the defined applications.

C. To evaluate the flexibility and upgradability of the proposed system with regard to possible alterations or expansions of defined applications.

D. To evaluate the impact of the proposed system on University facilities (e.g., space, utilities, lighting, sound conditioning, air conditioning).

E. To evaluate the need for compatibility of the proposed system with other systems.

F. To evaluate the impact of the proposed system on existing information systems, both automated and manual, and on workloads for the unit as well as for the campus.

G. To ensure that cost effective alternatives have been considered.

H. To ensure that equipment of the type proposed is the appropriate solution for the application requested.

In order to coordinate and expedite the acquisition (gifts, purchases, rent/ lease) of word processing and related peripheral equipment and software on the Ball State University campus, it is prudent and necessary to implement the following Office Systems Equipment Acquisition Policy.

Exhibit A-2 An example of the mission statement of an advisory committee for office systems (courtesy of Ball State University, Muncie, Indiana).

APPENDIX B

OFFICE AUTOMATION FEASIBILITY QUESTIONNAIRE

CONFIDENTIAL

OFFICE AUTOMATION
TECHNICAL/SPECIALIST QUESTIONNAIRE

NAME _____ POSITION _____

DIVISION/DEPARTMENT _____ DATE OF HIRE _____

REPORTS TO _____

GENERAL:

1. Describe your major responsibilities, by priority.

_____

_____

_____

_____

_____

_____

2. Indicate the number of support staff to whom you can delegate work:

_____ clerical support

_____ secretary

_____ word processing operator

_____ other (identify) _____

RECORDS MANAGEMENT:

3. Whose files do you maintain? Where are the files located? _____

_____

_____

Exhibit B-1 A sample of an office automation questionnaire for technical specialist applications. This type of questionnaire could also be used for management applications.

4. Do you follow any standard company filing procedures? _____
   If not, how do you file (e.g., client or vendor name, product line, geographical location, subject matter, chronological, etc.)?

   _____

   _____

5. How much file cabinet space or what number of drawers is required for
   your current files?

   _____

   Do you purge files annually and transfer to storage? _____
6. Do any of the people you support handle their own files? If so, how
   many?

   _____

7. Do you keep a followup file? _____
8. Do you have any filing backlog now? If yes, how much uninterrupted
   time would it take to eliminate this backlog?

   _____

9. Do you follow a corporate records retention schedule? _____ If not,
   how many years are you required to keep records in the office and who
   sets this requirement?

   _____

   _____

10. Are you presently microfilming any records? _____ If so, who is per-
    forming this function and how often?

    _____

11. Do you have a collection of periodicals or similar materials? _____

    _____

    If so, are these routed among the personnel in your department? _____

    _____

    If so, are they indexed, and where are they filed? _____

    _____

Exhibit B-1 (*Continued*)

12. Do you access files which are shared by other support staff?

_____

professionals? _____ How many people access common files? _____

13. What other files do you use? _____

_____

TELECOMMUNICATIONS:

14. How many principles do you handle telephones for? _____ List the principals' names and extension numbers.

_____

_____

_____

_____

_____

15. How many calls do you place each day? _____ How many calls do you receive each day? _____

16. How many of the above calls do you conclude yourself? _____ How many require:

call back _____ a lengthy message taken _____ no action

_____

17. Do you have backup to your telephone while you are away?

_____

Who covers your telephone? _____

18. How many estimated hours per day is your telephone not covered? _____

Exhibit B-1 (_Continued_)

MATHEMATICAL REQUIREMENTS:

19. Do you perform calculations? _____ If so, how many hours per day? _____

20. How do you handle your calculations?

calculator _____ hours/day

computer _____ hours/day

word processor _____ hours/day

pencil _____ hours/day

adding machine _____ hours/day

MAIL RESPONSIBILITY:

21. Please check the functions that best explain your responsibility for mail handling:

do not handle _____

deliver unopened _____

log _____

open _____

stamp _____

read for review and followup _____

read for review and highlight for principal _____

attach routing tag _____

handle personally _____

respond to letter _____

assign priority _____

attach relevant file and deliver to principal _____

Exhibit B-1 (*Continued*)

22. How many people do you handle mail for? List names and titles:

_____

_____

_____

23. List documents that you receive and have full responsibility for reading, filing, or destroying (for example, trade journals; book updates; advertising clipping, etc.).

_____

_____

_____

_____

REFERENCE MATERIAL:

24. Itemize manuals you refer to in your position (for example, word processing manual, desk manual, standards and procedures manual, etc.).

_____

_____

_____

_____

25. How many copies of each manual are you responsible for updating?

_____

_____

_____

_____

26. What lists or logs do you maintain (for example, mailing lists, telephone numbers or directories, equipment serial numbers, supplies inventory, etc.)?

_____

_____

_____

Exhibit B-1   (_Continued_)

27. Do you access a database? _____ If so, how often and for what purposes?

_____

_____

_____

28. Suggestions for improving maintenance of reference material?

_____

_____

_____

_____

REPLICATION:

29. Do you use a photocopier? _____

If so, how often during one day? _____

30. Do you use a color copier? _____

If so, how often? _____

31. Are you requested to prepare visuals? _____

flip charts _____

slides _____

overhead transparencies _____

32. How often do you get these requests? _____

_____

33. Where are copiers located in your office? _____

_____

Exhibit B-1 (*Continued*)

ADMINISTRATIVE DETAIL:

34. Check equipment presently required or used in your job:

_____ telephone   _____ Telex

_____ telephone answering   _____ facsimile
          device
                                          _____ dictation equipment
_____ speaker telephone
                                          _____ central dictation
_____ intercom   equipment

_____ copier   _____ calculator

35. Which of the following areas would you like to see improve?

_____ calendaring/followup (tickler), docketing

_____ meeting arrangements

_____ travel arrangements

_____ word processing

_____ dictation

_____ mail (internal)

_____ mail (external)

SUGGESTIONS:

36. Please use the rest of this form and the other side if needed to note any suggestions you have for improvements in the systems, procedures, or methods used in your job.

Exhibit B-1 (_Continued_)

APPENDIX C

IMPLEMENTATION PLAN

Careful planning for successful implementation is a critical part of an office automation project. Many items are necessary to achieve this success.

Implementation Function	Space Planner	Management Support Manager	Personnel Dept	Equipment Vendor	Mary M Ruprecht & Associates
RESPONSIBILITY CHART					
Departmental feedback					X
Develop RFPs		X			*
Order equipment		X			
Selection of management support staff		X	X		*
Restructure reporting relationships		X	X		*
Modify job descriptions		X	X		*
Develop procedures		X			*
Office layout space design; order furniture and supplies	X	X		X	*
Installation of equipment		X		X	
Training on word processing equipment		X		X	
Training secretaries and managers on dictation equipment		X		X	
Store documents from phase-in areas		X		*	
On-line phase-in implementation		X			*
Ongoing updating of procedures		X			
Management reports		X			
Training sessions for management support staff		X			X

* As needed.

Exhibit C-1 A sample of a responsibility chart listing the functions to be performed and a space to designate the personnel responsible for each function. Variations of this approach can be useful to the person accountable for implementing change.

APPENDIX D

JOB DESCRIPTIONS

Establishing appropriate job descriptions for the automated office is an important key to the success of office automation implementation.

INTERNAL CONSULTANT

FUNCTION

Under administrative supervision from a designated supervisor, to participate in and be responsible for the completion of the analysis of departmental or college word processing needs. To act as a consultant in the design, implementation, maintenance, and evaluation of automated office information systems and to participate in the analysis of complex integrated information processing systems problems and the development of problem solutions.

ORGANIZATIONAL RELATIONSHIPS

This position reports to the Assistant Director of Administrative Information and Services Systems.

DUTIES AND RESPONSIBILITIES

Perform comprehensive studies and analyses of office information equipment functions, methods, and procedures and make recommendations concerning the feasibility of revising existing operations or acquiring new equipment and software for office information systems solutions. Write documentation of studies and analyses.

Act as coordinator for the campus-wide development of word processing and related systems, and as coordinator for specific feasibility studies.

Coordinate and lead training programs and workshops to extend users' knowledge of automated office information equipment capabilities, techniques, and concepts. Maintain a reference area for automated office information systems. Write and distribute information about automated office information systems.

Assist departments and colleges with the selection of processing and peripheral equipment, its implementation, and reevaluation. Conduct user surveys and evaluations of equipment.

Review and approve recommendations for word processing and peripheral systems' design changes and improvements.

Serve as liaison with regard to word processing and peripheral systems between Administrative Information Systems and Services and departments and colleges.

Participate in training programs, seminars, and classes to extend knowledge and capability in office information systems design and implementation. Maintain a professional knowledge of and attitude toward automated office systems development and user needs by reading journals, attending presentations, etc.

Exhibit D-1 An example of an internal consultant job description, indicating the types of new jobs being created because of office automation (courtesy of Susannah Ganus, University of Illinois).

Supervise designated employees. Organize and direct the activities of subordinate employees in all phases of office systems analyses, surveys, and evaluations.

Perform related duties as assigned.

1. KNOWLEDGE REQUIRED FOR THE JOB

    The position requires knowledge of automated office information systems concepts and equipment. Requires ability to analyze office information processing requirements and relate those requirements to specific solutions. Requires ability to plan and coordinate overall development of word processing and peripheral systems. Requires ability to communicate technical information to users.

    The incumbent must possess:

    A. Extensive knowledge of automated office information systems concepts, terminology, capacities, and techniques.

    B. Extensive knowledge of available technology in automated office information systems.

    C. Extensive knowledge of office management concepts in relation to efficient office procedures and implications of introduction of new equipment, procedures, and office organization.

    D. Extensive knowledge of techniques required to conduct and analyze in-depth office information processing feasibility studies.

    E. Proficiency in public speaking and written communication.

    F. Knowledge of project implementation procedures for both word processing and data processing systems.

2. RESPONSIBILITY

    A. Supervisory Controls

    Under the supervision of the Assistant Director of Administrative Information Systems and Services, the incumbent will initialize, develop, and follow through on projects with regard to automated office information systems development. The incumbent will supervise and review the work of subordinate employees. The incumbent is expected to manage his/her own time.

    B. Guidelines

    The employee will consider alternative techniques and choose the most suitable method to satisfy requirements considering known problems, efficient usage, anticipated enhancements, new hardware and software, and user expectations.

3. DIFFICULTY

    A. Complexity

    This position requires the integration of many skills to complete specific and general tasks of analyzing and designing automated office

Exhibit D-1 (*Continued*)

information systems. The incumbent must understand the consequences of the proposed designs on the overall development and implementation of automated office information systems. The incumbent must be able to develop and modify recommendations for procedure and policy formation regarding office information systems development. The incumbent must apply proper mathematical, statistical, and office management knowledge and techniques in analyzing problems and selecting appropriate solutions. The incumbent must anticipate the short- and long-range effects of daily decisions.

B. Scope and Effect

The implementation of automated office information systems for a particular user has a visible and often critical impact on college, department, or office policies and procedures, as well as on the campus-wide development of automated office systems. The incumbent will bear the responsibility for the correct interpretation of users requirements, and appropriate analysis and solution identification.

4. PERSONAL RELATIONSHIPS, PERSONAL CONTACTS, AND PURPOSE

The incumbent will use formal meetings, one-to-one discussions, telephone contacts, and informal office visits with user personnel to develop and analyze requirements and to resolve problems.

The incumbent will act as liaison and participate in technical presentations by vendors to users.

The incumbent will conduct, participate in, or attend formal meetings and presentations and engage in telephone and informal discussions with vendors and other technical personnel to keep abreast of new developments in order to fully understand possible effects of current or proposed hardware and software on user systems.

The incumbent will coordinate and participate in formal meetings of AISS and user personnel to explain the design and operation of particular solutions and to solicit suggestions for improving the solution under review.

The incumbent will coordinate and lead workshops and seminars for user personnel.

The incumbent will have technical meetings with his/her supervisor and will participate in meetings for the purposes of planning with other AISS personnel. The incumbent will have informal meetings and one-to-one discussions with subordinate employees to plan, supervise, and review their work.

Exhibit D-1 (*Continued*)

Job Description

DIRECTOR OF INFORMATION SYSTEMS

I. JOB SUMMARY

Plans, organizes, and directs the Information Systems Department, developing and implementing systems to meet the current and future needs of the office in accordance with established policies of the organization.

II. PERFORMANCE REQUIREMENTS

A. Responsibilities and Authorities

1. Evaluates and recommends computer hardware and software to support the immediate and future requirements of the organization.

2. Plans, coordinates, controls, and directs the study, development, and implementation of new or improved management and information systems.

3. Evaluates and recommends new or modified physical plant requirements to support current and future needs of computer management.

4. Directs the modification and enhancement of existing computer applications as required and approved.

5. Develops, publishes, and assures conformance to specific work and documentation standards for information systems.

6. Develops operating budgets and control procedures for conformance to budget limitations.

7. Interviews, hires, evaluates, and terminates department personnel as necessary.

8. Coordinates activities of the Information Systems Department with those of other departments to ensure efficient service.

9. Performs special studies as directed.

10. Performs other duties as directed.

B. Physical Effort

Little physical effort required; however, position requires periodic intermittent sitting, standing, and/or walking.

C. Mental Effort

Work performed is varied in nature and requires a high degree of concentration and attention to accuracy and detail for a prolonged period of time.

III. QUALIFICATIONS

A. Education

Baccalaurate degree in computer science.

Exhibit D-2 A sample of a title and a job description modified to meet the new demands for controlling technology.

B. Experience

Five (5) years experience in computer science with some supervisory experience preferred.

C. Job Knowledge

Requires previous similar job experience and a knowledge and understanding of the principles, procedures, methodologies, and application in a computer science, for example, analytical ability, sophisticated mathematical ability, high degree of knowledge of procedures, and/or methods related to data processing.

IV. RESPONSIBILITY FOR SUPERVISION

A. Number of Employees Supervised

Direct supervision of the Information Systems Operations Manager and three (3) Systems Analysts. Indirectly supervises all office personnel in the Information Systems Department.

B. Complexity of Supervision

Work supervised is technical and complex and involves a moderate degree of revision and the adaptation of practices and procedures.

V. CONTACT RESPONSIBILITY

Involves interdepartmental, intradepartmental, and external contact and communication where subjects discussed include the handling and conveying of confidential information and a comprehensive understanding of the organization's goals, procedures, and policies.

VI. WORK ENVIRONMENT

Works in a well-lighted and ventilated environment with no apparent direct exposure to physical hazards.

VII. RESPONSIBLE TO

Vice President

Exhibit D-2   (*Continued*)

LIFE INSURANCE COMPANY

Position Description

Date: February, 1981

Written By:

Approved By: _____

_____

Hay Job Number:

Previous Job Number: 0712054

Previous Job Title: Word Processing Supervisor

Position: Word Processing Supervisor

Incumbent:

Division: Data Processing

Department: Office Services

Reports To: Administrator-Word Processing

Position Purpose:

This position is responsible for supervising the employees and day-to-day operations of the Word Processing Center for both shifts. Ensures high volume workflow is on a cost effective basis. Resolves customer problems and coordinates new system procedures. Oversees the training and development of all Word Processing staff.

Dimensions:

Total Staff Supervised:
Annual Staff Payroll:
Annual Operating Budget:
Equipment Owned by Word Processing:
Annual Cost of Equipment Leased, Service Contracts, and Supplies:
Average Pages per Month, Transcription:
Average Pages per Month, Prerecorded Letters:
Average Pages per Month, Administrative Messages:

Nature and Scope:

Position Location:

This position reports to the Administrator-Word Processing. Reporting to this position are the following: Night Supervisor (1), Coordinator-Word Processing (2), Coordinator Administrative Support Center (2), Assistant Text Processor (0-6), Text Processor (0-6), Senior Text Processor (0-6), Word Processor (0-32.5), Advanced Word Processor (0.32.5), and Senior Word Processor (0-32.5).

Personal Duties:

The incumbent is responsible for ensuring that daily workflow is properly directed to the appropriate area for the most efficient utilization of equipment and staff. This position coordinates the operations

Exhibit D-3   An example of the increasing complexity of a word processing supervisor's role, as illustrated in a life insurance corporation job description.

for both the day and night shifts. The incumbent is responsible for resolving equipment problems and adjusting workload to maintain the best possible service to the customers.

This individual ensures the development of the Word Processing staff. Develops individual career paths through counseling the participants of present and future needs for training programs; works with staff members in setting and achieving goals both individually as well as a group; prepares performance appraisals and reviews with staff members. This position is obligated to keep abreast of changes and customer activities that would impact current Word Processing procedures and communicates all pertinent information to the staff. The incumbent counsels staff regarding personnel problems, provides input regarding equipment and staff needs for budget preparation; interviews and hires candidates for employment in any given Word Processing area; responsible for promotion and merit review process.

In addition, this position is responsible for monitoring and insuring the timely processing of all work submitted to the Word Processing area. The incumbent is responsible for the preparation of daily work measurement reports of the staff's scheduled and actual time, utilizing it as a management control tool. This position prepares and/or maintains Word Processing records on workload, production rate, and equipment maintenance and submits various routine reports and results of special studies conducted.

Subordinate Activities:

The incumbent achieves accountabilities with the assistance of the following direct reporting positions.

Night Supervisor–Word Processing (1)—Supervises the second shift operation of the Word Processing Center. Assumes responsibility for production of staff and proper training.

Coordinator–Word Processing (2)—Trains employees on procedures and equipment, maintains procedural manuals for assigned functions, and develops formats for new applications on the equipment.

Coordinator–Administrative Support Services (2)—Coordinates the operation of the satellite support area. Is responsible for workflow, production of staff, and training. Accepts and prioritizes work submitted for processing.

Senior Text Processor (0 to 6)—Confers with customer translating request into format capable of being produced on OS/6 equipment. Determines capabilities to meet customer's time schedule. Input information in OS/6.

Advanced Word Processor (0 to 32.5)—Transcribes a wide variety of materials from dictating equipment throughout the Company; works independently and assists less experienced staff.

Major Challenges:

The Word Processing Supervisor is challenged to maintain an effective, well-balanced operating workflow on a daily basis within the Word Processing areas. This position is further challenged with resolving problems of subordinates, including but not limited to disciplinary problems, and developing the staff to obtain higher level positions within the area.

Controls:

This position has the authority to supervise the functions of the Word Processing areas. In addition to this, the incumbent completes performance appraisals, recommends merit increases, hires and pro-

Exhibit D-3   *(Continued)*

motes staff. Major and more sensitive personnel problems such as terminations and nonbudgeted expenditures are handled in unison with the incumbent's superior.

Contacts:

The incumbent has frequent contacts with customer departments of Word Processing and other departments for special projects on an as needed basis. This position has frequent contact with vendors, sales representatives, and staff from other companies' Word Processing areas.

Measurement:

Achievement of this position's accountabilities may be measured by the efficient supervision of the Word Processing area along with the ability to maintain high production while meeting client's needs, and the effective supervision of employees by counseling, motivating, and objectively evaluating.

Requirements:

To successfully perform in this position, the incumbent needs a proven knowledge of word processing as can be gained by two to three years experience as a coordinator or night supervisor. Excellent supervisory and interpersonal skills. This position requires the ability to plan, organize, and resolve problems. In-depth understanding of equipment operations and applications.

Principal Accountabilities:

1. Contributes to the personal and technical development of the staff.
2. Ensures good rapport is established with all customers, both assigned clients and special projects.
3. Updates and maintains procedure manuals for all areas of Word Processing and prepares reports of production for Word Processing and any special projects.
4. Coordinates the workflow to accommodate special projects or requests and provides service on a timely basis.
5. Ensures the effective utilization of the Word Processing areas by selecting, developing, and motivating the staff.

Exhibit D-3 (*Continued*)

APPENDIX E

PERFORMANCE GUIDELINES AND MEASUREMENT

Evaluating performance within the automated office is critical in order to monitor continued productivity improvements. Sample performance appraisal forms are provided for a variety of positions within the modern office.

PERFORMANCE PLAN

1 = Unacceptable; on notice.
2 = Marginal; must improve.
3 = Acceptable; improvement expected.
4 = Good.
5 = Excellent.

Name _____

Title ____Administrative Secretary____

Responsibility	Objective	Actual Achievements	Level of Achievement				
			1	2	3	4	5
Mail	Distribute promptly and correctly; handle mail to completion without instructions, whenever possible.						
Filing	File correctly; locate documents rapidly; update files regularly.						
Telephone	Handle calls correctly and pleasantly; handle calls to completion without instructions, whenever possible.						
Work Coordination	Work with WP Center to meet priorities; proofread for manager(s) signature.						
Work Organization	Organized work station, work methods, and work procedures enabling complete coordination with all managers on a timely basis and in an orderly manner.						
Special Projects	Accomplish projects and reports on time with little direction from manager(s).						
Judgment	Create original ideas; avoid preconceived ideas; communicate well; make sound decisions; adapt well to changing situations						
Personal	Pleasant manner and appearance; good attitude displayed in office; work well with others; good working relationship with manager(s); accepts counseling and guidance; keeps emotional or personal interests from influencing work.						

Exhibit E-1 Expected productivity standards for a nonexempt office automation staff. These can be used as guidelines for projecting performance standards.

Performance Plan, page 2

Name _____

SUMMARY:

1. Employee Strengths:

2. Significant accomplishments:

3. Areas of improvement:

4. Plan for accomplishing improvement:

5. Employee career interests:

6. Employee interview comments:

Review agreed upon _____   _____
                          (date)

                                             _____

Signed _____   _____
              (Employee)
                                             Overall rating _____

                                             Promotability _____

Exhibit E-1   (*Continued*)

PERFORMANCE PLAN

1 = Unacceptable; on notice.
2 = Marginal; must improve.
3 = Acceptable; improvement expected.
4 = Good.
5 = Excellent.

Name _____

Title ____Word Processing Secretary____

Responsibility	Objective	Actual Achievements	\multicolumn{5}{c}{Level of Achievement}
			1	2	3	4	5
Quantity of Work	500 lines/day minimum 800 lines/day acceptable 1000–1500 lines/day excellent						
Quality of Work	Neat, clean copy; accurate transcription.						
Work Coordination	Work with administrative secretaries to meet priorities in center; good followthrough on meeting priorities and making revisions.						
Work Organization	Organized work station, work methods, and work procedures enabling complete coordination with all managers on a timely basis and in an orderly manner.						
Job Knowledge	Good grammar, punctuation, and spelling skills.						
Judgment	Create original ideas for improving the word processing system; make sound decisions with respect to meeting priorities; adapt well to changing procedures in the entire concept.						
Personal	Pleasant manner and appearance; good attitude displayed in office; work well with others; good working relationship with manager(s); accepts counseling and guidance; keeps emotional or personal interests from influencing work.						

Exhibit E-1 (*Continued*)

Performance Plan, page 2

Name _____

SUMMARY:

1. Employee Strengths:

2. Significant accomplishments:

3. Areas of improvement:

4. Plan for accomplishing improvement:

5. Employee career interests:

6. Employee interview comments:

Review agreed upon _____   _____
                        (date)

                                            _____

Signed _____   _____
              (Employee)
                                            Overall rating _____

                                            Promotability _____

Exhibit E-1 (*Continued*)

PERFORMANCE APPRAISAL FOR WORD PROCESSING SPECIALIST

Attribute	Description	Weight	Score	Points
Quality & Quantity	Error ratio, proofing skills, grammar and transcription skills	30	_____	_____
Position Knowledge	Proper formatting of work, operation of equipment and understanding of work flow	35	_____	_____
Attitude	Cooperation, flexibility, interaction with clients, QC	20	_____	_____
Attendance = Marginal	0–2 days +100% = Outstanding 3–4 days = 90% = Excellent 5–7 days = 80% = Very Good 8–11 days = 70% = Satisfactory 12 or more = 60% = Marginal	15	_____	_____

Employee's Signature _____

Evaluator's Signature _____

Date _____

Dept. Head's Initials _____

Exhibit E-2 A performance appraisal plan with criteria and weighting established by employees in their QC (quality commitment) group.

PRICE BROTHERS COMPANY PERFORMANCE AND SALARY REVIEW

EMPLOYEE _____ DEPT. _____

POSITION _____

PERFORMANCE RATING	MARG.	F –	FAIR	F +	G –	GOOD	G +	O –	OUTS.	O +	D –	DIST.
Quantity of Work												
Quality of Work												
Timeliness of Work												
Initiative												
Need for Supervision												
Leadership Skills												
Cooperation												
OVERALL RATING												

RATER COMMENTS	EMPLOYEE COMMENTS
Recommended salary adjustment: From _____ To _____ (Signed)	I have reviewed this rating with my supervisor. (Signed)

APPROVALS		
First Approval	Division	Industrial Relations

Exhibit E-3 A sample of a comprehensive performance and salary review based on performance criteria (used by Price Brothers Company).

RECOMMENDED SALARY ADJUSTMENTS

EFFECTIVE _____

REVIEWER _____   DIVISION _____

EMPLOYEE	GP		RATE	AMT. INCR.	% INCR.	% MID.	PERF.	NEW RANGE		
								MIN.	MID.	MAX.
		OLD								
		NEW								
		OLD								
		NEW								
		OLD								
		NEW								
		OLD								
		NEW								
		OLD								
		NEW								
		OLD								
		NEW								
		OLD								
		NEW								
		OLD								
		NEW								
		OLD								
		NEW								
		OLD								
		NEW								
		OLD								
		NEW								

APPROVALS

REVIEWER
SUPERVISOR _____   DIVISION _____
REC'D. IND. REL. _____   FEEDBACK TO DIVISION _____

Exhibit E-3 (*Continued*)

GUIDELINES FOR RATING EMPLOYEE PERFORMANCE

1. The performance rating should be completed before considering your recommendation for a salary increase. A standard form is used for rating performance to make it easy for you to summarize your evaluation of each employee and to provide uniformity in reporting evaluations.

2. Accountabilities should be the primary basis for rating performance. Study the accountability statements on existing job descriptions. Discuss them with the employee to assure mutual understanding. Edit the statements as necessary and send edited copies to the Compensation Administrator.

3. Use all available quantitative and qualitative measurements to evaluate how well each accountability is being met. Review with the employee for additional measurement suggestions.

4. Translate performance measurements to the "Performance and Salary Review" form. Independently rate each of the seven performance factors. Strength or weakness in one factor should have no bearing on the rating of another factor. A strength in one area should be acknowledged even though overall performance may be weak. The opposite is also true.

5. After rating each factor separately, give the employee's performance an "Overall Rating." This is not necessarily an eyeball average of the other seven ratings because some aspects of performance are more important than others in this particular position. The purpose of the performance review is to describe how effectively the employee does *this* job, consider where in the pay range for this job he should be paid, and what he and his supervisor can do to help improve his overall performance. The rates should include specific recommendations for development action under "Rater Comments."

6. Performance can be rated at one of twelve levels. There are five major ratings with plusses and minusses in between to use if you are not quite sure which of the major headings is appropriate. The five major headings are defined as follows:

   Marginal
   Performance is clearly below the normally acceptable level. Employee may be inexperienced in the job. Must either improve on this rating or move out of the position in a relatively short time.

   Fair
   Performance comes close to well done but the need for further development is recognizable.

   Good
   Performance is satisfactory, sufficient, well done. All aspects of the job are performed at the level normally expected.

   Outstanding
   Performance is clearly better than well done. Some aspects of performance may be distinguished.

Exhibit E-3   *(Continued)*

Distinguished

Exceptionally outstanding performance is clearly obvious—the top one or two percent.

The "Rater Comments" block on the form provides space to explain your ratings or to make additional remarks about the employee's performance or development plans.

7. Based on performance rating, present salary, and resources available for increases, recommend an appropriate salary adjustment. The "Recommended Salary Adjustment" form shows the employee's present ("old") salary and percent of midpoint. As a general rule of thumb, the following correlation should exist between employee performance and percent of midpoint:

Marginal	80% to 88% of midpoint
Fair	89% to 96%
Good	97% to 104%
Outstanding	105% to 112%
Distinguished	113% to 120%

When an employee is being paid less than is indicated by his performance rating, it may be necessary to make the correction over more than one review period. The table given above will help you equitably distribute the resources available for increases among the employees you are reviewing this year.

8. Enter the new salary information on the "Recommended Salary Adjustments" sheet and forward the sheet to your supervisor as soon as it is complete for all reviews due. (Keep the "Performance and Salary Review" forms until after your review meetings are held with employees.)

9. Your supervisor will forward the salary adjustment sheet according to the routing established by the division. You will be notified when the sheet arrives in corporate Industrial Relations and the increases are approved. *The form must arrive in Industrial Relations by the 10th of the month in which the increases are to be effective.*

10. As soon as approval is received, meet with each reviewed employee to review his rating and establish goals and plans for the next rating period. Also communicate the approved salary increase at this time. It is important to have this meeting before the increase occurs in the employee's paycheck. If the proper kind of communication is taking place on a day-to-day basis, this meeting should contain no surprises nor cause undue strain for either party. The meeting is an opportunity to summarize the strengths and weaknesses of the employee's performance and work out with the employee specific plans for improvement.

11. The review form also provides space for the employee to make comments if he/she has any. His signature indicates that he has reviewed the information on the form with his supervisor. It does not necessarily mean that he agrees with it. The employee's signature is as important as the rater's.

Exhibit E-3 (*Continued*)

A missing signature could delay processing the salary increase through Industrial Relations and Payroll.

12. Immediately following the last review meeting, forward the review form through channels designated by division to corporate Industrial Relations.

CAUTION

▶ Both forms are highly *confidential* and must be handled accordingly.

▶ A delay in transmitting either form to Industrial Relations could result in a delay in the approved salary increase's inclusion in the employee's paycheck.

R.H. Givens
January, 1982

PRICE BROTHERS COMPANY

SUMMARY OF PROCEDURE FOR
PERFORMANCE AND SALARY REVIEW

1. Rate employee performance on "Performance and Salary Review" form for each employee due for review this month.

2. Determine salary recommendation to be made in each case.

3. Submit "Recommended Salary Adjustments" sheet for approvals.

4. After receiving notification of approval from Industrial Relations and before pay day, conduct review meetings with employees.

5. Send review forms (signed by the rater and the employee) through designated channels to corporate Industrial Relations.

IMPORTANT:

▶ Solicit employee participation.

▶ Maintain confidentiality.

▶ Be prompt.

If you need a copy of *"Guidelines for Rating Employee Performance,"* please call Industrial Relations, extension 8839 or 8808.

R.H. Givens
January, 1982

Exhibit E-3 *(Continued)*

GUIDELINES FOR SELECTION

Date _____

Name _____

Position Applied for _____

		Rate	Score
Clerical Skills	(30)	____	____
Interpersonal Skills	(25)	____	____
Responsibility and Maturity	(20)	____	____
Organizational Ability	(15)	____	____
Communication Skills	(10)	____	____

Clerical Skills

Mag card, printer, copier, CRT, Mag A, OS/6, *manual dexterity,* proofing, grammar, spelling, *logical thinking.*

Interpersonal Skills

Work with variety of individuals, clients, and co-workers.

Responsibility and Maturity

Flexibility.
Thorough job, complete on time.
Work under pressure.
Self-starter.

Organizational Ability

Work alone or as part of team.
Control and/or adapt to interruptions, changes, disorder.

Communication Skills

Listen effectively.
Appropriate vocabulary.

Hobbies/activities in leisure time:
Kind of work dislike/like:
Why are you working?
What appeals to you about this kind of work?

Explain Area

1. Produce documents.
2. Work with machines.
3. Majority of time in particular area.
4. Brainwork, correct, assembly.

Exhibit E-4 An example of the guidelines used for selection of a word processing specialist who will be evaluated on the job as shown in Exhibit E-2.

Selection Standards

1. Clerical Skills
   A. Use office equipment such as mag card, typewriter, copier, printer, CRT.
   B. Produce finished typewritten copy from rough drafts on appropriate equipment.
   C. Maintain attention to detail.
   D. Demonstrate knowledge of common formats for correspondence and variety of copy typing work.
2. Communication Skills
   A. Listen effectively.
   B. Receive written or oral instructions.
   C. Use vocabulary appropriate to situation.
   D. Respond clearly and directly.
   E. Describe or explain information, instruction, or ideas to others.
3. Responsibility and Maturity
   A. Do thorough job on each task and complete assignments on time.
   B. Recognize problems and enlist outside assistance when necessary.
   C. Maintain composure, effectiveness, and flexibility under pressure.
4. Interpersonal Skills
   A. Work cooperatively with a variety of individuals.
   B. Interface effectively with users and co-workers.
   C. Exhibit appropriate sensitivity to feelings of others.
   D. Recognize strengths and limitations of self and others.
   E. Focus on task or performance rather than personality when relating to users or co-workers.
5. Organizational Ability
   A. Organize work autonomously or as part of a team.
   B. Control and/or adapt to interruptions, changes, disorder, repetition without losing efficiency or composure.
   C. Plan, organize, and monitor activities according to priorities.
   D. Recognize strengths and limitations of self and others.

1. You will be working with several other individuals as part of a team. One member of your team is an excellent worker, but you abhor her style of dress. What would you do?
2. There are general guidelines for completing the assigned work. These guidelines can be changed after discussion in the Quality Commitment meetings and after final approval from management. One of your team members is not working according to the established guidelines. What would you do?
3. Within each team, there is a co-ordinator who is responsible for maintaining the work flow, receiving incoming work out of the normal routine, and resolving problems within the team. One of your team members is not carrying his/her share of the workload. This opinion is not yours alone, it is shared by other members of the team also. What would you do?

Exhibit E-4 (*Continued*)

JOB EVALUATION RECORD

JOB TITLE: _____WORD PROCESSOR_____   TOTAL POINTS: _____

DEPARTMENT: _____   WAGE GROUP: _____

JOB NO.: _____   EFFECTIVE DATE: _____

FACTOR	LEVEL	POINTS	COMMENTS
Experience			
Education			
Complexity			
Effect of Errors			
Supervision			
Contacts			
Mental Effort			
Physical Effort			
Surroundings			
Hazards			

Any Additional Explanation:

Date of this rating by the committee _____ Signed _____

Those attending meeting: 1. _____

2. _____

3. _____

4. _____

Exhibit E-5 A traditional approach to measuring the performance of a word processor.

APPENDIX F

REQUEST FOR PROPOSAL AND EQUIPMENT EVALUATION CHECKLISTS

Vendor proliferation throughout the equipment marketplace makes it increasingly difficult to select the appropriate equipment for specific applications. Considerations for evaluating and selecting equipment are provided along with selection criteria checklists and forms to assist in the equipment evaluation and acquisition process.

REQUEST FOR PROPOSAL (RFP) CONTENT CHECKLIST

Contents

 I. Introduction
 II. General Comments
 III. System Requirements
   A. Assumptions
   B. Hardware
     1. Configuration
     2. System Features
 IV. Proposal Requirements
   A. Purpose
   B. General Information
   C. Proposal Outline
 V. Proposal Evaluation
   A. Procedure
   B. Evaluation Criteria
 VI. Contract Process
   A. Preliminary Negotiations
   B. Final Contract

SYSTEM FEATURES TO BE INCORPORATED
IN REQUEST FOR PROPOSAL (RFP)

 A. Input of Documents to Include:
   —Character/mark requirements [type style(s) or font(s)]
 B. Formatting and Display Features:
   —Screen size and color
   —Display buffer (memory) size in characters
   —Vertical and horizontal scrolling
   —Character size control (can display characters be enlarged)
   —Displays (line space, format statement, underscore)
   —Formatting technique
   —Menu prompts
   —System security (passwords?)
   —Screen brightness control

Exhibit F-1 A sample of the information to be requested from a vendor when selecting equipment.

    —Merging technique

    —Move/delete features

    —Automatic widow adjust

    —Cursor movement techniques

D. Special keys and special features:

    —Character, line, paragraph, and page search technique

    —Block move (movement of large blocks of text)

    —Global search and replace technique

    —Automatic pagination and wraparound

    —Hyphenation or internal dictionary capabilities

    —Automatic centering

    —Statistical and numerical features

    —Spelling error detection?

    —Sub/superscripts

E. Printing of documents:

    —Type of printer (character, line, matrix, etc.)

    —Quality of output (provide sample print styles)

    —Printing technique (fabric, carbon, etc.)

    —Allowable distance from central processing

    —Noise level

    —Paper sheet feeders (do you have; will printer handle?)

    —Number of carbon sets that will adequately print

    —Speed of printer

    —Extent of printout queuing

    —Carriage paper width

F. Review and maintenance of stored documents:

    —Document indexing techniques (name, author, number, etc.)

    —Method of addition, deletion, modification, and search of document index

    —Method of retrieval (print and/or display)

    —Search techniques available (author, number, date created)

    —Storage capacity of storage media (pages, characters/page)

    —Technique used to alert operator to fullness of storage

G. Keyboard:

    —Available keyboard formats

    —Numeric key pad

    —Location of special keys

    Note: Please provide illustrations of keyboard.

Exhibit F-1 *(Continued)*

H. Communication:
—Can the system communicate to a mainframe database?
—Identify line protocols and line formats
—Describe code structures and end-to-end protocols
—Networking functions for features addressed by word processing software for future expansion to other offices
—Does the system have a 2400-baud or greater transmission rate?

RFP RESPONSE EVALUATION CRITERIA

PRICE
—Equipment
—Maintenance

EASE OF OPERATION

FEATURES

MODULARITY

MAINTENANCE

INSTALLATION SUPPORT

TRAINING

VENDOR

MEDIA CONVERSION

REFERENCES

Exhibit F-1 (*Continued*)

VENDOR AND EQUIPMENT CHECKLIST

A. Review Equipment Requirements.

B. Determine Equipment Alternatives.

C. Check Local Maintenance:
   1. Check customer references for specific unit that may be installed.
   2. The degree of investigation for maintenance cannot be overemphasized.

D. Check Vendor Installation Support.

E. Training.
   1. Amount of free training.
   2. Learning curve involved in training on new equipment.

F. Equipment Demonstration.
   1. Prepare a short document for keying and editing.
   2. System evaluation.
      A. hardware (keyboard, video, printer, etc.).
      B. ease of operation.
      C. revision capabilities.
      D. retrieval of stored text.
      E. additional features (footnotes, hyphenation, etc.).
   3. Review storage media.
      A. minimize manual handling of media.
      B. minimize storage costs per page.
      C. worst to best—mag card, cassette, floppy diskette, hard disk.

G. Evaluate Production Capabilities.
   1. Is the machine a true multifunction (split keyboard) unit (simultaneous keying of information while printing)?
   2. Document queueing technique.
   3. Print speed and quality.

H. Expansion Capabilities.

I. Cost.

J. Installation.
   1. Electrical requirements.
   2. Space requirements.
   3. Humidity and static considerations.
   4. Work stations.
   5. Soundproofing required.
   6. Storage of media.
   7. Lighting.

Exhibit F-2 This vendor and equipment checklist indicates items to be researched prior to attending equipment demonstrations.

FIFTEEN QUESTIONS TO ASK BEFORE BUYING

1. What functions do I want to perform? What do I want the word processor to do (e.g., correspondence typing, automatic letter writing, long-document revision)?
2. How much typing do we do (pages per day, week, month)?
3. How much money is budgeted for this equipment?
4. How much training do I need?
5. How much training are the vendors willing to provide?
6. Do I want to write my own programs?
7. Do I want to perform some tasks other than typing (e.g., data processing, electronic mail)?
8. Do I want to be able to buy software from outside sources? Does the system offer a popular operating system (e.g., CP/M) so plenty of software will be available?
9. What is the word processing vendor's reputation for service?
10. How much data storage do I need? Will it require floppy disks or hard disks?
11. What kind of printer quality do I need?
12. What kind of printer speed do I need?
13. What size display do I want?
14. How many workstations will I need?
15. Will I want to share resources (such as printers or files) with other workstations?

Exhibit F-3   Sample questions to be asked of a vendor (Courtesy of Amy D. Wohl).

EQUIPMENT DEMONSTRATION CHECKLIST

1. Can each name put into the database be retrieved
   —by geographic location?
   —by age?
   —by area of specialty?
   —by rate?

2. Can all terminals access the database? retrieve the information on the screen? and queue the printer?

3. How can you protect your confidential information in the system? by special security/password? by code? or at all?

4. How long does it take for an operator of the system to become proficient?

5. Can you demonstrate menu prompting for training and do you provide self-teach manuals? Is there an error message booklet?

6. How many man-hours of training will you provide each operator?

7. How many hours from the time you are called for service before we can expect to see an engineer on-site?

8. If we decide to transfer the existing database at a future date, what assistance do you provide in media conversion? possibly to another brand computer?

9. Can you handle simple accounting information with this system (e.g., simple timekeeping, income and expense statements, projections)? If so, how would it be indexed and retrieved while maintaining security?

10. If this accounting is available, what, if any, is the additional cost?

11. In the event I should decide to expand my system, how many terminals and printers would the mainframe accommodate?

12. If I decided to purchase the equipment this week, how soon can I expect it to be delivered? When would the first payment be expected? What kind of a discount can we expect if payment is made in cash?

13. How many fields will each record sort?

14. Can you sort the information in ascending and descending order?

15. What is the "ease of operation" in selecting, sorting, and merging and can any of the fields of information from each record be merged with a form?

16. How does paragraph assembly work for word processing?

17. Does the software that accompanies the equipment have all of the word processing features (e.g. automatic footnoting, super/subscript, global search, etc.)?

18. How large is the system's dictionary, if one exists?

19. Can the system merge a data processing and word processing document?

Exhibit F-4 Questions to be asked during an equipment demonstration.

APPENDIX G

PROCEDURES AND CONTROL FORMS

Procedures are the heart of a system and are essential to consistency in training and the successful ongoing operation of any system. In addition, control forms and work request forms are critical to providing benchmark statistics against which to measure and control workloads.

Sample work request forms, personnel request forms, and logging forms are provided as guidelines in developing management tools.

⬡ ROCHE	WEEKLY LINE LOG SHEET												

DEPARTMENT: _____

NAME: _____   WEEK OF: _____ 198-

Document	Origi-nator	No. of Pages	Fr.	Eng.	Machine Dicta-tion	Long Hand	Copy Type	Lines Returned	Lines Rekeyed	Prere-corded	Tables Setup	Statistics and Programs
1.												
2.												
3.												
4.												
5.												
6.												
7.												
8.												
9.												
10.												
11.												
12.												
13.												
14.												
15.												
16.												
17.												
18.												
19.												
20.												
21.												
22.												
TOTALS												

Exhibit G-1 A sample weekly log sheet to monitor an ongoing workload (used by Roche).

```
┌─────────────────────────────────────────────────────────────────┐
│                                                                   │
│   ⬡ROCHE⬡            SECRETARIAL SERVICES                         │
│                         WORK SHEET                                │
│                                                                   │
│   FROM: _____  DEPT: _____   │
│                                                                   │
│   DATE REQUIRED: _____                        │
│                                                                   │
│   DESCRIPTION: _____   │
│                                                                   │
│              Draft _____   Final _____                    │
│                                                                   │
│              Spacing:  single _____  1½ _____  double _____ │
│                                                                   │
│              Page numbering:  yes _____   no _____            │
│                                                                   │
│   STORAGE:        Temporary _____*                              │
│                                                                   │
│                   Permanent _____                               │
│                                                                   │
│                   Semi-permanent (6 months) _____               │
│                                                                   │
│   * Since you are not given a "white slip" with temporary jobs,   │
│   could you please return this work sheet with your draft at all  │
│   times.                                                          │
│                                                                   │
│   SPECIAL INSTRUCTIONS:                                           │
│                                                                   │
└─────────────────────────────────────────────────────────────────┘
```

SECRETARIAL SERVICES WORK SHEET

⬡ROCHE⬡

FROM: _____ DEPT: _____

DATE REQUIRED: _____

DESCRIPTION: _____

Draft _____   Final _____

Spacing: single _____ 1½ _____ double _____

Page numbering: yes _____   no _____

STORAGE: Temporary _____*

Permanent _____

Semi-permanent (6 months) _____

* Since you are not given a "white slip" with temporary jobs, could you please return this work sheet with your draft at all times.

SPECIAL INSTRUCTIONS:

_____

_____

_____

_____

_____

* *

<u>For Secretarial Services use only</u>

Completed by: _____   Name of diskette: _____

Text name: _____

* *

<u>For Secretarial Services use only</u>

Completed by: _____   Name of diskette: _____

Text name: _____

Exhibit G-2 An example of work request forms for monitoring an ongoing workload (used by Roche).

⟨ROCHE⟩　　　SECRETARIAL SERVICES
　　　　　　　WORK SHEET—STANDARD LETTERS

FROM: _____   DEPT: _____

DATE REQUIRED: _____

REQUEST FOR LETTER NO. _____

NAME: _____

ADDRESS: _____

_____

Zip code: _____

VARIABLES:

1. _____

2. _____

3. _____

4. _____

5. _____

_____

SPECIAL INSTRUCTIONS:

_____

_____

_____

_____

cc or sc to: _____

_____

Mrs. Allan, please ☐

LABEL: yes ☐   no ☐

Exhibit G-3 Another example of work request forms for monitoring ongoing workload (used by Roche).

USE BALL POINT PEN

02-5366
Rev. 9-77

METHODIST HOSPITAL OF INDIANA, INC.
COPY CENTER REQUISITION

Department _____ Account # _____ Date _____

Completion Date Requested _____ Requested By _____

No. of Originals _____ PHONE _____

No. of Copies Needed
of Each Original _____

CHECK THE FOLLOWING SPECIFICATIONS NEEDED:

Collated?	☐			Other Instructions: _____	
$8\frac{1}{2} \times 11$ Plain	☐	Yellow (small)	☐	_____	
$8\frac{1}{2} \times 11$ Punched	☐	Yellow (Large)	☐	_____	
$8\frac{1}{2} \times 14$	☐	3×5 Card	☐	_____	
Letterhead	☐	5×8 Card	☐	500 COPY LIMIT	

PLEASE KEEP BLUE COPY FOR DEPARTMENTAL RECORDS

DEPARTMENTAL COPY

Exhibit G-4 A sample requisition form for a copy center (used by Methodist Hospital of Indiana).

WORD PROCESSING EFFECTIVENESS SURVEY

The following survey is designed to seek your opinion regarding how effectively the word processing centers are meeting your needs as a faculty member or administrator. Your candid response will enable us to judge how well we are doing and where we need to improve. Please return your completed questionnaire to Judy Mellesmoen by May 18.

1. Do you use the services of the word processing centers?

   _____ yes

   _____ no

   If yes, Tower Hall _____ or the Science Building _____

2. How frequently do you use word processing services?

   _____ daily

   _____ twice a week

   _____ once a week

   _____ less than once a week

3. If you have chosen not to utilize word processing services, is there a specific reason? Please comment.

4. How much time does it generally take for the center to complete and return your work?

   _____ same day

   _____ next day

   _____ two days

   _____ more than two days

5. Please describe the type of work you are sending to the center.

   _____ short, original input (one-time correspondence, 1-page class handouts, etc.)

   _____ medium-sized projects (3-10 page exams, 4-15 page reports, etc.)

   _____ large projects (heavy numbers of form letters, large reports, heavy statistical or scientific projects)

   _____ other (please describe) _____

Exhibit G-5 Follow-up effectiveness surveys are used to assess the efficient use of new systems three to six months after implementation (used by the College of St. Scholastica, Duluth, Minnesota).

6. Please rate and comment on the quality of the work being produced in the center.

   (a) Appearance

           Excellent   Good   Fair   Poor

   Comment:

   (b) Accuracy

           Excellent   Good   Fair   Poor

   Comment:

7. Is the center staff able to incorporate changes or revisions you make in the first draft more effectively and quickly than through the traditional method of typing?

   _____ yes

   _____ no

8. Have you used the central dictation system?

   _____ yes

   _____ no

   If yes, please rate the quality of the work you have received back from the center.

           Excellent   Good   Fair   Poor

   Comments:

9. Did you attend the dictation orientation session held earlier this spring?

   _____ yes

   _____ no

   If you did not attend, did you request copies of the handouts that were passed out at the sessions?

   _____ yes

   _____ no

10. Have you reviewed the Word Processing Procedures Manual that was given to faculty/staff recently?

    _____ yes

    _____ no

    Do you have any suggestions to make this manual more effective?

11. Are you a faculty member or administrative staff member? _____
12. Other comments or suggestions you would like to share.

Exhibit G-5 *(Continued)*

INDEX